T0325778

Semantic Web Science and Real-World Applications

Miltiadis D. Lytras
The American College of Greece, Greece

Naif Aljohani
King Abdulaziz University, Saudi Arabia

Ernesto Damiani
Khalifa University, UAE

Kwok Tai Chui
City University of Hong Kong, Hong Kong

A volume in the Advances in Web Technologies and Engineering (AWTE) Book Series

Published in the United States of America by
  IGI Global
  Information Science Reference (an imprint of IGI Global)
  701 E. Chocolate Avenue
  Hershey PA, USA 17033
  Tel: 717-533-8845
  Fax: 717-533-8661
  E-mail: cust@igi-global.com
  Web site: http://www.igi-global.com

Copyright © 2019 by IGI Global. All rights reserved. No part of this publication may be reproduced, stored or distributed in
any form or by any means, electronic or mechanical, including photocopying, without written permission from the publisher.
Product or company names used in this set are for identification purposes only. Inclusion of the names of the products or
companies does not indicate a claim of ownership by IGI Global of the trademark or registered trademark.

                    Library of Congress Cataloging-in-Publication Data

Names: Lytras, Miltiadis D., 1973- editor. | Aljohani, Naif, 1983- editor. |
  Damiani, Ernesto, 1960- editor. | Chui, Kwok Tai, editor.
Title: Semantic web science and real-world applications / Miltiadis D.
  Lytras, Naif Aljohani, Ernesto Damiani, and Kwok Tai Chui, editors.
Description: Hershey, PA : Information Science Reference, 2019.
Identifiers: LCCN 2018019093| ISBN 9781522571865 (hardcover) | ISBN
  9781522571872 (ebook)
Subjects: LCSH: Semantic Web--Research. | Ontologies (Information retrieval)
Classification: LCC TK5105.88815 .S439 2019 | DDC 025.042/7--dc23 LC record available at https://lccn.loc.
gov/2018019093

This book is published in the IGI Global book series Advances in Web Technologies and Engineering (AWTE) (ISSN:
2328-2762; eISSN: 2328-2754)

British Cataloguing in Publication Data
A Cataloguing in Publication record for this book is available from the British Library.

The views expressed in this book are those of the authors, but not necessarily of the publisher.

For electronic access to this publication, please contact: eresources@igi-global.com.

Advances in Web Technologies and Engineering (AWTE) Book Series

Ghazi I. Alkhatib
The Hashemite University, Jordan
David C. Rine
George Mason University, USA

ISSN:2328-2762
EISSN:2328-2754

MISSION

The **Advances in Web Technologies and Engineering (AWTE) Book Series** aims to provide a platform for research in the area of Information Technology (IT) concepts, tools, methodologies, and ethnography, in the contexts of global communication systems and Web engineered applications. Organizations are continuously overwhelmed by a variety of new information technologies, many are Web based. These new technologies are capitalizing on the widespread use of network and communication technologies for seamless integration of various issues in information and knowledge sharing within and among organizations. This emphasis on integrated approaches is unique to this book series and dictates cross platform and multidisciplinary strategy to research and practice.

The **Advances in Web Technologies and Engineering (AWTE) Book Series** seeks to create a stage where comprehensive publications are distributed for the objective of bettering and expanding the field of web systems, knowledge capture, and communication technologies. The series will provide researchers and practitioners with solutions for improving how technology is utilized for the purpose of a growing awareness of the importance of web applications and engineering.

COVERAGE

- Radio Frequency Identification (RFID) research and applications in web engineered systems
- Security, integrity, privacy, and policy issues
- Case studies validating Web-based IT solutions
- Information filtering and display adaptation techniques for wireless devices
- Strategies for linking business needs and IT
- Web systems engineering design
- IT education and training
- Data analytics for business and government organizations
- Metrics-based performance measurement of IT-based and web-based organizations
- Quality of service and service level agreement issues among integrated systems

IGI Global is currently accepting manuscripts for publication within this series. To submit a proposal for a volume in this series, please contact our Acquisition Editors at Acquisitions@igi-global.com or visit: http://www.igi-global.com/publish/.

The Advances in Web Technologies and Engineering (AWTE) Book Series (ISSN 2328-2762) is published by IGI Global, 701 E. Chocolate Avenue, Hershey, PA 17033-1240, USA, www.igi-global.com. This series is composed of titles available for purchase individually; each title is edited to be contextually exclusive from any other title within the series. For pricing and ordering information please visit http://www.igi-global.com/book-series/advances-web-technologies-engineering/37158. Postmaster: Send all address changes to above address. Copyright © 2019 IGI Global. All rights, including translation in other languages reserved by the publisher. No part of this series may be reproduced or used in any form or by any means – graphics, electronic, or mechanical, including photocopying, recording, taping, or information and retrieval systems – without written permission from the publisher, except for non commercial, educational use, including classroom teaching purposes. The views expressed in this series are those of the authors, but not necessarily of IGI Global.

Titles in this Series

For a list of additional titles in this series, please visit: www.igi-global.com/book-series

Dynamic Knowledge Representation in Scientific Domains
Cyril Pshenichny (ITMO University, Russia) Paolo Diviacco (Istituto Nazionale di Oceanografia e di Geofisica Sperimentale, Italy) and Dmitry Mouromtsev (ITMO University, Russia)
Engineering Science Reference • copyright 2018 • 397pp • H/C (ISBN: 9781522552611) • US $205.00 (our price)

Innovations, Developments, and Applications of Semantic Web and Information Systems
Miltiadis D. Lytras (American College of Greece, Greece) Naif Aljohani (King Abdulaziz University, Saudi Arabia) Ernesto Damiani (University of Milan, Italy) and Kwok Tai Chui (City University of Hong Kong, Hong Kong)
Engineering Science Reference • copyright 2018 • 473pp • H/C (ISBN: 9781522550426) • US $245.00 (our price)

Handbook of Research on Biomimicry in Information Retrieval and Knowledge Management
Reda Mohamed Hamou (Dr. Tahar Moulay University of Saida, Algeria)
Engineering Science Reference • copyright 2018 • 429pp • H/C (ISBN: 9781522530046) • US $325.00 (our price)

Global Perspectives on Frameworks for Integrated Reporting Emerging Research and Opportunities
Ioana Dragu (Babes-Bolyai University, Romania) Adriana Tiron-Tudor (Babes-Bolyai University, Romania) and Szilveszter Fekete Pali-Pista (Babes-Bolyai University, Romania)
Business Science Reference • copyright 2018 • 160pp • H/C (ISBN: 9781522527534) • US $135.00 (our price)

Novel Design and the Applications of Smart-M3 Platform in the Internet of Things Emerging Research and Opportunities
Dmitry Korzun (Petrozavodsk State University (PetrSU), Russia) Alexey Kashevnik (St. Petersburg Institute for Informatics and Automation of the Russian Academy of Sciences (SPIIRAS), Russia & ITMO University, Russia) and Sergey Balandin (FRUCT Oy, Finland & St. Petersburg State University of Aerospace Instrumentation (SUAI), Russia)
Information Science Reference • copyright 2018 • 150pp • H/C (ISBN: 9781522526537) • US $145.00 (our price)

Developing Metadata Application Profiles
Mariana Curado Malta (Polytechnic of Oporto, Portugal & Algoritmi Center, University of Minho, Portugal) Ana Alice Baptista (Algoritmi Center, University of Minho, Portugal) and Paul Walk (University of Edinburgh, UK)
Information Science Reference • copyright 2017 • 248pp • H/C (ISBN: 9781522522218) • US $170.00 (our price)

Game Theory Solutions for the Internet of Things Emerging Research and Opportunities
Sungwook Kim (Sogang University, South Korea)
Information Science Reference • copyright 2017 • 221pp • H/C (ISBN: 9781522519522) • US $130.00 (our price)

701 East Chocolate Avenue, Hershey, PA 17033, USA
Tel: 717-533-8845 x100 • Fax: 717-533-8661
E-Mail: cust@igi-global.com • www.igi-global.com

Table of Contents

Detailed Table of Contents

Chapter 1

Jie Zhao, Anhui University, China
Jianfei Wang, Anhui University, China
Jia Yang, University of Science and Technology of China, China
Peiquan Jin, University of Science and Technology of China, China

In this chapter, we study the problem of extracting company acquisition relation from huge amounts of webpages, and propose a novel algorithm for a company acquisition relation extraction. Our algorithm considers the tense feature of Web content and classification technology of semantic strength when extracting company acquisition relation from webpages. It first determines the tense of each sentence in a webpage, where a CRF model is employed. Then, the tense of sentences is applied to sentences classification so as to evaluate the semantic strength of the candidate sentences in describing company acquisition relation. After that, we rank the candidate acquisition relations and return the top-k company acquisition relation. We run experiments on 6144 pages crawled through Google, and measure the performance of our algorithm under different metrics. The experimental results show that our algorithm is effective in determining the tense of sentences as well as the company acquisition relation.

Chapter 2

Cristhian Figueroa, Universidad Antonio Nariño, Colombia
Iacopo Vagliano, Leibniz Information Centre for Economics, Germany
Oscar Rodríguez Rocha, Université Côte d'Azur, France
Marco Torchiano, Politecnico di Torino, Italy
Catherine Faron Zucker, Université Nice Sophia Antipolis, France
Juan Carlos Corrales, Universidad del Cauca, Colombia
Maurizio Morisio, Politecnico di Torino, Italy

Data published on the web following the principles of linked data has resulted in a global data space called the Web of Data. These principles led to semantically interlink and connect different resources at data level regardless their structure, authoring, location, etc. The tremendous and continuous growth of the Web of Data also implies that now it is more likely to find resources that describe real-life concepts. However, discovering and recommending relevant related resources is still an open research area. This chapter studies recommender systems that use linked data as a source containing a significant amount of available resources and their relationships useful to produce recommendations. Furthermore, it also presents a framework to deploy and execute state-of-the-art algorithms for linked data that have been re-implemented to measure and benchmark them in different application domains and without being bound to a unique dataset.

Chapter 3

Alfredo D'Elia, University of Bologna, Italy
Paolo Azzoni, Eurotech Group, Italy
Fabio Viola, University of Bologna, Italy
Cristiano Aguzzi, University of Bologna, Italy
Luca Roffia, University of Bologna, Italy
Tullio Salmon Cinotti, University of Bologna, Italy

The research activity in the IoT field caused a proliferation of information brokers with different features and targeted at different information abstraction levels. The OSGI Semantic Information Broker (SIB) is a portable and extendable solution for providing an IoT system with semantic support, a publish subscribe paradigm, and expressive primitives for information modeling. In this chapter the authors explain the main reasons for defining a new SIB version, substituting the previously used RedSIB, its main features and comparative evaluation against both ad hoc and standard benchmarks. Furthermore, recently defined primitives and experimental work on the portability to mobile devices and resiliency are proposed and discussed.

Chapter 4

Eliot Bytyçi, University of Prishtina, Kosovo
Besmir Sejdiu, University of Prishtina, Kosovo
Arten Avdiu, South East European University, Kosovo
Lule Ahmedi, University of Prishtina, Kosovo

The Internet of Things (IoT) vision is connecting uniquely identifiable devices to the internet, best described through ontologies. Furthermore, new emerging technologies such as wireless sensor networks (WSN) are recognized as essential enabling component of the IoT today. Hence, the interest is to provide linked sensor data through the web either following the semantic web enablement (SWE) standard or the linked data approach. Likewise, a need exists to explore those data for potential hidden knowledge through data mining techniques utilized by a domain ontology. Following that rationale, a new lightweight IoT architecture has been developed. It supports linking sensors, other devices and people via a single web by mean of a device-person-activity (DPA) ontology. The architecture is validated by mean of three rich-in-semantic services: contextual data mining over WSN, semantic WSN web enablement, and linked WSN data. The architecture could be easily extensible to capture semantics of input sensor data from other domains as well.

Chapter 5

Pu Li, Zhengzhou University of Light Industry, China
Zhifeng Zhang, Zhengzhou University of Light Industry, China
Lujuan Deng, Zhengzhou University of Light Industry, China
Junxia Ma, Zhengzhou University of Light Industry, China
Fenglong Wu, Zhengzhou University of Light Industry, China
Peipei Gu, Zhengzhou University of Light Industry, China
Yuncheng Jiang, South China Normal University, China

Linked Data, a new form of knowledge representation and publishing described by RDF, can provide
more precise and comprehensible semantic structures. However, the current RDF Schema (RDFS) and
SPARQL-based query strategy cannot fully express the semantics of RDF since they cannot unleash the
implicit semantics between linked entities, so they cannot unleash the potential of Linked Data. To fill
this gap, this chapter first defines a new semantic annotating and reasoning method which can extend
more implicit semantics from different properties and proposes a novel general Semantically-Extended
Scheme for Linked Data Sources to realize the semantic extension over the target Linked Data source.
Moreover, in order to effectively return more information in the process of semantic data retrieval, we
then design a new querying model which extends the SPARQL pattern. Lastly, experimental results show
that our proposal has advantages over the initial Linked Data source and can return more valid results
than some of the most representative similarity search methods.

Chapter 6

Ali A. Amer, Taiz University, Yemen

In distributed database systems (DDBS), the utmost purpose of data distribution and replication aims at
shrinking transmission costs (TC), including communication costs, and response time. In this chapter,
therefore, an enhanced heuristic clustering-based technique for data fragmentation and replicated based
allocation is efficaciously presented. This work is mainly sought to further enhance an existing technique
so TC is to be significantly minimized. In fact, the approached enhancement is applied by suggesting
different replication scenarios. Off these scenarios, one scenario is to be selected based on competitive
performance evaluation process. DDBS performance is measured via its being exposed on objective
function (TC). Despite the fact that this work is mildly improved, yet evaluation results show that it has
been promising, particularly as TC being the foremost design objective of DDBS System. Experimental
results have been analyzed under all presented scenarios as an internal evaluation and are vividly provided
to demonstrate the undeniable impact of data replication on DDBS performance.

Chapter 7

Imen Jemili, University of Carthage, Tunisia
Dhouha Ghrab, National School for Computer Science, Tunisia
Abdelfettah Belghith, King Saud University, Saudi Arabia
Mohamed Mosbah, University of Bordeaux, France

Operating under duty-cycle mode allows wireless sensor networks to prolong their lifetime. However, this working pattern, with the temporary unavailability of nodes, brings challenges to the network design, mainly for a fundamental service like flooding. The challenging task is to authorize sensors to adopt a duty-cycle mode without inflicting any negative impact on the network performances. Context-awareness offers to sensors the ability to adapt their functional behavior according to many contexts in order to cope with network dynamics. In this context, the authors propose an Enhanced-Efficient Context-Aware Multi-hop Broadcast (E-ECAB) protocol, which relies on multi contextual information to optimize resources usage and satisfy the application requirements in a duty-cycled environment. The authors proved that only one transmission is required to achieve the broadcast operation in almost all situations. Simulation results show that E-ECAB achieves a significant improvement compared to previous work in terms of throughput and end-to-end delay without sacrificing energy efficiency.

Chapter 8

Badia Bouhdid, University of Manouba, Tunisia
Wafa Akkari, University of Manouba, Tunisia
Abdelfettah Belghith, King Saud University, Saudi Arabia
Sofien Gannouni, King Saud University, Saudi Arabia

Although recursive localization approaches are efficiently used in wireless sensor networks (WSNs), their application leads to increased energy consumption caused by the important communication overhead necessary to achieve the localization task. Indeed, localization information coverage increases iteratively as new nodes estimate their locations and become themselves new reference nodes. However, the uncontrollable number evolution of such nodes leads, especially in high density networks, to wasted energy, important communication overhead and even impacts the localization accuracy due the adverse effects of error propagation and accumulation. This chapter proposes an efficient recursive localization (ERL) approach that develops a new reliable reference selection strategy to ensure a better distribution of the reference nodes in the network. ERL improves localization accuracy without incurring any additional cost. It allows conserving the energy and consequently prolonging the WSN life time.

Chapter 9

Daniel Fernández-Álvarez, University of Oviedo, Spain
José Emilio Labra Gayo, University of Oviedo, Spain
Daniel Gayo-Avello, University of Oviedo, Spain
Patricia Ordoñez de Pablos, University of Oviedo, Spain

The proliferation of large databases with potentially repeated entities across the World Wide Web drives into a generalized interest to find methods to detect duplicated entries. The heterogeneity of the data cause that generalist approaches may produce a poor performance in scenarios with distinguishing features. In this paper, we analyze the particularities of music related-databases and we describe Musical Entities Reconciliation Architecture (MERA). MERA consists of an architecture to match entries of two sources, allowing the use of extra support sources to improve the results. It makes use of semantic web technologies and it is able to adapt the matching process to the nature of each field in each database. We have implemented a prototype of MERA and compared it with a well-known music-specialized search engine. Our prototype outperforms the selected baseline in terms of accuracy.

Posting sarcastic messages on social media like Twitter, Facebook, WhatsApp, etc., became a new trend to avoid direct negativity. Detecting this indirect negativity in the social media text has become an important task as they influence every business organization. In the presence of sarcasm, detection of actual sentiment on these texts has become the most challenging task. An automated system is required that will be capable of identifying actual sentiment of a given text in the presence of sarcasm. In this chapter, we proposed an automated system for sarcasm detection in social media text using six algorithms that are capable to analyze the various types of sarcasm occurs in Twitter data. These algorithms use lexical, pragmatic, hyperbolic and contextual features of text to identify sarcasm. In the contextual feature, we mainly focus on situation, topical, temporal, and historical context of the text. The experimental results of proposed approach were compared with state-of-the-art techniques.

Retrieving personalized care plans from a guideline repository is an ever-increasing need in the medical world, not only for physicians but also for empowered patients. In this chapter, we continue our long-lasting research on ontology-based personalized access to very large collections of multi-version documents by addressing a novel challenge: dealing with multi-version clinical guidelines but also with a multi-version ontology used to support personalized access to them. Efficiency is ensured by a newly introduced annotation scheme for guidelines and solutions to cope with the evolution of ontology structure. The tests performed on a prototype implementation confirm the goodness of the approach. Finally, the chapter proposes an exhaustive analysis of the state of the art in this field and, in the final part, a discussion where we expand our vision to related research themes and possible further developments of our work.

Twitter is one of the primary online social networks where users share messages and contents of interest to those who follow their activities. To effectively categorize and give audience to their tweets, users try to append appropriate hashtags to their short messages. However, the hashtags usage is very small and very heterogeneous and users may spend a lot of time searching the appropriate hashtags. Thus, the need for a system to assist users in this task is very important to increase and homogenize the hashtagging usage. In this chapter, the authors present a hashtag recommendation system on microblogging platforms by leveraging semantic features. Furthermore, they conduct a detailed study on how the semantic-based model influences the final recommended hashtags using different ranking strategies. Moreover, they propose a linear and a machine learning based combination of these ranking strategies. The experiment results show that their approach improves content-based recommendations, achieving a recall of more than 47% on recommending 5 hashtags.

Ontology or domain specific vocabulary is indispensable to a semantic web-based application; therefore, its evaluation assumes critical importance for maintaining the quality. A modular ontology is intuitively preferred to as a monolithic ontology. A good quality modular ontology, in turn, promotes reusability. This chapter is directed at summarizing the efforts towards ontology evaluation, besides defining the process of evaluation, various approaches to evaluation and underlying motivation. In particular, a modular ontology's cohesion and coupling metrics have been discussed in detail as a case study. The authors believe that the body of knowledge in this chapter will serve as a beginning point for ontology quality engineers and at the same time acquaint them with the state-of-art in this field.

Preface

Semantic web is 20 years old and has gained much attention in recent years. There have been many exciting developments on the concept, requirement and standard of late in the semantic web and technology space in academia and industries. The era of big data leads to consideration of the adoption of artificial intelligence and internet of things techniques to facilitate today's semantic web science applications. Thus, the semantic web thus becomes younger as a new research area in artificial intelligence and internet of things are based on the semantic web.

We are happy delivering this volume with the support from international experts and editors. This book is a manifestation of some of the most interesting aspects of theoretical and applied research covering complementary facets of the semantic web science and real-world applications, for instance:

- Extracting the company acquisition relations in webpage
- Linked data-based recommendation system
- OSGi semantic information broker implementation for Internet of Things
- Semantic sensor web architecture for Internet of Things
- Semantically-enhanced annotation and reasoning for linked data extension
- Data replication impact on distributed database
- Context-awareness of duty-cycled broadcast wireless sensor networks
- Recursive localization for high density wireless sensor networks
- Musical entities reconciliation architecture for recording linkage in music related database
- Sarcasm detection in twitter data
- Multi-version ontology-based personalization of clinical guidelines for patient centric healthcare
- Leveraging semantic features for time-sensitive hashtag recommendation on twitter network
- Advanced evaluation on ontology quality

This book covers the discussion on the semantic web science and real-world applications via 13 chapters. The summary of each chapter is given as follows.

The first chapter focuses on the algorithm for company acquisition relations extraction from webpage. The key steps of the algorithm are (i) The tense of every sentence is scanned in a webpage using conditional random fields; (ii) The tense is acted as input for sentence classification in order to evaluate the semantic strength of the candidate sentences in describing company acquisition relation; and (iii) The candidate acquisition relations are ranked and only the top-k are shown. This effectiveness of the proposed algorithm is evaluated using 6000 webpages.

It can be seen that data is published on the web freely and thus joining dataset of different domains is challenged by heterogeneity of linked data. Chapter 2 proposes a framework named AlLied for executing and deploying existing algorithms for recommendation of related linked data. Authors also investigate the approach to select the best algorithm in special application and whether there is a unique algorithm that is able to perform well in ubiquitous applications.

In Chapter 3, semantic information broker based IoT system is proposed. It is interoperable, portable and extendable solution which supports semantics, publish expressive primitives and subscribe paradigm for modelling the knowledge. Authors suggest an essential future work that security should be addressed to provide availability, integrity and confidentiality of data.

Attention is also drawn to IoT system in Chapter 4 that an architecture is proposed for linked data following the linked data standard or semantic web enablement standard. Performance evaluation is made on three scenarios (i) linked wireless sensor network data; (ii) semantic wireless sensor network web enablement; and (iii) contextual data mining over wireless sensor network. Future work could be supplementing each sensor in order to reflect the peculiarities of the certain domain and devices at the input, as well as services acquired at the output in the context of IoT.

Chapter 5 defines a new semantic reasoning and annotating approach for extension of implicit semantics into SPARQL pattern which is targeted for linked data sources. In the future, machine learning is believed to play an important role in semantic mapping, relatedness assessment between entities in linked data, RDF documents retrieval, clustering and classification.

Response time and communication cost are important criteria in evaluating the successfulness of distributed database system. Chapter 6 modifies the heuristic clustering-based method to fragment data. Key replicated based data allocation scenarios are considered named non-replicated based data allocation scenario, full replicated based data allocation scenario and mixed replicated based data allocation scenario. It is worth noting that the data replication will lead to poor performance in distributed database system when it comes to heavily query of update activities.

Authors in Chapter 7 propose an enhanced-efficient (end-to-end delay and throughput) context-aware multi-hop broadcast protocol which relies on multi contextual information to optimize resources usage and satisfy the application requirements in a duty-cycled environment. It has been demonstrated that one transmission is sufficient to maintain normal broadcast operation in general applications

Chapter 8 shares an idea of efficient recursive localization that develops a new reliable reference selection strategy to ensure a better distribution of the reference nodes in the network. In other words, nodes having better (lower) residual errors choose smaller periods. The algorithm improves localization accuracy without scarifying additional cost. In addition, it allows conserving the energy and consequently prolonging the WSN life time.

Data heterogeneity hinders the development on the detection of duplicated entries. Authors in Chapter 9 propose a semantically based musical entities reconciliation architecture that matches entries of two sources so that more support sources can be utilized to enhance the performance of entries detection. Further investigation is recommended to see if the proposed architecture can be applied in big data environments.

In Chapter 10, an automated system for sarcasm detection in social media text using six supervised algorithms is proposed. It is capable to analyze the various types of sarcasm occurs in Twitter data based on contextual, hyperbolic, pragmatic and lexical features. Nevertheless, authors have pointed out that semi-supervised and unsupervised classification algorithms are more useful in certain application like text regional languages.

Chapter 11 continues the research on ontology-based personalized access to very large collections of multi-version documents by addressing a novel challenge: dealing with multi-version clinical guidelines but also with a multi-version ontology used to support personalized access to them. It proposes an exhaustive analysis of the state of the art in this field.

Then, Chapter 12 deals with a hashtag recommendation system on microblogging platforms by leveraging semantic features. Then, authors conduct a detailed study on how the semantic-based model influences the final recommended hashtags using different ranking strategies. At last but not least, a linear and machine learning based combination of these ranking strategies are proposed.

In the last chapter, authors comprehensively present the various facets of ontology evaluation. It is the process of determining the quality of the ontology on the basis of some pre-defined criteria. It is often done to determine which out of all the ontologies developed for the particular domain better conceptualizes the knowledge of the domain.

Miltiadis D. Lytras
The American College of Greece, Greece

Naif Aljohani
King Abdulaziz University, Saudi Arabia

Ernesto Damiani
Khalifa University, UAE

Kwok Tai Chui
City University of Hong Kong, Hong Kong

Chapter 1
Company Acquisition Relations Extraction From Web Pages

Jie Zhao
Anhui University, China

Jianfei Wang
Anhui University, China

Jia Yang
University of Science and Technology of China, China

Peiquan Jin
University of Science and Technology of China, China

ABSTRACT

In this chapter, we study the problem of extracting company acquisition relation from huge amounts of webpages, and propose a novel algorithm for a company acquisition relation extraction. Our algorithm considers the tense feature of Web content and classification technology of semantic strength when extracting company acquisition relation from webpages. It first determines the tense of each sentence in a webpage, where a CRF model is employed. Then, the tense of sentences is applied to sentences classification so as to evaluate the semantic strength of the candidate sentences in describing company acquisition relation. After that, we rank the candidate acquisition relations and return the top-k company acquisition relation. We run experiments on 6144 pages crawled through Google, and measure the performance of our algorithm under different metrics. The experimental results show that our algorithm is effective in determining the tense of sentences as well as the company acquisition relation.

INTRODUCTION

Web has been the most important information source in the world. It has been widely accepted that webpages include useful competitive intelligence for enterprises (Zhao and Jin, 2009). Enterprise competitive intelligence refers to the intelligence related with competitors, competitive environment, and competitive strategies, among which the competitive strategies is the most difficult type of competitive intelligence to obtain in real applications. The competitive strategies about a certain company usually

DOI: 10.4018/978-1-5225-7186-5.ch001

Copyright © 2019, IGI Global. Copying or distributing in print or electronic forms without written permission of IGI Global is prohibited.

hide in a lot of phenomenon. For example, the future developing strategy of a company, e.g., IBM, may be reflected by its acquirement actions. There is a real case regarding IBM. Recently, this company is advancing its development on big data analysis (IBM, 2015). But if we check the acquirement history of IBM in recent years, we can find that since 2009 it keeps buying companies on data analysis, such as SPSS, Emptoris, and Netzza. Thus, if we can extract the company acquirement relation about concerned competitors from the Web and detect their early intends in strategical development, it will be helpful to conduct deeply analysis on enterprise competitive intelligence (Zhao and Jin, 2010a).

Company acquirement relation can be represented as a triple *<ORG1, verb_tense, ORG2>*, where *ORG1* is the acquirer while *ORG2* is the acquiree and *verb_tense* refers to the tense of the acquiring action. The *verb_tense* usually indicates the state of the acquirement relation. For instance, in a sentence saying "*IBM has acquired Algorithmics*", we can detect that there exists an acquirement relation between IBM and Algorithmics and this action has been actually completed due to the verb tense "has acquired".

Compared with traditional techniques in relation extraction, the extraction of company acquirement relation in the Web has two key issues:

1. How to detect the tense of a sentence?

In English sentences, the sentence tense has an important impact on the effectiveness of company acquirement relations extraction. For example, the sentence "IBM has acquired Algorithmics" is with the tense of present perfect, which indicates the validness of the acquirement relation between IBM and Algorithmics. However, in a sentence with future tense such as "IBM will acquire Algorithmics", the acquirement relation may not be valid. Another challenging issue is that some sentences imply negative semantics, e.g. "IBM rumored to acquire Algorithmics".

2. How to determine the semantic strength of sentences?

Web information usually has multiple styles, as different Web information sources have differing format when describing events or news. Some typical sources of Web information are blog, BBS (Bulletin Board System), Wikipedia, and news pages. Besides, webpages may differ in the time factor, e.g., the publication dates of webpages are usually different. As a result, there are various forms of company acquirement relations in the Web, so we cannot simply detect them by analyzing one Web page. The more reasonable way is to check a set of related webpages and detect their semantic strength in asserting the validness of a possible company acquirement relation. This problem is essentially an issue of classification, as we have to find the webpages showing positive semantics and others showing negative semantics, and then make further decision on the validness of company acquirement relations.

Traditional ways in relation extraction only considered the limited characters of sentences, such as morphology and syntax (Zhou et al., 2005; Zhang et al., 2005; García and Gamallo, 2011), and lacked the analysis on the tense of sentences as well as the semantic strength of sentences in determining the validness of relations. Some recent works showed that the tense of sentences has a very important impact on relation extraction (Zhao and Jin, 2010b). Therefore, we introduce the tense of sentences into the extraction of company acquirement relations.

In this paper, aiming at solving the challenging problems in extracting company acquirement relations from the Web, we present a new algorithm. The idea of our algorithm is to introduce the tense of sentences into the extraction process. In particular, we first label the tense of each sentence in each Web page, and then apply the resulted tenses into the classification of the semantic strength of sentences. After that, we get the acquiree candidates and conduct a ranking procedure to output the top-k company acquirement relations. The main contributions of the paper can be summarized as follows:

1. We propose a new tense-based algorithm to extract company acquirement relations from the Web. Compared with previous approaches, our algorithm takes into account the tense of sentences in webpages, and can improve the efficiency of relation extraction (Section 3).
2. In order to detect the tense features of sentences, we propose to use the CRF-based method to label the tense of sentences. To the best of our knowledge, this is the first work that labels the tense of sentences. (Section 4)
3. In order to determine the semantic strength of sentences, we design a classification model integrating different features including the tense of sentences, semantic features, and morphology (Section 5). Based on the classification results, we construct a list of acquiree candidates and return the top-k candidates as the most possible companies acquired by the given company (Section 6).
4. We conduct experiments on a real data set consisting of 6144 webpages crawled by Google API, and measure the performance in terms of tense labeling, classification, and top-k acquirement relation extraction. The experimental results show that the proposed algorithms have good performance regarding all the metrics (Section 6).

RELATED WORK

As an important task in information extraction, relation extraction has attracted much attention from the research community. In general, most of the related work considers the issue of relation extraction as a learning problem. Therefore, machine learning plays a critical role in relation extraction.

Basically, supervised methods for relation extraction mainly concentrate on two aspects: kernel optimization (Reichartz et al., 2010; Yap & Baldwin, 2009) and feature selection (Chan & Roth, 2010). Talaika et al. (2015) showed how deep linguistic structures can be represented suitably for model learning in entity relation extraction. Chen et al. (2015) selected six types of candidate features and explored the optimal extraction performances depending on the utilization of candidate features and different constraint conditions. Distant supervised method does not require a lot of manual tagging and can be used in large corpus (Tresp et al., 2016; Kirschnick et al., 2016; Zhang et al., 2012). Wang et al. (2011) leveraged the knowledge learned from previously trained relation detectors and the experimental results on Wikipedia and ACE (Automatic Content Extraction) data have confirmed that background knowledge-based topics generated from the Wikipedia relation repository can significantly improve the performance over the state-of-the-art relation detection approaches. Nowadays neural network methods have a profound impact on information extraction. Convolutional neural network architecture relies on two levels of attention, in order to better discern patterns in heterogeneous contexts (Wang et al., 2016).

Unsupervised learning adapts to the resolution of large-scale information extraction (Tandon et al., 2016). Bollegalaet al. (2010) firstly figured out the semantic relation classification in a social network system, and then made use of a dual representation of semantic relation to extract numerous relations efficiently from unlabeled data and improved the performance of existing relational similarity measures. Differing from supervised and unsupervised approaches, semi-supervised methods reduce the cost of manual tagging by using seed selection and expansion in entity relation extraction (Luan et al., 2014).

Zhu et al. (2009) proposed a statistical extraction framework Statistical Snowball (StatSnowball) to deal with bootstrapping-based relation extraction. The experiment results confirmed that StatSnowball can achieve high recall without sacrificing the performance of precision during iterations with a small number of seeds.

Company acquirement relations are one type of business relations in real commercial environments. Business relations can be divided into two kinds, namely external business relations and international business relations. For internal business relations, we can find the cues for those types of relations from Wikipedia or the authoritative website of companies. However, the external business relations are usually deeply hidden in the Web, and more challenging issues have to be solved. This is because the external business relations are more classified as they often represent the future or near-future developing strategies of companies. In case that the developing strategies of a company are discovered by its competitors, it will be much harmful to the company. Presently, internal business relations have been widely studied, such as company headquarters detection, position relations extraction, and tax relations extraction (Agichtein and Gravano, 2009; Liu, Jin, and Yue, 2009; Ma, 2009). However, there are few works concerning about external business relations extraction, especially company acquirement relations.

Some works on external business relations extraction concentrated on discovering competitors from the Web (Valkanas et al., 2017). They defined a lot of strict patterns to find competitors' information mentioned in webpages. Compared with those works, we use simpler patterns, e.g., "Company name + Relation indicating verb", and only for the data crawling task. Zhao and Jin (2010b) studied the tense in webpages, and conducted experiments to test the values of tense in relation extraction. Our algorithm is firstly motivated by this idea. However, they only considered the future tense in the process of relation extraction, and paid no attention to other tenses, such as past tense and perfect tense. According to our analysis and experimental results, various tenses can have different impact on the effectiveness of relation extraction. Besides, they only considered the tense of exact one verb in a sentence, which was ineffective in treating those sentences containing negative verbs, e.g., "IBM rumored to acquire Algorithmics."

Relation extraction has been widely studied in recent years and several algorithms have been proposed. They can be mainly classified into two types: pattern-based algorithms (Agichtein and Gravano, 2009; Liu, Jin, and Yue, 2009) and machine learning algorithms (Zhou et al., 2005; Zhang et al., 2005; Xi et al., 2008). The pattern-based algorithms are effective for webpages with many structural properties such as tables, lists, and bullets, but are not suitable for unstructured texts. Moreover, they only took into account the textual pattern and did not consider much on other semantic information such as morphology and tense. The machine learning algorithms consist of two major approaches, one is based on feature vectors (Zhou et al., 2005; Xi et al., 2008), and the other is based on kernel functions (Zelenko and Aone, 2003; Culotta and Sorensen, 2004). The kernel function-based approach transforms the problem of feature selection into the constructing issue of a kernel function. It can well treat the features with long distances and structures. The problem of this approach is that the training process is very time consuming and therefore it is not suitable for large-scale data analysis. The feature vector-based approach, which is also used in this paper, focuses on the selection of effective features. Zhou et al. (2005) claimed to use different features in relation extraction and analyzed the influences of composed features to the performance of relation extraction. This work was further advanced by Xi et al. (2008), where the researchers demonstrated that composed features were more effective for semantic relations extraction. However, they did not introduce new features to improve the performance. Our approach differs from their work in that we not only consider composed features but also introduce a new feature, namely the tense of sentences, which has been experimentally demonstrated to be more effective and efficient.

FRAMEWORK OF EXTRACTING COMPANY ACQUIREMENT RELATIONS FROM THE WEB

The framework of extracting company acquirement relations from the Web is shown in Fig.1, which mainly includes the following modules.

Web Crawler

In this module, we utilize Google API to obtain a set of webpages. Specially, we employ a keyword-based approach to crawl the webpages, e.g., "IBM + buy | acquire". This method is reasonable in Web platform, because there is duplicated information in the Web so that we need not to get the whole dataset but can only use a subset of webpages containing meaningful information.

Sentence Extraction

In this module, we extract the sentences for further processing. In detail, we analyze the crawled webpages and use a pattern-based approach to get the sentences, which are the candidates for the next modules on acquiree extraction and tense labeling.

Acquiree Extraction

In this module, we detect the companies that are candidates of acquirees. In this chapter, we use the NER (Named Entity Recognition) tool (Stanford NER tool, 2015) from Stanford University to accomplish this task. Note that there are some other available NER tools such as NERD (http://nerd.eurecom.fr/) that also has high precision on named entity recognition. This paper does not focus on improving the performance of named entity recognition; thus, other NER tools can also be used in this stage.

Figure 1. Framework of extracting company acquisition relations from the Web

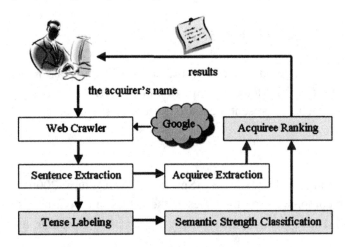

Tense Labeling

In this module, we label the extracted sentences outputted by the above module "Sentence Extraction." Through this module, we get the tense features of each extracted sentence. The details of this module will be discussed in Section 4.

Semantic Strength Classification

In this module, we perform the classification on extracted sentences on the basis of the tense features as well as other ones including the syntax and morphology of sentences. Each type of classified sentences implies a different level of positive contributions to the acquirement relations existing between the given acquirer and the extracted acquiree. The details of this module will be discussed in Section 5.

Acquiree Ranking

In this module, we rank the acquirees according to the semantic strength determined by the module "Semantic Strength Classification," and return the top-k acquirees as the final results. Those companies are of the most possibility to having been acquired by the given acquirer. The details of this module will be discussed in Section 6.

Figure 2 shows the general procedures of our algorithm to extract company acquirement relations. In this algorithm, we first prepare the set of webpages via Google API (line 1-2). Then we use a pattern-based approach to extract the candidates of the sentences to be further processed (line 3). Next, for each extracted sentence, we first use a sub-routine *TLS* (Tense Labeling of Sentences) to get the tense features of the sentence (line 5), and then use the sub-function *FeatureSelection* to extract the syntax and morphology features of the sentence (line 6). Through the sub-routine *NamedEntityRecognition*, we use the NER tool from Stanford University (Stanford NER tool, 2015) to recognize all the companies (line 7), which forms the candidates of acquirees. Finally, we use the routine *ClassLabeling* to perform the semantic strength classification on the sentences (line 8-9), and output the top-*k* acquirees (line 11).

The details about tense labeling, semantic strength classification (*ClassLabeling*) as well as acquiree ranking (*Rank*) will be discussed in Sections 5 and 6.

TENSE LABELING OF SENTENCES

In this paper, we employ the CRF model to accomplish the tense labeling task for each sentence. The basic idea is to transform the task of tense features extraction into a CRF-based labeling problem. Therefore, the tense labels in each sentence represent the tense features of the sentence.

The CRF Model

The CRF (Conditional Random Field) model (Sutton and McCallum, 2006) is an undirected graph model in which we can compute the probabilities of the values in output nodes in case that the values of input nodes are given. The input nodes are typically a series of observations, e.g., $X = X_1, X_2, ..., X_n$,

Figure 2. Algorithm of extracting company acquisition relationships

---

Algorithm *ExtractingCAR*

Input: *A*: the acquirer's name, *K*: the number of expected results

Output: *B_list*: The list of the Top-*k* A's acquirees.

1: Sending "A + buy OR acquire OR bought" to Google;

2: Saving the returned pages into *page_list*;

3: Processing *page_list* to get the sentences set *ST*;

4: For each sentence *S* in *ST* {

5: *S1 = TLS(S)*; // tense labeling

6: *FeatureList = FeatureSelection(S1)*; // get the features of S1

7: *B = NamedEntityRecognition(S)*; // get the acquiree candidates using NER

8: *label=ClassLabeling(Featurelist)*; // semantic strength classification (Section 4)

9: add <*A, B, label*> to candidate list *CL*;

10: }

11: *B_list = Rank(CL, K)*; // acquiree ranking and return top-K results

12: Return B_list;

End *ExtractingCAR*

---

while the output nodes represent a series of labels, e.g., $Y = Y_1, Y_2, ..., Y_n$. For the tense labeling problem, those observations $X = X_1, X_2, ..., X_n$ refer to the features of sentences, such as word sequences and part of speech (POS), and the out nodes $Y = Y_1, Y_2, ..., Y_n$ are the tense labels that we want to identify.

The CRF model is improved on the traditional HMM (Hidden Markov Model). HMM uses the following formula (1) to model the probability distribution of an input (observation) *x* and an output (label) *y*, i.e., *p(x,y)*.

$$p(x, y) = p(y \mid x) \cdot p(x) \tag{1}$$

However, CRF models *p(y|x)* instead of *p(x,y)*. There are two reasons for this change. First, the HMM model does not consider the interactions among inputted features, so it cannot capture the dependency among features during the modeling process. Second, the conditional probability *p(y|x)* contains enough information for the prediction of the outputted labels. As a result, CRF uses the following formula (2) to compute the conditional probability *p(y|x)*.

$$p(y \mid x) = \frac{1}{z} \exp\left(\sum_{k=1}^{K} \lambda_k f_k \left(y_{j-1}, y_j, x_j \right) \right) \tag{2}$$

In Formula (2), z is the normalization factor, which is defined in Formula (3).

$$z = \sum_{y'} \exp\left(\sum_{k=1}^{K} \lambda_k f_k \left(y'_{j-1}, y'_{j}, x_j \right) \right) \tag{3}$$

In the *exp* function shown in Formula (3), we need to sum up all the weighted features. The parameter λ_k, as the weight of f_k, can be determined through a training procedure.

When using CRF to solve the problem regarding the tense labeling of sentences, suppose the sentences and their POS features are provided, we compute the tense labeling series with the highest probabilities, namely $y^* = \arg\max_y \left(y \mid x \right)$. This means that we have to get the values of $p(y|x)$ for all y. This process is very time-consuming because it causes lot of exponential computation. So in this paper, we use the efficient *Viterbi* algorithm and dynamic planning approach to find the tense labels with the highest probabilities (Sutton & McCallum, 2006).

Tense Labeling of Sentences

The tense labeling of sentences aims at detecting the tense of each sentence in a Web page. The tense of a sentence is typically determined by the verbs in the sentence. For example, in the sentence "*IBM announced a definitive agreement to acquire Algorithmics.*", the verb "*acquire*" indicates that there is an acquirement relation between IBM and Algorithmics. For the validness of this relation, we can further find that another verb "*announced*" is close to acquire and with a past tense, based on which we can draw the conclusion that this acquirement relation is very possible to be true. Thus we give the following definitions.

Definition 1: *Relation Indicating Verb (verb_A).* A relation indicating verb is a verb or verb group in a sentence that describes some kind of relation.

For the acquirement relations, some examples of relation indicating verbs are *acquire, buy, bought, is buying, will acquire,* etc.

Definition 2: *Key Verb (key_verb).* The key verb in a sentence is the verb closest to *verb_A*.

The key verb has big influence on the validness of relations. For instance, in the sentence "*Oracle rumored to buy HP.*", the key verb "*rumored*" indicates that the acquirement between Oracle and HP is not valid.

To tell the positive of negative semantics of the key verb in a sentence, we construct a word table in this paper, which maintains a set of positive verbs and negative verbs. Typical positive verbs are *agree, announce,* etc., while typical negative verbs are *refuse, rumor,* etc.

Based on the above definitions, we use CRF to perform the tense labeling work. The general idea is illustrated in Fig.3. Given a series of observations, namely $< w_1, w_2, ..., w_N >$ and $< p_1, p_2, ..., p_N >$, in which w_i refers to a word and p_i is the POS of w_i, the tense labels of $< w_1, w_2, ..., w_N >$ are produced through the CRF model and denoted as $< t_1, t_2, ..., t_n >$, where $n \leq N$. According to English grammar,

Figure 3. Illustration of the CRF-based tense labeling

Word List: $w_1,\ w_2,\ w_3,\ \cdots,\ w_N$

Part of Speech: $p_1,\ p_2,\ p_3,\ \cdots,\ p_N$

Tense Labeling: $t_1,\ t_2,\ t_3,\ \cdots,\ t_n$

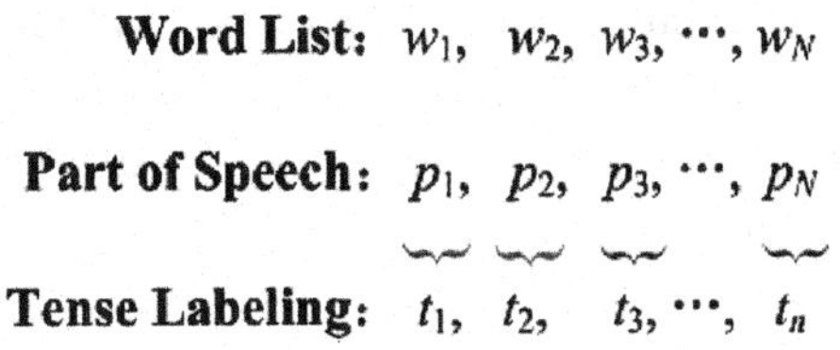

the tense label t_i can be *past, past_perfect, past_progressive, present, present_perfect, present_progressive,* and *future*. Generally, the semantic strength of the past or perfect tense is higher than the present strength, as the past or perfect tense means that the event has occurred. We append a symbol A after t_i, i.e., t_i_A, to indicate that the labeled word is a relation indicating verb.

Figure 4 shows an example of the tense labeling result. In this example, the tense label "*null*" shows that the corresponding word is not a verb. "*future_A*" indicates that the labeled word group "*will acquire*" is a relation indicating verb of future tense.

SEMANTIC STRENGTH CLASSIFICATION OF SENTENCES

Most of traditional algorithms for relation extraction are focused on one Web page, e.g., a news page. However, a single Web page may not clearly describe an acquirement relation. Besides, the validness of the extracted relations will be much influenced by the unique properties of the Web page, such as the publication date. On the contrast, our algorithm is designed to treat a set of webpages. Particularly, we consider the semantic strength of all the sentences from different webpages that report some acquirement relation, and use a classification approach to determine the overall validness of the results.

The semantic strength of sentences is influenced by many factors. After a careful analysis on webpages, we choose the following factors to measure the semantic strength, which are the tense of *verb_A*, the tense of *key_verb*, entity type, and sentence pattern. The features used in the classification are shown in Table 1.

According to the features listed in Table 1, we first input them into the CRF model and classify the sentences into four categories, which are denoted as *label_-1, label_0, label_1,* and *label_2*. Different

Figure 4. Example of CRF-based tense labeling

Sample sentence: *"IBM will acquire Algotithmics."*

Word List	IBM	will	acquire	Algorithmics
Part of Speech	NNP	MD	VB	NNP
Tense Labeling	null	future_A		null

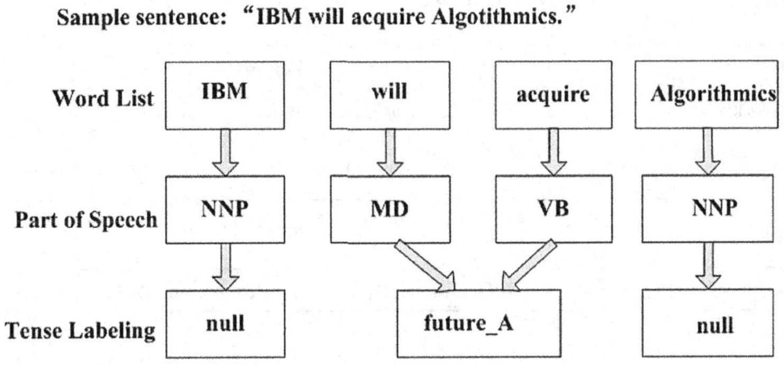

categories represent different semantic strength of the sentence for the extracted relation. Basically, *label_*-1 is of the weakest semantic strength, while *label_2* is of the highest. An example of semantic strength classification is shown in Table 2, where the features used are *<NE_type1, NE_type2, key verb, key verb tense, before word, before word tense, verb_A tense, positive number, negative number, Q>* whose meanings are listed in Table 1.

ACQUIREES RANKING

The acquriees ranking procedure is to conduct a ranking process on the extracted acquirees and return the top-k ones, so that we can get the most valid results and filter those incredible acquirement relations.

Definition 3: *Acquiree Grade.* For a company B in the list of extracted acquirees candidates, the grade of B is determined by the function *grade(B)*:

$$grade(B) = \sum_{i \in \{-1,0,1,2\}} \left(label\_i * count \left(label\_i \right) \right) \qquad (4)$$

Table 1. Features selected for classification

Symbol	Feature	Description
NE_type	Entity type	ORG, PERSON, LOCATION, OTHERS
verb_A	Relation Indicating verb	buy, acquire, bought, etc.
verb_A tense	The Tense of Relation Indicating verb	present_A, past_A, present_perfect_A, past_A, future_A, etc.
key verb	Key verb	The verb closest to verb_A
key verb tense	The tense of key verb	present, present_perfect, past, future, etc.
before word	The word located before the verb_A	The word located before the verb_A
before word tense	The tense of the before word	The tense of the before word
positive number	The count of positive words	agreement, announce, agree, etc.
negative number	The count of negative words	not, rumor, pending, refuse, etc.
Q	Question sentence	1 for question sentences, 0 for the opposite cases

Table 2. An example for semantic strength classification

Sentence	Features	Category
Oracle rumored to buy Algorithmics.	<ORG, ORG, rumored, past, to, null, present_A, 0, 1, 0>	*label_*-1
Oracle announced a definitive agreement to acquire Sun.	<ORG, ORG, announced, past, to, TO, present_A, 2, 0, 0>	*label_2*
Will Oracle buy Algorithmics?	<ORG, ORG, NULL, NULL, NULL, NULL, present_A, 0, 0, 1>	*label_0*
Oracle says to acquire Sun.	<ORG, ORG, says, present, to, To, present_A,0, 0, 0>	*label_1*

In Formula (4), we consider all the sentences that mention the company *B*. In particular, we sum up each category to get the total grade of B. For each category, we simple take *label_i* as *i* in the computation. *count(label_i)* is the total count of sentences that are classified as *label_i*.

For example, if there are 1000 sentences mentioning the company B, and 100 sentences are classified as *label_-1*, 200 sentences are *label_0*, 300 sentences are *label_1*, and 400 sentences are *label_2*, then the grade of B is: $grade(B) = (-1 * 100) + (0 * 200) + (1 * 300) + (2 * 400) = 1000$.

In order to filter those incredible acquirement relations, we suppose that acquirees that satisfy the following rule will be removed from the list.

$$\sum_{i \in \{-1,0\}} count(label\_i) \geq \sum_{i \in \{1,2\}} count(label\_i) \tag{5}$$

PERFORMANCE EVALUATION

In this section, we discuss the details of performance measurement. As there are a huge number of companies in the world, it is not feasible to involve all the companies in the experiment. Moreover, as only some giant companies may have a lot of acquirement actions, so we will focus on some specific companies such as IBM and Oracle in order to obtain a meaningful dataset.

Data Set

The dataset used in our experiment was collected via Google API in terms of the keyword-based queries. We used two types of queries to obtain the dataset: the first one is "Year + Company Name + buy", e.g., "2012 + IBM +buy", and the other is "Year + Company Name +acquire". There are six independent years used in our queries, namely 2007, 2008, 2009, 2010, 2011, and 2012. As some small companies have few acquirement actions, we manually select eight companies (Oracle, Microsoft, IBM, Google, HP, BP, Chevron, and BMW) and collect the related webpages of them. Those eight companies spread over different industries. For each company, we finally get 768 webpages. This is because the Google API can only return 64 pages each time, and we totally issue 12 queries for each company (one company, six years, two keywords) so as to obtain 12*64=768 webpages. Therefore, our dataset contains totally 6144 webpages. In the experiment, we extracted 4564 sentences for further company recognition and tense labeling, among which 2564 sentences were used as the training set while the other 2000 sentences were used for testing.

Although there exist other ways to prepare the dataset, our method is reasonable due to the duplication of information in the Web. For example, the information about IBM's buying Algorithmics may appear in many webpages, but with different words. From the perspective of acquirement relation extraction, we only need to find the valid relations but are not necessary to process all the involved webpages. This is not only time-consuming but also not practical as it is hard to crawl all the webpages mentioning the acquirement relations concerned.

Tense Labeling of Sentences

Our first experiment is to measure the performance of tense labeling. As we discussed in the previous sections, tense labeling is the foundation of our algorithm. Two metrics are used in the measurement, namely precision and recall.

To begin with, we label the 4564 sentences in the training set, and test the precision of the remaining 2564 sentences. In the experiment, we use the CRF++: Yet Another CRF Toolkit (CRF++, 2015) developed by Taku Kudo to conduct tense labeling. CRF++ is a simple, customizable, and open source implementation of CRF for labeling data. It has been demonstrated as one of the most effective implementation of CRF.

Table 3 shows the different precision and recalls of tense labeling for relation indicating verbs and key verbs as well as question sentences when using different features. In the experiment, we annotated 5220 verbs, among which 2080 verbs are relation indicating ones. This is because in some sentences there are two or more acquirement relations. Moreover, we extracted 150 question sentences.

The first column in Table 3, namely *Verb_Tense*, is the labeling precision and recall for the tense of verbs in sentences, the second column (*Verb_A_Tense*) shows the results for the tense labeling for relation indicating verbs, while the third column is the labeling results for question sentences. As Table 3 shows, we got the best performance for both *Verb_Tense* and *Verb_A_Tense* when using composed features. For the question sentences, as the symbol "?" can be easily distinguished from other verbs, so we got high precision and recall up to 100% when using the word sequence feature. However, the performance rapidly degraded when using the POS feature. This is due to the fault of the POS tagging tool (Stanford Postagging tool, 2015), in which the symbol "?" was tagged as ".". However, much other punctuation was also tagged as ".", which influenced the effectiveness of the CRF-base tense labeling.

Results on Semantic Strength Classification

To test the performance of semantic strength classification, we still use the manually annotated 4564 sentences. We randomly select 2564 sentences among them as the training set, and the rest are used for testing.

Table 4 shows the features used in this experiment and the results of semantic strength classification are described in Table 5. Based on the results in Table 5, we can choose the features with best performance of classification.

Table 3. Result of CRF-based tense labeling

TesneFeature	Verb_tense	Verb_A_tense	Q
Word Sequence	Recall = 73.87% Precision = 86.89%	Recall = 97.87% Precision = 99.46%	Recall = 100% Precision = 100%
POS (Part-Of-Speech)	Recall = 82.22% Precision = 82.54%	Recall = 83.51% Precision = 83.95%	Recall = 12.82% Precision = 100%
Word Sequence + POS	Recall = 94.87% Precision = 94.54%	Recall = 98.40% Precision = 99.46%	Recall = 100% Precision = 100%

Table 4. Features used in the experiment on semantic strength classification

Symbol	Features
S1	Entity type
S2	Word sequence
S3	Tense
S4	Positive and negative words
S5	S1+S2
S6	S1+S2+S3
S7	S1+S3+S4
S8	S1+S2+S3+S4

Table 5. Result of semantic strength of sentences

Feature	Correct	Wrong	Precision
S1	1133	867	56.68%
S2	1484	516	74.23%
S3	1705	295	85.27%
S4	1386	614	69.32%
S5	1557	443	77.83%
S6	1785	215	89.26%
S7	1896	104	94.78%
S8	1908	92	95.40%

As shown in Table 5, we got the best result of 85.27% precision when applying the S3 feature, i.e., the tense feature. When considering composed features such as S6, S7, and S8, we all got good performance, especially when using the S8 feature. Although the S7 feature also reached satisfied performance, it was a bit worse than the S8 feature due to the omission of the word sequence feature (S2) in S7.

Extracting Company Acquirement Relations

To measure the performance of the extraction on company acquirement relations, we asked two students in our university to evaluate the extracted results. The two students are required to first go to Wikipedia or the website of the extracted company to find corresponding acquirement relations. If not found, they are demanded to send a query like "A acquire B" or "A buy B" to Google and judge the validness of the acquirement relation based on the returned webpages by Google. The extracted acquirement relation is regarded as valid only if both of them agree on the relation; otherwise it is denoted as invalid.

In our experiment, we extracted 290 acquirees from the 6144 webpages, among which 268 are evaluated as valid ones. The acquirees that are wrongly detected all had low grades, which indicated that our ranking algorithm was feasible and effective. Table 6 shows the extracted top-5 acquirees for the eight given companies.

Table 6. Results on extracting company acquisition relations

Oracle	Microsoft	IBM	Google
RightNow	Skype	Algorithmics	Motorola Mobility
Endeca	*Facebook*	Q1 Labs	**Motorola**
FatWire	Hotmail	Platform Computing	Zagat
Sun	Visio	Micromuse	Neotonic Software
InQuira	WebTV Networks	DWL	Adscape Media

HP	BP	Chevron	BMW
Autonomy	ARCO	Atlas Energy	Husqvarna Motorcycles
Fortify	Sohio	Unocal	Hans Glas Company
ArcSight	Cellulosic Biofuels Unit	Texaco	Rover Group
Palm	Amoco	ex-Barrie Smith B8	John Cooper Works
EDS	Burmah-Castrol	*Reliance Petroleum*	Dixi Company

In the second column of Table 6, there is an acquirement relation between Microsoft and Facebook. This is because in our algorithm we remain the sentences mentioning partial acquirement relations. For example, the sentence "In 2007, Microsoft acquired a 1.6% stake in Facebook" indicates that there are partial acquirement relation between Microsoft and Facebook. This type of relations is finally extracted in our algorithm, which is emphasized with italic fonts, such as Facebook. Generally, the partial acquirement relations are also of competitive values. The wrongly detected acquirees are denoted with underline fonts, e.g., Motorola in the third column.

There is a very interesting phenomenon in our experiment. We find that the company Chevron has ambiguous names. In Wikipedia, it refers to an American energy company. However, Chevron is also a company engaging in car racing in England. For the American company, it has acquired Alas Energy and Unocal, while the English company has acquired other companies such as ex-Barrie Smith B8. This issue is somehow common in the Web. A possible way is to add a domain keyword into the Google search process, or to introduce a disambiguation procedure into the company recognition. We will advance this issue in our future work.

CONCLUSION AND FUTURE WORK

In this paper, we presented an effective algorithm to extract company acquirement relations from webpages. The main contribution of the paper was that we introduced the tense feature into the extraction of company acquirement relations. Specially, we used the CRF model to label the tense of sentences, and further applied the tense of sentences into the classification on the semantic strength of sentences. Based on the classification results, we conducted a ranking procedure and returned the top-k acquirees. Our experiments on real dataset crawled from Google demonstrated the effectiveness and efficiency of our approach.

There are a number of future works related with the study of this paper. First, as company acquirement relations are closely related with time and location information (Zhao et al., 2014; Lin et al., 2014; Zhao et al., 2010), it is worthy to extract the exact time and location information for company acquirement relations. Second, we will work on extracting other kinds of relations from the Web. Extracting the semantics of Web information has been an effort that has attracted a number of studies in recent years.

As many rich relationships exist among Web entities, it is helpful to extract such relations that can be used for decision making tasks. The company acquisition relationship studied in this paper is only one kind of semantic relations in the Web. There are many other relations that worth future studies, e.g., extracting the customer relationships from the Web and finding suppliers of a specific company in the Web. Finally, we will study the data quality of webpages, as incredible Web information will degrade the precision of the algorithm. Therefore, we need to develop an algorithm to evaluate the credibility of the extracted acquirement relation and further improve the effectiveness of our method.

ACKNOWLEDGMENT

This work is partially supported by the National Science Foundation of China under the grant (61672479 and 71273010) and the Doctor Start-up Fund of Anhui University. Peiquan Jin is the corresponding author.

REFERENCES

Agichtein, E., & Gravano, L. (2009). Snowball: extracting relations from large plain-text collections. In *Proc. of ICDL*, New York, NY (pp. 85-94).

Bollegala, D. T., Matsuo, Y., & Ishizuka, M. (2010). Relational duality: unsupervised extraction of semantic relations between entities on the web. In *Proceedings of the International Conference on World Wide Web*, Raleigh, North Carolina, April (pp. 151-160). 10.1145/1772690.1772707

Chan, Y. S., & Roth, D. (2010). Exploiting background knowledge for relation extraction. In *Proceedings of the 23rd International Conference on Computational Linguistics* (pp. 152-160).

Chen, Y., Zheng, Q., & Chen, P. (2015). Feature assembly method for extracting relations in Chinese. *Artificial Intelligence*, 228(C), 179-194. Retrieved from http://crfpp.googlecode.com/svn/trunk/doc/index.html

Culotta, A., & Sorensen, J. (2004), Dependency tree kernels for relation extraction. In *Proc. of ACL*, Barcelona, Spain (pp. 423-429).

García, M., & Gamallo, P. (2011). Evaluating various linguistic features on semantic relation extraction. *Proc. of RANLP*, Hissar, Bulgaria (pp. 721-726).

IBM. (2015), *Bring big data to the enterprise*. Retrieved from http://www-01.ibm.com/software/data/bigdata/

Kirschnick, J., Hemsen, H., & Markl, V. (2016). JEDI: Joint Entity and Relation Detection using Type Inference. In *Proceedings of the Annual Meeting of the Association for Computational Linguistics* (pp. 61-66). 10.18653/v1/P16-4011

Lafferty, J., McCallum, A., & Pereira, F. (2001). Conditional random fields: probabilistic models for segmenting and labeling sequence data. In *Proc. of ICML*, New York, NY (pp. 282-289).

Lin, S., Jin, P., Zhao, X., & Yue, L. (2014). Exploiting temporal information in Web search. *Expert Systems with Applications*, *41*(2), 331–341. doi:10.1016/j.eswa.2013.07.048

Liu, Y., Jin, P., & Yue, L. (2009). Extracting position relations from the web. In *Proc. of WIDM*, Hong Kong, China (pp. 59-62). 10.1145/1651587.1651601

Luan, M., Tsang, I. W., Ming, K., Chai, A., & Hai, L. C. (2014). Robust Domain Adaptation for Relation Extraction via Clustering Consistency. In *Proceedings of the 52nd Annual Meeting of the Association for Computational Linguistics* (pp. 807-817).

Ma, Z., Sheng, O. R. L., & Pant, G. (2009). Discovering company revenue relations from news: A network approach. *Decision Support Systems*, *4*(47), 408–414. doi:10.1016/j.dss.2009.04.007

Reichartz, F., Korte, H., & Paass, G. (2010). Semantic relation extraction with kernels over typed dependency trees. In *Proceedings of the 16th ACM SIGKDD International Conference on Knowledge Discovery and Data KDD'10* (pp. 773-782). 10.1145/1835804.1835902

Sha, F., & Pereira, F. (2003). Shallow parsing with conditional random fields. In *Proc. of NAACL*, Edmonton, Canada (pp. 134-141).

Stanford NER tool. (2015). Retrieved from http://nlp.stanford.edu/ner/index.shtml

Stanford Postagging Tool. (2015). Retrieved from http://nlp.stanford.edu/software/tagger.shtml

Sutton, C., & McCallum, A. (2006), An introduction to conditional random fields for relational learning, In L. Getoor & B. Taskar (Eds.), Introduction to Statistical Relational Learning. Cambridge: MIT Press.

Talaika, A., Biega, J., Amarilli, A., & Suchanek, F. (2015). IBEX: harvesting entities from the web using unique identifiers. In Proceedings of WebDB (pp. 13-19).

Tandon, N., Hariman, C., Urbani, J., Rohrbach, A., Rohrbach, M., & Weikum, G. (2016). Commonsense in parts: mining part-whole relations from the web and image tags. In *Proceedings of the Thirtieth AAAI Conference on Artificial Intelligence* (pp. 243-250).

Tresp, V., Overhage, J., Bundschus, M., Rabizadeh, S., Fasching, P., & Yu, S. (2016). Going digital: A survey on digitalization and large-scale data analytics in healthcare. *Proceedings of the IEEE*, *104*(11), 2180–2206. doi:10.1109/JPROC.2016.2615052

Valkanas, G., Lappas, T., & Gunopulos, D. (2017). Mining competitors from large unstructured datasets. *IEEE Transactions on Knowledge and Data Engineering*, *29*(9), 1971–1984. doi:10.1109/TKDE.2017.2705101

Wang, C., Fan, J., Kalyanpur, A., & Gondek, D. (2011). Relation extraction with relation topics. In *Proceedings of the International Conference on Empirical Methods in Natural Language Processing* (pp. 1426-1436).

Wang, L., Cao, Z., Melo, G. D., & Liu, Z. (2016). Relation Classification via Multi-Level Attention CNNs. In *Proceedings of the Annual Meeting of the Association for Computational Linguistics* (pp. 1298-1307).

Yap, W., & Baldwin, T. (2009). Experiments on pattern-based relation learning. In *Proceedings of the 18th ACM Conference on Information and Knowledge Management* (pp. 1657-1660).

Zelenko, D., Aone, C., & Richardella, A. (2003). Kernel methods for relation extraction. *Journal of Machine Learning Research*, *3*(6), 1083–1166.

Zhang, C., Hoffmann, R., & Weld, D. S. (2012). Ontological smoothing for relation extraction with minimal supervision. In *Proceedings of the Twenty-Sixth AAAI Conference on Artificial Intelligence* (pp. 157-163).

Zhang, M., Su, J., & Wang, D., Zhou, g., & Tan. C. (2005). Discovering relations from a large raw corpus using tree similarity based clustering. In *Proc. of IJCNLP*, Jeju Island, Korea (pp. 378-389).

Zhao, J., & Jin, P. (2009). *Towards the extraction of intelligence about competitor from the web*. In *Proc. of The Second World Summit on the Knowledge Society*, Crete, Greece (pp. 118–127). doi:10.1007/978-3-642-04754-1_13

Zhao, J., & Jin, P. (2010a). Conceptual modeling of the competitive intelligence hiding in the internet. *Journal of Software*, *5*(4), 378–386.

Zhao, J., Jin, P., & Liu, Y. (2010b). Business relations in the web: Semantics and a case study. *Journal of Software*, *5*(8), 826–833. doi:10.4304/jsw.5.8.826-833

Zhao, J., Jin, P., Zhang, Q., & Wen, R. (2014). Exploiting location information for web search. *Computers in Human Behavior*, *30*, 378–388. doi:10.1016/j.chb.2013.04.023

Zhao, X., Jin, P., & Yue, L. (2010). Automatic temporal expression normalization with reference time Dynamic-Choosing. In *Proc. of COLING*, Beijing, China (pp. 1498-1506).

Zhou, G. D., Su, J., Zhang, J., & Zhang, M. (2005). Exploring various knowledge in relation extraction. In *Proc. of ACL* (pp. 427-434).

Zhu, J., Nie, Z., Liu, X., Zhang, B., & Wen, J. R. (2009). StatSnowball: a statistical approach to extracting entity relationships. In *Proceedings of the International Conference on World Wide Web*, Madrid, Spain (pp. 101-110). 10.1145/1526709.1526724

Chapter 2

Executing, Comparing, and Reusing Linked–Data–Based Recommendation Algorithms With the *Allied* Framework

Cristhian Figueroa
Universidad Antonio Nariño, Colombia

Iacopo Vagliano
Leibniz Information Centre for Economics, Germany

Oscar Rodríguez Rocha
Université Côte d'Azur, France

Marco Torchiano
Politecnico di Torino, Italy

Catherine Faron Zucker
Université Nice Sophia Antipolis, France

Juan Carlos Corrales
Universidad del Cauca, Colombia

Maurizio Morisio
Politecnico di Torino, Italy

ABSTRACT

Data published on the web following the principles of linked data has resulted in a global data space called the Web of Data. These principles led to semantically interlink and connect different resources at data level regardless their structure, authoring, location, etc. The tremendous and continuous growth of the Web of Data also implies that now it is more likely to find resources that describe real-life concepts. However, discovering and recommending relevant related resources is still an open research area. This chapter studies recommender systems that use linked data as a source containing a significant amount of available resources and their relationships useful to produce recommendations. Furthermore, it also presents a framework to deploy and execute state-of-the-art algorithms for linked data that have been re-implemented to measure and benchmark them in different application domains and without being bound to a unique dataset.

DOI: 10.4018/978-1-5225-7186-5.ch002

Copyright © 2019, IGI Global. Copying or distributing in print or electronic forms without written permission of IGI Global is prohibited.

INTRODUCTION

The Web of Data has emerged as a way to make the Web machine-readable, relying on structured data that follow the Linked Data principles (Moyano, Sicilia, & Barriocanal, 2018). Thanks to the rise of the Web of Data, users are more likely to find resources that describe or represent real-life concepts.

However, due to the increase in the amount of structured data published on the Web, discovering and recommending related resources is still an open research area (Ricci, Rokach & Shapira, 2011). This problem can be addressed by analyzing the categories of resources, their explicit references to other resources and by combining both approaches (Figueroa, Vagliano, Rodríguez Rocha & Morisio, 2015). Accordingly, many works are addressing this problem, typically focusing on specific application domains and datasets. In contrast, we seek a solution which can fit more than one domain and dataset and we intend to generalize existing approaches. In this context, the research described in this chapter aims to answer the following research questions:

- How can we choose state-of-the-art algorithms for discovering and recommending resources from the web based on the characteristics of a given application domain and a given dataset?
- How can we benchmark the existing algorithms to select the one that best suits specific discovering and recommendation needs?
- How can we develop an algorithm that is dynamically adaptable to the characteristics of the dataset and independent of the application domain?

This chapter presents a framework named *AlLied* for deploying and executing recommendation algorithms based on Linked Data. This framework allows developers and researchers to test different configurations of these algorithms in a range of application domains and datasets. Additionally, *AlLied* provides a set of APIs to be exploited as the primary component for Recommender Systems (RS)' architectures: developers do not need to deal with the execution platform of the algorithms but only focus their efforts either on selecting the algorithm that best fits their needs or on writing a customized one.

After conducting an in-depth analysis of the state-of-the-art recommendation algorithms executed in *AlLied*, the authors proposed a generic resource discovery and recommendation algorithm named ReDyAl which dynamically adapts itself to the characteristics of the dataset and the application domain.

This chapter additionally provides an overview of the research problem in discovering and recommending resources as well as the various existing types of RS. It gives a detailed review of the Linked Data based RS and summarizes the results of an evaluation of ReDyAl deployed in the *AlLied* framework. Finally, this chapter shows how it is possible to choose the more appropriate state-of-the-art resource recommendation algorithms for a given application domain and dataset by measuring its performance and accuracy.

BACKGROUND

Recommendation Problem

The recommendation problem is finding an item which maximizes the utility of the item for a given user. A formal definition is described in Equation 1 (Adomavicius & Tuzhilin, 2005).

$$\forall u \in U i^{\mathrm{max},u} = \arg\max_{i \in I} f\left(i, u\right) \tag{1}$$

U is the set of users considered by the recommender system and *I* the set of items; they can be both extremely large. The utility function f: $U \times I \rightarrow R$ represents the usefulness of an item $i \in I$ for a given user $u \in U$, where R is a totally ordered set (e.g. nonnegative numbers within a given range).

The utility of an item is often represented by a rating, which indicates how a particular user liked a given item (Di Noia & Ostuni, 2015). For instance, a user gave the movie *The Green Mile* the rating 4 out of 5. The utility is not defined on the whole $U \times I$ space, but only a subset is available. In fact, only a portion of ratings is known for each user. Thus, a recommender system has to assess the utility function from the available data and use it to predict unknown values. Typically, the recommendations are provided by selecting for each user the best *N* items, i.e. the items with the highest utility (top-*N* recommendations).

Recommendation Techniques

Recommender Systems (RS) are software tools and techniques to suggest items or objects (films, music, news, people, messages, etc.) (Ricci, Rokach, & Shapira, 2011). The most popular classes of RS are content-based, collaborative filtering, knowledge-based, and hybrid. Content-based algorithms provide recommendations to a user based on their previous preferences and the content of items (e.g., keywords, size, pixels, genre, etc.) (Lops, Gemmis, & Semeraro, 2011). Collaborative-filtering (CF) approaches consider the ratings that users with similar preferences gave to the same items (Felfernig, Jeran, Ninaus, Reinfrank, & Reiterer, 2013). Knowledge-based infer similarities between user requirements and items' features described in a knowledge base (Dell'Aglio, Celino, & Cerizza, 2010). Hybrid techniques combine one or more approaches to compensate weaknesses of single methods. For example, CF methods suffer from the issue known as "new user," which is the difficulty of generating recommendations because of the lack or insufficiency of ratings that a new user may have issued. This problem, however, is not a limitation for content-based methods since the prediction of the new items is not focused on user ratings but the description of the features of these items (Ricci et al., 2011).

Knowledge-based RS have some advantages over other types (Dell'Aglio et al., 2010). First, these algorithms require few information about user profiles. Second, they are less subject to the "cold start" problem (new users or items do not contain enough ratings) (Tomeo, Fernández-Tobías, Cantador, & Di Noia, 2017). Third, they can explain recommendations. The main problems of knowledge-based RS are the significant computational complexity due to the processing of large amounts of data, and the high effort required to construct and maintain the knowledge base. Furthermore, the knowledge base depends on the application domain and may require frequent updates.

A new kind of knowledge-based RS known as "linked data-based RS" (Figueroa, Vagliano, Rodrí-guez Rocha, & Morisio, 2015), or semantics-aware RS (de Gemmis, Lops, Musto, Narducci, Semeraro, 2015; Di Noia & Ostuni, 2015), has emerged. These RS suggest items relying on datasets published on the Web of Data (Damljanovic, Stankovic, & Laublet, 2012). Unlike traditional knowledge-based RS, linked data-based RS use datasets built, modeled, and maintained by different organizations and communities around the world. These datasets may contain knowledge from different domains and sources in the Web of Data. Linked data-based RS still struggle to generate recommendations with an acceptable accuracy for end users. The causes include the need for information from both user profiles and descriptions of the items; the necessity of knowledge bases to be frequently updated and maintained; high computational complexity; and the required manual extraction of a subset of the knowledge bases representing a portion specialized on a domain of interest.

More research on how to apply the different techniques of RS and the web of data in real-world situations is required (Musto, Lops, de Gemmis, & Semeraro, 2017; Park, Kim, Choi, & Kim, 2012). The main objective of the work addressed in this chapter is to develop a linked data-based RS to recommend resources dynamically analyzing their relationships and considering the knowledge of the Web of Data.

RELATED WORK

This work classifies the related studies into four main types based on their recommendation algorithms: graph-based, machine learning, memory-based, and probabilistic. Though, there are also other methods that are less used.

Graph-Based Methods

The Web of Data can be analyzed from the perspective of its graph structure (Moyano et al., 2018). Graph-based algorithms exploit this structure for computing relevance scores for items represented as nodes in a graph. Algorithms in this category are classified into semantic exploration and path-based.

- *Semantic Exploration* techniques explore the graph structure of datasets using structural relationships to compute distances and generate recommendations. For example, *HyProximity* (Damljanovic et al., 2012) exploits hierarchical links among Wikipedia categories in DBpedia, while dbRec (Kitaya, Huang, & Kawagoe, 2012; Passant, 2010a; Yang et al., 2013) is a music recommender system, which mainly relies on the number of direct and indirect links between two resources. ReDyAl (Vagliano et al., 2016) combines these two approaches and generalize them to be applied to any dataset and domain. Other methods are based on page rank (Blanco, Cambazoglu, Mika, & Torzec, 2013; Narducci, Musto, Semeraro, Lops, & de Gemmis, 2013; Nguyen et al., 2015), semantic clustering (Ko, Kim, Ko, & Chang, 2014), feature selection (Musto, Basile, Lops, de Gemmis, & Semeraro, 2017), and the Vector Space Model (VSM) (Khrouf & Troncy, 2013; Narducci et al., 2013; Ostuni et al., 2013).
- *Path-based* algorithms use information about semantic paths within a graph structure to compute similarities useful to produce recommendations. For example, spreading activation (Cheekula,

Kapanipathi, Doran, & Jain, 2015; Chicaiza, Piedra, López-Vargas, & Tovar-Edmundo, 2014; Hajra, Latif, & Tochtermann, 2014; Marie, Gandon, Legrand, & Ribière, 2013), random walk (Cantador, Konstas, & Jose, 2011); path-weights for vertex discovery (Strobin & Niewiadomski, 2014). Modern methods combine machine learning to learn the best path to consider relying on learning to rank (Di Noia, Ostuni, Tomeo, & Di Sciascio, 2016) or deep learning (Palumbo, Rizzo, & Troncy, 2017; Rosati, Ristoski, Di Noia, De Leone, & Paulheim, 2016) techniques.

Machine Learning

These algorithms use techniques to analyze, predict and classify data extracted from datasets. This allows them to learn from data to produce recommendations. Algorithms in this type are classified in Supervised learning and unsupervised learning (Portugal, Alencar, & Cowan, 2018):

- **Supervised Learning:** A model is prepared through a training process and correct answers to produces predictions (Welling, 2011). These algorithms predict class labels from attributes. For example, kNN (Ahn & Amatriain, 2010; Ristoski, Loza Mencía, Paulheim, & Menc, 2014), decision trees (Khrouf & Troncy, 2013; Ostuni, Di Noia, Di Sciascio, & Mirizzi, 2013; Ristoski et al., 2014), logistic regression (Moreno et al., 2014; Narducci et al., 2013; Ostuni et al., 2013; Zhang, Wu, Sorathia, & Prasanna, 2014), Support Vector Machines (SVM) (Di Noia, Mirizzi, Ostuni, & Romito, 2012; Kushwaha & Vyas, 2014; Ostuni, Di Noia, Mirizzi, Di Sciascio, & Noia, 2014), random forest (Narducci et al., 2013; Ostuni et al., 2013), naive Bayes (Schmachtenberg, Strufe, & Paulheim, 2014) and bayesian classifiers (Lopes, Leme, Nunes, & Casanova, 2014).
- **Unsupervised Learning:** Unlike in the supervised learning, input data is not labelled and does not have a known result, so the aim of these algorithms is to try to discover the structure or distribution of the data (Welling, 2011). For example, K-Means (Manoj Kumar, Anusha, & Santhi Sree, 2015; Moreno et al., 2014), fuzzy-C means, self-organizing map (SOM); principal component analysis (PCA) (V. V. Ostuni et al., 2014).

Memory-Based

Memory-based algorithms recommends items based on the entire collection of previously rated path queries. For example, rating prediction (Kushwaha & Vyas, 2014; Moreno et al., 2014; Narducci et al., 2013); singular value decomposition (SVD) (Ko & Son, 2015; Moreno et al., 2014; Rowe, 2014); implicit feedback; and matrix factorization (Lommatzsch, Kille, Albayrak, & Berlin, 2013).

Probabilistic

These algorithms exploit probabilistic techniques applied to linked data such as Latent Dirichlet Allocation (LDA) (Hopfgartner & Jose, 2010; Khrouf & Troncy, 2013; Zhang et al., 2014), Random Indexing (RI) (Damljanovic et al., 2012), Bayesian ranking (Lopes, André et al., 2014), and beta probability distribution (Maccatrozzo, Ceolin, Aroyo, & Groth, 2014).

Others

Other types of algorithms exist. For example, evolutionary computation, automated planning, semantic reasoning, social network analysis (SNA), and text mining on user review.

- **Evolutionary Computation:** This class include stochastic methods inspired from natural evolution such as genetic algorithm (Khrouf & Troncy, 2013; Lommatzsch, Kille, Albayrak et al., 2013), biological classification (Chawuthai, Takeda, & Hosoya, 2015) and particle swarm optimization (Juang, Tung, & Chiu, 2011).
- **Automated Planning:** These methods use artificial intelligence to create strategies that are executed by intelligent agents such as (Gordea, Lindley, & Graf, 2011).
- **Semantic Reasoning:** These techniques are based on rules to infer logical consequences from a set of asserted facts or axioms (Calì, Capuzzi, Dimartino, & Frosini, 2013; Cantador, Castells, & Bellogín, 2011; Ozdikis, Orhan, & Danismaz, 2011). Some approaches combine reasoning with context-awareness (Karpus, Vagliano, & Goczyła, 2017; Karpus, Vagliano, Goczyła, & Morisio, 2016).
- **Social Network Analysis:** These algorithms exploit relationships found in social networks related to items and users (Lopes, André, et al., 2014; Lopes, Leme et al., 2014).
- **Semantic Annotation of User Review:** New approaches are emerging, which combine semantic annotation of user reviews with additional information from the Linked Data cloud (Vagliano, Monti, Morisio, & Scherp).

Linked data-based RS still have some issues. Graph-based algorithms for RS suffer from high computational complexity for exploiting semantic features due to the large data and inconsistency of datasets (Damljanovic et al., 2012; Passant, 2010a). Machine learning algorithms are time-consuming for the training phase, and some of them only use linked data just for representation, so they do not take into account the intrinsic semantic structure of datasets (Arturo et al., 2014; Ostuni et al., 2013; Ristoski et al., 2014). Other algorithms require user's profile information to produce recommendations, they suffer from the cold-start problem (Kushwaha & Vyas, 2014; Lommatzsch, Kille, & Albayrak, 2013; Moreno et al., 2014). Finally, existing hybrid recommendation techniques are not organized in a conceptual architecture based on their functionalities. This conceptual architecture would be useful to execute and test various configurations of algorithms for creating novel RS (Lommatzsch, Kille, & Albayrak, 2013; Lommatzsch, Kille, Kim, & Albayrak, 2013; Moreno et al., 2014).

AlLied: A FRAMEWORK FOR EXECUTING RESOURCE RECOMMENDATION ALGORITHMS BASED ON LINKED DATA

AlLied is a framework to select, evaluate, and create algorithms to recommend resources from Linked Data belonging to different application domains. This framework integrates the algorithms to execute specific tasks in the process of recommendation (i.e., resource generation, ranking, categorization, and presentation). Accordingly, the framework is suitable to compare the results of different configurations of these algorithms and to enable the development of innovative applications on top of it.

The work described in this chapter focuses on algorithms that rely only on linked data, but it is not limited to them. In fact, developers can extend it to consider other approaches in combination with Linked Data. The recommendation process of *AlLied* is shown in Figure 1.

- **Resource Generation:** The first step is intended to generate a set of candidate resources (CR) that maintain semantic relationships with an initial resource (IR). The semantic relations may be direct or indirect links between two resources in a dataset.
- **Results Ranking:** This step sorts the candidate resources generated in the previous one by considering the semantic similarity with the initial resource. Different semantic similarity measures can be used to calculate the semantic similarity between pairs of resources.
- **Grouping:** The list of ranked candidate resources generated in the previous step may be too general, that is, a recommendation may include resources from unrelated domains of knowledge. For this reason, this optional third step groups these resources already ranked into meaningful clusters that represent common knowledge domains.
- **Results Presentation:** Finally, the results of the last step are graphically presented through different facets to allow the end-users to visualize the recommendations.

Implementation

The framework *AlLied* is composed of three subsystems (Figure 2):

- **KB Management:** Is related to the Knowledge Base Layer as it provides the interfaces needed to access to local or remote Linked Data datasets. The components of this subsystem include 1) a query controller to execute queries on the local/remote datasets; 2) a category tree which is a hierarchical structure that allows the algorithms to perform hierarchical-dependent operations; and 3) local and remote datasets which are the source of the structured data.
- **RS Management:** Not only provides mechanisms for retrieving, searching, discovering and ranking resources, but also performs management tasks such as creating new connections to other remote/local datasets. It contains the main components of the RS as it is the central subsystem. It also controls the execution process of the RS. This subsystem includes the RS Executor to control the execution of recommendation algorithms, the Dataset manager to access the functionalities provided by the KB Management, the RS Controller to manage the recommendation algorithms as well as the datasets of the KB Management subsystem.

Figure 1. Steps of the recommendation process.
Source: (Figueroa et al., 2017)

Figure 2. Diagram of the implementation of the AlLied framework.
Source (Figueroa, 2017)

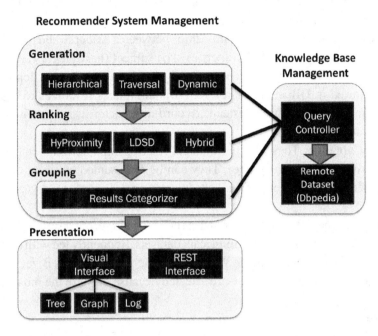

- **RS Presentation:** this subsystem provides the user interface.

Each subsystem contains functional components. These functional components are located in a set of layers for each subsystem conforming to their functionality. For example, the layers generation, ranking, and grouping are responsible for the recommender system management activities, and the knowledge base core layer oversees accessing the datasets and the presentation layer for showing the results to the users.

Knowledge Base Management

This subsystem represents the data layer of the *AlLied* framework. It is the primary data source containing knowledge about resources and their structural relationships. The knowledge base may be a tuple (R, T, L).composed of resources (R), categories (T), and links (L):

- **Resources:** Are representation of real-world ideas and objects such as persons, cities, movies, or topics.
- **Categories:** Are classes which hierarchically group resources. For instance, DBpedia provides information about the hierarchical relationships in three different classification schemata: Wikipedia Categories, YAGO Categories[1], and WordNet Synset Links[2]. This implementation uses the Wikipedia categories to describe the hierarchical information of resources and their relationships. Wikipedia categories are concepts of the Simple Knowledge Organization System (*SKOS*[3]) vocabulary.
- **Relationships:** Are the links (also known as properties) connecting resources or categories along the whole dataset. Any knowledge base may contain three types of relationships.

- ◦ **Resource-Resource:** These are the traversal relationships between resources, which are those links between resources that do not refer to hierarchical classifications. Most of the links of DBpedia belong to this type.
- ◦ **Resource-Category:** These are relationships between a resource and a category. They can be represented by using the SKOS properties skos:subject (hasCategory) and skos:isSubjectOf (IsCategoryOf). However, skos:subject and skos:isSubjectOf are deprecated and consequently not used in DBpedia. Therefore, DBpedia relates resources to their Wikipedia categories using dcterms:subject instead. Accordingly, dcterms:subject is used in AlLied for both relationships.
- ◦ **Category-Category:** These are hierarchical relationships between categories within a hyponymy structure (a category tree). They can be represented by using the SKOS properties skos:broader (isSubCategoryOf) and skos:narrower (isSuperCategoryOf).

By default, AlLied uses the DBpedia dataset as the knowledge base, but developers can easily extend it to other datasets. DBpedia is one of the most significant datasets, frequently fed with data from Wikipedia, and one of the most interlinked datasets in the Web of Data (Schmachtenberg, Bizer, & Paulheim, 2014). The Wikipedia categories (SKOS concepts) were selected because they are the most linked in DBpedia.

Generation Layer

This layer aims at discovering resources related to a given one through semantic relationships. Given an initial resource (or a set of initial ones) it generates a set of candidate resources located at a predefined distance. For this layer, three generators were implemented based on the semantic relationships found in the Linked Data through SPARQL queries (Ayala, Przyjaciel-Zablocki, Hornung, Schätzle, & Lausen, 2014).

Traversal Generator

The Traversal generator looks for resources that are directly related to a given initial resource and those found through a third resource (indirect relationships). Its implementation is inspired in the *dbrec* recommender (Passant, 2010b).

Hierarchical Generator

The hierarchical generator generates a set of candidate resources located at a specified distance in a hierarchy of categories taken from a category tree described in a dataset. The implementation of this module is inspired by (Damljanovic et al., 2012), which obtains candidate resources navigating a tree of Wikipedia categories.

The hierarchical generator firstly extracts categories of an initial resource (<inURI>) and then looks for broader categories until a maximum distance (which may be user-defined) is reached. This maximum distance is the hierarchical distance of a broader category from its base categories. It is inversely proportional to the specificity of a category (the higher the distance the lower the specificity of a category).

After extracting categories, this module retrieves subcategories for all the broader categories at maximum distance (it descends one level into the category tree) to increase the possibility for finding more candidate resources. Then, the algorithm obtains candidate resources for each category (including sub-categories). Therefore, the module creates a "category graph", including the initial resource, its category tree, and the candidate resources retrieved for each category. For example, *Figure 3* shows an example of the category graph for the resource <http://dbpedia.org/resource/Mole_Antonelliana>.

Dynamic Generator

It is a "hybrid" generator, which takes advantage of both the traversal and the hierarchical approaches, giving priority to the existing interlinking between resources, that is, one of the four principles of Linked Data (Bizer, Heath, & Berners-Lee, 2009). The innovative algorithm of this generator is explained in section *A Dynamic Algorithm for Recommendation.*

Ranking Layer

This layer uses semantic similarity functions to rank the candidate resources obtained in the previous layer. This layer sorts the candidate resources according to the values of a semantic similarity function, which measures the similarity between the initial resource and each candidate resource. The framework in its current implementation includes (but is not limited to) three ranking algorithms.

Figure 3. Example of a category graph for the resource "Mole Antonelliana" (candidate resources are not included for space reasons).
Source (Figueroa et al., 2017)

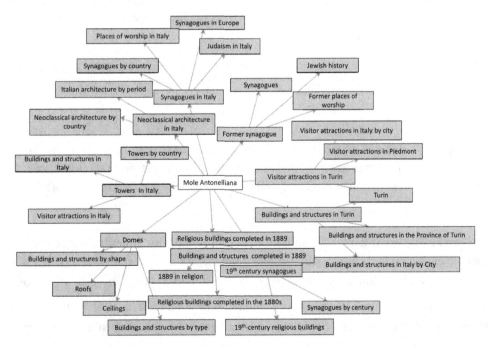

Traversal LDSD Ranking

The traversal LDSD ranking algorithm calculates the Linked Data Semantic Distance *(LDSD)* This measure that was initially proposed by (Passant, 2010a), is based on the number of indirect and direct links between two resources. The similarity of two resources $\left(r_1, r_2\right)$ is measured in Equation (2) as the basic form of the *LDSD* distance.

$$LDSD\left(r_1, r_2\right) = \frac{1}{1 + Cd_{out} + Cd_{in} + Ci_{out} + Ci_{in}} \tag{2}$$

In the LDSD equation, Cd_{out} is the number of direct input links (from r_1 to r_2), Cd_{in} is the number of direct output links, Ci_{in} is the number of indirect input links, and Ci_{out} is the number of indirect output links.

Unlike the implementation developed by Passant, which is limited to links from a specific domain, the LDSD function implemented in *AlLied* considers all resources from the dataset. However, it can be customized to defined types of links belonging or not to a specific domain by adding a set of *forbidden links*. Two SPARQL queries count direct and indirect input and output links between an initial resource and a resource of the set of candidate resources.

HyProximity Ranking

The *HyProximity* ranking algorithm is based on the similarity measure defined by (Stankovic, Breitfuss, & Laublet, 2011). This measure can be used to calculate both traversal and hierarchical similarities. The *HyProximity* in its general form is shown in Equation (3) as the inverted distance between two resources, balanced with a pondering function.

$$hyP\left(r_1, r_2\right) = \frac{p\left(r_1, r_2\right)}{d\left(r_1, r_2\right)} \tag{3}$$

In this equation, d is the distance function between two resources and p is a weighting function used to give a level of importance to different distances. Based on the structural relationships (hierarchical and traversal), different distances and weighting functions may be used to calculate the *HyProximity* similarity.

- **Hierarchical HyProximity:** The definition of this similarity function relies on the work of (Stankovic et al., 2011). It was calculated using the maximum distance of categories of the hierarchical generator algorithm such that: $d\left(ir, cr_i\right) = \max Level$. Here ir is the initial resource and cr_i is each one of the candidate resources generated in the hierarchical algorithm. The weighting function is defined in Equation (4), which is an adaptation of the informational content function

(Seco, Veale, & Hayes, 2004). In this equation, $hypo(C)$ is the number of descendants of category C and C is the total number of categories in the category Graph of C.

$$p(C) = 1 - \frac{\log(hypo(C) + 1)}{\log(C)} \tag{4}$$

- ○ This function was selected because it minimizes the complexity of calculation of the informational content with regard to other functions that employ an external corpus (Hadj Taieb, Ben Aouicha, Tmar, & Hamadou, 2011).
- **Traversal HyProximity:** In this similarity function $d(ir, cr_i) = \max Level$ if the generator of resources is hierarchical, otherwise $d(ir, cr_i) = 1$ for resources connected to the initial resource through direct traversal links or $d(ir, cr_i) = 2$ for indirect traversal links. The weighting function is defined in Equation (5): $p_{trav}(r_1, r_2)$ depends on the number of resources n connected over a specific property and the total number of resources of the dataset, M.

$$p_{trav}(r_1, r_2) = -\log\frac{n}{M} \tag{5}$$

Nonetheless, in *AlLied*, this algorithm is not limited to a specific property, and optionally can be configured to support a set of forbidden links or allowed links in a similar way as shown in the *Generation Layer*. The number of direct and indirect links was calculated with SPARQL queries. The value of M was fixed to the number of resources contained in DBpedia.

Grouping Layer

Since this implementation of the framework relies on DBpedia, which is a general-purpose dataset, the results obtained may contain an inherent ambiguity due to the generality of the data used to produce recommendations. Moreover, a single ranked list of recommendations may not always be an excellent way to show this kind of general results because users may require results arranged according to their personal needs or knowledge domain. The grouping layer addressed this requirement, because it provides mechanisms to group the results obtained from the ranking layer into meaningful clusters that represent domains of knowledge.

Currently, the grouping layer relies on Algorithm 1 (Box 1). This algorithm provides a mechanism to efficiently clusters the recommended items. Although in the current implementation of *AlLied* the resulting clusters correspond to Wikipedia categories, custom clusters can be easily defined by aggregating many categories or relying on other category schemas, such as YAGO categories.

Algorithm 1 receives as input a set of ranked candidate resources (CR), an initial resource $inURI$ and optionally an initial category graph (Gc_{in}) if the latter is already available. If Gc_{in} is not given, then the algorithm creates a new category graph Gc containing categories for the initial resource and the set of candidate resources until a maximum distance $(\max Level)$ (Lines 1 - 5). In this implementation

Box 1. Hierarchical classification algorithm

Require:	*CR, inURI, maxLevel*, optionally Gc_{in}
Insure:	A Category graph G_c
1.	**if** $Gc_{in} = null$ **then**
2.	$Gc = createCategoryGraph(CR, MaxLevel)$
3.	**else**
4.	$Gc = Gc_{in}$
5.	**end if**
6.	$C_{maxLevel} = getMaxLevelCategories(Gc)$
7.	**for each** pair of categories $(c_i, c_j) \in C_{maxLevel}$ **do**
8.	$C_{lcb} = getLesCommonBroaderCategory(c_i, c_j)$
9.	Add c_{lcb} to Gc
10.	Add edge (c_i, c_{lcb}) and edge (c_j, c_{lcb}) to Gc
11.	**end for**
12.	intersectCategories (Gc)
13.	*deleteEmptyCategories(Gc)*
13.	**return** Gc

(Source: Figueroa et al., 2017)

$\max Level$ is set to 2 because with this value it is possible to obtain a reasonable relationship between the number of categories and the time consumed.

Afterward, the algorithm extracts categories at the highest distance $\left(C_{maxLevel}\right)$ and creates pairs of categories combining the elements of $C_{\max Level}$ (Lines 6 - 7). Next, the function *getLessCommonBroaderCategory*, which is based on the less common ancestor, is executed to find a set of broader categories subsuming the categories of $C_{\max Level}$. These new broader categories are then added to Gc including their edges, i.e. $\left(c_i, c_{lcb}\right)$ and $\left(c_j, c_{lcb}\right)$ (Lines 8 - 11).

Presentation Layer

Developers can easily integrate *AlLied* to any application that requires recommendations based on linked data. The current implementation includes three main interfaces that provide mechanisms to present results to the final user: a web interface, a standalone interface, and a RESTful interface. These are described elsewhere (Vagliano et al., 2016; Figueroa, 2017).

A DYNAMIC ALGORITHM FOR RECOMMENDATION

ReDyAl (Vagliano et al., 2016) is an algorithm that was developed considering the different types of relationships between data published according to the Linked Data principles. It aims to discover related resources from datasets that may contain either "well-linked" resources as well as "poor-linked" resources. A resource is said to be "well-linked" if it has many links higher than the average number of links in the dataset; otherwise, it is "poor-linked." The algorithm can dynamically adapt its behavior to find a set of candidate resources to be recommended, giving priority to the implicit knowledge contained in the Linked Data relationships.

The execution of *ReDyAl* contains three stages: 1) discovering related resources by analyzing the interlinking between them; 2) Examining the categorization of the given initial resource and discovering similar resources located in common categories; and 3) intersecting the results of the previous stages, given priority to those found in the first stage.

Figure 4 shows a flowchart of the *ReDyAl* algorithm, which receives as input an initial resource by specifying its corresponding URI $\left(inURI\right)$, and three values ($\min T$, $\min C$, $\max Dis\tan ce$) for configuring its execution. $\min T$ is the minimum number of links (or triples involving the initial resource) to consider a resource as "well-linked" If the initial resource is "well linked", traversal interlinking has a higher priority in the generation of candidate resources, otherwise the algorithm gives priority to the hierarchical relationships. $\min C$ is the minimum number of candidate resources that the algorithm is expected to generate, while $\max Distance$ limits the distance (number of hierarchical levels) that the algorithm considers in the category tree. The value of $\max Distance$ may be defined

Figure 4. Flowchart of ReDyAl.
Source (Figueroa et al., 2017)

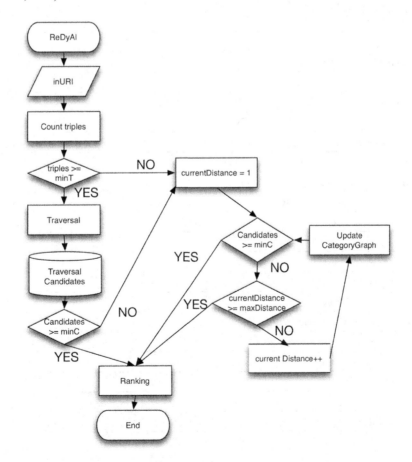

manually and it is useful when there are not enough candidate resources from the categories found at a certain distance (i.e., the number of candidate resources retrieved is lower than *minC*). In this case, the algorithm increases the distances to find more resources, and if the *maxDistance* value is reached with less than *minC* candidate resources, the algorithm ranks only the candidate resources found until that moment. Additionally, the algorithm may receive a list of "forbidden links" (*FL*) to avoid searching for candidate resources over a predefined list of undesired links.

ReDyAl (Algorithm 2 [Box 2]) starts by retrieving a list of allowed links from the initial resource. Allowed links are those that are not specified as forbidden $\left(FL\right)$ and that are explicitly defined in the initial resource. If there is a considerable number of allowed links, i.e., the initial resource is well-linked,

Box 2. ReDyAl algorithm

Require:	*inURI, minT, minC, FL, maxDistance*
Ensure:	A set of candidate resources *CR*
1.	$L_{in} = readAllowedLinks(inURI, FL)$
2.	**if** $|L_{in}| \geq minT$ **then**
3.	**for all** $l_k \in L_{in}$ **do**
4.	$DR_{lk} = getDirectResources(l_k)$
5.	$IR_{lk} = getIndirectResources(l_k)$
6.	**Add** DR_{pk} **to** CR_{tr}
7.	**Add** CR_{pk} **to** CR_{tr}
8.	**end for**
9.	**if** $|CR_{tr}| \geq minC$ **then**
10.	**return** CR_{tr}
11.	**else**
12.	$currentDistance = 1$
13.	$Gc = createCategoryGraph (inURI, currentDistance)$
14.	**while** $currentDistance \leq maxDistance$ **do**
15.	$Cr_{hi} = getCandidateResources(Gc)$
16.	**if** $|CR_{hi}| \geq minC$ **then**
17.	Add CR_{tr} and CR_{hi} to CR
18.	**return** CR
19.	**end if**
20.	increase *currentDistance*
21.	$updateCategoryGraph(currentDistance)$
22.	**end while**
23.	Add CR_{tr} and CR_{hi} to CR
24.	**end if**
25.	**end if**
26.	**return** CR

Source (Figueroa et al., 2017)

the algorithm obtains a set of candidate resources located through direct $\left(DR_{l_k} \right)$ or indirect links $\left(IR_{l_k} \right)$ (Lines 1-8). Next, the algorithm counts the number of candidate resources generated until this point $\left(CR_{tr} \right)$, and if it is greater than or equal to $\min C$ the execution terminates returning the results (Lines 9-10). Otherwise, the algorithm generates a category graph $\left(Gc \right)$ with categories of the first distance. Subsequently, it applies iterative updates on the categories at a distance n from the initial resource to obtain broader categories until at least one of two conditions is fulfilled: either, the number of candidate resources is enough $\left(CR > \min C \right)$, or the maximum distance is reached $\left(currentDistance > \max Distance \right)$. At each iteration, candidate resources $\left(CR_{hi} \right)$ are extracted from the broader categories of maximum distance (Lines 14- 23). In any case the algorithm combines these results with the results obtained in Lines $3 - 8$ (Adding CR_{tr} and CR_{hi} to CR). Finally, the set CR of candidate results is returned (Line 26).

EVALUATION

AlLied enables the comparative evaluation of any new algorithm to state-of-the-art algorithms. Using *AlLied*, the *ReDyAl* algorithm was evaluated concerning accuracy and novelty. This evaluation aimed to answer the following questions:

RQ1: Which of the considered algorithms is more accurate?
RQ2: Which of the considered algorithms provides the highest number of novel recommendations?

This section compares *ReDyAl* with algorithms that rely exclusively on Linked Data to produce recommendations.

Experiment

A user study was conducted involving 109 participants. The participants were mainly students of Politecnico di Torino (Italy) and University of Cauca (Colombia) enrolled in IT courses. The average age of the participants was 24 years old and they were 91 males, 14 females, and 4 did not provide any information about their sex. Although the proposed algorithm is not bounded to any particular domain, this evaluation was focused on movies because in this domain a quite large amount of data is available on DBpedia. Additionally, finding participants was not too difficult, since no specific skills are required to be able to express an opinion about movies. The evaluation was conducted as follows. A list of 20 recommendations generated from a given initial movie was presented to the participants. For each recommendation two questions were asked:

Q1: Did you already know this recommendation? Possible answers were yes, yes but I haven't seen it (if it is a movie) and no.
Q2: Is it related to the movie you have chosen? Possible answers were I strongly agree, I agree, I don't know, I disagree, I strongly disagree. Each answer was assigned respectively a score from 5 to 1.

Each list of 20 recommendations was pre-computed. Recommendations were generated for each of the 45 initial movies with the four different algorithms implemented within *AlLied*. Then, the recommendations generated by each algorithm were merged in a list of 20 recommendations to be shown to the participants.

The authors developed a website[4] to collect the answers from the participants. The participants were able to choose an initial movie from a list of 45 movies selected from the IMDB[5] top 250 list. The first 50 movies were considered, and five movies were excluded because they were not available in DBpedia. When a participant selected an initial movie, the tool provided the corresponding list of recommendations with the questions mentioned above. Participants were able to evaluate recommendations from as many initial movies as they wanted. As a result, the recommendations of the lists for 40 out of 45 initial movies were evaluated by at least one participant and each movie was evaluated by an average of 6.18 participants. The dataset with the initial movies and the lists of recommendations is available online[6].

About the questions stated at the beginning of this section, to answer RQ1, the Root Mean Squared Error (RMSE) (Shani & Gunawardana, 2011) was computed and to answer RQ2 the ratio between the number of evaluations. For the RMSE measure, scores given by the participants were normalized in the interval [0, 1] and considered as a reference. Then these scores were compared with the similarities computed by each algorithm, since each algorithm ranks its recommendations by using its own semantic similarity function.

RESULTS

The results of the evaluation are summarized in Figure 5, which compares the algorithms to their RMSE and novelty.

The "sweet spot" area represents the conditions in which an algorithm has a good trade-off between novelty and prediction accuracy. In effect, presenting a high number of recommendations not known to the user is not necessarily good because it may prevent him to assess the quality of the recommendations: for example, having in the provided recommendation a movie which he has seen and which he liked may increase the trust of the user in the RS.

Concerning the RQ1, *HyProximity* accounted the lowest RMSE measures (with 25% and about 36% for the hierarchical and traversal versions respectively). Though, these results are less significant due to the low number of answers to Q2 for these algorithms (this means that the RMSE was computed over a low number of recommendations). For both *ReDyAl* and dbrec the RMSE is roughly 45%. Concerning RQ2, the two versions of *HyProximity* account for the highest values (hierarchical approximately 99%, while traversal about 97%). The high values of novelty mean that the algorithm can recommend more novel objects that have not been noticed by the user before, however, these low values in performance scored by *HyProximity* hierarchical and traversal imply that most of these novel results are not relevant. In this regard, *ReDyAl* and dbrec scored good values for novelty accounting respectively for about 60% and 45%. while presenting also good values for performance.

HyProximity generated recommendations based in both traversal and hierarchical algorithms, which only obtained few answers to Q2. Table 1 shows that most of the recommendations generated were unknown to the users. As a consequence, the results for both algorithms are less definitive than for the other algorithms. This is especially meaningful for RQ1, since only the evaluations for which the answer to Q1 was either yes or yes but I haven't seen it (if it is a movie) were considered for computing the accuracy

Figure 5. Accuracy and novelty of the algorithms
Source (Figueroa et al., 2017)

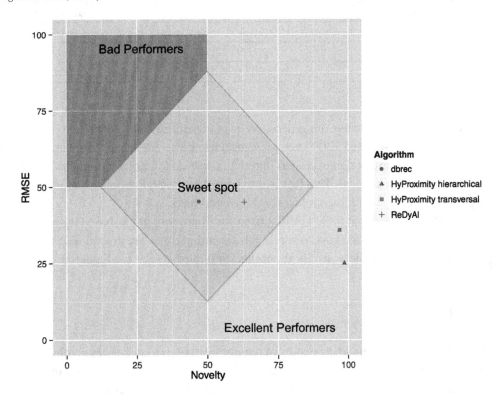

measures. Furthermore, the Fleiss' kappa measure was evaluated for assessing the agreement of the participants answering Q2. The recommendations that were not evaluated by at least one participant were excluded. The scored value for the Fleiss' kappa was 0.79; which corresponds to a substantial agreement.

Figure 5 shows also that *ReDyAl* and dbrec provide a good trade-off among accuracy and novelty (sweet spot area), although *ReDyAl* performs better in novelty. *HyProximity* hierarchical and *HyProximity* traversal seems to be excellent performers since their RMSE is low and their novelty is high. However, it should be noticed that RMSE was computed on few evaluations. A further analysis of these two algorithms is needed to verify if the user can benefit from such a high novelty and if novel recommendations are relevant. In addition, more research is needed on poorly-linked resources, since the choice of the initial films focused on selecting well-known films could ease the evaluation from participants. On poorly-linked resources *ReDyAl* and *Hyproximity* hierarchical are expected to score good values of the accuracy of the recommendations, since they can rely on categories, while dbrec and *HyProximity* traversal are likely to provide much less recommendations since they only rely on direct links between resources.

About the execution time, *ReDyAl* scored the best relationship candidate resources-execution time with a value of 3.7 resources per millisecond and the worse was scored by dbrec (0.28). These results showed, that generating candidate resources dynamically, not only allows improving the accuracy and novelty but also the execution time.

Table 1 shows the results of the performance for the ranking layer algorithms. The algorithms evaluated were the *ReDyAl*, dbrec, and *HyProximity* hierarchical. The ranker algorithms were tested with a fixed number of candidate resources; otherwise it is not possible to compare the algorithms. Though,

Table 1. Performance for generation layer algorithms

Generator Algorithm	Time (ms)	Candidate Films
ReDyAl	1911.3	7069.0
dbrec	5379.2	11513.1
HyProximity hierarchical	15637.5	4404.5

this is not a realistic situation because the generation layer algorithms may generate a different number of candidate resources. We selected 23000 resources because it was the mean value among the generation algorithms. This experiment demonstrated that the fastest ranking algorithm was *ReDyAl* and the lowest was *HyProximity* hierarchical. This fact was expected as the *HyProximity* hierarchical computes the similarity values based on both hierarchical and traversal links.

These results demonstrated that there is still a need for improving graph-based algorithms because, although the accuracy measures are good enough, the execution times are not suitable to quickly serve recommendations to users. For more details about this study please refer to (Figueroa, 2017).

DISCUSSION

Linked Data empowers RS to expand the results of recommendations to resources coming from different data sources and types. For example, the evaluation of the algorithms implemented in *AlLied* recommended resources about movies, however many of the results were not only resources of this type but also about producers, actors, cities, etc. This feature is an advantage in the case of RS that require the use of heterogeneous information, for example, in the domain of tourism, the recommended items may not be only points of interest such as museums, but also important personalities living in the city, typical foods, among others. Furthermore, linked data-based RS are useful to present explanations of the recommendations, because of the graph structure of the datasets in which the items are interlinked. In this case, following the links of the graph to which the recommended items belong is enough.

One of the features of the *AlLied* is that RS developed on top of it do not require user profile information to generate recommendations, they only need to consider the relationships of the concepts extracted from a resource with the concepts on the same or other existing structured datasets. Nonetheless, the knowledge of Linked Data should not be limited only to exploit relationships among items, but also to enrich data about items and users and to generate implicit knowledge about them and their relationships. In this way, RS would be able to produce personalized recommendations relying on the derived implicit knowledge.

AlLied is the first framework for Linked Data based RS that splits the recommendation process into meaningful phases embodied by layers. Each layer represents one task of the recommendation process that may be executed by various algorithms. In this way, *AlLied* allows developers to create and evaluate different configurations and combinations of algorithms at each layer to develop novel RS based on Linked Data. Hence, these RS are more suitable to users' requirements, applications, domains, and contexts.

Concerning the performance, obtaining resources with a reasonable degree of accuracy while keeping low-execution times is still subject to research. This work encourages other scientists to study this interesting type of RS using *AlLied*. Its layered architecture allows developers to create compositions of recommendation algorithms and to determine the most suitable combinations for the desired context.

It is also useful for the reproducibility of the results for the research community of RS because algorithms for recommendation are classified in the corresponding *AlLied*'s layer. Hence, these may be tuned to improve the accuracy and performance of the overall RS for a specific application. This is especially important taking into account that the difficulty to reproduce results is widely agreed in the community.

This study demonstrated that some of the algorithms for RS are more suitable to generate candidate resources under certain conditions of the initial resource. For example, if the initial resource contains a minimum number of links (properties) to other resources it should be desirable to execute the traversal algorithm that is specialized on finding related resources through the traversal links. In consequence, a new algorithm named ReDyAl was designed to automatically choose the best algorithm to recommend resources based on the relations of the initial resource. This algorithm demonstrated its ability to generate novel recommendations, which is useful when users do not want to receive recommendations about items they already know or have previously consumed.

FUTURE RESEARCH DIRECTIONS

The graph-based algorithms studied in this chapter were explicitly developed to deal with Linked Data datasets. They take advantage of the relationships among the items represented through resources of the Web of Data. Nevertheless, the execution time of the graph-based algorithms is still an open issue because they far exceed the performance of machine learning algorithms. Therefore, a logical evolution of this study is the combination of graph-based algorithms with machine learning algorithms. This evolution can make possible to obtain accurate results in an execution time adapted to the needs of the end users. Research and experimentation are still needed in RS based on Linked Data, to explore more techniques from the vast amount of machine learning algorithms to determine which of them are more suitable to deal with Linked Data datasets.

Furthermore, a recent method known as "Propagated Linked Data Semantic Distance (PLDSD)" for the traversal ranking, improves the results of the algorithms based on the semantic distance LDSD proposed initially by Passant. The PLDSD uses the Floyd-Warshall algorithm to expand semantic distance calculations beyond resources that are just one or two links (Alfarhood, Labille, & Gauch, 2017). The implementation of this measure into the *AlLied* framework means an improvement of the traversal ranking algorithm because unlike the LDSD, it extends the number of items considered for the calculation of the semantic distance.

In the same way, it is necessary a broad study of more types of algorithms such as evolutionary computation, automated planning, among others to analyze their relevance under different domains, which is required to increase the available set of techniques for each layer of the *AlLied* framework. This study may lead to an improvement of the performance and accuracy of the *ReDyAl* algorithm while maintaining its novelty.

Another issue which is gaining interest is mining microblogging data and text reviews. Opinion mining and sentiment analysis techniques can support recommendation methods that take into account the evaluation of aspects of items expressed in text reviews. Extracting information from the raw text in the form of Linked Data can ease its exploitation and the integration.

A closely related research area is exploratory search. It refers to cognitive consuming search tasks such as learning or topic investigation. Exploratory search systems also recommend relevant topics or concepts. An open question not addressed in this work is how to leverage the data semantics richness for successful exploratory search.

Finally, a current problem with the knowledge published in linked data is the poor quality of data. It is demonstrated that data extracted from semi-structured or even structured sources, often contains inconsistencies as well as misrepresented and incomplete information (Zaveri, Maurino, & Equille, 2014). A next step for improving the results of the algorithms implemented in *AlLied* is to develop an additional layer for addressing data quality in both local and remote datasets.

CONCLUSION

This chapter reviewed state-of-art Linked Data based recommendation algorithms and presented *AlLied*, a framework for deploying and executing these algorithms. *AlLied* allows developers to create and evaluate different configurations and combinations of algorithms at each layer to develop novel RS based on Linked Data. Hence, these RS are more suitable to users' requirements, applications, domains, and contexts. It is also useful for the reproducibility of the results for the research community of RS because algorithms for recommendation are classified in the corresponding *AlLied*'s layer. Hence, these may be tuned to improve the accuracy and performance of the overall RS for a specific application.

Additionally, a hybrid algorithm named ReDyAl is presented. This algorithm dynamically integrates both traversal and hierarchical approaches for discovering resources. The ReDyAl algorithm was designed based on the analysis of state-of-the-art algorithms that were implemented within the *AlLied* framework. The current version of this framework contains a set of three state-of-the-art traversal and hierarchical algorithms and the ReDyAl algorithm.

In this work, a user study was conducted to analyze the ReDyAl algorithm and a set of state-of-the-art algorithms re-implemented within *AlLied*. This framework facilitated the study a common framework contained all the algorithms involved, and the results of the generated recommendations were aligned.

The study demonstrated that, although ReDyAl improved the novelty of the results discovered, the accuracy of the algorithm was not the highest due to its inherent complexity.

Future work includes studying the relevance under different domains and improving the accuracy of ReDyAl while maintaining its novelty. This can lead us to discover resources faster and make the algorithm usable for real-time applications.

ACKNOWLEDGMENT

The first author was supported by the fellowship No 511 from the Administrative Department of Science, Technology and Innovation (COLCIENCIAS) of Colombia.

REFERENCES

Adomavicius, G., & Tuzhilin, A. (2005). Toward the next generation of recommender systems: A survey of the state-of-the-art and possible extensions. *IEEE Transactions on Knowledge and Data Engineering*, *17*(6), 734–749. doi:10.1109/TKDE.2005.99

Ahn, J., & Amatriain, X. (2010). Towards Fully Distributed and Privacy-Preserving Recommendations via Expert Collaborative Filtering and RESTful Linked Data. In *2010 IEEE/WIC/ACM International Conference on Web Intelligence and Intelligent Agent Technology* (Vol. 1, pp. 66–73). IEEE. 10.1109/WI-IAT.2010.53

Alfarhood, S., Labille, K., & Gauch, S. (2017). PLDSD: Propagated linked data semantic distance. In *Proceedings - 2017 IEEE 26th International Conference on Enabling Technologies: Infrastructure for Collaborative Enterprises, WETICE 2017* (pp. 278–283). doi:10.1109/WETICE.2017.16

Ayala, V. A. A., Przyjaciel-Zablocki, M., Hornung, T., Schätzle, A., & Lausen, G. (2014). Extending SPARQL for Recommendations. In Proceedings of Semantic Web Information Management on Semantic Web Information Management (pp. 1–8). doi:10.1145/2630602.2630604

Bizer, C., Heath, T., & Berners-Lee, T. (2009). Linked Data - The Story So Far. *International Journal on Semantic Web and Information Systems*, *5*, 1–22. doi:10.4018/jswis.2009081901

Blanco, R., Cambazoglu, B. B., Mika, P., & Torzec, N. (2013). Entity recommendations in web search. In The Semantic Web–ISWC 2013 (pp. 33–48). doi:10.1007/978-3-642-41338-4_3

Calì, A., Capuzzi, S., Dimartino, M. M., & Frosini, R. (2013). Recommendation of text tags in social applications using linked data. In International Conference on Web Engineering, LNCS (Vol. 8295 LNCS, pp. 187–191). doi:10.1007/978-3-319-04244-2_17

Cantador, I., Castells, P., & Bellogín, A. (2011). An enhanced semantic layer for hybrid recommender systems: application to news recommendation. *International Journal on Semantic Web and Information Systems*, *7*(1), 44–78. doi:10.4018/jswis.2011010103

Cantador, I., Konstas, I., & Jose, J. M. (2011). Categorising social tags to improve folksonomy-based recommendations. *Journal of Web Semantics*, *9*(1), 1–15. doi:10.1016/j.websem.2010.10.001

Caraballo, A. A. M., Arruda, N. M., Nunes, B. P., Lopes, G. R., & Casanova, M. A. (2014). TRTML - A Tripleset Recommendation Tool Based on Supervised Learning Algorithms. In V. Presutti, E. Blomqvist, R. Troncy et al. (Eds.), The Semantic Web: ESWC 2014 Satellite Events SE - 58 (pp. 413-417). Springer International Publishing. doi:10.1007/978-3-319-11955-7_58

Chawuthai, R., Takeda, H., & Hosoya, T. (2015). Link Prediction in Linked Data of Interspecies Interactions Using Hybrid Recommendation Approach. In T. Supnithi, T. Yamaguchi, J.Z. Pan (Eds.), Semantic Technology SE - 9 (Vol. 8943, pp. 113–128). Springer International Publishing. doi:10.1007/978-3-319-15615-6_9

Cheekula, S. K., Kapanipathi, P., Doran, D., & Jain, P. (2015). Entity Recommendations Using Hierarchical Knowledge Bases. In *Proceedings of the 4th Workshop on Knowledge Discovery and Data Mining Meets Linked Open Data co-located with 12th Extended Semantic Web Conference (ESWC 2015)*. Retrieved from http://ceur-ws.org/Vol-1365/

Chicaiza, J., Piedra, N., López-Vargas, J., & Tovar-Edmundo. (2014). Domain Categorization of Open Educational Resources Based on Linked Data. In *Knowledge Engineering and the Semantic Web*, (January).

Damljanovic, D., Stankovic, M., & Laublet, P. (2012). Linked Data-Based Concept Recommendation: Comparison of Different Methods in Open Innovation Scenario. In E. Simperl, P. Cimiano, A. Polleres, O. Corcho, & V. Presutti (Eds.), *The Semantic Web: Research and Applications,* Heraklion, Crete, Greece (pp. 24–38). Springer Berlin Heidelberg. Retrieved from http://link.springer.com/chapter/10.1007/978-3-642-30284-8_9 doi:10.1007/978-3-642-30284-8_9

Dell'Aglio, D., Celino, I., & Cerizza, D. (2010). *Anatomy of a Semantic Web-enabled Knowledge-based Recommender System. In 4th international workshop Semantic Matchmaking and Resource Retrieval in the Semantic Web, at ISWC,* Bonn, Germany. (Vol. 667, pp. 115–130). Retrieved from http://citeseerx.ist.psu.edu/viewdoc/download?rep=rep1&type=pdf&doi=10.1.1.204.3679

Di Noia, T., Mirizzi, R., Ostuni, V. C., & Romito, D. (2012). Exploiting the web of data in model-based recommender systems. In *6th ACM conference on Recommender systems - RecSys '12* (p. 253). New York, NY: ACM Press. 10.1145/2365952.2366007

Felfernig, A., Jeran, M., Ninaus, G., Reinfrank, F., & Reiterer, S. (2013). Toward the Next Generation of Recommender Systems: Applications and Research Challenges. In *Multimedia Services in Intelligent Environments* (pp. 81–98). Springer. Retrieved from http://link.springer.com/chapter/10.1007/978-3-319-00372-6_5#

Figueroa, C. (2017). *Recommender Systems based on Linked Data*. Politecnico di Torino - Universidad del Cauca; doi:10.6092/polito/porto/2669963

Figueroa, C., Vagliano, I., Rocha, O. R., Torchiano, M., Zucker, C. F., Corrales, J.-C. C., & Morisio, M. (2017). Allied: A framework for executing linked data-based recommendation algorithms. *International Journal on Semantic Web and Information Systems*, *13*(4), 134–154. doi:10.4018/IJSWIS.2017100107

Figueroa, C., Vagliano, I., Rodríguez Rocha, O., & Morisio, M. (2015). A systematic literature review of Linked Data-based recommender systems. *Concurrency and Computation*, *27*(17), 4659–4684. doi:10.1002/cpe.3449

Gordea, S., Lindley, A., & Graf, R. (2011). Computing Recommendations for Long Term Data Accessibility basing on Open Knowledge and Linked Data. In *RecSys 2011 Workshop on Human Decision Making in Recommender Systems affiliated with the 5th ACM Conference on Recommender Systems,* Chicago, IL (pp. 1–8). Retrieved from http://ceur-ws.org/Vol-811/paper8.pdf

Hadj Taieb, M. A., Ben Aouicha, M., Tmar, M., & Hamadou, A. B. (2011). New information content metric and nominalization relation for a new WordNet-based method to measure the semantic relatedness. In *2011 IEEE 10th International Conference on Cybernetic Intelligent Systems (CIS)*. doi:10.1109/CIS.2011.6169134

Hajra, A., Latif, A., & Tochtermann, K. (2014). Retrieving and Ranking Scientific Publications from Linked Open Data Repositories. In *Proceedings of the 14th International Conference on Knowledge Technologies and Data-driven Business* (p. 29:1--29:4). New York, NY: ACM. 10.1145/2637748.2638436

Hopfgartner, F., & Jose, J. M. (2010). Semantic user profiling techniques for personalised multimedia recommendation. *Multimedia Systems*, *16*(4–5), 255–274. doi:10.100700530-010-0189-6

Juang, Y.-T., Tung, S.-L., & Chiu, H.-C. (2011). Adaptive fuzzy particle swarm optimization for global optimization of multimodal functions. *Information Sciences*, *181*(20), 4539–4549. doi:10.1016/j.ins.2010.11.025

Khrouf, H., & Troncy, R. (2013). Hybrid event recommendation using linked data and user diversity. In *Proceedings of the 7th ACM conference on Recommender systems - RecSys '13* (pp. 185–192). New York, NY: ACM Press. 10.1145/2507157.2507171

Kitaya, K., Huang, H.-H., & Kawagoe, K. (2012). Music Curator Recommendations Using Linked Data. In *Second International Conference on the Innovative Computing Technology (INTECH 2012)*, Casablanca (pp. 337–339). IEEE. 10.1109/INTECH.2012.6457799

Ko, H., Kim, E., Ko, I.-Y., & Chang, D. (2014). Semantically-based recommendation by using semantic clusters of users' viewing history. In *2014 International Conference on Big Data and Smart Computing (BIGCOMP)* (pp. 83–87). IEEE.

Ko, H., & Son, J. (2015). Multi-Aspect Collaborative Filtering based on Linked Data for Personalized Recommendation. In *Proceedings of the 1st Workshop on New Trends in Content-based Recommender Systems co-located with the 8th ACM Conference on Recommender Systems (RecSys 2014)* (pp. 49–50). 10.1145/2740908.2742780

Kushwaha, N., & Vyas, O. P. (2014). SemMovieRec: Extraction of Semantic Features of DBpedia for Recommender System. In *Proceedings of the 7th ACM India Computing Conference* (p. 13:1--13:9). New York, NY: ACM. 10.1145/2675744.2675759

Lommatzsch, A., Kille, B., & Albayrak, S. (2013). Learning hybrid recommender models for heterogeneous semantic data. In *Proceedings of the 28th Annual ACM Symposium on Applied Computing - SAC '13* (p. 275). New York, NY: ACM Press. 10.1145/2480362.2480420

Lommatzsch, A., Kille, B., Albayrak, S., & Berlin, T. U. (2013). A Framework for Learning and Analyzing Hybrid Recommenders based on Heterogeneous Semantic Data Categories and Subject Descriptors. In *10th Conference on Open Research Areas in Information Retrieval*, Lisbon, Portugal (pp. 137–140). ACM.

Lommatzsch, A., Kille, B., Kim, J. W., & Albayrak, S. (2013). An Adaptive Hybrid Movie Recommender Based on Semantic Data. In *Proceedings of the 10th Conference on Open Research Areas in Information Retrieval* (pp. 217–218). Paris, France, Le Centre De Hautes Etudes Internationales D'informatique Documentaire. Retrieved from http://dl.acm.org/citation.cfm?id=2491748.2491795

Lopes, G. R., André, L., Rabello Lopes, G., Paes Leme, L., Pereira Nunes, B., Casanova, M., & Dietze, S. (2014). Two Approaches to the Dataset Interlinking Recommendation Problem. In Web Information Systems Engineering – WISE 2014 SE (pp. 324–339). doi:10.1007/978-3-319-11749-2_25

Lopes, G. R., Leme, L. A. P. P., Nunes, B. P., & Casanova, M. A. (2014). RecLAK: Analysis and recommendation of interlinking datasets. In CEUR Workshop Proceedings (Vol. 1137).

Lops, P., De Gemmis, M., & Semeraro, G. (2011). Content-based Recommender Systems: State of the Art and Trends. In Recommender Systems Handbook (pp. 73–105). doi:10.1007/978-0-387-85820-3

Maccatrozzo, V., Ceolin, D., Aroyo, L., & Groth, P. (2014). A Semantic Pattern-Based Recommender. In V. Presutti, M. Stankovic, E. Cambria, I. Cantador, A. Di Iorio, T. Di Noia, … A. Tordai (Eds.), *Semantic Web Evaluation Challenge: SemWebEval 2014 at ESWC 2014, Anissaras, Crete, Greece, May 25-29, 2014, Revised Selected Papers* (pp. 182–187). Cham: Springer International Publishing. 10.1007/978-3-319-12024-9_24

Manoj Kumar, S., Anusha, K., & Santhi Sree, K. (2015). Semantic Web-based Recommendation: Experimental Results and Test Cases. *International Journal of Emerging Research in Management & Technology*, 4(6), 215–222. Retrieved from http://www.ermt.net/docs/papers/Volume_4/6_June2015/V4N6-252.pdf

Marie, N., Gandon, F., Legrand, D., & Ribière, M. (2013). Discovery Hub: a discovery engine on the top of DBpedia. In *3rd International Conference on Web Intelligence, Mining and Semantics - WIMS '13* (p. 1). New York, NY: ACM Press. 10.1145/2479787.2479820

Moreno, A., Ariza-Porras, C., Lago, P., Jiménez-Guarín, C. L., Castro, H., & Riveill, M. (2014). Hybrid Model Rating Prediction with Linked Open Data for Recommender Systems. In *SemWebEval 2014 at ESWC 2014, Anissaras, Crete, Greece, May 25-29, 2014, Revised Selected Papers* (pp. 193–198). 10.1007/978-3-319-12024-9_26

Moyano, A. N., Sicilia, M. A., & Barriocanal, E. G. (2018). On the graph structure of the web of data. *International Journal on Semantic Web and Information Systems*, 14(2), 70–85. doi:10.4018/IJSWIS.2018040104

Musto, C., Basile, P., Lops, P., de Gemmis, M., & Semeraro, G. (2017). Introducing linked open data in graph-based recommender systems. *Information Processing & Management*, 53(2), 405–435. doi:10.1016/j.ipm.2016.12.003

Musto, C., Lops, P., de Gemmis, M., & Semeraro, G. (2017). Semantics-aware Recommender Systems exploiting Linked Open Data and graph-based features. *Knowledge-Based Systems*, 136, 1–14. doi:10.1016/j.knosys.2017.08.015

Narducci, F., Musto, C., Semeraro, G., Lops, P., & de Gemmis, M. (2013). Exploiting Big Data for Enhanced Representations in Content-Based Recommender Systems. In C. Huemer & P. Lops (Eds.), *14th International Conference, EC-Web 2013, Prague, Czech Republic, August 27-28, 2013. Proceedings* (Vol. 152, pp. 182–193). Springer Berlin Heidelberg. 10.1007/978-3-642-39878-0_17

Nguyen, P. T., Tomeo, P., Di Noia, T., Di Sciascio, E., Di Noia, T., & Di Sciascio, E. (2015). An Evaluation of SimRank and Personalized PageRank to Build a Recommender System for the Web of Data. In *Proceedings of the 24th International Conference on World Wide Web* (pp. 1477–1482). Republic and Canton of Geneva, Switzerland: International World Wide Web Conferences Steering Committee. 10.1145/2740908.2742141

Ostuni, V. C., Di Noia, T., Di Sciascio, E., & Mirizzi, R. (2013). Top-N recommendations from implicit feedback leveraging linked open data. In *Proceedings of the 7th ACM conference on Recommender systems - RecSys '13* (pp. 85–92). New York, NY: ACM Press. 10.1145/2507157.2507172

Ostuni, V. C. C., Gentile, G., Di Noia, T., Di Noia, T., Mirizzi, R., Romito, D., & Di Sciascio, E. (2013). Mobile movie recommendations with linked data. In *IFIP WG 8.4, 8.9, TC 5 International Cross-Domain Conference, CD-ARES 2013, Regensburg, Germany, September 2-6, 2013. Proceedings* (Vol. 8127 LNCS, pp. 400–415). 10.1007/978-3-642-40511-2_29

Ostuni, V. V., Di Noia, T., Mirizzi, R., Di Sciascio, E., & Di Noia, T. (2014). A Linked Data Recommender System Using a Neighborhood-Based Graph Kernel. In M. Hepp & Y. Hoffner (Eds.), *E-Commerce and Web Technologies SE - 10* (pp. 89–100). Springer International Publishing; doi:10.1007/978-3-319-10491-1_10

Ozdikis, O., Orhan, F., & Danismaz, F. (2011). Ontology-based recommendation for points of interest retrieved from multiple data sources. In *International Workshop on Semantic Web Information Management - SWIM '11* (pp. 1–6). 10.1145/1999299.1999300

Park, D. H., Kim, H. K., Choi, I. Y., & Kim, J. K. (2012). A literature review and classification of recommender systems research. *Expert Systems with Applications*, *39*(11), 10059–10072. doi:10.1016/j.eswa.2012.02.038

Passant, A. (2010). dbrec - Music recommendations using DBpedia. In International Semantic Web Conference (pp. 209-224). Springer. doi:10.1007/978-3-642-17749-1_14

Portugal, I., Alencar, P., & Cowan, D. (2018). The use of machine learning algorithms in recommender systems: A systematic review. *Expert Systems with Applications*, *97*, 205–227. doi:10.1016/j.eswa.2017.12.020

Ricci, F., Rokach, L., & Shapira, B. (2011). Introduction to Recommender Systems Handbook. In *Recommender Systems Handbook* (pp. 1–35). Springer; doi:10.1007/978-0-387-85820-3_1

Ristoski, P., Loza Mencía, E., Paulheim, H., & Menc, E. L. (2014). A Hybrid Multi-strategy Recommender System Using Linked Open Data. In V. Presutti, M. Stankovic, E. Cambria, I. Cantador, A. Di Iorio, T. Di Noia, … A. Tordai (Eds.), Semantic Web Evaluation Challenge SE - 19 (Vol. 475, pp. 150–156). Springer International Publishing. doi:10.1007/978-3-319-12024-9_19

Rowe, M. (2014). Transferring Semantic Categories with Vertex Kernels: Recommendations with SemanticSVD++. In P. Mika, T. Tudorache, A. Bernstein et al. (Eds.), *13th International Semantic Web Conference*, *Riva del Garda, Italy, October 19-23. Proceedings, Part I* (Vol. 8796, pp. 341–356). Springer International Publishing. doi:10.1007/978-3-319-11964-9_22

Schmachtenberg, M., Bizer, C., & Paulheim, H. (2014). Adoption of the Linked Data Best Practices in Different Topical Domains. In P. Mika, T. Tudorache, A. Bernstein et al. (Eds.), The Semantic Web – ISWC 2014 SE - 16 (Vol. 8796, pp. 245–260). Springer International Publishing. doi:10.1007/978-3-319-11964-9_16

Schmachtenberg, M., Strufe, T., & Paulheim, H. (2014). Enhancing a Location-based Recommendation System by Enrichment with Structured Data from the Web. In *Proceedings of the 4th International Conference on Web Intelligence, Mining and Semantics (WIMS14) - WIMS '14* (pp. 1–12). 10.1145/2611040.2611080

Seco, N., Veale, T., & Hayes, J. (2004). An Intrinsic Information Content Metric for Semantic Similarity in WordNet. In *European Conference on Artificial Intelligence*.

Stankovic, M., Breitfuss, W., & Laublet, P. (2011). Discovering Relevant Topics Using DBPedia: Providing Non-obvious Recommendations. In *2011 IEEE/WIC/ACM International Conferences on Web Intelligence and Intelligent Agent Technology* (pp. 219–222). IEEE. 10.1109/WI-IAT.2011.32

Strobin, L., & Niewiadomski, A. (2014). Recommendations and Object Discovery in Graph Databases Using Path Semantic Analysis. In L. Rutkowski, M. Korytkowski, R. Scherer, R. Tadeusiewicz, L. Zadeh, & J. Zurada (Eds.), *13th International Conference, ICAISC 2014, Zakopane, Poland*, June 1-5, *Proceedings, Part I* (Vol. 8467, pp. 793–804). Springer International Publishing. 10.1007/978-3-319-07173-2_68

Tomeo, P., Fernández-Tobías, I., Cantador, I., & Di Noia, T. (2017). Addressing the Cold Start with Positive-Only Feedback Through Semantic-Based Recommendations. *International Journal of Uncertainty, Fuzziness and Knowledge-based Systems*, 25(Suppl. 2), 57–78. doi:10.1142/S0218488517400116

Vagliano, I., Figueroa, C., Rodriguez, O., Torchiano, M., Faron-Zucker, C., & Morisio, M. (2016). *ReDyAl: A Dynamic Recommendation Algorithm based on Linked Data. In 3rd Workshop on New Trends in Content-based Recommender Systems - CBRecSys 2016* (pp. 31–39). Boston, MA, USA: CEUR Workshop Proceedings; Retrieved from http://ceur-ws.org/Vol-1673/paper6.pdf

Welling, M. (2011). *A First Encounter with Machine Learning*. Donald Bren School of Information and Computer Science - University of California Irvine. Retrieved from https://www.ics.uci.edu/~welling/teaching/ICS273Afall11/IntroMLBook.pdf

Yang, R., Hu, W., Qu, Y., Li, G., Wang, P., Yu, B., … Qu, Y. (2013). Using Semantic Technology to Improve Recommender Systems Based on Slope One. *Semantic Web and Web Science*, 2(1), 11–23. doi:10.1007/978-1-4614-6880-6_2

Zaveri, A., Maurino, A., & Equille, L.-B. (2014). Web Data Quality: Current State and New Challenges Amrapali. *International Journal on Semantic Web and Information Systems*, 10(2), 1–6. doi:10.4018/ijswis.2014040101

Zhang, Y., Wu, H., Sorathia, V., & Prasanna, V. K. (2014). Event recommendation in social networks with linked data enablement. In *ICEIS 2013 - Proceedings of the 15th International Conference on Enterprise Information Systems* (Vol. 2, pp. 371–379). Retrieved from http://www.scopus.com/inward/record.url?eid=2-s2.0-84887649972&partnerID=tZOtx3y1

ADDITIONAL READING

Alfarhood, S., Labille, K., & Gauch, S. (2017). PLDSD: Propagated linked data semantic distance. In *Proceedings - 2017 IEEE 26th International Conference on Enabling Technologies: Infrastructure for Collaborative Enterprises, WETICE 2017* (pp. 278–283). doi:10.1109/WETICE.2017.16

Figueroa, C., Ordoñez, H., Corrales, J.-C., Cobos, C., Wives, L. K., & Herrera-Viedma, E. (2016). Improving business process retrieval using categorization and multimodal search. *Knowledge-Based Systems*, *110*, 49–59. doi:10.1016/j.knosys.2016.07.014

Moyano, A. N., Sicilia, M. A., & Barriocanal, E. G. (2018). On the Graph Structure of the Web of Data. *International Journal on Semantic Web and Information Systems*, *14*(2), 70–85. doi:10.4018/IJSWIS.2018040104

Musto, C., Lops, P., de Gemmis, M., & Semeraro, G. (2017). Semantics-aware recommender systems exploiting linked open data and graph-based features. *Knowledge-Based Systems*, *136*, 1–14. doi:10.1016/j.knosys.2017.08.015

Portugal, I., Alencar, P., & Cowan, D. (2018). The use of machine learning algorithms in recommender systems: A systematic review. *Expert Systems with Applications*, *97*, 205–227. doi:10.1016/j.eswa.2017.12.020

Rocha, O. R., Vagliano, I., Figueroa, C., Cairo, F., Futia, G., Licciardi, C. A., & Morando, F. (2015). Semantic annotation and classification in practice. *IT Professional*, *17*(2), 33–39. doi:10.1109/MITP.2015.29

Sabou, M., Aroyo, L., Bontcheva, K., Bozzon, A., & Qarout, R. K. (2018). Semantic web and human computation: The status of an emerging field. *Semantic Web*, 1–12.

Tomeo, P., Fernández-Tobías, I., Cantador, I., & Di Noia, T. (2017). Addressing the Cold Start with Positive-Only Feedback Through Semantic-Based Recommendations. *International Journal of Uncertainty, Fuzziness and Knowledge-based Systems*, *25*(Suppl. 2), 57–78. doi:10.1142/S0218488517400116

Zhang, X., Lin, E., & Lv, Y. (2018). Multi-Target Search on Semantic Associations in Linked Data. *International Journal on Semantic Web and Information Systems*, *14*(1), 71–97. doi:10.4018/IJSWIS.2018010103

KEY TERMS AND DEFINITIONS

Linked Data: They are a set of good practices or principles for publishing and linking structured data on the Web. Linked Data provide the means to make the Semantic Web a reality.

Linked Data Datasets: They are sets of structured data using the principles of the linked data. Much of them are interlinked so it is possible to not only exploit the knowledge of a single dataset but also the power of the semantic interconnection among them.

Linked Data Endpoints: they are mechanism used in Linked Data to provide access to the available datasets. Endpoints may be interfaces to execute queries to the datasets in a similar way as in a database.

Resource Description Framework (RDF): This framework is a recommendation of the W3C that provides a generic graph-based data model for describing resources, including their relationships with other resources. The graph data model of the RDF framework is composed of triples or statements. Each triple contains a subject, a predicate, and an object.

Linked Data based RS: A kind of knowledge-based RS which uses linked data as source of data to infer relationships or to represent items and users, with the aim to improve the recommendation process.

Recommender System (RS): A kind of algorithms or frameworks designed to recommend items of interest for an end user. These items can belong to different categories or types, e.g. songs, places, news, books, films, events, etc.

The Web of Data: Unlike the World Wide Web that consists of human-readable documents linked via hyperlinks, the "Web of Data" refers to a global space of structured and machine-readable data.

ENDNOTES

[1]   http://www.mpi-inf.mpg.de/departments/databases-and-information-systems/research/yago-naga/yago/
[2]   https://wordnet.princeton.edu/
[3]   http://www.w3.org/2004/02/skos/
[4]   http://natasha.polito.it/RSEvaluation/
[5]   http://www.imdb.com/chart/top
[6]   http://natasha.polito.it/RSEvaluation/faces/resultsdownload.xhtml

APPENDIX: BACKGROUND OF THE RESEARCH UNIT

The research described in this chapter was conducted in collaboration of two Ph.D. programs. The Ph.D. Course in Telematics Engineering (Universidad del Cauca), and the Ph.D. Course in Computers and Systems Engineering (Politecnico di Torino). The former focus on telematics systems and services oriented to the development of the Information and Communication Technologies (ICT). The latter addresses computer and systems engineering, with main interest in automation, informatics and operational research. The Ph.D. advisors were: Prof. Juan Carlos Corrales (Universidad del Cauca), whose research areas are services composition and data analysis; and Prof. Maurizio Morisio (Politecnico di Torino) whose interests lie in finding, applying and evaluating the most suitable techniques and process to produce better software faster.

Additionally, the research was supported by the Wimmics joint research team between Inria Sophia Antipolis - Méditerranée and I3S (CNRS and Université Nice Sophia Antipolis). Wimmics stands for Web-Instrumented Man-Machine Interactions, Communities, and Semantics, and their challenge is to bridge formal semantics and social semantics on the web.

Chapter 3
The OSGI SIB:
A Resilient Semantic Solution for the Internet of Things

Alfredo D'Elia
University of Bologna, Italy

Paolo Azzoni
Eurotech Group, Italy

Fabio Viola
University of Bologna, Italy

Cristiano Aguzzi
University of Bologna, Italy

Luca Roffia
University of Bologna, Italy

Tullio Salmon Cinotti
University of Bologna, Italy

ABSTRACT

The research activity in the IoT field caused a proliferation of information brokers with different features and targeted at different information abstraction levels. The OSGI Semantic Information Broker (SIB) is a portable and extendable solution for providing an IoT system with semantic support, a publish subscribe paradigm, and expressive primitives for information modeling. In this chapter the authors explain the main reasons for defining a new SIB version, substituting the previously used RedSIB, its main features and comparative evaluation against both ad hoc and standard benchmarks. Furthermore, recently defined primitives and experimental work on the portability to mobile devices and resiliency are proposed and discussed.

DOI: 10.4018/978-1-5225-7186-5.ch003

Copyright © 2019, IGI Global. Copying or distributing in print or electronic forms without written permission of IGI Global is prohibited.

INTRODUCTION

This chapter extends the work proposed in (D'Elia, Viola, Roffia, Azzoni, & Cinotti, 2017) about the implementation of a OSGI-based semantic information broker (SIB) and the comparison with the "red SIB", the previous SIB implementation inspired by M3(Ovaska, Cinotti & Toninelli, 2012) technology. The OSGI SIB has been extended with further functionalities (D'Elia, Aguzzi et al., 2017) focused on the dependability and on the resiliency to abrupt client disconnections.

The interest on Semantic Web technologies applied to the Internet of Things (IoT) (Barnaghi, Wang, Henson, & Taylor, 2012; Kovatsch, Hassan & Mayer, 2015) has been the main topic of several international research projects and academic research activities, aimed at improving IoT solutions with semantic technologies. The Semantic Web was conceived to change the Web and drive it towards the original vision that Tim Berners Lee had in mind: a web of data (Berners-Lee, Hendler, Lassila et al., 2001). Semantic Web technologies allow to represent (i.e., RDF - Resource Description Framework, http://www.w3.org/RDF/, OWL - Web Ontology Language Reference, W3C Recommendation, 10 February 2004, http://www.w3.org/TR/owl-ref/) and retrieve (i.e., SPARQL - SPARQL 1.1 Overview W3C Recommendation 21 March 2013, http://www.w3.org/TR/sparql11-overview/) semantically enriched information, thus they have a high level of generality and inter-disciplinarity. One of the most interesting field of application is that of collaborative agents offering advanced services for private users and enterprises. The Semantic Web also applies to classification, abstraction, mining and reasoning over large amount of data. Information about energy consumption, user profiles, environmental monitoring, financial data and other similar data sources can be analyzed by smart software agents and used to perform context-aware operations (where context can be defined as "any information that can be used to characterize the situation of an entity, where an entity can be a person, a place or physical or computational object" (Abowd et al., 1999)).

In 2008, the ARTEMIS joint undertaking funded the FP7 European Project SOFIA (Smart Objects for Intelligent Applications) to develop a platform for sharing semantic information for the widest possible range of devices and agents. Since the conclusion of SOFIA, the platform has been adopted, evaluated and extended in several European research projects (e.g., CHIRON, IoE, RECOCAPE, IMPRESS, ARROWHEAD, CONNECT) in partnership with industrial players. Some of these projects are still ongoing and new projects proposals are currently in preparation to continue from the previous results. The multipurpose architecture conceived in SOFIA and called Smart-M3 represents one of the most important attempt to adopt the Semantic Web in IoT (smart environments) and has become one of the European reference platforms mentioned in the IoT oriented call for proposals. Smart-M3 follows a publish-subscribe model and proposes a simple approach based on two components and their communication protocol (Figure 1). The Semantic Information Broker (SIB) stores and shares the semantic information that is exchanged by smart objects of the Smart-M3 ecosystem. KPs (Knowledge Processors) run in the smart objects, process the information, update it, query the SIB and subscribe to the information stored in the SIB to be always up to date. KPs communicate with the SIB through the SSAP protocol (Smart Space Access Protocol). The SIB is not bound to a specific implementation and it is generally intended as a software able to read, process and produce SSAP messages, while coherently managing the semantic knowledge base (KB) stored in the SIB itself. As shown in Figure 1, the SIB can be seen as a wrapper over a SPARQL endpoint to enable the publish-subscribe mechanism.

The Smart-M3 architecture has been used in many heterogeneous application domains, and the growing interest of the community brought to the development of SIB versions more performant and featured than

Figure 1. Smart-M3 Architecture

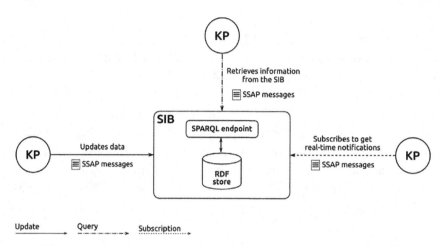

the original implementation of Sofia project. In recent years, the research community improved many aspects of the Smart-M3 original platform including, for example, the programming model, the SSAP protocol, the supported standards and the SIB core itself. The KPs can be implemented using a richer set of programming languages (Java, C#, Python, Javascript, PHP, C), are agnostic to the transport channel and may run on different platforms, but are bound to communicate with the SIB through the SSAP.

This paper describes a SIB implementation based on the OSGi framework, built on top of the authors experience on the development of the Smart-M3 platform for smart space applications (Bedogni et al., 2013; Manzaroli et al., 2010; Morandi, Roffia, D'Elia, Vergari, & Cinotti, 2012; Ovaska, Cinotti, & Toninelli, 2012; Vergari et al., 2011). OSGi and Java provide interesting advantages in terms of portability, productivity and compatibility with existing libraries and frameworks. OSGi is widely diffused both in the research and in the industrial communities because it offers a reliable Service Oriented Architecture (SOA) decoupling the atomic software entities called bundles. A complex software like the SIB can be decomposed into components, which can be implemented with bundles interacting through service calls: according to the "separation of concerns" principle, each bundle becomes a module with a well-defined interface. This paper focus on several improvements of the original Smart-M3 architecture and related implementation. (i) We improved the flexibility of a Smart-M3 based architecture: it is possible to define many bundle sets optimized for different situations that can be started-stopped or substituted even at runtime without interruptions to service provision. (ii) We implemented and evaluated of a new functionality of the SIB core, the persistent SPARQL update primitive (PU), to implement rule like facilities. (iii) We provides a porting on Android of the SIB, obtained with a minimal effort from the Linux version, thanks to the Java and OSGi portability. The introduction of mobile devices as host of a SIB increments the number of application domains where Smart-M3 based solutions can be used to provide environmental intelligence and advanced smart services in the Internet of Things. (iv) In the OSGi SIB novel modules and mechanisms have been added to provide information dependability and deal with abrupt losses of client connection, in particular with regard to a coherent management of subscriptions. (v) Eventually, the Smart-M3 implementation based on OSGi represents also a benefit for the OSGi framework itself. Currently, OSGi specifications do not address interoperability issues at the information level, therefore the introduction of native interoperability technologies represents an important improvement of the OSGi platform.

BACKGROUND

Several Semantic Web based interoperability platforms have tried to provide an answer to the level of interoperability, dynamicity, flexibility, expressivity and extendibility required in the development of IoT applications: e.g. the Task Computing Environment (TCE) (Masuoka, Parsia, & Labrou, 2003), the Context Broker Architecture for Pervasive Computing (CoBrA) (Chen et al., 2004; Chen, Finin, & Joshi, 2005), the Context Aware Platform (CAP) (Lamorte et al., 2007), Semantic Space (X. Wang, Dong, Chin, Hettiarachchi, & Zhang, 2004), the Semantic middleware for IoT (Song, Cardenas, Masuoka, & others, 2010), the Smart objects awareness and adaptation Model (SoaM) (Vazquez, de Ipiña, & Sedano, 2007), Amigo (Thomson, Bianco, Mokhtar, Georgantas, & Issarny, 2008), Web of things (Zhong et al., 2016; Gyrard et al., 2016.), etc.. The main drawback of Semantic Web technologies concerns the low level of performance, that makes it difficult to achieve the responsiveness and scalability required in real IoT applications. The main reason for the poor performance is that Semantic Web technologies have been conceived to process data sets consisting of big amounts of Resource Description Framework (RDF) triples (e.g., Open Linked Data project - Connect Distributed Data across the Web, http://linkeddata. org/): the information contained in these data sources evolves constantly, but it evolves at a much slower rate compared to the rate of elementary changes occurring in the physical environment.

Research approaches aiming at adopting Semantic Web technologies to promptly react to changes in the physical environment have been investigated and can be framed within the research topics known as Stream Reasoning (Bazoobandi, Beck & Urbani, 2017), Linked Stream Data Processing (Esposito et al., 2015) and Content-Based Publish-Subscribe (Eugster, Felber, Guerraoui, & Kermarrec, 2003). With reference to semantic publish-subscribe systems, in (Kjær & Hansen, 2010) a model of ontology-based publish-subscribe that uses the Semantic Web Rule Language to define event dissemination and its implementation is presented. In (J. Wang, Jin, & Li, 2004) the authors define an event as an RDF graph and propose their own subscription language and matching algorithm, while in (Chirita, Idreos, Koubarakis, & Nejdl, 2004) a solution to incorporate publish-subscribe capabilities in an RDF-based P2P network is presented. A similar approach is proposed in (Shi, Yin, Li, Qian & Dong, 2007), where events and subscriptions are described as RDF graphs and a fast graph-matching algorithm is presented. To the best of our knowledge, a first attempt to use SPARQL as subscription language with notifications and events expressed using XML was presented in (Skovronski, 2007. In (M Murth, 2008), Murth et al.) focus their attention on coordination problems, expressing subscriptions as RDF graph patterns (i.e., corresponding to SPARQL basic graph patterns) and introducing the idea of "continuous insertion" (i.e., described as a SPARQL CONSTRUCT form) as a way to generate new events when specific events occur (i.e., the Persistent Update primitive implemented in the OSGi SIB). The same authors also present a formal model based on first order logic and temporal propositional logic, a heuristic to optimize the notifications latency (Martin Murth & Kühn, 2009) and knowledge-based interaction patterns based on a set of Semantic Space API Operations (Martin Murth & Kuhn, 2010).

The application of publish subscribe systems to IoT is an hot topic in the current research panorama. It is possible to find many recent articles ranging from entire IoT systems to single parts or specific procedures. It is also very common to feel a stronger and stronger sensibility of the authors to the system robustness because in a complex IoT system it is unacceptable that the failure of a single part prevents the whole system from providing its functionalities. In (Antonić, Marjanović, Pripužić, & Žarko, 2016) the big data originated by the large number of sensors is kept under control thanks to a smart use of the publish subscribe paradigm: instead of sending every observation to the cloud, a local processing is made on mobile devices and only the aggregated data relevant to the applications is transmitted. In (Gündogan, Kietzmann, Schmidt, & Wählisch, 2018) the authors propose a resilient publish subscribe solution robust for typical IoT scenarios with a large node number where the main actors are resource constrained devices working in a condition of intermittent connectivity. In this work the analysis about resiliency is not made at the level of the single data loss, but centered on the capability of the system to recover from unexpected situations both at system level (see last will in 5,1) and at client level (see subscriptions resiliency in 5.2). A different analysis centered on the broker resiliency is made in (Sen, & Balasubramanian, 2018) where the authors propose an IoT architecture which aims at resiliency by properly decoupling the connection management from the connection handling.

With reference to Smart-M3, we compare the OSGi implementation with the RedSIB, the C implementation of the SIB component that is currently the most used. The RedSIB implementation extends the Smart-M3 original implementation (Morandi et al., 2012). It is based on RedLand RDF libraries (Beckett, 2002) and it can use one of the RDF storages supported by RedLand (e.g., hashes, Berkeley DB, Virtuoso (Erling & Mikhailov, 2009). The SSAP protocol (Honkola, Laine, Brown, & Tyrkko, 2010) has been extended to support two new primitives (i.e., SPARQL UPDATE and SPARQL SUBSCRIBE). RedSIB can also be deployed on low cost single core platforms (e.g., on a RaspberryPi). Smart-M3 had a considerable impact on research and literature inspiring works from a large community in different applicative fields like library generation (Lomov, Vanag, & Korzun, 2011), blogging (Korzun et al., 2011), electric mobility (Bedogni et al., 2016), maintenance (D'Elia et al., 2010; Pantsar-Syväniemi et al., 2011), advertisement (Hamza et al., 2014), application development (Palviainen & Katasonov, 2011), healthcare (Vergari et al., 2010). These works led to different SIB implementations derived from the original idea such as solutions integrated in Eclipse (Gómez-Pimpollo & Otaolea, 2010) optimized for embedded devices (Eteläperä, Kiljander, & Keinänen, 2011), or for the web of things (Roffia et al., 2018). The OSGi SIB implementation presented in this chapter differs from the original and from the other implementations because, as explained in the rest of the chapter, it is mainly focused on portability, modularity and extensibility.

OSGi SIB IMPLEMENTATION

The new implementation of the SIB described in this chapter has been conceived to satisfy the practical requirements of real applications. The choice to adopt the OSGi for the implementation of Smart-M3 architecture represents a strategic step in order to develop an interoperability platform able to address requirements such as portability, modularity and extensibility. The OSGi framework, with a service-oriented architecture and a modular approach, allows to optimize costs, provides agility and flexibility, ensuring systems evolution during their entire lifecycle. Moreover, OSGi based applications can integrate in a system easily and dynamically, without writing custom specific integration code and without extra costs. The OSGi applications framework (Open Services Gateway initiative - http://www.osgi. org) provides a programming model for developing, assembling and deploying modular applications based on Java EE technologies. It defines a standardized, component-oriented computing environment for general networked services that is intended to significantly increase the quality of the produced software. OSGi was designed as a services gateway for set-top boxes and, since its introduction in 1998, it has become broadly adopted in industrial application. It has been extensively used in several domains (e.g., automotive, mobile and fixed telephony, industrial automation, gateways & routers, private branch exchanges) and, today, it is supported in many integrated development environments (e.g., IBM Websphere, SpringSource Application Server, Oracle Weblogic, Sun's GlassFish,Eclipse, and Redhat's JBoss) by key companies (e.g., Oracle, IBM,Samsung, Nokia, IONA, Motorola, NTT, Siemens, Hitachi, Ericsson). OSGi provides the environment for running many different applications implemented with a strong component-based SOA oriented model: the framework provides a set of comprehensive and advanced features for installing, starting, stopping, updating, and uninstalling applications dynamically. Furthermore, the framework is adaptive, because bundles can find out what capabilities are available on the system through a service registry and can adapt consequently the functionality they provide. The dynamicity, modularity and flexibility of this SOA framework have been introduced to cover where the Java platform lacks and improve it. The specification defines a security model, an application lifecycle management model, a service registry, an execution environment and modules. The bundle is the basic building block when developing and deploying an application. An OSGi application emerges from a set of bundles, of different types, to provide a coherent business logic.

The software architecture of the OSGi SIB is shown in Figure 2. The blocks correspond to bundles, the oriented arrows are service calls while inside the blocks the bundle names are indicated with bold characters and the dependencies are written in italic.

The novel SIB architecture is strongly based on the OSGi modular approach that reduces the complexity, in terms of system architecture and components development. This approach contributes to the rationalization of applications and exploits components reuse, both at system level and at developer community level. The OSGi SIB components have been designed as configurable OSGi Declarative Services, exposing service API and raising events. Following the OSGi development model, the services offered by the SIB are provided on a per bundle basis. There is not a one to one mapping between services and bundles and, in many cases, a set of bundles represents a service. The binary version of bundle(s) and the service API are the only elements required for application development and, in some cases, services require multiple implementations. Currently, the OSGi SIB runs on an open source OSGi implementation called Equinox (release 3.7.2), from the Eclipse Foundation. This implementation is very simple and potentially ensures a wide diffusion of the SIB in terms of application contexts, operating systems and devices.

The architecture of the new SIB implementation is illustrated in figure 2. The module implemented to manage the communication with the KPs is the TCP bundle. If a message is sent from a KP to the SIB, the TCP bundle reads its content and adds a reference to the message to be processed in a queue managed by the Message Handler bundle (i.e., see AddMessage in Figure 2). The Message Handler bundle receives requests as generic strings, then it delegates the SSAP bundle to transform these requests into a structured internal representation. The Message Handler bundle associates the structured requests with an internal identifier through the GetToken service of the Token Handler bundle, and asks to the SIB bundle to process the request and to provide an appropriate response. When the SIB bundle processes a message, different data flows are possible depending on occurred errors (i.e., the KP making the request does not occur in the list of the Joined KPs managed by the Join bundle) and notifications to be sent (as it will be verified through the services exposed by the Subscription bundle). In all the cases, the SIB bundle generates an internal representation of the messages to be sent back. Messages are serialized by the SSAP bundle through the CreateResponse primitive and sent back to KPs by the callback function of the TCP bundle. The Tools bundle is a reference for the other bundles, it does not expose any service, but exports the relevant classes used to represent the main internal entities like the input-output messages, the notifications, the subscription template and so on. The RDF store is managed by the SIB

Figure 2. OSGi SIB software architecture

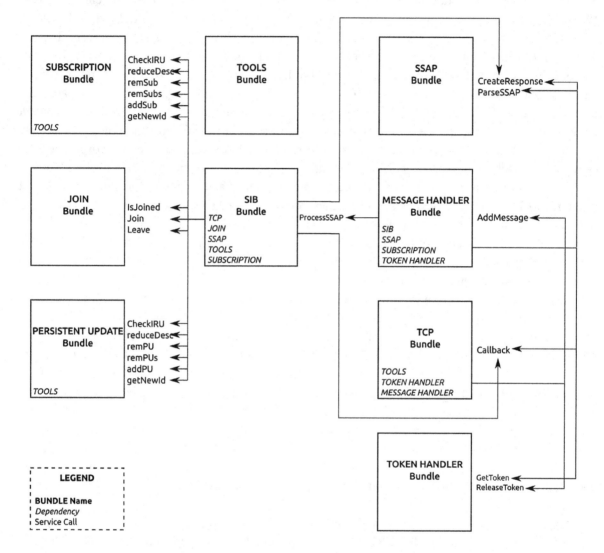

bundle: for this purpose, the well-known Jena libraries (Jena, 2007) have been used to have a solid and well maintained interface toward the stored information. In the Jena framework are also included the ARQ libraries and the TDB libraries, used respectively to efficiently manage SPARQL queries/updates and to store persistent data on the disk.

From the developer perspective, all the services registered to the framework can be called without worrying of service availability (e.g., the SSAP bundle always exposes the ParseSSAP service and if a message is currently under the parsing process the framework will take care of the synchronization issues).

The modular decomposition of the SIB may bring to many considerations and analysis. In this chapter the discussion is limited to the five major contributions identified in the introduction (i.e., flexibility, new functionalities and mobile version of the OSGi SIB). Flexibility is inherent in the modular nature of OSGi based systems and it can be best appreciated with regard to transport and protocol. New transport technologies can be supported by adding new bundles with the same interface of the TCP bundle:

Bluetooth, ZigBee, COAP - Constrained Application Protocol - http://datatracker.ietf.org/doc/draft-ietf-core-coap/, the Knowledge Sharing Protocol (KSP) (Kiljander, Morandi, & Soininen, 2012), or other relevant transport technologies can be substituted or juxtaposed to TCP bundle with the safe addition of modules that can be developed independently by specific area experts. Beside supporting new transport methods, future scenarios may require modification of data serialization (e.g., the migration from XML to JSON in order to limit the dimension of the messages). In this case a new version of the SSAP bundle will be enough to complete the migration to the new message serialization format.

Concerning new functionalities, these can be achieved by adding new bundles or extending existing ones. In the next section we describe a new feature, the persistent SPARQL Update (PU), which has been implemented by adding one bundle and by doing modifications localized in the SIB bundle and in the SSAP bundle.

Persistent Update

The persistent update (PU) is a new primitive specifying a SPARQL 1.1 update which is executed once when it is sent to the SIB and then acting persistently on the RDF store until it is deactivated. In general, a SPARQL update is made up of three clauses: delete, insert and where. The insert and the delete clauses contain variables which are bound by the SPARQL endpoint at the query execution time. The triples inserted or removed by a SPARQL update depend on the RDF store content (i.e., the same SPARQL update may have different effects on the RDF store if launched at different times) so the PU semantics can be considered similar to that of a rule. The rule "If A is a friend of B then A knows B" can be translated in the PU as:

```
INSERT { ?a <#knows> ?b } WHERE { ?a <#friendOf> ?b }
```

which acts on the RDF store promptly and persistently: every time a statement about friendship between two people is asserted, the PU checks if also the assertion about being acquaintances is present and if not, it inserts it in the semantic store. The expressivity of PUs is high, so they can be used for heterogeneous tasks like generating alarms in front of sensor observations, proposing personalized advertisements depending on user profiles and context, ontology alignment, data abstraction and so on. The implementation of the PU consisted of three phases. First, the SSAP protocol has been modified to support the messages related to the new primitive. Four messages have been added to the SSAP specification: MakePU request is sent from a KP to the SIB and it encapsulates the SPARQL update that will be persistently executed. The corresponding response is the MakePU response message which contains the PUID (i.e., a unique identifier used from the KPs to refer to a specific PU). The RemovePU request is sent from a KP to delete a PU through its PUID. If the deletion is correctly performed, then a RemovePU response message is sent back to the KP. Second, an OSGi bundle has been implemented to perform all the logic necessary for the PU management; the corresponding calls to its services have been added in the SIB bundle. The third phase of the PU implementation consisted in a performance optimization to limit the overhead due to PUs execution. This optimization has been the critical part of the PU integration and will be more detailed later in the persistent update evaluation section.

Java SIB for Android

The OSGi SIB was conceived to ensure flexibility and portability. The portability of Java VM and of the OSGi Framework allowed to easily install and run SIBs on Linux platforms (i.e., like the reference implementation that is bound to Linux dependencies), but also on Windows and MAC OS. A more difficult task was to port the OSGi SIB on mobile devices like tablets and smartphones. The porting on mobile devices is a relevant result because it extends the scenarios covered by Smart-M3 with new features and potentialities, increasing dramatically the potential diffusion of the OSGi SIB. Healthcare, electric mobility, social services and many other domains may benefit from a mobile SIB capable to store and share data in a semantic (i.e., interoperable) format. In the healthcare domain, for example, end users equipped with wearable sensors could store their biometrical parameters on their personal smartphone in a semantically rich format. Stored data, together with other information on the mobile SIB (e.g., the user profile and data observed from the internal equipment of the device) can be elaborated at run time or offline by medical personnel or by interoperable services to protect the end user health.

As the OSGi SIB is written in Java, the porting to a mobile platform was directed towards the Android OS, whose Dalvik virtual machine supports most of the Java language. We found that the OSGi SIB does not work without modifications on Android 4.2 or less, so we implemented a new Java SIB version specific to solve this portability issue, leaving to future works the porting of the main OSGi SIB distribution. The main encountered issues were:

- **Dynamic Class Loading:** Poorly supported in Dalvik VM and often used in OSGi framework;
- **I/O:** To be redirected from Java console or managed in a way specific for the Android OS;
- **Number of Methods:** Some of the imported packages, like ARQ, contain too many methods for the Dalvik virtual machine.

The dynamic class loading problem was solved simplifying the software architecture into the one shown in Figure 3 not based on OSGi bundles but on simple Java classes and threads. An Android Activity has been implemented for Input-Output operations and the SIB manager thread coordinates with other three main threads (TCP-IP, MessageHandler and Store) to provide the typical SIB functionalities. Thanks to the use of symbolic links and auxiliary libraries, the deployed packages meet the Dalvik VM requirements.

EVALUATION

While frameworks, benchmarks and methods for performance evaluation of Semantic Web systems have been proposed in the literature (Bizer & Schultz, 2009; Garcia-Castro & et al., 2013; Guo, Pan, & Heflin, 2005; Guo, Qasem, Pan, & Heflin, 2007; Angles et al., 2014), these methods are not suitable to evaluate the OSGi SIB with reference to its specific features and advantages (i.e., SPARQL subscription and SPARQL persistent update). To this end, we defined a benchmark inspired by a smart public lighting system that will be described later on in this section. This benchmark has been adopted to compare the OSGi SIB and the RedSIB in terms of (i) subscriptions notification latency, (ii) time to update the RDF store (also in presence of active subscriptions) and to evaluate the OSGi SIB specific persistent SPARQL update primitive. On the other hand, the SPARQL query performance are evaluated on an

Figure 3. Android SIB software architecture

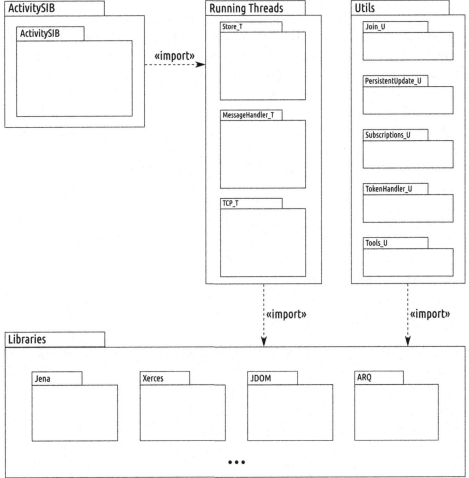

existing benchmark (Schmidt, Hornung, Lausen, & Pinkel, 2009) in order to obtain results that can be compared with other solutions and can be useful to further evaluate the overhead introduced by the OSGi SIB on the underpinning RDF store.

Smart Lighting System Benchmark

The benchmark designed to evaluate the OSGi SIB implementation is inspired by the public lighting system of a city with large, medium, small and very small roads (i.e., roads with up to 100, 50, 25 and 10 lamp-posts). Each post is supposed to be equipped with a lamp and two sensors (i.e., temperature and presence). Each road and each lamp within a road are identified by a URI respectively in the form: ROAD_URI_X and LAMP_URI_X_Y, where X is a road identifier, while Y is a lamp identifier within a road (i.e., Y varies from 1 to NLAMP, where NLAMP is the amount of lamp-posts in road X). Each lamp is characterized by a status (i.e., ON, OFF, BROKEN), a dimming value (i.e., 0-100%) and a type (i.e., LED, TRADITIONAL). Each post is identified by its geographical position (i.e., latitude and longitude), while each sensor is represented by a set of properties: the type (e.g., TEMPERATURE, PRESENCE), the unit of measurement (e.g., °C), the value (e.g., 32, True, False) and a timestamp (i.e., expressed as Unix time extended to μs).

Table 1 provides the details about the ontology and the SPARQL endpoint RDF store size (i.e., number of RDF triples) of a city with 9500 posts (i.e., 42 triples are needed to describe a single lamp-post).

The benchmark considers the following primitives, where X indicates the index of a road, while Y indicates the index of a lamp post within a road:

```
Update U1 (i.e., set to "n" the dimming value of lamp Y within road X)
PREFIX   unibo: <http://www.unibo.it/benchmark#>
DELETE   { unibo:LAMP_URI_X_Y unibo:hasDimmingValue ?dimming }
INSERT   { unibo:LAMP_URI_X_Y unibo:hasDimmingValue "n" }
WHERE    { unibo:LAMP_URI_X_Y unibo:hasDimmingValue ?dimming }
Update U2 (i.e., the presence sensor of lamp Y within road X detects a pres-
ence)
PREFIX   unibo: <http://www.unibo.it/benchmark#>
DELETE   { unibo:SENSOR_URI_X_Y unibo:hasSensorDataValue ?value }
INSERT   { unibo:SENSOR_URI_X_Y unibo:hasSensorDataValue "true" }
WHERE    { unibo:SENSOR_URI_X_Y unibo:hasSensorDataValue ?value }
```

Subscription S1 (i.e., subscribe to changes of the dimming value of any lamp within road X)

```
PREFIX   unibo: <http://www.unibo.it/benchmark#>
SELECT   ?lamp ?dimming
WHERE    { unibo:ROAD_URI_X unibo:isConnectedTo ?post .
?post unibo:hasLamp ?lamp .
?lamp unibo:hasDimmingValue ?dimming}
```

Persistent update PU1 (i.e., if a presence sensor of any lamp of road X detects a presence then all the lamps of road X are turned on)

```
PREFIX   unibo: <http://www.unibo.it/benchmark#>
DELETE { ?lamp unibo:hasDimmingValue ?dimming }
INSERT   { ?lamp unibo:hasDimmingValue "100" }
WHERE    { unibo:ROAD_URI_X unibo:isConnectedTo ?post .
unibo:ROAD_URI_X unibo:isConnectedTo ?postUpdate .
?postUpdate unibo:hasLamp ?lamp .
?lamp unibo:hasDimmingValue ?dimming .
?post unibo:hasSensor ?sens .
?sens unibo:hasSensorData ?data .
?data unibo:hasSensorDataValue "true" .
?data unibo:hasMeasurand unibo:PRESENCE }
```

Test Bench

Both the SIB instances (OSGi and RedSIB) run on the same server machine (12 CPUs Intel(R) Xeon(R) CPU E5-2430 v2 @ 2.50GHz 6 Cores, 64 GB RAM, Ubuntu Server 15.04) on a dedicated Virtual Machine (Ubuntu 12.04 LTS, 32 GB RAM, 8 CPUs) while the KPs are written using the Python API and run on a Samsung RC530 PC (CPU Intel i7-2670QM eight core 2.2 GHz, 8 GB RAM, Linux Mint 17 Qiana). The RedSIB is tested using both hash-tables in RAM and Virtuoso. Instead, the OSGi is evaluated using Jena running in RAM. KPs are connected to the SIB through a 100Mbps LAN connection. In all the tests (except for the ones on the notification latency of subscriptions and persistent updates), the time has been measured from the start of a KP request to the delivery of a reply. Timing components can be expressed as:

$$T = Trequest + Telaboration + Treply$$

where Trequest represents the time spent by the KP to build an SSAP message and transmit it to the SIB, Telaboration is the time required by the SIB to elaborate the request, Treply is the time interval required to send the response message from the SIB to the KP, including the time spent by the KP to parse the message.

Insert Time Evaluation

The first test measures the time required to insert a block of n lamp-posts (i.e., with n in the range [1..100]). Taking into account that a lamp-post is represented by 42 RDF triples, the number of inserted RDF triples varies from 42 to 4,2K. Insert time is a relevant metric to compare SIB performance because it is almost independent from the RDF store content. Moreover, insertions are quite common in the IoT (e.g., a new sensor node joins a Wireless Sensor Network), so the tests results will reflect SIB responsiveness in real conditions, not limited to lab environment. When the number of triples to insert grows,

Table 1. Smart lighting benchmark knowledge base summary

Road Type	N$_{LAMP}$/Road	Roads	OWL Ontology T-BOX Content	
			Classes	27
			Individuals	26
			Object Properties	16
			Datatype Properties	8
			Lamp-Post Instances	
			Lamp-Posts (Sensors)	**RDF Triples**
Very small	10	100	1K (2K)	35K
Small	25	100	2.5K (5K)	88K
Medium	50	100	5K (10K)	175K
Large	100	10	1K (2K)	35K
Total		**310**	**9.5K (19K)**	**334K**

both Trequest and Telaboration increase, since a longer message will be built and sent, a longer time is needed for the parsing phase and a higher number of triples must be inserted. Treply is not affected by the block size because, according to the SSAP specifications, the reply is always the same (i.e., a confirmation message) and does not depend on the number of inserted triples. The results (see Figure 4) show that the OSGi SIB outperforms the other two SIB implementations and this is more evident as the number of inserted lamp-posts increases. The gap with the RedSIB with Virtuoso is clear and it can be expected as it uses a persistent on-disk store.

To evaluate the scalability with the number of active subscriptions, the test is performed also in presence of active subscriptions (i.e., from 10 to 100 with steps of 10 subscriptions), where none of these is triggered. Figure 5 shows how all the SIB implementations scale very well with the number of active subscriptions and, at the same time, are not affected by the size of the update (i.e., 1, 10, 100 lamp-posts). The RedSIB Virtuoso trend with 100 lamp-posts is not shown in Figure 5 just because of readability reasons as its values span from 5673 ms, with 10 subscriptions, to 5840 ms, with 100 subscriptions. This means that also RedSIB with Virtuoso scales well with the number of active subscriptions.

Subscriptions Notification Latency Evaluation

Subscriptions represent a relevant feature of the SIB which allows reactivity to context changes and reduce network traffic by avoiding resource demanding solutions based on polling. At the same time, subscriptions allow KPs to be notified of any relevant changes in the RDF store, allowing them to keep track of the context evolution. The drawback of this approach is represented by the fact that subscriptions require more resources and processing time to be executed, server-side. A SIB implementation should be characterised by a negligible impact on performance due to subscriptions. More precisely, subscriptions require, in principle, an unavoidable effort (i.e., required for every operation which modifies the RDF store) to check if an RDF store update may trigger a notification and, if this happens, an additional effort to determine the content of notification. We evaluated the former effort in Figure 5, where the scalability

Figure 4. Time to insert a block of n lamp-posts without any active susbcription or persistent update

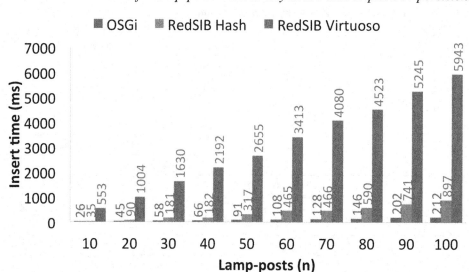

Figure 5. Time to insert a block of 1, 10, 100 lamp-posts with n active subscriptions

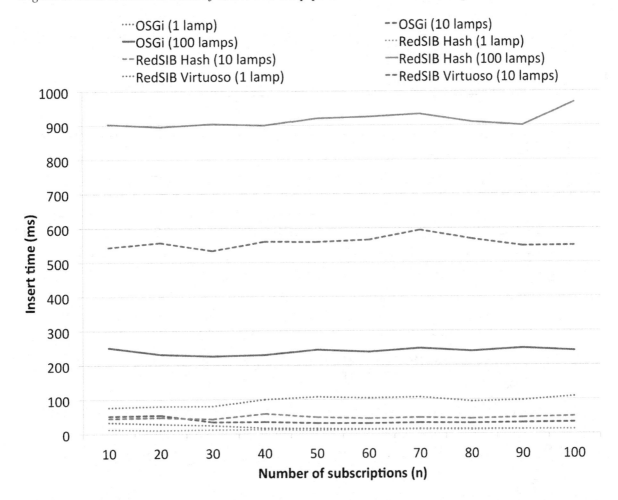

with the number of active subscriptions (i.e., not triggered) has been proved. Instead, the following test aims at measuring the latency of notifications. An increasing number of subscriptions (see S1 in the bechmark definition) is spanned over roads of different sizes (see Table 2).

Several updates of the dimming value of a single lamp (see U1 in benchmark definition), always triggering the same subscription (i.e., if the update changes the dimming value of LAMP_X_Y only the subscription to ROAD_X is triggered), are executed and the average latency taken from when the updates are issued to when the corresponding notifications are received (on the KP side) is measured. The test is repeated four times considering each time, as triggered subscription, a subscription to a road of different size (i.e., very small, small, medium, large).

As shown in Figure 6, the OSGi SIB outperforms the other two SIB implementations. If the number of active subscriptions is less than 40, no difference can be appreciated between the OSGi and RedSIB hash (excluding the case of RedSIB hash with the triggered subscription on a large road). The RedSIB Virtuoso performance, using a persistent store, performs well if the triggered subscription is on a very small road. Instead, considering the large road case, the RedSIB performance decrease both using hash-tables and Virtuoso as RDF store.

Table 2. Subscriptions distribution

Road Size				Total Number of S1 Subscriptions
Very Small	**Small**	**Medium**	**Large**	
3	3	3	1	10
6	6	6	2	20
9	9	9	3	30
12	12	12	4	40
15	15	15	5	50
18	18	18	6	60
21	21	21	7	70
24	24	24	8	80
27	27	27	9	90
30	30	30	10	100

Figure 6. Notification latency versus number of active subscriptions

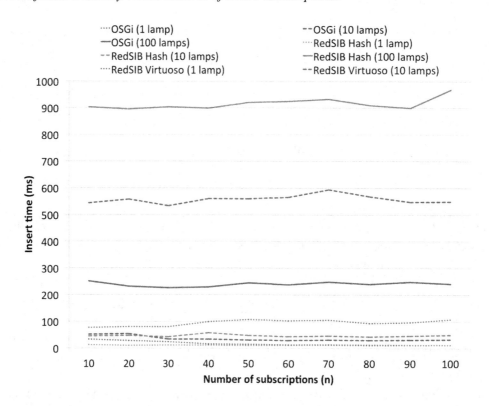

Figure 7. Time to insert a block of 1 or 10 lamp-posts with n active persistent updates

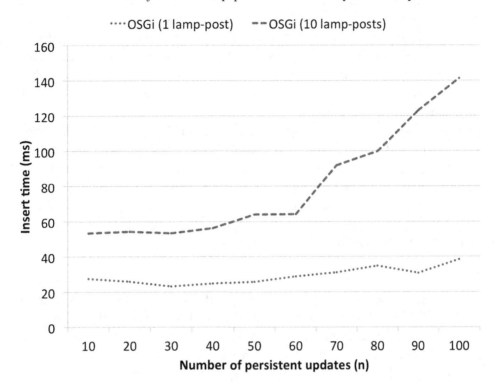

Persistent Updates Evaluation

A naive implementation of PUs consists in letting the PU bundle run his business logic for every operation implying a RDF store modification. This means that, for every insertion or removal, all the PUs must be executed at least once (excluding PUs firing other PUs), even if no modifications to KB will be performed after the execution of all the PUs. This implementation leads clearly to performance issues because the SIB, that is intended to share context data among many interacting entities, should be responsive and efficient. In fact, PUs must be executed only when necessary (i.e., when the conditions in the WHERE clause change). To improve performances, we proposed an optimization of the naive PU execution which, similarly to what happens with subscriptions, makes a pre-analysis of the incoming updates in order to filter the PUs that are not sensitive to the triples modified by such updates. This optimization makes it possible to have many PUs active at the same time, with a negligible impact on performance only due to triggered PUs, or with an acceptable performance reduction when the RDF store modifications does not trigger any PU.

Like for the subscriptions, following this approach we can state that in principle also for the PUs an unavoidable effort to check if updates have to be performed must be spent, such as an additional effort must be considered only if the PU is triggered by some modification on the KB. Figure 7 shows the unavoidable impact evaluated inserting a different number of lamp-posts (i.e., 1 or 10) and increasing the number of active persistent updates, where none of them is triggered.

A second additional component of this impact depends on the RDF store content, on the PU query and on the SPARQL engine used (i.e., Apache Jena). To evaluate the effort needed when a PU is triggered, we measure the notification latency of a subscription triggered by that PU. The test considers the persistent update PU1, the update U2 and the subscription S1 (see benchmark definition). When the presence sensor Y of a lamp-post within the road X detects an object, PU1 is activated, it turns on all the lamps of road X and subscription U1 is triggered. The test measures the elapsed time from the instant when the presence sensor updates its data to the instant when a notification of S1 is received. The test is performed several times and average latencies are calculated considering four roads of different size (i.e., very small, small, medium and large).

Results analysis shows a not negligible impact of not triggered PUs on insert time: this impact must be taken into consideration and reduced as much as possible in future releases as it limits the usage of more PUs at the same time. Figure 8 instead shows a good performance of a single triggered PU. In this case, the latency increases with the road size mainly because of the dimension of the notification: a very small road notification produces up to 10 results, while a large road notification produces up to 100 results.

SP²B Benchmark Evaluation

Schmidt et al. in (Schmidt et al., 2009) propose a SPARQL performance benchmark based on the DBLP scenario and composed by a set of seventeen queries with different selectivity, query size and output size. DBLP (http://dblp.uni-trier.de) is a web service offered by the University of Trier and Schloss Dagstuhl that provides bibliographic information about computer science journals and proceedings. This benchmark, called SP²B (SPARQL Performance Benchmark) has been specifically designed for the SPARQL evaluation, so the proposed queries address language specific issues. The benchmark is provided with a data generator that produces an N3 file with n triples, where n can vary from a minimum of 10k up to a maximum of 25M triples. The following tables report the average time elapsed to perform the queries by the OSGi SIB. Such queries have been evaluated with a data set composed respectively by 10K and 50K triples. The first column in Table 3 contains the query identifier, while for the two data sets both the expected number of results and the query time are reported (queries Q12a, Q12b and Q12c are SPARQL ASK queries, so they only expect result is True or False). $T_{request}$ is almost the same for each query, since the differences related to the length of the queries can be neglected. The relevant time components here are $T_{elaboration}$ and T_{reply} respectively influenced by the complexity of the query and by the number of results.

Figure 8. Time to receive a notification fired by a persistent update subscribed to roads of different size

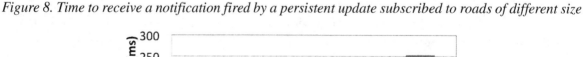
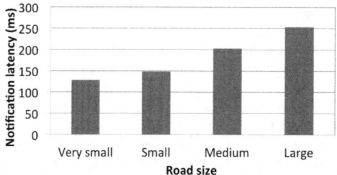

OSGI SIB EXTENDED FEATURES

The first implementation of the OSGi SIB has been further extended to make the M3 architecture resilient to unstable connections, and therefore suitable for a wider range of scenarios characterized by stronger constraints. Three different classes of scenarios, where such architectural solution would play a fundamental role, have been identified:

- **Frequent Temporary Disconnections:** E.g. consider a scenario where a drone is responsible for surveillance operation in a wide area partially covered by network connectivity. The drone flies in and out the areas covered by network services and it is not possible (without specific addons) to deal with the temporary disconnections to grant a resilient application. This happens because relevant information to be notified to the drone may be never received as when the drone exits from a covered area, subscriptions fall, and notifications are lost.
- **Local Image of a Shared Subgraph:** Semantic clients often maintain an image of the shared subgraph used to interoperate. The subscriptions grant the synchronization of the local copies with the centralized one, allowing the local consistency and coherence of data and the global proper operation of the application. In this class of scenarios, the disconnections or temporary failures of some of the interacting agents may be destructive for the whole application, depending on the criticality level determined by losing the synchronization between the different images of the target subgraph.

Table 3. SP²B query times with 10K and 50K triples data sets

Query	10K Triples Data Set		50K Triples Data Set	
	Query Time (s)	Expected Results	Query Time (s)	Expected Results
Q1	0.022	1	0.011	1
Q2	0.219	147	0.807	965
Q3a	0.125	846	0.401	3647
Q3c	0.014	0	0.028	25
Q3b	0.010	9	0.021	0
Q4	9.181	23226	>300	104746
Q5a	0.774	155	22.569	1085
Q5b	0.324	155	10.684	1085
Q6	0.623	229	24.707	1769
Q7	0.146	0	5.183	2
Q8	0.049	184	0.062	264
Q9	0.025	4	0.041	4
Q10	0.045	166	0.116	307
Q11	0.021	10	0.020	10
Q12a	0.009	True	0.027	True
Q12b	0.014	True	0.009	True
Q12c	0.007	True	0.009	True

- **Security and Monitoring:** E.g., in surveillance application, presence sensors or cameras may be connected with a semantic broker and cooperate with other devices or processes, like RFID readers and context reasoners, to detect unwanted accesses to restricted areas or potentially dangerous situations. The sensors may also be dedicated to send relevant observations about the status of equipment that are critical for security, to ensure a prompt maintenance in case of failures or wear. In these scenarios the failure of one device may impact on the whole system, affecting the awareness of happening relevant situations or of events happened in the past. In these scenarios, it is important to store all the observations and to keep track of the whole context, capturing both the present and past events in their chronological evolution. A temporarily disconnection of an agent should not prevent its ability to detect even past events (i.e. undesired accesses) once it reconnects. It should then be able to access the information acquired by sensors and be informed about their timestamps. In predictive maintenance applications both the observations about parameters out of bound and their frequency in time are relevant. If some observations cannot be received as notification because of a disconnection it is necessary to recover not only the observation's values or their numbers, but also the specific instants in which they were generated.

To properly manage similar scenarios, architectural changes and add-ons have been applied to the original implementation of the OSGI SIB and are currently available as prototypes. The main topics to describe about the new features are the introduction of the last will primitive and the different levels of resiliency for subscriptions.

Last Will

The last will (LW) is a primitive used in the MQTT protocol to execute a final action when a client disconnects. MQTT is a broker-centric protocol exploiting the publish-subscribe paradigm (Eugster, Felber, Guerraoui, & Kermarrec, 2003). Despite being architecturally similar to Smart-M3, application based on MQTT ecosystem is bound to a lower level of information and it is so not applicable to the same scenarios of smart-M3. In fact, the data model is too simple to describe complex scenarios or situations. While in Smart-M3 the data model is an oriented, labeled graph with nodes and arcs semantically referenceable by means of an ontology, in MQTT there is just a tree of topics in which branches and leaves contains a textual entry. The research challenge faced while modifying the original architecture and primitive set was to enjoy the benefits of LW in a more advanced information world, where the last will provides higher expressivity and more flexibility of use. The details of the work done to implement the new primitive are reported in (D'Elia, Aguzzi et al., 2017). The application of the LW to a semantic KB and its inclusion in the Smart-M3 architecture improves the overall reliability and provides new dynamics that can be exploited by developers with simpler code. The advantages are twofold: first, each agent specifying a LW, inherently instantiates a persistent connection with the central KB that can be used to verify its temporary or definitive unavailability. Second, when a connection is not working properly, it is the LW itself that may automatically start recovery procedures to solve the lack of resources due to the agent unavailability. The last will primitive was implemented with minimal delay on other operations in fact, as shown in figure 9 the insertion time of triples is mainly independent from the number of active last will. this because the architecture of the OSGI SIB allowed to build the mechanisms related to the last will management outside from the main data flow.

Subscriptions Resiliency

When facing a hostile environment the applications based on the publish-subscribe paradigm are strongly affected by the issues related to temporary disconnections, in particular if a subscribed agent is maintaining a local copy of a subgraph that is continuously and collaboratively edited by multiple agents. Obviously if a disconnection occurs, there is loss of synchronization between the local and remote copy of the subgraph and, furthermore, recovery operations are impossible during the disconnection phase. However, it is at least possible to improve the overall system resiliency with modifications to the subscription management, in order to recover automatically the current and even the past subgraph states. While the LW is an instrument that can be used to make the system aware of the disconnection and to take automatic recovery actions, the improvement of the subscriptions resiliency level is related to the recovery at client side, in order minimize the information lost during the disconnection and to resynchronize it with the current context seamlessly.

In general subscriptions are managed through the scheme in Figure 10 where the subscription message contains a query to the main store; it returns as answer the whole query result, and finally notifications are sent from the server for each new result (triples added matching the query) or obsolete results (triples removed). On the client side the developer implements the application code using Smart Space access

Figure 9. Response time for an insert of 50 triples in absence of disconnections and with growing number of active last wills
(D'Elia, Aguzzi, et all, 2017).

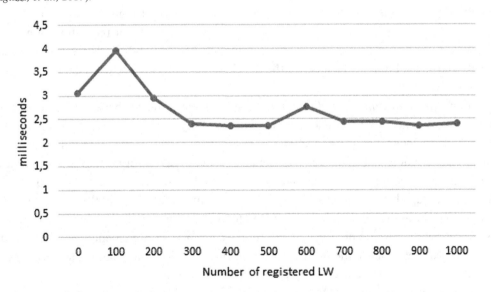

Figure 10. Main modules at client and server side involved in subscriptions.

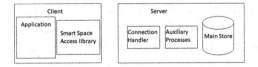

libraries, specific libraries conceived to hide the low level details: the application makes subscriptions and it is notified by means of the Smart Space access libraries, which manage the interaction with the SIB at transport level and may run helper processes managing local objects and data structures. On the server side the connection handler is responsible of detecting the disconnection and identifying the affected clients. The auxiliary processes run all the required procedures to manage the subscriptions, storing in a local memory the required data structures and building the notification messages. The main objective is to have a system where the developer is unaware of the internal details so that he can focus on the application.

Five levels of subscription resiliency have been identified. In the following list we consider as main use cases the one in which an image in the application of a subgraph in the main store must be maintained as synchronized as possible (requirement satisfied at resiliency level 3), and the use case of monitoring events which may be relevant for the security (requirement satisfied at resiliency level 5):

Level 1: *simple subscription.* If a disconnection happens the client and the server deallocate all the resources bound to the subscriptions. On the server side it is possible to use a lazy policy which require cheap resources, i.e. when a notification can't be sent all the subscriptions with that specific client are deallocated. Using this basic resiliency level, the synchronization between the subgraph image in the client and the real graph in the store is lost and the developer must take care of the code necessary to restart the subscription and resynchronize with the store. The events occurred during the disconnection phase are, in part, lost from the application perspective.

Level 2: *subscription with reconnection.* The server does not remove the resources related to the subscriptions if communication problems arise, the libraries automatically recover the connection when possible. The disconnection is detected through beacons sent at regular intervals. This solution makes it simpler from the developer perspective to build the code for the application recovery at reconnection. The re-synchronization between the local image and the subgraph in the store can be made automatic but is still a load for the developer. The events occurred during the disconnection are partially lost.

Level 3: *reconnection and state rebuild.* A summary of all the differences between the target sub-graph states before and after the reconnection are automatically sent to the client. After some study it was possible to detect a strategy to apply this resiliency level with modification only on the client library. This solution makes the re-synchronization automatic with no burden for the developer. The events occurred during the disconnection are partially lost, because a comparison of the target and local subgraph before and after the disconnection inherently lack all the triples that are added and removed during the disconnection. In an application for monitoring access to structures the presence sensors will state presence and eventually remove the statement when the intruder exits the monitored area. If both the event happens during the disconnection of the intruder detection agent, it is not possible to detect the intrusion after the reconnection.

Level 4: *reconnection and history.* At this level, server-side modification allows temporary substitution of the disconnected client with a thread server side, using local memory to store all the notifications that would have been sent to the client. When the reconnection happens, all the notifications are sent and the client can continue its operations. As for level 3, the resynchronization is automatic with no burden for the developer. No events are lost, but their temporal information is lost. Notifications are strongly connected with the instant in which they are sent, so sending them later allow to determine that an event happened, but not when it happened, if it happened before or after another notification or its frequency in time.

Level 5: *reconnection and chronological history.* Processes server side don't simply store the notifications, but enrich them with timestamp information. The notifications are sent with a special message which envelope both the notifications and their timestamp, so that on client side it is possible to reconstruct the whole history of the subgraph. This resiliency level requires strong modifications both server side and client side: it introduces a new data model for the notifications happened during the disconnection period and, moreover, it implies effort and resources from the libraries and from the developer in the applicative code, so it is advisable to use this kind of subscriptions only if required by the applicative use case.

Level 1 is the starting point of our research, already implemented in [D'Elia, Viola, Roffia, Azzoni, & Cinotti, 2017], while Level 5 allows the maximum recovery after a disconnection. However, Level 5 needs lot of resources and its adoption in real scenarios must be motivated by strong application requirements. Level 3 was recognized as a fair improvement to the basic simple subscriptions and it is currently used as default subscription resiliency level.

CONCLUSION

In this paper the authors presented an OSGi implementation of a semantic information broker (SIB), which represents the core component of the Smart-M3 interoperability platform. The main motivations are based on the interest that the research and industrial community demonstrated on the Smart-M3 based services and programming model. Besides making a solution fully compatible with existing legacy applications based on the RedSIB implementation, the OSGi SIB includes a new and expressive primitive, the SPARQL Persistent Update, which allows to integrate rules into Smart-M3 applications. It was also presented a specific SIB implementation for the Android OS conceived to increase the number of envisioned scenarios, including also those where interoperable data and services are required on mobile devices. This demonstrated the portability of the OSGI SIB solution. With reference to the proposed benchmarks, the evaluation revealed good performance both for insert and query operations. The OSGi SIB scales with the number of active subscriptions, granting at the same time a low latency on notifications.

As stated in (Bellavista, Corradi, Fanelli, & Foschini, 2012; Gubbi, Buyya, Marusic, & Palaniswami, 2013; Perera, Zaslavsky, Christen, & Georgakopoulos, 2014; Suo, Wan, Zou, & Liu, 2012), security in context aware systems is still an open issue. In this chapter, the resiliency aspect was taken in consideration by proposing a new primitive and extending the subscription mechanisms. Future work on the OSGi SIB will focus on support for security mechanisms in order to provide confidentiality, integrity and availability of data (the so-called CIA Triad). This task will be achieved through the development of a proper set of bundles implementing a security infrastructure that exploits Semantic Web technologies to define powerful, efficient and effective access control methods.

REFERENCES

Abowd, G. D., Dey, A. K., Brown, P. J., Davies, N., Smith, M., & Steggles, P. (1999). Towards a better understanding of context and context-awareness. In Handheld and ubiquitous computing (pp. 304–307). doi:10.1007/3-540-48157-5_29

Angles, R., Boncz, P., Larriba-Pey, J., Fundulaki, I., Neumann, T., Erling, O., ... Toma, I. (2014). The linked data benchmark council: A graph and RDF industry benchmarking effort. *SIGMOD Record, 43*(1), 27–31. doi:10.1145/2627692.2627697

Antonić, A., Marjanović, M., Pripužić, K., & Žarko, I. P. (2016). A mobile crowd sensing ecosystem enabled by CUPUS: Cloud-based publish/subscribe middleware for the Internet of Things. *Future Generation Computer Systems, 56*, 22–607. doi:10.1016/j.future.2015.08.005

Barnaghi, P., Wang, W., Henson, C., & Taylor, K. (2012). Semantics for the Internet of Things: Early Progress and Back to the Future. *International Journal on Semantic Web and Information Systems, 8*(1), 1–21. doi:10.4018/jswis.2012010101

Bazoobandi, H. R., Beck, H., & Urbani, J. (2017). Expressive stream reasoning with laser. In *International Semantic Web Conference* (pp. 87-103). Cham: Springer.

Beckett, D. (2002). The design and implementation of the Redland RDF application framework. *Computer Networks, 39*(5), 577–588. doi:10.1016/S1389-1286(02)00221-9

Bedogni, L., Bononi, L., Di Felice, M., D'Elia, A., Mock, R., Morandi, F., ... Vergari, F. (2016). An Integrated Simulation Framework to Model Electric Vehicle Operations and Services. *IEEE Transactions on Vehicular Technology, 65*(8), 5900–5917. doi:10.1109/TVT.2015.2453125

Bellavista, P., Corradi, A., Fanelli, M., & Foschini, L. (2012). A survey of context data distribution for mobile ubiquitous systems. *ACM Computing Surveys, 44*(4), 24. doi:10.1145/2333112.2333119

Berners-Lee, T., Hendler, J., & Lassila, O. (2001). The semantic web. *Scientific American, 284*(5), 28–37. doi:10.1038cientificamerican0501-34 PMID:11341160

Bizer, C., & Schultz, A. (2009). The Berlin SPARQL Benchmark. *International Journal on Semantic Web and Information Systems, 5*(2), 1–24. doi:10.4018/jswis.2009040101

Chen, H., Finin, T., & Joshi, A. (2005). *Semantic web in the context broker architecture.*

Chen, H., Finin, T., Joshi, A., Kagal, L., Perich, F., & Chakraborty, D. (2004). Intelligent agents meet the semantic web in smart spaces. *IEEE Internet Computing, 8*(6), 69–79. doi:10.1109/MIC.2004.66

Chirita, P.-A., Idreos, S., Koubarakis, M., & Nejdl, W. (2004). Publish/subscribe for rdf-based p2p networks. In The Semantic Web: Research and Applications (pp. 182–197). Springer.

D'Elia, A., Aguzzi, C., Viola, F., Antoniazzi, F., & Cinotti, T. S. (2017). Implementation and evaluation of the last will primitive in a semantic information broker for IoT applications. In*IEEE 3rd International Forum on Research and Technologies for Society and Industry (RTSI)*, Modena (pp. 1-5) 10.1109/RTSI.2017.8065947

D'Elia, A., Roffia, L., Zamagni, G., Vergari, F., Toninelli, A., & Bellavista, P. (2010). Smart applications for the maintenance of large buildings: How to achieve ontology-based interoperability at the information level. In *Proceedings - IEEE Symposium on Computers and Communications* (pp. 1077–1082).

D'Elia, A., Viola, F., Roffia, L., Azzoni, P., & Cinotti, T. S. (2017). Enabling Interoperability in the Internet of Things: A OSGi Semantic Information Broker Implementation. *Int. J. on Semantic Web and Information Systems*, *13*(1), 147–167. doi:10.4018/IJSWIS.2017010109

Erling, O., & Mikhailov, I. (2009). RDF Support in the Virtuoso DBMS. In *Networked Knowledge-Networked Media* (pp. 7–24). Springer. doi:10.1007/978-3-642-02184-8_2

Esposito, C., Ficco, M., Palmieri, F., & Castiglione, A. (2015). A knowledge-based platform for Big Data analytics based on publish/subscribe services and stream processing. *Knowledge-Based Systems*, *79*, 3–17. doi:10.1016/j.knosys.2014.05.003

Eteläperä, M., Kiljander, J., & Keinänen, K. (2011). Feasibility Evaluation of M3 Smart Space Broker Implementations. In *2011 IEEE/IPSJ 11th International Symposium on Applications and the Internet (SAINT)* (pp. 292–296). 10.1109/SAINT.2011.56

Eugster, P. T., Felber, P. A., Guerraoui, R., & Kermarrec, A.-M. (2003). The many faces of publish/subscribe. *ACM Computing Surveys*, *35*(2), 114–131. doi:10.1145/857076.857078

Garcìa-Castro, R. (2013). *Web Semantics: Science, Services and Agents on the World Wide Web.*

Gómez-Pimpollo, J. F., & Otaolea, R. (2010). Smart Objects for Intelligent Applications-ADK. In *2010 IEEE Symposium on Visual Languages and Human-Centric Computing (VL/HCC)* (pp. 267–268). 10.1109/VLHCC.2010.52

Gubbi, J., Buyya, R., Marusic, S., & Palaniswami, M. (2013). Internet of Things (IoT): A vision, architectural elements, and future directions. *Future Generation Computer Systems*, *29*(7), 1645–1660. doi:10.1016/j.future.2013.01.010

Gündogan, C., Kietzmann, P., Schmidt, T. C. & Wählisch M. (2018). HoPP: Robust and Resilient Publish-Subscribe for an Information-Centric Internet of things.

Guo, Y., Pan, Z., & Heflin, J. (2005). LUBM: A Benchmark for OWL Knowledge Base Systems. *Journal of Web Semantics*, *3*(2-3), 158–182. doi:10.1016/j.websem.2005.06.005

Guo, Y., Qasem, A., Pan, Z., & Heflin, J. (2007). A Requirements Driven Framework for Benchmarking Semantic Web Knowledge Base Systems. *Knowledge and Data Engineering. IEEE Transactions on*, *19*(2), 297–309. doi:10.1109/TKDE.2007.19

Gyrard, A., Patel, P., Datta, S., & Ali, M. (2016, October). Semantic web meets internet of things (iot) and web of things (wot). In *The 15th International Conference on Semantic Web (ISWC)*.

Hamza, H. S., Enas Ashraf, A. K., Nabih, M. M. A., Ahmed, M., Alaa, S., Hosny, K., … Attallah, A. (2014). SALE--An Innovative Platform for Semantically Enriching Next Generation Advertising Services. *Social Media and Publicity, 53.*

Honkola, J., Laine, H., Brown, R., & Tyrkko, O. (2010). Smart-M3 information sharing platform. In The IEEE symposium on Computers and Communications (pp. 1041–1046). doi:10.1109/ISCC.2010.5546642

Jena, A. (2007). semantic web framework for Java.

Kiljander, J., Morandi, F., & Soininen, J.-P. (2012). Knowledge sharing protocol for smart spaces. *International Journal of Advanced Computer Science and Applications, 3*(9). doi:10.14569/IJACSA.2012.030915

Kjær, K. E., & Hansen, K. M. (2010). Modeling and Implementing Ontology-Based Publish/Subscribe Using Semantic Web Technologies. In *2010 15th IEEE International Conference on Engineering of Complex Computer Systems (ICECCS)* (pp. 63–71).

Korzun, D. G., Galov, I. V., Kashevnik, A. M., Shilov, N. G., Krinkin, K., & Korolev, Y. (2011). Integration of Smart-M3 applications: Blogging in smart conference. In Smart Spaces and Next Generation Wired/Wireless Networking (pp. 51–62). Springer.

Kovatsch, M., Hassan, Y. N., & Mayer, S. (2015, October). Practical semantics for the Internet of Things: Physical states, device mashups, and open questions. In *2015 5th International Conference on the Internet of Things (IOT)* (pp. 54-61). IEEE.

Lamorte, L., Licciardi, C. A., Marengo, M., Salmeri, A., Mohr, P., & Raffa, G., … Cinotti, T. S. (2007). A platform for enabling context aware telecommunication services. In *Third Workshop on Context Awareness for Proactive Systems*, Guildford, UK.

Lomov, A. A., Vanag, P. I., & Korzun, D. G. (2011). Multilingual ontology library generator for Smart-M3 application development. In *Proc. 9th Conf. of Open Innovations Framework Program FRUCT and 1st Regional MeeGo Summit Russia--Finland* (pp. 82–91).

Manzaroli, D., Roffia, L., Cinotti, T. S., Azzoni, P., Ovaska, E., Nannini, V., & Mattarozzi, S. (2010). Smart-M3 and OSGi: The interoperability platform. In *2010 IEEE Symposium on Computers and Communications (ISCC)* (pp. 1053–1058).

Masuoka, R., Parsia, B., & Labrou, Y. (2003). Task computing--the semantic web meets pervasive computing. In *The Semantic Web-ISWC 2003* (pp. 866–881). Springer. doi:10.1007/978-3-540-39718-2_55

Morandi, F., Roffia, L., D'Elia, A., Vergari, F., & Cinotti, T. S. (2012). RedSib: a Smart-M3 semantic information broker implementation. In *Proc. 12th Conf. of Open Innovations Association FRUCT and Seminar on e-Tourism* (pp. 86–98). 10.23919/FRUCT.2012.8122091

Murth, M., & Kühn, E. (2008). A Semantic Event Notification Service for Knowledge-Driven Coordination. In *Proc. of 1st Int'l. workshop on emergent semantics and cooperation in open systems (ESTEEM), cooperation with the 2nd Int'l. Conf. on Distributed Event-Based Systems (DEBS 2008), Rome, Italy*.

Murth, M., & Kuhn, E. (2010). Knowledge-based interaction patterns for semantic spaces. In *2010 International Conference on Complex, Intelligent and Software Intensive Systems (CISIS)* (pp. 1036–1043). 10.1109/CISIS.2010.31

Murth, M., & Kühn, E. (2009). A heuristics framework for semantic subscription processing. In The Semantic Web: Research and Applications (pp. 96–110). Springer. doi:10.1007/978-3-642-02121-3_11

Ovaska, E., Cinotti, T. S., & Toninelli, A. (2012). The Design Principles and Practices of Interoperable Smart Spaces. In Advanced Design Approaches to Emerging Software Systems: Principles, Methodologies and Tools (pp. 18–47). Hershey, PA: IGI Global. doi:10.4018/978-1-60960-735-7.ch002

Palviainen, M., & Katasonov, A. (2011). Model and ontology-based development of smart space applications. In *Pervasive Computing and Communications Design and Deployment: Technologies, Trends, and Applications* (pp. 126-149).

Pantsar-Syväniemi, S., Ovaska, E., Ferrari, S., Cinotti, T. S., Zamagni, G., & Roffia, L. … Nannini, V. (2011). Case study: Context-aware supervision of a smart maintenance process. In *Proceedings - 11th IEEE/IPSJ International Symposium on Applications and the Internet, SAINT 2011* (pp. 309-314).

Perera, C., Zaslavsky, A., Christen, P., & Georgakopoulos, D. (2014). Context aware computing for the internet of things: A survey. *IEEE Communications Surveys and Tutorials*, *16*(1), 414–454. doi:10.1109/SURV.2013.042313.00197

Roffia, L., Azzoni, P., Aguzzi, C., Viola, F., Antoniazzi, F., & Salmon Cinotti, T. (2018). Dynamic Linked Data: A SPARQL Event Processing Architecture. *Future Internet*, *10*(4), 36. doi:10.3390/fi10040036

Schmidt, M., Hornung, T., Lausen, G., & Pinkel, C. (2009). SP^ 2Bench: a SPARQL performance benchmark. In *IEEE 25th International Conference on Data Engineering ICDE'09* (pp. 222–233).

Sen, S., & Balasubramanian, A. 2018. A highly resilient and scalable broker architecture for IoT applications. In *2018 10th International Conference on Communication Systems & Networks (COMSNETS)* (pp. 336-341).

Shi, D., Yin, J., Li, Y., Qian, J., & Dong, J. (2007). An RDF-Based Publish/Subscribe System. In *Third International Conference on Semantics, Knowledge and Grid* (pp. 342–345).

Skovronski, J. (2007). *An ontology-based publish-subscribe framework*. ProQuest.

Song, Z., Cardenas, A., Masuoka, R., & … (2010). Semantic middleware for the Internet of Things. In *Internet of Things* (pp. 1–8). IOT. doi:10.1109/IOT.2010.5678448

Suo, H., Wan, J., Zou, C., & Liu, J. (2012). Security in the internet of things: a review. In *2012 International Conference on Computer Science and Electronics Engineering (ICCSEE)* (Vol. 3, pp. 648–651). 10.1109/ICCSEE.2012.373

Thomson, G., Bianco, S., Ben Mokhtar, S., Georgantas, N., & Issarny, V. (2008). Amigo aware services. In *Constructing Ambient Intelligence* (pp. 385–390). Springer. doi:10.1007/978-3-540-85379-4_43

Vazquez, J. I., de Ipiña, D., & Sedano, I. (2007). Soam: A web-powered architecture for designing and deploying pervasive semantic devices. *International Journal of Web Information Systems*, *2*(3/4), 212–224. doi:10.1108/17440080780000301

Vergari, F., Bartolini, S., Spadini, F., D'Elia, A., Zamagni, G., Roffia, L., & Cinotti, T. S. (2010). A smart space application to dynamically relate medical and environmental information. In *Proceedings of the Conference on Design, Automation and Test in Europe* (pp. 1542–1547). 10.1109/DATE.2010.5457056

Vergari, F., Cinotti, T. S., D'Elia, A., Roffia, L., Zamagni, G., & Lamberti, C. (2011). An integrated framework to achieve interoperability in person-centric health management. *International Journal of Telemedicine and Applications*, *2011*, 5. doi:10.1155/2011/549282 PMID:21811499

Wang, J., Jin, B., & Li, J. (2004). An ontology-based publish/subscribe system. In *Proceedings of the 5th ACM/IFIP/USENIX international conference on Middleware* (pp. 232–253).

Wang, X., Dong, J. S., Chin, C. Y., Hettiarachchi, S. R., & Zhang, D. (2004). Semantic Space: An infrastructure for smart spaces. *Pervasive Computing*, *3*(3), 32–39. doi:10.1109/MPRV.2004.1321026

Zhong, N., Ma, J., Huang, R., Liu, J., Yao, Y., Zhang, Y., & Chen, J. (2016). Research challenges and perspectives on Wisdom Web of Things (W2T). In *Wisdom Web of Things* (pp. 3–26). Cham: Springer. doi:10.1007/978-3-319-44198-6_1

Chapter 4
A Semantic Sensor Web Architecture in the Internet of Things

Eliot Bytyçi
University of Prishtina, Kosovo

Besmir Sejdiu
University of Prishtina, Kosovo

Arten Avdiu
South East European University, Kosovo

Lule Ahmedi
University of Prishtina, Kosovo

ABSTRACT

The Internet of Things (IoT) vision is connecting uniquely identifiable devices to the internet, best described through ontologies. Furthermore, new emerging technologies such as wireless sensor networks (WSN) are recognized as essential enabling component of the IoT today. Hence, the interest is to provide linked sensor data through the web either following the semantic web enablement (SWE) standard or the linked data approach. Likewise, a need exists to explore those data for potential hidden knowledge through data mining techniques utilized by a domain ontology. Following that rationale, a new lightweight IoT architecture has been developed. It supports linking sensors, other devices and people via a single web by mean of a device-person-activity (DPA) ontology. The architecture is validated by mean of three rich-in-semantic services: contextual data mining over WSN, semantic WSN web enablement, and linked WSN data. The architecture could be easily extensible to capture semantics of input sensor data from other domains as well.

DOI: 10.4018/978-1-5225-7186-5.ch004

Copyright © 2019, IGI Global. Copying or distributing in print or electronic forms without written permission of IGI Global is prohibited.

INTRODUCTION

Internet of Things (IoT) paradigm has been around since almost two decades but its meaning has undergone significant changes. Initially, the term was envisioned as a way to link supply chain with radio frequency identification (RFID) (Ashton, 2009). Nowadays, IoT's vision is to connect to the Internet not only computers, tablets or smartphones but also other physical objects and devices surrounding us, such as sensors, actuators, etc. – which, through unique identifiers are able to interact with each other to reach common goals in everyday life like in environmental monitoring, e-health, domotics, or in automation and industrial manufacturing just to mention few (Atzori, 2010; Giusto, 2010).

That creates a triangle device – person - activity with relations drawn between people and devices. Furthermore, it should be further explored in order to infer important knowledge like are activities of people but also their devices. That requires meaning interpretation, which can be obtained by semantics. Therefore, using ontologies to describe the conceptualization of this certain domain is necessary. Some researchers argue that sensor networks are the most essential components of the IoT, with most of the sensors today deployed as wireless (Perera, 2014). According to a recent BBC report, the global market for sensors is expected to grow fast to almost double by 2021, with wireless sensor devices[1] nearly triple its current market by 2021. Ericsson[2] on the other side predicts that IoT sensors and devices are expected to exceed mobile phones as the largest category of connected devices in 2018. Hence, new emerging technologies such as *WSN*s (wireless sensor networks) are an imperative in this domain conceptualization. That may implicate adding new ontological constructs and constraints on top of the existing ontologies.

A standard already exists, SWE (Lefort, 2011), (Bröring, 2012), conceived by the Open Geospatial Consortium[3] (OCG) that supports publication on the Web of (potentially heterogeneous) WSN related data following a single standard schema. WSN data may thus get accessed with ease via a single web, the so-called Web Enabled WSN (Rouached 2012) (Udayakumar, 2012), leading provisionally to lower cost and better quality communication between sensors.

On the other side, there is an ever growing vast amount of data from a diversity of domains being published as *Linked Data* (Bizer, 2009), (Lee, 2006), namely open semantically described and interlinked data that are made available for access through the Web. It may thus be easier and time effective to build applications using Linked Data. Moreover, applications may gain from new knowledge potentially derived from semantic descriptions including interlinks. As more open rich-in-semantics linked sensor data are published on the Web, best practices are evolving too, such as the proposed six step model to create and publish linked data (Hyland, 2011, Cygankia, 2014) and as well the best practices for publishing Linked Data published by World Wide Web Consortium (W3C)[4].

Finally, given the increasing interest to provide linked sensor data through the Web following either the SWE standard or the Linked Data approach, there is obviously also need to further explore such data in order to check for potentially new knowledge. *Data mining* techniques may aid in exploring massive datasets, especially if utilized by ontologies imposing certain modeling on data and their semantic annotations.

The work presented here is part of a major project INWATERSENSE[5] (Ahmedi, 2013), which consists of a WSN deployed in a river in Kosovo for monitoring its water quality. WSN has two main components: static component – deployed in a specific location at the river, and the mobile component – used to measure in different locations throughout the river. Both components contain several sensors, which measure different quality parameters such as: pH, temperature, dissolved oxygen, etc. As an umbrella of the project, an environmental monitoring portal was introduced. The portal supports modeling and management of both, the observational stream data on water quality coming from wireless sensors – dynamic data, as well as of the data describing the WSN itself, its devices and the corresponding site allocation data – static data (Ahmedi, 2015).

Following the trends and rationale discussed above, as well as the experience gained while working with the real-life WSN system within the INWATERSENSE project, a new lightweight IoT *architecture* has been developed and is presented in this paper. It supports linking sensors and other devices, as well as people at the input via a single web by mean of a *device-person-activity* ontology referred to as DPA. At the output, multiple services are readily supported, here exemplified through three typical services, contextual data mining over WSN, semantic WSN web enablement, and linked WSN data. The main contribution behind the proposed architecture with the ontology in the middle acting as a Semantic Web (Lee, 2001) crossroad may thus be summarized into:

- The ease of service provision via a single schema Web in conformity to the existing SWE standards which base on sensor data but also on the participating people as actors with certain activities related to sensors at the input.
- The richness of service provision due to semantics encapsulated by mean of ontology.
- The support for multiple diverse services at the output, from data mining to web services to linked data and even more services via a common Web.

The remainder of this article is organized as follows. In the next section, related work is discussed, followed by a section on the proposed IoT architecture. After that, the DPA ontology describing the concepts presented in the architecture, i.e. devices, people, as well as activities relating them is introduced in detail. Then, the platform for the IoT with its three sample rich-in-semantic services is provided. Finally, in last part, conclusions and future work are discussed.

RELATED WORK

In support of working with sensor data, semantic web has already been utilized to enable rich modeling and querying or even reasoning over sensor data annotated with meta-descriptions in form of ontologies: In (Calbimonte, 2011), the SSN[6] and SWEET[7] ontologies are used to model sensor data and to allow a federated query system among them. An enriched ontology WSSN (Bendadouche, 2012) to the existing SSN, adds new concepts such as communication, data flow and state. In (Phuoc, 2011), a Linked Stream Middleware (LSM) provides wrappers for real time data collecting and publishing, a web interface to publish data and a SPARQL[8] endpoint for querying sensor data. OpenIoT (Soldatos, 2015) is another platform that enables the semantic interoperability of IoT services in the cloud. It includes the sensor middleware that eases the collection of data from virtually any sensor, a wide range of visual tools that enable the development and deployment with almost zero programming and has the ability to handle mobile sensors, thereby enabling the emerging wave of mobile crowd sensing applications. As part of the INWATERSENSE project, in (Ahmedi, 2013), the INWS[9] ontology which builds on top of the SSN[10] ontology models WSNs for water quality monitoring, whereas in (Jajaga, 2017a, Jajaga 2016) and (Jajaga, 2017b), a reasoning framework uses a Jess production rule system or a Semantic Web rule language C-SWRL respectively over the INWS's stream sensor data. In (Keßler, 2010), linking sensor data using Linked Data principles is seen as promising approach in order to make data available to users that are not in line with SWE standards. Even though it makes querying more difficult, by enabling annotations with timestamp and location, still it makes explicit what meta-data describes. An Semantic Sensor Network Model (Rezan,2015) proposed to be applied in IoT in order to be applicable in all types of sensors during different stages of sensor data processing for information abstraction. Using semantic web techniques and machine learning methods, the model converts the raw sensor data into higher-level abstractions to be understood by human or machine. The model increases the abstraction level of the data collected by the sensors but it does not make available the data resulting of data abstraction in the Linked Open Data (LOD) cloud.

Apart from semantic web alone, combination of semantics and data mining, or semantics and SWE, or SWE and data mining have all been explored as well, as is recalled next.

In (Aggarwal, 2013), bringing together semantic web and data mining in the context of IoT with a focus on sensors as interconnected devices is presented. Sensors produce vast amount of data, which need to be linked first, and then described in a standardized way by reusing existing infrastructure and in the end analyzing the data. By this, authors conclude that practical data mining applications can be build, since real world sensors ontologies exist, query mechanisms as well and the availability of linked sensor data. Moreover, the authors of (Medvedev, 2017), propose that the data mining methods, due to their complexity, to be implemented on the cloud. They propose a web based solution, which not only makes the data mining process simpler but aswell is easy understandable and easy to use.

In (Sheth, 2008), semantic sensor web (SSW) is described as a synthesis of sensor data and semantic metadata. SSW represents an approach by Open Geospatial Consortium (OGC) and Semantic Web Activity of the W3C to provide meaning for sensor data. Core suit of services developed and maintained by OGC under *SWE* framework comprises of Observations and Measurements (O&M), Sensor Model Language (SML), Sensor Planning Service (SPS) and Sensor Observation Service (SOS) amongst other. In (Henson, 2009), a construction of a Semantic Sensor Observation Service (SemSOS) based on the SWE standards is discussed. They have modelled the domain of sensors and sensor observations in a suite of ontologies, adding semantic annotations to the sensor data, using the ontology models to reason over sensor observations, and extended an open source SOS implementation with their semantic knowledge base. They extend the open source implementation of SOS from 52North[11]. 52North's SOS is an open source software implementation of the Open Geospatial Consortium's Sensor Observation Service standard[12], which is designed to be highly modular, and adaptable to arbitrary suitable sensor data sources, transport protocols, etc.

In (Lee, 2015), an extension of the *SWE* framework in order to support standardized access to sensor data is described. The system also introduces a web-based data visualization and statistical analysis service for data stored in the SOS by integrating open source technologies such as WEKA[13] API for data mining tasks. Furthermore, as future work they list the extension of SOS server with a semantics, since the lack of semantically rich mechanism is seen as a significant issue, which makes it hard to explore related concepts, subgroups of sensor types, or other dependencies between the sensors and the data they collect. Authors believe that by integrating SOS with semantics will enable for querying high-level knowledge of the environment as well as the raw sensor data. Moreover, that would also facilitate knowledge sharing and exchange, and automated processing of web resources. In (Conover, 2008), Sensor Management for Applied Research Technologies (SMART), a project developed to present the capabilities of OGC SWE for observation and forecasting is presented. A major component of the system is Phenomena Extraction Algorithm (PEA), a data mining algorithm for detection of anomalies amongst other.

In (Liefde, 2016), is designed a conceptual system architecture that uses the semantic web to improve sensor data discovery as well as the integration and aggregation of sensor data from multiple sources. This conceptual system architecture is presented containing two web processes: (1) A process for harvesting and harmonising SOS metadata, which are stored as linked data in a semantic knowledge base, and (2) A process for discovering, retrieving and processing observation data by translating a logical query to SOS requests, using a semantic knowledge base with linked sensor metadata.

In (Pradilla, 2016), is proposed a SOS implementation, that fits small sensors networks environments and that does not require very robust systems to operate, thus providing a standard and agile platform. This implementation of the SOS provides independence from manufactures and heterogeneous sensors networks, increasing interoperability because information is transmitted in a standard structure and through well-defined software interfaces.

To the best of our knowledge, there is yet no combination of all three abovementioned ground concepts, namely of semantic web (including linked data), SWE, and data mining explored at one place for harnessing sensor data or any other data produced by devices people have interest to relate to in the context of the IoT, which is what characterizes the approach presented in this paper.

InWaterSense PROJECT

The InWaterSense project (Ahmedi, 2013), consists of a WSN deployed in a river in Kosovo. WSN has two main components: static component – deployed in a specific location at the river, and the mobile component – used to measure in different locations throughout the river. Both components contain several sensors, which measure different parameters such as: pH, temperature, dissolved oxygen, etc.

Main aim of the project is to apply recent advanced practices stemming from ICT in water quality monitoring for healthy environment. The specific objectives of the project to serve the overall objectives mentioned above are following: build a WSN infrastructure in the river Sitnica for monitoring water quality with the aim of providing a best practice scenario for expanding it to other surface water resources as well in the country; monitor water quality in the river Sitnica supported by the WSN in order to make the quality data available to the community and the decision makers for determining the current health of the river; transform the existing WSN for WQM into an intelligent platform to operate almost autonomously, and support more functionality as envisioned by the future Internet and intelligent systems. The intelligent behavior of the system is aimed to present a novelty in research in the field.

In accordance with the project aims and objectives, a WSN system was developed consisting of three types of nodes: sensing, gateway and central monitoring node. Sensing nodes, included static wireless sensor nodes, auto-sampler nodes and mobile wireless sensor nodes. Main aim of the sensor nodes was to collect data about the above mentioned parameters and send them to central monitoring node through the gateway node. In order to present the meassurements, an intelligent system was developed (Ahmedi, 2015). Besides, presenting the meassurements through a portal, the system was equipped with expert module, which according to expert data and rules, infers new knowledge about the water parameters.

PROPOSED SEMANTIC DEVICE-PERSON-ACTIVITY ARCHITECTURE

Semantic Device-Person-Activity architecture is presented in Figure 1. In the core of the architecture lies the ontology, which describes the main concepts involved: devices, people and their activities. The ontology may get fed by a WSN deployed, like for example in a river. Every person and device involved, has a specific Uniform Resource Identifier (URI) or RFID tag, which can link to other relevant information about the person or device.

In a perfect scenario, measurements from sensors, after collected, are to be validated and presented to the public. The validation should be performed by the corresponding agency responsible for environmental monitoring, Of course, in cases where there are non-validated data, the system should not transmit those to the public. SWE plays an important role in not letting that happen. It links through ontology to the sensor data, and then further, through the SOS web services, describes the way sensor data are presented to the Web. Furthermore, our architecture extends on data mining of sensor data, through the addition of context ontologies for the given domain, in this case the water domain and its quality sensing. Besides, Linked Data further provides an additional value to the system by making sensor data annotated with semantics available to all interested parties, regardless of their OGC SWE standards conformity.

Even though the architecture is showcased for the water domain, it is generic and adaptable to any other domain like e-health, domotics, or automation and industrial manufacturing just to mention few, with devices and people interacting towards gathering and processing data for the sake of useful rich-in-semantics services at the output. Taking healthcare systems as an example of another domain with sensors acquiring useful data about patients, therapies, pharmaceutics, and doctors, including also people interacting with the system, the proposed architecture may at the output support provision of services like patient actual health, most expertise of doctors, certain pharmaceutics in doubt for patients' worst health, and similar.

Figure 1. Proposed Architecture

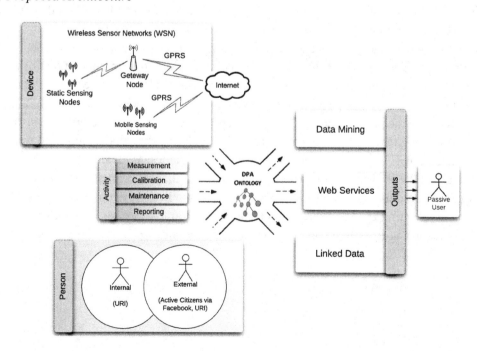

Hence, the DPA ontology presented is aimed to serve as a Semantic Web crossroad in the middle of the architecture which supports modeling and semantically annotating and interlinking any input data of three DPA (device-person-activity) parties and in turn enables distinct rich-in-semantics services at the output. Although the architecture illustrated assumes WSN in the place of devices, it is generic and adaptable for any arbitrary device at the input in the context of the IoT infrastructure.

DPA ONTOLOGY

Concepts belonging to the architecture are formally specified through the DPA ontology, presented in Figure 2, which describes relations between Device, Person and Activity, and as well time and place of the occurrence of such encounter. The ontology presents an extension of the INWATERSENSE project ontology – INWS ontology (hence of the SSN ontology as well) to generalize it for supporting other devices along sensors constituting the IoT, then also people involved and their activities related to those devices. Therefore, few new concepts are added or other ones reused from existing ontologies, described in following. *Instant* is the main class describing the time occurrence, which is reused from the Time[14] ontology. It has a specific data property, *hasTimestamp*, describing the exact time and date of the occurrence. Another concept, *Place*, is as well reused from DBpedia[15] and which through object property *closeTo* describes the vicinity of one location to another. Besides that, data properties *hasLatitude* and *hasLongitude*, describe the coordinates of the specific location.

Modeling Devices in and Around WSN

In the DPA ontology, one of the main parts of it deals with the description of devices of the WSN. As seen in Figure 3, the main class *PhysicalObject* represents the root. *PhysicalObject* is reused from SSN[16] ontology. Its sole subclass is:

- **Platform:** Which is as well reused from the SSN ontology, also reused in INWS[17] ontology, represents the main entity, in which other components can be attached. Its subclasses are:
  - **SensingNode:** Reused from the INWS ontology, represents all sensors attached to the system.

Figure 2. The DPAOntology: Its subclass hierarchy

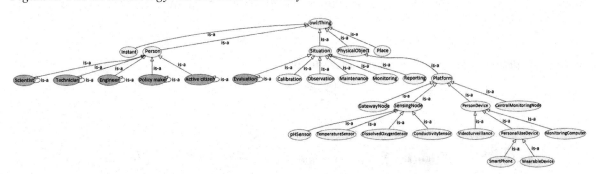

Figure 3. Modeling of devices: The subclass hierarchy

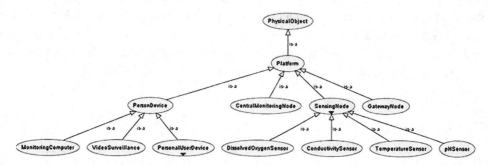

- ◦ **CentralMonitoringNode and GatewayNode:** Also reused from INWS. Sensors measure the specified parameters and send back data through the gateway node to the central monitoring node as the end point (a remote server) for further research.
- ◦ **PersonDevice:** Which is a new construct in our ontology, describes devices used by persons involved in the WSN. It has three direct subclasses: *MonitoringComputer* represents the device of the person that evaluates the data, while *PersonalUserDevice* represent the personal device of the person such as smartphone (SmartPhone class) or any portable wearable device (WearableDevice class). *VideoSurveillance* on in other hand represents the cameras attached to the WSN or any video report by the public, willing to contribute to the monitoring of water quality in general.

Properties of the *PhysicalObject* class are: *isCalibrated* which describes if the sensors are calibrated, *hasCamera* describing if the smartphone has a camera, as well as *hasDeviceID* and *hasDeviceStatus* identifying and describing the status of device respectively. The device ID represents in fact an RFID of the device in best case scenario under the assumption there are RFID tags available and manageable to attach to every singular device belonging to the input system.

Modeling Person in and Around WSN

Another important part of the ontology is person modeling, shown in Figure 4. The WSN captured involves a number of parties into its functionality. First of all, there is *Technician* directly involved with measuring required parameters. *Technician* is part of the internal structure of person involved and therefore described by the *internalPerson* object property. Another person part of the *internalPerson* property is *Engineer*, dealing with all the malfunctions of the system and more importantly the calibration of the sensors.

Figure 4. Modeling of person: The subclass hierarchy

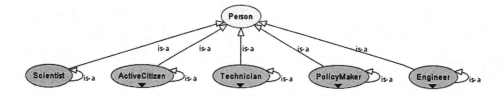

Other people involved, *ActiveCitizen*, *PolicyMaker* and *Scientist*, are all part of the external people involved with activities around the system and therefore described by the *externalPerson* property. *ActiveCizitizen* represents all people willing to contribute voluntarily to the water quality monitoring by sending video or picture of the possible pollution around the river. *PolicyMaker* represents other institutional people dealing with the water quality monitoring, which validates the data measured by sensors, whereas *Scientists* involve researchers that are willing to use data for their research.

All people represented in the ontology have a unique ID, described as data property *hasPersonID*, which distinguishes them from each other. That property is used as well as part of context inference, which let us understand if data can be released for public or not. If the data are validated, then the person ID would change to the ID of the *PolicyMaker*, therefore understanding that data are valid and can be used by other parties.

Besides that, there is another property involving *Person*, *hasActivity* property, which describes the situation that involves the person in.

Modeling Activities in and Around WSN

Another part of the ontology describes the concepts related to the activities of the actors involved in the system. As seen in Figure 5, the top class in the activities part is *Situation*, which is reused from DUL[18] SSN ontology. Its subclasses are:

- **Calibration:** Performed for the system and which models the calibration process.
- **Evaluation:** Modeling the validation of the data.
- **Maintenance:** Modeling the maintenance process of the system.
- **Monitoring:** Modeling the monitoring of the system performance.
- **Observation:** Reused from SSN ontology, with its properties *isMeasured* and *meassurementID*.
- **Reporting:** Modeling a report from active citizens, with property *isReported*.

SEMANTIC MULTI-SERVICE WSN PLATFORM FOR THE IOT

The WSN platform as any other device constituting the IoT modeled through the DPA ontology intertwines several services, making thus the platform of the most IoT essence. First of all, by using the ontology it enables inferring contextual data, which are mined and provide more valuable insight then by using only raw data. Then, from another perspective, it allows for semantic WSN web enablement and further more linking WSN data through the URI. In the rest of this section, each service will be discussed separately in details accompanied with a possible scenario for each of them.

Figure 5. Modeling of activities: The subclass hierarchy

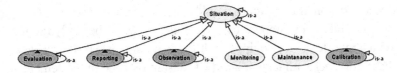

Service 1: Contextual Data Mining Over WSN Supported by Ontology

Data produced by sensors are accounted as raw data. Those direct sensor measurements are saved in a database for further analysis. Before the analysis, data has to be prepared and preprocessed for the process. This involves usage of filters, removal or substitution of missing data and discretizing or division of data into several bins. After that, by usage of state of the art algorithms, one will be able to extract valuable association rules.

Assocation rule mining is the process of discovering interesting relationship hidden in large dataset (Tan, Steinbach, Karpatne, & Kumar, 2013). The result can be represented in form of association rules. Initially the process was used to discover frequent item sets on transaction databases but recently it gained momentum also on ontological derived data. With the usage of this simple technique, one could find rules, presented in the form $X \Rightarrow Y$, known also as antecedent (left part) and consequent (right part). Rules have to satisfy two constraints: support – defined as the fraction of transactions in a transaction database that satisfies the union of items in the consequent and antecedent of the rule and confidence describes the ratio between the support of the rules and the support of the antecedent (Agrawal, Imieliński, & Swami, 1993). The process of finding the rules involves finding frequent patterns or large itemsets and then by using the large itemsets to generate the desired rules (Agrawal & Ramakrishnan, 1994). In order to find possible candidate itemsets, one needs to compare each candidate against every transaction, which tend to be a very expensive approach (Tan, Steinbach, Karpatne, & Kumar, 2013).

Apriori (Agrawal, 1996) and its derivatives, is one of the most used algorithms for the association rule mining, but it is also a very effective one due to the fact that it eleminates some candidate itemsets without counting their support. The items that are frequently associated together are discovered by Apriori and thus also emphasizing the fact that the items subsets are frequent aswell. That is performed by Apriori in two steps: candidate generation step and candidate evaluation step. The first step finds the items that meet the condition of minimum support set by the user, while the second step filters candidate with insufficient support.

Association rules describe the relation between several components. Those components can be raw data or even metadata – semantically enriched data. Even though association rules are used a lot in order to get those relations between raw data, only in the last few years the relations between metadata has been started to be drawn. That rose an interesting research area of semantically enriched metadata evaluation through association rules. Therefore, in our case, the process of the association rules over raw data is compared to the process of the association rules on metadata.

The same process applied on raw data will be identically conducted on the data extracted from ontologies. According to several authors (Abedjan, 2013, Bytyçi, 2016), semantically enriched data will provide further comprehension of the raw data. That enrichment is done through usage of ontologies used to describe concepts involving device, person, and activity, and their relations in the process. All of them are modelled into the ontology. By populating the ontology with data and then using a reasoner, further number of relations would be obtained. In Figure 6, a part of the process that results in rules obtained over semantic data is presented. As per case of raw data, data are preprocessed and prepared for the data mining process and in the end the resulted rules are obtained.

A possible case scenario from this approach would be knowing which information should be released for general public to perceive. Let's suppose that a technician, who does only the measurements, does the measurement with a mobile device equipped with sensors in a part of the river. Measurements will be sent to the database, together with technician ID, timestamp of the measurement and coordinates of

Figure 6. Association rules on semantic data

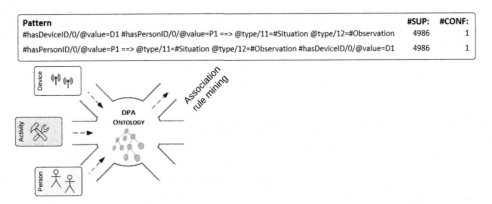

Pattern	#SUP:	#CONF:
#hasDeviceID/0/@value=D1 #hasPersonID/0/@value=P1 ==> @type/11=#Situation @type/12=#Observation	4986	1
#hasPersonID/0/@value=P1 ==> @type/11=#Situation @type/12=#Observation #hasDeviceID/0/@value=D1	4986	1

the place. Now, according to the activity occurred, it can be concluded that a measurement is performed, which is obvious. But, in the other hand, when ID of the person changes to another value, for example from technician to engineer or someone else, depending on that, one can conclude if a validation of data has occurred or calibration has occurred or even if a reporting from somebody outside (an active citizen) has been performed.

In order to achieve that, the ontology is saved into appropriate format for further mining with association rules. Beforehand, as in the case of raw data, metadata will be preprocessed, where several supervised methods will be used such as normalization or discretization. Then, the Apriori algorithm (Agrawal, 1996) will be used over enriched sensor data. Results obtained are then compared to the results obtained by same Apriori algorithm in raw data.

Some of the raw data association rules, with the highest confidence, are presented in Table 1. There are only few strong relations derived. One of them, describes a strong relation between a person with a specific ID and a device with a specific ID. But, there is no other rules, not amongst the parameters itself or parameters and devices and people, indicating a relation. Of course, on the raw part of the data, there is no description of the activity that have occurred. The activity is derived as the context in the ontology, as a relation between person and device. For example, the measurement activity is reasoned from the person ID and device ID. So, if the person ID belongs to a technician and device ID to the equipment used for measurement, then it would be possible to infer which activity is performed. That would be of great benefit, since in the case of validated data, it would enable withholding the not validated data, and not let them release to the public.

On the other hand, when association rules are applied on context ontology, an overwhelming number of rules are derived. For argument, we have presented in Table 2 only a couple of them, which in fact

Table 1. Association rules on raw data

Pattern	#SUP	#CONF
DeviceID=D1 ==> PersonID=P1	4991	1
PersonID=P1 ==> DeviceID=D1	4991	1
Temperature='\'(5.666667-10.333333]\'' DeviceID=D1 ==> PersonID=P1	1798	1
Temperature='\'(5.666667-10.333333]\'' PersonID=P1 ==> DeviceID=D1	1798	1

Table 2. Association rules on context ontology data

Pattern	#SUP	#CONF
#hasDeviceID/0/@value=D1 #hasPersonID/0/@value=P1 ==> @type/11=#Situation @type/12=#Observation	4986	1
#hasPersonID/0/@value=P1 ==> @type/11=#Situation @type/12=#Observation #hasDeviceID/0/@value=D1	4986	1

back up our initial claim – a strong relation between device-person-activity triple of concepts. It should be emphasized that the number of rules derived from the DPA context ontology data is significantly higher, i.e., more than 10 times the number of rules derived from applying the same algorithm but on raw data. The most interesting among derived rules is the one that creates a connection not only between person and device, but also the activity. Therefore, one can relate the person with the specific ID to the situation or activity conducted by him, through a specific device. This specific rule, acclaims the aid of the semantics by the usage of context in deriving new rules, strengthening even more the claim in a previous work (Bytyçi, 2016).

Service 2: Semantic WSN Web Enablement

WSNs are part of many research areas lately, which can be attributed to the development of sensors in particular or even to the paradigm of the IoT in general. Furthermore, sensor networks are being enabled through the Sensor Web providing thereby solutions to the web enabled WSN (Rouached, 2012) (Udayakumar, 2012). OGC defines standardization for the Sensor Web named Sensor Web Enablement (SWE). Sensor Web Enablement is a framework and a set of standards that allow exploitation of sensors and sets of sensors connected to a communication network. SWE is founded on the concept of "Web Sensor" and aims at making them accessible using standard protocols and application interfaces (Pradilla, 2016). SWE is divided into two parts (Echterhoff, 2011):

1. **SWE Information Model:** Is comprised of conceptual language encodings that permits sensor observations visibility on the Internet. The SWE information model includes the following specifications: *O&M* - Standard models and XML Schema for encoding observations and measurements from a sensor, both archived and real-time. *Sensor Model Language (SensorML)* - describes sensors systems and processes associated with sensor observations. *Transducer Model Language (TransducerML or TML)* - describes transducers and supporting real-time streaming of data to and from sensor systems.
2. **SWE Service Model:** Is a set of Web Service specifications that allow a client to search and find the required information. The SWE Service model includes the following specifications: *SOS* - Standard web service interface for requesting, filtering, and retrieving observations and sensor system information. This is the intermediary between a client and an observation repository or near real-time sensor channel. *SPS* - a web service interface for requesting user-driven acquisitions and observations. *Sensor Alert Service (SAS)* - a web service interface for publishing and subscribing to alerts from sensors. *Web Notification Services (WNS)* - a web service interface for asynchronous delivery of messages.

The goal of SWE is to enable all types of Web and/or Internet-accessible sensors, instruments, also imaging devices to be accessible and controllable via the Web where applicable. The vision is to define and approve the standards foundation for "plug-and-play" Web-based sensor networks. Usually a sensor location is a critical parameter for sensors on the Web, and OGC is the world's leading geospatial industry standards organization (Botts, 2011).

In this paper, the focus is on *SOS*. The SOS standard is applicable to use cases in which sensor data need to be managed in an interoperable way. This standard defines a Web service interface which allows querying observations, sensor metadata, as well as representations of observed features (Bröring, 2012). SOS has three mandatory "core" operations (Na, 2007):

- **GetObservation:** Provides access to sensor observations and measurement data via a spatio-temporal query that can be filtered by phenomena
- **DescribeSensor:** Enables querying of metadata about the sensors and sensor systems available by an SOS server.
- **GetCapabilities:** Provides access to metadata and detailed information about the operations available by an SOS server.

Following the IoT architecture suggested, a prototype system in Java is developed, which implements standards like SWE, respectively version 2.0 of the SOS standard (SOS 2.0 relies on the OGC O&M) to encode data gathered by sensors (Bröring, 2012)). Figure 7 shows the system architecture covering this service as a valuable output of the architecture.

In the following, the *GetObservation* operation is used to explain the functioning of the system stepwise. Given that the *GetObservation* function is the heart of the SOS (Henson, 2009), it is chosen among the three mandatory SOS operations to next describe the process of obtaining information about the sensor observations: Client posts a request to a web portal to read the measurements that have been conducted, specifying thereby optionally different filters such as: the time period within which mea-

Figure 7. System Architecture of IoT Web Services

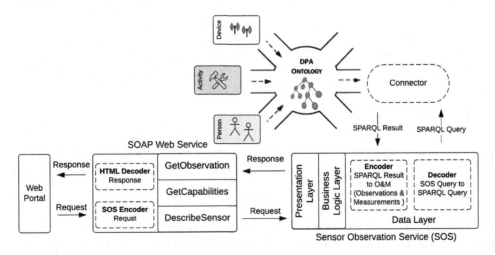

surements are made; phenomens like: temperature, electrical conductivity, pH, dissolved oxygen (DO), turbidity, biochemical oxygen demand (BOD), etc, measurement locations, sensors, etc. Such a request must be translated (encoded) into an SOS query of the *GetObservation* operation which is enabled through the Simple Object Access Protocol (SOAP) web service. The encoded client's request into SOS query is then transmitted to the SOS server. The SOS on Business Logic Layer makes the validation of the request. If the request is not valid then returns an exception report, otherwise forwards it to the Data Layer (the Decoder) which further decodes it, namely the SOS query into a SPARQL query. Depending on the filters that SOS query contains, the SPARQL query is generated dynamically applying these filters. The SPARQL query is executed over the ontology, in this case the DPA ontology, to extract required information (the measurements). It is worth mentioning that for the execution of the SPARQL query over the ontology, the Java library called Jena[19] Ontology API has been used. The result of the SPARQL query which is in format XML is converted (encoded) through the Encoder into O&M format of the OGC, because the response form *GetObservation* must be encoded in O&M. The response through SOS server conveys to the SOAP web services, in which through the HTML Decoder is done the decoding of the response from O&M format to HTML table format and is displayed to the client on the web portal.

An Example GetObservation Operation in SemDAP

Next, an example demonstrating a *GetObservation* request and its SOS query encoded, as well as its corresponding SPARQL query and the *GetObservation* response is provided.

GetObservation Request

An example request includes finding all the measurements made on locations Plemetin or Mitrovica, for phenomena such as temperature and electrical conductivity which have been measured from sensors Sensor1_Temp, Sensor2_Cond, Sensor3_Temp or Sensor4_Cond within the time period from 2016-01-19 14:00:00 and 2016-01-19 14:05:00. An abstract of the *GetObservation* request is presented below:

```
GetObservation(
(featureOfInterest:= Plemetin OR Mitrovica) AND
(observedProperty:= Temperature OR Conductivity) AND
(procedure:= Sensor1_Temp OR Sensor2_Cond OR Sensor3_Temp OR Sensor4_Cond) AND
(temporalFilter:= BETWEEN 2016-01-19T14:00:00 AND 2016-01-19T14:05:00.000))
```

SOS Query

The request on *GetObservation* operation encoded into an SOS query is shown in Figure 8.

The given *GetObservation* request, its SOS query, contains following properties as defined in (Bröring, 2012) (Cox, 2011):

- **temporalFilter:** Specifies a filter for a time property of requested observations.
- **featureOfInterest:** Pointer to a feature of interest for which observations are requested.
- **observedProperty:** Pointer to an observedProperty for which observations are requested.

Figure 8. Example GetObservation Request as SOS query

```
<sos:GetObservation xmlns:sos=... service="SOS" version="2.0.0"...>
  <sos:temporalFilter>
    <fes:During>
      <fes:ValueReference>phenomenonTime</fes:ValueReference>
      <gml:TimePeriod gml:id="tp_1">
        <gml:beginPosition>2016-01-19T14:00:00.000+01:00</gml:beginPosition>
        <gml:endPosition>2016-01-19T14:05:00.000+01:00</gml:endPosition>
      </gml:TimePeriod>
    </fes:During>
  </sos:temporalFilter>
<sos:featureOfInterest>http://inwatersense.uni-pr.edu/ontologies/inws-
core.owl#Plemetin</sos:featureOfInterest>
<sos:featureOfInterest>http://inwatersense.uni-pr.edu/ontologies/inws-
core.owl#Mitrovica</sos:featureOfInterest>
<sos:observedProperty>http://inwatersense.uni-pr.edu/ontologies/inws-
core.owl#Temperature</sos:observedProperty>
<sos:observedProperty>http://inwatersense.uni-pr.edu/ontologies/inws-
core.owl#Conductivity</sos:observedProperty>
<sos:procedure>http://inwatersense.uni-pr.edu/ontologies/inws-
core.owl#Sensor1_Temp</sos:procedure>
<sos:procedure>http://inwatersense.uni-pr.edu/ontologies/inws-
core.owl#Sensor2_Cond</sos:procedure>
<sos:procedure>http://inwatersense.uni-pr.edu/ontologies/inws-
core.owl#Sensor3_Temp</sos:procedure>
<sos:procedure>http://inwatersense.uni-pr.edu/ontologies/inws-
core.owl#Sensor4_Cond</sos:procedure>
  <sos:responseFormat>http://www.opengis.net/om/2.0</sos:responseFormat>
</sos:GetObservation>
```

- **Procedure:** Pointer to a procedure for which observations are requested. It defines a filter for the procedure property of the observations.
- **responseFormat:** Identifier of desired responseFormat for the requested observations (Default is O&M 2.0 [OGC 10-004r3/ISO 19156] identified by the value http://www.opengis.net/om/2.0).

SPARQL Query

The *Decoder SOS Query to SPARQL Query* component of the proposed system will decode the request from *GetObservation* SOS queryinto SPARQL query, depicted in Figure 9, which will then be executed over the DPA ontology to generate the required result.

Figure 9. Example SPARQL Query

```
PREFIX ...
SELECT ?sos ?hasTimestamp ?hasConductivity ?hasTemperature ?hasLocation
WHERE {
?sos inws:hasTimestamp ?hasTimestamp.
?sos inws:hasTemperature ?hasTemperature.
?sos inws:hasConductivity ?hasConductivity.
?sos inws:hasLocation ?hasLocation.
?sos inws:hasDeviceID ?hasDeviceID.
FILTER ( ?hasTimestamp >= "2016-01-19T19:14:00"^^xsd:dateTime &&
         ?hasTimestamp <= "2016-01-19T19:14:05"^^xsd:dateTime ).
FILTER (?hasLocation = "Mitrovica" || ?hasLocation = "Plemetin").
FILTER (?hasDeviceID = "Sensor1_Temp" || ?hasDeviceID = "Sensor2_Cond" ||
        ?hasDeviceID = "Sensor3_Temp" || ?hasDeviceID = "Sensor4_Cond" ).

}
```

GetObservation Response

Encoder SPARQL Result to O&M will encode the result of SPARQL in the O&M standard because the response format of *GetObservation* request (SOS 2.0) must be encoded according (Cox, 2011) to O&M. Figure 10 shows an excerpt of the *GetObservation* response.

Service 3: Linked Open WSN Data

As part of the lifecycle of LOD, there are three main phases required for creating and publishing data following this paradigm, which will in this section be discussed in the context of our proposed architecture.
Initialy, the guidelines are explained for publishing Linked WSN Data (Lee, 2006):

- **URIs and Naming:** Assigning URIs for sensor descriptions; each sensor description is published with a unique URI that refers to it descriptions. The naming of sensors can follow similar conventions that are used for HTML pages or other resources on the current Web.
- **Providing HTTP Access:** The Linked WSN Data can be made available through HTTP access by publishing descriptions by providing SPARQL endpoints to query and access the data. Sensor observation and measurement data can be also made available through HTTP interfaces via sensor observation service.
- **Providing Meaningful Descriptions:** WSN Data can include RDF descriptions according to ontologies designed to represent sensor features and attributes.
- **Linking to Other URI's:** To describe sensor data using the basic sensor ontology, the terminology can be chosen from publicly available Linked Open Data but in our case we use DPA ontology to publish our Linked WSN Data . This enables construction of sensor descriptions that are already linked to other resources based on different features.

When talking about generating the LOD, it should be noted that in our case those data are generated by sensor measurements, as presented in Figure 11.

Figure 10. Example GetObservation response

```
<sos:GetObservationResponse ...>
  <observationData>
    <om:OM_Observation gml:id="o1">
      <om:type xlink:href="http://www.opengis.net/def/observationType/OGC-OM/2.0/OM_Measurement"/>
      <om:phenomenonTime>
        <gml:TimeInstant gml:id="phenomenonTime_1">
          <gml:timePosition>2016-01-19T14:00:00.000+01:00</gml:timePosition>
        </gml:TimeInstant>
      </om:phenomenonTime>
      <om:resultTime xlink:href="#phenomenonTime_1"/>
      <om:procedure xlink:href="http://inwatersense.uni-pr.edu/ontologies/inws-
core.owl#Sensor1_Temp"/>
      <om:observedProperty xlink:href="http://inwatersense.uni-pr.edu/ontologies/inws-
core.owl#Temperature"/>
      <om:featureOfInterest xlink:href="http://inwatersense.uni-pr.edu/ontologies/inws-
core.owl#Mitrovica"/>
      <om:result xsi:type="gml:MeasureType" uom="C">15.3</om:result>
    </om:OM_Observation>
  </observationData>

    ...

</sos:GetObservationResponse>
```

Figure 11. Publishing process of sensor data as Linked Open Data

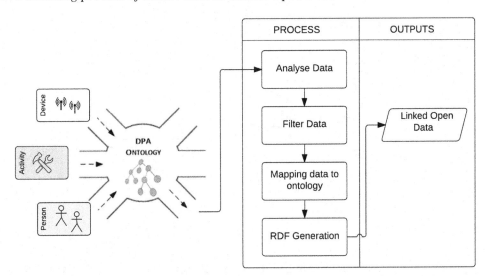

The initial step of creating the LOD includes several methods. One of the initial methods is analysis of data. Since sensors generate a lot of data with some being also not relevant for publishing as Linked Open Data, one needs to analyze the data and filter the ones suitable for the process of creation of LOD. Thus it is crucial to know the content of data generated from sensors. After that, as part of filtering, parts of dataset to be published as LOD are extracted.

The next phase after data analysis and filtering is the mapping of data to an ontology. It incorporates our sensor architecture, which in addition related to the DPA ontology is presented in Figure 12. In this phase, it is of imperative importance that a proper ontology is being used, involving concepts and relations between data.

As it is requirement of the Semantic Web community, the ontology should either extend one or more existing ontologies, or be defined from the scratch in cases the structure of data is not fully supported by the existing ontologies. The mapping schema between data and ontology can be created by linking data to respective classes in ontology or can be generated automatically by usage of a specific tool. An example of such a mapping tool is D2RQ[20] generate-mapping tool, which creates a D2RQ mapping file by analyzing the schema of an existing database (some graphical details are shown in Figure 13). Created mapping file, maps each table of the database to a new RDFS class that is based on the table's name, and maps each column to a property based on the column's name. In our case mapping is created manually according to DPA ontology (example presented in Figure 12), even though this mapping file can be used as it is or can be customized, as needed (Bizer, 2004).

Figure 12. Mapping data example

```
map:sensorvalues_Temperature a d2rq:PropertyBridge;
d2rq:belongsToClassMap map:sensorvalues;
d2rq:property vocab:sensorvalues_Temperature;
d2rq:propertyDefinitionLabel "sensorvalues Temperature";
d2rq:column "sensorvalues.Temperature";
d2rq:datatype xsd:integer;
```

Figure 13. Server Architecture

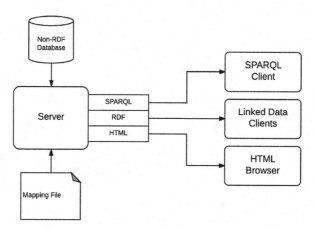

The next phase in the process of creating LOD is conversion of data to LOD. Even though several approaches for converting data to LOD are mentioned, they might be grouped in two main approaches: generating RDF and using RDF Storage to access them, or on the fly conversation. In the first approach, LOD are converted from sensor data and stored in a triple store which can be queried via SPARQL queries as shown in Figure 9. This is the approach that we have used. In Figure 9, the SPARQL example is shown, used for retrieving all sensor measurements for specified location, time and device. In the second approach, sensor data are stored in database and converted in RDF on the fly when they requested. An example of it would be the D2RQ-query tool that allows executing SPARQL queries against a D2RQ-mapped relational database from the command line. This can be done with or without a D2RQ mapping file. If a mapping file is specified, then the tool will query the virtual RDF graph defined by the mapping and if no mapping file is specified, then the tool will use the default mapping in D2RQ to generate-mapping for the translation (Bizer, 2004).

For the different components of proposed model, Water Sensor Observation Service requires URIs as link of observations to the LOD. Those URIs are assigned to the components such as sensorvalues[21] by appending the component type such us Conductivity[22]to the URI identifying the authority. The Component sensorvalues[22] refers links to all sensor descriptions. Consequently, Conductivity[23] refers the description of a conductivity sensor and links to the produced observations.

An example showing the relation of a person to LOD is when the involved person authenticates himself through his/her Facebook account which has a specific URI (for example arten.avdiu.3[23]), which may link to other relevant information about the person. Also, for each involved device, a URI containing RFID tag[24] is generated, which as well may link to other relevant information about the device.

For each activity of the actors involved in the system is similarly assigned an URI, such as Situation[25], or a specific feature may be accessed by appending identifiers of those resources to the base URI. For example, the reference Reporting[26] points to all reports made by the person[26].

DISCUSSION AND FUTURE WORK

Even though the IoT was introduced initially to connect RFID device information to the internet, it has evolved through the years. Now, the IoT is envisioned as an infrastructure that intelligently links living and non-living things to the Internet, creating enormous amount of useful data through their intercommunication to our everyday life. In line with its aim, our proposed lightweight architecture enables the triangular ontological relation between device, person, and activity conducted by both. With the help of web semantics as the center of the architecture, and by usage of new evolving technologies such as context-aware data mining techniques, semantic-enriched sensor web enablement standards and linked data methods, our approach achieves the interlinking of the previous under the umbrella of IoT. Although the architecture suggested is illustrated to work in the domain of WSN data at the input, it is generic as to capture the semantics of input sensor or even other devices' data from other domains, but still similarly gain due to services provided at the output. This denotes the most contribution of this paper, with a generic architecture and the triangle DPA ontology in line with the IoT vision in the middle as a crossroad towards multitude of useful services at the output. The architecture is moreover distinguished for its ease of service provision via a single Web, and for the richness of service provision due to semantics encapsulated by mean of ontology in the middle of the architecture.

It is achieved, by using data mining techniques, to find hidden relation between data, previously coated by the semantics of the given context. The association rule mining is the technique used, previously used in transactional databases, but that had recently gained momentum also in usage of the techniques in ontology enriched data. The number of rules generated is higher than without using the aid of the context ontology but the most important input of the usage of context ontology is on the new knowledge derived.

Furthermore, by using SWE, or in case of devices other than sensors at the input, their corresponding Web-enabled standards, it creates a peculiar prototype to connect the sensors, or certain other devices, via a semantic web. And in the end, by integrating them to linked data, it facilitates for further global querying and analyzing.

Despite previous work existing in provision of either of these services alone or in certain twin combinations as discussed in the related work, none has achieved to present a generic lightweight architecture modeling the triple device-person-activity of actors at the input, and a *triple of services or even more* at the output benefiting from such an architecture.

In the future, with aim on evolving the architecture, each component will be further supplemented to reflect the peculiarities of the certain domain and devices at the input, as well as services acquired at the output in the context of IoT.

REFERENCES

Abedjan, Z., & Naumann, F. (2013). Improving rdf data through association rule mining. *Datenbank-Spektrum*, *13*(2), 111–120. doi:10.100713222-013-0126-x

Aggarwal, C. C., Ashish, N., & Sheth, A. (2013). The internet of things: A survey from the data-centric perspective. In Managing and mining sensor data (pp. 383-428). Springer US. doi:10.1007/978-1-4614-6309-2_12

Agrawal, R., Mannila, H., Srikant, R., Toivonen, H., & Verkamo, A. I. (1996). Fast discovery of association rules. *Advances in knowledge discovery and data mining, 12*(1), 307-328.

Ahmedi, L., Jajaga, E., & Ahmedi, F. (2013, October). An ontology framework for water quality management. In *Proceedings of the 6th International Conference on Semantic Sensor Networks-Volume 1063* (pp. 35-50). CEUR-WS.org.

Ahmedi, L., Sejdiu, B., Bytyçi, E., & Ahmedi, F. (2015). An integrated web portal for water quality monitoring through wireless sensor networks. *International Journal of Web Portals, 7*(1), 28–46. doi:10.4018/IJWP.2015010102

Ashton, K. (2009). That 'internet of things' thing. *RFiD Journal, 22*(7), 97–114.

Atzori, L., Iera, A., & Morabito, G. (2010). The internet of things: A survey. *Computer Networks, 54*(15), 2787–2805. doi:10.1016/j.comnet.2010.05.010

Bendadouche, R., Roussey, C., De Sousa, G., Chanet, J. P., & Hou, K. M. (2012). Extension of the semantic sensor network ontology for wireless sensor networks: The stimulus-WSNnode-communication pattern. In *5th International Workshop on Semantic Sensor Networks in conjunction with the 11th International Semantic Web Conference (ISWC)* (pp. 16-p).

Berners-Lee, T., Hendler, J., & Lassila, O. (2001). The semantic web. *Scientific American, 284*(5), 28–37. doi:10.1038cientificamerican0501-34 PMID:11341160

Bizer, C., Heath, T., & Berners-Lee, T. (2009). Linked data-the story so far. In *Semantic Services, Interoperability and Web Applications: Emerging Concepts* (pp. 205-227).

Bizer, C., & Seaborne, A. (2004, November). D2RQ-treating non-RDF databases as virtual RDF graphs. In *Proceedings of the 3rd international semantic web conference (ISWC2004)*. Springer.

Botts, M., Percivall, G., Reed, C., & Davidson, J. (2006, October). OGC sensor web enablement: Overview and high level architecture. In *International conference on GeoSensor Networks* (pp. 175-190). Springer Berlin Heidelberg.

Bröring, A., Echterhoff, J., Jirka, S., Simonis, I., Everding, T., Stasch, C., ... Lemmens, R. (2011). New generation sensor web enablement. *Sensors, 11*(3), 2652–2699. doi:10.3390110302652 PMID:22163760

Bröring, A., Stasch, C., & Echterhoff, J. (2012). OGC sensor observation service interface standard. *Open Geospatial Consortium Interface Standard*, 12-006.

Bytyçi, E., Ahmedi, L., & Kurti, A. (2016). Association Rule Mining with Context Ontologies: An Application to Mobile Sensing of Water Quality. In *Metadata and Semantics Research: 10th International Conference, MTSR 2016 Proceedings*, Göttingen, Germany, November 22-25 (pp. 67-78). Springer International Publishing.

Calbimonte, J. P., Jeung, H., Corcho, O., & Aberer, K. (2011, October). Semantic sensor data search in a large-scale federated sensor network. In *Proceedings of the 4th International Conference on Semantic Sensor Networks* (pp. 23-38). CEUR-WS. org.

Compton, M., Barnaghi, P., Bermudez, L., García-Castro, R., Corcho, O., Cox, S., ... Taylor, K. (2012). The SSN ontology of the W3C semantic sensor network incubator group. *Journal of Web Semantics*, *17*, 25–32. doi:10.1016/j.websem.2012.05.003

Conover, H., Goodman, H. M., Zavodsky, B., Regner, K., Maskey, M., Lu, J., ... Berthiau, G. (2008). Intelligent Assimilation of Satellite Data into a Forecast Model Using Sensor Web Processes and Protocols. In *Earth Science Technology Conference*.

Cox, S. (2011). Observations and measurements-xml implementation (OGC document).

Cygankiak, R. (2014). *Best practices for publishing linked data*. World Wide Web Consortium.

Devaraju, A., & Kauppinen, T. (2012). Sensors tell more than they sense: Modeling and reasoning about sensor observations for understanding weather events. *International Journal of Sensors Wireless Communications and Control*, *2*(1), 14–26. doi:10.2174/2210327911202010014

Echterhoff J. (2011) Open Geospatial Consortium. OpenGIS SWE Service Model Implementation Standard. *Open Geospatial Consoritum*, 155.

Giusto, D., Iera, A., Morabito, G., & Atzori, L. (Eds.). (2010). *The internet of things: 20th Tyrrhenian workshop on digital communications*. Springer Science & Business Media.

Henson, C. A., Pschorr, J. K., Sheth, A. P., & Thirunarayan, K. (2009, May). SemSOS: Semantic sensor observation service. In *International Symposium on Collaborative Technologies and Systems CTS'09* (pp. 44-53). IEEE.

Hyland, B., & Wood, D. (2011). The joy of data-a cookbook for publishing linked government data on the web. In *Linking government data* (pp. 3–26). Springer New York. doi:10.1007/978-1-4614-1767-5_1

Jajaga, E., & Ahmedi, L. (2017b). C-SWRL: SWRL for Reasoning over Stream Data information. In *SDI Workshop, IEEE ICSC 2017*.

Jajaga, E., Ahmedi, L., & Ahmedi, F. (2016). StreamJess: Enabling Jess for Stream Data Reasoning and the Water Domain Case (Demo paper). In *20th International Conference on Knowledge Engineering and Knowledge Management (EKAW2016)*, Bologna.

Jajaga, E., Ahmedi, L., & Ahmedi, F. (2017a). (in press). StreamJess: Stream Data Reasoning System for Water Quality Monitoring. *International Journal of Metadata, Semantics and Ontologies*.

Keßler, C., & Janowicz, K. (2010, November). Linking sensor data-why, to what, and how? In *Proceedings of the 3rd International Conference on Semantic Sensor Networks* (pp. 48-63). CEUR-WS.org.

Le-Phuoc, D., Quoc, H. N. M., Parreira, J. X., & Hauswirth, M. (2011). The linked sensor middleware–connecting the real world and the semantic web. In *Proceedings of the Semantic Web Challenge*.

Lee, T. B. (2006). Linked data. Retrieved from http://www.w3.org/DesignIssues/LinkedData.html

Lee, Y. J., Trevathan, J., Atkinson, I., & Read, W. (2015). The integration, analysis and visualization of sensor data from dispersed wireless sensor network systems using the SWE framework. *Journal of Telecommunications and Information Technology*, (4), 86.

Lefort, L., Henson, C., Taylor, K., Barnaghi, P., Compton, M., Corcho, O., ... & Neuhaus, H. (2011). Semantic sensor network xg final report. *W3C Incubator Group Report, 28.*

Liefde, I., Vries, M., & Meijers, B. (2016, June). Exploring the use of the semantic web for discovering, retrieving and processing data from sensor observation services [master thesis]. Delft University of Technology, Netherlands.

Medvedev, V., Kurasova, O., Bernatavičienė, J., Treigys, P., Marcinkevičius, V., & Dzemyda, G. (2017). A new web-based solution for modelling data mining processes. *Simulation Modelling Practice and Theory, 76,* 34–46. doi:10.1016/j.simpat.2017.03.001

Na, A., & Priest, M. (2007). *Sensor observation service.* Implementation Standard OGC.

52. North Sensor Web Community. (n.d.). Retrieved from http://52north.org

Perera, C., Zaslavsky, A., Christen, P., & Georgakopoulos, D. (2014). Context aware computing for the internet of things: A survey. *IEEE Communications Surveys and Tutorials, 16*(1), 414–454. doi:10.1109/SURV.2013.042313.00197

Pradilla, J., Palau, C., & Esteve, M. (2016). *SOSLITE: Lightweight Sensor Observation Service (SOS) for the Internet of Things (IOT). ITU Kaleidoscope.* Barcelona: Trust in the Information Society.

Rezvan, M., Barekatain, M., Zaeri, A., & Taghandiki, K. (2015). Applying an innovative semantic sensor network model in internet of things. In *Proceedings of the International Conference on Information and Communication Technology Convergence* (pp. 324–328). 10.1109/ICTC.2015.7354556

Rouached, M., Baccar, S., & Abid, M. (2012, June). RESTful sensor web enablement services for wireless sensor networks. In *2012 IEEE Eighth World Congress on Services* (pp. 65-72). IEEE. 10.1109/SERVICES.2012.48

Schmachtenberg, M., Bizer, C., Jentzsch, A. & Cyganiak, R. (2014). Linking open data cloud diagram 2014.

Sheth, A., Henson, C., & Sahoo, S. S. (2008). Semantic sensor web. *IEEE Internet Computing, 12*(4), 78–83. doi:10.1109/MIC.2008.87

Soldatos, J., Kefalakis, N., Hauswirth, M., Serrano, M., Calbimonte, J. P., Riahi, M., ... Skorin-Kapov, L. (2015). Openiot: Open source internet-of-things in the cloud. In *Interoperability and open-source solutions for the internet of things* (pp. 13–25). Cham: Springer. doi:10.1007/978-3-319-16546-2_3

Spahiu, N., Ahmedi, L., & Bouju, A. (2010). Implementation of sensor observation services to monitor moving objects [master thesis]. University of Prishtina, Kosovo, and University of La Rochelle, France.

Udayakumar, P., & Indhumathi, M. (2012). Semantic web based Sensor Planning Services (SPS) for Sensor Web Enablement (SWE). arXiv:1207.5310

ENDNOTES

[1]   http://www.bccresearch.com/market-research/instrumentation-and-sensors/wireless-sensors-technologies-report-ias019c.html

[2]   https://www.ericsson.com/res/docs/2016/ericsson-mobility-report-2016.pdf

[3]   www.opengeospatial.org/

[4]   https://www.w3.org/TR/ld-bp/

[5]   http://inwatersense.uni-pr.edu/

[6]   http://purl.oclc.org/NET/ssnx/ssn

[7]   http://sweet.jpl.nasa.gov/2.3/sweetAll.owl

[8]   http://www.w3.org/TR/sparql11-query/

[9]   http://inwatersense.uni-pr.edu/ontologies/inws-core.owl

[10]   http://purl.oclc.org/NET/ssnx/ssn

[11]   52north.org

[12]   http://52north.org/swe

[13]   www.cs.waikato.ac.nz/ml/weka

[14]   http://www.w3.org/2006/time#

[15]   http://dbpedia.org/ontology/#

[16]   http://purl.oclc.org/NET/ssnx/ssn

[17]   http://inwatersense.uni-pr.edu/ontologies/inws-core.owl

[18]   http://www.loa-cnr.it/ontologies/DUL.owl#

[19]   jena.apache.org/documentation/ontology/index.html

[20]   d2rq.org

[21]   http://inwatersense.uni-pr.edu/data/sensorvalues

[22]   http://inwatersense.uni-pr.edu/data/sensorvalues#Conductivity

[23]   https://web.facebook.com/arten.avdiu.3

[24]   http://inwatersense.uni-pr.edu/vocab/sensorvalues_DeviceID/334bte3g5

[25]   http://inwatersense.uni-pr.edu/data/Situation

[26]   http://inwatersense.uni-pr.edu/data/Situation/Reporting

Chapter 5
Semantic Extension for the Linked Data Based on Semantically Enhanced Annotation and Reasoning

Pu Li
Zhengzhou University of Light Industry, China

Junxia Ma
Zhengzhou University of Light Industry, China

Zhifeng Zhang
Zhengzhou University of Light Industry, China

Fenglong Wu
Zhengzhou University of Light Industry, China

Lujuan Deng
Zhengzhou University of Light Industry, China

Peipei Gu
Zhengzhou University of Light Industry, China

Yuncheng Jiang
*South China Normal University,
China*

ABSTRACT

Linked Data, a new form of knowledge representation and publishing described by RDF, can provide more precise and comprehensible semantic structures. However, the current RDF Schema (RDFS) and SPARQL-based query strategy cannot fully express the semantics of RDF since they cannot unleash the implicit semantics between linked entities, so they cannot unleash the potential of Linked Data. To fill this gap, this chapter first defines a new semantic annotating and reasoning method which can extend more implicit semantics from different properties and proposes a novel general Semantically-Extended Scheme for Linked Data Sources to realize the semantic extension over the target Linked Data source. Moreover, in order to effectively return more information in the process of semantic data retrieval, we then design a new querying model which extends the SPARQL pattern. Lastly, experimental results show that our proposal has advantages over the initial Linked Data source and can return more valid results than some of the most representative similarity search methods.

DOI: 10.4018/978-1-5225-7186-5.ch005

Copyright © 2019, IGI Global. Copying or distributing in print or electronic forms without written permission of IGI Global is prohibited.

INTRODUCTION

With the increasing amount of information, how can we find meaning in these terabytes (Kusiak, 2017)? To answer this question, we should consider from two aspects: On one hand, the World Wide Web (WWW) must be more structured and machine-readable contrasting with the traditional Web. Driven by these demands, semantic web (SW) (Berners-Lee et al., 2001) is proposed and widely used, which aims to develop techniques to incorporate semantics into Web design. On the other hand, confronting the sea of online information, users prefer to get knowledge which is more clear and meaningful rather than pages with unstructured text. To counter this requirement, there is a need for new querying techniques to improve traditional keyword-based search (Tran et al., 2011).

From the WWW Consortium's vision of the Web of Linked Data (Rahoman & Ichise, 2018), SW presents a revolutionary opportunity for deriving value from data and activity has gained momentum with the widespread publishing of structured data as RDF (Klyne & Carroll, 2014). In recent years, an increasing number of data providers like (Bollacker et al., 2007; He et al., 2018; Hoffart et al., 2013; Lehmann et al., 2015; Nebot & Berlanga, 2016; Wiemann & Bernard, 2016; Zhang et al., 2017) have published and connected their data into Web of Linked Data and, ultimately, into the SW. Promoted by the eager demand, many Linked Data-oriented techniques have been researched such as (Assaf et al., 2016; Auer et al., 2014; Nguyen & Ichise, 2017; Sande et al., 2016; Santipantakis et al., 2017; Yang et al., 2017).

The aforementioned developments bring the upsurge to the query for Linked Data. So, the works presented in this paper will make a further study on Linked Data querying from semantics. The rest of the chapter is organized as follows. Section 2 briefly reviews related works and highlights the difference between our study and these exiting works. Section 3 introduces some preliminaries about Linked Data and provides our research questions and research methodology. In Section 4 we present some new notions to depict the properties between different predicates and establish the Semantic Matrix for Predicates (SM_p). The Semantically-Extended Scheme for Linked Data Sources (SES_{LDS}) and the details of rules about semantically-enhanced reasoning strategy are presented in Section 5. In Section 6 we design a well-defined framework as the formalized expression of our query model and present the details of processing algorithms of our querying method. Section 7 is devoted to evaluating our method. Finally, we draw our conclusion and outline the future work in Section 8.

RELATED WORK

In April 1998, the first draft of the RDF Schema (RDFS) specification was published as a W3C Working Note (Ciobanu et al., 2016). The focus of the work was to extend the RDF vocabulary and detect some semantics of user-defined relationships between classes and properties. As being heavily modified in later versions, the subsequent RDFS specification was accepted as a W3C Recommendation in early 2004 (Dan & Guha, 2004) and remained ever since (Klyne & Carroll, 2014). RDFS extends RDF with four key terms (Kejriwal & Miranker, 2015) and makes more detailed description about the RDF Semantics (Hayes et al., 2004).

The list of four relationships and some of their corresponding rules are shown in Table 1. The interested reader can see Section 7 in (Hayes et al., 2004) for all.

Table 1. A selection of RDF(S) relationships and rules

Relationship Name	Rule ID	If Contain	Then Add
rdfs:domain (dom)	rdfs2	$(?p, dom, ?c) \wedge (?x, ?p, ?y)$	$(?x, rdf{:}type, ?c)$
rdfs:range (ran)	rdfs3	$(?p, ran, ?c) \wedge (?x, ?p, ?y)$	$(?y, rdf{:}type, ?c)$
rdfs:subPropertyOf(sPO)	rdfs5	$(?p_1, sPO, ?p_2), \wedge (?p_2, sPO, ?p_3),$	$(?p_1, sPO, ?p_3)$
rdfs:subPropertyOf(sPO)	rdfs7	$(?p_1, sPO, ?p_2) \wedge (?x, ?p_1, ?y)$	$(?x, ?p_2, ?y)$
rdfs:subClassOf (sCO)	rdfs9	$(?c_1, sCO, ?c_2) \wedge (?x, rdf{:}type, ?c_1)$	$(?x, rdf{:}type, ?c_2)$
rdfs:subClassOf (sCO)	rdfs11	$(?c_1, sCO, ?c_2) \wedge (?c_2, sCO, ?c_3)$	$(?c_1, sCO, ?c_3)$

Considering RDFS entailment is layered on top of simple entailment, the W3C began devoting to designing a more expressive language which would extend upon RDFS with richer entailment regimes and more semantics. Web Ontology Language (OWL) (Mcguinness & Harmelen, 2004), a new ontological language, was developed in 2004 and subsequently extended into OWL 2 (Golbreich et al., 2009) as a W3C Recommendation in 2009.

Relative to RDFS, OWL can also be serialized as RDF triples notwithstanding it is a much more complicated standard. It is unnecessary to draw the whole OWL standard into consideration because some reasoning tasks over OWL 2 are undecidable (e.g., OWL 2 Full ontology) (Harth et al., 2014). So, we summarize a subset of OWL 2 only for pertinent aspects. A selection of the rules defined in OWL 2 is listed in Table 2. The more details can be found at Section 4.3 in Ref. (Golbreich et al., 2009).

The analyses in Ref. (Harth et al., 2014) indicate that the rules such as those enumerated in Table 2 can be applied directly over arbitrary RDF datasets to derive inferences. The combination of RDFS plus certain OWL primitives is often referred to colloquially as RDFS++ (Matinfar et al., 2014).

Despite many of Linked Data sources in Linked Data cloud such as DBpedia, YAGO, GeoNames, Freebase have adopted part or all of aforementioned rules and can derive out some implicit semantics through reasoning, the result set returned by SPARQL which is recognized as the standard query language for RDF data is often inadequate. The cause lies in the fact that the rules both in RDFS and OWL 2 are mainly face to a specific single predicate, so the relevant reasoning strategies can merely deduce those implicit RDF triples which are bound with the same predicate. To put it another way, the rules described in above tables cannot efficiently express the semantics between different predicates, thus it is conceivable that we would not obtain much more valid answers which are also reasonable from semantics if we just take these existing rules into consideration.

Moreover, the goal of Linked Data query processing is an online execution of declarative queries over the SW, by relying only on the Linked Data principles (Bizer et al., 2009). Aiming to unleash the potential of SW, a number of general methods for querying Linked Data have been developed.

Early querying methods like Sindice (Oren et al., 2008) and Falcons (Cheng & Qu, 2009) are based on key words. Since SPARQL (W. E. Zhang et al., 2018) can be used to express queries across diverse data sources, it becomes the foundation of many recent researches about Linked Data querying. The devices in (Umbrich et al., 2011; Wagner et al., 2012) use index-based source selection and provide source ranking, while the techniques mentioned in (Hartig, 2013; Miranker et al., 2012) are traversal-based query execution approaches without source ranking. Moreover, some domain-oriented or datasource-oriented methods are presented to further pursue the accuracy and efficiency. NAGA (Mahdisoltani et al., 2014) provides best-effort heuristics to return and rank the relevant RDF triples from YAGO (Hoffart et al.,

Table 2. A selection of OWL 2 relationships and rules

Rule ID	If Contain	Then Add
eq-sym	(?x, owl:sameAs, ?y)	(?y, owl:sameAs, ?x)
eq-trans	(?x, owl:sameAs, ?y)∧ (?y, owl:sameAs, ?z)	(?x, owl:sameAs, ?z)
eq-rep-s	(?s, owl:sameAs, ?s')∧ (?s, ?p, ?o)	(?s', ?p, ?o)
eq-rep-p	(?p, owl:sameAs, ?p')∧(?s, ?p, ?o)	(?s, ?p', ?o)
eq-rep-o	(?o, owl:sameAs, ?o')∧(?s, ?p, ?o)	(?s, ?p, ?o')
eq-diff1	(?x, owl:sameAs, ?y)∧ (?x, owl:differentFrom, ?y)	false
prp-dom	(?p, rdfs:domain, ?c)∧ (?x, ?p, ?y)	(?x, rdf:type, ?c)
prp-rng	(?p, rdfs:range, ?c)∧ (?x, ?p, ?y)	(?y, rdf:type, ?c)
prp-fp	(?p,rdf:type, owl:FunctionalProperty) ∧ (?x, ?p, ?y1)∧ (?x, ?p, ?y2)	(?y1, owl:sameAs, ?y2)
prp-symp	(?p, rdf:type, owl:SymmetricProperty) ∧ (?x, ?p, ?y)	(?y, ?p, ?x)
prp-trp	(?p, rdf:type, owl:TransitiveProperty) ∧ (?x, ?p, ?y)∧ (?y, ?p, ?z)	(?x, ?p, ?z)
prp-eqp1	(?p_1, owl:equivalentProperty, ?p_2)∧ (?x, ?p_1, ?y)	(?x, ?p_2, ?y)
prp-pdw	(?p_1, owl:propertyDisjointWith, ?p_2) ∧ (?x, ?p_1, ?y)∧ (?x, ?p_2, ?y)	false
prp-inv1	(?p_1, owl:inverseOf, ?p_2)∧ (?x, ?p_1, ?y)	(?y, ?p_2, ?x)
prp-inv2	(?p_1, owl:inverseOf, ?p_2)∧ (?x, ?p_2, ?y)	(?y, ?p_1, ?x)
cax-sco	(?c_1, rdfs:subClassOf, ?c_2)∧ (?x, rdf:type, ?c_1)	(?x, rdf:type, ?c_2)
cax-eqc1	(?c_1, owl:equivalentClass, ?c_2)∧ (?x, rdf:type, ?c_1)	(?x, rdf:type, ?c_2)
cax-dw	(?c_1, owl:disjointWith, ?c_2)∧ (?x, rdf:type, ?c_1)∧(?x, rdf:type, ?c_2)	false
scm-sco	(?c_1, rdfs:subClassOf, ?c_2)∧(?c_2, rdfs:subClassOf, ?c_3)	(?c_1, rdfs:subClassOf, ?c_3)
scm-spo	(?p_1, rdfs:subPropertyOf, ?p_2) ∧ (?p_2, rdfs:subPropertyOf, ?p_3)	(?p_1, rdfs:subPropertyOf, ?p_3)

2013). By using SPARQL and SPIN, Lo Bueand Machi (Lo Bue & Machi, 2015) study on integrating and querying over tourism domain datasets via interlinking techniques. MEQLD (Tran & Nguyen, 2015) investigates to improve the mapping extension of lexical entities into DBpedia's components for creating query in SPARQL. Besides, other current works focus on mapping visual method to SPARQL (Haag et al., 2015), optimizing query results over several heterogeneous Linked Data sources (Taelman, 2016), as well as automatically generating SPARQL query (Alec et al., 2016).

To give a brief overview about the main contributions of the above related works and our studies, the main capacities and features of these similar systems are listed in Table 3.

OUR RESEARCH QUESTIONS AND METHODOLOGY

In this section, we will analyze the limitations of the basic SPARQL pattern and present our research questions and the corresponding methodology. Previously, we must introduce some basic concepts for easier understanding subsequent discussions. See especially (Auer et al., 2014; Bizer et al., 2009; Harris & Seaborne, 2010; Klyne & Carroll, 2014; Suchanek et al., 2008) for further details.

Table 3. The brief overview about related works and our studies

Name	Use Method	Publish Year	Data Source/ Domain-Oriented	Support Ranking	Matching Strategy	Result Type	Main Focus
Sindice/ Falcons	keyword matching	2008-09	No	Yes	Syntactic	RDF documents	Keyword-based querying strategy
Umbrich's/ Wagner's	SPARQL	2011-12	No	Yes	Syntactic	RDF documents	Index-based querying strategy
Hartig's/ Miranker's	SPARQL	2012-13	No	No	Syntactic	RDF triples	Traversal-based querying strategy
NAGA	SPARQL+ time+location	2014	Yes	Yes	Syntactic+ spatio-temporal computing	RDF triples	Querying over YAGO data source
Lo Bue's	SPARQL+ SPIN	2015	Yes	No	Syntactic+interlink	RDF documents	Integrating tourism domain datasets
MEQLD	SPARQL	2015	Yes	No	Syntactic	RDF triples	Entities mapping extension to DBpedia
Haag's	SPARQL	2015	No	No	Syntactic	RDF triples	Visual query mapping method
Taelman's	SPARQL	2016	No	No	Syntactic	RDF triples	Query results optimizing over heterogeneous sources
Alec's	SPARQL	2016	No	No	Syntactic	RDF triples	SPARQL query automatically generating
our work	SEQM$_{LD}$	now	No	No	Syntactic+ semantic reasoning	RDF triples	Integrating semantic extension into SPARQL

Preliminaries

RDF and SPARQL

RDF defines a data format for representing information in the Web and can be considered as a general model for graph-structured data encoded as triples in the form of subject-predicate-object (s, p, o).

Definition 1: (RDF Term, RDF Triple, RDF Graph). Given three pairwise disjoints sets: a set of URIs *U*, a set of literals *L*, and a set of blank nodes *B*, we call elements of $U \cup B \cup L$ *RDF terms T* . A triple (s, p, o)$\in (U \cup B) \times U \times T$ is called an *RDF triple* or a *fact*. A finite set of triples is called *RDF graph G*. The mapping $Sig(G):G \rightarrow T$ is a finite set which contains all labels cited in every RDF triple in *G*.

As the standard query language for RDF data, SPARQL can be used to express queries across diverse data sources. The following notions define the *triple pattern* and *basic graph patterns* which are core features of SPARQL.

Definition 2: (Triple Pattern, Basic Graph Pattern). Let *V* be a set of variables, $V \cap T = \Phi$ where *T* is a set of *RDF terms*. A *triple pattern* is formed as $tp=(s, p, o) \in (U \cup V) \times (U \cup V) \times (U \cup L \cup V)$. We denote variables by a leading question mark symbol (e.g., $?x \in V$). The function vars(*tp*) maps a triple pattern *tp* to the set of all variables mentioned in *tp*. A set of triple patterns is called *basic graph pattern* (BGP) $B=\{tp_1,...,tp_n\}$.

We introduce a function μ which is a partial mapping $\mu: V \rightarrow T$, where dom(μ) denotes the domain of μ. The function can be applied to triple patterns, written as $\mu(tp)$, and replace all $?x \in \text{dom}(\mu) \cap \text{vars}(tp)$ in *tp* by $\mu(?x)$.

Linked Data

We now depict the definition of Linked Data by four principles which are known as the "*Linked Data principles*".

Definition 3: (Linked Data). *Linked Data* is simply about using the Web to create typed links between data from different sources. The publication of Linked Data on the WWW should comply with the following four principles:

- ◦ Use URIs as names for things;
- ◦ Use HTTP URIs so that people can look up those names;
- ◦ When someone looks up a URI, provide useful information, using the standards (RDF, SPARQL);
- ◦ Include links to other URIs, so that they can discover more things.

Figure 1 is downloaded from the homepage of Linked Data cloud[1] and shows the fundamental structure about the composition of Linked Data.

YAGO Dataset

The YAGO knowledge base is already an important member of Linked Data project, which is based on a data model that slightly extends RDF. YAGO is a large ontology with high coverage and precision which comprises entities and predicates automatically derived from Wikipedia[2] and WordNet (Alrababah et al., 2017).

Currently, YAGO contains about 100 manually defined predicates, more than 2 million extracted entities and 120 million facts. Incredibly, for such a large knowledge base, YAGO has an overall precision of 95% confirmed by manual evaluation.

In consideration of its superiorities such as large data size, feasible hierarchy, and high precision, we will use YAGO as target data source in our experiments to validate the effectiveness of our SEQM_{LD} presented in this paper.

Our Research Questions

To further illustrate the main limitations of RDFS++ as well as the current SPARQL-based querying methods and describe our research questions, we provide a simple example as the motivation in this section.

Example 1: (A query in YAGO[3]). Consider two query requests as follows:

Figure 1. The Linked Data cloud

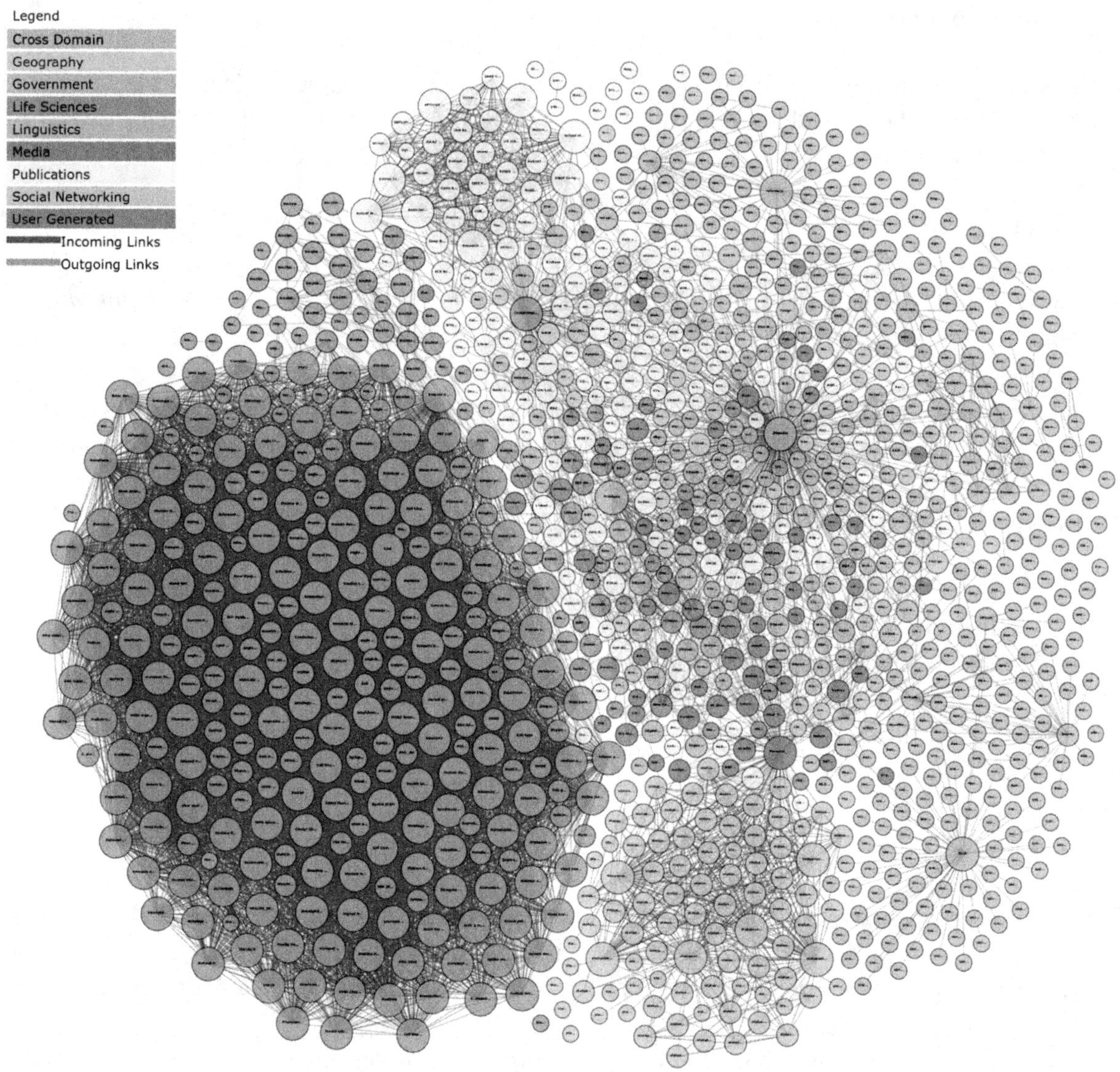

Q_1=(George W. Bush, isPoliticianof, ?*place*) and

Q_2=(?*person*, isPoliticianof, United States)

The outcome of Q_1 by YAGO is μ_1(?*place*)=Texas, while μ_2(?*person*)=Φ for Q_2.

Obviously, μ_1 is a valid answer for Q_1, but not complete. While the *null* of μ_2 is inconformity with our cognition. Should George W. Bush and Barack Obama not be two politicians of United States? If we want to get the valid answers for Q_2, we have to translate it into the following tedious format:

Q'_2={(?*person*, isPoliticianof, ?*place*), (?*place*, isLocationIn, United States)}

Figure 2. A fragment of RDF graph about the entity "George W. Bush"

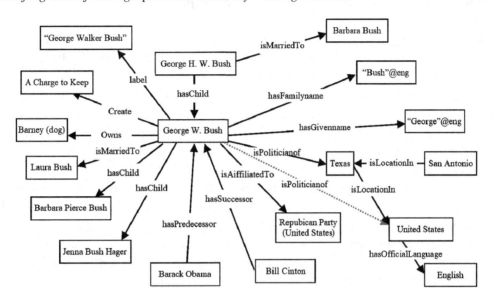

To analyze the cause of this incompleteness, we check the dataset of YAGO, and draw a RDF graph which loads the entity "George W. Bush" as a central node (see Figure 2).

In Figure 2, we know that there is only one fact (George W. Bush, isPoliticianof, Texas) which is matched by the triple pattern in Q_1. Thus we achieve the mapping $\mu_1 = \{?place \rightarrow \text{Texas}\}$ as a valid answer. However, there is an additional fact (Texas, isLocationIn, United States) which indicates Texas is a state of United States. Due to this semantic subsumption, we ought to have an implicit fact (George W. Bush, isPoliticianof, United States) labeled by the dotted directed edge. Obviously, this deduced fact should be a new valid answer for both Q_1 and Q_2.

Remark 1: Figure 2 is not the whole RDF graph about the entity "George W. Bush" in YAGO. Some other facts are not shown in Figure 2(e.g., (George W. Bush, wasBornOnDate, 1946-07-06) and (George W. Bush, owns, India(cat)), etc.). Considering these omitted facts either have the unique explanation or have the isomorphic form in Figure 2, this simplification is ineffective for our following study.

Although this example admittedly takes some liberties, it serves to illustrate some of the shortcomings of the current reasoning rules when we apply them into the target Linked Data source for querying. The SPARQL querying strategy are mainly based on the syntax matching between BGP and the target RDF graph, but do not fully reveal the properties and semantics of the predicates. This limitation leads to the incompleteness of the query results. That is why we provide a formal definition about the semantically-enhanced annotation strategy (i.e., SM_p) for Linked Data sources as well as SPARQL pattern and take this issue as the research question in this paper.

Conceptualization of Our Research Methodology

From Table 3, we know that despite adopting different querying strategies and Linked Data sources, most of the existing querying methods for Linked Data are all based on SPARQL. However, the above motivating example indicates that RDF triples may have some implicit semantics reflected by the properties of predicates, while the execution of SPARQL query aims at finding the matching triples whose forms are consistent with the query pattern in syntactic level. So, when we want to get the satisfactory answers, the existing SPARQL-based querying methods may perform powerless or have to translate the requirement complicatedly if we only use the current reasoning rules given in Tables 1 and 2 without changing the original knowledge structure and size of the target Linked Data source.

To solve these limitations, the purpose of this paper is to establish a Semantically-Extended Scheme for Linked Data Sources (SES_{LDS}) and present a new query model ($SEQM_{LD}$) which extends the SPARQL pattern. Concretely, we strengthen the current reasoning rules for RDF-based data source and extend the ability of query expression by analyzing the hierarchies and properties of the entities and relevant predicates in triple patterns. Meanwhile, we design algorithms to implement SES_{LDS} and $SEQM_{LD}$. The steps of our research methodology are shown in Figure 3.

Figure 3. The steps of our research methodology

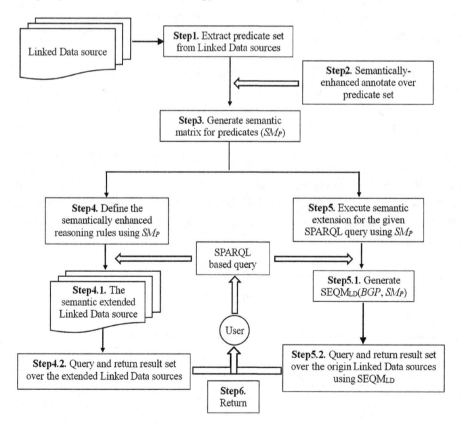

According to Figure 3, the key variables and main contributions of our research are as follows:

1. We further analyze the semantic properties of predicates in Linked Data sources and present some new notions to depict these properties.
2. We establish a well-defined semantically-enhanced annotation strategy and design the Semantic Matrix for Predicates (SM_p).
3. We define new semantically-enhanced rules based on SM_p for Linked Data sources and propose a Semantically-Extended Scheme for Linked Data Sources (SES_{LDS}).
4. We present the notion of Semantically-Extended Query Model for the Linked Data ($SEQM_{LD}$) and provide a framework as the formalized expression of our query model.
5. We develop algorithms to implement our $SEQM_{LD}$ and provide the architecture of the implementation about $SEQM_{LD}$.
6. We analyze the properties for all predicates in YAGO and build the relevant SM_p. Moreover, we create a list of *BGP*s as new benchmark and then use the benchmark to evaluate the effectiveness and generality of our $SEQM_{LD}$ by comparing with some of the most representative similarity search methods.

SEMANTIC MATRIX FOR PREDICATES (SM$_p$)

In this section We firstly give some basic definitions to describe the semantic properties of the binary predicates in RDF triples. Then we give a formal definition about SM_p.

The Semantic Properties About Predicates

Definition 4: (Semantic Equal Predicate). Given a RDF graph G, a finite set of RDF terms $T=Sig(G)$, a binary predicate $p \in T$. We say that p is a *Semantic Equal Predicate*, denoted as SEP, if for every RDF triple $t=(x, p, y) \in G$, the entities x and y represent the same individual in real world.

Definition 5: (Semantic Symmetry Predicate).Given a RDF graph G, a finite set of RDF terms $T=Sig(G)$, a binary predicate $p \in T$. We say that p is a *Semantic Symmetry Predicate*, denoted as SSP, if for every RDF triple $t=(x, p, y) \in G$, the fact $t'=(y, p, x)$ is also reasonable from semantics.

Definition 6: (Semantic Transmission Predicate). Given a RDF graph G, a finite set of RDF terms $T=Sig(G)$, a binary predicate $p \in T$. We say that p is a *Semantic Transmission Predicate*, denoted as STP, if for RDF triples $t_1=(x_1, p, y_1) \in G$, and $t_2=(x_2, p, y_2) \in G$ where $y_1=x_2$, the fact $t'=(x_1, p, y_2)$ is also reasonable from semantics.

Definition 7: (Semantic Inversion Predicates). Given a RDF graph G, a finite set of RDF terms $T=Sig(G)$, and two different binary predicates $p_1, p_2 \in T$ ($p_1 \neq p_2$). We call p_1 and p_2 are mutual *Semantic Inversion Predicates*, denoted as SIP, if for every RDF triple $t=(x, p_1, y) \in G$, the fact $t'=(y, p_2, x)$ is also reasonable from semantics.

However, these concepts are quite insufficient for our $SEQM_{LD}$. Because these notions just express the semantic properties of predicates, but do not demonstrate how to apply these properties to queries.

Therefore, to guarantee the effectiveness of our $SEQM_{LD}$, we need to further analyze the semantic properties between different predicates. Thus, we have the following notions.

Definition 8: (SEP Extendable Predicate). Let G be a RDF graph, $p \in Sig(G)$ be a predicate, and $r \in Sig(G)$ be a SEP. We say that p is a SEP *extendable predicate* about r, denoted as P_{SEP}, if for every fact $t=(x, p, y) \in G$, any of the following conditions holds:

- if $(x, r, w) \in G$ or $(w, r, x) \in G$, then (w, p, y) is reasonable from semantics,
- if $(y, r, z) \in G$ or $(z, r, y) \in G$, then (x, p, z) is reasonable from semantics.

Definition 9: (SSP Extendable Predicate). Let G be a RDF graph, $p \in Sig(G)$ be a predicate, and $r \in Sig(G)$ be a SSP. We divide into the following two situations:

- p is called a *subject* SSP *extendable predicate* about r, denoted as SP_{SSP}, if for every fact $t=(x, p, y) \in G$, only the following condition (i) holds.
- p is called an *object* SSP *extendable predicate* about r, denoted as OP_{SSP}, if for every fact $t=(x, p, y) \in G$, only the following condition (ii) holds.
  - if there is $(x, r, w) \in G$ or $(w, r, x) \in G$, then (w, p, y) is reasonable from semantics,
  - if there is $(y, r, z) \in G$ or $(z, r, y) \in G$, then (x, p, z) is reasonable from semantics.

Definition 10: (STP Extendable Predicate). Let G be a RDF graph, $p \in Sig(G)$ be a predicate, and $r \in Sig(G)$ be a STP. We divide into the following four situations:

- p is called a *subject*-(*inside*) STP *extendable predicate* about r, denoted as $SP^{(in)}_{STP}$, if for every fact $t=(x, p, y) \in G$, only the following condition (i) holds.
- p is called a *subject*-(*outside*) STP *extendable predicate* about r, denoted as $SP^{(out)}_{STP}$, if for every fact $t=(x, p, y) \in G$, only the following condition (ii) holds.
- p is called an *object*-(*inside*) STP *extendable predicate* about r, denoted as $OP^{(in)}_{STP}$, if for every fact $t=(x, p, y) \in G$, only the following condition (iii) holds.
- p is called an *object*-(*outside*) STP *extendable predicate* about r, denoted as $OP^{(out)}_{STP}$, if for every fact $t=(x, p, y) \in G$, only the following condition (iv) holds.
  - If there is $(w, r, x) \in G$, then (w, p, y) is reasonable from semantics,
  - If there is $(x, r, w) \in G$, then (w, p, y) is reasonable from semantics,
  - If there is $(z, r, y) \in G$, then (x, p, z) is reasonable from semantics,
  - If there is $(y, r, z) \in G$, then (x, p, z) is reasonable from semantics.

Remark 2: Considering the predicates in both RDF graph and BGP are directed, we have some additional remarks about Definitions 8-10:

- In Definition 8, because of the inherent equivalence of SEP, we need not consider its position and direction for each entity.
- In Definition 9, due to the symmetry but inequivalence, most of the SSP can be just extended by subject or object from semantics. For instance, in Figure 2, the predicate "isMarriedTo" is a SSP. We can define "hasChild" as a SP_{SSP} about "isMarriedTo". There are two facts: $t_1 =$ (George W. Bush, hasChild, Barbara Pierce Bush) and $t_2 =$ (George W. Bush, isMarriedTo, Laura Bush). According to the condition of SP_{SSP} in Definition 9, we can infer a new conclusion $t_{1\&2} =$ (Laura Bush, hasChild, Barbara Pierce Bush), which is undoubted because both George W. Bush and Laura Bush are parents of Barbara Pierce Bush.

However, if we define "hasChild" as an OP_{SSP} about "isMarriedTo", it may lead to some semantic mistakes. There is another fact $t_3 =$ (George H.W. Bush, hasChild, George W. Bush) in Figure 2. According to the condition of OP_{SSP} in Definition 9, we can obtain $t_{2\&3} =$ (George H.W. Bush, hasChild, Laura Bush) from t_2 and t_3. But $t_{2\&3}$ is invalid obviously, because George H.W. Bush is not Laura Bush's father but her father-in-law.

Figure 4. A fragment of RDF graph about the entity "Texas"

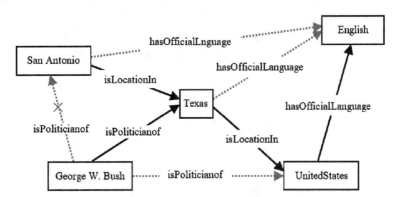

(3) In Definition 10, the complexity of the situations is ascribed to the direction and asymmetry of STP. We cannot only consider the position of an entity in a given RDF triple but also check the linking direction of its relevant STP.

Hereafter, we will give a further interpretation about Definition 10 and illustrate the third note in Remark 2through the following example.

Example 2: (A RDF graph with STP extendable predicate). Assume that there is a fragment of RDF graph which include four facts $\{t_1, t_2, t_3, t_4\}$, where t_1=(George W. Bush, isPoliticianof, Texas), t_2=(San Antonio, isLocationIn, Texas), t_3=(Texas, isLocationIn, United States), and t_4=(United States, hasOfficialLanguage, English) as given in Figure 4. According to the semantic subsumption in geography, we can define the predicate "isLocationIn" as a STP.

From t_1 and t_3, we can derive the valid conclusion (George W. Bush, isPoliticianof, United States) which is drawn as a dotted directed edge in Figure 4, denoted as $t_{1\&3}$. Complying with the condition in Definition 10, the predicate "isPoliticianof" is an $OP^{(out)}_{STP}$ about "isLocationIn". However, we cannot determine the soundness of $t_{1\&2}$=(George W. Bush, isPoliticianof, San Antonio) which is inferred from t_1 and t_2, denoted as $t_{1\&2}$. Because Texas contains many other cities such as Dallas, Houston and so on, and we are not sure which city George W. Bush had ever been worked at as a leader. So, the predicate "isPoliticianof" is not an $OP^{(in)}_{STP}$ about "isLocationIn". See the dotted directed edge with a symbol "×" in Figure 4.

In same manner, the predicate "hasOfficialLanguage" can be defined as a $SP^{(in)}_{STP}$ about "isLocationIn" correspondingly.

The Formal Definition About SM$_P$

To discover more implicit candidates and extend Linked Data sources in semantic level more effectively, we will present a formal definition about the Semantic Matrix for Predicates (SM$_P$) as the basis of our following studies.

Definition 11 (Semantic Matrix for Predicates). Given a RDF graph G, let $R=\{r_1, r_2, ..., r_n\}$ be a set of predicates which contains all predicates appeared in RDF triples of G, $P \subseteq R$ be a subset of predicates which are defined as Definitions 4-7 (i.e., $P=\{p_1, p_2, ..., p_m\}$, where $p_i \in R \wedge ((p_i$ is a SEP)$\vee(p_i$ is a SSP)$\vee(p_i$ is a STP)$\vee(p_i$ is a SIP)) and $m \leq n$). The set $W=\{w_1, w_2, ..., w_m\}$ is the corresponding value set of P, where $w_i \in \{$SEP, SSP, STP, S*I*P$\}$ (e.g., if p_i is a SEP, then w_i=SEP). The $n \times m$ matrix called a *Semantic Matrix for Predicates* w.r.t. G, denoted as SM_P, can be defined over $R \times P$ as follows:

$$SM_P=(r_1, r_2, ..., r_n)^T \times (p_1, p_2, ..., p_m) = \begin{bmatrix} A_{11} & \cdots & A_{1m} \\ \vdots & \ddots & \vdots \\ A_{n1} & \cdots & A_{nm} \end{bmatrix}.$$

where the value of A_{ij} is assigned according with any of the following conditions:

1. if $r_i = p_j$ and $w_j \neq S\!I\!P$, then $A_{ij} = w_j$,
2. if $r_i = p_j$ and $w_j = S\!I\!P$, then $A_{ij} = null$,
3. if $r_i \neq p_j$, then $A_{ij} \in \{null, S\!I\!P, P_{\text{SEP}}, SP_{\text{SSP}}, OP_{\text{SSP}}, SP^{(in)}_{\text{STP}}, SP^{(out)}_{\text{STP}}, OP^{(in)}_{\text{STP}}, OP^{(out)}_{\text{STP}}\}$,
4. if $r_i \neq p_j$, and $A_{ij} = S\!I\!P$, then $A_{ji} = S\!I\!P$.

Example 3: (A SM_P for Figure 2). According to the RDF graph in Figure 2, Table 4 gives evaluations to some of predicates from semantics.

$$SM_P = \begin{bmatrix} & & & & & P_{\text{SEP}} \\ & & & & SP_{\text{SSP}} & P_{\text{SEP}} \\ & & & & SP_{\text{SSP}} & P_{\text{SEP}} \\ & & & & & P_{\text{SEP}} \\ & & & SP^{(in)}_{\text{STP}} & & P_{\text{SEP}} \\ & & \text{SIP} & & & P_{\text{SEP}} \\ & \text{SIP} & & & & P_{\text{SEP}} \\ & & & & & P_{\text{SEP}} \\ & & & \text{STP} & & P_{\text{SEP}} \\ & & & & \text{SSP} & P_{\text{SEP}} \\ & & OP^{(out)}_{\text{STP}} & & & P_{\text{SEP}} \\ & & & & & \text{SEP} \\ & & & & & P_{\text{SEP}} \end{bmatrix}$$

Then we construct the SM_P w.r.t. the RDF graph in Figure 2. Here, we arrange the sequence of predicates in alphabetical order. The more details about predicates are given in Table 5, where the highlighted area is exact the SM_P.

In the aforementioned matrix, we can get the evaluation $SM_P[11][3] = OP^{(out)}_{\text{STP}}$ (Here, the positions of the elements are from logic not mean the physical address). From Table 5, we can find out the corresponding predicates and the semantics between them (i.e., "isPoliticianof" is a $OP^{(out)}_{\text{STP}}$ about "isLocationIn"). This conclusion is consistent with Example 2.

Table 4. The semantic properties of predicates in Figure 2

	hasPredecessor	hasSuccessor	isLocationIn	isMarriedTo	Label
SEP					√
SSP				√	
STP			√		
SIP	√ (hasSuccessor)	√(hasPredecessor)			

Table 5. The semantic explanation about the SM_p w.r.t. the RDF graph in Figure 2

	hasPredecessor	hasSuccessor	isLocationIn	isMarriedTo	label
Create					P_{SEP}
hasChild				SP_{SSP}	P_{SEP}
hasFamilyname				SP_{SSP}	P_{SEP}
hasGivenname					P_{SEP}
hasOfficialLanguage			$SP^{(in)}_{STP}$		P_{SEP}
hasPredecessor		SIP			P_{SEP}
hasSuccessor	SIP				P_{SEP}
isAiffiliatedTo					P_{SEP}
isLocationIn			STP		P_{SEP}
isMarriedTo				SSP	P_{SEP}
isPoliticianof			$OP^{(out)}_{STP}$		P_{SEP}
label					SEP
Owns					P_{SEP}

SEMANTICALLY-EXTENDED SCHEME FOR LINKED DATA SOURCES

With semantically-enhanced annotation strategy as the foundation, a Linked Data source can be extended by a given SM_p through semantically-enhanced reasoning. In this section we focus on discussing the reasoning rules and the relevant algorithm.

The Reasoning Rules Based on SM_p

Based on the above discussion, we now give the definition and corresponding reasoning rules Based on SM_p as follows:

Definition 12: (Semantically-Extended Scheme for Linked Data Sources). Given a Linked Data source *D* which can be seen as a dataset composed of RDF triples, *D'* is the corresponding dataset as the outcome of the semantically-enhanced reasoning over *D* under the given SM_p, where SM_p is a Semantic Matrix for Predicates in Definition 11. The *Semantically-Extended Scheme for Linked Data Sources*, denoted as SES_{LDS}, is a mapping $f: D \rightarrow D'$, where for each element A_{ij} and its matching pair $<r_i, p_j>$ in SM_p (see Definition 11), f utilize the following list of rules shown in Table 6.

Table 6. The semantically-enhanced reasoning rules Based on SM_P

Rule ID	The Value of A_{ij}	If Contain	Then Add
SES_{LDS}-sep	A_{ij}=SEP	(?x, ?r_i, ?y)	(?x, owl:sameAs, ?y)
SES_{LDS}-ssp	A_{ij}=SSP	(?x, ?r_i, ?y)	(?y, ?r_i, ?x)
SES_{LDS}-stp	A_{ij}= STP	(?x, ?r_i, ?y) ∧ (?y, ?r_i, ?z)	(?x, ?r_i, ?z)
SES_{LDS}-sip	A_{ij}=SIP	(?x, ?r_i, ?y)	(?y, ?p_j, ?x)
SES_{LDS}-psep-1	$A_{ij}=P_{SEP}$	(?x, ?r_i, ?y)∧ ((?x, ?p_j, ?z)∨(?z, ?p_j, ?x))	(?z, ?r_i, ?y)
SES_{LDS}-psep-2	$A_{ij}=P_{SEP}$	(?x, ?r_i, ?y)∧((?y, ?p_j, ?z)∨(?z, ?p_j, ?y))	(?x, ?r_i, ?z)
SES_{LDS}-spssp	$A_{ij}=SP_{SSP}$	(?x, ?r_i, ?y)∧((?x, ?p_j, ?z)∨(?z, ?p_j, ?x))	(?z, ?r_i, ?y)
SES_{LDS}-opssp	$A_{ij}=OP_{SSP}$	(?x, ?r_i, ?y)∧((?y, ?p_j, ?z)∨(?z, ?p_j, ?y))	(?x, ?r_i, ?z)
SES_{LDS}-spstp-in	$A_{ij}=SP^{(in)}_{STP}$	(?x, ?r_i, ?y)∧(?z, ?p_j, ?x)	(?z, ?r_i, ?y)
SES_{LDS}-spstp-out	$A_{ij}=SP^{(out)}_{STP}$	(?x, ?r_i, ?y)∧(?x, ?p_j, ?z)	(?z, ?r_i, ?y)
SES_{LDS}-opstp-in	$A_{ij}=OP^{(in)}_{STP}$	(?x, ?r_i, ?y)∧(?z, ?p_j, ?y)	(?x, ?r_i, ?z)
SES_{LDS}-opstp-out	$A_{ij}=OP^{(out)}_{STP}$	(?x, ?r_i, ?y)∧(?y, ?p_j, ?z)	(?x, ?r_i, ?z)

The Algorithm for SES$_{LDS}$

Based on the above discussion, we now give the definition and corresponding reasoning rules Based on SM_P as follows:

According to the architecture given in Figure 3, we present an algorithm for SES$_{LDS}$ in order to implement deeper-layer semantic extension in Linked Data sources.

For a given Linked Data source and its corresponding SM_P, we firstly utilize the first three rules in Table 6 which represent the properties of the specific predicate itself to achieve the initial extension just as the aforementioned strategies defined in RDFS and OWL 2 (see Tables1 and 2). In the subsequent step, we make the further extension for the target source with the rest rules which reason between different predicates. The high-level overview of pseudo-codes is shown in Algorithm 1.

SEMANTICALLY-EXTENDED QUERY MODEL FOR THE LINKED DATA

In this section we will propose a novel framework for our SEQM$_{LD}$ and give a formal definition about SEQM$_{LD}$. Moreover, we will present the details of processing algorithms of this new querying method.

The Framework for SEQM$_{LD}$

According to the above discussion, we define the notion of SEQM$_{LD}$ as follows:

Definition 13: (Semantically-Extended Query Model for the Linked Data). Let D be a finite dataset of Linked Data represented as a RDF graph, $E(F)$ be a finite set of all possible elements of query results specific to some query formalism F. A *Semantically-Extended Query Model for the Linked*

Algorithm 1. The Implementation of SES$_{LDS}$

```
Function: SES_LDS(D, SM_p)
Input: A Linked Data source D, a SM_p=R×P=A_n×_m over D
Output: The closure of D, denoted as D'
Initialization: D'=D
(1) while |D'|≥|D| //Ensure results derived by the second cycle trigger the
first batch
(2)    for i=0 to m-1 // Semantically-enhanced reasoning over the predicate it-
self
(3)       if P_i=SEP    then apply rule(SES_LDS-sep) to D'
(4)       if P_i=SSP    then apply rule(SES_LDS-ssp) to D'
(5)       if P_i=STP    then apply rule(SES_LDS-stp) to D'
(6)    end for
(7)    for i=0 to n-1    // Semantically-enhanced reasoning using SM_p
(8)       for j=0 to m-1
(9)          if A_ij=SIP                    then apply rule(SES_LDS-sip) to D'
(10)         if A_ij=P_SEP         then apply rule(SES_LDS-psep-1) + (SES_LDS-psep-2) to D'
(11)         if A_ij=SP_SSP                   then apply rule(SES_LDS-spssp) to D'
(12)         if A_ij=OP_SSP                   then apply rule(SES_LDS-opssp) to D'
(13)         if A_ij=SP^(in)_STP                then apply rule(SES_LDS-spstp-in) to D'
(14)         if A_ij=SP^(out)_STP                 then apply rule(SES_LDS-spstp-out) to D'
(15)         if A_ij=OP^(in)_STP                 then apply rule(SES_LDS-opstp-in) to D'
(16)         if A_ij=OP^(out)_STP        then apply rule(SES_LDS-opstp-out) to D'
(17)      end for
(18)   end for
(19) end while
(20) return D'
```

Data, denoted as $SEQM_{LD}$, is a tuple $Q= (B, SM_p)$, which is a total mapping $Q: D \rightarrow E((B, SM_p))$, where B is a BGP in Definition 2, and SM_p is a semantic matrix for predicates in Definition 11.

With SEQM$_{LD}$ as the foundation, a SPARQL-based *BGP* can be extended by a given SM_p. Applying SEQM$_{LD}$, we may obtain some implicit consequences.

The Algorithms for SEQM$_{LD}$

Now we focus on discussing the implementation problem about the semantic extension of query. Firstly, to realize the abstract SEQM$_{LD}$, we will design some concrete algorithms. Afterwards, we give the architecture of the implementation about the querying method using SEQM$_{LD}$.

To design the algorithm for SEQM$_{LD}$, we first discuss the characteristics of BGP. Every triple pattern in a given *BGP* has one or two variables (if a triple pattern has three variables in all of units such as

($?x$, $?p$, $?y$), this query may be meaningless). Besides, considering the majority of query requirements about Linked Data aim at searching subject or object in a RDF triple rather the predicate, in this paper our study just focus on the situations which the variables are formed as ($?x$, p, e), (e, p, $?x$) or ($?x$, p, $?y$).

According to the different properties of predicates, we firstly give some basic sub-algorithms. Then, we integrate these sub-algorithms into a complete algorithm for SEQM$_{LD}$. The high-level overview of pseudo-codes is shown in Algorithms 2-5.

Here, we design Algorithm 5 in one single-variable triple pattern case (i.e. ($?x$, p, e) or (e, p, $?x$)) for simplicity. If there are more than one variable or triple pattern in *BGP*, we can circularly execute Algorithm 5 and calculate the intersections of the results for the shared variable.

Algorithm 2. Finding all relevant entities about entity e and excluding the set of entities EX from the queried dataset of Linked Data D, where e is linked by a SEP p in a triple pattern.

```
Function: SE(e, p, EX)
Input: An entity e, a SEP p, and a set of excepted entities EX
Output: The answer set of all relevant entities A
Initialization: A=A'=Φ, checked= EX
(1)        t₁=(?x, p, e), t₂=(e, p, ?x)
(2)        A=A'=(µ(t₁)∪µ(t₂))\ checked
(3)        while(A'≠Φ)
(4)              e'=an element of A'
(5)              checked =checked∪{e'}          //prevent the endless-cycle
(6)              A=A∪SE(e', p, checked)
(7)              A'=A'\{e'}
(8)        end while
(9)        return A
```

Algorithm 3. Finding all relevant entities about entity e from the queried dataset of Linked Data D, where e is linked by a STP p in a triple pattern and e is an object.

```
Function: ST_object(e, p)
Input: An entity e, a STP p
Output: The answer set of all relevant entities A
Initialization: A=A'=Φ
1.         t=(?x, p, e)
2.         A=A'=µ(t)
3.         while(A'≠Φ)
4.         e'= an element of A'
5.         A=A∪ST_object(e', p)
6.         A'= A' \ {e'}
7.         end while
8.         return A
```

Algorithm 4. Finding all relevant entities of entity e from the queried dataset of Linked Data D, where e is linked by a STP p in a triple pattern and e is a subject.

```
Function: ST_subject(e, p)
Input: An entity e, a STP p
Output: The answer set of all relevant entities A
Initialization: A=A'=Φ
1.          t=(e, p, ?x)
2.          A=A'=μ(t)
3.          while(A'≠Φ)
4.          e'= an element of A'
5.          A=A∪ST_subject(e', p)
6.          A'= A' \ {e'}
7.          end while
8.          return A
```

Algorithm 5. Finding the relevant query result set about a given BGP and a corresponding SM_p from the queried dataset of Linked Data D.

```
Function: SEQM_LD(BGP, SM_p)
Input: A BGP (e.g., a single-term query t), a semantic matrix for predicates
SM_p
Output: The answer set of all relevant entities A
Initialization: A=B=Φ, k=i=0, n=the column length of SM_p, len=-1
//len=-1 ensure that the while-cycle is executed at least once
(1)        A=μ(t)
(2)        k=the row-id of r in SM_p, where r∈Sig(t) is not the variable (the
same below)
(3)        while (len≠|A|)          //avoid the result omission caused by col-
umn-order of SM_p
(4)            len=|A|
(5)            for i=0 to n-1
(6)                p=the corresponding predicate for the i-th column
of SM_p[k][i]
(7)                if SM_p[k][i]=SEP
(8)                    A=A∪SE(e, r, Φ), where e∈Sig(t) is not the
variable
(9)                else if SM_p[k][i]=SSP
(10)                   A=A∪μ(?x, r, e)∪μ(e, r, ?x)
(11)                else if SM_p[k][i]=STP
```

continued on following page

Algorithm 5. Continued

(12)   **if** e is object in t **then** A=A**UST_object**(e, r)

(13)   **else** A=A**UST_subject**(e, r)

(14)   **else if** $SM_p[k][i]$=SIP

(15)   **if** e is object in t **then** A= AUμ(e, p, ?x)

(16)   **else** A=AUμ(?x, p, e)

(17)   **else if** $SM_p[k][i]$=P_{SEP}

(18) B=B**USE**(e, p, Φ)

(19)   **for** every element b_j in B

(20)   **if** e is object in t **then** A=AUμ(?x, r, b_j)

(21)   **else** A=AUμ(b_j, r, ?x)

(22)   **end for**

(23)   **for** every element a_j in A

(24) A=A**USE**(a_j, p, Φ)

(25)   **end for**

(26)   **else if** $SM_p[k][i]$=SP_{SSP}

(27)   **if** e is object in t

(28)   **for** every element a_j in A

(29) A=AUμ(?x, p, a_j)Uμ(a_j, p, ?x)

(30)   **end for**

(31)   **else** B=μ(?x, p, e)Uμ(e, p, ?x)

(32)   **for** every element b_j in B

(33) A=AUμ(b_j, r, ?x)

(34)   **end for**

(35)   **else if** $SM_p[k][i]$=OP_{SSP}

(36)   **if** e is object in t

(37) B=μ(?x, p, e)Uμ(e, p, ?x)

(38)   **for** every element b_j in B

(39) A=AUμ(?x, r, b_j)

(40)   **end for**

(41)   **else for** every element a_j in A

(42) A=AUμ(?x, p, a_j)Uμ(a_j, p, ?x)

(43)   **end for**

(44)   **else if** $SM_p[k][i]$=$SP^{(in)}_{STP}$

(45)   **if** e is object in t

(46)   **for** every element a_j in A

continued on following page

Algorithm 5. Continued

```
(47)                                                    A=AUST_object(a_j, p)
(48)                                        end for
(49)                            else B= ST_subject(e, p)
(50)                                    for every element b_j in B
(51)                                        A=AUμ(b_j, r, ?x)
(52)                                    end for
(53)                    else if SM_p[k][i]=SP^(out)_STP
(54)                            if e is object in t
(55)                                    for every element a_j in A
(56)                                        A=AUST_subject(a_j, p)
(57)                                    end for
(58)                            else B= ST_object(e, p)
(59)                                    for every element b_j in B
(60)                                        A=AUμ(b_j, r, ?x)
(61)                                    end for
(62)                    else if SM_p[k][i]=OP^(in)_STP
(63)                            if e is subject in t
(64)                                    for every element a_j in A
(65)                                        A=AUST_object(a_j, p)
(66)                                    end for
(67)                            else B= ST_subject(e, p)
(68)                                    for every element b_j in B
(69)                                        A=AUμ(?x, r, b_j)
(70)                                    end for
(71)                    else if SM_p[k][i]=OP^(out)_STP
(72)                            if e is subject in t
(73)                                    for every element a_j in A
(74)                                        A=AUST_subject(a_j, p)
(75)                                    end for
(76)                            else B= ST_object(e, p)
(77)                                    for every element b_j in B
(78)                                        A=AUμ(?x, r, b_j)
(79)                                    end for
(80)                    end if
(81)              end for
(82)        end while
(83)        return A
```

Figure 5. The Architecture of the Implementation about SEQM$_{LD}$

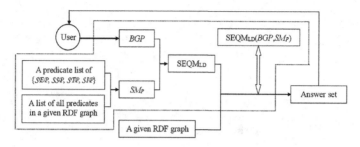

Figure 6. The partial semantic extension result of Figure 2 deduced by SES$_{LDS}$

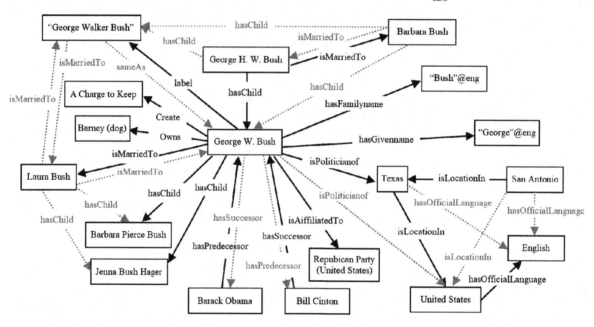

Table 7. The semantic extension result of Figure 5 deduced by SES$_{LDS}$

The Size of the Original Linked Data Source	The semantic extension result deduced by SES$_{LDS}$						
	The Number of Existing Knowledge	The Number of Implicit Knowledge Deduced by SES$_{LDS}$	The Number of Valid Implicit Knowledge	The Overall Size	Novelty	Extra Coverage	Soundness
17	17	29	29	46	63.04%	170.59%	100%

The Architecture of the Implementation About SEQM$_{LD}$

A querying system applying SEQM$_{LD}$ requires a concrete process for implementing the execution. For such a purpose, we will construct the architecture of the implementation about our SEQM$_{LD}$ as being illustrated in Figure 5.

EVALUATION

To validate the effectiveness of our SES_{LDS} as well as $SEQM_{LD}$, in this section we will be interested in the query results with the real-world Linked Data sources in our experiments. Up to now, the standardization of experimental practice in keyword-based query which orients normal text and pages has come a long way. But in contrast, there is not an equivalent body of methodologies and datasets for the evaluation of the reasoning over RDF-based Linked data sources and the corresponding SPARQL-based query methods. So, we must do our best to choose the better experimental object.

The Visual Assessment for SES_{LDS}

To validate the effectiveness of our SES_{LDS} presented in this paper, in this section, we are interested in the semantic extension results conducted on given Linked Data sources. We design a visual assessment and evaluate the feasibility and soundness of SES_{LDS} as well as the corresponding algorithm.

As the visual assessment for SES_{LDS}, we implement Algorithm 1 on a simple Linked Data source which can be represented as a RDF graph shown in Figure 2. The annotations about the semantic properties of the corresponding predicates are shown in Table 5. The partial semantic extension result which is as the output of Algorithm 1 is given in Figure 6. The dotted directed edges with the relevant predicate names denote the implicit semantics deduced by our SES_{LDS}. Because of the semantic equivalency of *SEP*, the entities linked by a given *SEP* will have same topological structure after the reasoning of SES_{LDS}. So, to ensure the legibility, we filter out some results extended by the *SEP* "label" and its corresponding P_{SEP}.

Through the measuring of the experiments, we aggregate and analyze the semantic extension result deduced by SES_{LDS}. The whole statistics are shown in Table 7.

Along this line, we define the following three formulas to evaluate the feasibility and soundness of our SES_{LDS}. The first two analogous methods can be found in Ref. (Ponzetto & Strube, 2011).

$$Novelty = \frac{|\text{The overall size} \setminus \text{The original size}|}{|\text{The overall size}|}$$

$$ExtraCoverage = \frac{|\text{The overall size} \setminus \text{The original size}|}{|\text{The original size}|}$$

$$Soundness = \frac{|\text{The number of valid implicit knowledge}|}{|\text{The overall size} \setminus \text{The original size}|}$$

From the "Novelty" and "ExtraCoverage" shown in Table 7, we conclude that the SES_{LDS} can discover much more implicit knowledge and effectively extend the original Linked Data source. Further, by adjudicating the validity of the implicit knowledge deduced by SES_{LDS}, the "Soundness" shows that the algorithm for SES_{LDS} can ensure the rationality of these triples if the original Linked Data source and its corresponding SM_p are well designed.

Here, we must note that, the visual assessment method is only applicable for the mini-type Linked Data sources, because in this case the number of RDF triples is relatively small, so we can easily get the extended tag graph and evaluate the soundness of all implicit knowledge deduced by SES_{LDS}. However, under Big Data environment, most of Linked Data sources are very large and contain millions of RDF triples. Faced with these massive data, we cannot evaluate all triples and draw a vivid graph. Moreover, from the user's point of view, the expansion scheme for the whole Linked Data Source is meaningless especially when the purpose of the user is to search some specific content. In most cases, the query request often has only a few conditions, and the related knowledge scale is very small compared with the overall scale of the whole Linked Data Source. So only the reasoning and extensions which execute over the related knowledge are really meaningful. The user will not care about the extension results of other irrelevant knowledge. This is why we continue to study the semantic extension of query for the Linked Data (i.e. $SEQM_{LD}$).

Along this line, in the following sections, we shift our eyes to the assessment for $SEQM_{LD}$.

Selecting Data Source and Building SM$_p$

Since the Linked Data community include many members of data sources and different data sources have very different structures such as the taxonomy, hierarchy, entities and predicates and so on, so $SEQM_{LD}$ cannot be applied to every data source in Linked Data cloud and make a parallel comparison between them.

A sensible and feasible strategy to evaluate the effectiveness of our $SEQM_{LD}$ is to select one of data sources from Linked Data cloud and implement the algorithm of $SEQM_{LD}$ over this target data source. Then we compare the consequences returned by $SEQM_{LD}$ and some existing SPARQL-based querying methods.

Promoted by this motivation, we choose YAGO as our experiment object which has high coverage and precision with clear taxonomy and hierarchy. Since our experimentation need an evaluated version, we download the latest-evaluated English version 2.5.3[4]of YAGO2 in June 2015 (2.2 GB compressed, more than 92 GB uncompressed). Without GeoNames[5], this enormous corpus consists of about 124 million facts for 2.6 million entities and 126 manually defined predicates, extracted from Wikipedia and WordNet. The average accuracy of the facts in YAGO2 is up to 95%confirmed by human evaluation. This stunning accuracy provides a secure guarantee for our experimental results.

To construct our $SEQM_{LD}$, we first analyze the predicates defined in YAGO. There are 126 manually defined predicates in YAGO, but not all predicates are meaningful for $SEQM_{LD}$. One of the prominent advantages of YAGO is that it uses fact identifiers (IDs) which represent one fact with unambiguous semantics. Exceptionally, some of facts with particular predicates do not have their IDs. For instance, as an extension of study of Example 1, we summarize all relevant facts about the entity "George W. Bush" using the whole 126 predicates. The statistic results are shown in Table 8 and Table 9.

As being shown in Table 8 and 9, the total number of relevant facts is 9336, but only 29 facts with concrete IDs which merely accounted for 0.3%. The rest of those which have no IDs highlighted in above tables are all ambiguous and less comprehensible. For example, the fact (George W. Bush, linksTo, Bill Clinton) is certainly true as everyone knows. But what is the detail of this link? In view of the semantic characteristics of our $SEQM_{LD}$, we expel these no-ID facts and their corresponding predicates as well.

Table 8. The number of facts where "George W. Bush" is subject

Creat	hasChild	hasFamilyName	hasGivenName	label	isAffiliatedTo	hasWebsite	isMarriedTo
4	2	1	1	145	1	3	1
type	linksTo	isPoliticianOf	redirectedFrom	owns	wasBornIn	wasBornOnDate	prefLabel
69	365	1	85	3	1	1	1
Summation: 684			With ID: 22 ("label" has two facts with ID)			Without ID: 662	

Table 9. The number of facts where "George W. Bush" is object

hasChild	hasPredecessor	hasSuccessor	isMarriedTo	label	linksTo	prefLabel
2	2	2	1	1	8645	1
Summation: 8652		With ID: 7 (facts with "label" and "prefLabel"are same as in Table 4, so we do not count these 2 facts in summation in Table 5)			Without ID: 8645	

In addition, since the main concern of SEQM$_{LD}$ focuses on the semantic relationship between individuals in real world, so we are indifferent to the predicates which represent the properties of predicates (e.g., domain, range, subjectStartRelation, subjectEndRelation, permanentRelationToObject, permanentRelationToSubject, objectStartRelation, objectEndRelation, and so on).

Through filtering, we discard the 13 of 126 predicates in YAGO and retain the rest 113 ones. According to the previous definitions, we assign different semantic properties to these predicates and establish the corresponding SM_p for YAGO. A subset of the SM_p for YAGO is shown in Table 5. The whole SM_p for YAGO as well as some relevant data are available at the homepage of the author.

The Design for BGP

In what follows, we will provide some *BGP*s as the query set for our SEQM$_{LD}$ and its competitors. To the best of our knowledge, unlike evaluating the traditional keyword-based querying techniques, there is no standard query set for the measurement of SPARQL-based query. So, we have to provide these queries as new benchmark by ourselves. We construct 12 natural-language-composed questions and translate them into *BGP*s with RDF format. The whole query list is shown in Table 10. A sample query and the corresponding *BGP* can be obtained from Table 11.

The Competitor and the Comparison

As being discussed in Section 2, YAGO has a function-rich querying interface, NAGA, which uses SPARQL-based querying strategy and presents a feasible ranking approach for query results. So, we compare our SEQM$_{LD}$ with this state-of-the-art system.

All 12 queries were submitted to both SEQM$_{LD}$ and NAGA. The total number of answers for each query is counted and shown in Table 12. Specifically, it is easy to see from Table 5 that if a predicate r is defined as a SEP, all else predicates can be named as a P_{SEP} about r because of the semantic equiva-

Table 10. The whole query list for experimentation

Query ID	Query Requirements
Q1	Who had won prize of Nobel Prize in Physics and was born in Europe?
Q2	The city which is located in Florida and has official language of American English?
Q3	What is the official language of London?
Q4	Which place regards George W. Bush as a politician?
Q5	Who are known as the politicians of United States and was born in Texas?
Q6	Who are parents of George Walker Bush?
Q7	Who are parents of Barack Obama?
Q8	Whose predecessor is Bill Clinton?
Q9	The battle of World War II which happened in China?
Q10	What are Ken Gemes interested in?
Q11	Who is interested in Philosophy of history?
Q12	Who directed the movie "Jaws" and which prize does she/he have won?

Table 11. A sample query and the corresponding BGP

Query ID	Query Requirements	The Corresponding *BGP*
Q1	Who had won prize of Nobel Prize in Physics and was born in Europe?	(*?who*, hasWonPrize, Nobel_Prize_in_Physics), (*?who*, wasBornIn, *?where*), (*?where*, isLocatedIn, Europe)

Table 12. The number of answers returned by NAGA and SEQM$_{LD}$

Query ID	NAGA	SEQM$_{LD}$	
		Without SEP	With SEP
Q1	4	97	194
Q2	Φ	235	470
Q3	Φ	1	2
Q4	1	2	4
Q5	Φ	4	8
Q6	Φ	2	4
Q7	1	2	4
Q8	4	4	4
Q9	14	51	102
Q10	1	48	96
Q11	10	11	22
Q12	3	3	12

lence. Hence, to make clearer comparison, we distinguish the querying result set returned by $SEQM_{LD}$ between two different subsets. One of the subsets does not extend the entities in the output of $SEQM_{LD}$ using SEP (i.e., remove the for-cycle from (23) to (25) in Algorithm 5), while the other retains all the steps of Algorithm 5.

The corresponding column chart for Table 12 is shown as Figure 7 and Figure 8, while Figure 8 makes a local amplification for some queries whose result sets include answers less than 25.

From the experimental results shown in above two figures, we can conclude that, in most cases, our $SEQM_{LD}$ can return more answers than NAGA even taking no account of those results extended by SEP.

In what follows, we will evaluate the quality of the answers returned by our $SEQM_{LD}$. Since the elaborate design of YAGO, most of the facts in this huge data set are rational. If the answer set is not null,

Figure 7. The total number of answers for each query

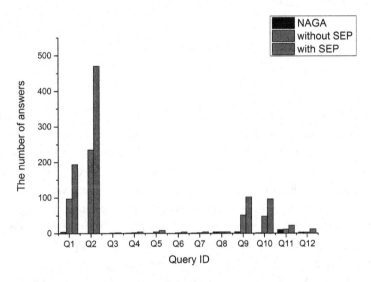

Figure 8. A local amplification for Figure 7

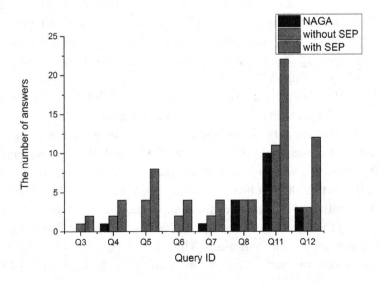

the elements in the answer set are proper for the query requirement with a high probability. Therefore, notwithstanding that NAGA provides a meticulous scheme for answers ranking, the results ranked below are also legitimate. So we take no account of the issue for ranking in our experiments.

Based on unranked answer sets as the research object, we do not take the measurement criteria such as *MAP* (mean average precision) and *P@k* (precision at *k*), but adopt the well-known metrics *Precision* (*P*), *Recall* (*R*), and *F₁ measure* (*F₁*) (Manning et al., 2008). The corresponding formulas are defined as:

$$P = \frac{\text{The number of valid answer returned}}{\text{The number of returned answer}} = P(\text{valid}|\text{returned}),$$

$$R = \frac{\text{The number of valid answer returned}}{\text{The number of valid answer}} = R(\text{returned}|\text{valid}),$$

$$F_1 = \frac{2PR}{P + R}$$

An important task for us to compute the assessment metrics (*P*, *R*, and *F₁*) is that we need to know complete and valid query results about each of the 12 test queries in YAGO. An ideal method is to traverse all relevant facts in data source and evaluate the soundness of all these facts in semantic level by manual. However, for such a huge data source, the aforesaid method is too difficult to apply. So, we introduce an approximate estimation to simulate and substitute the ideal value.

Based on the definitions and analysis in previous sections, we can infer that the outcome of $SEQM_{LD}$ using SEP is very close to the real complete and valid result set. So, we extend the data in last column of Table 12 with all valid equivalent entities deduced by SEP with unique IDs.

Nevertheless, there may be some mistake when we execute the extension. For example, for Q7, the result set of "without SEP" is $A=\{(?who\rightarrow\text{Barack Obama, Sr.}), (?who\rightarrow\text{Ann Dunham})\}$. If we extend A with SEP and include all valid equivalent entities into the result set, for "Barack Obama, Sr.", there are 3 equivalent entities with IDs such as "Barack Obama @eng", "Baraka Obama", and "Barack Obama, Sr. @eng". Coincidently, the entity "Barack Obama" is also has an equivalent entity "Barack Obama @ eng" with a fact ID. Though the ID of each matching fact is different, we cannot distinguish this ambiguity literally and will get a wrong conclusion from the extended fact ("Barack Obama @eng" hasChild, Barack Obama) which implies Barack Obama is a child of himself.

What is more, due to the high but not absolute accuracy of YAGO, there are some facts with incorrect semantics. If our $SEQM_{LD}$ executes over these facts, the error may be magnified and transferred into the extended results. To ensure the soundness of the approximate estimation for the complete and valid results, we must analyze the results returned by $SEQM_{LD}$ and filter out the ambiguities manually. For each entity in the answer set, we resubstitute it into the corresponding query in Table 10, and decide on a score by 1 and 0, whether the result is reasonable from semantics (1), or unreasonable (0). The score of each result is confirmed by human evaluation. In addition, to reduce subjectivity, we have a random sample of 20% of the results evaluated by 3 judges instead of one and accept the majority. The odd number of judges is to avoid equal judgments. The same tactic is applied to the judgments over the results of NAGA. The whole summaries about the evaluation are shown in Tables 13-16.

Table 13. The judgments over the results of NAGA and SEQM$_{LD}$

Query ID	NAGA		SEQM$_{LD}$ (Without SEP)		SEQM$_{LD}$ (With SEP)		All Valid Results
	All Results	Valid Results	All Results	Valid Results	All Results	Valid Results	
Q1	4	4	97	97	194	194	228
Q2	0	0	235	235	470	470	822
Q3	0	0	1	1	2	2	2
Q4	1	1	2	2	4	4	6
Q5	0	0	4	4	8	8	10
Q6	0	0	2	2	4	4	5
Q7	1	1	2	2	4	3	4
Q8	4	3	4	3	4	3	4
Q9	14	14	51	37	102	74	79
Q10	1	1	48	34	96	68	69
Q11	10	10	11	11	22	22	23
Q12	3	3	3	3	12	12	12

Table 14. Quality of results by Precision (P)

Query ID	NAGA	SEQM$_{LD}$ (Without SEP)	SEQM$_{LD}$ (With SEP)
Q1	100.00%	100.00%	100.00%
Q2	0.00%	100.00%	100.00%
Q3	0.00%	100.00%	100.00%
Q4	100.00%	100.00%	100.00%
Q5	0.00%	100.00%	100.00%
Q6	0.00%	100.00%	100.00%
Q7	100.00%	100.00%	75.00%
Q8	75.00%	75.00%	75.00%
Q9	100.00%	72.55%	72.55%
Q10	100.00%	70.83%	70.83%
Q11	100.00%	100.00%	100.00%
Q12	100.00%	100.00%	100.00%

From the above experimental results in Table 13, we know that, for a given query, our SEQM$_{LD}$ can excavate out more implicit candidates than the traditional SPARQL-based querying strategy over a concrete Linked Data source. If we introduce the SEP into results, the answer sets will contain richer outcomes.

There are two exceptional cases, Q8 and Q12, whose results of both NAGA and SEQM$_{LD}$ "without SEP" are equal. For Q8, notwithstanding the predicates "hasPredecessor" and "hasSuccessor" are declared as SIP for each other, we don't get additional results by our SEQM$_{LD}$. The cause is the configuration about the domain of these two predicates. Unlike our normal perception, the domains of these two predicates are all "Statement" (i.e., fact IDs), rather than "person" which is their ranges. So we cannot

Table 15. Quality of results by Recall (R)

Query ID	NAGA	SEQM$_{LD}$ (Without SEP)	SEQM$_{LD}$ (With SEP)
Q1	1.75%	42.54%	85.09%
Q2	0.00%	28.59%	57.18%
Q3	0.00%	50.00%	100.00%
Q4	16.67%	33.33%	66.67%
Q5	0.00%	40.00%	80.00%
Q6	0.00%	40.00%	80.00%
Q7	25.00%	50.00%	75.00%
Q8	75.00%	75.00%	75.00%
Q9	17.72%	46.84%	93.67%
Q10	1.45%	49.28%	98.55%
Q11	43.48%	47.83%	95.65%
Q12	25.00%	25.00%	100.00%

Table 16. Quality of results by F measure (F_1)

Query ID	NAGA	SEQM$_{LD}$ (Without SEP)	SEQM$_{LD}$ (With SEP)
Q1	3.45%	59.69%	91.94%
Q2	0.00%	44.47%	72.76%
Q3	0.00%	66.67%	100.00%
Q4	28.57%	50.00%	80.00%
Q5	0.00%	57.14%	88.89%
Q6	0.00%	57.14%	88.89%
Q7	40.00%	66.67%	75.00%
Q8	75.00%	75.00%	75.00%
Q9	30.11%	56.92%	81.77%
Q10	2.86%	58.12%	82.42%
Q11	60.61%	64.71%	97.78%
Q12	40.00%	40.00%	100.00%

get more answers by reversing the subject and object in a triple pattern when the predicate is a SIP but the domain and range belong to different categories. For Q12, the two referred predicates "directed" and "hasWonPrize" do not have any semantic relationship with other predicates except the P_{SEP}. So, if we overlook the extension of the output by the SEP, there are no more semantically-extended answers to return.

What's more, since the targeted design scheme of the 12 queries, NAGA cannot return any result for some queries such as Q2, Q3, Q5, and Q6. The purpose we devise these queries is not only to indicate the well performance of SEQM$_{LD}$, but also to unfold the user-friendly usability of SEQM$_{LD}$. For instance, if a user want to know the father of George Walker Bush (see Q6), she/he must format the query exactly as (*?who*, hasChild, George W. Bush). If the user does not know the abbreviation but use the full name as "George Walker Bush", there will no result returned by NAGA even if the data source contains a semantic-valid fact (George H.W. Bush, hasChild, George W. Bush). This is also the reason why we design the two similar queries Q6 and Q7. Though the only difference of these 2 queries is merely on the people's names, the results returned by NAGA are entirely different. Obviously, our SEQM$_{LD}$ offers a lower threshold and looser form standard for users and makes the querying interface much easier to use. As shown in Table 14, the precision of the results for each query is quite gratifying. In most cases, the answers can fulfill the requirement of the query no matter they are returned by NAGA or SEQM$_{LD}$. This outstanding performance should be attributed to the high accuracy of the facts in YAGO. However, we can perceive the conspicuous descent of precision for Q7, Q9, and Q10 when SEQM$_{LD}$ is utilized. All these declines derive from the features of facts and the design of the SM_p in SEQM$_{LD}$. We have interpreted the reason for Q7 when we introduce how to obtain the approximation about the complete and valid result. While for Q9, the decrease is caused by the duplication. Because of the geographic features of battles, some results are formed with two geographic names such as <Battle of Beiping-Tianjin>. This entity has two different relevant facts (Battle of Beiping-Tianjin, isLocatedIn, Beiping), (Battle of Beiping-Tianjin, isLocatedIn, Tianjin) which are considered as two distinct results extended by SEQM$_{LD}$. Different from the previous discussions, most of the results of Q10 are returned by the semantic extension. The major contribution is from the STP "influences" and the $OP^{(in)}_{STP}$ "isInterestedIn" about "influences". But we suppose that not all things that influence an entity can be interested by a person who is interested in this entity. So, we just reserve those entities which belong to the same category with the given entity for the complete valid answer set of Q10.

Notwithstanding that the precision may decline over the results for some queries returned by our SEQM$_{LD}$, the percentages are still relatively high and acceptable when we consider the increasing number of results.

Now, we shift our eyes to the recall of the result sets. From Table 15, we can clearly realize that our SEQM$_{LD}$ can return much more valid answers especially when we extend the results with SEP. If the predicates in a query do not have any semantic relationship with other predicates, the answers return by SEQM$_{LD}$ are same as those of NAGA (see Q8 and Q12). These experiment results illustrate that SEQM$_{LD}$ is a generalization and extension for the traditional SPARQL-based querying strategy.

Finally, let us make a discussion about F_1 shown in Table 16. We can conclude from Table 16 that, with a few exceptions (e.g., Q8 and Q12), the values of F_1 for SEQM$_{LD}$ exceed those for NAGA. Although these queries in Table 10 are merely the tip of the iceberg for the query requirements in real-world, their results remain reflect the superiority and practicability of SEQM$_{LD}$.

CONCLUSION AND PhD CONTRIBUTION

Due to the arrival of Big Data, more and more structured data are published and integrated into Linked Data community. However, in view of the basic reasoning strategies for RDF triples mainly derive from RDF(S) and OWL 2 rules and focus on the properties of the specific predicate itself, these strategies cannot fully comprehend and discover the deeper implicit knowledge in Linked Data sources. What is more, the traditional search engines and SPARQL-based querying strategy mainly rely on the syntax-based representations. Such reasoning rules and querying methods have been limited due to the ignorance of the semantics between predicates. So, they cannot fully comprehend and return the extra implicit knowledge. Hence, finding a feasible and expressive scheme to enhance the current reasoning rules and make an extension for SPARQL-based querying strategy over this gigantic Linked Data space are urgently waiting to be solved.

In this paper, a novel Semantically-Extended Scheme for Linked Data Sources (SES_{LDS}) is proposed by taking the semantic features between different predicates into consideration. Concretely, we introduce a semantic matrix SM_P by analyzing the hierarchies and properties between predicates in semantic level. Afterwards, we design the reasoning rules and corresponding algorithm for our SES_{LDS} in order to strengthen the ability of reasoning presented in RDF(S) and OWL 2. Moreover, to accommodate real-time queries, a new querying method has been employed by integrating semantic extension into SPARQL pattern. We propose a novel query model $SEQM_{LD}$ by applying the SM_P into BGP in order to strengthen the expression ability of the existing SPARQL pattern. Then we design algorithms for our $SEQM_{LD}$. The experimental results indicate that our proposal displays a better performance than the original data sources in terms of semantic extension and some SPARQL-based querying systems.

Along this line, we will list some topics as our future works in Linked Data as well as Semantic Web areas:

1. We will aim to introduce some machine learning technologies into the construction of $SEQM_{LD}$. We want to find a method which can automatically establish the SM_P by assessing the semantic similarity between predicates with human supervision and training.
2. Along our previous studies (Li et al., 2010; Shi et al., 2010) and some other related researches (Codescu et al., 2017; Kureychik & Semenova, 2017), we plan to study on ontology-model extracting and modular linking for Linked Data sources.
3. To ensure semantic consistency of the data sources, we will further investigate the semantic integration for heterogeneous Linked Data sources based on my previous studies (Li et al., 2016; Li, Jiang, et al., 2017).
4. By extending our research in (Jiang et al., 2016; Jiang et al., 2015; Li et al., 2018; Li, Xiao, et al., 2017), we will continually study the issue about the semantic mapping and relatedness assessment between entities in Linked Data.
5. Last but not least, referring the researches introduced in (Auer et al., 2014; Harth et al., 2014), we try to do some works on RDF documents retrieval, classification and clustering.

ACKNOWLEDGMENT

The authors would like to thank the anonymous referees for their valuable comments as well as helpful suggestions from Editor-in-Chief (Professor Miltiadis D. Lytras) and Managing Editor (Kwok Tai Chui) which greatly improved the exposition of the chapter. The works described in this chapter are supported by PhD research fund of Zhengzhou University of Light Industry under Grant No. 0215/13501050015; The National Natural Science Foundation of China under Grant Nos. 61772210 and 61272066; The Program for New Century Excellent Talents in University in China under Grant No. NCET-12-0644; The Natural Science Foundation of Guangdong Province of China under Grant No. S2012030006242; The Project of Science and Technology in Guangzhou in China under Grant Nos. 2014J4100031 and 201604010098.

REFERENCES

Alec, C., Reynaud-Delaitre, C., & Safar, B. (2016). A model for linked open data acquisition and SPARQL query generation. In O. Haemmerle, G. Stapleton, & C. F. Zucker (Eds.), *Graph-Based Representation And Reasoning* (Vol. 9717, pp. 237–251). Cham: Springer. doi:10.1007/978-3-319-40985-6_18

Alrababah, S. A. A., Gan, K. H., & Tan, T. P. (2017). Mining opinionated product features using WordNet lexicographer files. *Journal of Information Science*, *43*(6), 769–785. doi:10.1177/0165551516667651

Assaf, A., Senart, A., & Troncy, R. (2016). Towards an objective assessment framework for linked data quality: Enriching dataset profiles with quality indicators. *International Journal on Semantic Web and Information Systems*, *12*(3), 111–133. doi:10.4018/IJSWIS.2016070104

Auer, S., Bryl, V., & Tramp, S. (2014). *Linked open data-creating knowledge out of interlinked data: Results of the LOD2 Project*. Springer.

Berners-Lee, T., Hendler, J., & Lassila, O. (2001). The semantic Web: A new form of Web content that is meaningful to computers will unleash a revolution of new possibilities. *Scientific American*, *284*(5), 34–43. doi:10.1038cientificamerican0501-34 PMID:11396337

Bizer, C., Heath, T., & Berners-Lee, T. (2009). Linked data: The story so far. *International Journal on Semantic Web and Information Systems*, *5*(3), 1–22. doi:10.4018/jswis.2009081901

Bollacker, K., Cook, R., & Tufts, P. (2007). Freebase: A shared database of structured general human knowledge. In *Proceedings of the 22nd AAAI Conference on Artificial Intelligence*, Vancouver, British Columbia, July 22-26 (pp. 1962-1963). AAAI Press.

Cheng, G., & Qu, Y. (2009). Searching linked objects with Falcons: Approach, implementation and evaluation. *Semantic Services Interoperability & Web Applications Emerging Concepts*, *5*(3), 49–70.

Ciobanu, G., Horne, R., & Sassone, V. (2016). A descriptive type foundation for RDF Schema. *Journal of Logical and Algebraic Methods in Programming*, *85*(5), 681–706. doi:10.1016/j.jlamp.2016.02.006

Codescu, M., Mossakowski, T., & Kutz, O. (2017). A Categorical Approach to Networks of Aligned Ontologies. *Journal on Data Semantics*, *6*(4), 155–197. doi:10.100713740-017-0080-0

Dan, B., & Guha, R. V. (2004). RDF vocabulary description language 1.0: RDF schema. *W3C Recommendation 10 February 2004*. Retrieved from http://www.w3.org/TR/2004/REC-rdf- schema-20040210/

Golbreich, C., Wallace, E. K., Patel-Schneider, P. F., Golbreich, C., Wallace, E. K., & Patel-Schneider, P. F. (2009). OWL 2 Web Ontology Language New Features and Rationale. *W3C Recommendation*. Retrieved from http://www.w3.org/TR/2009/REC-owl2-new-features-20091027/

Haag, F., Lohmann, S., Siek, S., & Ertl, T. (2015). QueryVOWL: A visual query notation for linked data. In F. Gandon, C. Gueret, S. Villata et al. (Eds.), Semantic Web: Eswc 2015 Satellite Events (pp. 387-402). Cham: Springer Int. Publishing Ag. doi:10.1007/978-3-319-25639-9_51

Harris, B. S., & Seaborne, A. (2010). SPARQL 1.1 query. *W3C*. Retrieved from http://www.w3.org/TR/2009/WD-sparql11-query-20091022

Harth, A., Hose, K., & Schenkel, R. (2014). *Linked data management*. CRC Press/Taylor & Francis. doi:10.1201/b16859

Hartig, O. (2013). An overview on execution strategies for linked data queries. *Datenbank-Spektrum*, *13*(2), 89–99. doi:10.100713222-013-0122-1

Hayes, P., & McBride, B. (2004). RDF Semantics. *W3C Recommendation*. Retrieved from http://www.w3.org/TR/2004/REC-rdf-mt-20040210/

He, Y. Q., Xiang, Z. S., Zheng, J., Lin, Y., Overton, J. A., & Ong, E. (2018). The eXtensible ontology development (XOD) principles and tool implementation to support ontology interoperability. *Journal of Biomedical Semantics*, *9*(1), 3. doi:10.118613326-017-0169-2 PMID:29329592

Hoffart, J., Suchanek, F. M., Berberich, K., & Weikum, G. (2013). YAGO2: A spatially and temporally enhanced knowledge base from Wikipedia. *Artificial Intelligence*, *194*, 28–61. doi:10.1016/j.artint.2012.06.001

Jiang, Y. C., Li, P., & Aftab, A. (2016). A framework for semantic similarity estimation in formal concept analysis. *Journal of South China Normal University*, *48*(3), 44–52.

Jiang, Y. C., Zhang, X. P., Tang, Y., & Nie, R. H. (2015). Feature-based approaches to semantic similarity assessment of concepts using Wikipedia. *Information Processing & Management*, *51*(3), 215–234. doi:10.1016/j.ipm.2015.01.001

Kejriwal, M., & Miranker, D. P. (2015). An unsupervised instance matcher for schema-free RDF data. *Journal of Web Semantics*, *35*, 102–123. doi:10.1016/j.websem.2015.07.002

Klyne, G., & Carroll, J. J. (2014). Resource Description Framework (RDF): Concepts and abstract syntax. *W3C Recommendation*. Retrieved from https://www.w3.org/TR/2014/REC-rdf11-concepts-20140225/

Kureychik, V., & Semenova, A. (2017). Combined Method for Integration of Heterogeneous Ontology Models for Big Data Processing and Analysis. In *Proceedings of the 15th International Conference on Service Oriented Computing, ICSOC 2017* (pp. 302-311), Springer Publishers. 10.1007/978-3-319-57261-1_30

Kusiak, A. (2017). Smart manufacturing must embrace big data. *Nature*, *544*(7648), 23–25. doi:10.1038/544023a PMID:28383012

Lehmann, J., Isele, R., Jakob, M., Jentzsch, A., Kontokostas, D., Mendes, P. N., ... Bizer, C. (2015). DBpedia-A large-scale, multilingual knowledge base extracted from Wikipedia. *Semantic Web*, *6*(2), 167–195.

Li, P., Jiang, Y. C., & Wang, J. (2016). Modular ontology reuse based on conservative extension theory. *Journal of Software*, *27*(11), 2777–2795.

Li, P., Jiang, Y. C., Wang, J., & Yin, Z. L. (2017). Semantic Extension of Query for the Linked Data. *International Journal on Semantic Web and Information Systems*, *13*(4), 109–133. doi:10.4018/IJSWIS.2017100106

Li, P., Shi, Y. X., & Jiang, Y. C. (2010). Tourism domain ontology construction based on ε-connections. *Computer Engineering*, *36*(22), 274–276.

Li, P., Xiao, B., Akram, A., Jiang, Y. C., & Zhang, Z. F. (2018). SESLDS: An Extension Scheme for Linked Data Sources Based on Semantically Enhanced Annotation and Reasoning. *International Journal of Intelligent Systems*, *33*(2), 233–258. doi:10.1002/int.21926

Li, P., Xiao, B., Ma, W. J., Jiang, Y. C., & Zhang, Z. F. (2017). A graph-based semantic relatedness assessment method combining wikipedia features. *Engineering Applications of Artificial Intelligence*, *65*, 268–281. doi:10.1016/j.engappai.2017.07.027

Lo Bue, A., & Machi, A. (2015). Open data integration using SPARQL and SPIN: A case study for the tourism domain. In M. Gavanelli, E. Lamma, & F. Riguzzi (Eds.), *Advances In Artificial Intelligence* (Vol. 9336, pp. 316–326). Berlin: Springer-Verlag Berlin. doi:10.1007/978-3-319-24309-2_24

Mahdisoltani, F., Biega, J., & Suchanek, F. (2014). Yago3: A knowledge base from multilingual Wikipedias. In *Proceedings of the 7th Biennial Conference on Innovative Data Systems Research, CIDR 2015*. Asilomar, CA.

Manning, C. D., Raghavan, P. Sch., & Tze, H. (2008). *Introduction to Information Retrieval*. Cambridge University Press. doi:10.1017/CBO9780511809071

Matinfar, F., Nematbakhsh, M. A., & Lausen, G. (2014). Discovery of RDFs. *International Journal of Pattern Recognition and Artificial Intelligence*, *28*(2), 17. doi:10.1142/S0218001414500037

McGuinness, D. L., & Harmelen, F. (2004). OWL Web ontology language: overview. *W3C Recommendation*. Retrieved from http://www.w3.org/TR/2004/REC-owl- features-20040210/

Miranker, D. P., Depena, R. K., Jung, H., Sequeda, J. F., & Reyna, C. (2012). Diamond: A SPARQL query engine, for linked data based on the Rete match. In *Proceedings of the Workshop on Artificial Intelligence meets the Web of Data (AImWD) at ECAI*. IOS Press Amsterdam.

Nebot, V., & Berlanga, R. (2016). Statistically-driven generation of multidimensional analytical schemas from linked data. *Knowledge-Based Systems*, *110*, 15–29. doi:10.1016/j.knosys.2016.07.010

Nguyen, K., & Ichise, R. (2017). Automatic schema-independent linked data instance matching system. *International Journal on Semantic Web and Information Systems*, *13*(1), 82–103. doi:10.4018/IJSWIS.2017010106

Oren, E., Delbru, R., Catasta, M., Cyganiak, R., Stenzhorn, H., & Tummarello, G. (2008). Sindice.com: A document-oriented lookup index for open linked data. *International Journal of Metadata, Semantics and Ontologies*, *3*(1), 37–52. doi:10.1504/IJMSO.2008.021204

Ponzetto, S. P., & Strube, M. (2011). Taxonomy induction based on a collaboratively built knowledge repository. *Artificial Intelligence*, *175*(9), 1737–1756. doi:10.1016/j.artint.2011.01.003

Rahoman, M. M., & Ichise, R. (2018). A proposal of a temporal semantics aware linked data information retrieval framework. *Journal of Intelligent Information Systems*, *50*(3), 573–595. doi:10.100710844-017-0483-2

Sande, M. V., Verborgh, R., Dimou, A., Colpaert, P., Mannens, E., & Walle, R. V. D. (2016). Hypermedia-based discovery for source selection using low-cost linked data interfaces. *International Journal on Semantic Web and Information Systems, 12*(3), 79–110. doi:10.4018/IJSWIS.2016070103

Santipantakis, G., Kotis, K., & Vouros, G. A. (2017). OBDAIR: Ontology-Based Distributed framework for Accessing, Integrating and Reasoning with data in disparate data sources. *Expert Systems with Applications, 90*, 464–483. doi:10.1016/j.eswa.2017.08.031

Shi, Y. X., Li, P., Xiao, B., Wei, T. T., & Jiang, Y. C. (2010). Semantic query expansion method for tourism domain. *Computer Engineering, 36*(18), 43–45.

Suchanek, F. M., Kasneci, G., & Weikum, G. (2008). YAGO: A Large Ontology from Wikipedia and WordNet. *Journal of Web Semantics, 6*(3), 203–217. doi:10.1016/j.websem.2008.06.001

Taelman, R. (2016). Continuously self-updating query results over dynamic heterogeneous linked data. In H. Sack, E. Blomqvist, M. Daquin, C. Ghidini, S. P. Ponzetto, & C. Lange (Eds.), *Semantic Web: Latest Advances And New Domains* (Vol. 9678, pp. 863–872). Cham: Springer Int Publishing Ag. doi:10.1007/978-3-319-34129-3_55

Tran, P. N., & Nguyen, D. T. (2015). Mapping expansion of natural language entities to DBpedia's components for querying linked data. In *Proceedings of the International Conference on Ubiquitous Information Management and Communication* (pp. 1-5). ACM. 10.1145/2701126.2701212

Tran, T., Herzig, D. M., & Ladwig, G. (2011). SemSearchPro-Using semantics throughout the search process. *Journal of Web Semantics, 9*(4), 349–364. doi:10.1016/j.websem.2011.08.004

Umbrich, J., Hose, K., Karnstedt, M., Harth, A., & Polleres, A. (2011). Comparing data summaries for processing live queries over linked data. *World Wide Web, 14*(5-6), 495–544. doi:10.100711280-010-0107-z

Wagner, A., Duc, T. T., Ladwig, G., Harth, A., & Studer, R. (2012). Top-k linked data query processing. In *Proceedings of the 9th Extended Semantic Web Conference, ESWC 2012* (pp. 56-712). Springer.

Wiemann, S., & Bernard, L. (2016). Spatial data fusion in spatial data infrastructures using linked data. *International Journal of Geographical Information Science, 30*(4), 613–636. doi:10.1080/13658816.2015.1084420

Yang, F., Wu, D. Z., Lin, L. M., Yang, J., Yang, T. H., & Zhao, J. (2017). The integration of weighted gene association networks based on information entropy. *PLoS One, 12*(12), 19. doi:10.1371/journal.pone.0190029 PMID:29272314

Zhang, L. Y., Ren, J. D., & Li, X. W. (2017). OIM-SM: A method for ontology integration based on semantic mapping. *Journal of Intelligent & Fuzzy Systems, 32*(3), 1983–1995. doi:10.3233/JIFS-161553

Zhang, W. E., Sheng, Q. Z., Qin, Y. R., Taylor, K., & Yao, L. N. (2018). Learning-based SPARQL query performance modeling and prediction. *World Wide Web-Internet and Web Information Systems, 21*(4), 1015–1035.

ENDNOTES

[1]   http://lod-cloud.net/

[2]   http://www.wikipedia.org/

[3]   https://gate.d5.mpi-inf.mpg.de/webyagospotlx/WebInterface

[4]   http://www.mpi-inf.mpg.de/departments/databases-and-information-systems/research/yago-naga/yago/

[5]   http://www.geonames.org/

Chapter 6
Data Replication Impact on DDBS System Performance

Ali A. Amer
Taiz University, Yemen

ABSTRACT

In distributed database systems (DDBS), the utmost purpose of data distribution and replication aims at shrinking transmission costs (TC), including communication costs, and response time. In this chapter, therefore, an enhanced heuristic clustering-based technique for data fragmentation and replicated based allocation is efficaciously presented. This work is mainly sought to further enhance an existing technique so TC is to be significantly minimized. In fact, the approached enhancement is applied by suggesting different replication scenarios. Off these scenarios, one scenario is to be selected based on competitive performance evaluation process. DDBS performance is measured via its being exposed on objective function (TC). Despite the fact that this work is mildly improved, yet evaluation results show that it has been promising, particularly as TC being the foremost design objective of DDBS System. Experimental results have been analyzed under all presented scenarios as an internal evaluation and are vividly provided to demonstrate the undeniable impact of data replication on DDBS performance.

INTRODUCTION

In most DDBS and cloud-based DDBS applications and services, the storing and retrieving of data are integral essential activities of nature of application at hand. As a matter of fact, with continuous access and retrieval for data, the design of DDBS (that some application uses) can have a great impact (positively/negatively) on DDBS metrics including performance, throughput, and even scalability and availability of DDBS system as a whole. Therefore, the necessity for an effective partitioning technique that is able to find balance between DDBS metrics while applied efficiently in large-scale DDBS is still the hot spot in DDBS research community.

In fact, partitioning data into separate partitions is set to make data more easily to be managed for access and retrieval at the same time. However, the partitioning technique has to be designed critically to maximize the utilities of data being partitioned while minimizing adverse effects that occasionally comes along data partitioning. On the other hand, it is widely known, in literature that data partitioning along with data replication are bound to help enhance DDBS scalability, reduce Transmission Costs (TC),

DOI: 10.4018/978-1-5225-7186-5.ch006

Copyright © 2019, IGI Global. Copying or distributing in print or electronic forms without written permission of IGI Global is prohibited.

and promoting performance of system in total (Adel et al., 2017). Nevertheless, it is worth indicating that combining a careful data partitioning and intelligently-designed data replication in one single work can bring several other advantages as follows:

- **To Enhance DDBS Scalability:** As database system is being scaled up, it is set to finally reach a physical hardware limit in terms of capacity, as instance. However, when data is being scattered and replicated across multiple partitions, and each partition allocated to a single site, hardware limititations can be wisely exploited to great extent.
- **To Enhance Performance:** When data access is being frequently accessed as a whole for little information needed, it can be hold a significant bearing on DDBS performance. However, when data is partitioned and properly replicated over network sites, DDBS system is meant to be highly effective. Moreover, parallel access can be leveraged chiefly for activities that reach more than one partition. To minimize latency and TC while maximize response time, each partition must be allocated near the application (or in the site) that uses it greatly frequently.
- **To Enhance Availability:** As a matter of fact, dividing data and placing partitions into multiple sites (data replication is adopted) seeks to circumvent a single point of failure that often might be happening. In the sense that If one site fails, or site is under maintenance, other site(s) is set to have other copy of the same required data (unlike the scenario of non-replication as in this case the data in that partition would surely be unavailable for users' operations/activities). So, to reduce the possibility of site(s) being unable to provide data (getting into deadlock), the number of partitions have to be cautiously increased (replicated) as needed.

Another benefit can be observed in terms of: enhancing security specifically for data classified as sensitive; maximizing administrative efficiency in terms of data management and monitoring. Finally, data partitioning and replication helps distribute the load over many sites (instead of single one site), which consequently reduces TC and improves performance at the same time. Giving reader(s) a flavour of how all these factors (chiefly data replication) could affect DDBS performance would be highly appreciated, though.

In this chapter, thus, we are trying to expose reader(s) on DDBS design in terms of vertical partitioning of data and replication-based data allocation as well, while listing the come-along benefits which is already drawn above. In section (2), the state of art is being briefly yet usefully discussed. The enhanced work's methodology for (Adel et al. 2017), with the major aim of significantly reducing TC to most great extent, including heuristics and fragmentation and allocation costs models, is introduced in sections (3, 4, and 6))). In section (7), experimental results have been presented in detail. Brief yet clearly-drawn discussion for results is given in section (8) showing the highly positive impact of data replication, in terms of TC minimization as all data allocation scenarios considered. Finally, conclusions of this chapter are provided in section (9).

Related Work

It is a rule of thumb in DDBS that the better the DDBS design is, the higher DDBS performance is to be guaranteed. However, for DDBS design issue the most effective strategies recorded in literature were the data partitioning (Vertical, Horizontal or Mixed) and data allocation, chiefly if replication is adopted intelligently, as discussed in Nashat and Amer, 2018. In our work of (Nashat and Amer, 2018), a comprehensive taxonomy has been given. More than one hundred references (Chapters, Papers, Reports, Books, etc.) in DDBS design were thoroughly investigated in both static and dynamic environments. The issues of data fragmentation, data allocation and data replication were the key pillars using which references investigated. The core purpose of this survey was concentrating on finding the gabs and faults from which most of works in literature recorded to be suffering from. Then, by observing these faults and disadvantage, more effective methods might be produced for improving the performance of DDBS on the light of available taxonomy. TC minimization (including communication costs) was the key objective to which much of work sought to meet, chiefly by maximizing data locality. However, much of these works never provided a clear definition for TC which is a huge drawback.

Based on this taxonomy, our efforts in this work has been directed toward enhancing (Adel et al. 2017) so DDBS performance is to be sustainably kept high. Moreover, comprehensive optimization is also expected to be released within the same efforts in purpose of finding the best fitting technique for DDBS design. The intended technique is meant to help minimizing TC while giving an obvious definition for TC. It is worth indicating that those criteria involved in this taxonomy are also considered in this work (of this chapter), and tackled properly. TC is being minimized by increasing data locality while communication overhead is somehow lessened by adopting partial replication scenario.

On the other hand, while (Raouf et al., 2017) presented an enhanced system to perform initial-stage fragmentation and data allocation along with replication at run time over cloud environment. Site clustering was addressed as well to promote DDBS throughputs by increasing data locality. (Adel et al., 2017) sought to effectively help solving DDBS design at initial stage, a three-fold vertical fragmentation and allocation technique was developed. In fragmentation phase, query-based clustering algorithm is created with the aim of producing disjoint fragments. Fragments, in its turn, were then padded into solution space. As overlapping schemes, fragments needed to be passed into refinement process to generate non-overlapping schemes, which examined by proposed fragmentation evaluator (Chakravarthy et al., 1994). In second phase, data allocation algorithm was evolved to assign data into their appropriate sites. Several different techniques had been compiled into this work in the sake of promoting DDBS Design. Among these techniques: a hierarchical clustering method to cluster queries under consideration, refinement process, fragmentation evaluator, network sites clustering, and data fragments allocation along with considering data replication (Wiese, 2017) on two scenarios.

Meanwhile, in (Amer and Sewisy, 2017), an extension version for (Abdalla, 2014) was drawn. The extended version suggested incorporating site clustering algorithm, for network sites, and mathematically-based cost-effective data allocation and replication model into (Abdalla, 2014). Moreover, different data allocation scenarios were considered that data replication is conducted using proposed replication model (Wiese, 2016). A significant enhancement has been observed in terms of overall DDBSs performance through decreasing transmission costs among network sites. Constraints of clusters and sites are also considered to stimulate the real-world DDBS as well as strengthen the proposed work efficiency. However, no experiments had been done to prove that claim with exception of one single exclusively-done experiment. This experiment was basically to illustratively demonstrate work's mechanism. By the same token, as follow-up optimization for Amer and Sewisy, 2017, Amer et al., 2018 comes as perfect extension while proving the effectiveness of this technique with respect of minimizing TC and promoting DDBS performance.

This extended work is evaluated internally and externally against (Abdalla, 2014) on the basis of drawn objective function of (Amer et al., 2018) which is originally taken from (Abdalla, 2014) and significantly amended to reflect actual reality of transmission costs (Sewisy et al., 2017). Results, on the other hand, were confidently proven that (Amer et al., 2018) had outperformed (Abdalla, 2014) in terms of hugely mitigating transmission costs and massively promoting overall DDBS throughputs.

In (Raouf et al., 2018), CB-DDBS architecture over a cloud environment has been developed. This architecture is claimed that its design allows clients to access DDBS from anywhere. Moreover, through replication scenario, DDBSMs is allowed to work in parallel to process the client's queries. Site clustering was also integrated into this work. However, it appears that the proposed OFRAR Algorithm was hugely driven by POEA algorithm, (Abdalla et al., 2014). Authors of this work never indicated this inspiration, though. For data migration, each cluster leader was given the control to migrate and/or replicate independently of other cluster leaders. However, selecting leader of each cluster was not practical enough to be adopted in an efficient environment as almost of DDBSs over globe have the same specification for all of its members (nodes), specifically in P2P network. The performance of CB-DDBS architecture and the proposed OFRAR Algorithm were examined in two environments (simulated environment and "proposed" Amazon cloud environment). Experimental results show that CB-DDBS architecture was able to reduce execution time needed for the transactions to reach relative data in sites. The total execution time to execute all queries required by all sites was claimed to be more optimal compared with previous algorithms without giving a clear definition for either execution time measure or communication costs equations.

(Luong et al., 2018) proposed vertical fragmentation technique based on k-Means rough clustering technique. Distance and similarity were merged with upper and lower approximations to enhance algorithm. For each object, algorithm was able to calculate focuses of object to determine its cluster based on lower approximation or upper approximation of each cluster. Several experiments carried out and results using KR rough clustering technique showed that: (1) With a small number of clusters k (say, k = 6 as given in this work), k-Means algorithm has large total time, satisfactory error average cost and memory cost. Meanwhile, KR rough clustering algorithm optimizes all three criteria. (2) As number of clusters k, gets increased (k = 13, or, k = 15), KR algorithm clearly observed to optimize all three criteria in comparison with normal k-Means algorithm. Error average cost of KR, on the other hand, was recorded to be high as both upper and lower approximations are to be considered during the process of updating the new focus. This work claimed that complexity of KR is usually given as O (n) which is more optimal than k-Means clustering algorithm. In k-means clustering algorithm (Jun & Kobayashi, 2010), complexity is O (t*n*k), in which t is number of iterations, k is number of clusters, and n is number of objects on the set D to be clustered. However, from researcher points of view, such claim needs to be further verified.

In (Abdalla et al., 2014), communication costs and response time were the key factor by which it originally existed. Vertical fragmentation and two-phase allocation model was presented and mathematically proved to be an effective. However, Abdalla et al. 2014 did not support a clear definition for response time. The replication problem was cautiously addressed so that update costs got into consideration. The replication of data was based on the rule of thumb in DDBS that says: if fragment/attribute is queried more frequently than it is modified, then replication is advisable. Moreover, partial data duplication is made as more than one cluster have the same update cost value for the updated attribute that one of the copies still being accessed even if other copies have failed. Finally, in (Mostafa Mahi et al. 2018), a Particle Swarm Optimization based method is proposed with the aim of minimizing Transmission Cost (TC) for each site, fragment dependency and the each inter – fragment dependency. The main purpose was to solve Data Allocation Problem by utilizing and adaptation (PSO) algorithm. Fragments were allocated to sites using PSO algorithm and its performance had been evaluated on several test problems and compared with others work in literature with superiority recorded for Mostafa Mahi et al. 2018.

VERTICAL FRAGMENTATION HEURISTIC

In this chapter, the vertical fragmentation (VF) is set to be generated in the same way used in (Adel et al., 2017). A set of query clusters are produced by which disjointed data fragments are to be created. Like (Adel et al., 2017), the information given below is the only information needed to perform VF at initial stage of DDBS design.

- Db $(R_1, R_2, ..., R_n)$: set of considered relations of Database.
- $R_i (A_1, A_2, ..., A_n)$: is the data schema which is composed of *n* attributes.
- Q $(Q_1, Q_2, ..., Qs)$: a set of data queries that supposedly run against R_i.
- F $(F_1, F_2, ..., F_t)$: F_i is the frequency of each query Q_i over sites, to be given by DBA.

VF Heuristics

As drawn in (Adel et al., 2017), the proposed work is a three-fold technique. In the first phase, the set of most-frequently-used queries (Q) are sorted in sequential order of their attributes (A). Such sort would help satisfy an accurate clustering process by mathematically expressing them in numerical patterns using List of Attribute Significance values (ASL), and Query Attribute Coded Matrices (QACM). Moreover, such ordering is indispensable because hamming distance profoundly requires it to precisely distinguish the difference values between numerical patterns of queries.

Each ASL value accumulates access cost for each attribute over its owner queries. Therefore, each attribute is to be replaced by its corresponding ASL value in a step to build QACM. In QACM, the original queries would be expressed numerically (numerical patterns) rather than alphabetically, Table 8. Consequently, the differences values among patterns are to be unmistakably computed by applying hamming distance metric (Norouzi et al., 2013) on QACM.

Finally, Query Difference Matrix (QDM), is the sole parameter needed to activate hierarchical clustering process. The clustering process is set to be iteratively applied until no pattern excluded from being centroid. The least difference value is used as metric to blend similar patterns together in each loop, equations (6 and 7). This process is bound to keep comparing each pair of patterns in bottom-up approach till all pattern "query" clusters formed in space called solution space. Solution space, on its turn, would contain all combinations of partitioning schemes resulted from clustering process.

On the other hand, solution space is the virtual container for all results of all loops of hierarchical clustering. However, in order for all query clusters "solutions" of clustering process to be contained in solution space, clustering process needs |Q/QN| loop. Where QN is the number of considered queries in each cluster, and CN is the number of query clusters initiated at the first loop. As a matter of fact, the idea of creating solution space is proposed in order for not to exclude any partition schema since each schema might be an optimal solution, as it is demonstrated on performance evaluation of this work.

In the second phase, refinement process seeks to produce non-overlapping schemes from those over-lapping contained in solution space. For each schema, each shared attribute (A_i) is examined among all partitions of the same query cluster. Normally, attribute will be assigned to the partition of the highest access to it. However, if A_i equally required by more than one partition, it shall be assigned interchange-ably to all partitions in the same Partitioning Schemes (PS). Doing such placement iteratively, all schemes combinations are set to be generated, Table 16. It is worth mentioning that during refinement process if it happens to have schema duplication, only one copy is set to be kept.

The third phase is the filtering process which comes with complex computation as per the evaluative function of non-overlapping schemes (Fragments, N). The process of evaluation is accomplished using Fragmentation Evaluator, FE (Chakravarthy et al., 1994). Usually, the partition comes with the lowest FE value, it is the successful partitioning schema which would be considered for allocation process.

PROPOSED FRAGMENTATION MODEL

Fragmentation Cost Model

Fragmentation Cost Functions

As drawn in (Adel et al., 2017), based on queries under consideration, the Attribute Access Matrix (AAM) is concluded. Each AAM_{ij} indicates whether attribute A_i is approached by query Q_k. Moreover, suppose that Query Frequency Matrix (QFM) is given by Database Administrator DBA. Each QFM_{ij} refers to the number of times each query released from its relevant site S_j. Therefore, based on these requirements, vertical fragmentation technique would be processed as per the following cost functions:

$$TFQ_{kx} = \sum_{k=1}^{q}\sum_{j=1}^{m}QFM_{kj}, x = 1 \tag{2}$$

$$AUM_{ki} = \sum_{j=1}^{m}\sum_{k=1}^{q}TFQ_{kx} * AAM_{kj}, x = 1 \tag{3}$$

$$ASL_{k} = \sum_{i=1}^{n}\sum_{k=1}^{q}AUM_{ki} \tag{4}$$

$$QACM_{ik} = \sum_{i=1}^{n}\sum_{k=1}^{q}ASL_{k} \tag{5}$$

$$Similarity(Q_{k1}, Q_{k2}) = \sum_{k1=1}^{q}\sum_{k2=1}^{q}\left(1 - dif\left(P\left((Q_{k1}), P(Q_{k2})\right)\right)\right) \tag{6}$$

$$where\, P(Q)\, means\, the\, numerical\, pattern(Q)$$

$$QDM_{k1k2} = \sum_{k1=1}^{q}\sum_{k2=1}^{q}Similarity\left(Q_{k1}, Q_{k2}\right) \tag{7}$$

Fragmentation Evaluator (FE)

In this chapter, FE proposed in (Chakravarthy et al., 1994) including its both measures is adopted to evaluate generated clusters (Schemes). The measures used to evaluate schemes are: irrelevant local access and relevant remote access. While the irrelevant local access for attributes produced by local processing, the access cost of the relevant remote attributes gives the net access costs of remote attributes stored at else site other than the original site of query under consideration. For the first component, "square-error" criterion is calculated as presented in (Jain and Dubes, 1998). The general purpose is to obtain that schema, for a fixed number of clusters, of minimal square-error. Therefore, as per most of algorithms used for vertical fragmentation, in particular that of (Navathe and Ra, 1989), the optimal fragmentation schema determined by its square error. For the first term of FE, the square-error of the entire partition scheme containing a certain number of "*nf*" fragments are given by:

$$E_{nf}^2 = \sum_{i=1}^{nf} \sum_{q=1}^{Q} \left[TFQ * |Al_{ik}| \left(1 - \frac{|Al_{ik}|}{NA_i} \right) \right] \tag{8}$$

where $|Al_{ij}|$ is Number of attributes in F_i locally accessed by Q_k, and NA_{ikj} is The entire number of attributes in fragment F_i distantly accessed, in regard to F_j, by Q_k.

For the second term of FE, given set of partitions, for each application running on partition compute the ratio of the number of remote attributes to be accessed is the total number of attributes in each remote partitions, as follows:

$|Ad_{ikj}|$ is Number of attributes in F_i distantly accessed, in regard to fragment F_j, by query Q_k

$$E_{ad}^2 = \sum_{i=1}^{nf} \sum_{q=1}^{Q} \left[\sum_{j=1}^{m} TFQ_{qi}^i * |Ad_{ik}| * \left(\frac{|Ad_{ik}|}{NA_{iqk}} \right) \right] \tag{9}$$

where NA is the whole number of attributes of relation under consideration. Finally, the final form of FE is given by,

$$FE = E_{nf}^2 + E_{Ad}^2 \tag{10}$$

It is worth remembering that, the higher PE value is, the worse DDBS performance is and vice versa.

CLUSTERING METHODOLOGY

Query Clustering Technique

In this chapter, as (Adel et al., 2017), the process of query clustering basically counts on the average distances between their corresponding numerical patterns. The similarity function is inspired by the similarity between objects which is computed using the Euclidian and Manhattan metric. The hamming distance metric (Norouzi et al., 2013), is used to calculate the differences between patterns of queries. Then, those patterns are being clustered using the idea of least difference value, as shown in equations (6 and 7). It is worth referring that the function of $\left(Difference\left(P(Q_{k1}), P\left(Q_{k2}\right)\right)\right)$, seeks to find the dissimilarity value using hamming distance metric. The distance functions and the similarity measure, on the other hand, are "inversely proportional" in [0, 1]. In the sense that the bigger distance between each pair of patterns of queries is, the smaller similarity is, and vice versa.

Query Description

Each query represents the foundation stone using which the overall partitioning process would be completely accomplished. It contains the attributes used as initial requirements for query clustering and consequently for data fragmentation. Additionally, it could be fallen in four types of applications: read, create, update and delete.

Cluster Projection Statement

Let Cq be the targeted cluster of queries so that $Cq = \{Q_1 = \pi_{A_1\sigma_c(R)}, Q_2 = \pi_{A_2\sigma_c(R)}, ..., Q_n = \pi_{A_n\sigma_c(R)}\}$, where R is the intended relation to be partitioned. Therefore, each query Q_i represented as $Q_i = \pi_{A_i\sigma_c(R)}$. Thus, each query cluster needs to be projected to give the intended fragment so that all attributes (A_i) that appear in all queries Q_j of Cq shall be contained in Cq. Therefore, query cluster could be expressed as $Cq = \left\{A_1 \cup A_2 \cup ... A_n\right\}$. Needless to say, that each A_i belongs to Q_j and attribute duplication is removed.

Sites Clustering Technique

Site clustering has been made using the threshold-based algorithm (Abdalla et al. 2014). This method is entirely based on the least average communication cost between sites to decide site's belonging if it has the same distance with many clusters. Needless to say, that as network sites clustered, the communication costs within and between clusters are of key importance for the fragment allocation phase chiefly in the non-replication scenario.

As a rule of thumb, the optimal way to get this cost is to have the cheapest path between the clusters. However, this method is an NP-complete problem (Huang and Chen, 2001). So, the symmetry average communication cost would be used as it has been proved to be rapid, reliable and an efficient. In the sense that the cost matrix is assumed to be a symmetric between sites and cost between the same sites is considered to be a zero or, in other words, it is neglected, Table 1. The same presumption goes to cluster matrix, Table 2.

Table 3, on the other hand, is formed based on having pre-determined threshold value (thv = 6) with the help of communication cost matrix (CMS) presented in Table 1. The network sites would be grouped (according to the clustering algorithm) as displayed in Table 3.

Where CCM_{ij} is the communication cost unit between cluster C_i and cluster C_j, CMS_{ij} is the communication cost unit between site S_i and site S_j, measured in "ms/byte" units, and bandwidths fall in; 64 kbps, 128 kbps and 512 kbps, and COM_{ij} is CMS_{ij} if S_i and S_j at the same cluster; otherwise, it is CCM_{ij}.

PROPOSED ALLOCATION AND REPLICATION MODEL

The fundamental aim of allocation model is to mainly shrink communication costs, equation (1), by placing the data fragment in the site, or near the site, in which they are most frequently accessed (Adel et al. 2017).

Table 1. Communication Costs between clusters (CMS)

Site#	Site 1	Site 2	Site 3	Site 4	Site 5	Site 6
Site 1	0	10	8	2	4	6
Site 2		0	7	3	5	4
Site 3			0	3	2	5
Site 4				0	11	5
Site 5					0	5
Site 6						0

Table 2. Communication Costs between clusters (CCM)

Cluster/Cluster	C_1	C_2	C_3
C_1	0	3.5	5
C_2	3.5	0	5
C_3	5	5	0

Table 3. Site Grouping (Clusters)

Site#	Site 1	Site 2	Site 3	Site 4	Site 5	Site 6
C 1	1	1	1	0	0	0
C 2	0	0	0	1	1	0
C 3	0	0	0	0	0	1

Allocation Requirements

Given that there is set of N attributes $A = \{A_1, A_2, ..., A_n\}$ required by set of K queries $Q = \{Q_1, Q_2, ..., Q_k\}$, these queries would be clustered into Q query clusters $Cq_1, Cq_2, ..., CQ_{cn}$, to be assigned to a set of M network sites $S=\{S_1, S_2, ..., S_m\}$ which are grouped into cm clusters $Cs = \{Cs_1, Cs_2, ..., CS_{cn}\}$ in a fully connected network. Let $F = \{F_1, F_2, ..., F_m\}$ be the set of disjoint fragments obtained from clustering process. Allocation model mainly seeks to find the optimal distribution of each query cluster (F) over clusters Cs, and consequently on cluster's own sites individually. Hence, the allocation problem may be expressed mathematically by a function from the set of fragments to the set of clusters of sites, equation 11.

Allocation Scenarios and Phases

The allocation process is done in two phases in such a way that the allocation is performed as fragment by fragment instead of attribute by attribute. The advantage of this scenario is that it will guarantee optimal placement for each fragment as well as reducing allocation time.

Scenario 1: Phase 1

In the first phase, each fragment would be allocated to all clusters of sites as fragment replication adopted. The rationale behind this replication is to decrease response time and minimize transmission costs. In other words, this step comes in favour of increasing data locality and availability.

Scenario 2: Phase 1

This scenario has been performed based on the proved-to-be-effective theory of (Abdalla, 2014) so that each fragment shall be allocated to the cluster of maximum access cost. The Total Access Cost of each sites' Cluster (TACC) would be used as measure of fragments assignment over clusters. TACC, however, is the maximum cost needed to reach fragments' attributes individually. Such allocation is bound to lessen communication cost.

Phase 2 for Both Scenarios 1 and 2

The net cost for each site S_j, to access all attributes of F_i would be the criterion of allocation. In the sense that the Total Access Cost for each Site ($TACS_{ij}$), to access these attributes together, needs to be properly calculated. TACS matrix is formed using SAAM and CMS matrices, equation (13). Among all members of TACS matrix, site of the largest access value for specific fragment is the primary candidate storage site for this relevant fragment, as shown in Decision Allocation Matrix.

Scenario 3 (Mixed Replication, Full and Partial)

In the first phase, each fragment would be allocated to all clusters of sites as fragment replicated using full replication scenario, fragments are given for more than one single site in each cluster as per certain calculated threshold. This threshold, however, could be simply calculated by taking average of maximum transmission costs and minimum transmission costs in each cluster. Then, each site succeeds to surpass threshold, is to be candidate for holding copy of fragment at question. This scenario proves to be highly effective chiefly as update queries grows slowly and slightly reflecting the real world DDBS behavior. However, it proves to behave worse as update queries grows quickly and significantly (which is unreal case in real world DDBS)

Allocation Cost Functions

$$SAAM = \sum_{k=1}^{q}\sum_{j=1}^{m}\sum_{i=1}^{n} AAM_{ik} * QFM_{ji} \tag{12}$$

$$TACS = \sum_{j1=1}^{m}\sum_{i=1}^{n}\sum_{j=1}^{m} SAAM_{ij1} * CMS_{ji} \tag{13}$$

$$TACC = \sum_{j1=1}^{m}\sum_{i=1}^{n}\sum_{j=1}^{m} SAAM_{ij1} * CCM_{ji} \tag{14}$$

Equation (12), seeks to build the Site Attribute Access Matrix (SAAM), using which the total access cost matrix for all sites (TACS) is precisely computed with the help of equation (12). Lastly, equations (13) and (14) paves the way to draw the final allocation of fragments over cluster of sites as second scenario of allocation being under consideration.

Data Replication Model

This model simply adopts and slightly modifies the data replication problem "DRP" presented in (Wiese, 2017) as follows: There are M clusters/sites and each cluster/site have a maximum capacity C. Meanwhile, there are N fragments and each fragment has size *Fsize*. These fragments shall be assigned to the minimum number of clusters/sites without exceeding the maximum capacity. It worth noting that X_{ik} points to fragment F_I located in cluster C_k or (site S_k), and Y_k indicate to that cluster/site m already in use. Thus, an integer linear program (ILP) to represent this problem presented as follows;

$$Minimize \sum_{k=1}^{m} y_k \tag{15}$$

$$\sum_{i=1}^{N} X_{ik} = 1, k = 1,...,m \tag{16}$$

$$\sum_{k=1}^{m} C_i X_{ik} \leq C_{yk}, i = 1,...,m \tag{17}$$

$$X_{ik} \in \{0,1\}, k = 1,\ldots,m; i = 1,\ldots,n \tag{18}$$

$$Y_{ik} \in \{0,1\}, k = 1,\ldots,m; i = 1,\ldots,n \tag{19}$$

Equation (15) is to minimize the number of clusters/sites used as places of allocation; while equation (16) means that each fragment has to be assigned to exactly one cluster (in case that non-replicated scenario adopted). Equation (17) means that the capacity of each cluster/site shall not be violated; and the last two equations denote that the variables are binary (0, 1) linear program. Like (Adel et al., 2017), Table 4 describes three constraints of sites, represented in virtual capacity (in Megabyte), lower limit and upper limit of attribute allowed to each site.

EXPERIMENTAL RESULTS

This work of this chapter uses the same requirement of (Adel et al., 2017). Moreover, we have performed simulation in the same environment of (Adel et al., 2017). Just queries under consideration and their frequencies over network sites are needed. These frequencies can be explicitly provided by administrator of *DDBSs* or could be generated using a numerical generator. As mentioned earlier, several techniques have been compiled into one single effective tool. The virtual network is assumed to be fully-connected of six sites. It is worth indicating that this single experiment is given in details in (Adel et al., 2017). However, for convenience of readers, we here provide the most important steps used to generate fragments.

In order for the experiments to be conducted, an employee dataset is proposed in accordance to description drawn in Table 5. Dataset consists of six attributes and filled out with 300 records. For

Table 4. Site Constraints

Site	S_1	S_2	S_3	S_4	S_5	S_6
Capacity (MB)	16000	11000	9000	10000	11000	16000
LA	1	1	1	1	1	1
UA	12	14	11	7	10	14

Table 5. Employee database description

Attributes	Symbol	Type	Length (Bytes)
Emp-no	A1	Nominal	4
Emp-name	A2	Categorical	30
Job-id	A3	Categorical	4
Salary	A4	Numerical	3
Loaction	A5	Categorical	5
Dept-id	A6	Nominal	4

computation simplicity and to the limit space of this chapter, the attributes: Emp-no, Emp-name, Job-id, Salary, Location and Dept-id referred to as A_1, A_2, A_5, A_6, A_5, and A_6 respectively.

Assume that there are eight queries under consideration as the most frequently running queries, say 40% to 80% of all database queries, against Employee database.

Q_1: Select A_1, A_2, A_5, A_6 from Employee where A_1 in (1234, 261, 1239) and A_3= "Mang222";

Q_2: Select A_3, A_5 from Employee where A_5 in ('site 1', 'site 3', 'site 6');

Q_3: Select A_2, A_4, A_5 from Employee;

Q_4: Select A_1, A_3, A_6 from Employee where A_6 ='dept2';

Q_5: Select A_1, A_2, A_5 from Employee where A_2 = "Jane" and A_5 in ('site 2','site 5');

Q_6: Select A_3, A_4, A_6 from Employee where A_4 > 4500;

Q_7: Select A_2, A_6 from Employee where A_1>1234;

Q_8: Select A_1, A_3, A_5, A_6 from Employee;

In fact, attribute occurrence is of key concern because the ultimate goal is to tie up all queries of high similarities with each other in each cluster. In other words, the concern is to identify whether attribute appears in query or not. If it appears, it would be treated as required "accessed" attribute by relevant queries. Based on this assumption along with these queries, the query attribute matrix "Attribute Access Matrix" is formed. AAM_{kj}, Table 6, expresses whether query Q_k requires attribute A_j or not.

Additionally, the only information needed is QFM (Table 7), presumably provided by DB administrator. Each value (QFM_{kj}) indicate to the number of times each query Q_k issued from its original site S_j.

Using the same procedure drawn in (Adel et al., 2017) along with drawn-above matrices and fragmentation costs model of this work, Query Difference Matrix (QDM), Table 8, will be produced, equations 6 and 7. Each QDM_{ij} represents the difference value between numerical patterns of Q_i and Q_j. The number of initial cluster is uncontrollable. In the sense that it is undergone to the algorithm mechanism itself in every step of its process cycle.

Table 6. Attribute Access Matrix (AAM)

Query/ Attribute	A_1	A_2	A_3	A_4	A_5	A_6
Q_1	1	1	0	0	1	1
Q_2	0	0	1	0	1	0
Q_3	0	1	0	1	1	0
Q_4	1	0	1	0	0	1
Q_5	1	1	0	0	1	0
Q_6	0	0	1	1	0	1
Q_7	0	1	0	0	0	1
Q_8	1	0	1	0	1	1

Table 7. Query Frequency Matrix (QFM)

Query/Site	S_1	S_2	S_3	S_4	S_5	S_6	TQF
Q_1	2	0	0	0	1	3	6
Q_2	2	2	0	0	3	0	7
Q_3	0	0	3	3	0	0	6
Q_4	0	0	0	1	0	3	4
Q_5	0	2	0	0	0	2	4
Q_6	0	1	1	3	0	0	5
Q_7	2	0	0	1	0	0	3
Q_8	0	1	1	0	2	1	5

Hierarchical Clustering Process

In the very beginning, the first cluster determined for pattern pair of the smallest value of QDM. In this example, there are two pairs of query patterns (Q1 and Q5) and (Q4 and Q8), either one could be used as initial cluster. Supposedly, (Q1 and Q5) is chosen as first cluster with Q1 as centroid. Then, QACM will subsequently be updated as per the newly-formed cluster, Table 9.

Table 8. Query Difference Matrix (QDM)

Query	Q_1	Q_2	Q_3	Q_4	Q_5	Q_6	Q_7	Q_8
Q_1	0	4	3	3	1	5	2	2
Q_2	4	0	3	3	3	3	4	2
Q_3	3	3	0	6	2	4	3	5
Q_4	3	3	6	0	4	2	3	1
Q_5	1	3	2	4	0	6	3	3
Q_6	5	3	4	2	6	0	3	3
Q_7	2	4	3	3	3	3	0	4
Q_8	2	2	5	1	3	3	4	0

Table 9. QDM (first step, Q_{15} formed)

Query	Q_{15}	Q_2	Q_3	Q_4	Q_6	Q_7	Q_8
Q_{15}	0	4	2	3	5	2	2
Q_2	4	0	3	3	3	4	2
Q_3	2	3	0	6	4	3	5
Q_4	3	3	6	0	2	3	1
Q_6	5	3	4	2	0	3	3
Q_7	2	4	3	3	3	0	4
Q_8	2	2	5	1	3	4	0

From Table 11, it is clear that (Q4 and Q8) will still be the best to be chosen as the second cluster. Therefore, two query clusters CQ15 and CQ48 have been formed so that Q1, or Q5, is the centroid of Q15 while Q4, or Q8, is the centroid of Q48. After getting second cluster, the updated matrix would be as shown in Tables 10 and 11.

Then, as hierarchical clustering process goes on, both clusters Q1573 and Q4826 are produced as the final results of the clustering process, table 12 and table 13. These results, for first loop, would be automatically kept in solution space.

As (Adel et al., 2017), in this example, clustering process would need four, |eight/two|, loops to have all solutions added to solution space, Table 14. Each loop has to reach stable state to consider its produced solutions, though.

Table 10. QDM (second step, Q_{48} formed)

Query	Q_{15}	Q_2	Q_3	Q_{48}	Q_6	Q_7
Q_{15}	0	4	2	2	5	2
Q_2	4	0	3	2	3	4
Q_3	2	3	0	5	4	3
Q_{48}	2	2	5	0	2	3
Q_6	5	3	4	2	0	3
Q_7	2	4	3	3	3	0

Table 11. Query Distribution over Clusters

Cluster/Query	Q_1	Q_2	Q_3	Q_4	Q_5	Q_6	Q_7	Q_8
CQ_{15}	1				1			
CQ_{48}				1				1

Table 12. QDM (final results)

Query	Q_{1573}	Q_{4826}
Q_{1573}	0	2
Q_{4826}	2	0

Table 13. Final Distribution of Queries over Clusters

Cluster/Query	Q_1	Q_2	Q_3	Q_4	Q_5	Q_6	Q_7	Q_8
CQ_{1357}	1		1		1		1	
CQ_{2468}		1		1		1		1

Table 14. Solution Space

Solution #	Cluster #	Queries contained
Solution 1	Cq_1	Q_{1573} Q_{2468}
Solution 2	Cq_2	Q_{12357} Q_{468}
Solution 3	Cq_3	Q_{13578} Q_{246}
Solution 4	Cq_4	Q_{13567} Q_{248}

4.2. Refinement Process

The input parameters are all overlapping Partitioning Schemes (PS), contained in solution space that are already produced. Then, for each PS, its attributes have to be examined attribute by attribute to decide to which partition, within PS, it would be allocated, Table 15. The Attribute Allocation Decision (AAD) for attributes over query clusters drawn in equation 21

$$AAD = \begin{cases} Cq_k, & A_i \text{ highly required by } Cq_k \text{ For each } Cq_k, k = 1,...,NC \text{ cluster} \\ Otherwise & A_i \text{ replicated interchangeably over partitions} \end{cases} \quad (21)$$

From Table 15, it is manifestly clear that Cq_2 has been disregarded since its entire schemes is another copy of Cq_1.

Fragmentation Evaluator (FE)

The last stage of fragmentation technique, is FE. All non-overlapping PS gained from refinement process are taken into FE. The importance of the evaluation process is to determine the optimal, successful, PS among all PS under consideration. The results of FE process is drawn in Table 16, and depicted in figure 1.

Table 15. Refinement Process Results

PS Number	Over-lapping PS	Non-overlapping PS
1		(A_1, A_2, A_4, A_5) (A_3, A_6)
2	QC_1 $(A_1, A_2, A_4, A_5, A_6)$ $(A_1, A_3, A_4, A_5, A_6)$	(A_2, A_5) $(A1, A_3, A_4, A_6)$
3		(A_1, A_2, A_5) $(A3, A_4, A_6)$
4		(A_2, A_4, A_5) (A_1, A_3, A_6)
5	QC_3 $(A_1, A_2, A_5, A_6, A_4, A_3)$ $(A_3, A_5, A_1, A_6, A_4)$	$(A_1, A_2, A_4, A_5, A_6)$ (A_3)
6		(A_1, A_2, A_5, A_6) (A_3, A_4)
7	QC_4 $(A_1, A_3, A_5, A_6, A_4, A_2)$ (A_3, A_5, A_6, A_1)	(A_2, A_4, A_5, A_6) (A_1, A_3)

Table 16. Partitioning Schemes

PS Number	PS	E^2_L	E^2_M	PE Value
1	$(A_1, A_2, A_4, A_5)\ (A_3, A_6)$	199	292	491
2	$(A_2, A_5)\ (A_1, A_3, A_4, A_6)$	244	315	559
3	$(A_1, A_2, A_5)\ (A_3, A_4, A_6)$	234	283	517
4	$(A_2, A_4, A_5)\ (A_1, A_3, A_6)$	184	266	450
5	$(A_1, A_2, A_4, A_5, A_6)\ (A3)$	230	158	388
6	$(A_1, A_2, A_5, A_6)\ (A_3, A_4)$	222	237	459
7	$(A_2, A_4, A_5, A_6)\ (A_1, A_3)$	252	307	559

Figure 1. Partitioning Schemes

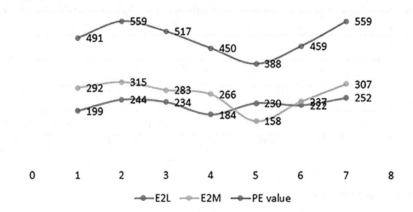

It is very clear that (from Table 16 and Figure 1) the successful schema is the PS_5, since it is of the lowest PE value. This schema is evaluated as per equations (8, 9 and 10), NA means that no access possible to that attribute, as follows:

For Local Access:

Cost of F_1 + cost of F_2 = (29 + 49 + 43 + 19 + 19 + 30 + 11 + 30) + (zero) = 230

For Remote Access:

Cost of F_1 + cost of F_2 = (0+ 10+ 0+ 3+ 0+ 6 + 0 + 8) + (NA+49+NA+32 +NA+50+NA+NA)

= 27 + 131 = 158

So, the total access cost is: 230 + 158 = 388

Allocation Process

Using QFM and AAM along with equation 12, Site Attribute Access Matrix (SAAM) is to be built. Every $SAAM_{ij}$ row describes the total cost for each site Sj, through its own queries, to reach certain Attribute Ai, Table 17.

Then, by multiplying SAAM with communication cost matrix between sites, Total Access Cost Matrix (TACS) is created as shown in Table 18.

After that, using successful schema, the attribute allocation to query clusters is presented in Table 19.

As a result, the final fragments represented by the next SQL statements:

$DataF_1 = Cq_1$: Select A_1, A_2, A_4, A_5, A_6 from Employee; size $(DataF_1) = 13800$ byte.

$DataF_2 = Cq_2$: Select A_3 from Employee; size $(DataF_2) = 1200$ byte.

The first Allocation Scenario (Fragments Replicated Over Cluster Of sites)

Table 17. Site Access Attribute Matrix (SAAM)

Site/Attribute	A_1	A_2	A_3	A_4	A_5	A_6
S_1	2	4	2	0	4	4
S_2	3	2	3	1	5	2
S_3	1	3	2	4	4	2
S_4	1	4	4	6	3	5
S_5	3	1	5	0	5	2
S_6	9	5	4	0	6	7

Table 18. Total Access Cost Matrix (TACS)

Site/Attribute	A_1	A_2	A_3	A_4	A_5	A_6
S_1	106	86	98	54	144	96
S_2	81	98	87	46	126	107
S_3	91	85	79	25	116	100
S_4	94	59	94	15	120	77
S_5	81	101	91	79	112	120
S_6	49	72	79	54	104	77

Table 19. Attribute Allocation over Query Clusters

Cluster/Attribute	A_1	A_2	A_3	A_4	A_5	A_6
CQ_1	1	1		1	1	1
CQ_2			1			

This scenario has been done the same procure of (Adel et al. 2017). In phase (1): Fragment will be directly allocated to all clusters using replication principal as shown in Table (20). In phase (2): Using Total Access Cost (TACS$_{ij}$), the site of the largest access cost is the primary candidate storage site for relevant fragment given that no site constraint violated, as shown in Decision Allocation Matrix, Table 20.

From Table 20, by comparing the TACS of all sites for each cluster, it is clear that F_1 assigned to S_1 in CS_1, S_4 in CS_2 and S_6 of CS_3. While F_2 allocated to S_1, $CS_2.S_4$ and $CS_3.S_6$, respectively. The final allocation for fragments drawn in Tables 21.

The Second Allocation Scenario (No Fragment Replication)

The same procedure drawn in (Adel et al., 2017) has been applied to allocate fragments. In Phase (1): fragments are to be allocated to all clusters using non-replication principal so as to each fragment must be allocated to the cluster of maximum access cost as shown in Tables 22, 23. In Phase (2): The Decision Allocation will be made over sites in each cluster, drawn in Table 24.

Then, the competition to have these fragments allocated over sites will be accomplished among all sites of each relevant cluster. Each fragment will be directly assigned to the site of highest access cost, Table 24.

Table 20. Decision Allocation Matrix

Sites' Cluster/ Fragment	Sites/ Attributes	A_1	A_2	A_5	A_4	A_6	Total Cost (F_1)	A_3	Total Cost (F_2)
CS$_1$	S$_1$	106	86	144	54	96	486	98	98
	S$_2$	81	98	126	46	107	458	87	87
	S$_3$	91	85	116	25	100	417	79	79
CS$_2$	S$_4$	94	59	120	15	77	365	94	94
	S$_5$	81	101	112	79	120	493	91	91
CS$_3$	S$_6$	49	72	104	54	77	356	79	79

Table 21. The final fragments distribution (Scenario 1)

Fragment/Sites' Cluster	CS$_1$			CS$_2$		CS$_3$
	S$_1$	S$_2$	S$_3$	S$_4$	S$_5$	S$_6$
F$_1$	1			1		1
F$_2$	1				1	1

Table 22. Phase-1 Final Allocation over Cluster of Sites

Cluster #	A_1	A_5	A_2	A_4	A_6	Total Cost of F_1	A_3	Total Cost of F_2
C$_1$	857.5	920	1332	546	1074.5	4730	1042.5	1042.5
C$_2$	1218	1301.5	8171	770.5	1445.5	12906.5	1319	1319
C$_3$	2265	2146	3090	1135	2500	11136	2245	2245

Table 23. Fragment Allocation over Cluster of Sites (Scenario 2)

Fragment	F₁	F₂
Cluster	2	1

Table 24. Fragment Allocation over Sites (Scenario 2)

Sites' Cluster/Fragment	Sites/Attributes	A_1	A_2	A_5	A_4	A_6	Total Cost (F₁)	A_3	Total Cost (F₂)
CS₁	S₁	106	86	144	54	96	486	98	98
	S₂	81	98	126	46	107	458	87	87
	S₃	91	85	116	25	100	417	79	79
CS₂	S₄	94	59	120	15	77	365	94	94
	S₅	81	101	112	79	120	493	91	91
CS₃	S₆	49	72	104	54	77	356	79	79

The Third Allocation Scenario (Full Fragment Replication Over Clusters, Yet Partially Over Sites in Each Cluster)

This procedure is distinctly drawn for this chapter. In Phase (1): fragments are to be allocated to all clusters using Full replication principal so as to each fragment must be allocated to each cluster as shown Tables 25, 26. In Phase (2): The Decision Allocation will be made over sites that surpass threshold value, in each cluster, drawn in Table 27.

Then, the competition to have these fragments allocated over sites will be accomplished among all sites of each relevant cluster. Each fragment will be directly assigned to the site of highest access cost, Table 27.

Table 25. Phase-1 Final Allocation over Cluster of Sites

Cluster #	A_1	A_5	A_2	A_4	A_6	Total Cost of F₁	A_3	Total Cost of F₂
C₁	857.5	920	1332	546	1074.5	4730	1042.5	1042.5
C₂	1218	1301.5	8171	770.5	1445.5	12906.5	1319	1319
C₃	2265	2146	3090	1135	2500	11136	2245	2245

Table 26. Fragment Allocation over Cluster of Sites (Scenario 3)

Fragment	F₁	F₂
Cluster	1,2,3	1,2,3

Table 27. Fragment Allocation over Sites (Scenario 3), (Adel et al 2017).

Sites' Cluster/Fragment	Sites/Attributes	A_1	A_2	A_5	A_4	A_6	Total Cost (F_1)	A_3	Total Cost (F_2)
CS_1	S_1	106	86	144	54	96	486-surpass	98	98-surpass
	S_2	81	98	126	46	107	458 -surpass	87	87-surpass
	S_3	91	85	116	25	100	417	79	79
CS_2	S_4	94	59	120	15	77	365	94	94
	S_5	81	101	112	79	120	493	91	91
CS_3	S_6	49	72	104	54	77	356	79	79

DISCUSSION

This enhanced works comes basically with the aim of meeting several objectives. Off these objectives: (1) increasing data locality to the greatest possible extent so that data placed and replicated in the site(s) where it is highly and frequently required; (2) providing data availability effectively through suggesting several allocation scenarios including the presented Mixed Allocation Scenario (MAS). As a result, communication costs and response time are set to be substantially subsided. Therefore, to support our claims, an internal evaluation has been done. Five Allocation Scenario has been considered as follows: (1) Full Replication Based Allocation Scenario (FAS); (2) Mixed Replication based Allocation Scenario (MAS); (3) Non-replication Allocation Scenario (NAS); Random Non-replication Scenario and whole Relation Allocation Scenario. All these scenarios are approached in detail in the drawn above Allocation Cost Model as well as in (Adel et al. 2017). Furthermore, to address these scenarios professionally while simulating the real world DDBS Application, eleven problems have been considered as shown in Table 28. The first problem, however, is separately done, and exclusively restricted for retrieval queries like the way it was addressed in (Adel et al. 2017).

On the other hand, the rest of problems addressed, has been varied in the space of queries under consideration. A mixture of retrieval and update queries have been merged and carefully tackled and fluctuated in one single space called query space. Retrieval queries rate and update queries rate have been meticulously varied from one problem to another, so all scenarios are to be properly tested under several circumstances. This variation in query space allow us to automatically decide upon the best fitting scenario for data allocation (highest TC-reducing Scenario) which is the key goal this work comes to satisfy. The evaluation process is being made in terms of rate in which TC, as objective function of (Adel et al., 2017), is being minimized. It is worth indicating that DDBS performance has been measured by the rate of TC recorded over network while queries are being processed and answered. So, the minimum rate of TC is the highest performance DDBS is, and the best scenario of data allocation is. Briefly, for the first experiment in Table 28, Figures 2 and 3 come to illustrate that MAS scenario prove to be by far the best scenario.

Table 28. Fragment Allocation over Sites (Scenario 3), [Present]

Sites' Cluster/Fragment	Sites/Attributes	A_1	A_2	A_5	A_4	A_6	Total Cost (F_1)	A_3	Total Cost (F_2)
CS_1	S_6	49	72	104	54	77	356	79	79
	S_2	81	98	126	46	107	458	87	87
CS_2	S_4	94	59	120	15	77	365	94	94
	S_1	106	86	144	54	96	486	98	98
CS_3	S_3	91	85	116	25	100	417	79	79
	S_5	81	101	112	79	120	493	91	91

Figure 2. First Experiment, TC Costs Rate as per single experiment conducted in (Adel et al. 2017) with MAS superiority

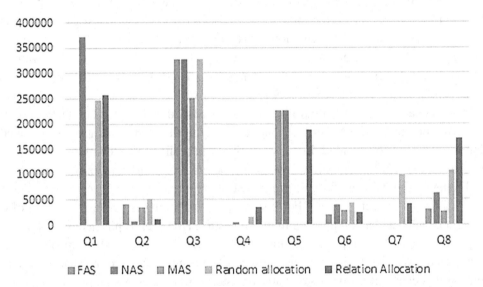

Figure 3. First experiment, DDBS performance (Total TC Rate Minimization)

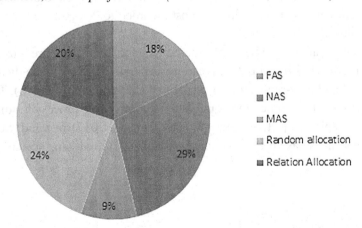

CONCLUSION

Given the current explosion of data as well as the ever-increasing growth of distributed databases-based web applications (or distributed off-line application) later this decade, the ability to handle data effectively is being of high importance to be considered for most information systems including DDBSs, chiefly at initial stage of design. Moreover, given the amount of developed DDBS design approaches in literature, the focus and interest in this area is highly likely to be continuing to grow with exploration of new applications that heavily depends on DDBS. On the other hand, it is worth referring that finding an efficient design for DDBS and distribute databases beyond a single availability site/region takes a considerable efforts and exhausting planning as well as careful engineering investment. However, having this goal achieved, it is unbelievably powerful tool to delightedly serve DBA as well as final users with high response for their queries accompanied with low latencies and towering availability.

In this chapter, therefore, as key pillars for DDBS design, we have tried to closely cover the principles of data allocation and replication and their impact on DDBS performance is investigated in a brief simple, yet concise manner. The manner of presentation of data replication effects is very obvious, self-explained while the intuition with figures and simple-yet-clear explanations is provided. In other words, we have tried to avoid having reader(s) involved in intimidating, lengthy and hard-to-follow notations, processes and diagrams. As consequent, from the thoroughly drawn above discussion of this work, several important benefits of data allocation replication have been simply deduced as follows: (1): Data availability has been improved (chiefly for partition of critical data) by ensuring allocating partitions in replicated manner so the point of failure is to be avoided. In the sense that data replication is being used as a pre-emptive measure against failure; (2) Minimizing response time where cross-partition joins are necessary, query parallelism has been exploited and fully utilized; (3) Data replication used to scale up network particularly as physical limit has been reached. For instance, if partitioning is at the exact level of database, partitions might be allocated and replicated in multiple sites. However, if physical limitations are being a problem, partitions have to be replicated in multiple sites. On the other hand, as update queries are being grown increasingly, several key disadvantages are concluded. The key drawback represented in the negative impact that data replication has on data consistency as it takes time for changes to be reflected on all partition copies over network sites. That why DDBS performance hugely suffers from undeniable deterioration as before changes being reflected, many partitions observed to hold different data values for the same copy. In the sense that an additional cost recorded to come along with synchronizing any changes occurring to the partition at hand.

Five data allocation scenarios have been considered while three of them are replicated based. These scenarios are: Mixed replicated based data allocation scenario (MAS), Full replicated based data allocation scenario (FAS) and Non-replicated based data allocation scenario (NAS). To show how much negative or positive impact data replication could have, a competitive process for these scenarios have been performed with keeping objective function of (Adel et al. 2017) in mind. Several experiments under different circumstances have been conducted so the best TC-reducing scenario is to be chosen.

ACKNOWLEDGMENT

The author would like to express his sincere appreciation to the Research Unit of Computer Science Department at Taiz University (YEMEN) for the physical materials dedicated to help complete this work successfully. Additionally, author would like to heartedly express his indescribable gratitude for both, Prof. Dr. Taha Morsi Elgindy, and Prof. Dr. Adel A. Sewisy (Assiut University / Egypt) for their valuable insights and directions whilst doing this work. For their constructive and informative suggestions, author' thanks is to be sincerely extended to the Editors of this book, namely, Miltiadis D. Lytras, Naif Aljohani, Ernesto Damiani and Kwok Tai Chui. Last but not least, the author thanks those respected unknown reviewers for their invaluable comments that otherwise this research article would not be released. Finally, we would like to greatly thank the staff of IGI Global for providing us with excellent support in the publication of this chapter.

REFERENCES

Abdalla, H. I., Amer, A. A., & Mathkour, H. (2014). A Novel Vertical Fragmentation, Replication and Allocation Model in DDBSs. *Journal of Universal Computer Science, 20*(10), 1469–1487. Retrieved from http://www.jucs.org/jucs_20_10/a_novel_vertical_fragmentation and https://pdfs.semanticscholar.org/4538/62e6e68f24836fcdfc92f66db14b682adda8.pdf

Abdallaha, H. I., Amer, A. A., & Mathkour, H. (2014). Performance optimality enhancement algorithm in DDBS (POEA). *Computers in Human Behavior, 30*, 419–426. doi:10.1016/j.chb.2013.04.026

Abdel Raouf, A. E., Badr, N., & Tolba, M. F. (2017). Distributed Database System (DSS) Design Over a Cloud Environment. In Multimedia Forensics and Security (pp. 97-116). Cham: Springer. Retrieved from https://link.springer.com/chapter/10.1007/978-3-319-44270-9_5

Abdel Raouf, A. E., Badr, N. L., & Tolba, M. F. (2018). Dynamic data reallocation and replication over a cloud environment. *Concurrency and Computation.* doi:10.1002/cpe.4416

Amer, A. A., & Sewisy, A. A. (2017). An Extended Approach for Synchronized Data Partitioning and Distribution in Distributed Database Systems (DDBSs). *International Journal of Economics and Management Systems, 2*, 161–170. Retrieved from http://www.iaras.org/iaras/home/caijems/an-extended-approach-for-synchronized-data-partitioning-and-distribution-in-distributed-database-systems-ddbss

Amer, A. A., Sewisy, A. A., & Elgendy, T. M. (2017). An optimized approach for simultaneous horizontal data fragmentation and allocation in distributed database systems (DDBSs). *Heliyon (London), 3*(12). doi:10.1016/j.heliyon.2017.e00487

Chakravarthy, S., Muthuraj, J., Varadarajan, R., & Navathe, S. B. (1994). An objective function for vertically partitioning relations in distributed databases and its analysis. *Journal Distributed and Parallel Databases, 2*(2), 183-207. Retrieved from http://dl.acm.org/citation.cfm?id=180313

Hassan, I. Abdalla. (2014). A synchronized design technique for efficient data distribution. *Computers in Human Behavior, 30*, 427–435. Retrieved from http://www.sciencedirect.com/science/article/pii/S0747563213001374

Luong, V. N., Le, V. S., & Doan, V. B. (2018). Fragmentation in Distributed Database Design Based on KR Rough Clustering Technique. In P. Cong Vinh, N. Ha Huy Cuong, & E. Vassev (Eds.), *Context-Aware Systems and Applications, and Nature of Computation and Communication ICCASA 2017.* Cham: Springer. Retrieved from https://link.springer.com/chapter/10.1007/978-3-319-77818-1_16 doi:10.1007/978-3-319-77818-1_16

Mahi, M., Baykan, O. K., & Kodaz, H. (2018). A new approach based on particle swarm optimization algorithm for solving data allocation problem. *Applied Soft Computing*, *62*, 571–578. doi:10.1016/j.asoc.2017.11.019

Nashat, D., & Amer, A. A. (2018). A Comprehensive Taxonomy of Fragmentation and Allocation Techniques in Distributed Database Design. *ACM Computing Surveys*, *51*(1), 12.

Norouzi, M., Fleet, D. J., & Salakhutdinov, R. (2013). Hamming Distance Metric Learning. University of Toronto. Retrieved from https://papers.nips.cc/paper/4808-hamming-distance-metric-learning.pdf

Sakuma, J., & Kobayashi, S. (2010). Large-scale k-means clustering with user-centric privacy-preservation. *Knowledge and Information Systems*, *25*(2), 253–279. Retrieved from https://link.springer.com/article/10.1007%2Fs10115-009-0243-x

Sewisy Adel, A., Amer Ali, A., & Abdalla Hassan, I. (2017). A novel query-driven clustering-based technique for vertical fragmentation and allocation in distributed database systems. *International Journal on Semantic Web and Information Systems*, *13*(2). Retrieved from http://www.igi-global.com/article/a-novel-query-driven-clustering-based-technique-for-verti-cal-fragmentation-and-allocation-in-distributed-database-systems/176732

Wiese, L., Waage, T., & Bollwein, F. (2017). A Replication Scheme for Multiple Fragmentations with Overlapping Fragments. *The Computer Journal*, *60*(3), 308–328. http://ieeexplore.ieee.org/document/8187838/

APPENDIX

The next figures (4-13) briefly and vividly illustrate the amount of TC produced over network sites as queries being answered, in both work, for experiment that done exclusively in this work (8 queries, 6 sites). The behaviour of both work over all scenarios is being monitored and recorded as queries walking through fragments to obtain the results of issued queries.

Figure 4. Adel et al. 2017- TC values as per FAS scenario

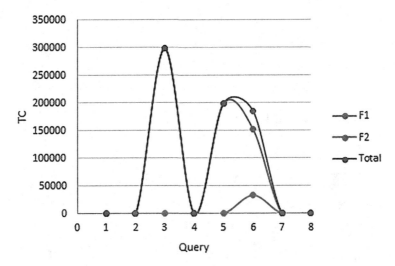

Figure 5. Present - TC values as per FAS scenario

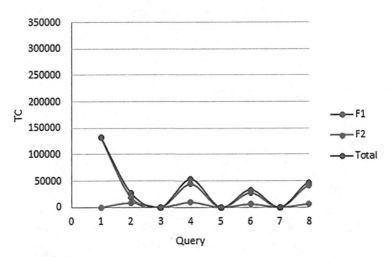

Figure 6. Adel et al. 2017- TC values as per MAS scenario

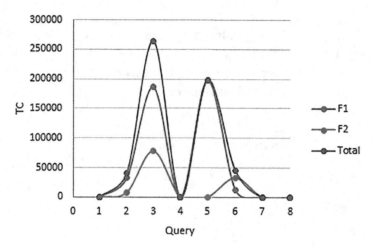

Figure 7. Present - TC values as per MAS scenario

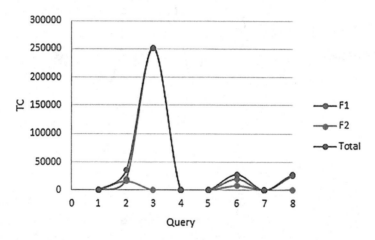

Figure 8. Adel et al. 2017- TC values as per NAS scenario

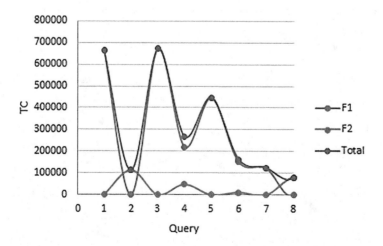

Figure 9. Present - TC values as per NAS scenario

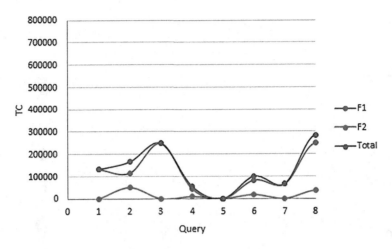

Figure 10. Adel et al. 2017- TC values as per Random Allocation scenario

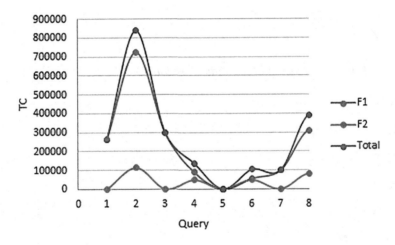

Figure 11. Present - TC values as per Random Allocation scenario

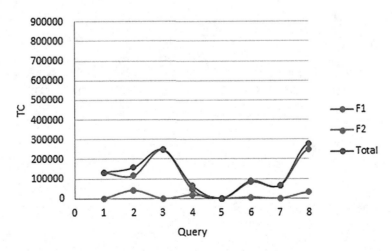

Figure 12. Adel et al. 2017- TC values as per Whole Relation scenario

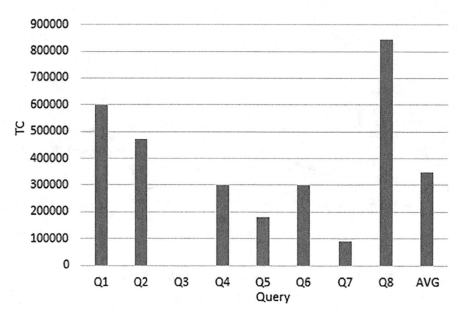

Figure 13. Present - TC values as per Whole Relation scenario

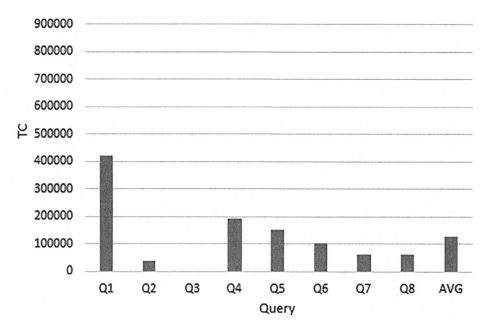

Chapter 7
Leveraging Context–Awareness in Duty–Cycled Broadcast Wireless Sensor Networks

Imen Jemili
University of Carthage, Tunisia

Dhouha Ghrab
National School for Computer Science, Tunisia

Abdelfettah Belghith
King Saud University, Saudi Arabia

Mohamed Mosbah
University of Bordeaux, France

ABSTRACT

Operating under duty-cycle mode allows wireless sensor networks to prolong their lifetime. However, this working pattern, with the temporary unavailability of nodes, brings challenges to the network design, mainly for a fundamental service like flooding. The challenging task is to authorize sensors to adopt a duty-cycle mode without inflicting any negative impact on the network performances. Context-awareness offers to sensors the ability to adapt their functional behavior according to many contexts in order to cope with network dynamics. In this context, the authors propose an Enhanced-Efficient Context-Aware Multi-hop Broadcast (E-ECAB) protocol, which relies on multi contextual information to optimize resources usage and satisfy the application requirements in a duty-cycled environment. The authors proved that only one transmission is required to achieve the broadcast operation in almost all situations. Simulation results show that E-ECAB achieves a significant improvement compared to previous work in terms of throughput and end-to-end delay without sacrificing energy efficiency.

INTRODUCTION

The attractive features of wireless sensor networks (WSN) promote their deployment in a large variety of domains, and recently they are increasingly becoming a key building block for realizing the vision of smart cities. In fact, WSNs are infiltrating our daily life through the elaboration of many systems and Internet of Things platforms for smart home monitoring, home automation, assisted living and

DOI: 10.4018/978-1-5225-7186-5.ch007

Copyright © 2019, IGI Global. Copying or distributing in print or electronic forms without written permission of IGI Global is prohibited.

environment monitoring making our life easier and more comfortable. The sensors technology and sensor networking can play a primary role in supporting these Internet of Things (IoT) applications by gathering and delivering raw context information appropriately, according to the constraints imposed by the application and the environment, for further process and analysis. In such fields, heterogeneous applications can coexist within the same remote network resulting to more fluctuations and heterogeneous demands. These contextual and technical requirements may differ significantly considering the diversity and heterogeneity of targeted domains involving WSNs.

To cope with such dynamics and heterogeneity, these resource constrained networks need autonomy to smartly adapt their operations to changing situations while taking into account nodes and network constraints. To fully enable such a functional behavior, context-awareness, broadly recognized as an important paradigm in pervasive and mobile computing environments, offers great opportunities by providing systems with full awareness of current environment context (Perera et al., 2014). This paradigm has been defined in (Salber et al., 1998) as "…the ability to provide maximum flexibility of a computational service based on real-time sensing of context…" In (Abowd et al., 1999), the authors defined context sensitive systems and applications as "…those that respond to changes in their environment. Typically these responses are designed to improve a systems' performance or to make its behaviour more relevant to the situation in which it is being used…"

A context-aware system requires acquiring contextual information from various sources; in this context, WSNs are considered among the main appliances to gather and send contextual information to the processing station (Taherkordi et al., 2008, Borges et al., 2013) in order to identify the corresponding situation and behave accordingly. For their large deployment, an autonomic network management is required to enable sensor nodes to self-behave with less human interventions. In relation with autonomic networks, context-awareness was defined in (Agoulmine et al., 2006), as "…perception and cognitive reaction to an event or more generically to a condition, relevant to the same intelligent node or, respectively to the environment. Context-awareness is a foundation for the rest of the operational features: self-configuring, self-healing, self-optimizing, and self-protecting…" In the same context, authors in (Jennings et al., 2007) define the notion of adaptability, one of most the important operations in autonomic networks, as "…the capability to adapt the functionality of the system in response to changes in user requirements, business rules, and/or environmental conditions…"

Defined, in (Ganz et al., 2011), as "…the information which is not related to the real sensing operation and information…" the sensor node context may concern any information characterizing the situation of the sensor and providing knowledge about other entities within the environment, such as the current battery status, location, radio information and its capabilities (Ghrab et al., 2016). Context can include also collected information from the environment, shared between nodes in the network, cross-layer information, etc. Sensed data or captured events may to be part of the node's context since, sometimes, the data content or the relevance of data can also be considered as contextual parameters useful to handle recent applications with heterogeneous traffic demands. Authors in (Makris et al., 2013), provide more generalized definition that considers the context as "…a collection of measured and inferred knowledge rather than just a set of values with no underlying understanding of what these values ultimately mean…" As context can be deduced from observing network activity (De et al., 2012), or estimated through analyzing the history of some parameters, such as traffic load (Ghrab et al., 2015), this definition can be approved in the context of WSNs. In this chapter, the authors suggest a more generalized definition for context-awareness in WSNs as "…the ability to adapt sensor nodes functional behavior and decision making to changing contexts at different layers. They define the context in WSNs "as any information measured or inferred, local or gathered that can have impact on the operational behavior of sensor nodes and the network performances…" Such contextual information can be exploited, at different levels, to enable the automatic adaptation of nodes behavior according to current context changes and satisfy needed requirements.

To overcome the intrinsic constraints of WSNs imposing many challenges to be handled for their large deployment, WSNs move from a main appliance to gather contextual parameters for ubiquitous computing to a system that exploits context-awareness to optimize resources use and to improve the operating protocols performances while meeting the QoS (Quality of Service) application requirements. The integration of context-awareness paradigm promises more autonomy to sensor nodes and consequently more sophisticated applications. In fact, energy remains the most challenging issue in such networks, as the nature of sensor nodes and hostile sensing environments preclude battery replacement as a feasible solution while providing a long lifetime for these networks. Recently, some efforts have explored energy harvesting solutions to recharge batteries, such as using solar power. However, the trade-off between energy efficiency and equipment cost can influence the decision of equipping sensor nodes with additional harvesting modules, such as solar cells. Besides, the recourse to such solutions is not always possible depending on sensors location or weather conditions. Thus, to reduce energy waste, much of the current research rely on duty-cycle mode (Alfayez et al., 2015), where nodes are put into a dormant state whenever possible and kept active only to receive or transmit a packet. Putting sensors into a sleep mode can significantly prolong the network lifetime. Nevertheless, the temporary unavailability of nodes can result in losing connectivity which may affect the communication performances related mainly to latency and throughput. In fact, we must take into account waiting times at intermediate nodes since a sender node must wait the wake-up of neighbors to be able to deliver the pending packet. Consequently, this working pattern brings challenges to the network design, mainly for a fundamental service like network flooding. Performing such operation under a duty-cycle mode constitutes a difficult task in an asynchronous environment, where involved nodes wake up independently of each other and follow different activity schedules. Besides, resource limitations of sensors and links unreliability, in combination with various performance demands of different applications, impose many challenges in designing efficient communication protocols for duty-cycled WSNs.

It is worthwhile to investigate appropriate benefits in the network performances and to examine feasibility of broadcasting services in duty-cycled WSN while considering context awareness. Thus, through the Enhanced-Efficient Context-Aware Broadcast protocol (E-ECAB), the authors highlight how the combination of a duty-cycle mechanism and a context-aware paradigm can improve system performances and maintain desired characteristics for supporting certain application requirements such as throughput and end-to-end delay. The key novelty of this work lies in exploiting multi relevant contextual information to adapt node behavior and adjust scheduling for communications in duty-cycle WSNs. Combining several context values may generate a more powerful understanding of the current situation. While energy level and traffic load are the most frequently used contextual attributes, other attributes like communication history and medium conditions may also be relevant and useful. Through the E-ECAB, the authors explore further kinds of context information and investigate the potential performance gains.

The rest of this paper is organized as follow. In Section 2, the authors discuss related work. The details of the proposed duty-cycled MAC protocol are introduced in Section 3. In Section 4, the authors provide an analytical study to prove the upper bound for broadcast count. In Section 5, E-ECAB with similar state-of-the-art previous approaches are evaluated to highlight the improvements brought by the integration of context-awareness. Finally, discussion and future directions are introduced in Section 6.

RELATED WORK

Many duty-cycled protocols are proposed in the literature, mainly classified into synchronous and asynchronous approaches. Synchronous approaches reserve a portion of the active state to synchronize all nodes to a global active/sleep schedule to allow neighboring nodes to communicate during the common active periods (Carrano et al., 2014). In (Tong et al., 2017), the authors proposed an Adaptive Data Collection (ADC) protocol, relying on the RTF/CTF (Request-to-Forward/Clear-to-Forward) handshake schedule synchronization and topology control and maintenance. In ADC, all nodes are divided into different grades based on their communication hop distances towards the sink. ADC offers a pipelined forwarding so that a relaying node can forward a received packet in a short time to reduce the end-to-end packet delivery latency. Each sensor node periodically experiences three consecutive statuses, receiving a data packet from a previous sender (R), transmitting a data packet to its next-hop receiver (T) and sleeping (S). To cope with the network traffic load, ADC can adaptively utilize the sleeping slots in status S to achieve a Dynamic Duty-Cycling (DDC) based on DDC flag of exchanged RTF packets, which will be set if a node has more than one packet to be transmitted. However, it allows at the most one node to schedule data packet transmission in a cycle, when multiple nodes, with data packets to send, lie in the interference range of each other or the next-hop forwarder of each node lies in the interference range of the remaining nodes (Singh et al., 2017). To reduce these shortcomings, JRAM (Singh et al., 2017) enables up to k nodes to schedule data packet transmission in a cycle in similar situations. It provides k chances to a node to schedule data packet transmission in a cycle by partitioning the network nodes into k disjoint sets (DSs) and then using a novel cycle structure. Achieving broadcast over synchronous duty-cycled network is simpler since nodes can easily exchange packets during their common active period. However, extra complexity and overhead are required for synchronization. Being unable to have a fully independent duty-cycle prevents also each node to adapt to the current surrounding conditions, in a distributed way.

On the other hand, supporting broadcast is more challenging in an asynchronous environment. As each sensor node wakes up and operates independently according to its own duty-cycle schedule, a sender can't guarantee the simultaneous wake-up of all the intended receivers. To be able to communicate, we have to ensure that neighbors always have overlapped active periods. In this context, two techniques are suggested: sender-based and receiver-based techniques. The former relies on low power listening (LPL), where each node periodically samples the channel and each sender transmits a long preamble larger than the listen period of nodes to guarantee that all neighbors are notified about the subsequent transmission (Carrano et al., 2014). Demand Sleep MAC (DS-MAC) is designed to reduce latency (Wang et al., 2015). It attempts to transmit a series of short token packets, including the target address, to wake up the receiver, which avoids the overhearing problem of preamble-based protocols. DS-MAC allows nodes to adjust their sleep time adaptively according to the amount of the received data packets in order to ensure efficient and effective communications with the dynamic traffic load. Nodes put the prediction field into ACK packets. Knowing the receiver's wake up time, the sender needs to wake up slightly before the receiver and can then decrease sending time of preamble. In (Morshed et al., 2014), the authors proposed TR-MAC, an energy-efficient preamble sampling protocol allowing nodes to maximize sleeping time and to wake up periodically independent of other nodes to sample the channel for any ongoing activity. Initially, the sender node operating in unsynchronized link state sends preamble accompanying a small data packet together and repeats this procedure until it receives an acknowledgement. As the nodes can remember each other next wake up time, it moves to the synchronized link state.

Being aware of the receiver's next wake up, the sender can schedule its packet transmission. In (Morshed et al., 2016), the authors proposed a traffic-adaptive duty cycle adaptation mechanism in order to provide responsiveness to traffic rate variations for TR-MAC protocol. Cao et al. (Cao et al. 2017) proposed a distributed concurrent broadcast layer for flooding in asynchronous duty-cycled networks, called Chase. Based on a distributed random inter-preamble packet interval adjustment approach, Chase can satisfy the signal timing and strength requirements for concurrent transmission while decreasing contentions and collisions. When such requirements cannot be satisfied due to physical constraints, a light-weight signal pattern recognition-based approach is proposed to extend the wake-up time for packet delivery. However, a destination must receive multiple preamble packets to successfully recover original flooding payload, which may further increase delivery delay, and the optimal preamble packet length varies for different senders. Chase++ was introduced in (Cao et al. 2018) to improve the efficiency of concurrent broadcast under different size of flooding payload by converting long flooding payload to some short-encoded payload blocks.

The second technique consists in remaining active enough time waiting the reception of beacons from receivers announcing their wake-up. RI-MAC (Sun et al., 2008) is the first receiver-initiated MAC protocol for unicast communication over asynchronous duty-cycled WSNs. Similarly, in (Duan et al., 2015), the authors presented a Wakeup Adapting Traffic (WAT). It enables the receiver to adjust its wakeup interval dynamically based on the traffic loads. WAT divides the interval range of wakeup interval into three partitions according to the categories of traffic load status: low traffic load, normal traffic load and high traffic load. Nodes wake up independently using a wakeup interval, randomly generated in the corresponding interval range, to reduce idle waiting and minimize wireless collisions. These solutions may be efficient in the case of one hop broadcasting. However, they lack efficiency with multi-hop broadcasting, as they can lead to more overhearing and higher latency. In Opportunistic Flooding (Guo et al., 2014), each node makes probabilistic forwarding decisions based on the delay distribution of next-hop nodes. Only opportunistic early packets are forwarded via the links outside of the energy-optimal tree to reduce flooding delays and the level of redundancy. In (Cheng et al., 2018), the authors investigated the flooding tree construction problem to minimize the flooding cost and flooding delay in asynchronous low-duty-cycled WSNs with unreliable links. They present a distributed Minimum-Delay Energy-efficient flooding Tree (MDET) algorithm to construct an energy optimal tree with flooding delay bounding. To avoid predefined static duty-cycles shared among neighbors, L-MAC (Dinh et al., 2016) is designed for low data rate periodic reporting applications where a data collection tree is normally used to gather data from sensors. It exploits beacon messages of receiver-initiated MAC protocols to enable nodes to coordinate their wakeup time with their parent nodes without incurring extra communication overhead. In each wakeup interval, if a child node wakes up before its parent node and receives a beacon when the parent wakes up, the node computes the offset between its wakeup time and that of its parent. Then, it compensates this offset by re-calculating its sleep period in order to wake-up closely earlier than its parent node. L-MAC seeks to expand wakeup interval in proportion to data rate. The authors in (Aby et al., 2015) designed a self-adaptive low activity cycle knowledge-based MAC (SLACK-MAC) where the nodes adapt their activation times depending on their neighborhood by exploiting the history information of successful frame exchanges.

Other multi-hop broadcast protocols are also based on an adaptive duty-cycling. ADB (Sun et al., 2009) is designed based on RI-MAC to support multi-hop broadcast through redundant transmissions towards each intended neighbor. ADB includes information about the progress of broadcast, mainly the sender neighbors not reached yet and the respective quality of links. If a receiver can reach one of these neighbors with better link quality, it has to inform the source in the acknowledgement beacon. Hence, the source will delegate the broadcast to this neighbor. If all its neighbors are reached or delegated, the sender returns to sleep immediately. A similar approach is adopted in (Xu et al., 2018), where authors allow some early wake-up nodes to postpone their wake-up slots to opportunistically overhear the broadcasting messages sent by their neighbors. As authors assume that each node is aware of the working schedules of all its neighboring nodes within two hops, any sender can distinguish between two kinds of receivers, DelayedReceivers and InstantReceivers. The sender will send the message to each InstantReceiver, and will also inform DelayedReceivers about InstantReceivers through short beacon packets. Thus, any DelayedReceiver will go to sleep immediately and defer its message receiving time by setting a timer to wake up itself at the next active state of the InstantReceiver. The authors formulated the Receiver-Constrained Minimum Cost Single-hop Broadcast Problem (RC-MCSB), extended to find an efficient broadcasting schedule and to provide an adaptive control on the tradeoff between average broadcasting delay and total energy consumption for broadcasting to meet various performance requirements through an efficient bottom-up algorithm. In (Duc et al., 2017), the authors tackled the minimum-transmission broadcast (MTB) problem in synchronous duty-cycled environments. They proposed a Broadcast Redundancy Minimization Scheduling (BRMS), executed at a central node having full awareness of the whole network topology and the active time slot of every node. BRMS identifies one set of covering nodes for all nodes active at a particular time slot, which minimizes the number of broadcast transmissions. Then, it constructs a forest of sub-trees based on the relationship between each forwarding node and its corresponding receivers. A broadcast tree is constructed ultimately by connecting all sub-trees with a minimum number of connectors. To reduce redundancies, a pruning method is also introduced. (Le et al., 2017) introduced a novel strategy of Collision-Tolerant Scheduling that aims to reduce broadcast latency by allowing collisions at secondary nodes to speed up the broadcast process for primary ones. To ensure receiving of the broadcast packets by all nodes, the protocol allows additional transmissions to nodes experiencing a collision. Structured into a tree topology, primary nodes are defined as internal nodes, whereas secondary nodes are defined as the leaf nodes. Authors in (Ghrab et al., 2015, Ghrab et al., 2016) introduced ECAB, an efficient context-aware multi-hop broadcasting protocol performed over an adaptive asynchronous duty-cycled network. The basic idea of ECAB is to modify the behavior of nodes and adjust their duty-cycling schedules in a distributed manner by exploiting efficiently acquired awareness, specially related to neighborhood activity and traffic load, to enhance the broadcast operation without penalizing the network performances. Nodes adopt a fixed cycle where they alternate between active and inactive periods following two possible schedules. The decision about keeping the same scheduling or modifying it is taken after observing the traffic for a period of three cycles. Gathered information allows senders to compute the adequate instances for packets sending with minimal number of transmissions. In (Dong et al., 2017), the authors proposed a Prediction-Based Asynchronous MAC protocol (PBA-MAC) to support heavy traffic load in WSNs. PBA-MAC is a receiver-based duty-cycle MAC protocol which introduces a predictive wakeup mechanism, a backcast-based retransmission mechanism to avoid persistent collisions and an exponential advance mechanism to handle the prediction error caused by the latency of operation system and the clock drift. The predictive wakeup mechanism allows a sender to compute next wakeup time of target receiver R, based on prediction information shared by this latest, including the parameters of pseudo-random number generator of R, the seed and the current time of R. Based on such awareness, the sender can adjust its wake-up. To compensate prediction error, a sender may advance its wakeup by a short time T, selected as a tradeoff among packet delay, power consumption and successful reception of wakeup beacon.

PROTOCOL OVERVIEW

To the best of the author's knowledge, E-ECAB (Jemili et al., 2017) is the first MAC layer design for flooding in duty-cycled WSNs, taking into account multi-contextual information and even wireless medium characteristics as unreliable links and collision occurrence. The aim is to exploit any relevant information helping nodes to improve the execution performance and to fine tune their behavior according to the network dynamics. Through passive listening and control packets exchange, each node becomes able to gather different kinds of information. The contexts considered in our protocol are related to: neighborhood, traffic load, medium, and history.

The authors consider an asynchronous network where nodes wake up at different times. Each node adopts a fixed cycle where an active period is followed by an inactive period. The active period could be maximal, noted PA_{max}, or minimal, noted PA_{min}, as well as the inactive period could be maximal, noted PI_{max}, or minimal, noted PI_{min}. Each cycle is divided into slots (*e-ecab_slot*), where PA is equal to **x** *e-ecab_slot* and PI is equal to **y** *e-ecab_slot*. A slot time for E-ECAB represents the required time to transmit 1 beacon and 1 data packet after a back-off time before each packet transmission. The slot is computed as follow:

$$E - ECAB_{slot} = Average_{Backoff} + Tx_{beacon} + Average_{Backoff} + TX_{data} \tag{1}$$

Where Tx_{beacon} is the required time to send a beacon frame and Tx_{data} represents the time needed to broadcast a data packet.

In the deployment phase, authors assume that nodes wake up within a period of length PI_{min}. To ensure the correct functioning of the protocol, the lengths of the active and inactive periods should respect the following rules:

$$PA\max > PI\max$$

$$PI\min < PA\min$$

$$PI\min < \frac{1}{2}PA\max$$

Nodes must observe continuously their execution context in order to detect the conditions under which some behavioral adaptations are required. In the next subsections, the authors will describe the behavior of a node in different situations to reveal the impact of the acquired awareness on the broadcast operation and the network performances.

Neighborhood Awareness

Nodes With No Neighborhood Awareness

In a newly deployed sensor network, nodes have scarce information about their surrounding environment. In fact, nodes have no knowledge about the nodes' distribution or wake-up patterns. Thus, they should follow a default duty-cycle scheduling and adopt a default behavior. Since nodes have only limited knowledge about their neighborhood, the default duty-cycle must allow nodes to be active for a maximal period, noted PA_{max}, which guarantees the well reception of neighbors' beacons, followed by a minimal inactive period. At the beginning of the active period, each node sends a beacon frame to notify its neighbors that it is ready to receive pending data. A beacon frame should include all required information helping neighbors to make their own decision about the scheduling to adopt and the packet transmission instants to choose. A beacon frame includes the node ID (IDentifier) and the scheduling adopted by the sender node enabling neighbors to be aware of its next wake-up and sleep times. Two specific fields give more information about the node behavior:

- The field, noted *default state*, indicates if the node follows the default scheduling or a modified one. When this bit is set to 1, the node adopts the default scheduling.
- The field, called *beacon request*, is set to 1 when the node asks its neighbors to send beacons more frequently. Such a situation arises, for example, when a new source is introduced in an already operational network.

Each node remains awake during the active period waiting for the neighbors' beacons and data packets. The neighborhood knowledge, acquired by means of the beacons exchange, allows nodes to have a local view about the surrounding environment. Through the time, the beacon frame will include also the neighbors' list of each node.

To make a broadcast operation, the transmitter needs to reach all its neighbors. So, to ensure the well reception of its beacons by all its neighbors, the source node should send its frame twice. These two operations are required at the deployment phase to allow stations to acquire more rapidly local neighborhood awareness. Each node should continue working with the default scheduling until acquiring enough knowledge enabling it to adjust its scheduling.

At the beginning of the active period, a node sends its first beacon to inform its active neighbors about its wake-up and its adopted scheduling. The second beacon transmission will be scheduled after a period equals to PI_{min}. By delaying the instant of the second packet transmission, the source node will be able to reach the remaining receivers despite their asynchronous wake ups. Whenever the data is urgent, the sender can broadcast the data packet just after the second beacon transmission or it can simply send a beacon piggybacked in data (after a period equals to PI_{min} from the cycle beginning). When a node receives a data packet, it behaves like a source node in order to forward data to its neighbors.

Nodes With Neighborhood and Duty-Cycling Awareness

Thanks to the passive listening during active periods and the beacon exchange, nodes acquire more knowledge about their neighborhood. In fact, besides the node scheduling, each beacon includes the set of already known neighbors. Such awareness allows the sender node to schedule the packet broadcast according to neighbors' availability. Based on neighbors' scheduling, each node computes the appropriate instants to broadcast its data packet in order to decrease latency as well as the broadcast count. To reduce the number of duplicated copies, the node has to select overlapping periods including the maximum number of active neighbors not already reached.

As detailed in Algorithm 1, the authors compute the overlapping intervals between the active periods of the different receivers. They first consider the neighbor node that turns to sleep the first and according to its scheduling, the authors compute the overlapped interval between its active period and the active periods of the other active neighbors. They postpone the broadcast operation while considering the wake-up of the latest node during this overlapping period to target the maximum number of receivers with the same transmission. These covered nodes are removed from the list L of receivers. Then, the same instructions are repeated with the remaining nodes until reaching all the neighbors. The adequate instants to perform the broadcast are within the computed intervals. The number of required iterations corresponds to the number of broadcast operations for the same packet to cover all neighbors.

According to neighbors scheduling modifications, the node is able to adjust its behavior according to the new network changes and computes each time the appropriate overlapping intervals for packets broadcast.

A New Source With No Knowledge in a Network With Neighborhood and Duty-Cycling Awareness

In order to unburden the network from an extra control overhead, nodes, working with neighborhood and duty-cycling awareness, reduce the frequency of beacons exchange. In fact, each node, following the adequate scheduling for the actual conditions, sends beacons once each three cycles if there is no adjustment. In case of duty-cycling adjustment, beacon sending becomes more frequent enabling the node to inform rapidly the neighborhood about modifications.

Algorithm 1. Overlap intervals computing algorithm

```
L: the list of the receivers; Δ=transmission time
D(ni): the beginning of the active period of the node n_i;
F(ni): the end of the active period of the node n_i;
Pj:the overlap interval number j ;
Lj: the remaining of receivers not yet reached;
Int j=0
While  L ≠ Ø do
j++;
Pj=[Dj,Fj];
Fj=min{ F(ni) ;ni ∈ L}
Dj=max{ D(ni) / ni ∈ L and D(ni)+Δ <Fj}
Lj={ni ∈ L / D(ni) > Dj and F(ni)<Fj }
L=L\Lj
End While
```

For newly introduced nodes, beacons exchanged by neighbors should be more frequent in order to allow these nodes to collect information about their neighborhood. Thus, such a node should adopt the default scheduling and stays awake even during the inactive period. It should send beacons many times during a cycle, to cover all its neighbors, generally following different schedules. The first beacon is sent at the beginning of the active period to notify active neighbors about its wake up. The remaining neighbors will be active either after a period of a minimal length PI_{min} or a period of maximal length PI_{max}, according to the adopted scheduling. Hence, in order to cover the remaining neighbors, two other beacons should be sent after PI_{min} and PI_{max}. To acquire information about them, it pleads with neighbors to send beacons more frequently through a specific field in the beacon frame.

To broadcast a data packet, the new source, unaware about the neighbors scheduling, should send its data frame twice, one should be sent after PI_{min} and the second after PI_{max}.

Traffic Load Awareness

In a WSN, the traffic volume and pattern can vary significantly both across the deployment area and through the time, depending on the application and sensed data nature. For a periodic reporting after data gathering, involved nodes may have a regular and low traffic rate, while for an event-driven application, network may experience a large burst of traffic affecting a lot of nodes. Such traffic variability may concern many WSN applications and different nodes may have different traffic volumes and rates. Thus, each node should adjust its scheduling to meet the different traffic requirements since ignoring such traffic dynamic leads to poor network performances. In this context, traffic aware scheduling adjustment can substantially improve network performances through enhancing the packet delivery ratio and system overall throughput while reducing channel access and energy consumption.

E-ECAB allows nodes to adjust their scheduling in order to cope with the network dynamicity without penalizing performances, based on traffic load observation during a predefined period. Nodes could adopt two possible schedules, either $\left[PA\max; PI\min\right]$ to enhance throughput in heavy loaded period or $\left[PA\min; PI\max\right]$ in lightly loaded environment to reduce energy wasting due to idle listening and traffic overhearing. The decision of following one of these two schedules is taken locally based on traffic load observation during three cycles. To smoothly switch to the new schedule, each node should keep working with the old one until advertising all its neighbors. The aim is to avoid losing logical connectivity with surrounding neighbors due to an unexpected schedule modification. As exposed in Figure 1, thanks to the beacon sent during the last cycle, the node announces the upcoming modification and will

Figure 1. Observation period

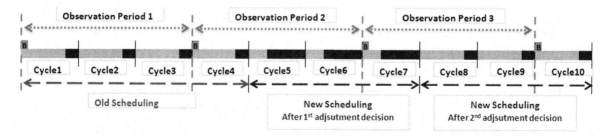

follow the new scheduling during the next three cycles, since the observation period begins upon sending the beacon.

To be able to decide locally and adjust its scheduling, each node gathers the required information related to network load over three cycles. Each node computes the average idle time Ti and the average busy time Tb as follows:

$$Ti = \frac{1}{3} \sum_{J=1}^{3} \left(Paj - \left(Trxj + Ttxj + \Delta cj \right) \right) \tag{2}$$

$$Tb = \frac{1}{3} \sum_{J=1}^{3} \left(Trxj \right) \tag{3}$$

where Trxj is the total receiving time, Ttxj is the total transmitting time and Δcj is the collisions duration, calculated during cycle j.

Then, it calculates the new length of the active period Pa as follow:

$$Pa_{new} = PA_{min} \cdot \left(1 - \frac{T_i}{T_i + T_b} + \frac{T_b}{T_i + T_b} \right) + Q.N.\Delta tx \tag{4}$$

Q refers to the number of pending packets and announced by neighbors, N is the number of required transmissions to broadcast one packet to all neighbors and Δtx is the transmission time of one data packet.

If $Pa_{new} < PA_{min}$, the minimal activity period is then sufficient for the light traffic activity within the neighborhood. As such, the node adopts the schedule [PA_{min}; PI_{max}] to cut down energy consumptions in idle listening. Otherwise, it opts for the schedule [PA_{max}; PI_{min}] since the high network activity in surrounding zone requires more time to be able to send and receive pending packets. In this way, E-ECAB tries to remedy to the data delivery latency issue by adopting a dynamic duty-cycle working pattern.

Medium Awareness

Reliable flooding is a difficult task in WSNs due to wireless link unreliability. This situation is stressed by the fact that an event can excite many sources simultaneously. Duplicate sensing results in redundant transmissions incurring a serious medium contention problem. In asynchronous duty-cycled networks, a broadcast operation needs multiple unicast transmissions to cover all neighbors according to their specific activity. To recover lost packets in case of acknowledgment absence, these approaches rely on piggybacking within data retransmission. This acknowledgment indicates to the sender that there was no collision or data-loss in the radio channel and the packet was successfully transmitted without fearing any collision or interference. In case of a data loss, the sender node tries to resend its packet according to its scheduling algorithm. Thus, for an increased reliability, loss recovery through data packet retransmissions sacrifices both latency and energy.

The authors aim to remedy to packet loss without performance penalties. They rely on collecting substantial information from neighboring nodes to decide whether a retransmission is necessary. Without reducing the reliability of packet delivery, the node has to piggyback the information about received data during the previous period in the beacon. To confirm the receipt of the message, each neighbor node has to include the sequence number and the source of its last received frame in its subsequent beacon. In this way, the sender node will be aware of the good reception of sent data frames. According to data importance, a sender node schedules a data retransmission. The sender node must also specify in the data packet header the data context, to invoke receiver to send an explicit acknowledgement in the beacon during the following period. This is required especially when nodes decrease the beacon transmission rate to reduce the control overhead.

Besides, reducing the risk of packet losses due to collisions contributes to improve reliability. The authors introduce some enhancements allowing subsequent nodes to schedule broadcasts according to neighbor implication in transmission, so that they do not interfere with each other. When a broadcast message is received for the first time, a node has to schedule a transmission for the message so that the message can be quickly delivered to its active neighbors. To resolve simultaneous forwarding operations by subsequent nodes, a source node must inform its immediate neighbors whether it will be involved in more duplicate transmissions to cover other remaining neighbors. To this end, it has to mark a specific field, noted 'more data' (set to 1), if it has scheduled more transmissions for the same packet. The subsequent node modifies its behavior to avoid throttling the sender transmissions. It will delay its current transmission, in such a way to schedule broadcasts without interfering with each other. To differentiate the treatment when sending a packet, a source node must compute a random backoff timer between zero and a predefined boundary B1, whereas, a subsequent neighbor generates a random backoff in the range of B1 to B2, with B1 < B2. As the random computed delay is decremented according to the defined unslotted CSMA/CA (Carrier Sense Multiple Access with Collision Avoidance), the authors assure that source node transmits before its neighbor nodes, which have already received its broadcasted packet. As such, the authors reduce the number of contending nodes for channel access and consequently reduce the risk of packet loss due to collision. A node also announces to its subsequent neighbors the number of waiting data packets, information used to compute the new scheduling by subsequent neighbors.

History Awareness

Context history may be relevant for many applications, based on periodic sensing and reporting data to the sink. For these applications, the sensor readings are collected at a constant sampling frequency then the gathered data will be forwarded towards the sink in a multi-hop fashion. The adoption of history for scheduling adjustment is inspired by recent research outcomes (Khader et al., 2009) suggesting that a forwarder node has to wake up and sleep "just at the right time," which is at the nominal arrival time of the next periodic packet minus some safety margin to avoid packet loss due to a late waking up. To this end, forwarder nodes have to acquire knowledge of the traffic period and its jitter in a distributed way. The authors adopt a similar approach in E-ECAB, where the source node indicates in the header of each packet the data context, mainly periodic or irregular traffic. For periodic traffic, the source can also specify the traffic periodicity. For periodic data, upon receiving a broadcast message, the node has to store the reception cycle associated to each source, in addition to the source ID and the traffic periodicity. With such information, the node will be able to compute the next expected cycle for the next data reception. At the end of each observation period, each node has to check if in the next observation period, a periodic traffic is planned and to take into account the eventual receptions and transmissions when computing the appropriate scheduling for the next period. The formula 4 is modified as follows:

$$Pa_{new} = PA_{\min} \cdot \left(1 - \frac{T_i}{T_i + T_b} + \frac{T_b}{T_i + T_b}\right) + Q.N.\Delta tx + SRCnbr.\left(Trx.Prednbr + Ttx\right) \qquad (5)$$

SRCnbr refers to the number of sources having periodic traffic during the next observation period, Prednbr is the number of predecessors, Trx is the reception time of one data packet and Ttx is the time of transmission.

ANALYTICAL STUDY

The broadcast count of both beacons and data transmissions, defined as the minimal number of transmissions of the same packet needed to cover all neighboring nodes, constitutes a main metric to measure the efficiency of a MAC broadcast protocol in duty-cycled environments. In this section, the authors discussed the upper bound of the one hop broadcast count while considering the three potential situations:

Situation 1: Nodes without neighborhood awareness
Situation 2: Nodes with neighborhood awareness
Situation 3: Novel source introduced in a network with neighborhood awareness

To reason about the broadcast count of these three situations, the authors have to prove the existence of an overlapping interval of time, noted l, between a source node S and its neighbors. As the broadcast operation involves all adjacent nodes, the length of the interval separating the wake-up time of the node that wakes up the last and the sleep time of the node that turns to sleep the first constitutes the period where the source can reach all neighbors for packet broadcast, which should satisfy the following constraints:

$$l \geq 1\, slot\, and\, l \leq PA\max \qquad (6)$$

Theorem 1: For nodes operating without neighborhood awareness, the one hop broadcast count for beacons transmission is equal to 2; while the one hop broadcast count for data transmission is equal to 1.

Lemma 1: When adopting the default scheduling at the deployment phase, it exists an interval of time in each cycle, where the source node and its neighboring nodes are active simultaneously.

Proof of Lemma 1: When considering a broadcast operation initiated by a source node, three cases can occur:

Case 1: The source node wakes up the last one among its neighbors, all immediate receivers are already awake

Case 2: The source node wakes up the first one among its neighbors and has to wait until the wake up of the latecomer node to transmit its packet.

Case 3: There are N1 and N2 two neighboring nodes of the source S where N1 wakes up the first node among the source neighbors and N2 the node that wakes up the last among the source neighbors.

As exposed above, the two worst cases for a broadcast operation triggered by a source S are relative to case 1 and case 2, where the source wakes up the first and has to wait the other neighbors awakening

Figure 2. Overlapping interval for case 1

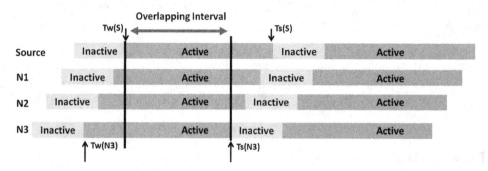

Figure 3. Overlapping interval for case 2

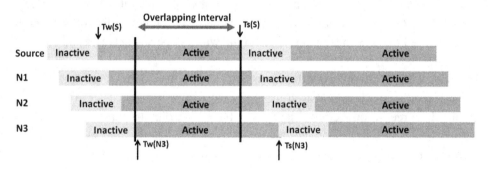

Figure 4. Overlapping interval for case 3

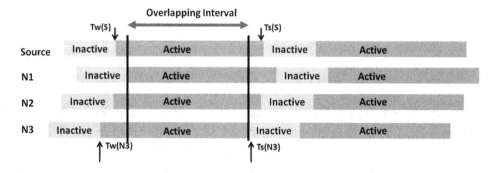

or the source wakes up the last and has lesser time for packet transmission. The authors have to prove the existence of one overlapping interval l, satisfying the constraints of equation (6). These two cases are discussed below:

Case 1: The source node wakes up the last one among its neighbors

The authors assume that the source node S wakes up at t =Tw(S) and turns to sleep at Ts(S). And, for each node N where N belongs to S neighborhood, they denote by Tw(N) the wake-up time of node N and Ts(N) the time when it turns to sleep.

At the deployment phase, all nodes lack knowledge about neighbors and their scheduling. To gather rapidly some relevant contextual information, each node adopts the default scheduling, allowing nodes to be active for a maximal active period PAmax and to sleep for a minimal inactive period PImin. Recall also that the authors assume that all nodes wake up initially within PImin interval. Thus, the interval separating the wake-up times of the source and the latecomer neighbor is equal to:

$$Tw(S) - Tw(N) \leq PI\min \tag{7}$$

The overlapping interval will be computed as follows:

$$l = Ts(N) - Tw(S) = \left[Tw(N) + PA\max\right] - Tw(S) \tag{8}$$

Since

$$Tw(S) - Tw(N) \leq PI\min$$

Then

$$Tw(N) - Tw(S) \geq -PI\min$$

$$Tw(N) - Tw(S) + PA\max \geq PA\max - PI\min$$

$$\left[Tw(N) + PA\max\right] - Tw(S) \geq PA\max - PI\min$$

$$Ts(N) - Tw(S) \geq PA\max - PI\min$$

$$l \geq PA\max - PI\min \tag{9}$$

Since

$$PA\max > 2PI\min$$

$$PA\max - PI\min > PI\min$$

Consequently

$$l > PI\min \tag{10}$$

Besides,

$$L - PA\max = Ts(N) - Tw(S) - PA\max$$
$$= [Tw(N) + PA\max] - Tw(S) - PA\max$$
$$= Tw(N) - Tw(S)$$

Since S wakes up after N, thus:

$$Tw(N) - tw(S) < 0$$

$$L - PA\max < 0$$

$$l < PA\max \tag{11}$$

Given (9) and (11), the authors proved that an overlapping interval l, which lasts at least $PA\max - PI\min$ and at most PAmax, exists allowing the source node to cover all its neighbors simultaneously.

Case 2: The source node wakes up the first one among its immediate neighbors.

As source wakes up the first among its neighbors, it has to wait until receiving the wakeup beacon of the latecomer neighbor to be able to reach all nodes with minimal transmissions:

$$l = Ts(S) - Tw(N) = [Tw(S) + PA\max] - Tw(N) \tag{12}$$

Similar to case 1, the authors pursue the same reasoning to prove the existence of an overlapping interval, among the activity periods of the source node and its neighbors, which extends over $PA\max - PI\min$ At least and PAmax at most, as shown in Figure 3.

Proof of Theorem 1: As E-ECAB adopts a receiver-based approach, each node should send a beacon upon its wake-up to inform its neighboring nodes. However, due to network asynchrony, only active nodes will receive this first beacon, while the still inactive ones will miss this transmission. At the deployment phase, each node must send other beacons to cover remaining neighbors to let them acquire neighborhood knowledge faster. To ensure the well reception of additional beacons by all its neighboring nodes while reducing the number of transmissions, a source node should send its beacons when a maximum number of neighbors are active. Based on *Lemma 1*, the authors proved that an overlapping interval exists, where the source and all one-hop nodes are active simultaneously. As inactive nodes will wake up at most after PImin, a source sends its second beacon after PImin period to reach all remaining neighbors. Consequently, the broadcast count for beacons transmission is 2.

For data packets, the aim is to assure the broadcast operation with a minimal number of transmissions. As all neighboring nodes are active simultaneously during the overlapping interval, broadcasting data during this interval is sufficient to be received by the intended receivers. Consequently, the broadcast count for data transmission is 1.

Theorem 2: Upon acquiring neighborhood awareness, the one hop broadcast count for beacons transmission is equal to 2 and the one hop broadcast count for data transmission is equal to 1.

Lemma 2: When operating with neighborhood knowledge, there is an interval of time, in each cycle, where the source node and its adjacent nodes are active simultaneously.

Proof of Lemma 2: E-ECAB adopts successive cycles with fixed length. Each cycle is arranged as two consecutive periods: an active period followed by an inactive period. After collecting enough information about neighbors' scheduling and observing their activities, nodes can adopt two possible schedules [PAmax; PImin] or [PAmin; PImax] to cope with current network state:

$$cycle = PA\max + PI\min = PA\min + PI\max \tag{13}$$

Even after n cycles with scheduling adjustment, the difference between wake-up times of the different nodes remains equal to PImin. In fact, during a giving cycle n $(n > 0)$, the authors assume that the source node wakes up at t = Tw[n](S) and turns to sleep at Ts[n](S) and they denote by Tw[n](N) the wake up time of any node N, belonging to S neighbors, and Ts[n](N) the time when it turns to sleep.

When the source wakes up the first among its neighbors or the last one, within PImin interval, constitutes the worst case for packet broadcast:

$$\left| Tw\big[0\big]\big(S\big) - Tw\big[0\big]\big(N\big) \right| \leq PI\min \tag{14}$$

Let note $Tw\big(S\big) = Tw\big[0\big]\big(S\big)$ and $Tw\big(N\big) = Tw\big[0\big]\big(N\big)$ the authors should prove by recurrence that $Tw\big[n\big]\big(S\big) - Tw\big[n\big]\big(N\big) = Tw\big(S\big) - Tw\big(N\big)$.

For $n=1$, nodes initially adopt default scheduling for at least 3 cycles, relative to the observation period, until acquiring enough neighborhood awareness, so we have:

$$Tw\big[1\big]\big(S\big) - Tw\big[1\big]\big(N\big) = \Big[Tw\big[0\big]\big(S\big) + PA\max + PI\min\Big] - \Big[Tw\big[0\big]\big(N\big) + PA\max + PI\min\Big]$$
$$= Tw\big[0\big]\big(S\big) - Tw\big[0\big]\big(N\big) = Tw\big(S\big) - Tw\big(N\big) \tag{15}$$
$$= PI\min$$

Let call *i* the cycle where nodes are aware about their scheduling. As the cycle length is fixed, the authors can prove by recurrence that:

$$
\begin{aligned}
Tw[i](S) - Tw[i](N) &= \\
&= \left[Tw[i-1](S) + PA\max + PI\min\right] - \left[Tw[i-1](N) + PA\max + PI\min\right] \\
&= Tw[i-1](S) - Tw[i-1](N) \\
&= \left[Tw[i-2](S) + PA\max + PI\min\right] - \left[Tw[i-2](N) + PA\max + PI\min\right] \\
&= ... = Tw(S) - Tw(N) = PI\min
\end{aligned}
\tag{16}
$$

As the assumption related to node wakeup within PImin interval is made for all nodes, the authors assume that for each cycle $n > 0$, $Tw[n](S) - Tw[n](N) = Tw(N1) - Tw(N2)$. where N1 and N2 belong to S neighborhood.

The authors have to demonstrate that the upper bound PImin is also valid for neighboring nodes wakeups; they consider the two possible scenarios among neighbors according to scheduling adjustment:

Case 1: Nodes N1 and N2 change their scheduling to [PAmin; PImax] during the cycle n, then the difference between their next wake up during the cycle $n+1$ is equal to:

$$
\begin{aligned}
Tw[n+1](N1) - Tw[n+1](N2) &= \\
&= \left(Tw[n](N1) + PA\min + PI\max\right) - \left(Tw[n](N2) + PA\min + PI\max\right) \\
&= Tw[n](N1) - Tw[n](N2) \\
&= \left(Tw[n](N1) + cycle\right) - \left(Tw[n](N2) + cycle\right) \\
&= ... = Tw(S) - Tw(N)
\end{aligned}
\tag{17}
$$

Case 2: Node N1 changes its scheduling to [PAmin; PImax] and the node N2 keeps the default scheduling during the cycle n, then the difference between their next wake up during the cycle $n+1$ is equal to:

$$
\begin{aligned}
Tw[n+1](N1) - Tw[n+1](N2) &= \\
&= \left(Tw[n](N1) + PA\min + PI\max\right) - \left(Tw[n](N2) + PA\max + PI\min\right) \\
&= \left(Tw[n](N1) + cycle\right) - \left(Tw[n](N2) + cycle\right) \\
&= Tw[n](N1) - Tw[n](N2) = Tw(S) - Tw(N) = PI\min
\end{aligned}
\tag{18}
$$

To compute the length of the overlapping interval, the best case is when all nodes keep the scheduling with maximal active period; in such situation, bounds proved in *theorem 1* are valid. The worst case, illustrated in Figure 5, is when all nodes are active for a minimal period by adopting the $\left[PA\min, PI\max\right]$ scheduling. Assuming N1 and N2 are two neighboring nodes of the source S, where N1 wakes up the last and N2 turns to sleep the first, the overlapping interval l is computed as follows:

$$
l = Ts(N1) - Tw(N2) = \left(Tw(N1) + PA\min\right) - Tw(N2)
\tag{19}
$$

Figure 5. Overlapping interval for the worst case

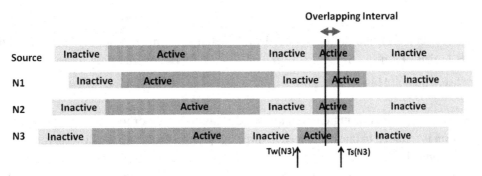

Since

$$Tw\big(N2\big) - Tw\big(N1\big) \le PI\min$$

Then

$$Tw\big(N1\big) - Tw\big(N2\big) \ge -PI\min$$

so

$$\big(Tw\big(N1\big) + PA\min\big) - Tw\big(N2\big) \ge PA\min - PI\min \; since \; PA\min > PI\min$$

Then

$$PA\min - PI\min > 0 \tag{20}$$

$$Ts\big(N1\big) - Tw\big(N2\big) - PA\min = \big(Tw\big(N1\big) + PA\min\big) - Tw\big(N2\big) - PA\min = Tw\big(N1\big) - Tw\big(N2\big)$$

Since node N1 wakes up before node N2, thus:

$$Tw\big(N1\big) - Tw\big(N2\big) < 0$$

Then

$$Ts\big(N1\big) - Tw\big(N2\big) - PA\min < 0$$

$$Ts\big(N1\big) - Tw\big(N2\big) < PA\min \tag{21}$$

Based on (20) and (21), the authors proved the existence of an overlapping interval bounded by PAmin and $PA\min - PI\min$. Since $PA\min - PI\min > 0$, the overlapping interval length will be, in the worst case, equal at least to one slot.

Proof of Theorem 2: After acquiring enough knowledge about neighborhood, the frequency of beacons transmission is reduced to one beacon each three cycles upon wake up to alleviate the network from additional control packets. However, each node has to notify all its immediate neighbors in case of scheduling adjustment. Sharing such updates allows adjacent nodes to keep accurate information about neighbors scheduling and to be able to send broadcast packets appropriately during the right overlapping interval. Hence, as the authors mentioned in the previous proof, to rapidly notify active neighbors a first beacon is sent upon node wake up. Then, to notify the remaining neighbors, the given node must send another beacon during the overlapping interval where all neighboring nodes are active simultaneously, as proved in *Lemma 2*. Hence, a beacon sent during this interval can be received by all the neighbors. Consequently, the broadcast count for beacons transmission is 2.

For data packets, based on *Lemma 2*, the authors proved that there is an interval of time where neighboring nodes are active at the same time. So, it is sufficient to broadcast data packet, once, within this interval.

Theorem 3: *The one hop broadcast count for beacons and data transmission in the case of a novel source introduced in a network with neighborhood awareness is equal to 3.*

Proof of Theorem 3: When a source node is newly introduced in the network, its neighboring nodes are either adopting $\big[PA\max, PI\min\big]$ or $\big[PA\min, PI\max\big]$ scheduling. At source wake up, neighboring nodes are either active or inactive:

- If all the neighbors are active, a transmission upon waking up can reach all of them.
- If all its neighbors are inactive, two cases arise:
  - **Case 1:** Nodes adopting $\big[PA\max, PI\min\big]$ will wake up at most after PImin. So, in this case: $Tw\big(N\big) - Tw\big(S\big) < PI\min$.
  - **Case 2:** Nodes adopting $\big[PA\min, PI\max\big]$ will wake up at most after PImax. So, in this case: $Tw\big(N\big) - Tw\big(S\big) < PI\max$

Thus, the source node must send 3 beacons to ensure the well reception by all the neighbors: the first beacon is sent upon wakeup, the second one after PImin and the third one after PImax. To reach all its neighbors, such novel source has to send its data packets three times.

EVALUATION

To highlight the efficiency of context-awareness in optimizing duty-cycled network performances for broadcasting operations, the authors conducted extensive simulations using the OMNET++ simulator (Varga, 2010) under various network settings. To quantify the improvements brought by context-awareness, we compare E-ECAB against ADB, a receiver-based duty-cycle mechanism relying on unicast transmissions for broadcast operations and delegation rule based on link quality. To highlight the enhancements incorporated into E-ECAB, we evaluate 3 versions of ECAB: (1) two variants of ECAB using only neighborhood awareness: ECAB-MAX, adopting the scheduling $[PA\max, PI\min]$ and ECAB-MIN working with $[PA\min, PI\max]$ scheduling to point out the impact of traffic load awareness (2) ECAB exploiting mainly neighborhood and traffic load awareness.

The authors focus on the following criteria during the evaluation phase:

- **Energy Consumption:** The average energy consumed per node during the simulation time.
- **Consumed Energy per Packet:** The average energy consumed by the entire network to deliver a data packet to its destination. It represents the average consumed energy per node divided by the total number of received packets.
- **Broadcast Latency:** The elapsed time from the instant of the data packet generation until its reception time.
- **Packet Delivery Ratio:** The percentage of successfully delivered packets to the sink (without counting redundancy) over the total number of sent data packets.
- **Control Overhead:** The signalling overhead during the entire simulation, which includes beacon frames transmitted from all nodes and the acknowledgments required by unicast transmissions for ADB.

The simulations mainly focus on two scenarios inspired from real applications:

1. For event-driven applications, traffic is generated right upon the event happening. This event can excite many neighboring nodes and trigger flooding throughout the whole network. Each node within the circle of center (x,y) and with radius Rs (sensing range) should send one packet to the sink to report the event. To vary the degree of workload, the authors varied Rs in order to increase the number of source nodes in the target area.
2. For applications relying on periodic sensing and reporting towards the sink, sensor sources send periodically packets to the sink. To simulate this case, many sources are scattered in the network, flooding periodically a data packet towards the sink.

To simulate different degrees of workload in the network, the authors start first by fixing one source of periodic traffic while varying the data generation periodicity. In a second step, they vary the number of sources while fixing the traffic generation rate to 1 packet each 10 cycles for each source. For the scenario inspired from event-driven applications, the authors generate an event each 10 cycles. For the second scenario, source nodes, scattered in the network, generate periodically a data packet each 10 cycles at different times.

Table 1. Simulation parameters

Parameter	Value
Transmission range	10m
$(PA_{max}, PA_{min}, PI_{max}, PI_{min})$	(7, 3, 6, 2) slots
Slot duration	0.000556s
Battery capacity	10 mAh
(Rxpower, txpower, sleep)	(15, 20, 0,03) mA

For the two scenarios, the authors generate several topologies with 200 nodes, uniformly distributed in a simulation area 180m*70m.The Table 1 resumes the parameters adopted during the evaluation phase:

Figure 6 exposes the impact of the variation of traffic generation rate for a single source, while Figures 12 and 13 portray the impact of data load variation, due to the increase of sources, on delivery ratio. E-ECAB achieves higher throughput than the other protocols. E-ECAB adjusts efficiently its scheduling to cope with the load variation. In fact, as expected, the knowledge of traffic pattern successfully enhances the delivery ratio, since E-ECAB predicts the incoming periodic traffic arrivals and each node adopts the appropriate scheduling required to transfer as soon as possible the broadcast traffic.

Even in loaded environment, network activity awareness and traffic pattern usage allow nodes to cope with traffic load changes by adjusting beforehand dynamically the scheduling to [PA_{max}, PI_{min}] when required, behaving like ECAB-MAX. The flooding process becomes less effective with ADB due to collisions and node congestion. When using ADB in heavy traffic condition, data packets will be blocked at the sending queue, as contention for medium access increases among neighboring nodes. ADB relies

Figure 6. Throughput as a function of the traffic generation rate (number of cycles)

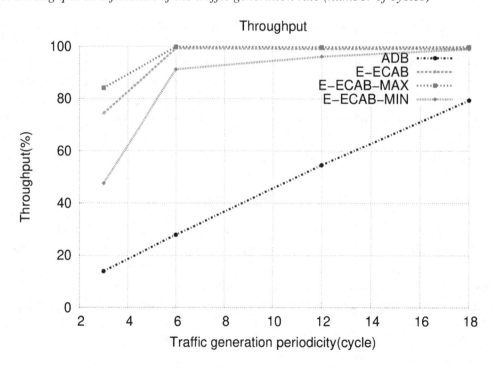

Figure 7. Control overhead as a function of the traffic generation rate (number of cycles)

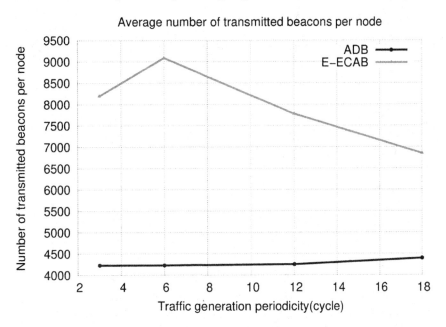

Figure 8. Energy consumption as a function of the traffic generation rate (number of cycles)

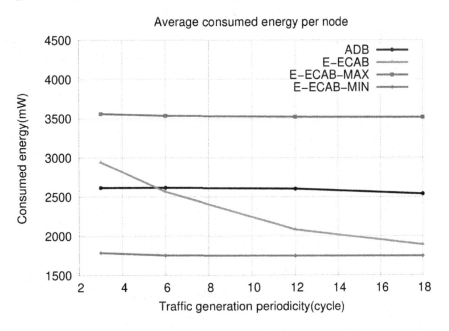

on multi unicast transmissions to reach all neighbors. The broadcast storm, resulting from simultaneous transmissions from neighboring nodes excited by the same event (Figure 12), increases contention and collisions in the network. Besides, the traffic control load throttles data packets forwarding, as exposed on Figures 7, 14 and 15. In ADB, each node has to send a beacon upon wake-up to notify its immediate neighbors to send pending packets. Besides, each unicast transmission must be acknowledged, these

Figure 9. Consumed energy per packet as a function of the traffic generation rate (number of cycles)

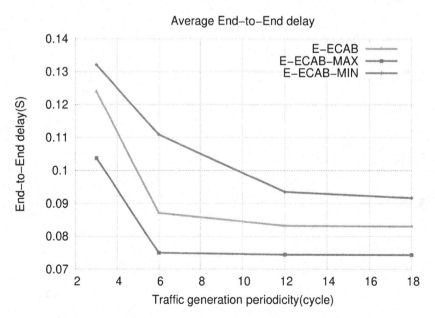

Figure 10. Broadcast latency as a function of the traffic generation rate (number of cycles)

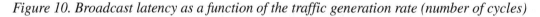

acknowledgments constitute a heavy signaling overhead, increasing with traffic load and with network density. As portrayed on Figures 7, 14 and 15, the authors notice the effectiveness of ECAB and E-ECAB in reducing the control overhead. In fact, once the required context knowledge is acquired, each node reduces the transmission of beacons to alleviate network from additional overhead. This tacitly leaves more bandwidth for data packets, which explains that E-ECAB and its variants deliver more data packets than ADB.

Figure 11. Broadcast latency compared to ADB as a function of the traffic generation rate (number of cycles)

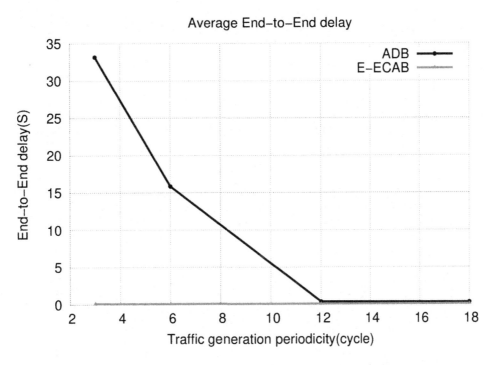

Figure 12. Throughput as a function of the number of sources (case scattered sources)

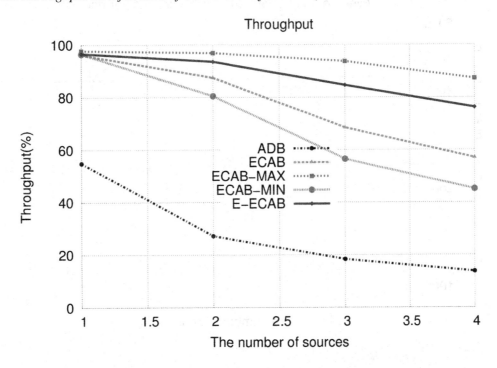

Figure 13. Throughput as a function of the number of sources (case neighboring sources)

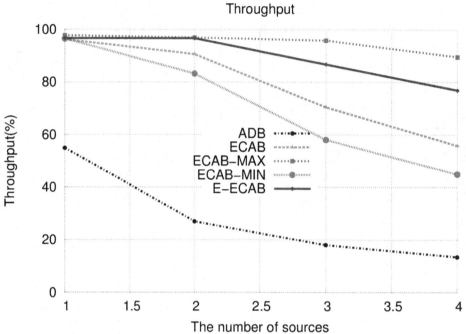

Figure 14. Control overhead (case scattered sources)

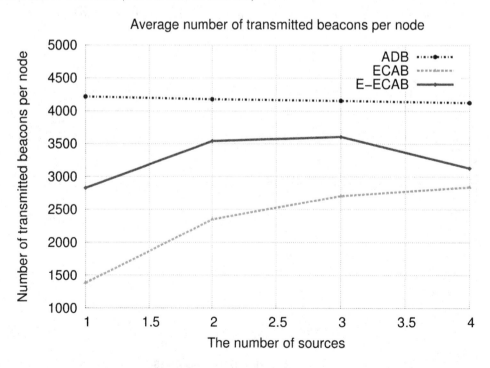

Figure 15. Control overhead (case neighboring sources)

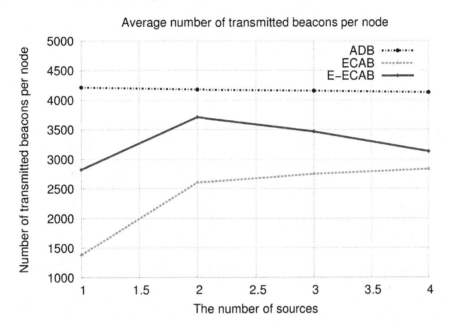

Thank to this behavior, E-ECAB and all its variants achieve a reduced end-to-end delay, as it is shown on Figures 10, 11, 16 and 17. E-ECAB and ECAB-MAX outperform the other protocols because they follow the scheduling $[PA_{max}, PI_{min}]$, allowing nodes to handle more efficiently burst traffic and congestion situations. In fact, nodes have enough time to forward pending data packets towards subsequent nodes, instead of waiting for neighbor's wake-up. Although E-ECAB and ECAB-MAX spend more

Figure 16. End-to-end Delay (case scattered sources)

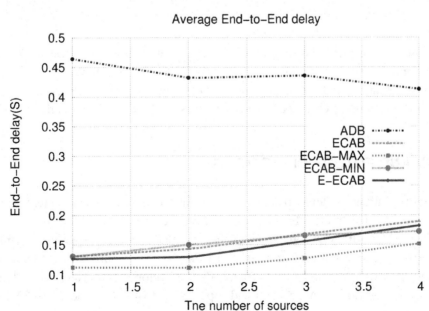

Figure 17. End-to-end Delay (case neighboring sources)

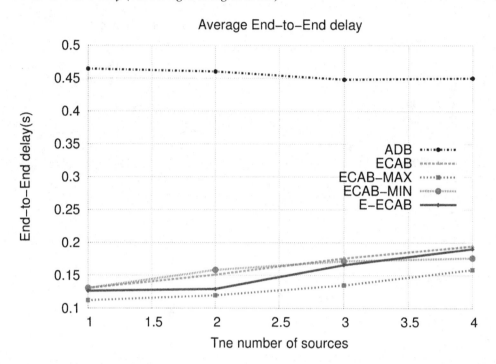

time in active mode than ECAB and ECAB-MIN, E-ECAB substantially outperforms ECAB-MAX in terms of reduced energy. The ability of E-ECAB to adjust more efficiently node scheduling to meet the traffic requirements also contributes to reduce energy consumption by allowing nodes to adopt [PA_{min}, PI_{max}] whenever they are not involved in communication or do not expect traffic arrivals. As portrayed in Figures 8, 18 and 19, energy consumption per node is slightly lower for E-ECAB than ECAB-MAX, especially for low data loads due to the better management of network resources and the efficient use of gathered contextual information. Besides, the additional mechanisms introduced by E-ECAB contribute in reducing the number of contending candidates for medium access and the risk of collision between data packets in case of subsequent transmissions. Results on energy consumption per packet are portrayed on Figures 9, 20 and 21. These results consolidate that E-ECAB outperforms others in achieving the best trade-off between throughput and energy. With ADB, a lot of energy is consumed due to redundant transmissions and receptions by each node, which explains the higher values obtained.

DISCUSSION AND FUTURE DIRECTIONS

As context-awareness allows systems to adapt their operations to the current context without explicit user intervention, many MAC protocols can be considered as context-aware MAC protocols, called also adaptive MAC protocols. Although context-awareness is a maturing area in pervasive computing, only few work devoted to the concept of context-awareness in WSNs were reported in the literature. With such paradigm, sensors are no longer considered as context data collectors, sensor can exploit some contextual information to adjust their functional behavior and cope with network dynamics. In WSNs, context data

Figure 18. Consumed energy per node (case scattered sources)

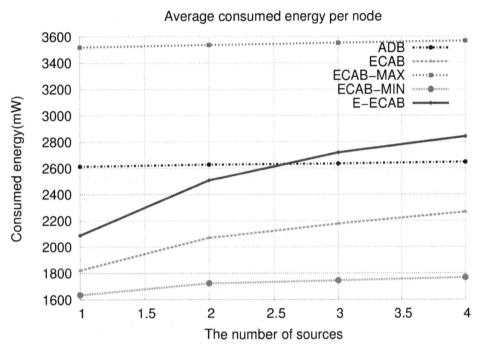

Figure 19. Consumed energy per node (case neighboring sources)

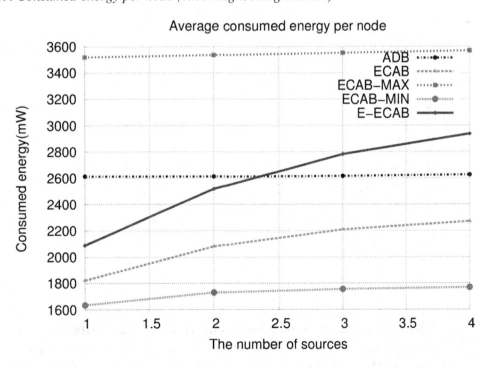

Figure 20. Consumed energy per packet (case scattered sources)

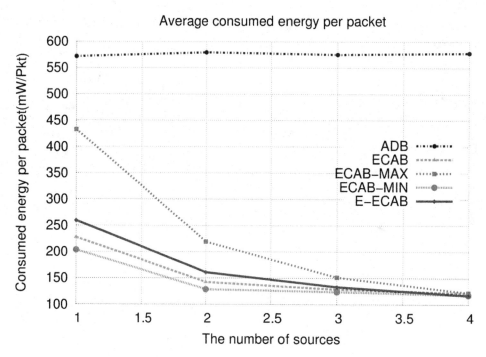

Figure 21. Consumed energy per packet (case neighboring sources)

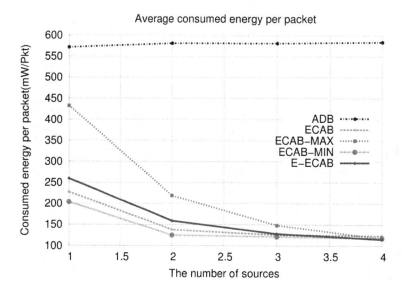

can include some parameters related to the node such as its residual energy, traffic rate, queue length, observed traffic load, its localization, other information related to its neighborhood and preferences related to the application requirements such as QoS (Quality of service). In fact, contextual information can be incorporated at the different stack layers of the wireless node to achieve diverse objectives. Exploiting such awareness at MAC level can be relevant to enhance poor performances, due to unreliable wireless links, node connectivity and network topology changes over time, mainly under duty-cycling operation mode (Ghrab et al., 2018). Some approaches were proposed to deal with unicast transmissions in such environments while adopting an adaptive duty-cycle to optimize energy or latency. Proposed broadcast MAC protocols focus mainly on reducing latency while relying on little contextual information.

Most of the duty-cycle MAC protocols, proposed in literature, rely on predefined sets of contexts, where energy, link quality (Sun et al., 2009), and neighborhood knowledge (Xu et al., 2018, Sun et al., 2009), are main used ones to mainly adjust the node scheduling or to adapt its behavior. For a flooding operation, all nodes are involved and must retransmit received packets in case of flooding. Each node must cooperate and participate in this flooding process even if its residual energy is critic. Thus, other contexts, besides energy, may be more relevant to enhance the multi-hop broadcast operation in a duty-cycled WSN. In addition to local contexts related to energy or transmission rate, many gathered or inferred contexts are still under-utilized or unexploited which may be pertinent to explore for duty-cycled networks. Simple prediction mechanisms, relying on neighbor scheduling knowledge or traffic load (Duan et al., 2015, Ghrab et al., 2015), were proposed to adjust node wake-up in order to reduce latency or energy consumption. History context may be a powerful mean to retrieve traffic pattern and the evolution of network conditions over time in order to anticipate the appropriate behavior (Jemili et al., 2017, Aby et al., 2015). Only few proposals exploit full awareness from multi-contextual information (Jemili et al., 2017, Dong et al., 2017), increasing consequently usability, effectiveness and scalability.

In addition, even for unicast transmission, a cross layer approach is highly recommended to optimize routing as well as channel access in such constrained networks. Interaction among layers allows a better understanding of the current context, thanks to local and gathered information about the sensor node and its environment, to adjust appropriately protocols behavior. For example, neighbor's activities knowledge provides required information to routing layer for best next hop selection among active ones to allow a fluid transfer, while residual energy and link quality can help MAC layer for packet transmission. Coping context-awareness with energy harvesting solutions may be fruitful for some IoT applications.

ACKNOWLEDGMENT

This work was financially supported by the PHC Utique program of the French Ministry of Foreign Affairs and Ministry of higher education and research and the Tunisian Ministry of higher education and scientific research in the CMCU project number 17G1417.

REFERENCES

Abowd, G. D., Dey, A. K., Brown, P. J., Davies, N., Smith, M., & Steggles, P. (1999). Towards a better understanding of context and context-awareness. In *Proceedings of the 1st International Symposium on Handheld and Ubiquitous Computing*, Karlsruhe, Germany, September 27–29 (pp. 304–307). Springer-Verlag. 10.1007/3-540-48157-5_29

Aby, A. T., Guitton, A., Lafourcade, P., & Misson, M. (2015, September). SLACK-MAC: Adaptive MAC protocol for low duty-cycle wireless sensor networks. In *International Conference on Ad Hoc Networks, San Remo, Italy*. Cham: Springer. 10.1007/978-3-319-25067-0_6

Agoulmine, N., Balasubramaniam, S., Botvich, D., Strassner, J., Lehtihet, E., & Donnelly, W. (2006). Challenges for autonomic network management.

Alfayez, F., Hammoudeh, M., & Abuarqoub, A. (2015). A Survey on MAC Protocols for Duty-cycled Wireless Sensor Networks. *Procedia Computer Science*, *73*, 482–489. doi:10.1016/j.procs.2015.12.034

Borges, V., & Jeberson, W. (2013). Survey of context information fusion for sensor networks based ubiquitous systems. arXiv:1309.0598

Cao, Z., Liu, D., Wang, J., & Zheng, X. (2017). Chase: Taming concurrent broadcast for flooding in asynchronous duty cycle networks. *IEEE/ACM Transactions on Networking*, *25*(5), 2872–2885. doi:10.1109/TNET.2017.2712671

Cao, Z., Wang, J., Liu, D., Miao, X., Ma, Q., & Mao, X. (2018). Chase++: Fountain-Enabled Fast Flooding in Asynchronous Duty Cycle Networks. In *IEEE Conference on Computer Communications INFOCOM 2018*, Honolulu, HI. IEEE.

Carrano, R. C., Passos, D., Magalhaes, L. C., & Albuquerque, C. V. (2014). Survey and taxonomy of duty cycling mechanisms in wireless sensor networks. *IEEE Communications Surveys and Tutorials*, *16*(1), 181–194. doi:10.1109/SURV.2013.052213.00116

Cheng, L., Niu, J., Luo, C., Shu, L., Kong, L., Zhao, Z., & Gu, Y. (2018). Towards minimum-delay and energy-efficient flooding in low-duty-cycle wireless sensor networks. *Computer Networks*, *134*, 66–77. doi:10.1016/j.comnet.2018.01.012

De, D., Tang, S., Song, W. Z., Cook, D., & Das, S. K. (2012). ActiSen: Activity-aware sensor network in smart environments. *Pervasive and Mobile Computing*, *8*(5), 730–750. doi:10.1016/j.pmcj.2011.12.005

Dinh, T., Kim, Y., Gu, T., & Vasilakos, A. V. (2016). L-MAC: A wake-up time self-learning MAC protocol for wireless sensor networks. *Computer Networks*, *105*, 33–46. doi:10.1016/j.comnet.2016.05.015

Dong, C. & Yu, F. (2017). A prediction-based asynchronous MAC protocol for heavy traffic load in wireless sensor networks. *International Journal of Electronics and Communications*.

Duan, R., Fang, D., & Chen, X. (2015, August). A wakeup adapting traffic and receiver-initiated duty cycle protocol for wsn. In *2015 IEEE Ubiquitous Intelligence and Computing and 2015 IEEE 12th Intl Conf on Autonomic and Trusted Computing and 2015 IEEE 15th Intl Conf on Scalable Computing and Communications and Its Associated Workshops (UIC-ATC-ScalCom)*, Beijing, China (pp. 1753-1759). IEEE. 10.1109/UIC-ATC-ScalCom-CBDCom-IoP.2015.318

Duc, T. L., Le, D. T., Zalyubovskiy, V. V., Kim, D. S., & Choo, H. (2017). Towards broadcast redundancy minimization in duty-cycled wireless sensor networks. *International Journal of Communication Systems*, *30*(6), e3108. doi:10.1002/dac.3108

Ganz, F., Barnaghi, P., Carrez, F., & Moessner, K. (2011, July). Context-aware management for sensor networks. In *Proceedings of the 5th International Conference on Communication System software and middleware*, Verona, Italy (p. 6). ACM.

Ghrab, D., Jemili, I., Belghith, A., & Mosbah, M. (2015, August). ECAB: An Efficient Context-Aware multi-hop Broadcasting protocol for wireless sensor networks. In *2015 International Wireless Communications and Mobile Computing Conference (IWCMC)*, Dubrovnik, Croatia (pp. 1023-1029). IEEE. 10.1109/IWCMC.2015.7289223

Ghrab, D., Jemili, I., Belghith, A., & Mosbah, M. (2016, April). Study of context-awareness efficiency applied to duty-cycled wireless sensor networks. In *2016 IEEE Wireless Communications and Networking Conference (WCNC)*, Doha (pp. 1-6). IEEE. 10.1109/WCNC.2016.7564865

Ghrab, D., Jemili, I., Belghith, A., & Mosbah, M. (2018). Context-aware MAC protocols in Wireless Sensor Networks. *Internet Technologies Letters, e43.*

Guo, S., He, L., Gu, Y., Jiang, B., & He, T. (2014). Opportunistic flooding in low-duty-cycle wireless sensor networks with unreliable links. *IEEE Transactions on Computers, 63*(11), 2787–2802. doi:10.1109/TC.2013.142

Jemili, I., Ghrab, D., Belghith, A., & Mosbah, M. (2017). Context-aware broadcast in duty-cycled wireless sensor networks. *International Journal on Semantic Web and Information Systems, 13*(3), 48–67. doi:10.4018/IJSWIS.2017070103

Jennings, B., Van Der Meer, S., Balasubramaniam, S., Botvich, D., Foghlú, M. Ó., Donnelly, W., & Strassner, J. (2007). Towards autonomic management of communications networks. *IEEE Communications Magazine, 45*(10), 112–121. doi:10.1109/MCOM.2007.4342833

Khader, O., Willig, A., & Wolisz, A. (2009, May). Distributed wakeup scheduling scheme for supporting periodic traffic in wsns. In *Wireless Conference, 2009. EW 2009. European*, Leipzig, Germany (pp. 287-292). IEEE. 10.1109/EW.2009.5357978

Le, D. T., Le Duc, T., Zalyubovskiy, V. V., Kim, D. S., & Choo, H. (2017). Collision-tolerant broadcast scheduling in duty-cycled wireless sensor networks. *Journal of Parallel and Distributed Computing, 100*, 42–56. doi:10.1016/j.jpdc.2016.10.006

Makris, P., Skoutas, D. N., & Skianis, C. (2013). A survey on context-aware mobile and wireless networking: On networking and computing environments' integration. *IEEE Communications Surveys and Tutorials, 15*(1), 362–386. doi:10.1109/SURV.2012.040912.00180

Morshed, S., Baratchi, M., & Heijenk, G. (2016, March). Traffic-adaptive duty cycle adaptation in TR-MAC protocol for Wireless Sensor Networks. In *Wireless Days (2016 WD)* (pp. 1–6). Toulouse, France: IEEE. doi:10.1109/WD.2016.7461501

Morshed, S., & Heijenk, G. (2014, September). TR-MAC: An energy-efficient MAC protocol exploiting transmitted reference modulation for wireless sensor networks. In *Proceedings of the 17th ACM international conference on Modeling, analysis and simulation of wireless and mobile systems*, Montreal, Canada (pp. 21-29). ACM. 10.1145/2641798.2641804

Perera, C., Zaslavsky, A., Christen, P., & Georgakopoulos, D. (2014). Context aware computing for the internet of things: A survey. *IEEE Communications Surveys and Tutorials, 16*(1), 414–454. doi:10.1109/SURV.2013.042313.00197

Salber, D., Dey, A. K., & Abowd, G. D. (1998). *Ubiquitous Computing: Defining an Hci Research Agenda for an Emerging Interaction Paradigm.* Atlanta, GA: Georgia Institute of Technology.

Singh, R., Rai, B. K., & Bose, S. K. (2017). A joint routing and MAC protocol for transmission delay reduction in many-to-one communication paradigm for wireless sensor networks. *IEEE Internet of Things Journal, 4*(4), 1031–1045. doi:10.1109/JIOT.2017.2724762

Sun, Y., Gurewitz, O., Du, S., Tang, L., & Johnson, D. B. (2009, November). ADB: an efficient multihop broadcast protocol based on asynchronous duty-cycling in wireless sensor networks. In *Proceedings of the 7th ACM Conference on Embedded Networked Sensor Systems*, Berkeley, CA (pp. 43-56). ACM. 10.1145/1644038.1644044

Sun, Y., Gurewitz, O., & Johnson, D. B. (2008, November). RI-MAC: a receiver-initiated asynchronous duty-cycle MAC protocol for dynamic traffic loads in wireless sensor networks. In *Proceedings of the 6th ACM conference on Embedded network sensor systems.* Raleigh, NC (pp. 1-14). ACM. 10.1145/1460412.1460414

Taherkordi, A., Rouvoy, R., Le-Trung, Q., & Eliassen, F. (2008, December). A self-adaptive context processing framework for wireless sensor networks. In *Proceedings of the 3rd international workshop on Middleware for sensor networks.* Oslo, Norway (pp. 7-12). ACM. 10.1145/1462698.1462700

Tong, F., & Pan, J. (2017). ADC: An adaptive data collection protocol with free addressing and dynamic duty-cycling for sensor networks. *Mobile Networks and Applications, 22*(5), 983–994. doi:10.100711036-017-0850-9

Varga, A. (2010). *OMNeT++ User Manual, Version 4.1.* Retrieved from www.omnetpp.org

Wang, G., Yu, J., Yu, D., Yu, H., Feng, L., & Liu, P. (2015). DS-MAC: An Energy Efficient Demand Sleep MAC Protocol with Low Latency for Wireless Sensor Networks. *Journal of Network and Computer Applications, 58*, 155–164. doi:10.1016/j.jnca.2015.09.007

Xu, L., Yang, G., Xu, J., Wang, L., & Dai, H. (2018). Achieving adaptive broadcasting performance tradeoff for energy-critical sensor networks: A bottom-up approach. *Computer Networks, 136*, 155–170. doi:10.1016/j.comnet.2018.03.007

Chapter 8
An Efficient Recursive Localization Approach for High–Density Wireless Sensor Networks

Badia Bouhdid
University of Manouba, Tunisia

Wafa Akkari
University of Manouba, Tunisia

Abdelfettah Belghith
King Saud University, Saudi Arabia

Sofien Gannouni
King Saud University, Saudi Arabia

ABSTRACT

Although recursive localization approaches are efficiently used in wireless sensor networks (WSNs), their application leads to increased energy consumption caused by the important communication overhead necessary to achieve the localization task. Indeed, localization information coverage increases iteratively as new nodes estimate their locations and become themselves new reference nodes. However, the uncontrollable number evolution of such nodes leads, especially in high density networks, to wasted energy, important communication overhead and even impacts the localization accuracy due the adverse effects of error propagation and accumulation. This chapter proposes an efficient recursive localization (ERL) approach that develops a new reliable reference selection strategy to ensure a better distribution of the reference nodes in the network. ERL improves localization accuracy without incurring any additional cost. It allows conserving the energy and consequently prolonging the WSN life time.

DOI: 10.4018/978-1-5225-7186-5.ch008

Copyright © 2019, IGI Global. Copying or distributing in print or electronic forms without written permission of IGI Global is prohibited.

INTRODUCTION

A Wireless Sensor Network (WSN) is a collection of tiny sensor nodes with non-rechargeable batteries (Sivakumar et al., 2018) and typically equipped with processing, sensing, power management and communication capabilities. These sensor nodes collaborate to form a Wireless Sensor Network (WSN). The essential objective of WSN is to observe, assemble and process the knowledge of sensor nodes within the network scope (Kaur et al., 2015). With the significant development and deployment of WSNs, associating the sensed data with its physical locations becomes a crucial requirement for different applications such as object tracking, environment monitoring, healthcare, intrusion detection, and habitat monitoring among others (Chow et al., 2018). Indeed, accurate positional information of the nodes also helps acquiring the value of location tagged parameters such as pressure, temperature, humidity and geographic coordinates from a given site (Pandey et al., 2017).

The simplest technique to localize a sensor node is to equip it with a Global Positioning System (GPS). However, its high cost and increased energy consumption makes it difficult to install in every node (Belghith et al., 2008), (Belghith et al., 2009) (Bouhdid et al., 2017). To overcome this weakness, other techniques, called collaborative localization techniques, were proposed (Niculescu et al., 2001), (Oliveira et al., 2009), (Ding et al., 2012), (Gui et al., 2015), (Li et al., 2015), (Ahmadi et al., 2016), (Darakech et al., 2018), (Bouhdid et al., 2018). They rely on the idea that sensor nodes with unknown locations (un-localized nodes) are guided by one or more sensor nodes with already known locations (either from GPS or by direct manual placement) for position estimation. The latter are called anchors or beacons. Based on the received information, the un-localized sensor nodes can compute their coordinates using distance measuring techniques (ranging techniques) (Paul et al., 2017). However, it is noticed that increasing the anchors number would also increase the deployment cost of the network (Mahjri et al., 2016). Moreover, these anchor nodes will also deplete their energy very quickly, which will drastically reduce the network lifetime and affect the network performance. Consequently, localization methods are designed such that the number of anchor nodes are reduced and explore instead and further the cooperation between nodes to enhance the localization (position) accuracy. One of the main cooperative approaches is the recursive localization approach, such as the Recursive Position Estimation (RPE) (Albowicz et al., 2001), where a node estimates its location based on the position information of three reference nodes. Once its position is estimated, it broadcasts its own location information to assist other nodes in estimating their positions. RPE makes full use of the connectivity of the network, and requires few anchors with the obvious advantages of simple localization method and easy realization.

Nevertheless, in such cooperative approaches, additional operational costs should be highlighted and investigated such as the amount of required communication overhead (signaling traffic) to exchange location data, the power consumption required to complete node localization, the time taken for the convergence of the localization algorithm, and resources (storage and computing) required to compute the positions of the different nodes within the network.

Motivation

Despite the importance of these additional operational costs that may negatively impact the network performances, they remain unexplored. In fact, most of the WSN localization approaches mainly focus rather on checking the localizability of a network and/or how to localize as many nodes as possible with high accuracy given a static and/or mobile set of anchors and distance measurements without considering the operational cost (individual cost, per node or the whole network localization cost) of the considered localization approach. These costs amount to how much expensive is to carry out the localization, and it is often motivated by realistic application requirements. Recently, as it is the case in (Halder et al., 2016), (Klogo et al., 2013) and (Paul et al., 2017) localization has been intensively dealt with by researchers for its contradictive goals. They have focused on how to tackle the problem of minimizing energy consumption, communication overhead as well as maintaining localization precision. Moreover, authors pointed out some factors that influence a localization approach and presented an overview on new challenges and metrics to be carried out in future research. For example, energy management in Wireless Sensor Networks is unavoidable issue in the application of WSN. To guarantee efficiency and durability in a network, the localization system must go beyond hardware solutions and seek alternative software solutions that allow the implementation of a better energy conservation strategy.

Contributions

This work revisits the Recursive Position Estimation (RPE) localization approach and proposes novel ways to optimize the aforementioned costs. To address these issues, this work aims to improve the functioning of RPE and propose an Efficient Recursive Localization approach (for) WSNs. In our approach, each unlocalized node estimates its location using three reference nodes. After estimating its localization, a localized node can be considered as a new reference node in the network. Practically, a high declared number of reference nodes are not desirable. For this reason, ERL implements a reference selection strategy to reduce the adverse effects of error propagation and accumulation, and to conserve the residual energy of the sensor nodes. The implemented strategy aims to provide suitably accurate results (relative to RPE) in a simple and decentralized way, with low communication overhead and time latency. Whilst requiring few number of anchors, and allowing incremental addition of nodes to serve and act as additional anchors in the network.

The reminder of the chapter is organized as follows. Section 2 introduces the Sensor Network Localization Problem. Section 3 presents the related works, analyzes its advantages and discusses their costs in terms of energy consumption, time latency, communication overhead and location accuracy. In section 4, the proposed solution is described in detail. Section 5 presents the performance evaluation of our contribution and its comparison to the original RPE algorithm by means of extensive simulations using OMNet++. Finally, conclusion is provided in section 5.

SENSOR NETWORK LOCALIZATION PROBLEM (SNLP)

In WSN the localization problem consists of identifying a node location with respect to a set of known reference positions. It is also referred to as location estimation or positioning. In this section we will introduce the main components of a localization system, and define the problem statement.

Localization System in WSNs

The localization process of sensor nodes in the network is bootstrapped with some input data. The most common input data are the location of a set of anchors. Other inputs are needed such the connectivity information, and the distances and or angle estimations between nodes in the network. All these inputs are exploited by the localization system with the main objective to determine the location of all sensor nodes residing within the network. These locations vary from absolute, to relative locations according to the need of the application (Risteska et al., 2016).

The localization system can be divided as proposed by (Boukreche et al., 2007) into three components: distance/angel estimation, this component is responsible for estimating the information about the distances and/or angles between sensor nodes. Conjointly with anchors positions this information will be used for the node position computation (second component) using computation methods. These two components are assisted by the localization algorithm component which determines how the available information will be manipulated in order to allow most or all of the nodes of a WSN to estimate their positions.

Distance/Angel Estimation

This estimation often relies on physical measurements, depending on the available hardware capabilities to determine angel and/or distance between two sensor nodes. On the other hand, network connectivity information, such as hop count, or neighborhood information, can lead to coarse-grained localization that may be sufficient in dense networks. As illustrated in Figure 1, according to the dependency of range measurement techniques for distance estimation, localization schemes can be classified into two main categories: range-based schemes and range-free schemes.

Position Computation

With enough information about distances and/or angles and positions of anchors or neighbors, an un-localized node can compute its own position using one of the computation methods. Such methods include trilateration, multi-lateration, triangulation, probabilistic approaches, bounding box. The choice of which method to use also impacts the final performance of the localization system. Such a choice depends on the information available and the processor limitations.

Localization Algorithm

This component explores the received data from the two other components to cover the rest of the network, by leading the localized nodes to help other un-localized nodes (cooperative localization) to estimate their positions, or by sending the collected location data of each unknown node to a central unit to perform the position computation (centralized localization). On the other hand, each node can independently determine its location with only limited communications with one-hop or multi-hop neighbor nodes (distributed localization).

Problem Statement

Consider a network N in real two dimensional space consisting of a set P of n points $p_i \in R^2$ *(i=1, ..., n)*, each point p_i can be:

- Anchor node: $a_k \in R^2, k = 1 \ldots m$

Figure 1. Localization system: Overview of measurement techniques

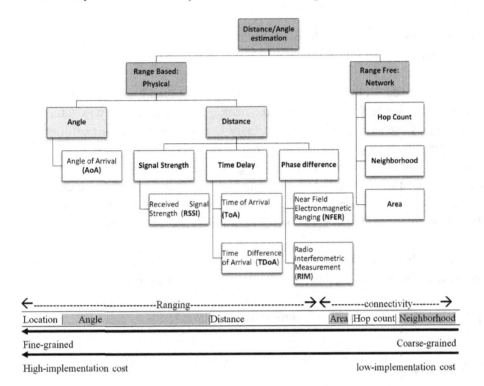

- Un-localized node: $u_i \in R^d, i = m + 1 \ldots n$

Each node p_i is located at a fixed position in R^2 and associates with a specific set of neighboring nodes within some specified transmission range r. For each point p_i P (i= 1, ..., n), its neighbor set $N_r(p_i)$ is defined as follows:

$$N(p_i) = \left\{ p_j \in P : d_{ij} < r \right\} \tag{1}$$

With d_{ij} denotes the Euclidian distance $\left\| p_i - p_j \right\|$ between a pair of points $(p_i, p_j) \in P \times P$ with i, j = 1, ..., n. Under these conditions, neighbor relationships can be conveniently described by an undirected connected graph $G = (V, E)$ with vertex set $V = \{1 \ldots n\}$ and edge set E. G connectivity depends on the transmission range.

The network localization problem with distance information is to determine the location of each node p_i in R^2 given the graph G, the positions of the anchors a_k, k= {$1 \ldots m$} in R^2 and the distance d_{ij}. between each neighbor pair (i, j) ∈E. The network N is said to be localizable if there is exactly one set of positions in R^2 for all nodes that is consistent with all available information about distances and positions.

Definitions

In a localization system, we distinguish five different states for nodes depending on their status and the role they are assuming.

- **Un-Localized Node State (U):** U nodes do not know yet their localization information. To allow these nodes to estimate their positions is the main goal of a localization system.
- **Settled Node State (S):** S nodes were initially U nodes, and got their estimated positions calculated by the localization system. The numbers of S nodes along with their position estimation errors are the main parameters for determining the quality of a localization system.
- **Anchors Node State (A):** A nodes are anchors whose initial positions are determined at the deployment process either manually or using a GPS. These nodes are also called beacons.
- **Virtual Anchor State (V):** V nodes are those S nodes that participate in the localization process and act as anchors.
- **Reference Node State (R):** R nodes are either A or V nodes. Localization information broadcasted by R nodes is to be used by U nodes to estimates their locations.

The system state transition graph is illuminated in figure1.

RELATED WORKS

Recursive Position Estimation

The recursive position estimation was proposed in (Albowicz et al., 2001). Nodes in the network collaborate to accomplish the localization task. In (Albowicz et al., 2001), authors took advantage of the recursive hierarchy to provide a framework for extending position estimations throughout a sensor network. System coverage increases iteratively as nodes with newly estimated positions join the anchors set. Each localized node broadcasts its location and its residual error computed using equation 2.

$$e_i = \sum_{k \in refset} \left(p_i - p_k - d_{ik} \right) \tag{2}$$

where e_i represents the residual error of node, $p_i - p_k$ the Euclidian distance between node i and reference node k, and d_{ik} the distance between nodes i and k measured using the RSSI. The value of the residual error is null for anchor nodes. This value is used as a measure of confidence of the estimated position. Each un-localized node selects three anchor nodes (called reference nodes and form the set *refset* in equation 2) from the set of received localization packets to compute its position. The three selected nodes are those having the smallest residual errors. Figure 3 portrays the time progression of the RPE recursive localization scheme.

The recursive localization scheme has been widely investigated and some variants and enhancements of the original scheme have been proposed (Oliveira et al., 2009), (Zhou et al., 2010).

Figure 2. State transition state graph of sensor node in a localization system, with

$$refset\left(u_i\right) = \left\{v_j \in V, a_j \in A \,\&\, d_{ij} < r; r : transmission\, range\right\}$$

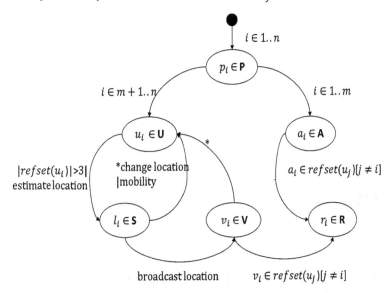

The hardware cost effectiveness of cooperative localization algorithms has motivated researchers to improve their localization accuracy, such as the works presented in: (Darakech et al, 2018), (Cui et al, 2018), (Wu et al, 2017), (Li et al. 2017), (Stanoev et al 2016). However, by exploring the cooperative nature of sensor nodes, a great attention needs to be given to other costs added by these algorithms during the localization process. These costs limit the efficiency of the network and degrade its performances. They concern the additional communication overhead required for the collaboration between nodes, and location packets exchange. As wireless sensor networks are typically constrained in terms of energy, optimizing the communication overhead of these schemes improves the network performance.

Figure 3. RPE Algorithm: (a) First, the anchors start the recursion by broadcasting its positions information of the beacon nodes. (b) Each un-localized node chooses its set of reference points. (c) The position computation is done. (d) The localized nodes broadcast its newly estimated position in order to help the other nodes in estimating their own positions.

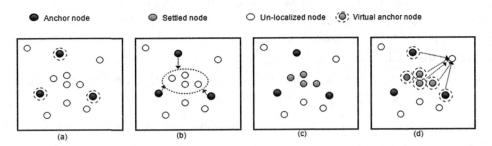

Algorithm 1. RPE

```
G: the input connected graph
A: the set of already localized sensor nodes
(Initially this set is the set of anchor nodes)
While (A does not contain all nodes)
identify nodes  a_i ∈ A from G
localize the sensor nodes in  N_{a_i}  for ∀  a_i
```

$$N_a = \bigcup_i N_{a_i}$$
$$A \leftarrow A \cup N_a .$$

Discussion and Motivations

Communication Cost

The use of the cooperative nature of sensors to provide network localization by the RPE algorithm, leads to increase the signalization overhead related to the localization process, especially with the increase of network density and size. These observations remain us to address quantitatively how well the RPE can be proved against the localization accuracy and signalization overhead (i.e. communication overhead).

In the RPE scheme, the un-localized node needs to be connected to at least three reference nodes, and its feasible set Bi can be reduced considering the intersection between circles centered on each connected reference (anchors or virtual anchors) r_k :

$$\forall pi \in P, Bi \begin{cases} \bigcap_{k=1}^{l} r_k, l \geq 3 \\ and \\ N_r \left(p_i \right) \neq \varnothing, d_{ik} < r \end{cases} \qquad (3)$$

Each settled node $si \in S$ is associated to its estimated position and its residual error (equation 2). A settled node si, can act as virtual anchor by broadcasting its location data (id, estimated position, residual error) to the set of its neighbors $N \left(s_i \right)$.

The total number of nodes that can act as references, R, within the networks at any instant is equal to the number of A nodes (the original anchors) which is constant equal to m, plus the current number of V nodes. Note that while the number of A nodes remains the same, the number of V nodes increases as we progress in the localization of the U nodes.

Let us denote by $N_a \left(u_i \right)$ the set of A nodes neighbors to the unlocalized node u_i, and by $N_v \left(u_i \right)$ the set of V nodes neighbors to node i. Recall that A and V nodes broadcast localization packets periodically. The node u_i receives $\left| N_a \left(u_i \right) \right| + \left| N_v \left(u_i \right) \right|$ localization packets. Among these packets, u_i selects three reference nodes, those having the least residual errors. The remaining received location packets $\left(\left| N_a \left(u_i \right) \right| + \left| N_v \left(u_i \right) \right| - 3 \right)$ are just ignored and not used in the RPE localization process for node u_i. This amounts to $\sum_{i=m+1}^{n}\left(\left|N_a\left(u_i\right)\right|+\left|N_v\left(u_i\right)\right|-3\right)$ unused received packets in the RPE localization process throughout the network. Let W denotes the percentage of ignored received packets, we readily have:

$$W = \frac{\sum_{i=m+1}^{n}\left(\left|N_a\left(u_i\right)\right|+\left|N_v\left(u_i\right)\right|-3\right)}{\sum_{i=m+1}^{n}\left(\left|N_a\left(u_i\right)\right|+\left|N_v\left(u_i\right)\right|\right)} * 100$$

with $\left(\left|N_a\left(u_i\right)\right|+\left|N_v\left(u_i\right)\right|\right) \gtrless 3$ for each node $i = m+1, ..., n$

Recall that the reception of a packet is power consuming, and as such the nodes consume additional energy to receive these location packets to be ignored, which directly impacts the network performance. Furthermore, the V nodes consume valuable energy for the transmission of these un-necessary (to be dropped by the receiver) location packets.

Impact of the Reference Node Number and Density on the Localization Accuracy

In literature, many researchers such as in (Chen et al., 2013), (Han et al., 2009) and (Aomumpai et al., 2011), explored how anchor nodes can be placed at specific location to improve the localization system performance. As depicted in Figures 4 the localization errors can be large due to anchor node placement and number. However, in the case of the recursive process, the virtual anchors number increases iteratively in an uncontrollable way. As a result, election algorithms are required to select a set of settled nodes to act as virtual anchors in the network. Also, a good strategy to maintain and control the distribution and the announcement of the reference nodes, which are initially, settled nodes.

Figure 4. Geographic error distribution for 4 scenarios (a) Geographic error: 3 anchors Poor distribution, (b) Geographic error: 3 Anchors Uniform distribution, (c) Geographic error: 10 anchors Poor distribution, (d) Geographic error: 10 anchors Uniform distribution

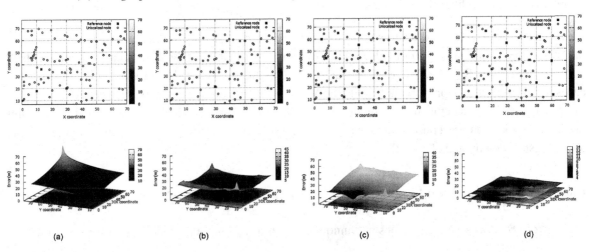

ERL: EFFICIENT RECURSIVE LOCALIZATION APPROACH FOR A WSN

Basic Idea

Implementing a strategy that optimizes the number of virtual anchor nodes for the recursive approach can ensure a much better outcome, while using the smallest number possible of virtual anchor nodes. Our conducted simulations of the RPE algorithm showed that the S nodes that are very close to each other and covered by the same set of R nodes, have approximately the same estimated position. However, all of them will be declared V nodes by the RPE. This induces a very high though unnecessary signaling overhead especially in high density network. As such, the RPE recursive scheme may hinder the network operation which tacitly leads to a slowdown of the localization process.

The proposed strategy restricts the number of S to be declared V nodes in areas where multiple S nodes are close to each other. In contrast, all these S nodes are declared V nodes by RPE.

In our proposed ERL, a U node waits for a predefined period, called the collecting period and denoted by τ_1 to collect as many location packets as possible. Recall that these location packets emanated from neighboring R nodes. The collecting period τ_1 starts at the reception of the first location packet. Upon the termination of this collecting period, node U selects three R nodes, those having the least residual error among all R nodes from which it has received the location packets. These three R nodes serve the U node to compute its location using trilateration. Once it calculates its position, node U converts to state S and becomes a settled node. Now as a settled node, it proceeds to check if it has the ability to also become a V node. To this end, it returns on the R nodes from which it has received the location packets during the last τ_1 period and checks whether it can switch to the R state.

To check the viability of an S node to become V node, we distinguish among its neighboring V nodes according to their remoteness (distance) from this receiving S node. Let $N_d\left(s_i\right)$ denotes the current set of V nodes at a distance d less than the transmission range r from S node s_i. That is:

$$N_r\left(s_i\right) = \left\{v_j \in V : d_{ij} < d\right\} \tag{4}$$

For instance, according to Figure 5 we have $N_r\left(s_0\right) = \left\{v_1, v_2, v_3\right\}$, $N_{\frac{r}{2}}\left(s_0\right) = \left\{v_2, v_3\right\}$ and $N_{\frac{r}{3}}\left(s_0\right) = \left\{v_3\right\}$.

Recall that to become an S node, this node should have received at least three location packets emanating from three different neighboring R nodes, otherwise it remains in state U as it cannot localize itself with less than three R nodes. We now consider the following two cases. The rationale behind these two cases is twofold: First to properly distribute the V nodes throughout the network and secondly to reduce the density of V nodes in the quest to reduce the signaling overhead within the network. This constitutes our V node selection procedure to reduce the signaling overhead, yet to allow the localization procedure to progress normally and efficiently.

Case 1: $d = \frac{r}{2}$: $N_{\frac{r}{2}}\left(s_i\right)$ is then the set of neighboring V nodes within half of the communication range r from **S** node s_i. Node s_i does not announce itself as a V node (i.e.; does not transmit a location

Figure 5. Set of neighbors of the settled node 0 (with node 1, node 2 and node 3 are virtual anchor)

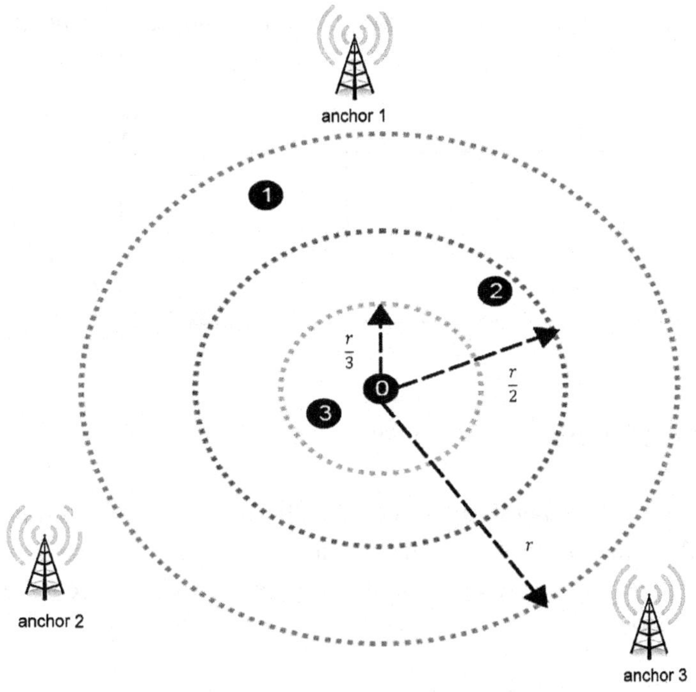

packet) when it receives a localization packet from a V node among the set $N_{\frac{r}{2}}\left(s_i\right)$. This allows the announcement of at least one V node per cell with radius $\frac{r}{2}$.

Case 2: $d = \frac{r}{3}$: $N_{\frac{r}{3}}\left(s_i\right)$ is then the set of neighboring V nodes within third of the communication range r from **S** node s_i. Node s_i does not announce itself as a V node (i.e.; does not transmit a location packet) when it receives a localization packet from a V node among the set $N_{\frac{r}{3}}\left(s_i\right)$. This allows the announcement of at least one V node per cell with radius $\frac{r}{3}$.

Algorithm Process

The algorithm is divided into four phases. In the first phase, Figure 6.a, the original anchors (the A nodes) start the recursion process by broadcasting their location data. In the second phase, each U node receives localization packets from its neighboring R node (anchors and/or virtual anchors), and determines its reference points set (the three reference nodes having the least residual errors). In the third phase, the node estimates its position and then becomes a new settled node (S node), Figure 6.b. A settled node may act as a new V node (virtual anchor) in the network and helps others U nodes to get localized, Figure 6.c. The localization data propagates within the network with the newly V broadcasting their data, Figure 6.d.

Figure 6. ERL operation progression: (a) Node A broadcast location packets (b) U nodes having received location packets from three or more R nodes become S (c) Some eligible S nodes become V nodes and transmit their locations packets (d) Consequently more U nodes become able to be localized and become S nodes.

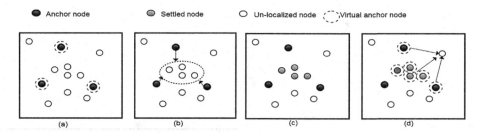

Phase 1: Starting the Recursion From Anchors

Each A node broadcasts its localization packet periodically during its reserved time slot in order to avoid collision with other A node transmissions. These A nodes are original anchors with known positions and therefore with a null residual error. As such, they will always be selected to be part of the reference set of any receiving U node.

Phase 2: Selecting References

U node receiving localization packets stores the received data and waits for the predefined time period τ_1 to collect as many localization packets as possible. At the end of period τ_1, the U node selects the three R nodes having the least residual errors among those from which it has received the localization packets. These three R nodes serve to estimate the location of the U node using trilateration. The choice of which set of R nodes to use (when there are more than three references) is an important issue in our proposed ERL algorithm. Not only we select the three R nodes having the least residual error but also the one having the largest distance between them. Recall that the location residual error is computed by a node upon its localization (when it becomes S node) based on the difference between the trilateration result and the RSSI outcome. It is important to choose reference nodes with accurate positions to lower the location error accumulation.

Phase 3: Estimating the Position of U Nodes

The third phase is to estimate the position of the un-localized node using Trilateration. The estimated position is the center of the intersection area of the three circles formed around the received positions of the three chosen R nodes. The residual position error is computed as the absolute value of the difference between the estimated position and the position calculated using the RSSI technique.

Phase 4: Becoming a Virtual Anchor

Unlike RPE and DPE, an S node cannot directly become a virtual anchor (a V node). In ERL, we exercise a selection procedure as explained before. We have set up two cases to distinguish among the V neighbors of a newly declared S node. If the S node s_i has not received any location packet from the set $N_d(s_i)$ whether we are using case 1 (that is $d = \frac{r}{2}$) or case 2 (that is $d = \frac{r}{3}$), then it is viable to act as a virtual anchor and becomes a V node. To this end, s_i prepares a location packet and start a randomization time period, denoted by τ_2. The length of randomization period τ_2 depends on the residual position error of node s_i. S nodes having better (lower) residual errors, choose smaller periods. If during this time period τ_2, node s_i receives a new location packet emanating from a distance less than d, it then stops the timer and cancels its transmission of the prepared location packet. Such a packet normally has emanated from a newly declared V node in the vicinity having a very low location residual error. Otherwise, s_i transmits its location packet at the end of time period τ_2. The fact that τ_2 is designed as an increasing function of the residual error of the S node, provides the priority for S nodes with lowest residual errors to become V nodes.

PERFORMANCE EVALUATION

The performance evaluation of our proposed ERL is conducted through simulations using OMNET++. We consider a network containing 400 sensor nodes, randomly distributed in an area of 100m x 100m. We use the RSSI technique as the distance estimation method implemented, and the trilateration method to estimate the locations of U nodes once they acquire three or more R nodes. The collecting period τ_1 is set to 100 milliseconds and the maximum randomization period τ_2 is set to 200 milliseconds. The node density, defined as the expected number of nodes within a given neighborhood. Node density is controlled by changing the communication range while keeping the area of deployment the same. We consider a communication range from 10 m to 21 m, which results in an average node density ranging from 4 to 17. In the evaluation performance of ERL, we consider both scenarios of case 1 and case 2 specified before:

ERL-Scenario 1: S nodes consider only location packets emanating from the V neighbors within radius $N_{\frac{r}{2}}$.

ERL-Scenario 2: S nodes consider only location packets emanating from the V neighbors within radius $N_{\frac{r}{3}}$.

Accuracy and Precision of Localization

The usual performance metric to evaluate the accuracy of a localization approach concerns the average sum of the residual errors between the estimated positions and the actual real node positions within the network. We portray on Figure 7 the average localization of ERL-Scenario 1, ERL-Scenario 2 and RPL

Figure 7. Localization accuracy using 5% of anchors

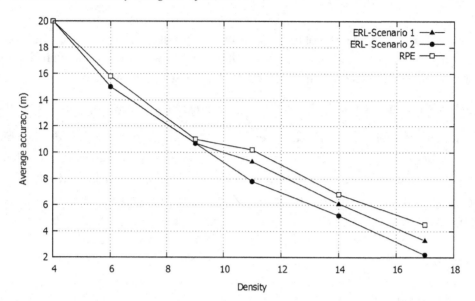

as a function of the density of nodes where 5% of the deployed nodes are original anchors (A nodes). Figure 8 portrays the same but with 10% of the deployed nodes are original anchors. We observe that for all three schemes, the location accuracy gets much better as the node density gets higher. Both ERL variants amount to a better average accuracy than that provided by RPL. We should recall here that RPE, by design, uses a much larger number of V nodes than ERL. Indeed, for a node density equals to 17, 90% of the initial U nodes became V nodes in RPE, while only 53% and 60% of the nodes acquired the V status in ERL-Scenario 1, ERL-Scenario 2 respectively. This certainly amounts to a much higher signaling overhead for RPE.

Figure 8. Localization accuracy using 10% of anchors

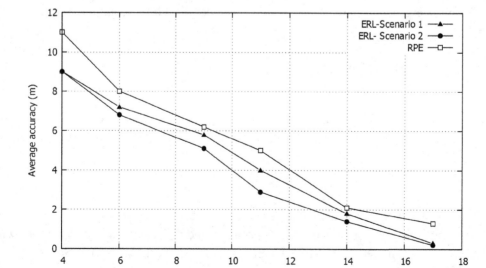

Number of Virtual Anchors in the Network

An increase in the network density results in more neighbors, and therefore more S nodes and consequently more V nodes. This is true for RPE as well as our proposed ERL. Figure 9, 10 and 11 portray the
proportion of declared V nodes (among the initial U nodes) in the network as a function of node density
and for different percentage of initial A nodes (5%, 10% and 20% respectively). We observe that RPE

Figure 9. Proportion of V nodes as a function of the node density using initially 5% A nodes

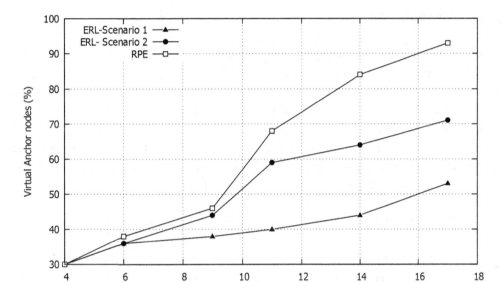

Figure 10. Proportion of V nodes as a function of the node density using initially 10% A nodes

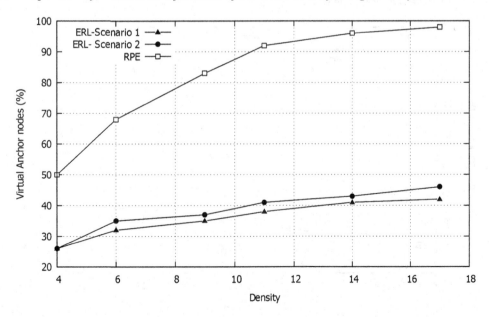

declares much more V nodes than both variants of ERL. Most importantly, we observe that the number of V nodes in RPE reaches the 100% of the initial U nodes, and this is faster for increased numbers of A nodes. Remarkably, we have the exact opposite for both variants of ERL. This is due to the inherent functioning of our proposed ERL variants which limit the number of R nodes per cell.

Besides using a much lower signaling overhead, ERL in both of its variants provides a balanced distribution of the declared V nodes throughout the network. The limitation of the number of V nodes as well as their even distribution throughout the network are attained due to the V nodes selection strategy adopted in our proposed ERL.

Average of Computation Time

The computing time spent by the localization algorithm until it converges, provides another valuable comparison metric. The computing time is plotted of Figure 12 as a function of the node density for RPE and the two ERL variants. The reduction of the number of V nodes in both ERL variants accelerated the localization progression and propagation and as such yielded a lower computing time. In contrast, in RPE many V nodes are declared and consequently much more location packets are sent, the majority of them are neglected as trilateration is done just using three R nodes. In our proposed ERL, many S nodes cancel their announcement because other V or A already exist within the neighborhood. This accelerates the localization data propagation and consequently the convergence time.

Communication Overhead

Communication or signaling overhead is directly related to the number of location packets transmitted throughout the networks. This is then directly related to the number of A and V nodes in the networks. Figures 13 and 14 portray the number of location packets transmitted throughout the network as a func-

Figure 11. Proportion of V nodes as a function of the node density using initially 20% A nodes

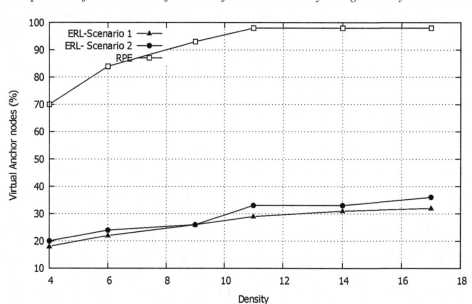

Figure 12. Average computing time for RPE, ERL-Scenario 1 and ERL-Scenario 2, using 5% anchors

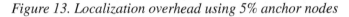

Figure 13. Localization overhead using 5% anchor nodes

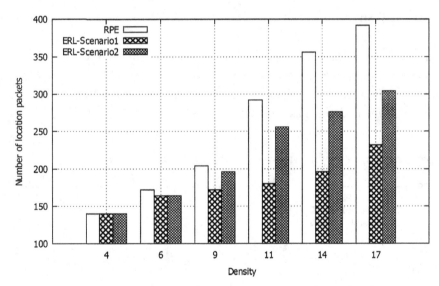

tion of the node density, for an initial number of anchors of 5% an 10% respectively. We observe that the signaling overhead increase as the node density increases. But this increase is much less both the ERL variants. An increase in the number of initially deployed anchors amounts to an increase of the declared V nodes in RPE but in a decrease in the number of declared V nodes in both ERL variants. This has been observed on Figures 9, 10, and 11. As such, going from 5% anchors to 10%, amounts to a remarkable gain in ERL signaling overhead compared to that of RPE.

Figure 14. Localization overhead using 10% anchor nodes

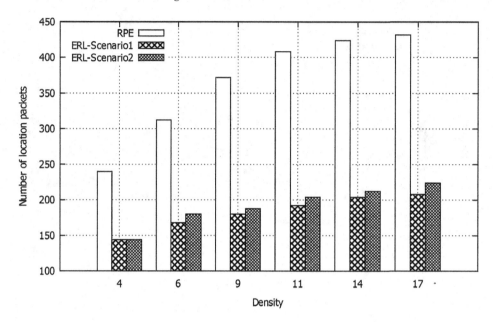

Energy Consumption

The energy consumption is paramount for the life of a WSN. To this end, we portrayed on Figures 15 and 16 the proportion of consumed energy by RPE and the two proposed ERL variants as a function of the node density, for 5% and 10% initial anchors respectively. The proportion of the energy consumed by the localization scheme is defined as follows:

Figure 15. Energy consumption of the network, using 5% of anchor nodes

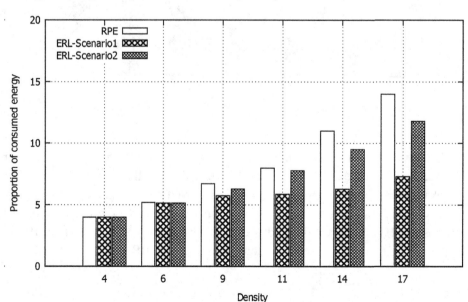

Figure 16. Energy consumption of the network, using 10% of anchor nodes

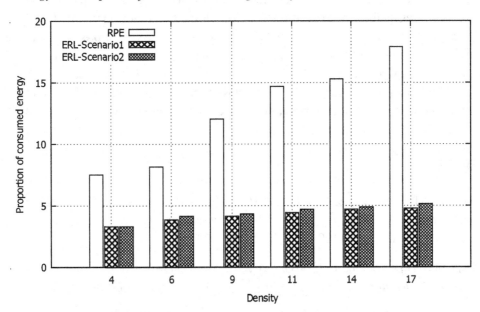

$$\text{Proportion of the energy consumed} = \frac{\sum_{i=1}^{n}\left[initialEnergy\left(node_i\right) - residualEnergy\left(node_i\right)\right]}{\sum_{i=1}^{m} initialEnergy\left(node_i\right)}100$$

$$(5)$$

We observe from both figures that the energy consumed increases as the node density increases since the number of V nodes increases too, though at different rates for RPE and ERL as was discussed earlier. We clearly notice that both ERL variants consume less energy than RPE. The energy consumption of both ERL variants is remarkably lower than that of RPE when we use 10% of the initial deployment as anchors.

Figure 15 shows that ERL-Scenario1 conserves around 50% of the energy consumed by RPE when a node density of 17 is deployed. Figure 16 shows that ERL-Scenario1 conserves around 75% of the energy otherwise consumed by RPE when a node density of 17 is deployed.

CONCLUSION

This work has presented and evaluated ERL, an efficient recursive localization approach. ERL is a distributed low overhead localization approach for WSNs that stands well for high density WSNs. Our solution implements a new selection strategy of virtual anchor nodes V that ensures an optimal distribution of these nodes in the network. Indeed, the declaration of a virtual anchor in the network is performed based on a randomization period. The latter depends on it's the position residual error of localized nodes S. Consequently, nodes having better (lower) residual errors choose smaller periods. The fact that this period is designed as an increasing function of the residual error of the S node provides the priority for S nodes with lowest residual errors to become V nodes. Simulations showed that ERL consistently outperforms RPE. Moreover, the performance evaluation not only discusses the precision and the accuracy of the presented solution but also takes in consideration various evaluation metrics that are critical for WSN, such as the energy consumption the communication overhead and time latency.

One should note that the performance of the proposed scheme, as well as RPE, should be evaluated with presence of node non-uniform distribution, connectivity irregularities and sparse network.

REFERENCES

Ahmadi, H., Viani, F., Polo, A., & Bouallegue, R. (2016). An improved anchor selection strategy for wireless localization of WSN nodes. In *2016 IEEE Symposium on Computers and Communication (ISCC)*, pages 108-113. DOI: 10.1109/ISCC.2016.7543723

Albowicz, J., Chen, A., & Zhang, L. (2001). Recursive position estimation in sensor networks. In *The 9th International Conference on Network Protocols* (pp. 35–41). doi:10.1109/ICNP.2001.992758

Aomumpai, S., & Prommak, C. (2011). On the Impact of Reference Node Placement in Wireless Indoor Positioning Systems. *International Journal of Computer, Electrical, Automation. Control and Information Engineering*, 5(12), 1704–1708. doi:10.1109/ECTICon.2014.6839894

Belghith, A., & Abid, M. A. (2009). Autonomic self-tunable proactive routing in mobile ad hoc networks. In *Proceedings of the IEEE International Conference on Wireless and Mobile Computing, Networking and Communications* (pp. 276-281). 10.1109/WiMob.2009.54

Belghith, A., Akkari, W., & Bonnin, J. M. (2008). Traffic Aware Power Saving Protocol in Multi-hop Mobile Ad-Hoc Networks. *Journal of Networks*, 2(4), 1–13. doi:10.4304/jnw.2.4.1-13

Bouhdid, B., Akkari, W., & Belghith, A. (2017). Low cost recursive localization scheme for high density wireless sensor networks. *International Journal on Semantic Web and Information Systems*, 13(3), 68–88. doi:10.4018/IJSWIS.2017070104

Bouhdid, B., Akkari, W., & Belghith, A. (2017). Energy-aware cooperative localization approach for wireless sensor networks. In *Proceedings of the IEEE 13th International Conference on Intelligent Computer Communication and Processing* (pp. 429-435). 10.1109/ICCP.2017.8117043

Boukerche, A., Oliveira, H. A. B. F., Nakamura, E., & Loureiro, A. A. F. (2007). Localization systems for wireless sensor networks. *IEEE Wireless Communications*, 14(6), 6–12. doi:10.1109/MWC.2007.4407221

Chen, C., & Lin, T. C. (2013). A Low-Cost Anchor Placement Strategy for Range-Free Localization Problems in Wireless Sensor Networks. *International Journal of Distributed Sensor Networks*, 1–12. doi:10.5121/ijcnc.2011.3607

Chow, J. C. K., Peter, M., Scaioni, M., & Al-Durgham, M. (2018). Indoor tracking, mapping, and navigation: algorithms, technologies, and applications. *Journal of Sensors*, 2018, 1–89. doi:10.1155/2018/5971752

Cui, L., Xu, C., Li, G., Ming, Z., Feng, Y., & Lu, N. (2018). A high accurate localization algorithm with DV-Hop and differential evolution for wireless sensor network. *Applied Soft Computing, 68*, 39–52. doi:10.1016/j.asoc.2018.03.036

Darakeha, F., Khanib, G. R. M., & Azmic, P. (2018). DCRL-WSN: A distributed cooperative and range-free localization algorithm for WSNs. *AEÜ. International Journal of Electronics and Communications*, 1–21. doi:10.1016/j.aeue.2018.05.015

Ding, Y., Tian, H., & Han, G. (2012). A Distributed Node Localization Algorithm for Wireless Sensor Network Based on MDS and SDP. In *Proceedings of the 2012 International Conference on Computer Science and Electronics Engineering* (pp. 624-628). 10.1109/ICCSEE.2012.93

Gui, L., Val, T., Wei, A., & Dalce, R. (2015). Improvement of range-free localization technology by a novel DV-hop protocol in wireless sensor networks. *Ad Hoc Networks, 24*, 55–73. doi:10.1016/j.adhoc.2014.07.025

Halder, S., & Ghosal, A. (2016). A survey on mobility-assisted localization techniques in wireless sensor networks. *Journal of Network and Computer Applications, 60*, 82–94. doi:10.1016/j.jnca.2015.11.019

Han, G., Choi, D., & Lim, W. (2009). Reference node placement and selection algorithm based on trilateration for indoor sensor networks. *Wireless Communications and Mobile Computing, 9*(8), 1017–1027. doi:10.1002/wcm.651

Kaur, H., & Bajaj, B. (2015). Review on localization techniques in wireless sensor. *International Journal of Computers and Applications, 116*(2), 4–7. doi:10.5120/20306-2348

Klogo, G. S., & Gadze, J. D. (2013). Energy constraints of localization techniques in wireless sensor networks (WSN): A Survey. *International Journal of Computers and Applications, 75*, 44–52. doi:10.5120/13143-0543

Li, J., & Lu, G. (2017). Sparse Anchor Nodes Cooperative Localization Algorithm for WSN. In *Proc. 2017 3rd IEEE International Conference on Computer and Communications (ICCC)* (pp. 368-372). 10.1109/CompComm.2017.8322573

Li, X., Yan, L., Pan, W., & Luo, B. (2015). Optimization of DV-hop localization algorithm in hybrid optical wireless sensor networks. *Journal of Heuristics, 21*(2), 177–195. doi:10.100710732-014-9257-y

Mahjri, I., Dhraief, A., Belghith, A., Drira, K., & Mathkour, H. (2016). A GPS-less framework for localization and coverage maintenance in wireless sensor networks. *TIIS, 10*(1), 96–116. doi:10.3837/tiis.2016.01.006

Niculescu, D., & Nath, B., B. (2001). Ad hoc positioning system (APS). In *Proc. of the IEEE GLOBECOM* (pp. 2926-2931). doi:10.1109/GLOCOM.2001.965964

Oliveira, H. A. B. F., Boukerche, A., Nakamura, E., & Loureiro, A. A. F. (2009). An efficient directed localization recursion protocol for wireless sensor networks. *IEEE Transactions on Computers, 58*(5), 677–691. doi:10.1109/TC.2008.221

Pandey, O. M., & Hegde, R. M. (2017). Node localization over small world WSNs using constrained average path length reduction. *Ad Hoc Networks*, *67*, 87–102. doi:10.1016/j.adhoc.2017.10.010

Paul, A. K., & Sato, T. (2017). Localization in Wireless Sensor Networks: A Survey on Algorithms, Measurement Techniques, Applications and Challenges. *Journal of Sensor and Actuator Networks*, *6*(4), 24. doi:10.3390/jsan6040024

Risteska, B. S. (2016). A taxonomy of localization techniques based on multidimensional scaling. In *2016 39th International Convention on Information and Communication Technology, Electronics and Microelectronics (MIPRO)*. doi:10.1109/MIPRO.2016.7522221

Sivakumara, P., & Radhika, M. (2018). Performance Analysis of LEACH-GA over LEACH and LEACH-C in WSN. *Procedia Computer Science*, *125*, 248–256. doi:10.1016/j.procs.2017.12.034

Stanoev, A., Filiposk, S., In, V., & Kocarev, L. (2016). Cooperative method for wireless sensor network localization. *Ad Hoc Networks*, *40*, 61–72. doi:10.1016/j.adhoc.2016.01.003

Wu, H., Mei, X., Chen, X., Li, J., Wang, J., & Mohapatr, P. (2017). A novel cooperative localization algorithm using enhanced particle filter technique in maritime search and rescue wireless sensor network. *ISA Transactions*, 1–8. doi:10.1016/j.isatra.2017.09.013 PMID:28969856

Zhou, Z., Cui, J. H., & Zhou, S. (2010). Efficient localization for large scale underwater sensor networks. *Ad Hoc Networks*, *8*(3), 267–279. doi:10.1016/j.adhoc.2009.08.005

Chapter 9

Overview of MERA:
An Architecture to Perform Record Linkage in Music–Related Databases

Daniel Fernández-Álvarez
University of Oviedo, Spain

José Emilio Labra Gayo
University of Oviedo, Spain

Daniel Gayo-Avello
University of Oviedo, Spain

Patricia Ordoñez de Pablos
University of Oviedo, Spain

ABSTRACT

The proliferation of large databases with potentially repeated entities across the World Wide Web drives into a generalized interest to find methods to detect duplicated entries. The heterogeneity of the data cause that generalist approaches may produce a poor performance in scenarios with distinguishing features. In this paper, we analyze the particularities of music related-databases and we describe Musical Entities Reconciliation Architecture (MERA). MERA consists of an architecture to match entries of two sources, allowing the use of extra support sources to improve the results. It makes use of semantic web technologies and it is able to adapt the matching process to the nature of each field in each database. We have implemented a prototype of MERA and compared it with a well-known music-specialized search engine. Our prototype outperforms the selected baseline in terms of accuracy.

DOI: 10.4018/978-1-5225-7186-5.ch009

Copyright © 2019, IGI Global. Copying or distributing in print or electronic forms without written permission of IGI Global is prohibited.

INTRODUCTION

Although the problem of entity reconciliation has been largely studied, it remains a challenging issue. New research trends related to entity reconciliation has appeared in the last decade. This includes the need of developing efficient algorithms to deal with Big Data (Castano, Ferrara, & Montanelli, 2018; Enríquez, Domínguez-Mayo, Escalona, Ross, & Staples, 2017), the challenge of linking individuals in domains in which preserving their privacy is a requirement (Pow et al., 2017) or the need to align ontologies in Linked Data scenarios (Achichi et al., 2016; Zahaf & Malki, 2018).

Different entity reconciliation environments rise different challenges. The specific context of music databases has not been deeply studied, despite the content related to this kind of datasets include a set of insightful features. Examples of fields usually contained in musical databases are titles, artist names, albums, genres, etc. Each one of these fields have some distinguishing peculiarities which cause that a certain real entity may be represented in different ways in different databases. For instance, there are many specific correct forms, or at least recognizable forms, in which we could express the name of an artist. This includes artistic names, civil names, names conventions ("The Beatles" vs "Beatles, the"), acronyms or common misspellings. When dealing with information related to genre, one may find that a certain song is specified as *pop* in a database, as *rock* in a second one and as *pop-rock* in a third one. Sometimes, the same genre is even named with different forms that are in fact expressing the same reality.

Our assumption is that finding general reconciliation rules between two databases is far from being trivial, as well as finding appropriate rules or strategies to conciliate each field of those databases. The result could drastically change if it is compared to the rules that may be used when handling a different pair of sources. Trying to establish general rules could drive into an unnecessary number of failures when identifying two records of different databases as forms of the same real entity. The inference of reconciliation rules in a particular case through the use of training data may be useful for covering issues such as misspellings, naming conventions or even noisy prefixes/suffixes, but it cannot handle cases in which the strings that represent the entities do not have common characters (example: "The King of Rock" should be recognized as "Elvis Presley").

Our main contribution is the specification of MERA architecture. MERA tries to adapt to all those scenarios using graph concepts and semantic web technologies. Our approach turns the information of one of the target databases into a custom RDF graph G containing all the information (name variations, alias, common misspellings ...) of every database record, as well as the relations between those records. The records of the second database are turned into complex queries that will be launched against G. The result of each query is the list of the most similar nodes to the target record according to:

- String-distance-based functions.
- Use of all the alternative identifying forms of a concept.
- Graph navigation in order to detect shared associated entities for disambiguation purposes.

MERA can use different reconciliation algorithms for each pair of databases and even for each field of those databases, trying to cover all the issues linked to the nature of the data. Our solution is able to reach better results with more prior knowledge of the data issues, since the user is the agent that specifies the algorithms to use. MERA allows configuring different properties that should be considered, the reconciliation algorithms to apply in each case, and the threshold of similarity that a result must reach to be accepted. It also provides mechanisms to incorporate ad-hoc algorithms in the reconciliation process.

Our approach is designed to involve several sources at a time during the linking process by merging them in a single and reusable RDF graph. MERA describes a graph schema in which every piece of information is qualified with its original source through reification techniques. This allows the algorithm to distinguish which nodes of the graph are potential matches between a given pair of sources and which ones are merely used to enrich the data and improve the matching process. This also allows ignoring the content of certain sources in another use of the built graph. The source code is available at https://github.com/DaniFdezAlvarez/wMERA.

STATE OF THE ART

Record linkage, also referred as object identification (Eshghi, Rajaram, Dagli, & Cohen, 2015), data-cleaning (Ilyas, Chu, & others, 2015), approximate matching (Lotker, Patt-Shamir, & Pettie, 2015), fuzzy matching (Lamarine, Hager, Saris, Astrup, & Valsesia, 2018), entity resolution (Altwaijry, Kalashnikov, & Mehrotra, 2017) or coreference resolution (Benatallah et al., 2017), is a widely-studied problem. Nevertheless, with the proliferation of huge databases in the Era of Big Data and the need of developing effective and scalable reconciliation systems, the scientific community still put much effort to solve the challenges of record linkage (Enríquez et al., 2017). The essence of the problem consists of identifying two or more elements that refer to the same reality. A basic use case is the detection of duplicate entries within a file or the detection of equivalents across two databases.

Research work about entity resolution has been largely based on Fellegi & Sunter (1969), which was inspired by the ideas introduced by Newcombe & Kennedy (1962). Record linkage is presented as a classification problem, where a pair of entities can be classified as "matching" or "non-matching". Several scientific communities have adopted that scheme to formulate the problem in its own way, producing many reusable techniques and technologies to solve it (Christen & Winkler, 2016). A systematic study of the type of techniques developed in the last seven years for reconciliation tasks in Big Data environments is provided in (Enríquez et al., 2017).

Since record linkage becomes a problem due to the lack of unique reliable identifiers, traditional approaches are highly based in string comparators. Being able to recognize different strings that represent the same real-world object has been, and still is, a major research project (Hall & Dowling, 1980; Yu, Li, Deng, & Feng, 2016). Despite there have been many works defining string similarity measures (Yu et al., 2016), it has been concluded that there is not such an algorithm or combination that can outperform all the rest in terms of accuracy and efficiency in every context (Harron, Goldstein, & Dibben, 2015), not even if we try to compare specific subsets of algorithms such as string-edit distance metrics(Peng, Li, & Kennedy, 2014). Even if this problem has been largely studied, it still remains as an active research field due to the increasing need of producing efficient comparison algorithms in Big Data environments (McCormack & Smyth, 2017).

Selecting the most accurate strategy to apply in order to get the best possible results is not a trivial task. Some research lines have put efforts in the design of methods to automatically detect which algorithm or combination of algorithms from a known set of possibilities works better for a particular scenario (Nguyen & Ichise, 2016). This can be done through providing training data containing a set of pairs qualified as "matching" or "non-matching" and applying automatic learning techniques.

The techniques used to determine the similarity between two records through applying string distance metrics over their attributes are known as content-based or Feature-Based Similarities (FSB). However, it was early demonstrated that FBS is not enough to properly determine if two entities match the same real object, especially when a disambiguation is needed (Kalashnikov & Mehrotra, 2006). In those scenarios, checking relations between entities in addition to entities' features may be a mechanism to improve matching. Traditional FBS approaches match each individual independently. By contrast, approaches in which relations between records are considered to produce a result are named context-based (Rahmani, Ranjbar-Sahraei, Weiss, & Tuyls, 2016) or collective entity resolution systems (Kouki, Pujara, Marcum, Koehly, & Getoor, 2017). The representation of relations between entities fits well in graph structures, so these kind of approaches are usually graph-based. Those graph-based approaches combined with FBS can outperform the matching quality of FBS standalone on different scenarios (Frontini, Brando, & Ganascia, 2015; Song, Luo, & Heflin, 2017; Zhu, Ghasemi-Gol, Szekely, Galstyan, & Knoblock, 2016). A recent study has pointed out that 26.23% of the publications of record linkage techniques in Big Data environments over the past seven years rely on graph-based approaches or are thought to be applied to graphs of Linked Data (Enríquez et al., 2017).

Some of the main tools used to improve the scalability of systems are the blocking or clustering techniques. When trying to find matches between entities of two databases A and B, i.e. that every a_i in A is a possible match for every b_j in B would lead to a quadratic complexity hardly scalable. Many approaches were early suggested to reduce that complexity via filtering the number of potential matches, such as sorting of records in order to keep similar contents together (Hernández & Stolfo, 1995), clustering of candidates with computationally cheap functions before employing more expensive methods to compare potential pairs(Chaudhuri, Ganjam, Ganti, & Motwani, 2003) or q-gram indexing (Baxter, Christen, & Churches, 2003). Current investigation lines are going deeper in the development of blocking techniques for large, heterogeneous and possibly semi-structured data (Efthymiou, Papadakis, Papastefanatos, Stefanidis, & Palpanas, 2017), as well as graph-like environments (de Assis Costa & de Oliveira, 2016; Fisher, Christen, Wang, & Rahm, 2015; Shin, Jung, Lee, & Kang, 2015), especially for Linked Open Data (Vidhya & Geetha, 2017).

Developing or designing a reconciliation system needs to include combinations of the algorithms mentioned and several other features. A great example could be *privacy preserving matching* (Gao, Cheng, Li, & Xia, 2018; Vatsalan, Sehili, Christen, & Rahm, 2017), handy when several organizations take part in the matching process but the information to be linked is sensible or should be encrypted. In addition, some extra challenges or decisions must be addressed, such as accepted input/output formats, mechanisms to interact with the user (API, library, web application ...), configuration options or the possibility of including extra algorithms/workflows.

We have explored a commercial patented system specialized in recognition of music metadata (Dunning, Kindig, Joshlin, & Archibald, 2011) and several well-known open-source approaches, including Dude (Draisbach & Naumann, 2010), D-Dupe (Kang, Getoor, Shneiderman, Bilgic, & Licamele, 2008), SILK (Volz, Bizer, Gaedke, & Kobilarov, 2009), BigMatch (Yancey, 2002), FEBRL (Christen, 2008), FRIL (Jurczyk, Lu, Xiong, Cragan, & Correa, 2008), Merge ToolBox (Schnell, Bachteler, & Reiher, 2009), NADEEF/ER (Elmagarmid et al., 2014), and MusicBrainz Piccard (Stutzbach, 2011). We have checked the features of those systems and we provide a qualitative comparison of them with MERA architecture, which is shown in Table 1.

Even though all of them tackle the challenge of entity matching, they are really heterogeneous. Table 1 also shows that MERA is the most flexible and configurable system among the music-specialized ones. In addition, to the best of our knowledge, none of the existing systems include the following MERA's features:

Table 1. Comparison of record linkage systems

		MERA	BigMatch	FEBRL	SILK	DUDE	D-Dupe	FRIL	Merge ToolBox	NADEEF/ER	CD Patent	MB Piccard
Main	Linkage	✓	✓	✓	✓	-	✓	✓	✓	✓	✓	✓
	Deduplication	-	✓	✓	-	✓	✓	-	✓	✓	-	-
Comparison algorithms	Include	✓	-	✓	✓	✓	✓	✓	✓	✓	✓	✓
	Let choose	✓	-	✓	✓	✓	✓	✓	✓	✓	-	-
	Let combine	✓	-	✓	✓	✓	✓	✓	-	✓	✓	✓
	Let implement	✓	-	✓	-	✓	✓	-	-	✓	-	-
Blocking techniques	Include	✓	✓	✓	✓	✓	✓	✓	✓	✓	✓	✓
	Let choose	✓	✓	✓	✓	✓	✓	✓	✓	✓	-	-
	Let combine	✓	✓	✓	✓	✓	✓	-	-	-	✓	-
	Let implement	✓	✓	✓	-	✓	✓	-	-		-	-
Training data	Include	-	-	✓	-	-	-	✓	-	-	-	-
	Let choose	-	-	✓	-	-	-	✓	-	-	-	-
	Let combine	-	-	✓	-	-	-	-	-	-	-	-
	Let implement	-	-	✓	-	-	-	-	-	-	-	-
Collective Matching		✓	-	-	-	-	✓	-	-	-	-	✓
Privacy preserving		-	-	-	-	-	-	-	✓	-	-	-
GUI		-	-	✓	✓	-	✓	✓	✓	✓	✓	✓
Multi-source		✓	-	-	-	-	-	-	-	-	✓	-
Alternative entity forms		✓	-	-	-	-	-	-	-	-	-	✓
Music specialized		✓	-	-	-	-	-	-	-	-	✓	✓

- Integration of several sources to be used during the reconciliation process in a reusable graph, with a scheme which maintains which pieces of information have been provided by which source(s).
- Identification of alternative textual forms of an entity during the matching process via configurable complex paths in a graph.

SYSTEM ARCHITECTURE

MERA defines a strategy to combine several categories of algorithms or heuristics to conciliate two sets of entities $A = \{a_0, a_1 \ldots a_n\}$ and $B = \{b_0, b_1 \ldots b_m\}$, where the entities of B are stored in an RDF graph G. Each record a_i is processed independently to find its most similar records in B. The user of MERA should be allowed to define a set of conditions that an entity b_j must fulfill to be considered as a possible match. Consequently, every entity a_i could be associated with none, one or several results, depending on the number of entities $b_j \in B$ that fit in the conditions. In case of having more than one result for the same entity a_i, those will be ranked regarding its degree of similarity with the target element.

If we think of MERA as a black box, the expected inputs and the received outputs are the following:

- **Input1:** Set of entities A = $\{a_0, a_1 \dots a_n\}$, for which every a_i will be processed independently.
- **Input2:** RDF graph containing the set of entities B = $\{b_0, b_1 \dots b_m\}$.
- **Input3:** Configuration data, in which MERA's options are specified.
- **Output:** Association of each element a_i with the elements in B that fit in the matching conditions. In case of having several results for an entity a_i, they will be presented sorted in decreasing order by degree of similarity with a_i.

MERA has been designed to achieve better results with more prior knowledge of the nature of the sources to conciliate, so the user can configure several parameters of the matching process like:

- List of normalization algorithms.
- List of comparison algorithms.
- List of blocking functions.
- Relevance of related contents/entities when applying disambiguation.
- Thresholds of similarity that two entities should reach to be considered matches.
- List of sources (white/black lists) to use during the matching process.
- Maximum number of candidate results per query.
- Maximum number of candidates at the end of blocking stages.
- Relations between entities that should be considered.
- Alternative forms of entities that should be considered.

Configuration related to algorithms or acceptance values can be applied at different hierarchical levels, i.e, the user could indicate, for example, that Levenshtein distance should be applied in every case with the exception of canonical names, which will be compared using exact match. He could even specify that the canonical name of CDs will be compared with exact match, but the canonical name of a group will use Jaccard similarity. In addition, MERA is designed to let the user implement new functions (normalization, comparison, blocking) that can be integrated into the base workflow.

The graph schema of MERA has been thought to let the user combine the knowledge of several sources during the matching process. Suppose a scenario in which we want to conciliate two sources *A* and *B*, where *A* contains civil names of artists and *B* contains artistic names. Also, we have access to a third source *C* which includes both civil and artistic names. In order to produce matches between *A* and *B*, we propose to to turn *B* records in a graph *G* and link records of *C* with nodes of *G*. The obtained results allow us to build an enriched graph *G'* containing all *B* records in nodes decorated with information of *C*. By this, making queries with entities of *A* against *G'* will potentially improve the result of making queries directly against *G*. *G'* may be reusable for different purposes, even to use separately the information of *B* and *C*. Each piece of information is associated with its original source, and MERA purpose a way of just using the data from certain sources during the matching process.

Query Structure

Records in *A* are turned into queries that may involve one or more entities at a time. A query in MERA context must specify a main type or main order *o*, a main content *m*, and a set *R* of typed refinements *r*, represented as pairs $r_i = (t_i, s_i)$. Let's consider a scenario in which we have a set *A* containing artists possibly associated to song titles. One of the artists of *A* is a_α ="Mike Chang", with no associated songs.

Another artist is a_β = "Kurt Hummel", and he has associated the song s_β = "For Good". Now, let's consider that we want to conciliate the artists of A with a graph G. For that, we must turn entities in A into queries. The resulting query $q_\alpha = (o_\alpha, m_\alpha, R_\alpha = \{r_\alpha*\})$ for a_α would be ("artist", "Mike Chang", $\{\lambda\}$). The resulting query $q_\beta = (o_\beta, m_\beta, R_\beta = \{r_\beta*\})$ for a_β would be ("artist", "Kurt Hummel", $\{$("song","For Good")$\}$).

As it can be seen, a MERA query q_i searches for a main raw string m_i associated to certain type o_i. Also, all the refinements or extra data provided for disambiguation purposes should also be labeled with a type.

MERA's Adaptable Algorithm

Algorithm 1 describes the MERA algorithm from the moment in which a Query q is received to the moment in which MERA returns its associated entities in Graph G. Table 2 contains the meaning of every macro used in Algorithm 1 (Box 1).

We have distinguished four parts in algorithm 1:

- **Blocking Stage:** C stores a set of blocking functions to filter candidates of G. All those functions are applied over G nodes to obtain a subset of nodes which will be compared with q.
- **Main Comparison:** Query q has a main type o and a main string content m. m is compared with all the alternative forms of the candidates obtained in *step 1*.
- **Refinements:** Query q may have a set of extra data or *refinements*. For each refinement r, G is navigated starting from the candidate nodes of *step 1*. If some coincidences good enough according to C are found, the obtained score is added weighted according to parameters in C to the respective candidate node score.
- **Filtering and Sorting Results:** The results associated with a query q are sorted in decreasing order. The user can define a maximum quantity k of results to be associated to a query q. If more results than k were found, only the k better are returned. Otherwise, all the results are returned.

String Comparison

In lines 11 and 20 of Algorithm 1, we use a macro f_{CMP} to represent the process in which the similarity between two strings s and t is obtained by using several comparison algorithms. f_{CMP} also receives a type o, expected to be the type of the entities that s and t represent. o must be specified for a potential accuracy profit, since different algorithms may be applied to conciliate s and t regarding their type o.

When mapping s and t to their degree of similarity r, once the set $P = \{P_0, P_1 \dots P_k\}$ of preprocessing techniques and the set $C = \{C_0, C_1 \dots Cl\}$ of comparison techniques has been selected based on the type o, the same workflow is followed in all cases, graphically described in Figure 1. s is turned into s' and t into t' pipping all algorithms P_i in P. That is, the input of P_0 is s and, in general terms, the input of P_i is the output of P_{i-1}. The final output s' is the output of P_k. Then, for each $C_i \in C$, we obtain every $R_i = C_i(s', t')$. The greater value of $\{R_0, R_1 \dots R_i\}$ is taken as the result r, having $f_{CMP}(s, t, o) = r$.

Blocking Function

MERA may employ several blocking functions at a time. However, we also include a blocking function that manages the concept of *an alternative form of an entity*, which consists of an adaptation of q-gram indexing and TF-IDF. The pseudo-code is included in Algorithm 2 (Box 2), and the macros are explained in Table 3.

Box 1. Algorithm 1: MERA Query

01: **Input:** Graph *G*
02: **Input:** Query *Q*
03: **Input:** Config *C*
%% **Blocking stage**
04: candidateNodes ← G.nodes
05: **for all** *fBLK* ∈ C.blockingFunctions **do**
06: candidateNodes ← *fBLK*(*q*, candidateNodes)
%% **Main Comparison**
07: tmpResults ← [λ]
08: **for all** aNode ∈ candidateNodes **do**
09: formScores ← {λ}
10: **for all** aForm ∈ aNode.alternativeForms **do**
11: formScores += *fCMP* (*q*.mainContent, aForm, *q*.type)
12: **if** max(formScores) ≥ *C*.minMainScore(*q*.order) **then**
13: tmpResults[aNode] = max(formScores)
%% **Refinements**
14: **for all** aRefType ∈ *q*.refinementTypes **do**
15: **for all** aCandidateRes ∈ tmpResults **do**
16: candidateRefs ← *G*.getRelated(aCandidateRes.node, aRefType)
17: **for all** aRefinement ∈ *q*.refinementsOfType(aRefType) **do**
18: formScores ← { λ }
19: **for all** aForm ∈ candidateRefs.alternativeForms **do**
20: formScores += *fCMP* (aRef, aForm, aRefType)
21: **if** max(formScores) ≥ *C*.minRefScore(*q*.order, aRefType) **then**
22: refScore ← max(formScores)·*C*.relevance(*q*.order, aRefType)
23: tmpResults[aNode] += refScore
%% **Filtering and sorting results**
24: results ← [λ]
25: *k* ← *C*.maxResults(*q*.order)
26: **for all** candidate ∈ tmpResults **do**
27: **if** candidate.score < *C*. minScore(*q*.order) **then**
28: results += candidate
29: sort(results)
30: **if** |results| ≤ *k* **then**
31: **return** results
32: **else**
33: **return** results[0:*k*]

Table 2. MERA Query

Structures			
Model	**Meaning**		
$\{\lambda\}$	Empty set		
$[\lambda]$	Empty dictionary of pairs (key $\rightarrow$ value)		
Functions			
Name	**Parameters**	**Return**	
fBLK	Query q, set of nodes S	Subset S' of S with the best matching candidates for q in S	
fCMP	String s_1, string s_2, type t	Similarity score between s_1 and s_2, applying algorithms associated to type t	
sort	Set or dictionary S	Sort S in descending order	
Methods			
Name	**Parameters**	**Invoked Over**	**Return**
minMainScore	Type of order o	Config C	Minimum score associated to o in C
getRelated	Node n, type t	Graph G	Nodes in G related with n with an edge of type t
refinementsOfType	Type t	Query q	Set of all the refinements in q of type t
minRefScore	Type of order o, type of entity t	Config C	Minimum score that an entity of type t should reach to be accepted when executing an order of type o.
relevance	Type of order o, type of entity t	Config C	Relevance factor of a refinement of type t when executing an order of type o.
Properties			
Name	**Invoked Over**	**Return**	
nodes	Graph G	All nodes in G	
blockingFunctions	Config C	Set of blocking functions	
alternativeForms	Node n	Alternative forms of n	
mainContent	Query q	Main string in q	
type	Query q	Type of the main content in q	
order	Query q	Type of order in q	
refinementTypes	Query q	Set of types of refinements in q	

Figure 1. Mapping two strings s and t into a real number r

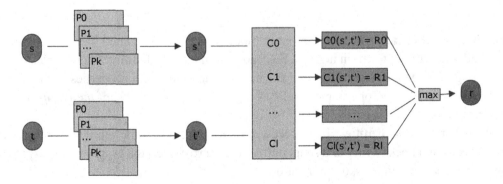

Box 2. Algorithm 2: MERA Blocking

01: Input: Query Q
02: Input: Index I
03: $N \leftarrow$ extractUniqueQrams(q.mainContent)
04: $Eidf = [\lambda]$
05: $Engr = [\lambda]$
06: for all $ni \in N$ **do**
07: $idfni \leftarrow I.\text{idf}(ni)$
08: for all $ei \in I.\text{entitiesWithQgram}(ni)$ **do**
09: $Eidf[ei] \leftarrow Eidf[ei]+\text{meraTfIdf}(ei, ni, idfni, I)$
10: $Engr[ei] \leftarrow Engr[ei] + 1$
11: result $\leftarrow \{\lambda\}$
12: for all $ei \in Engr$ **do**
13: if $Engr[ei] = |N|$ **then**
14: result $\leftarrow$ result $+ ei$
15: return result $\bigcup$ bestK($Eidf$)

The differences between the algorithm 2 and classical TF-IDF approaches based in q-grams are:

- We introduce the concept of an alternative form of an entity. An entity may be considered as a set of forms, and the algorithm takes care about how many forms contain a q-gram, instead of how many total times a q-gram is contained in all the entity forms.
- We manage the relevance of the q-grams in an entity with an accumulated TF-IDF score but also the number of q-grams contained in an entity e. If a certain entity contains all the q-grams of q.mainContent, then that entity is automatically included in the result set of candidates.

Graph Navigation

MERA is designed to match queries with graph nodes that represent entities. Finding a result requires the use of string similarity measures and graph navigation through the nodes' neighborhood. MERA uses two types of graph navigation when resolving a query: looking for alternative forms and looking for related entities.

- **Looking for Alternative Forms:** An entity (node) e may be associated with several identifying or pseudo-identifying forms in a graph, reachable from e through different properties or complex paths. E.g., a node that represents an artist may be identified with properties such as *canonical name, civil name, alias,* or complex paths as *all the identifying forms of the groups in which he participates*.
- **Looking for Related Entities:** If the received queries include some refinement regarding other entities (CD of a track, writer of a song, partner of an artist, etc.) the graph will be explored looking for coincidences in that kind of relations.

Table 3. MERA blocking

Structures		
Model	**Meaning**	
$\{\lambda\}$	Empty set	
$[\lambda]$	Empty dictionary of pairs (key $\rightarrow$ value)	
Functions		
Name	**Parameters**	**Return**
extractUniqueQgrams	String *s*	Set containing all the q-grams in *s*
meraTfIdf	entity ID *ei,*, q-gram *ni*, IDF score *idfni*, Index *I*.	$r = tf \cdot idfni$, where *tf* is the amount of forms of *ei* in which the q-gram *ni* appears
bestK	Dictionary *D*	Set containing *k* keys of pairs in *D* that are pointing to greater values. The parameter *k* is specified through configuration.
Methods		
Name	**Parameters**	**Invoked Over**	**Return**
idf	q-gram *ni*	Index *I*	Idf score of *ni* in *I*
entitiesWithNgram:	q-gram *ni*	Index *I*	Id of the entities in *I* that contain *ni*
Properties		
Name	**Invoked Over**	**Return**
nodes	Graph *G*	All nodes in *G*
blockingFunctions	Config *C*	Set of blocking functions
alternativeForms	Node *n*	Alternative forms of *n*
mainContent	Query *q*	Main string in *q*
type	Query *q*	Type of the main content in *q*
order	Query *q*	Type of order in *q*
refinementTypes	Query *q*	Set of types of refinements in *q*

Graph Schema

MERA is designed to be able to manage different sources, storing the origin of each piece of information in a single Graph *G*. The strategy employed is reification, where the nodes are not directly linked with their related contents (other entities of string properties), but auxiliary nodes are used as intermediaries. Those auxiliary nodes relate the subject and the object while they point to a third node that represents the origin of the information.

For example, let's suppose that we have a song *s* performed by an artist *a*. A natural way of representing this with an RDF graph is the triple $t = (s,$ "performer", $a)$. However, we also want to keep the information of *according to who s* is performed by *a*. Suppose that this information has been obtained from a dataset *d*. In general terms, a triple $t = (s, p, o)$ that has been obtained from a dataset *d* is transformed in three triples (s, p, n_{aux}), $(n_{aux}, target, o)$ and $(n_{aux}, dataset, d)$.

Let's say that we want to add the info of a new dataset denoted as *e* to graph *G* and, according to *e*, song *s* also has *a* as a performer. The resulting MERA graph is the one shown in Figure 2. The relation we want to represent is the same as in the previous case, i.e., the triple $(s,$ "performer", $a)$, but there is an already existing auxiliary node *aux* representing that link. Then, the triple $(aux,$ "dataset", $e)$ in *G* to indicate that dataset *e* also agrees about that link between *s* and *a*.

Figure 2. Auxiliary node with several datasets

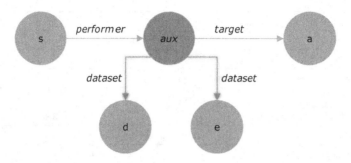

EVALUATION

We have implemented a prototype of MERA which includes the following characteristics:

- Graph navigation exploring alternative forms for each entity.
- Graph navigation exploring related entities.
- Configuration of relevancies when applying refinements to a query.
- Configuration of minimum acceptable values for each type when scoring a result.
- Blocking function adapted to alternative entity forms as described in section Blocking function.
- Usage of MERA RDF graph schema.
- Set of comparison algorithms of general-purpose.
- Set of text standardization functions.

The prototype has been used to conduct two kinds of experiments. On the one hand, intra-comparisons tests to evaluate which is the influence of the different features of MERA over the matching results. On the other hand, comparison of the results obtained by our prototype with the results of a baseline system matching the same sources.

Our experiments are all based on the reconciliation of a random slice of two different musical sources A and B against a third source C. The information of C has been introduced in a graph G and the entries of A and B have been used to build queries. The expected result for each query has been manually determined and annotated, which allowed us to measure the correctness of the results automatically obtained by MERA and the alternative approach. Source A is supposed to contain data of high quality (complete and with none or few misspellings) while source B is supposed to contain noisy data (user-entered and incomplete). However, every query thrown against G is formed by a song name and one or more names of associated artists/writers. The selected sources are:

- Source A of high quality: MusicBrainz (Stutzbach, 2011).
- Source B of noisy data: queries extracted from AOL dump (Arrington, 2006).
- Target source C: Discogs (Hartnett, 2015).

Some entries were randomly selected from the material of MusicBrainz and AOL to build queries. The same queries were used during all the experiments. Since the targeted source is the content of Discogs, the advanced search engine of Discogs itself has been used to compare with MERA. As well as our proposal, Discogs advanced search engine allows the user to perform rich queries in which every piece of information is labeled with a type of the musical domain (release, artist, writer, genre…). The types specified by Discogs are a closed set which does not fit exactly in the RDF schema of our prototype, but these differences are minor. None of the mappings between MERA's and Discogs's schemes are controverted.

Description of Sources

The experiments were executed under the following software/hardware conditions: Virtual Machine using Windows Azure cloud computing services, 64-bit Operating System: Windows Server 2012 R2, AMD Opteron (tm) Processor 4171 HE 2.10 GHz, 14 GB RAM and Python 2.7.3 64-bit.

Target Source: Discogs

We have used the source Discogs (Hartnett, 2015) to create a graph G containing a total of 500000 songs, as well as their associated artists and writers. The information has been extracted from a dump of Discogs published in 2015-01-01. That dump includes a set of musical releases containing one or more tracks and associated artist, with a total of 45458287 detected tracks among all the releases.

The scalability of our prototype is not enough to manage a graph with the data of the entire dump, since it completely works in main memory, so we have reduced that quantity to 500000, a number that we can handle but that is still a representative and a high enough slice. Those 500000 songs include 205 that has been manually detected to be the adequate answer to the queries used in the experiments. The rest of songs has been randomly selected from the dump file.

We also included in the graph all the artists and writers linked to each song. Discogs associates people to tracks/releases using different roles. We have mapped some of the original Discogs roles to our own roles to include these associated people in our graph. Discogs roles "Artist", "Featuring", and "Vocals" have been mapped to "artist", and "Written-By" has been mapped to "writer". The rest of Discogs roles have been ignored.

The final graph used in the experiments contains a total of 500000 songs and 624441 people.

Source of High Quality: MusicBrainz

The open music encyclopedia MusicBrainz (Hemerly, 2011) fits in our requirements of offering a great amount of data of high quality. We have randomly selected a set of works from this source and we have manually checked that they point to a work that also exists in the Discogs data dump. In order to generate a sample of MusicBrainz, the entire database was downloaded, and 300 recordings were randomly picked. Later, we manually looked for coincidences between these elements and song nodes in the graph formed by the partial content of Discogs. The first 100 coincidences were selected and used to build queries using the song title and the artists/writers associated to them in MusicBrainz. The average of associated artist/writers per song is 2.62.

Noisy Source: AOL Dump

In 2006, AOL Inc. released a file containing twenty million search keywords for over 650.000 users over a three-month period (Arrington, 2006). We have considered that musical-related searches found among this material could be a representative example of a noisy source, since all the inaccuracies have been introduced by random real users when doing real searches. The strategy to find musical content among the rest of searches followed the next steps:

- We explored all the items selecting those that contained the tokens "feat" and "featuring". We divided those items into two parts using the word "feat" as a separator, and we added each one to a set of noisy candidate keys N.

- We removed from N those words or sequences that are meaningless for our purposes, such as "to download", "ringtone", "free music", "song of", "video", etc. In case of finding "-" in a key, we divided the key into two pieces and we repeated the cleaning process with each part. All the results were added to a set of clean candidate keys C with 1203 elements.

- We revised manually each key in C in the context of its apparition in the log of AOL to check if they really were artists/songs or not. In addition, if we detected that some of the keys contained more than one artist/song at a time, we divided it in parts and considered them separately. At the end of this process 922 sequences (not unique) representing songs or artists were detected. We stored them in a set of found keys F.

- We put all the elements of F in a set of definitive keys D. Then, for every key k_i in F with a length greater than 3, we generated all the possible strings $S_i = \{s_0, s_1 \ldots s_k\}$ in a Levenshtein distance of one with k_i. For each $s_j \in S_i$, if s_j was found more than 5 times in the log of AOL, s_j was added to D. With this, we collected a group of detected musical entities that were queried by users as well as character variations of all of them that had a certain presence in the log of AOL. We removed from D meaningless sequences as the ones used in previous steps.

- We processed again the entire log looking for lines containing at least a key of D. We elaborated three different lists with the found elements, regarding if they contained a single key, between two and three keys or more than three. 327.904 user queries were detected.

- For each list, we picked random elements and checked if they were actual queries looking for musical content or false positives. We kept the first 35 real queries found in each least that included a song name and one or more artist names. We erased all the meaningless words or sequences of previous steps from the picked elements.

In every case, we respected the original appearance of each entity in the log of AOL. That is, we removed meaningless words, but no other changes were applied to the original content.

With this, we obtained a list of 105 items with material to build queries with noise introduced by real users. The average of associated artists per song was 1.44.

Evaluation

Evaluation of MERA Features

Some experiments designed to check the impact of MERA's proposals over scenarios with different level of data quality were executed. The tests evaluate the correctness of the results returned by our prototype with different configurations when executing a consistent set of queries against the very same source. In all cases, the entities to recognize were songs, and the information used was its title and associated artists. The sets of chosen features across the different experiments are shown in Table 4.

There are some other configuration parameters whose values have been fixed for all the experiments, including:

- Top results per query: 15.
- Minimum score for a song to be accepted: 0.50.
- Minimum score for an artist to be accepted: 0.65.
- Artist relevance when refining the result of a song: 0.80.
- Reconciliation string algorithms used in all cases: Levenshtein similarity.
- Pre-processing functions included: replacement of all non-ASCII characters by ASCII equivalents with Unicode normalization, lower-casing, deletion of punctuation marks, and deletion of redundant white spaces.

In absence of the MERA blocking function described in the Algorithm 2, the blocking strategy consisted on selecting the best 60 candidates based on accumulated TF-IDF score of q-grams. In case of being active MERA blocking, the candidates may exceed that number if there are enough individuals containing all the q-grams of the song provided in the query. The length of the q-grams was, in all cases, 3 characters.

This configuration allows relatively bad results to be ranked (at a low position) as possible matches, mainly because of the low threshold of acceptance for songs. An execution of MERA looking for safe matches should probably define higher values of acceptance. However, since we are purely evaluating the correctness of the results, in this case we prefer to prioritize exhaustiveness by sacrificing performance (the more accepted songs, the more comparisons will be performed). Needless to say, the usage of Levenshtein distance as the unique string similarity may cause false negatives when trying to match entities which are named using disordered tokens or abbreviations not recognized as alternative forms.

Table 4. Features used in experiments

Feature	Experiment ID				
	A	B	C	D	E
Considering alternative forms of entities	-	✓	-	✓	✓
Using information of related entities	-	-	✓	✓	✓
Using MERA blocking function	-	-	-	-	✓

The alternative forms considered for each entity when building the graph G were the following:

- **Artists:** Canonical name, civil name, alias and usual name variations such as abbreviations. All this information is provided by Discogs. When dealing with a group, also the canonical name of its integrating artists. When dealing with a person, the canonical name of the groups she belongs to.
- **Songs:** Canonical name. When this name has text between brackets (e.g., "Summer love (radio remix)"), also the same name without the information in brackets was considered as an alternative form.

MERA vs. Discogs Advanced Search

Among the available alternative matching systems mentioned, Discogs advanced search system[1] was selected as baseline mainly because of two reasons. On the one hand, in our experiments we aim to match entities of different sources with the content of Discogs. Then, it seems like the search engine of Discogs itself may be an appropriate tool to consider. On the other hand, the input information expected by the advanced search system of Discogs is pretty similar to the conceptual information expected by MERA. Most of the alternatives are general-purpose and do not accept a labeled input such as MERA expects. Despite it may be possible to adapt some of those systems to build conditions similar to our experiments, probably the closest systems to our design are the music specialized ones, such as Discogs search engine or MusicBrainz Piccard. Nevertheless, the former is designed to match entries with MusicBrainz database.

Discogs portal also offers a type of unlabeled search as a regular general-purpose search engine. However, this type of search is hardly comparable to MERA, especially when dealing with queries which have extra associated information further than the name of the core element to match. Because of this, only the advanced search system has been compared with our prototype.

As far as we know, Discogs has not released software separate from its web application to perform queries against its library. Due to that, our evaluation has consisted in introducing manually the contents of each query in the web form of advanced search and annotating the obtained results. Each query has been thrown using different slices of the whole information to check how the presence/absence of data affects the results. For instance, given a query to match a song called "Heart-Shaped Box", with "Nirvana" as artist and "Kurt Cobain" as writer, the results of using just the of the name of the song in the form, song plus artists, song plus writer, and all the information at a time have been annotated.

All the queries from both target sources were introduced in the Discogs system. In the case of AOL, which contains information already typed, artists were specified in the field with the label "By Artist". The information related to writers have been put into the field "Credit", which points to every other role different to "artist". However, in the case of AOL source, the content was typed a posteriori, then it is not clear if the user who originally wrote the query was referring to an artist, a writer or to any other role. Due to that reason, the information of people was introduced in both fields of the form, and just the best result obtained was annotated.

As we previously stated, the current version of our prototype operates just in main memory and cannot handle a graph containing the entire dump of Discogs. Nevertheless, the Discogs web search system always uses the entire information of the source. In order to produce comparable results, when we threw a query and the desired entry did not appear in the first position of the results, we checked each element which ranked better to determine if it were also included in our random slice of Discogs. All those entities that were not in our slice were excluded from the obtained list, and the expected entry was promoted to its corresponding rank without these elements. This decision could have affected the quality of the experiments if Discogs applied a blocking function with a maximum number of candidates, such as MERA does. However, there is not a maximum number of results when using the web search.

RESULTS AND DISCUSSION

Inclusion of MERA Features

Experiment A consisted of applying Levenshtein distance to conciliate sources without using any kind of graph navigation, i.e., just by comparing canonical titles of songs. The obtained results can be queried in Figure 3. In the chart, we have grouped the results of the queries in four different categories:

- Queries in which the correct entry appeared in first place.
- Queries in which the correct entry appeared in second or third place.
- Queries in which the correct entry appeared in fourth or worse place.
- Queries in which the correct entry did not even appear.

Under these conditions, 52% of MB's target results are ranked first. In AOL case, just 43.81%. The reasons we have found for these high rates of incorrect are mainly the same for both sources:

- The blocking function did not detect as candidate the target entry. This happens mostly when dealing with songs with a short name, with common words in G, or a combination of these two factors.
- Lack of alternative forms of song. The titles of AOL and MB may present a great difference with their corresponding title in Discogs according to Levenshtein distance, despite they point to the same reality. This is mainly because Discogs' content usually contains song titles with information between brackets, such as "Summer love (radio edition)" or "Summer love (remix DJ)".
- Ambiguity: Song names are not unique in some cases. If we do not explore related artist in order to decide the best result, there is not a reliable criterion to decide which entry should appear in first place.

Figure 3. Experiment A: No graph navigation

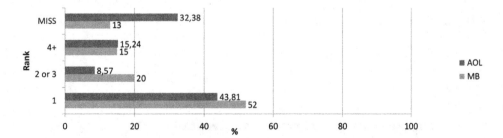

The conditions of experiments B and C allow us to solve issues derived from lack of alternative forms of songs and ambiguity respectively. These results are respectively shown in Figure 4 and Figure 5. As it can be checked, the inclusion of MERA's graph navigation strategies improve the results for both sources, increasing the rate of target entities ranked first and decreasing the rate of intermediate/ missed entries. The inclusion of related entities produces a positive impact on the results, improving the rate of first-ranked entities. Nevertheless, it has poor or even none impact in the rate of missed entries. This happens because most of the missed results are not accepted in blocking stage. MERA explores relations between entities that have passed the blocking cut, so intermediate results can improve their rank, but this does not affect at all to those that have not reached the comparison stage. On the other hand, in Experiment B we have added alternative forms that affect the TF-IDF of some target entities, which allow some missed results to pass the cut during the blocking stage and let them be evaluated by the comparison algorithms.

In Experiment D, we have applied both graph navigations at a time, i.e., we consider alternative forms and related entities during the matching process. This has a positive effect on the success rates for both sources. The results can be checked in Figure 6. In this case, the reasons to find a target entry missed or low-ranked are not the same for both sources:

Figure 4. Experiment B: Alternative forms

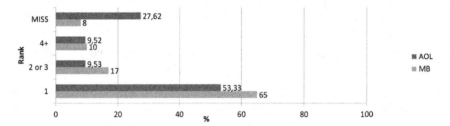

Figure 5. Experiment C: Related entities

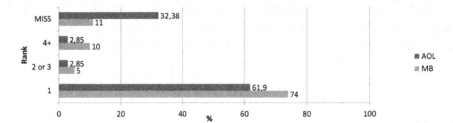

Figure 6. Experiment D: Complete graph navigation

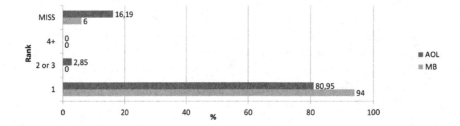

- **MusicBrainz:** There are 6 target entries not ranked first. One of them did not pass the cut of the blocking function because the song has a short name formed by common q-grams in Spanish: "El amor". The other five are all pieces of classical music in which it looks like Levenshtein distance cannot detect matches. An illustrative example of this is the query "Sonata for Piano no. 7 in C major, K. 284b/309: III. Rondeau. Allegretto grazioso". Its equivalent in Discogs express the same reality but with different naming conventions. Artist information has not been helpful in these cases since the classical composers provided by MusicBrainz for those pieces (Mozart, Beethoven...) are widely repeated across other tracks with similar names. Algorithms different to Levenshtein should be applied to match this kind of works.

- **AOL:** The under-ranked entries happen mainly because of the detection of versions of songs before the one we are looking for. The reason for the missed ones is, in most of the cases, that the target entry did not pass the cut of the blocking function. Some results are still missed because the song name contained heavy misspellings. An illustrative example is the string "ghostrider" trying to express the song "Ghost Writer".

When we include MERA blocking function in Experiment E, all the target results pass the blocking cut and the rate of first-ranked entries grows to 95% for MB and 94.29% for AOL. The under-ranked results are the same of Experiment E, since we have not change comparison techniques nor we used extra data. The obtained results are shown in Figure 7.

Nevertheless, this blocking function has a performance cost. We repeated 50 times the experiments E and D and our measurements indicate that the performance is 14.76% worse in experiment E compared with experiment D. This cost is not just because of the calculations needed to select the candidates in blocking stage, but because that approach may generate more candidates than the pre-configured top number. This leads to more operations during the comparison stage. We have measured how MERA blocking function exceeds the preconfigured number of candidates to be accepted in blocking stage in experiment E. That number had been set to 60, and we checked that the average number of candidates returned per entity has been 68.12. Also, 94.62% of the queries had exactly 60 results. However, we have detected that in some cases the function returned a number of candidates that exceed by large 60. This happened with queries formed by short names with common q-grams in G. While executing E, the query that produced the highest number of valid candidates in blocking stage was "So what" of the artist "Ciara", with a total of 326 detected candidates.

As shown in Figure 3, Figure 4, Figure 5, and Figure 6, if we do not use all the MERA features implemented in our prototype, the results of the clean source (MB) improve the results of the noisy

Figure 7. Experiment E: Using MERA blocking function

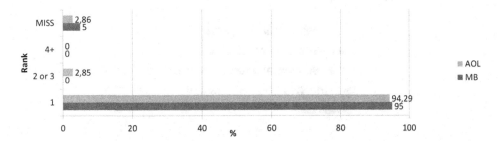

source (AOL). However, when using all them at a time, as it is shown in Figure 7, both sources present very similar results. Then, it can be concluded that noise introduced in entity names by real users does not have a notable impact over the quality of the matching process. Even if the rate of first-ranked elements is slightly higher with MB, AOL obtained a lower rate of missed songs (2.86% vs 5% of MB).

MERA vs. Discogs System

During the evaluation of MERA features in the previous experiments, we could check that the inclusion of an extra feature has a positive effect on the obtained results. This means that, in general terms, the more information is associated with a query, the more accurate are the results brought by MERA. However, Discogs search engine does not behave equally. The algorithms used by Discogs look for entries in which all the information introduced is included somehow. This may cause false negatives under the following conditions:

- When the information of the query exceeds the information of the target entity.
- When some of the elements of the query do not produce a match with some of the elements of the target entity due to misspellings or alternative names.

Due to that reason, using all the available information is not always the best approach to find the correct result with Discogs search engine. We have detected that 46.81% of the target entries using AOL material ranked worse with the inclusion in the query of some extra piece of information. In the case of MusicBrainz, this rate grows up to 64%.

Bearing that in mind, we present the results of our experiments using Discogs search engine segregated by the number and nature of the pieces of information used in each attempt to match an element of AOL/MusicBrainz with an entry in Discogs. We analyze separately the material of AOL and MusicBrainz.

AOL Against Discogs and MERA

In Figure 8 the results of using different strategies to match the very same element of the AOL material with its corresponding entry in Discogs are offered. Those strategies are identified with a label in the Y axis of the chart. Each label has the following meaning (in every case at least the song name was included in the query):

- **No Artist:** Just a song name.

Figure 8. AOL against Discogs and MERA

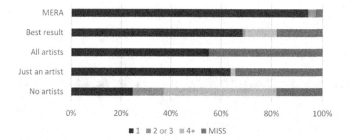

- **Just an Artist:** The associated artist who produced better results.
- **All Artist:** All the available artist, in case there are two or more.
- **Best Result:** Best obtained result using any of the previous strategies for each entry
- **MERA:** MERA results using its complete set of features. These statistics are the ones obtained in Experiment E.

Not all the queries fit in all the strategies. In the section of "All artists", just those entries with two or more associated people are considered. In every case, the offered results are relative to the number of cases which fit in the strategy.

Several conclusions can be extracted from the obtained data. Firstly, it seems like the best strategy to find the target entity for each query is using a single artist as extra information. The rate of queries which are resolved with the desired entry in the first position is 63.81% with just an artist, compared with the 55.17% obtained for all artists and the 24.76% with no extra information rather than song name. The reason behind this is the general strategy followed by Discogs search engine, in which all the information introduced in the search form must be part of an entry to be included in the results. Then, using an artist in the query usually works as a useful tool to decide the best entry among several songs with the same or similar name. However, including a piece of information which is not stored in Discogs causes a false negative.

As well as MERA, Discogs produced poor results of desired entities ranked in the first place when using just song names. Just 24.76% of the entities are successfully matched without providing artists. With MERA this number grows up to 43.81% without using alternative forms, as it is shown in Figure 3 (Experiment A). Despite MERA's rate is sensibly higher, none of the systems are accurate enough to consider that they produce good enough matches at the first attempt. Nevertheless, Discogs outperforms MERA in the rate of missed results using just a song name. 32.38% are missed with MERA, by 18.10% that are missed with Discogs. This difference is mainly caused because of the effects of the configured blocking function in Experiment A. The desired results did not pass the cut for MERA, while they are simply low-ranked using Discogs.

Not mattering the combination of information used, MERA outperforms the effectivity of Discogs. As it is shown in Figure 7 (Experiment E), when all the features of our prototype were active, MERA finds the desired result in 94.29% of the cases, compared with the 68.57% achieved by Discogs. The reason behind this is the different text reconciliation algorithms used. The Discogs search engine, based on ElasticSearch (Hartnett, 2015), do not follow a strategy of exact match, since it is capable of producing matches between titles with some missed or disordered tokens. However, is it heavily affected by misspellings or any other internal change in a token. An example of this is the query which expected match is the song Fine Young, of Cannibals. The input found in the dump of AOL for this recording was "fine young", of "canibals". A query which uses just the song name is resolved with the desired entry ranking first. However, when introducing "canibals" in the field of artist, no results are offered by the search engine because of a missing "n" in the group name. Another significant example is the query "'touch it'remix", with single quotes surrounding "touch it" and no blank between the final quote and "remix". The absence of a blank after the quote cause that no result is shown. Just by adding that white space to the original query, the first result obtained is the target one.

MusicBrainz Against Discogs and MERA

The results of using different sets of information of an entry of MusicBrainz to match it with its equivalent in Discogs using the web search engine are shown in Figure 9. Due to the nature of MusicBrainz information, it has been possible to test more combinations than in the case of AOL. All the people related to a song in MusicBrainz has an explicit role (main artist, writer, featurer, etc.). Then, it is clear where each piece of information should be placed in the search form, in opposition to the case of AOL were the roles of related people were a priori unknown. This lets us analyze in a separate way the effect of including pieces of information of different types in the form.

The different strategies are identified with a label in the Y axes. The labels have the following meaning (in every case at least the song name was included in the query):

- **No Artist:** Just a song name.
- **Just an Artist:** just the name of the artist who produced the best result.
- **All Artist:** All the names of all the artists at a time.
- **Just a Writer:** Just the name of the writer who produced the best result.
- **All Writers:** The name of all the writers at a time.
- **An Artist and a Writer:** The name of the artist and the writer which produce a better result, just in case there are at least an artist and a writer.
- **All the Information:** The name of every artist and every writer, just in case this number of related entities is greater or equal to three.
- **An Artist or a Writer:** The name of the artist or the writer who, by just himself, produced the best result.
- **Best Result:** For each entry in MusicBrainz, best result achieved by using any of the previous strategies.
- **MERA:** MERA results using its complete set of features. These statistics are the ones obtained in Experiment E.

Figure 9. MusicBrainz against Discogs and MERA

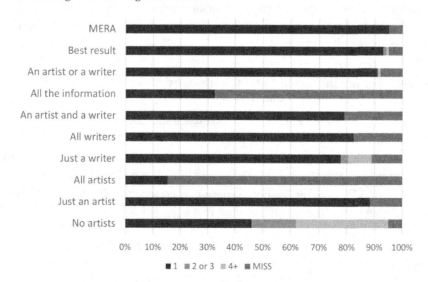

240

As in the case of AOL, not all the MusicBrainz entries fit in all the strategies. In every case, the offered results are relative to the number of cases which fits in the strategy.

One of the most relevant fact that can be extracted from our results is that, with a clean source and an adequate combination of artists and writers, the effectiveness of MERA and Discogs is quite similar. With all its features activated, our prototype was able to rank first the adequate entity 95% of the times, compared with the 93% scored by Discogs. Nevertheless, it is noticeable that the score of Discogs is obtained through considering the best attempt for each entry of MusicBrainz, instead of using a consistent strategy. Using a consistent strategy, the inclusion of a single artist in the query has revealed as the best approach to produce perfect matchings, with a success rate of 88.41%.

The results of using all the available information in a query may look shocking a priori: just 32.43% of the entries with several artists and writers associated produced a match, while 67.57% of the attempts did not return the target entity among the results (actually, all the results consisted of an empty list in those cases). This occurs because of using too much information. As we have already mentioned, a query with data more complete than the corresponding entry in Discogs causes a false negative.

Also, it is noticeable that the inclusion of an artist, with a success rate of 88.41%, have a more positive effect on the results than the inclusion of a writer, with a success rate of 77.78%. The reason for this result is that it is common to have songs versioned by different artists. In a well-documented source, such as Discogs, all these versions are connected to the same writer. Then, the search engine is capable of finding all these entries, but it does not have extra information to decide which of these versions is the target one. In opposition, specifying the artists of a given song works better as a disambiguation mechanism.

It is interesting to remark that despite MERA and Discogs have the same rate of missing results for AOL queries (5%), the reasons for failing are not the same for both approaches due to the different capabilities of the algorithms used. As we already mentioned, MERA failed to recognize pieces of classical music with long names and disordered tokens. This may be solved by integrating into MERA's pipeline an algorithm token-oriented such as Jaccard similarity. Nevertheless, further investigation needs to be done to check the effect on false positives due to that decision.

By contrast, Discogs is able to properly match some of these titles of classical music, but it fails with other entries due mainly to slight differences in song or artists' names. An insightful example of this is the query "Cholly (Funk Gettin' Ready to Roll)". The corresponding entry in Discogs for that query is stored with a blank after the single quote. The absence of a blank made the search engine to consider "Gettin'Ready" as a single token, which is not present in any title of the source, which makes the application to return an empty list of results. An example of a query which is solved with the desired entry under-ranked is "Feel Like Makin'Love", written by "Gene McDaniels". In this case, the absence of blank between "Makin" and "Love" does not motivate the failure, but the way of specifying the author of the song. The Discogs advanced search system considers alternative forms of artists, such as MERA does. When matching clean sources such as Discogs and MusicBrainz, an exact match with some of that forms is enough most of the times to recognize an artist. For instance, this writer is stored in the system with the forms of "Eugene McDaniels", "E. McDaniels" or just "McDaniels". However, in this case, the form "Gene McDaniels" used in MusicBrainz does not appear as a recognized alternative form, which causes that the correct entry appears under-ranked in the result list.

CONCLUSION AND FUTURE WORK

We have described MERA, the architecture of a highly configurable system for matching several data sources containing music-related information. The novel contributions of our approach are:

- A graph-based approach in which every piece of information maintains a list of source(s) that agrees on it, allowing the user to use this information for filtering contents.
- A configurable graph navigation system that looks for alternatives identifying forms of each entity involved in the matching process.

We have also proposed a blocking technique based on q-gram indexing and TF-IDF adapted to MERA's notion of alternative forms of an entity. We implemented a prototype of our system and we found that it was effective in more than 94% of the cases under the conditions of our experiments. Our prototype has performed similarly dealing with sources of high quality and with noisy sources composed of data handwritten by real users. We have compared our prototype with a well-known search engine music-specialized, outperforming its rate of correct matches.

Following current research trends in record linkage, we want to extend MERA to be compatible with Big Data environments by including parallel computing. We also plan to integrate automatic learning options in the workflow to let the user provide training data to deal with issues transversal to most record linkage scenarios, such as misspellings or naming conventions.

REFERENCES

Achichi, M., Cheatham, M., Dragisic, Z., Euzenat, J., Faria, D., Ferrara, A., ... & Jiménez-Ruiz, E. (2016). Results of the ontology alignment evaluation initiative 2016. In OM: Ontology Matching (pp. 73–129).

Altwaijry, H., Kalashnikov, D. V., & Mehrotra, S. (2017). Qda: A query-driven approach to entity resolution. *IEEE Transactions on Knowledge and Data Engineering*, 29(2), 402–417. doi:10.1109/TKDE.2016.2623607

Arrington, M. (2006). AOL proudly releases massive amounts of private data.

Baxter, R., Christen, P., & Churches, T. (2003). A comparison of fast blocking methods for record linkage. In ACM SIGKDD (Vol. 3, pp. 25–27).

Benatallah, B., Venugopal, S., Ryu, S. H., Motahari-Nezhad, H. R., Wang, W., & ... (2017). A systematic review and comparative analysis of cross-document coreference resolution methods and tools. *Computing*, 99(4), 313–349. doi:10.100700607-016-0490-0

Castano, S., Ferrara, A., & Montanelli, S. (2018). Matching Techniques for Data Integration and Exploration: From Databases to Big Data. In A Comprehensive Guide Through the Italian Database Research Over the Last 25 Years (pp. 61–76). Springer.

Chaudhuri, S., Ganjam, K., Ganti, V., & Motwani, R. (2003). Robust and efficient fuzzy match for online data cleaning. In *Proceedings of the 2003 ACM SIGMOD international conference on Management of data* (pp. 313–324). 10.1145/872757.872796

Christen, P. (2008). Febrl-: an open source data cleaning, deduplication and record linkage system with a graphical user interface. In *Proceedings of the 14th ACM SIGKDD international conference on Knowledge discovery and data mining* (pp. 1065–1068). 10.1145/1401890.1402020

Christen, P., & Winkler, W. E. (2016). Record Linkage. In Encyclopedia of Machine Learning and Data Mining.

de Assis Costa, G., & de Oliveira, J. M. P. (2016). A blocking scheme for entity resolution in the semantic web. In *2016 IEEE 30th international conference on Advanced Information networking and applications (AINA)* (pp. 1138–1145).

Draisbach, U., & Naumann, F. (2010). DuDe: The duplicate detection toolkit. In *Proceedings of the International Workshop on Quality in Databases (QDB)*.

Dunning, T. E., Kindig, B. D., Joshlin, S. C., & Archibald, C. P. (2011). *Associating and linking compact disc metadata*. Google Patents.

Efthymiou, V., Papadakis, G., Papastefanatos, G., Stefanidis, K., & Palpanas, T. (2017). Parallel meta-blocking for scaling entity resolution over big heterogeneous data. *Information Systems, 65*, 137–157. doi:10.1016/j.is.2016.12.001

Elmagarmid, A., Ilyas, I. F., Ouzzani, M., Quiané-Ruiz, J.-A., Tang, N., & Yin, S. (2014). NADEEF/ER: Generic and interactive entity resolution. In *Proceedings of the 2014 ACM SIGMOD international conference on Management of data* (pp. 1071–1074). 10.1145/2588555.2594511

Enríquez, J. G., Domínguez-Mayo, F. J., Escalona, M. J., Ross, M., & Staples, G. (2017). Entity reconciliation in big data sources: A systematic mapping study. *Expert Systems with Applications, 80*, 14–27. doi:10.1016/j.eswa.2017.03.010

Eshghi, K., Rajaram, S. S., Dagli, C., & Cohen, I. (2015). *Identifying related objects in a computer database*. Google Patents.

Fellegi, I. P., & Sunter, A. B. (1969). A Theory for Record Linkage. *Journal of the American Statistical Association, 64*(328), 1183–1210. doi:10.1080/01621459.1969.10501049

Fisher, J., Christen, P., Wang, Q., & Rahm, E. (2015). A clustering-based framework to control block sizes for entity resolution. In *Proceedings of the 21th ACM SIGKDD International Conference on Knowledge Discovery and Data Mining* (pp. 279–288). 10.1145/2783258.2783396

Frontini, F., Brando, C., & Ganascia, J.-G. (2015). Domain-adapted named-entity linker using Linked Data. In *Workshop on NLP Applications: Completing the Puzzle co-located with the 20th International Conference on Applications of Natural Language to Information Systems (NLDB 2015)*.

Gao, C., Cheng, Q., Li, X., & Xia, S. (2018). Cloud-assisted privacy-preserving profile-matching scheme under multiple keys in mobile social network. *Cluster Computing*, 1–9.

Hall, P. A. V., & Dowling, G. R. (1980). Approximate string matching. *ACM Computing Surveys, 12*(4), 381–402. doi:10.1145/356827.356830

Harron, K., Goldstein, H., & Dibben, C. (2015). *Methodological developments in data linkage*. John Wiley & Sons. doi:10.1002/9781119072454

Hartnett, J. (2015). Discogs. com. *The Charleston Advisor*, *16*(4), 26–33. doi:10.5260/chara.16.4.26

Hemerly, J. (2011). Making metadata: The case of MusicBrainz.

Hernández, M. A., & Stolfo, S. J. (1995). The merge/purge problem for large databases. *SIGMOD Record*, *24*(2), 127–138. doi:10.1145/568271.223807

Ilyas, I. F., Chu, X., & others. (2015). Trends in cleaning relational data: Consistency and deduplication. *Foundations and Trends®in Databases*, *5*(4), 281–393.

Jurczyk, P., Lu, J. J., Xiong, L., Cragan, J. D., & Correa, A. (2008). FRIL: A tool for comparative record linkage. *AMIA ... Annual Symposium Proceedings - AMIA Symposium. AMIA Symposium*, *2008*, 440. PMID:18998844

Kalashnikov, D. V., & Mehrotra, S. (2006). Domain-independent data cleaning via analysis of entity-relationship graph. *ACM Transactions on Database Systems*, *31*(2), 716–767. doi:10.1145/1138394.1138401

Kang, H., Getoor, L., Shneiderman, B., Bilgic, M., & Licamele, L. (2008). Interactive entity resolution in relational data: A visual analytic tool and its evaluation. *Visualization and Computer Graphics. IEEE Transactions On*, *14*(5), 999–1014. PMID:18599913

Kouki, P., Pujara, J., Marcum, C., Koehly, L., & Getoor, L. (2017). Collective entity resolution in familial networks. In *2017 IEEE International Conference on Data Mining (ICDM)* (pp. 227–236). 10.1109/ICDM.2017.32

Lamarine, M., Hager, J., Saris, W. H., Astrup, A., & Valsesia, A. (2018). Fuzzy Matching and Machine Learning approaches for large-scale, automated mapping of food diaries on food composition tables. *Frontiers in Nutrition*, *5*, 38. doi:10.3389/fnut.2018.00038 PMID:29868600

Lotker, Z., Patt-Shamir, B., & Pettie, S. (2015). Improved distributed approximate matching. *Journal of the Association for Computing Machinery*, *62*(5), 38. doi:10.1145/2786753

McCormack, K., & Smyth, M. (2017). A Mathematical Solution to String Matching for Big Data Linking. *Journal of Statistical Science and Application*, *5*, 39–55.

Newcombe, H. B., & Kennedy, J. M. (1962). Record linkage: Making maximum use of the discriminating power of identifying information. *Communications of the ACM*, *5*(11), 563–566. doi:10.1145/368996.369026

Nguyen, K., & Ichise, R. (2016). Linked data entity resolution system enhanced by configuration learning algorithm. *IEICE Transactions on Information and Systems*, *99*(6), 1521–1530. doi:10.1587/transinf.2015EDP7392

Peng, T., Li, L., & Kennedy, J. (2014). A Comparison of Techniques for Name Matching. *Journal of Computers*, *2*(1), 55–61.

Pow, C., Iron, K., Boyd, J., Brown, A., Thompson, S., Chong, N., & Ma, C. (2017). Privacy-preserving record linkage: An international collaboration between Canada, Australia and Wales. *International Journal for Population Data Science, 1*(1). doi:10.23889/ijpds.v1i1.101

Rahmani, H., Ranjbar-Sahraei, B., Weiss, G., & Tuyls, K. (2016). Entity resolution in disjoint graphs: An application on genealogical data. *Intelligent Data Analysis, 20*(2), 455–475. doi:10.3233/IDA-160814

Schnell, R., Bachteler, T., & Reiher, J. (2009). Privacy-preserving record linkage using Bloom filters. *BMC Medical Informatics and Decision Making, 9*(1), 41. doi:10.1186/1472-6947-9-41 PMID:19706187

Shin, K., Jung, J., Lee, S., & Kang, U. (2015). Bear: Block elimination approach for random walk with restart on large graphs. In *Proceedings of the 2015 ACM SIGMOD International Conference on Management of Data* (pp. 1571–1585). 10.1145/2723372.2723716

Song, D., Luo, Y., & Heflin, J. (2017). Linking heterogeneous data in the semantic web using scalable and domain-independent candidate selection. *IEEE Transactions on Knowledge and Data Engineering, 29*(1), 143–156. doi:10.1109/TKDE.2016.2606399

Stutzbach, A. R. (2011). MusicBrainz [review]. *Notes, 68*(1), 147–151. doi:10.1353/not.2011.0134

Vatsalan, D., Sehili, Z., Christen, P., & Rahm, E. (2017). Privacy-Preserving Record Linkage for Big Data: Current Approaches and Research Challenges. In Handbook of Big Data Technologies (pp. 851–895). Springer.

Vidhya, K. A., & Geetha, T. V. (2017). Resolving entity on a large scale: determining linked entities and grouping similar attributes represented in assorted terminologies. *Distributed and Parallel Databases, 35*(3–4), 303–332. doi:10.100710619-017-7205-1

Volz, J., Bizer, C., Gaedke, M., & Kobilarov, G. (2009). *Silk-A Link Discovery Framework for the Web of Data* (Vol. 538). LDOW.

Yancey, W. E. (2002). BigMatch: A program for extracting probable matches from a large file for record linkage. *Computing, 1*, 1–8.

Yu, M., Li, G., Deng, D., & Feng, J. (2016). String similarity search and join: A survey. *Frontiers of Computer Science, 10*(3), 399–417. doi:10.100711704-015-5900-5

Zahaf, A., & Malki, M. (2018). Methods for Ontology Alignment Change. In Handbook of Research on Contemporary Perspectives on Web-Based Systems (pp. 214–239). Hershey, PA: IGI Global. doi:10.4018/978-1-5225-5384-7.ch011

Zhu, L., Ghasemi-Gol, M., Szekely, P., Galstyan, A., & Knoblock, C. A. (2016). Unsupervised Entity Resolution on Multi-type Graphs. In *International Semantic Web Conference* (pp. 649–667).

ENDNOTE

[1] https://www.discogs.com/search/advanced

Chapter 10
Sarcasm Detection in Twitter Data:
A Supervised Approach

Santosh Kumar Bharti
Pandit Deendayal Petroleum University, India

Sathya Babu Korra
National Institute of Technology Rourkela, India

ABSTRACT

Posting sarcastic messages on social media like Twitter, Facebook, WhatsApp, etc., became a new trend to avoid direct negativity. Detecting this indirect negativity in the social media text has become an important task as they influence every business organization. In the presence of sarcasm, detection of actual sentiment on these texts has become the most challenging task. An automated system is required that will be capable of identifying actual sentiment of a given text in the presence of sarcasm. In this chapter, we proposed an automated system for sarcasm detection in social media text using six algorithms that are capable to analyze the various types of sarcasm occurs in Twitter data. These algorithms use lexical, pragmatic, hyperbolic and contextual features of text to identify sarcasm. In the contextual feature, we mainly focus on situation, topical, temporal, and historical context of the text. The experimental results of proposed approach were compared with state-of-the-art techniques.

INTRODUCTION

Sentiment analysis is a procedure to extract the attitude of a speaker or a writer concerning some target (Pang, 2002, PP. 79-86). Social media and social networking have fueled the online space, including Facebook, Amazon, Twitter, etc. as ratings, reviews, comments, etc. are everywhere. Social media content is growing rapidly with every passing day. With the large volumes of information generating daily, identifying clear and most consumer reliable information about their preferences has become very tough task nowadays. To get the correct and trusted information, individuals are showing interest towards analysis of social networking content. For every business, online reviews have become the

DOI: 10.4018/978-1-5225-7186-5.ch010

Copyright © 2019, IGI Global. Copying or distributing in print or electronic forms without written permission of IGI Global is prohibited.

deciding factor which can break or make a product in the marketplace. Sentiment analyzer is used as a tool to understand how consumers are reacting to an event or a new product through auditing social networking posts and comments.

Sarcasm is derived from the French word "Sarcasmor" that means "tear flesh" or "grind the teeth". In simple words, sarcasm is a way to speak bitterly. Macmillan Dictionary defines, "…sarcasm is an activity of saying or writing the opposite of what you mean, or of speaking in a way intended to make someone else feel stupid or show them that you are angry…" (Macmillan, 2007). For example: "it feels great being bored". In this example, the literal meaning of the sentence is different than what the speaker intends to say using sarcasm. While writing sarcasm in text, people often use only positive words to convey a negative opinion instead of real negative. However, the average human reader face problem in sarcasm detection for social media content such as tweets, reviews, blogs, online forums, etc.

In this paper, the tweets of Twitter are used as the dataset for sarcasm detection. Twitter is a microblogging social networking site where a user can read and post the messages. The Twitter allow posting a message of a limited length of 140 characters. Due to the limitations, the users often use symbolic and figurative texts to express their feelings such as @username, smilies, emoji, exclamation mark and interjection words. Recognition of these symbolic and figurative texts in tweets is the most tedious task in NLP. In the realm of Twitter, the author has observed several types of sarcastic tweets as shown in Table 1that occurred frequently.

The author has already discussed sarcasm type T_1, T_2 and T_3 in their previous article (Bharti, 2015). The remaining types of sarcastic tweets are as follows:

- Type T_4 depicts the users' likes and dislikes behavior while posting the tweets on Twitter. To learn the behavioral habit of a particular Twitter user, one can analyze and observe his likes and dislikes habit. Using these likes and dislikes lists of a particular user; one can analyze the sarcastic tweets from the particular user's account. For example, if any Sachin Tendulkar fan who likes to post the tweet about Sachin and his Twitter account consist a tweet like "I love to see Sachin's failure in batting" which contradict his like's habit so, one can be easily identify that given tweet is sarcastic.
- Type T_5says about tweets contradicting universal facts. For example, if any user has posted a tweet "sun is revolving around the earth" and the fact is earth revolves around the sun. In such cases, user is intentionally negating the universal facts in their tweet, and there is a high probability that the tweet is sarcastic.
- Type T_6 says about tweets that contradict temporal facts, which may change over a period. For example, "India had an amazing win in cricket world cup 2015 final", while the fact is Australia

Table 1. Different types of sarcastic tweets.

T_1	Sarcasm as a contradiction between positive sentiment and negative situation.
T_2	Sarcasm as a contradiction between negative sentiment and positive situation.
T_3	Tweets that starts with interjection word.
T_4	Sarcasm as a contradiction between likes and dislikes.
T_5	Sarcasm as a contradiction between tweet and theuniversalfacts.
T_6	Sarcasm as a contradiction between tweet and its temporal facts.
T_7	Positive tweet that contains a word and its antonym pair.

won the cricket world cup in 2015 and India won the cricket world cup in 2011. If this type of contradiction occurs, then the tweet will be sarcastic.

- Type T_7 discuss about the positive tweets that contains an antonym pair of adjective, verb, noun or adverb. For example, "when I am online, she is offline, and when she is online, I am offline, and I love this game so much" #sarcasm. In this example, online is an adjective and offline is the antonym of online. If any tweet contains an antonym pair of either adjective or adverb or verb and overall tweet sentiment is positive, then the tweet has high chance to be classified as sarcastic.

Ongoing research has discussed the only T_1 type of sarcastic tweet analysis as shown in Table 1. In this chapter, the author considered this as limitations over existing research and proposed an algorithm for every type of sarcastic tweet that occurs on Twitter as mentioned in Table 1 to identify it. The proposed algorithms cover almost all the occurrences of sarcastic tweets on Twitter and provide a complete framework for sarcasm detection in tweets.

RELATED WORK

Representing sarcasm in text is very difficult as it often carries opposite meaning of the actual sentences. Sarcasm arises from the figurative language where the meaning is opposite of what it looks. Relevant research works in sarcasm is presented in Table 2.

Sarcasm detection from the text is the most challenging task as the representation of sarcasm in text is clueless. The only author of the text can say confidently that they have written sarcastically. One can only try to identify it using the observation of sarcastic text using various features namely, lexical, pragmatic, hyperbolic, context, etc. The process of sarcasm detection in text started in 2007 by Kreuz and Caucci. They utilized lexical and syntactic features that play a vital role to recognize sarcasm and irony in the text. They also state that lexical feature such as interjections and punctuation could be useful to detect sarcasm in text. In recent times, sarcasm detection became the popular research area for researchers (Davidov, 2010; González, 2011; Kreuz, 2007; Liebrecht, 2013; Lunando, 2013; Rajadesingan, 2015; Riloff, 2013; Tsur, 2010). Research interest grew rapidly towards detection of sarcasm in social media, especially for Twitter data (tweets) and Amazon product reviews (Davidov, 2010; González, 2011; Riloff, 2013; Tsur, 2010). A consolidated summary presenting the literature on automatic sarcasm detection is shown in Table 3.

In the state-of-the-art techniques, researchers have used several classification techniques and features for sarcasm detection in the text. Based on this literature, sarcasm detection system can be classified into three categories based on classification approaches namely, supervised, unsupervised and semi-supervised approach as shown in Figure 1.

Supervised Learning

Supervised learning is the most common technique used for classification. In this approach, one needs a large corpus of the labelled training dataset. The performance of this approach depends on the quality of dataset and the feature engineering step. The supervised technique can be classified into three categories namely machine learning, rule-based learning and pattern-based learning.

Table 2. Relevant studies on sarcasm

Author(s)	Findings/Results
Jorgenson et al. (1984)	Sarcasm arises from figurative meaning as opposed to literal meaning.
Gibbs (1986)	Ease of processing and memory for sarcastic utterances depends crucially on how explicitly a speaker's statement echoes address or some other source's putative beliefs, opinions, or previous statement.
Kreuz & Glucksberg (1989)	Listeners recognize sarcasm when they perceive that a speaker is alluding to some antecedent state of affairs.
Gibbs & O'Brien (1991)	Verbal irony is either writing or saying the opposite of what is actually meant.
Giora (1995)	Sarcasm is a mode of indirect negation which requires processing of both the negated and implicated messages [30].
Kreuz & Roberts (1995)	Sarcasm is typically expressed verbally through the use of heavy tonal stress, and certain gestural clues such as rolling of the eyes.
Clark (1996)	Author does not explicitly state that the phrase is meant sarcastically, readers have few clues to pick up on the sarcasm, such as the context of the situation, known as common ground and the words being used to pick up on the sarcasm.
Utsumi (2000)	Use of extreme adjectives and adverbs in text, such as 'absolutely fantastic', is a way of implicitly displaying a negative attitude.
Utsumi (2002)	Cognitive model of how poetic effects are achieved by a work of literature, especially by individual figurative expressions such as metaphor and irony.
Kreuz & Link (2002)	Pragmatic factor of common ground can be projected by readers to characters that know each other in written text; the participants from the paper reading the excerpts are capable of reading sarcastic statements more quickly, and with a greater degree of certainty, than when the characters do not know each other.
Ivanko & Pexman (2003)	Direct action model of figurative language processing.
Gibbs & Colston (2007)	Irony in language and thought.
Bogard (2008)	A sarcastic sentence is sometimes expressed vocally with heavy stress to audibly give clue that the sentence is meant non-literally; this is sometimes mimicked in text by extending the letters that constitute a syllable, an example being "Riiiiight" as demonstrated.
Riloff et al. (2013)	Sarcasm as contrast between a positive sentiment and negative situation.
Liebrecht et al. (2013)	Sarcasm in text often expressed using positive or intensified positive words or phrases.
Rajadesingan et al. (2015)	Sarcasm in text is unusual behavior of a user.
Bharti et al. (2017)	Sarcasm is a gap between actual meaning and intended meaning.

Machine Learning

Machine learning-based supervised learning is the most useful approach for classification work. There are several standard machine learning classifiers are existing which perform better for text classification such as Naive Bayes, Support Vector Machine, Decision Tree, etc. Further, these classifiers are used to train using various text features such as lexical, pragmatic, hyperbolic, etc.

Liebrecht (2013) designed a machine learning model to detect sarcasm in Dutch tweets. Peng (2015) used a supervised approach to classify movie reviews into two classes after performing subjective feature extractions. Tayal (2014) utilized machine learning classifier to detect the sarcastic political tweets. Tungthamthiti (2014), explored concept level knowledge using the hyperbolic words in sentences and gave an indirect contradiction between sentiment and situation such as raining, bad weather that are conceptually the same. Therefore, if 'raining' is present in any sentence, then one can assume 'bad weather'. They built a system for sarcasm detection using SVM classifier and used this indirect contradiction feature for training.

Table 3. Relevant studies on automatic sarcasm detection.

Kreuz & Caucci (2007)	Lexical and syntactic features play a vital role to recognize sarcasm and irony in text. The role of different lexical factors, such as an interjection(e.g., gee or gosh) and punctuation symbols (e.g., ?).
Carvalho et al. (2009)	Irony detection can be achieved efficiently when one use the "oral or gestural clues" such as emoticons; onomatopoeic expressions for laughter; heavy use of punctuation marks; quotation marks and positive interjections of the utterances as features.
Tsur et al. (2010)	Motivation for using sarcasm in online communities and social networks.
Davidov et al. (2010)	Dependencies and overlap between different sentiment types represented by smileys and Twitter hashtags.
Gonzalez-Ibanez et al. (2011)	Impact of lexical and pragmatic factors on machine learning effectiveness for identifying sarcastic utterances.
Riloff et al. (2013)	Sarcasm as contrast between a positive sentiment and negative situation.
Liebrecht et al. (2013)	Sarcasm is signaled by hyperbole, using intensifiers and exclamations; in contrast, non-hyperbolic sarcastic messages often receive an explicit marker.
Maynard & Greenwood (2014)	Impact of sarcasm on sentiment analysis.
Justo et al. (2014)	Sarcasm detection task benefits from the inclusion of linguistic and semantic information sources.
Wallace et al. (2014)	Apart from lexical, pragmatic and hyperbole features, sometimes context beyond text is important for sarcasm detection in text.
Rajadesingan et al. (2015)	Behavioral context of author is important for sarcasm detection in text.
Bamman et al. (2015)	Conversation context is important for sarcasm classification in text.
Wang et al. (2015)	Sarcasm classification is a sequence labeling problem.
Joshi et al. (2016)	Harnessing the context incongruity to identify sarcastic tweets
Bharti et al. (2017b)	Harnessing newspaper as context for sarcasm detection in tweets.

Figure 1. Different classification techniques used for sarcasm detection in text.

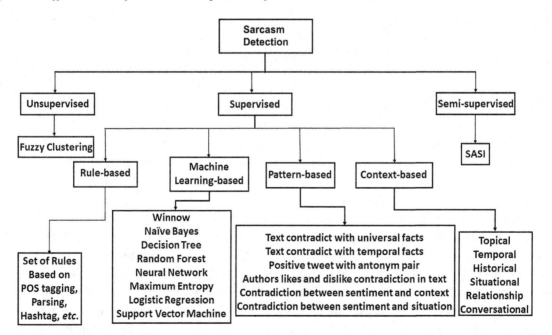

Rule-Based Learning

The rule-based approach is the most basic method used for sarcasm detection in the text. In this approach, we mainly focus on hyperbolic and syntactic features of the text. Lunando (2013) designed a rule-based classifier using syntactic and hyperbolic feature set. They proposed an algorithm and said that if a tweet starts with interjection word, then there is a high possibility to be classified as sarcastic.

Pattern-Based Learning

In literature, pattern-based learning is the most common approach used for sarcasm detection. In this approach, authors discovered a set of patterns. These patterns are given as follows:

- Sarcasm as a contradiction between sentiment and situation. In this pattern, a given text is said to be sarcastic, if the sentiment of the text is contradicted with its situation phrases. The authors have been evaluated this pattern in both directions namely, sarcasm as a contradiction between positive sentiment and negative situation (Riloff, 2013).
- Sarcasm as a contradiction between author's likes and dislikes. Using this pattern, a given text is said to be sarcastic, if the likes of text's author are contradicted with his/her dislikes (Rajadesingan, 2015).

Semi-Supervised Learning

In this approach, the dataset is partially labelled. It is a combination of both labelled and unlabeled dataset. Davidov (2010) designed a semi-supervised used classifier algorithm to detect sarcasm in a tweet and online reviews. It uses pattern-based (high-frequency words and content words) and punctuation-based to build a weighted k-nearest neighbor (kNN) classification model to perform sarcasm detection. Tsur (2010) observed that bigram based semi-supervised classification approach produce better results in detecting sarcasm in tweets and Amazon product reviews.

Unsupervised Learning

In this approach, there is no predefined labelled datasets are available. Clustering is a one of the most common unsupervised classification technique, in which it divides a set of objects into clusters (parts of the set) so that objects in the same cluster are similar to each other, and objects in different clusters are dissimilar. Mukherjee et al: designed an unsupervised classification model using clustering technique to detect sarcasm in microblogs such as tweets.

Similarly, sarcasm can also be classified into eight categories based on usage of text feature set in the past work of sarcasm detection. These eight categories are lexical, pragmatic, sentiment, pattern, hyperbole, semantic, syntactic and context. The details about text feature sets are shown in Figure 2.

Figure 2. Different feature sets used for sarcasm detection in text.

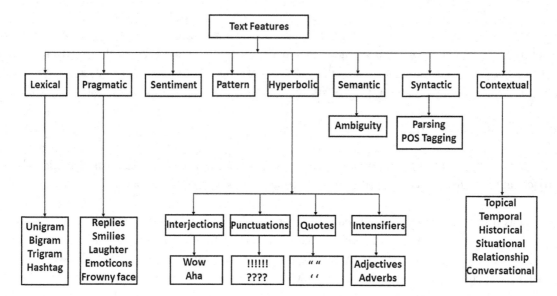

Lexical Feature Based Classification

Text properties such as unigram, bigram, n-grams, etc. come under the lexical features of the text. Many authors used these features to identify sarcasm such as Kreuz (1995) introduced this for the first time, and they observed that the lexical feature plays a vital role to detect irony and sarcasm in text like tweets. Kreuz (2007) in his subsequent work used this lexical feature along with syntactic features to detect sarcastic tweets. Davidov (2010) used pattern-based (high-frequency words and content words) and punctuation-based to build a weighted k-nearest neighbor (kNN) classification model to perform sarcasm detection. Tsur (2010) observed that bigram-based features produce better results to detect sarcasm in tweets and Amazon product reviews. González (2011) explored numerous lexical features (derived from LWIC (2001) and WordNet affect (2004)) to identify sarcasm. Riloff (2013) used a well-constructed lexicon-based approach to detect sarcasm, and for lexicon generation, they used unigram, bigram and trigram features. Barbieri (2014) considered seven lexical features to detect sarcasm through its inner structure such as unexpectedness, the intensity of the terms or imbalance between registers.

Pragmatic Feature Based Classification

Pragmatic is one of the powerful features to identify sarcasm in tweets as the user use symbolic and figurative text while writing tweets. Due to the limitation of character size (140) allowed in a Twitter message, a Twitter user often use smilies, emoticons, replies and @user pragmatic while writing tweets. Several authors used this feature in their research to detect sarcasm. Kreuz (2007) used the concept of pragmatic and observed that to detect sarcasm in textual data like tweets, pragmatic is one of the key features. Carvalho (2009) used pragmatic like emoticons and special punctuations to detect irony for newspaper text data. Subsequently, González (2011) further explored this feature with some more parameters like smiles and replies and developed a sarcasm detection system using the pragmatic features for Twitter data. Tayal (2014) also used the pragmatic feature in political tweets to predict which party will win in the upcoming election. Similarly, Rajadesingan (2015) used two unique, pragmatic features namely, psychological and behavioral to detect sarcasm in users' present and past tweets.

Sarcastic Pattern Based Classification

Sarcastic patterns are the special and unique feature to detect sarcasm in text alone. In this approach, one can observe the sarcastic dataset and identify the unique patterns for sarcastic text. Riloff (2013) started the pattern-based approach for sarcasm detection in tweets. They deployed a well-constructed lexicon-based pattern as "…sarcasm as a contradiction between positive sentiment and negative situation…" Bouazizi and Ohtsuki (2016) identified three patterns for sarcasm in tweets, namely sarcasm is a wit, sarcasm is an evasion and sarcasm is a whimper. Based on these three patterns, they proposed an efficient sarcasm detection system enhance the accuracy of sentiment analysis.

Hyperbolic Feature Based Classification

Hyperbole is another key feature which is often used in sarcasm detection for textual data. A hyperbolic text that contain one of the text properties such as punctuation, interjection, intensifier, quotes, etc. Previous authors used this hyperbole feature very nicely in their research to detect sarcasm in tweets. Utsumi (2000) discussed extreme adjective and adverb. The presence of these two in any text is called intensified text. Most often, it provides an implicit way to display negative attitudes i.e. sarcasm. Kreuz (2007) discussed the other hyperbolic term such as interjection and punctuation. They have shown how hyperbole is useful in sarcasm detection. Filatova (2012) used this hyperbole feature in document level text. According to them, phrase or sentence level is not sufficient for good accuracy and considered the text context in that document to improve the accuracy. Liebrecht (2013) explained hyperbolic feature nicely in their research with an example, the utterances "fantastic weather when it rains" is identified as sarcastic with more ease than the utterances "the weather is good when it rains". In this example, the hyperbole is indicated in italics. Lunando (2013), declared that the tweet contains interjection words such as "wow, aha, yay, etc." have a higher chance to be sarcastic. They developed a system for sarcasm detection for Indonesian social media. Tungthamthiti (2014), explored concept level knowledge using the hyperbole in sentences and found an indirect contradiction between sentiment and situation such as 'raining', 'bad weather' are conceptually same. Therefore, if raining is present in any sentence, then one can assume bad weather.

Context Feature Based Classification

The relationship between an author and audience followed by the immediate communicative context can be helpful to improve the sarcasm prediction accuracy (Bamman, 2015). Message level sarcasm detection on Twitter using a context-based model were used for sarcasm detection

(Wang, 2015). Chains of tweets that work in a context were considered. They introduce a complex classification model that works over an entire tweet sequence and not on one tweet at a time. Integration between linguistic and contextual features extracted from the analysis of embedded in multimodal posts was deployed for sarcasm detection (Schifanella, 2016). A framework based on the linguistic theory of context incongruity and an introduction of inter-sentential incongruity by considering the history of the posts in the discussion thread was considered for sarcasm detection (Joshi, 2015). A quantitative evidence of historical tweets of an author can provide additional context for sarcasm detection (Khattri, 2015).

Based on these two classifications on sarcasm detection, the author has formed a summary report on state-of-the-art related to sarcasm detection and is shown in Table 4. It provides methodologies (denoted as M_1, M_2), types of sarcastic tweets occurred on Twitter (denoted as T_1, T_2, T_3, T_4, T_5, T_6, and T_7), various features list (denoted as F_1, F_2, and F_3) and dataset from different domains (denoted as D_1, D_2, D_3, D_4, and D_5), mostly from Twitter *i.e.* tweets. The descriptions are given in Table 5.

PRELIMINARIES

Sentiment analyzer can classify opinions in social media as positive, negative and neutral.

But, the result of sentiment analyzer may be ambiguous for users in case of sarcastic opinions. Therefore, there is a need for an automatic system that can be able to classify actual positive/negative sentiment and sarcastic sentiment.

System Model

The contents of social media are growing rapidly with every passing day. However, getting relevant opinions or reviews about any social media entities is tedious and time-consuming tasks. Every user cannot read every review and identify the actual and sarcastic opinions manually. Additionally, an average human reader faces numerous problem to detect sarcasm in twitter data, product review, etc., which may mislead the individuals or organizations. To overcome this kind of problem, there is a need for a system which automatically identifies actual sentiments (positive/negative) and sarcastic sentiment. As per requirement, the author proposed a similar kind of system model as shown in Figure 3, which depicts

Figure 3. Proposed model for sarcasm detection while making a decision using users' opinions.

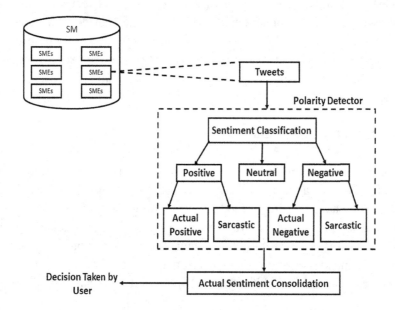

Table 4. State-of-the-art sarcasm detection system for text

State-of-the-Art	Methodologies			Types of Sarcastic Tweets							Various Feature List						Different Domains				
	M_1		M	T_1	T_2	T_3	T_4	T_5	T_6	T_7	F_1	F_2	F_3				D_1	D_2	D_3	D_4	D_5
	M_{11}	M_{12}											F_{31}	F_{32}	F_{33}	F_{34}					
Kreuz et al., 2007	√			√							√	√		√			√				
Chaumartin et al., 2007		√		√							√						√				
Carvalho et al., 2009	√			√							√						√	√			
Tsur et al., 2010		√		√							√							√			
Davidov et al., 2010		√		√							√						√				
Gonzálezet al., 2011	√	□		√							√	√					√				
Filatova et al., 2012	√	□	√	√							√			√			□	√			
Riloff et al., 2013	√	□	√	√							√						√				
Lunando et al., 2013	√	□		□		√					√		√				√				
Liebrecht et al., 2013	√	□		√							√			√			√				
Lukin et al., 2013	√	□	√	√							√						√				
Tungthamthiti et al., 2014	√	□		√						√	√			√			√				
Peng et al., 2014	√	□		□	√						√	√				√	√				
Raquel et al., 2014	√	□		√							√					√	√				
Kunneman et al., 2014	√	□		√							√	√	√	√			√				
Barbieri et al., 2014	√	□		√							√						√				
Tayal et al., 2014	√	□		√							√	√					√				
Nitin et al., 2014	√	□		□			√	√		√	√						√				
Pielage et al., 2014	√	□		√							√						√	√	√	√	√
Rajadesingan et al., 2015	√	□		√			√				√	√					√				
Bharti et al., 2015		□	√	√	√						√		√				√				
Schifanella et al., 2016	√	√		□							□						√	√			
Bharti et al., 2016		√		√	√	√	√	√	√	√	√		√	√			√	√			
Bharti et al., 2017b		□	√	√	√	√	√	√	√	√	√		√	√			√	√			
Al-Ghadhban et al., 2017	√	□		√							√	√					√				
Filatova et al., 2017		□	√	√	√						√		√				√				
Kuo et al., 2018	√	□		√							√						√				
Rajeswari et al., 2018	√	□		□		√					√		√				√				

three model entities, namely social media, social media entities and polarity detector to recognize the sentiments of any opinion in social media. Details of these three model entities are:

1. **Social Media (SM):** It is a platform to share feelings, opinions about any product or individuals through the online post. It may be a social networking website (Facebook, Twitter, Amazon, online discussion forum, online blogs etc.

2. **Social Media Entities (SME):** It may be anything (individuals, organizations, products, movies, games, etc.) where users are free to post or retrieve comments through social media.

Table 5. Methodologies, types of sarcastic tweets, features and domains used.

	Methodologies for Sarcasm Detection
M₁	Machine Learning based
M₁₁	Supervised
M₁₂	Semi-supervised
M₂	Corpus based
	Types of Sarcastic Tweets on Twitter
T₁	Sarcasm as a contradiction between positive sentiment and negative situation.
T₂	Sarcasm as a contradiction between negative sentiment and positive situation.
T₃	Tweets that starts with interjection word.
T₄	Sarcasm as a contradiction between likes and dislikes.
T₅	Sarcasm as a contradiction between tweet and the universal facts.
T₆	Sarcasm as a contradiction between tweet and its temporal facts.
T₇	Positive tweet that contains a word and its antonym pair.
	Various Feature List
F₁	Lexical- unigram, bigram, trigram, n-gram, #hashtag
F₂	Pragmatic- smilies, emoji, replies
F₃	Hyperbolic- interjection, intensifier, exclamation and question mark, quotes
F₃₁	Interjection word- yay, oh, wow, yeah, nah, aha, etc.
F₃₂	Intensifier- adverbs, adjectives
F₃₃	Exclamation and Question mark- !!!!!,????
F₃₄	Quotes- " ", ' '
	Different Domains of Text
D₁	Twitter data
D₂	Reviews
D₃	Blogs
D₄	Google books
D₅	Online forums

3. **Polarity Detector (PD):** An automated system which is capable to differentiate the actual sentiment with sarcastic sentiment in text.

In this work, the author considered users' opinions in social media, especially Twitter data (tweets) and product reviews as input to recognize sentiments. In the current scenario, individuals, as well as industries, are very much dependent on social media for their online marketing as well as social reputations. Individuals check their online reviews on social media before buying any item through online. Once they are satisfied with available reviews, then only, they buy. Organizations/industries are also very much dependent on these social media to know the status of their marketplace, and subsequently, they enhance the quality of their products. Hence, the proposed system model describes the usefulness of the social media for individuals as well as organizations in their decision making. Figure 3 shows the process of finding opinions from social media entities (current work considered tweets) automatically. One can collect post about any SMEs and pass it through polarity detector to get the correct opinions about the SMEs. Based on the result of the polarity detector, users can take the decision.

Parts-of-Speech (POS) Tagging

POS tagger divides sentences or paragraphs into words and assigns a corresponding part-of-speech tag to each word based on their relationship with adjacent and related words in a phrase, sentence, or paragraph. In this work, the author used a Hidden Markov Model (HMM) based POS tagger (Bharti, 2016) on identifying the correct POS tag value of a given sentence or phrase. For example, POS tag value for sentence "Love has no finite coverage" is love-NN, has-VBZ, no-DT, finite-JJ, and coverage-NN. POS tag value NN, JJ, VBZ and DT denote noun, adjective, verb and determiner respectively. The author followed Penn Treebank Tag set notations. It is a brown corpus style of tagging having 44 tags (Marcus, 1993).

Parsing

Parsing is a process of analyzing the grammatical structure, identifying its parts of speech and syntactic relations of words in sentences. When a sentence passed through a parser, then the parser divides the sentence into words and identifies the POS tag. With the help of POS tag and syntactic relation, it forms units like subject, verb, and object, then determines the relations between these units to generate a parse tree. In this work, the author used a Python-based package called TEXTBLOB for parsing. An example of parsing and parse tree for text "I love waiting forever for my doctor" is shown in Figure 4. Parsing output using TEXTBLOB is I/PRP/B-NP/O, love/NN/I-NP/O, waiting/VBG/B-VP/O, forever/RB/B-ADVP/O, for/IN/B-PP/B-PNP, my/PRP$/BNP/ I-PNP, doctor/NN/I-NP/I-PNP).

PROPOSED SCHEME

In this section, the author has proposed six algorithms to detect various types of sarcastic tweets that occur in Twitter. In literature survey, the author observed that sarcasm types T_2, T_3, T_5, T_6, T_7 as shown in Table 3 are not yet explored. Therefore, based on these limitations, the following set of algorithms are proposed.

1. Parsing-based algorithm for lexicon generation(PBALN) for types T_1 and T_2, the author has already discussed and implementedin their previous article (Bharti, 2015) to recognize sarcasm in Twitter data.

Figure 4. Parse tree for a tweet: I love waiting forever for my doctor.

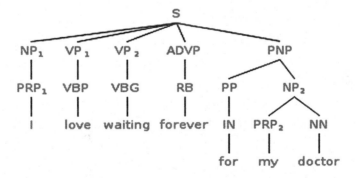

2. An algorithm, tweet startwith interjection words (TSIW)for type $T_{3,}$ the author has already discussed and implemented in their previous article (Bharti, 2015) to recognize sarcasm in Twitter data that starts with interjection words.

3. A behavioral based algorithm, Sarcasm as a contradiction between tweets and itslikes and dislikes(TCLD) is proposed here to detect sarcasm in a particular user's tweet that meets the requirements of type T_4.

4. An algorithm, sarcasm as a contradiction between tweet and theuniversal facts (CTUFs) is proposed to identify the sarcastic tweets that negate the universal facts intentionally as the requirement of type T_5.

5. An algorithm, sarcasm as a contradiction between tweet and its temporal facts (CTTFs)which identify the sarcastic tweets that negate the time-dependent facts intentionally as the requirement of type T_6.

6. An algorithm, positive tweet that contains a word and its antonym pair (PTCAP) that detects sarcasm in tweets that carry positive sentiments, and an antonym pair serves the requirement of type T_7.

Implementation details of Algorithm 1 (PBALN) and Algorithm 2 (TSIW) are already explained in author's previous article (Bharti, 2015). To present the complete structure of sarcasm detection in tweets, the author included these two algorithms in this current article.

Sarcasm as a Contradiction Between Tweets and Users' Like and Dislike (TCULD)

In this approach, users' behaviour on Twitter while posting tweets is used as a feature set for sarcasm detection. The feature set consists of users' likes and dislikes nature on any particular target such as individuals, organizations, places, etc. The step-wise procedure of this approach is given in Algorithm 3. It describes how to extract likes and dislikes lists of the individual Twitter user. To retrieve the learned lists of likes and dislikes, one can find all the tweets from a particular user's account and store as a corpus of tweets. Then feed the tweet corpus as an input to Algorithm 3. In the steps 1 to 10, the Algorithm 3 finds the sentiment value of all tweets in the corpus using Equations 1, 2 and 3. According to sentiment value, the algorithm segregates positive and negative sentiments tweets and store it in β_p andβ_n respectively.

$$P_R = \frac{PWP}{TWP} \tag{1}$$

$$N_R = \frac{PWP}{TWP} \tag{2}$$

$$Sentiment\ value = \frac{PWP}{TWP} \tag{3}$$

where,

Algorithm 1. Parsing-based algorithm for lexicon generation (PBALN)

Data: Corpus of tweets (C)

Result: Lexicon lists of sentiment (positive, negative) and situation (positive, negative).

Notation: *VP*: Verb Phrase, *NP*: Noun Phrase, *ADJP*: AdjectivesPhrase, *ADV P*: AdverbsPhrase, *PPF*: Parse PhraseFile, *TWPP*: Tweet-wise Parse Phrase, α: List of sentiments, β: List of situations, α_p: List of positive sentiment phrase, α_n: List of negative sentiment phrase, β_p: List of positivesituation phrase, β_n: List of negative situation phrase, η: Sentiment value, *P*: Phrase, T: Tweet.

Initialization: $\alpha = \{\ \Phi\ \}$, $\beta = \{\ \Phi\ \}$, $\alpha_p = \{\ \Phi\ \}$, $\alpha_n = \{\ \Phi\ \}$, $\beta_p = \{\ \Phi\ \}$, $\beta_n = \{\ \Phi\ \}$.

```
1:    For T in C do
2:         ω = determine_parse_phrase (T)
3:         PPF← PPF U ω
4:    End for
5:    For TWPP in PPF do
6:         τ = determine_token (TWPP)
7:         If (τ= NP || ADJP || (NP + VP)) then
8:              α←α U τ
9:         Else if (τ = V P || (ADVP + VP) || (VP + ADVP) || (ADJP + VP) || (VP + NP) || (VP
 +
ADVP + ADJP) || (VP+ADJP+NP) || (ADVP+ADJP+ NP)) then
10:              β←β U τ
11:         End if
12:    End for
13:    For P in α do
14:         η = calculate_sentiment_value (P)
15:         If η>0.0 then
16:              α_p←α_p U P
17:         Else if η<0.0 then
18:              α_n←α_n U P
19:         Else
20:              P is neutral.
21:         End if
22:    End for
23:    For P in β do
24:         η = calculate_sentiment_value (P)
25:         If η>0.0 then
26:              β_p←β_p U P
27:         Else if η<0.0 then
28:                   β_n←β_n U P
29:         Else
30:                   P is Neutral.
31:         End if
32:    End for
```

Algorithm 2. Tweet_Start_with_Interjection_Word (TSIW)

Data: Corpus of tweets that start with interjection words (C).

Result: Tweet classified as sarcastic or non-sarcastic.

Notation: *JJ*: Adjectives, *VB*: Verbs, *RB*: Adverbs, *NN*: Nouns, *INJ*: Interjections, T: Tweet, C: Corpus, α: Tagged_file, τ: Tags, β: Each tweet tag list, F_T: First_tag, S_T: Second_tag, A_T: Any tag other than F_T and S_T.

Initialization: $\alpha = \{\Phi\}$

```
1:    For T in C do
2:          ω = determine_tag (T)
3:          α←α Uω
4:    End for
5:    For β in α do
6:          τ= determine_each_token (β)
7:          F_T = calculate_first_tag (β)
8:          S_T = calculate_second_tag (β)
9: A_T = (β -(F_T +S_T))
10: If (F_T = INJ) && (S_T = JJ || RB) then
11:         Input tweet is classified as sarcastic.
12:         Else if (F_T = INJ) && (A_T= (RB + JJ) || (JJ+ NN) || (RB + VB)) then
13:         Input tweet is classified as sarcastic.
14:         Else if (F_T ≠ INJ) then
15:         Input tweet is invalid.
16:         Else
17:                 Input tweet is non-sarcastic.
18:         End if
```

Algorithm 3. Users' Likes_and_Dislikes_Contradiction_in_Tweets (TCULD)

Data: Corpus of tweets that start with interjection words (C).

Result: Tweet classified as sarcastic or non-sarcastic.

Notation: *NN*: Noun, T: Tweets, C: Corpus, α: Tagged_file, α_p: Positive sentiment tag file, α_n: Negative sentiment tag file, τ: tag, γ: Each tweet tag list, F_T: First_tag, β: Tweet_file, β_p: Positive sentiment tweet file, β_n: Negative sentiment tweet file, Ψ: User's_likes_list, Ω: User's_dislikes_list, η: Sentiment value.

Initialization: $\alpha_p = \{ \Phi \}$, $\alpha_n = \{ \Phi \}$, $\beta_p = \{ \Phi \}$, $\beta_n = \{ \Phi \}$, $\Psi = \{ \Phi \}$, $\Omega = \{ \Phi \}$

```
1:    for T in C do
2:            η = calculate_sentiment_value (T)
3:            If(η>0.0) then
4:                    β_p←β_p U T
```

continued on following page

Algorithm 3. Continued

```
5:              Else if (η<0.0) then
6:                   βₙ←βₙ U T
7:              Else
8:                   Invalid tweet.
9:              End if
10:     End for
11:     For T in βₚ do
12:          ω = determine_tag (T)
13:          αₚ←αₚ Uω
14:     End for
15:     For γ in αₚ do
16:          τ= determine_each_token (γ)
17:          F_T = calculate_first_tag (γ)
18:          If (F_T== PRP) then
19:               $ = determine_object_value(γ)
20:               Ψ ← Ψ U $
21:          Else
22:               $= determine_subject_value (γ)
23:               Ψ ← ΨU $
24:          End if
25:     End for
26:     For T in βₙ do
27:          ω = determine_tag (T)
28:          βₙ←βₙ Uω
29:     End for
30:     For γ in βₚ do
31:          τ = determine_each_token (γ)
32:          F_T = calculate_first_tag (γ)
33:          If (F_T = PRP) then
34:               $ = determine_object_value (γ)
35:               Ω ← Ω U $
36:          Else
37:               $= determine_subject_value (γ)
38:               Ω ← Ω U $
39:          End if
40:     End for
```

P_R= Positive_ratio,

N_R= Negative_ratio,

PWC= Positive words countin aphrase,

NWC= Negative words count in a phrase, TWC =Total words count in a phrase.

Further, steps 11 to 14, algorithm determine the POS tag information of all the positive tweets (β_p) and store it in positive tweets tagged file (α_p). Next, steps 15 to 25, the algorithm finds first tag (F_T) value from each tweet tagged file (γ). If F_T is matched with any of the personal pronouns such as I, we, etc. then retrieve the object of the tweet using Rusu (2007) Triplets approach (The triplets mean, it extracts the subject, verb and the object of any sentence) and add into likes list (Ψ). Otherwise, retrieve the subject value of that tweet using Rusu triplets approach and add it to Ψ. Similarly, in steps 26 to 40, steps 15 to 25 is repeated to obtain the dislikes list (Ω) from negative sentiment tweet file (β_n). For testing a tweet from same user's profile, one need to determine sentiment value (η) of a given input tweet and then retrieve subject or object of the same tweet using Algorithm 3. If the value of η is positive and subject/ object are in Ψ then, the given tweet is non-sarcastic. Otherwise, check its presence in Ω. If it is present in Ω, then the tweet is sarcastic. Similarly, if the sentiment value is negative and subject/object value is present in Ψ then, the given input tweet is sarcastic. Otherwise, the given input tweet is non-sarcastic. If the sentiment value is zero, then discard the tweet. In the same way, one can form Ψ and Ω for many users' profile and test for sarcasm in their respective tweets.

Sarcasm as a Contradiction Between Tweet and the Universal Facts (CTUFs)

In this approach, a corpus of universal facts is used as a context to determine a tweet is sarcastic or non-sarcastic. A sentence is said to be universal fact if the meaning of the sentence doesn't change. For instance: "Earth is spherical." Here, the meaning of the sentence will never change. The procedure of sarcasm detection in tweets using a set of universal facts is given in Algorithm 4.

In the steps 1 to 4, Algorithm 4 takes the corpus of universal facts as an input and produce <key, value> pair. To do so, the algorithm determines corresponding parse information of all the sentences in

Algorithm 4. Contradiction_between_Tweets_and_the_Universal_Facts (CTUFs)

```
Data: Corpus of universal facts (C).
Result: List of <key, value> pair.
Notation: $: Subject, O: Object, U: Verb, C: Corpus, T: Tweet, α: Parse_data, γ:
Each tweet tag list.
Initialization: α = {Φ}
1:   For T in C do
2:          ω = determine_parse_information (T)
3:          α←α U ω
4:   End for
5:   For γ in α do
6:          $ = determine_subject_value (γ)
7:          U = determine_verb (γ)
8:          O = determine_object_value (γ)
9:          forms <key, value> pair using $, U, O
10:         key← ($ + U)
11:         value←O
12:  End for
```

the corpus of universal facts using TextBlob python module and store it to parse_file (α). Next in steps 6 to 8, algorithm read parse information of every sentence (γ) in $\alpha$and extract the triplets i.e. subject, object and verb of every sentence from γ using Rusu (2007) Triplets extraction techniques. Furthersteps 9 to 11, it forms a <key, value> pair for every universal fact using triplet values. Here, subject ($) and verb ($\upsilon$) together treated as a 'key' and object ($\odot$) alone is treated as a `value'. The <key, value> pair is used as a context feature for sarcasm detection in tweets that contradict universal facts intentionally.

For the testing approach, one can find <key, value> pair of the testing tweet using Algorithm 4 and compare with the learned <key, value> pair. If 'key' of testing tweet match with 'key' of the learned list, then check 'value' of both. If both 'values' are matched then the tweet is non-sarcastic; otherwise, the tweets are classified as sarcastic.

Sarcasm as a Contradiction Between Tweet and Its TemporalFacts (CTTFs)

In TCTFs, the time-dependent fact is used to identify sarcasm. The time-dependent or temporal facts may change over the period. This type of facts is not permanent. For instance, "@MirzaSania becomes world number one. Great day for Indian Tennis". In this example, Sania Mirza is number one Tennis player now, but in the future,someone else may be number one.

In the steps 1 to 4, Algorithm 5 takes the corpus of temporal facts which contains time-stamp (T_s) of each fact as an input and produce <key, value> pair. To do so, the algorithm determines corresponding parse information of all the sentences in the corpus of universal facts using TextBlob python module and store it to parse_file (α). Next steps 6 to 8, algorithm read parse information of every sentence (γ) in $\alpha$and extract the triplets i.e. subject, object and verb of every sentence from γ using Rusu (2007) Triplets extraction techniques. Further, steps 9 to 11, it forms a <key, value> pair for every universal fact using

Algorithm 5. Contradiction_between_Tweet_and_its_Temporal_Facts (CTTFs)

```
Data: Corpus of temporal facts (C).
Result: List of <key, value> pair.
Notation: $: Subject, U: Verb,⊙: Object, T: Tweet, C: Corpus, α: Parse_data,γ:
Each tweet tag list, Γ: Time-stamp.
Initialization: α = {Φ}
1:    ForT in Cdo
2:         ω = determine_parse_information (T)
3:         α←α U ω
4:    End for
5:    Forγ in αdo
6:         $ = determine_subject_value (γ)
7:         U = determine_verb (γ)
8:         ⊙ = determine_object_value (γ)
9:         forms <key, value> pair using $, U,⊙
10:        key← ($ + U)
11:        value←(⊙ + Γ)
12:   End for
```

triplet values. Here, subject ($) and verb (U) together are treated as 'key' and object (O) along with time-stamp (T_S)are treated as a value. The <key, value> pair is used as a context feature for sarcasm detection in tweets that contradict temporal facts intentionally.

For the testing approach, one can find <key, value> pair of a testing tweet using Algorithm 5 and compare with the learned <key, value> pair. If 'key' of a testing tweet is matches with 'key' of the learned list, then check 'value' of both. If both 'values' match then the tweet is non-sarcastic otherwise, it is classified as sarcastic.

Positive Tweet That Contains a Word and Its Antonym Pair (PTCAP)

In this approach, the antonym pair is considered as a feature to identify sarcasm in positive sentiment tweets that contain an antonym pair of either an adjective or an adverb or a verb. Example: "From someone who loves @ScorpionCBS and HATES snakes, I'm about to enjoy these next 30 minutes...: #Sarcasm". In this tweet, love and hate are the antonym pair, and overall tweet sentiment is positive. To detect sarcasm in this type of tweet, Algorithm 6 finds the sentiment value from step 1 to 8 using equations 1, 2 and 3. If the sentiment value is higher than zero, append the tweets into a positive sentiment tweet file (β_p) otherwise the tweet is discarded. In the steps 9 to 12, it finds the POS tag for every tweet in β_p and stores all the tags in a tagged file (α). Next, in steps 13 to 28, it checks the tags of every tweet (γ) whether it contains either adjective, noun, adverb or verb in the α. If either of adjective, noun, adverb, or verb is present then check for the corresponding antonym. Suppose, if an adjective is found in the tweet, then it will check for the antonym of the same adjective. A similar strategy is followed, for a noun, adverb and verb. If any antonym pair were present then the tweet is sarcastic; otherwise, it is non-sarcastic.

RESULTS AND DISCUSSION

In this section, the author discussed the dataset used for experiment followed by the comparison of experimental results of proposed algorithms with state-of-the-arts.

Database Collection

To obtain the learned lists of sentiment and situation phrases using PBALN, the author has collected a corpus of 200000 tweets from the Twitter. Among these 200000 tweets, 100000 tweets are labelled as sarcastic, and rest of the 100000 tweets are non-sarcastic (regular tweets). The sarcastic labelled tweets were obtained using keywords which are more likely to found using love, amazing, good, hate, sad, happy, bad, hurt, awesome, excited, nice, great, sick, etc. Similarly, to obtain the users' likes and dislikes lists using algorithm TCULD, the author has retrieved all the tweets from around 50 different Twitter user's accounts. To fetch the <key, value> pairs using CTUFs and CTTFs from universal facts and temporal facts, a corpus of 10000 universal fact sentences and a corpus of 25000 temporal facts (the fact which may change over the period) sentences were collected. For testing, separate sets of tweets were collected for all the proposed algorithms. The testing sets are as follows:

Algorithm 6. Positive_Tweet_that_Contains_a_Word_and_its_Antonym_Pair (PTCAP)

Data: Corpus of tweets (C)
Result: Tweet classified as sarcastic or non-sarcastic.
Notation: *JJ*: adjective, *VB*: verb, *RB*: adverb, T: tweets, C: corpus, α: Tagged_file, τ: tag, γ: Each tweet tag list, β_p: Positive_sentiment_tweet_file, η: Sentiment_value.
Initialization: $\alpha = \{\Phi\}$, $\beta_p = \{\Phi\}$, *flag* = 0

```
1:      For T in C do
2:              η = calculate_sentiment_value (T)
3:              If (η>0.0) then
4:                      β_p←β_p U T
5:              Else
6:                      Invalid tweet.
7:              End if
8:      End for
9:  For T in β_p do
10:         ω = determine_pos_tagging (T)
11:         α←α U ω
12:     End for
13:     For γ in α do
14:         For τ in γ do
15:             If (τ = JJ || RB || VB || NN) then
16:                 check corresponding antonym value
17: If antonym found then
18:                     flag=1
19:                 break
20:                 End if
21:             End if
22:         End for
23:         If (flag=1) then
24:             Tweet is classified as sarcastic.
25: Else
26:             Tweet is classified as non-sarcastic.
27:         End if
28:     End for
```

1. For PBALN, a total of 3000 tweets is collected. Among these 3000 tweets, 1500 tweets were labelled with the hashtag #sarcastic and rest of the 1500 tweets were non-sarcastic as without the #sarcastic hashtag.
2. For TSIW, totally 3500 tweets are collected that starts with interjection word, among these tweets 1000 tweets that contain the sarcastic hashtag and 2500 regular tweets without any hashtag.
3. For TCULD, from each users' account 100 tweets were selected randomly.

4. For CTUFs, randomly 5000 tweets were collected.
5. For CTTFs, a total of 5000 tweets with time-stamp were collected randomly as testing set.
6. For PTCAP, a total of 50000 tweets were collected randomly.

In addition, each tweet was preprocessed by removing RT, hashtags, URL, @user, converting from upper cases to lower cases from the respective tweet corpus.

Experimental Results

1. ForPBALN, 1500 sarcastic tweets and 1500 regular tweets were tested. The observations are as follows:
   a. PBALN recognized 1070 tweets as sarcastic among 1500 tweets with sarcasm hashtag. However, the ground truth value was 1200.
   b. Similarly, PBALN recognized 425tweets as sarcastic among 1500 regular tweets (without any hashtag). However, the ground truth value was 360.
2. For TSIW, totally 3500 tweets were tested that starts with interjection word, among these 3500 tweets, 1000 were with the sarcastic hashtag and the remaining 2500 tweets were regular (without any hashtag). The observations are as follows:
   a. 830 tweets recognized as sarcastic among1000 tweets with sarcasm hashtag while ground truth value was 735.
   b. 999 tweets recognized as sarcastic among 2500 regular tweets while ground truth value was 1050.
3. In TCULD, about 100 tweets were tested from three different user's account. The observations are as follows:
   a. From the first user's account, the number of successfully identified tweets (for likes and dislikes) is 52.
   b. From the second user's account, the number of successfully identified tweets (for likes dislikes) is 55.
   c. From the third user's account, the number of successfully identified tweets (for likes and dislikes) is 61.
4. In CTUFs, a total of 5000 random tweets were tested. The observations areas follow:
   a. 78 tweets are identified as universal facts based.
   b. Algorithm produced correct <key, value> pairs for 31 tweets.
5. In PTCAP, a total of 5000 random tweets was tested. The observations are as follows:
   a. 20000 tweets are identified as positive.
   b. 135 tweets were containing antonym pair.
   c. Total 105 tweets are identified as sarcastic out of 135.
6. In CTTFs, around 5000 random tweets were tested. The observations are as follows:
   a. 91 tweets are identified as universal facts based.
   b. Algorithm produced correct <key, value> pairs for 31 tweets.

Comparison of the Results With State-Of-The-Arts

In this work, the author made the comparison with the help of various statistical parameters such as precision, recall and F1-measure. A standard formula used to calculate these parameters are shown in equations 4, 5, and 6 respectively.

$$\text{Precision} = \frac{T_p}{T_p + F_p} \tag{4}$$

$$\text{Recall} = \frac{T_p}{T_p + F_n} \tag{5}$$

$$\text{F1-measure} = \frac{2 * Precision * Recall}{Precision + Recall} \tag{6}$$

where,

T_p = True positive,
F_p = False positive,
F_n = False negative

Precision is a statistical parameter that shows and finds how much relevant information was identified. Similarly, recall determines how much retrieved information was relevant. F1-measure is a harmonic mean of precision and recall. To calculate precision and recall, one need to find the confusion matrix of tweets in different categories as shown in Table 4. With the help of the confusion matrix, precision, recall and F1-measure can be calculated using equations 4, 5, and 6 respectively. A result of precision, recall and F1-measure for tweets in different categories is shown in Table 5.

The author made a comparison of the proposed algorithms (PBALN, TSIW, TCULD, CTUFs, PTCAP, and CTTFs) with some of the state-of-the-arts as given in Table 5 and observed that the obtained result attains considerable improvements. Results of algorithms such as TSIW, TUCF, PTCAP and CTTFs are proposed for the first time.

CONCLUSION AND FUTURE DIRECTION

There is no formal structure of sarcasm. Due to this, analysis of sarcasm is difficult for researchers in any form of data such as text or voice. However, continuous research is going on in this era for betterment. In this paper, the author proposed six algorithms and tried to provide complete solutions for sarcasm detection in Twitter data i.e. tweets. They mainly focused on tweet structure and observed various types of sarcasm occurrences in tweets as shown in Table 3. Based on these sarcasm types, the author has proposed set of algorithms. Experimental results of the proposed algorithm attained significant accuracy as PBALN attains 0.90 precision and 0.85 F1-measure. Testing results of TSIW prove Lunando's state-

Table 6. Representation of error analysis of tweets in different categories using confusion matrix.

Tweets Categorization	T_p	F_p	F_n	T_n
1500 tweets with sarcasm hashtag	955	109	218	218
1500 tweets without sarcasm hashtag	270	150	90	990
1000 interjection tweets with sarcasm hashtag	706	120	26	146
2500 interjection tweets without sarcasm hashtag	772	227	272	1182
100 tweets from first user's account	52	4	20	24
100 tweets from second user's account	55	5	16	24
100 tweets from third user's account hashtag	61	05	22	12
78 tweets that based on universal facts	31	1	23	23
135 tweets that contains antonym pair	105	3	5	22
91 tweets that based on time dependent facts	41	3	25	22

Table 7. A comparison of proposed approaches with state-of-the-art.

Approaches	Precision (%)	Recall (%)	F-measure (%)
Barbieri system	87	86	87
Tungthamthiti system	75	75	75
Riloff with positive verb	27	44	34
with negative situation	28	37	32
Contrast (+VPs, -situation) unordered	10	55	17
Contrast (+VPs, -situation) ordered	08	69	14
Contrast (+preds, -situation)	12	62	21
Liebrecht system with 50/50	74	-	-
with 25/75 negative, positive ratio	55	-	-
PBALN with sarcastic tweets	**90**	82	**85**
PBALN without sarcastic tweets	65	76	70
TSIW sarcastic tweets	86	**97**	**91**
TSIW without sarcastic tweets	78	74	75
TCULD from first user's account	**92**	72	81
TCULD from second user's account	91	**77**	**84**
TCULD from third user's account	92	73	82
CTUFs based on universal facts	**96**	57	72
PTCAP tweets that contains antonym pair	**97**	**95**	**96**
CTTFs based on time dependent facts	**93**	62	74

ment "if tweet contains any interjection word such as "wow, aha, yay, etc." then that tweet has a higher chance to be classified into sarcastic as it attains 0.97 recalls and 0.91 F1-measure. TCULD attains 0.92 precision and 0.84 F1-measure. CTUFs and TCTDC reach the precision value 0.96 and 0.93 respectively, while PTCAP achieves 0.97, 0.95, 0.96 precision, recall, and F1-measure respectively.

Sarcasm detection in the images, audio clip and videos are still the uncharted areas to continue the research. The results of this research can be investigated using additional features such as emoticons, laughter acronyms and onomatopoeic expressions denoting laughter to improve the accuracy of the proposed classifiers. This research only confined to supervised approaches. In low-resourced languages, the supervised approaches may not be a perfect solution. In this scenario, the unsupervised approaches or semi-supervised approaches may be an alternate solution. In the future, the author will target in this field with text regional languages where semi-supervised and unsupervised techniques for classification will be useful.

REFERENCES

Al-Ghadhban, D., Alnkhilan, E., Tatwany, L., & Alrazgan, M. (2017). Arabic sarcasm detection in Twitter. In *2017 International Conference on Engineering & MIS (ICEMIS)* (pp. 1-7). IEEE.

Bamman, D., & Smith, N. A. (2015). Contextualized sarcasm detection on Twitter. In *International Conference on Web and Social Media 2015* (pp. 574–577). AAAI.

Barbieri, F., Saggion, H., & Ronzano, F. (2014). Modelling Sarcasm in Twitter, a Novel Approach. In *Proceedings of the 5th Workshop on Computational Approaches to Subjectivity, Sentiment and Social Media Analysis 2014* (pp. 50–58). ACL.

Bharti, S. K., Babu, K. S., & Jena, S. K. (2015). Parsing-based Sarcasm Sentiment Recognition in Twitter Data. In *Proceedings of the 2015 IEEE/ACM International Conference on Advances in Social Networks Analysis and Mining 2015* (pp. 1373-1380). ACM. 10.1145/2808797.2808910

Bharti, S. K., Babu, K. S., & Jena, S. K. (2017c). Harnessing Online News for Sarcasm Detection in Hindi Tweets. In *International Conference on Pattern Recognition and Machine Intelligence* (pp. 679-686). Cham: Springer. 10.1007/978-3-319-69900-4_86

Bharti, S. K., Pradhan, R. K., Babu, K. S., & Jena, S. K. (2017a). Sarcasm Analysis on Twitter Data Using Machine Learning Approaches. *Trends in Social Network Analysis: Information Propagation, User Behavior Modeling, Forecasting, and Vulnerability Assessment,* 51–76. doi:10.1007/978-3-319-53420-6_3

Bharti, S. K., Pradhan, R. K., Babu, K. S., & Jena, S. K. (2017b). Sarcastic Sentiment Detection Based on Types of Sarcasm Occurring in Twitter Data. *International Journal on Semantic Web and Information Systems, 13*(4), 89–108. doi:10.4018/IJSWIS.2017100105

Bharti, S. K., Vachha, B., Pradhan, R. K., Babu, K. S., & Jena, S. K. (2016). Sarcastic sentiment detection in tweets streamed in real time: A big data approach. *Digital Communications and Networks, 2*(3), 108–121. doi:10.1016/j.dcan.2016.06.002

Bogard, D. (2008). Living a dream. Retrieved from https://www.amazon.com/Living-Dream-D-Bogart/dp/1434380076

Carvalho, P., Sarmento, L., Silva, M. J., & De Oliveira, E. (2009). Clues for detecting irony in user-generated contents: oh...!! It's so easy;-). In *Proceedings of the 1st international CIKM workshop on Topic-sentiment analysis for mass opinion* (pp. 53-56). ACM. 10.1145/1651461.1651471

Chaumartin, F. R. (2007). UPAR7: A knowledge-based system for headline sentiment tagging. In *Proceedings of the 4th International Workshop on Semantic Evaluations* (pp. 422-425). ACL. 10.3115/1621474.1621568

Clark, H. H. (1996). Using language. In *Google books*. Cambridge University Press. doi:10.1017/CBO9780511620539

Davidov, D., Tsur, O., & Rappoport, A. (2010). Semi-supervised recognition of sarcastic sentences in twitter and amazon. In *Proceedings of the Fourteenth Conference on Computational Natural Language Learning* (pp. 107-116). ACL.

Filatova, E. (2012). Irony and Sarcasm: Corpus Generation and Analysis Using Crowdsourcing. In LREC (pp. 392-398).

Filatova, E. (2017). Sarcasm Detection Using Sentiment Flow Shifts. In *Proceedings of the Thirtieth International Florida Artificial Intelligence Research Society Conference* (pp. 264-269), AAAI.

Gibbs, R. W., & Colston, H. L. (2007). *Irony in language and thought: A cognitive science reader.* Psychology Press.

Gibbs, R. W. Jr, & O'Brien, J. (1991). Psychological aspects of irony understanding. *Journal of Pragmatics, 16*(6), 523–530. doi:10.1016/0378-2166(91)90101-3

Giora, R. (1995). On irony and negation. *Discourse Processes, 19*(2), 239–264. doi:10.1080/01638539509544916

González-Ibánez, R., Muresan, S., & Wacholder, N. (2011). Identifying sarcasm in Twitter: a closer look. In *Proceedings of the 49th Annual Meeting of the Association for Computational Linguistics: Human Language Technologies: short papers* (Vol. 2, pp. 581-586). ACL.

Ivanko, S. L., & Pexman, P. M. (2003). Context incongruity and irony processing. In *Discourse Processes* (Vol. 35, pp. 241–279). Taylor & Francis.

Joshi, A., Sharma, V., & Bhattacharyya, P. (2015). Harnessing context incongruity for sarcasm detection. In *Proceedings of the 53rd Annual Meeting of the Association for Computational Linguistics and the 7th International Joint Conference on Natural Language Processing* (Vol. 2, pp. 757–762), ACL.

Justo, R., Corcoran, T., Lukin, S. M., Walker, M., & Torres, M. I. (2014). Extracting relevant knowledge for the detection of sarcasm and nastiness in the social web. *Knowledge-Based Systems, 69*, 124–133. doi:10.1016/j.knosys.2014.05.021

Khattri, A., Joshi, A., Bhattacharyya, P., & Carman, M. J. (2015). Your sentiment precedes you: Using an author's historical tweets to predict sarcasm. In *6th workshop on computation approaches to subjectivity, sentiment and social media analysis (WASSA, 2015),*(pp. 25–30), ACL.

Kreuz, R. J., & Caucci, G. M. (2007). Lexical influences on the perception of sarcasm. In *Proceedings of the Workshop on computational approaches to Figurative Language* (pp. 1-4). ACL. 10.3115/1611528.1611529

Kreuz, R. J., & Glucksberg, S. (1989). How to be sarcastic: The echoic reminder theory of verbal irony. *Journal of Experimental Psychology. General, 118*(4), 374–386. doi:10.1037/0096-3445.118.4.374

Kreuz, R. J., & Link, K. E. (2002). Asymmetries in the use of verbal irony. *Journal of Language and Social Psychology, 21*(2), 127–143. doi:10.1177/02627X02021002002

Kreuz, R. J., & Roberts, R. M. (1995). Two cues for verbal irony: Hyperbole and the ironic tone of voice. *Metaphor and Symbol, 10*(1), 21–31. doi:10.120715327868ms1001_3

Kunneman, F., Liebrecht, C., van Mulken, M., & van den Bosch, A. (2014). Signaling sarcasm: From hyperbole to hashtag. *Information Processing & Management, 51*(4), 500–509. doi:10.1016/j.ipm.2014.07.006

Kuo, P. C., Alvarado, F. H. C., & Chen, Y. S. (2018). Facebook Reaction-Based Emotion Classifier as Cue for Sarcasm Detection. arXiv:1805.06510

Liebrecht, C., Kunneman, F., & Bosch, A. (2013). *The perfect solution for detecting sarcasm in tweets\# not. In Proceedings of the Association for Computational Linguistics* (pp. 29–37). ACL.

Liu, P., Chen, W., Ou, G., Wang, T., Yang, D., & Lei, K. (2014). Sarcasm Detection in Social Media Based on Imbalanced Classification. In *Web-Age Information Management* (pp. 459–471). Springer International Publishing. doi:10.1007/978-3-319-08010-9_49

Lukin, S., & Walker, M. (2013). Really? Well apparently bootstrapping improves the performance of sarcasm and nastiness classifiers for online dialogue. In *Proceedings of the Workshop on Language Analysis in Social Media* (pp. 30-40). ACL

Lunando, E., & Purwarianti, A. (2013). Indonesian social media sentiment analysis with sarcasm detection. In *2013 International Conference on Advanced Computer Science and Information Systems (ICACSIS)* (pp. 195-198). IEEE. 10.1109/ICACSIS.2013.6761575

Marcus, M. P., Marcinkiewicz, M. A., & Santorini, B. (1993). Building a large annotated corpus of English: The Penn Treebank. *Computational Linguistics, 19*(2), 313–330.

Maynard, D., & Greenwood, M. A. (2014). Who cares about sarcastic tweets? Investigating the impact of sarcasm on sentiment analysis. *In Proceedings of Language Resources and Evaluation Conference*, (pp. 4238–4243), ACL.

Pang, B., Lee, L., & Vaithyanathan, S. (2002). Thumbs up?: Sentiment classification using machine learning techniques. In *Proceedings of the ACL-02 conference on Empirical methods in natural language processing* (Vol. 10, pp. 79-86). Association for Computational Linguistics. 10.3115/1118693.1118704

Pennebaker, J. W., Francis, M. E., & Booth, R. J. (2001). Linguistic inquiry and word count: LIWC 2001. Lawrence Erlbaum Associates.

Rajadesingan, A., Zafarani, R., & Liu, H. (2015). Sarcasm detection on Twitter: A behavioral modeling approach. In *Proceedings of the Eighth ACM International Conference on Web Search and Data Mining* (pp. 97-106). ACM. 10.1145/2684822.2685316

Rajeswari, K., & ShanthiBala, P. (2018). Recognization of Sarcastic Emotions of Individuals on Social Network. *International Journal of Pure and Applied Mathematics, 18*(7), 253–259.

Riloff, E., Qadir, A., Surve, P., De Silva, L., Gilbert, N., & Huang, R. (2013). *Sarcasm as Contrast between a Positive Sentiment and Negative Situation* (pp. 704–714). EMNLP.

Rusu, D., Dali, L., Fortuna, B., Grobelnik, M., & Mladenic, D. (2007). Triplet extraction from sentences. In *Proceedings of the 10th International Multiconference Information Society* (pp. 8-12).

Schifanella, R., de Juan, P., Tetreault, J., & Cao, L. (2016). Detecting sarcasm in multimodal socialplatforms. In *Proceedings of the 2016 ACM on Multimedia Conference* (pp. 1136–1145), ACM. 10.1145/2964284.2964321

Strapparava, C., & Valitutti, A. (2004). WordNet Affect: an Affective Extension of WordNet. In LREC (Vol. 4, pp. 1083-1086).

Suzuki, S., Orihara, R., Sei, Y., Tahara, Y., & Ohsuga, A. (2017). Sarcasm Detection Method to Improve Review Analysis. In ICAART (Vol. 2, pp. 519-526).

Swami, S., Khandelwal, A., Singh, V., Akhtar, S. S., & Shrivastava, M. (2018). A Corpus of English-Hindi Code-Mixed Tweets for Sarcasm Detection. arXiv:1805.11869

Tayal, D. K., Yadav, S., Gupta, K., Rajput, B., & Kumari, K. (2014, March). Polarity detection of sarcastic political tweets. In *2014 International Conference on Computing for Sustainable Global Development (INDIACom)* (pp. 625-628). IEEE. 10.1109/IndiaCom.2014.6828037

Tsur, O., Davidov, D., & Rappoport, A. (2010). ICWSM-A Great Catchy Name: Semi-Supervised Recognition of Sarcastic Sentences in Online Product Reviews. In ICWSM (pp. 162–169). ACL

Tungthamthiti, P., Shirai, K., & Mohd, M. (2014). Recognition of Sarcasm in Tweets Based on Concept Level Sentiment Analysis and Supervised Learning Approaches. In *Proceedings of Pacific Asia Conference on Language, Information and Computing* (pp. 404–413). ACL.

Utsumi, A. (2000). Verbal irony as implicit display of ironic environment: Distinguishing ironic utterances from nonirony. *Journal of Pragmatics*, *32*(12), 1777–1806. doi:10.1016/S0378-2166(99)00116-2

Utsumi, A. (2002). Toward a cognitive model of poetic effects in figurative language. In *2002 IEEE International Conference on Systems, Man and Cybernetics* (Vol. 7, pp. 6–11). IEEE.

Verma, N., & Bhattacharyya, P. (2004). Automatic lexicon generation through WordNet. *GWC*, *2004*, 226–229.

Wang, Z., Wu, Z., Wang, R., & Ren, Y. (2015). Twitter sarcasm detection exploiting a context-basedmodel. *In International Conference on Web Information Systems Engineering 2015* (pp. 77–91). Springer.

Chapter 11

Towards Patient-Centric Healthcare:
Multi-Version Ontology-Based Personalization of Clinical Guidelines

Fabio Grandi
University of Bologna, Italy

Federica Mandreoli
University of Modena and Reggio Emilia, Italy

Riccardo Martoglia
University of Modena and Reggio Emilia, Italy

ABSTRACT

Retrieving personalized care plans from a guideline repository is an ever-increasing need in the medical world, not only for physicians but also for empowered patients. In this chapter, we continue our long-lasting research on ontology-based personalized access to very large collections of multi-version documents by addressing a novel challenge: dealing with multi-version clinical guidelines but also with a multi-version ontology used to support personalized access to them. Efficiency is ensured by a newly introduced annotation scheme for guidelines and solutions to cope with the evolution of ontology structure. The tests performed on a prototype implementation confirm the goodness of the approach. Finally, the chapter proposes an exhaustive analysis of the state of the art in this field and, in the final part, a discussion where we expand our vision to related research themes and possible further developments of our work.

INTRODUCTION

The adoption of reference ontologies and their deployment for the personalization of multi-version resources has been considered by several authors in the medical informatics domain (Grandi et al., 2012; Riaño et al., 2012; Tu et al., 2011, Wang et al., 2013) (but also in other application fields, e.g.,

DOI: 10.4018/978-1-5225-7186-5.ch011

Copyright © 2019, IGI Global. Copying or distributing in print or electronic forms without written permission of IGI Global is prohibited.

e-Government (Grandi et al., 2009)). In this work, as resources we consider clinical guidelines (Peleg, 2013), that is "best practices" encoding and standardizing health care procedures, either in textual or in executable format, and their personalization with respect to an ontology of diseases, patients or available hospital facilities they are applicable to. In practice, references to ontology classes are added to the computer encoding of resources (e.g., for which an XML (W3C, 2018a) format can conveniently be used) to introduce a sort of semantic indexing of contents representing their applicability, relevance or eligibility with respect to ontology classes. For instance, a given guideline (e.g., involving treatment of heart diseases) may contain different recommendations which are not uniformly applicable to the same classes of patients: one general therapy may be non-applicable to persons who suffer from some metabolic disorders (e.g., diabetes mellitus) or chronic diseases (e.g., kidney failure) or present some addictions (e.g., cocaine); one first-choice drug may not be administered to patients who are already under treatment with possibly interacting drugs (e.g., anticoagulants), or show genetic or acquired hypersensitivity or intolerance to some substances (e.g., patients with enzymatic defects or documented allergies), and so on. Hence, when dealing with a specific patient care case, a physician may be interested in retrieving a personalized version of a clinical guideline, that is a version tailored to his/her use needs by means of all the available personalization coordinates involving the patient's health state, anamnesis and characteristics (e.g., genetic, demographic or preferential) and local settings (including available hospital resources, diagnostic facilities and physicians' skills). Therefore, the personalized version will only contain recommendations which are safely and effectively applicable by the user to the patient's specific case. Furthermore, the emergence of patient-centered healthcare (NEJM Catalyst, 2017) and the development of patient-centered decision support systems (González-Ferrer et al., Melnick et al. 2017; 2013; Sacchi et al., 2013), with the involvement of empowered patients as final users, requires the adoption of also non strictly medical characteristics and individual preferences as further personalization coordinates (e.g., level of education, meal schedule and sleep habits).

To this purpose, we introduced in (Grandi et al., 2009; Grandi et al., 2012) a personalization query engine that, starting from a user-supplied list of ontology classes representing values of the semantic personalization coordinates, can exploit semantic indexing to retrieve the relevant contents only and produce a guideline version tailored to a specific use case. Notice that, coherently with ontology-based personalization solutions also proposed in other application fields (De Bra, 2017), we use the term "personalized" as referred to the user of the computer system, that is either the medical care provider or the empowered patient who follows the guideline.

However, in a dynamic environment, the management of this kind of semantic versioning is interleaved with temporal aspects. The fast evolution of medical knowledge and the dynamics involved in clinical practice imply the coexistence of multiple temporal versions of the clinical guidelines stored in a repository, which are continually subject to amendments and modifications. Therefore, it is crucial to reconstruct the consolidated version of a guideline as produced by the application of all the modifications it underwent so far, that is the form in which it currently belongs to the state-of-the-art of clinical practice and, thus, must be applied to patients today. However, also past versions are still important, not only for historical reasons: for example, a physician might be called upon to justify his/her actions for a given patient at a past time on the basis of the clinical guideline versions applicable to the pathology of patient and which were valid at that time.

Moreover, in a dynamic environment, the definition of domain ontologies themselves is also subject to modification as the medical knowledge, clinical environments and viable technologies evolve and, thus, also ontologies come out versioned as a consequence of updates periodically effected by domain

Figure 1. An overview of the multi-version ontology-based framework for personalized access to clinical guidelines

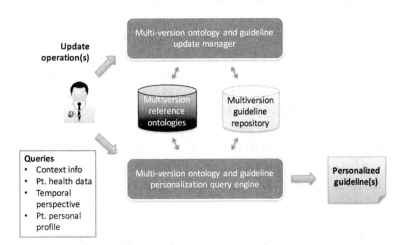

experts and knowledge engineers or even standardization committees. As we will exemplify in Section "Motivating Example", personalization of a guideline with respect to a past point in time must be affected by taking into account, in order to consider semantic indexing, the version of the reference ontology which was valid at the same time point. In other words, the selected guideline version and the ontology version used for personalization must be mutually temporally consistent. Since clinical guidelines have also been recently proposed to be used as evidence of the legal standard of care in medical malpractice litigation (Mackey & Liang, 2011; Ruhl & Siegal, 2017), enforcement of temporal consistency is crucial to assess the responsibility of physicians having followed the guidelines in the past (e.g., for an insurance controversy involving some damage due to treatment). In a patient-centric personalization scenario, where different responsibility levels might be ascribed either to the physicians and to the empowered patients, it is also crucial to reconstruct a temporally consistent historical perspective for both type of users.

In this chapter, we address the problem of dealing with multi-version ontologies in a framework for ontology-based personalized access to clinical guidelines in XML, extending the personalization approach proposed in (Grandi et al., 2009; Grandi et al., 2012). We provide an overview of the framework in Figure 1. The approach allows the semantic indexing of guideline contents with respect to ontology classes and exploits the IS-A relationship among such classes for granting personalized access. Efficiency is ensured by a numbering scheme for ontology classes encoding the IS-A hierarchy and an XML-based engine that exploits such encoding for fast reconstruction of the requested guideline versions. When the reference ontologies are subject to change, the numbering scheme becomes a problem: if the same class belongs to two ontology versions, its codes are very likely different as long as the two ontology versions have a different IS-A structure. To overcome this drawback this chapter introduces:

- A new annotation scheme for resources, based on ontology class identifiers which are independent of the encoding of the IS-A structure and an accessory data structure to bind the evolving IS-A encoding to time-invariant class identifiers;
- An efficient solution to cope with the evolution of the IS-A encoding when structural changes are applied to the ontology;

- A query processor that is able to efficiently solve XQuery-like requests with text, validity and applicability constraints when both guidelines and ontology are versioned.

The rest of the chapter is organized as follows. Next section provides useful details of the framework for ontology-based personalization proposed in (Grandi et al., 2009; Grandi et al., 2012); Sec. "Motivating Example" emphasizes the relevance of ontology versioning by means of a motivating example. Sec. "Representation and Management of Multi-version Ontology" presents the approach for the representation and management of multi-version ontologies while Sec. "Personalization Query Processing with Multi-version Ontology" addresses the problem from a query processing point of view. Sec. "Implementation Notes and Performance Evaluation" presents the main features of a prototyping solution we designed to assess the approach and the results we obtained on synthetic guidelines. Finally, related works and concluding remarks are addressed at Secs. "Related Work and Discussion" and "Conclusions", respectively.

A FRAMEWORK FOR ONTOLOGY-BASED PERSONALIZATION

Our personalization method is based on the adoption of reference domain ontologies and the introduction of semantic indexing of guideline contents with respect to ontology classes. Semantic indexing can then be used by personalization services to adapt generic resources to specific use cases, for example, to derive and enact individual and locally adapted care plans as proposed in (Grandi et al., 2012; Riaño et al., 2012; Tu et al., 2011). Notice that, in this chapter, we will adopt a single ontology (i.e., diseases) and a single time dimension (i.e., valid time (Jensen et al., 1998)) for the examples, in order to make them easier to follow, although multiple ontologies and multiple time dimensions can be supported in our approach as multiple semantic and temporal personalization dimensions, respectively. For instance, a reference ontology to be used for diseases can be derived from the ICD-10[1] international classification of diseases or from the SNOMED-CT[2] comprehensive healthcare terminologies.

The main ontology feature which is relevant for our personalization approach is the hierarchy of classes (taxonomy) induced by the IS-A relationship. Hence, we do not consider properties or other features and also follow the simplified assumption made in (Grandi et al., 2009; Grandi et al., 2012) that the class hierarchy underlying the ontology is tree-shaped, that is each node in the class hierarchy (but the root) has a single parent. Owing to the tree structure, nodes can be assigned a preorder and a postorder code, corresponding to the sequence in which nodes are visited during a preorder or postorder traversal of the tree. Such codes can be used for efficiently characterizing the descendants of a node:

N is a descendant of M iff M.Pre < N.Pre and N.Post < M.Post

with obvious meaning of the used dotted notation. For example, we can consider the sample ontology depicted in the left part of Figure 2, representing a portion of a taxonomy of diseases, where the (preorder, postorder) code pairs can be found in the top left of the depicted ontology classes.

The right part of Figure 2 represents a portion of the XML encoding of a multi-version clinical guideline with embedded semantic indexing to be used for personalization. It is made of an element "therapy" with two versions, the former (version 1) valid from T0 to T1 and applicable to class 3 (Myocardial ischemia) of the ontology to the left of Figure 2 and the latter (version 2) valid from T1 on and applicable to class 4 (Angina pectoris) of the ontology. The special time value UC (Until Changed) is used to represent the

Figure 2. A reference ontology and an XML guideline specification with temporal and semantic versioning

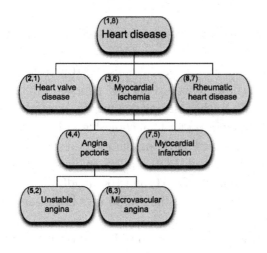

```
...
<therapy>
<version number="1">
  <pertinence>
    <valid from="T0" to="T1"/>
    <applies to="3"/>
  </pertinence>
    Contents of therapy-version 1
</version>
<version number="2">
  <pertinence>
    <valid from="T1" to="UC"/>
    <applies to="4"/>
  </pertinence>
    Contents of therapy-version 2
  <lifestyle>
  <version number="1">
    <pertinence>
      <applies also="2"/>
    </pertinence>
      Contents of lifestyle-version 1
  </version>
  </lifestyle>
</version>
</therapy>
...
```

To value of a right-unlimited time interval denoting a still valid version. The second version of element "therapy" contains a subelement "lifestyle", which inherits the validity of its parent element (from T1 on) and extends the applicability inherited from its parent also to class 2 (Heart valve disease) of the same ontology (i.e., the applicability of this "lifestyle" element is class 2 or class 4). The only version (version 1) defined for "lifestyle" is necessary in order to redefine the inherited semantic pertinence (notice that the "pertinence" XML element is defined as a subelement of the "version" XML element).

In our previous approach, as in Figure 2, preorder codes were directly adopted as node identifiers to be used as a reference to ontology classes for semantic indexing of the guidelines which are the object of personalization. Throughout the rest of the chapter, we will call this the baseline solution: preorder codes are, thus, embedded in the semantic markup of XML documents making up the guideline repository. When the reference ontologies are subject to change, this becomes a problem: if the same class belongs to two ontology versions, its preorder (and postorder) code is very likely different as long as the two ontology versions have a different structure. Hence, the ontology class identifiers are not time-invariant and the creation of a new ontology version also implies the creation of a new version of all the indexed guidelines, since all references to ontology classes embedded into a guideline have to be set to the new values of the class identifiers in the new guideline version in order to maintain semantic indexing. This may imply a huge amount of data to be updated even if a single class has been added to a reference ontology.

In this work, we will adopt a different approach, by introducing as proposed in (Grandi, 2013) time-invariant identifiers for reference to ontology classes and a separate management of preorder and postorder codes. In this way, the proposed encoding scheme implies an indirect reference from class identifiers used for semantic indexing of guidelines to preorder and postorder codes, which are used to support efficient query processing as described in Sec. "Personalization Query Processing with Multi-version Ontologies".

MOTIVATING EXAMPLE

In order to emphasize the relevance of ontology versioning in a personalization environment, we will introduce in this section a motivating example. To this end, let us consider the history of treatment, as recommended by guidelines, of a patient suffering from a cardiovascular disease (CVD) for which dyslipidemia is taken as one of the major risk factors. In order to reduce the risk, patients with high cholesterol levels are subject to a lipid-lowering therapy. We further assume that the first treatment guideline was published in 1994 and recommended a target serum level for total cholesterol (TC) of 270 mg/dL. In 1998, we further assume a new guideline was published, defining the target levels as 193 mg/dL for TC and 116 mg/dL for low-density lipoprotein cholesterol (LDL-C). We finally assume that a new guideline published in 2003 reduced the goals to 175 mg/dL for TC and 100 mg/dL for LDL-C. With some simplifications, this is more or less what really happened in the evolution of European guidelines, as witnessed in (Erhardt & Gotto, 2006).

In an ontology-based personalization environment like the one we consider in this work, the evolution of medical knowledge underlying clinical practice implies changes to the reference domain ontologies. In our example, this leads to modifications to the definition of a "high-cholesterol cardio vascular disease" in an ontology of pathologies like that of Figure 2. In particular, using DL-style ontology definitions, the evolution of the "HighCholesterolCVD" patient class definition consists of three versions: the first valid from 1994 to 1997 equivalent to:

HighCholesterolCVD = CardioVascularDisease ⊓ ∃hasTClevel.over270

the second valid from 1998 to 2002 equivalent to:

HighCholesterolCVD = CardioVascularDisease ⊓ ∃hasTClevel.over193 ⊓ ∃hasLDL-Clevel.over116

and the third valid from 2003 equivalent to:

HighCholesterolCVD = CardioVascularDisease ⊓ ∃hasTClevel.over175 ⊓ ∃hasLDL-Clevel.over100

In fact, by means of role value restrictions (in the form ∃R.A), we stated that the high TC and LDL-C cholesterol levels are defined starting from suitably defined data types (i.e., "over270" used in the first version, "over193" and "over116" used in the second version, "over175" and "over100" used in the last one).

In order to retrieve a CVD treatment guideline personalized to the case of a specific patient, the patient has first to be classified by the physician using the system, possibly with the help of a suitable reasoning service, with respect to the ontology of diseases. To this end, his/her medical records are matched against the HighCholesterolCVD definition in order to check whether the patient is an instance of the class. Hence, in our framework, in December 2000, a CVD patient with TC and LDL-C serum levels of 180 and 120 mg/dL, respectively, had not to be considered for a lipid-lowering therapy since, according to the ontology valid in December 2000, would not be classified as a high-cholesterol patient (cholesterol levels were already under the therapeutic target). However, if the patient was prescribed then a lipid-lowering drug like cerivastatin by a zealous physician and died of fatal rhabdomyolysis as an adverse effect of the drug[3], the physician behavior might go under investigation (e.g. for an insurance controversy). If the physician's behavior has to be judged today, the prescription of a statin drug could even seem appropriate, as the patient had out-of-target TC and LDL-C levels according to the definitions in the current ontology. However, the correct temporal perspective must be applied, and the definitions in the ontology version valid in December 2000 must be used to evaluate the decision of the physician taken at that time. Hence, as he/she prescribed to the patient a potent drug like cerivastatin without an actual classification as a high-cholesterol patient (w.r.t. definitions in the available guidelines), then a wrong decision or at least an excess of zeal could be acknowledged.

Therefore, the framework assumed in the previous Section must be extended to include representation and storage of ontologies in multi-version format and a query facility to extract a valid ontology version as a temporal snapshot from the multi-version repository. In brief, assuming ontologies are defined using the OWL language (W3C, 2018b) or a sublanguage of it and represented as RDF/XML documents, "The Valid Ontology" approach consists of adding a custom XML markup to OWL documents in order to mark the boundaries of versioned portions and add timestamps to versions in a way similar to that applied to guideline documents (as exemplified in the right part of Figure 2). The query engine already available in our framework can then be used to extract, as temporal snapshots (Jensen et al., 1998), individual ontology versions from their multi-version store.

Notice that the example presented above involved the evolution of an ontology class definition, which did not affect the ontology structure, only for the sake of providing a reasonably compact, significant and easy to understand example. In such a case, once the right ontology version has been selected and used for classification of the use case of interest, the personalization engine described in (Grandi et al., 2012) can be readily used for guideline personalization. But, in general, both class and property definitions can be versioned, also allowing IS-A hierarchies to arbitrarily evolve between versions. The real problem, that will be addressed in this work, is when the ontology evolution involves the class hierarchy, which is the foundation on which the whole building of our personalization method is based. Therefore, we will show in the next Section how the personalization framework must be upgraded in order to also cope with structural changes of an underlying reference ontology in an effective and efficient way.

REPRESENTATION AND MANAGEMENT OF MULTI-VERSION ONTOLOGIES

In this Section, we present our new semantic indexing scheme, based on the solutions introduced in (Grandi, 2013), which is used to link resource portions to ontology classes in the presence of a multi-version ontology. It consists of the introduction of time-invariant ontology class identifiers and on the representation of the ontology class hierarchy structure by means of an accessory data structure, which we will call code table. For example, we can consider our sample ontology of Figure 2 with the class identifiers redefined as depicted in the left part of Figure 3, where the corresponding preorder and postorder codes of nodes can be found in the table to the right. The structure of the class hierarchy is completely defined by the information present in the table.

The new class identifiers are time-invariant: for instance, "Myocardial Infarction" remains class C6 in all the ontology versions it belongs to, regardless of its position in the evolving class hierarchy. A different code table is indeed associated to each ontology version to represent its structure. The time-

Figure 3. A reference ontology with time-invariant class identifiers and the code table representing its structure

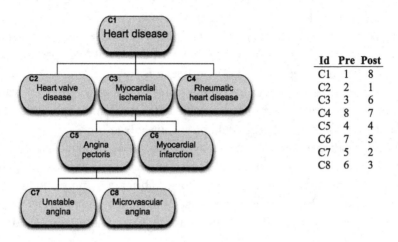

invariant class identifiers can then be used for semantic indexing of guidelines instead of preorder codes as in the right part of Figure 2.

In order to efficiently deal with the evolution of the code table when structural changes are applied to the ontology definition, three primitive operations have been defined to perform the: (1) insertion of a leaf node; (2) insertion of an intermediate node; (3) deletion of a node. Any complex modification of the structure of an ontology class hierarchy can be affected via a suitable sequence of such modification primitives. Moreover, it has also been shown how the whole evolution of a multi-version ontology can be stored in a single temporal table with schema *TreeRelation(Id, Pre, Post, From, To),* from which the individual code tables associated to single versions can be extracted as snapshots by means of a temporal query. The semantics of the *InsertUnder( ), InsertOver( )* and *DeleteNode( )* modification primitives have also been redefined in order to directly work on the *TreeRelation* temporal table in an efficient way. Full details on their definition can be found in (Grandi, 2013). In the Performance Evaluation section, for reference, we will also evaluate the ontology update costs paid in case such primitives are not used and, thus, the code table must be recomputed from scratch after the creation of each new ontology version.

For instance, assume our ontology created at time T0 is composed of a single version as depicted in Figure 3 (the *TreeRelation* initially contains the same tuples as the code table in the right part of the figure, each augmented with timestamps From=T0 and To=UC). Assume further that, at time T2, we want to create a new "ST elevation myocardial infarction" class as a subclass of C6 and evidence, among the guideline portions formerly applicable to the "Myocardial infarction" class, the ones which are more specifically applicable to the new "ST elevation myocardial infarction" class. The selection of such guideline portions, whose annotations have to be updated as shown in the following, can be largely automated (e.g., based on the presence of "ST elevation" or "STEMI" keywords) but, for fine tuning, requires validation by human experts, as for the annotation of the first created guideline version.

The new ontology version can be created via the execution of the following operation:

InsertUnder(C6, T2)

whose effects on the *TreeRelation* temporal table are shown in Figure 4. The new class has been assigned by the *InsertUnder* procedure a C9 time-invariant identifier, which must be used in the definition of the "ST elevation myocardial infarction" OWL class and in the markup of semantically indexed guidelines. Notice how, in the *TreeRelation* of Figure 4, the nodes C1, C3, C4 and C6 are represented through two tuples each, representing their versions belonging to the two ontology versions, respectively (e.g., the first version of C1 with preorder 1, postorder 8 and validity [T0,T2) belongs to the first ontology version, whereas the second version of C1 with postorder changed to 9 and validity [T2,UC) belongs to the second ontology version). Nodes represented through a single tuple (e.g., C2) have a single version with validity [T0,UC) shared by both ontology versions.

Therefore, the ontology version valid at a given time T can be retrieved by means of a classical temporal snapshot query over the temporal relation in Figure 4

```
SELECT Id,Pre,Post FROM TreeRelation
WHERE From<=T AND T<To
```

We can notice that the retrieved snapshot coincides with the code table of the first ontology version shown in Figure 2 if T0≤T<T2, whereas the outcome would be the code table of the second ontology version (with "ST elevation myocardial Infarction" class identified by C9) if T≥T2.

As far as the annotated guidelines are concerned, the existing guideline portions which were marked as applicable to C6 but which are more specifically applicable to the new "ST elevation infarction" class must be updated. For example, with reference to the guideline portion in the right part of Figure 2, assume this is the case of version 2 of the "therapy" element, as its contents have been reclassified as applicable to the new class C9. Then the guideline encoding must be updated as shown in Figure 5. In this way, the updated annotations in the figure say that the (unchanged) contents are still applicable to class C6 in the first ontology version valid in [T0, T2) but applicable to class C9 in the second ontology

Figure 4. The TreeRelation temporal table after the creation of the new ontology class

Id	Pre	Post	From	To
C1	1	8	T0	T2
C2	2	1	T0	UC
C3	3	6	T0	T2
C4	8	7	T0	T2
C5	4	4	T0	UC
C6	7	5	T0	T2
C7	5	2	T0	UC
C8	6	3	T0	UC
C1	1	9	T2	UC
C3	3	7	T2	UC
C4	9	8	T2	UC
C6	7	6	T2	UC
C9	8	5	T2	UC

Figure 5. Guideline contents update before (to the left) and after (to the right) the creation of a subclass C9 of C6 at time T1. The update is required since we assume the contents are more specifically applicable to the new class C9.

```
...
<version number="2">
  <pertinence>
    <valid from="T1" to="UC"/>
    <applies to="C6"/>
  </pertinence>
      Contents of therapy–version 2
  <lifestyle>
    ...
  </lifestyle>
</version>
...
```

→

```
...
<version number="2">
  <pertinence>
    <valid from="T1" to="T2"/>
    <applies to="C6"/>
  </pertinence>
  <pertinence>
    <valid from="T2" to="UC"/>
    <applies to="C9"/>
  </pertinence>
      Contents of therapy–version 2
  <lifestyle>
    ...
  </lifestyle>
</version>
...
```

version valid from T2 on. The existing guideline portions applicable to C6 but not specifically to the "ST elevation infarction" class, are left untouched indeed. Notice that, after such an update, by inheritance of the pertinence, the "lifestyle" subelement of Figure 2 remains applicable to C6 or C2 in [T1, T2) but becomes applicable to C9 or C2 in [T2,UC).

In the baseline solution where preorder codes are used as class identifiers, update of resources after an ontology changes are mandatory to preserve the basic functionalities of the personalization approach, as the semantic indexing would be irremediably lost without updating what links the resource portions to the ontology classes. On the contrary, in the solution based on time-invariant class identifiers proposed in this chapter, update of resources after an ontology change is aimed at improving the precision of the semantic indexing mechanism, by making the personalization approach benefit of the full available ontology. Hence, in some cases, it would not be strictly necessary to update the resources immediately after the ontology changes (e.g., updates could be affected in a lazy fashion). For instance, the existing portions which would be more specifically applicable to "ST elevation infarction" could still be retrieved as applicable to "Myocardial infarction", until the update is affected. However, in the performance comparison between our proposed solution and the baseline solution in Sec. "Personalization Query Processing with Multi-version Ontologies", we will take into account the costs of such resource updates, since sooner or later they have to be done for a finer tuning of the semantic indexing mechanism. Notice also that such updates involve a small fraction of the available resources, whereas even the whole resource repository might have to be often updated after an ontology change in the baseline solution.

In case the effected ontology modification is *InsertOver(Cy, T)* and Cx was the parent of Cy before T, then the existing guideline portions whose semantic annotations must be changed are the ones that were applicable to Cx but not to Cy and that result applicable to the newly created class, which is child of Cx and parent of Cy in the new ontology version. In case the modification is *DeleteNode(Cy, T)* and Cx was the parent of Cy before T, then the existing guideline portions whose semantic annotations must be changed are the ones that were applicable to the deleted class Cy and which remain applicable to Cx in the new ontology version.

PERSONALIZATION QUERY PROCESSING WITH MULTI-VERSION ONTOLOGIES

The semantic indexing of resources which links their contents to reference ontologies is designed to support personalization queries. To this purpose, and in order to show how query processing works in the presence of multi-version ontology, we consider the XQuery-like (World Wide Web Consortium [W3C], 2018c) query template which follows:

```
FOR $x IN document("resources.xml")
WHERE TEXT_CONSTRAINT($x,CC)
  AND VALID($x,T) AND APPLICABLE($x,Cx:depth)
RETURN $x
```

which is a simplified form of the template which is embedded in our prototype system. The function TEXT_CONSTRAINT() applies textual constraints to the contents of the resources to be retrieved. Textual constraints can include both structural and lexical constraints, being expressible as an XPath expression (Berglund et al., 2016) which can be used for matching keywords within the resource structured contents. The function VALID() extracts a temporal snapshot of the resources by selecting the content versions valid at time "T". Finally, the function APPLICABLE() effects a semantic slicing of the resources by selecting the content versions which are applicable to instances of ontology class "Cx" and of its ancestors up to "depth" levels (the expression "Cx:depth" can be called *navigational pattern*, with respect to the reference ontology). For example, the following query:

```
FOR $x IN document("guidelines.xml")
WHERE TEXT_CONSTRAINT($x, "//therapy//title/text(), anticoagulant")
  AND VALID($x, "2000-12-01")
AND APPLICABLE($x, "Myocardial infarction":1)
RETURN $x
```

asks the system to retrieve the guideline portions which contain the word "anticoagulant" in the title of some contents of the section "therapy" and that are applicable to the "Myocardial infarction" class or to its parent class in the ontology, using a temporal perspective as of December 1, 2000 (i.e., the version either of the guidelines and of the reference ontology to be used is the one valid at T="2000-12-01").

In the presence of multi-version ontologies, the first step in query processing is the determination of the ontology classes denoted by the navigational pattern "Cx:depth" and of the preorder and postorder codes of such classes. This information can be retrieved by first deriving the ontology version valid at time T from the TreeRelation temporal table. Then, table rows CX and CY must be retrieved in the snapshot ontology, where CX corresponds to the class whose identifier is "Cx" and CY corresponds to the ancestor of the class CX that can be reached in "depth" steps starting from CX (to this purpose, simple SQL statements as shown in (Grandi, 2013) can be used).

CX and CY data are then used, in the second query processing step, to select the qualifying resource contents through their preorder and postorder codes. In particular, a resource version qualifies if its semantic pertinence implies the navigational. Thanks to the properties of the preorder/postorder encoding, this notion of implication translates into verifying whether at least one of the ontology classes which make up the semantic pertinence of the resource is contained in the rectangular region defined in the preorder/postorder plane by the navigational. Such rectangular region, in which all and only the nodes in the inheritance path from CY to CX fall, can be determined as the Cartesian product [CY.Pre,CX.Pre] x [CX.Post,CY.Post] (i.e., the lower right corner of the rectangle is CX, whereas the upper left corner is CY). Owing to the fact that preorder and postorder codes associated to the same classes can be different in different ontology versions, we might have a different containment relationship to be checked for each ontology version.

For example, let us consider the multi-version ontology stored in our sample TreeRelation displayed in Figure 4 and the query navigational pattern "Myocardial infarction:1". Depending on the time "T" of interest, the CX and CY values are as summarized in the Table which follows:

Let us further consider the guideline portion in Figure 2, after the update shown in Figure 5. The element therapy(v1) is applicable to class C3 in [T0,T1); the element therapy(v2) is applicable to class C6 in [T1,T2) and to class C9 in [T2,UC); the element therapy(v2)/lifestyle(v1) is applicable to class C6 or class C2 in [T1,T2) and to class C9 or class C2 in [T2,UC). The relative positioning of such resource pertinences with respect to the regions individuated by the navigational pattern "Myocardial infarction:1" in the preorder/postorder plane for different time values is displayed in Figure 6.

Hence, at any time T∈[T0,T1), the only valid element therapy(v1) qualifies since its semantic pertinence is class C3 which has coordinates (3,6)) and is contained in the region individuated by "Myocardial infarction:1" (that is [3,5] x [7,6]). At any time T∈[T1,T2), the valid elements are therapy(v2), which qualifies since its semantic pertinence is class C6 (which has coordinates (7,5)) and is contained in the

Table 1. Evaluation of the navigational pattern "Myocardial infarction:1" in different versions of the ontology of Figure 4.

Time	Id	CX		Id	CY	
		Pre	Post		Pre	Post
[T0,T2)	C6	7	5	C3	3	6
[T2,UC)	C6	7	6	C3	3	7

Figure 6. Query processing in the preorder/postorder plane. Placement of candidate guideline elements is shown by blue circles with a solid border.

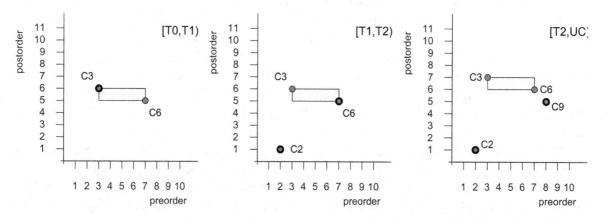

region individuated by "Myocardial infarction:1" (which is [3,5] x [7,6]), and its subelement therapy/lifestyle(v1), which also qualifies as it inherits the applicability class C6 from its parent (whereas its other applicability class C2 with coordinates (2,1) lays outside of the region). At any time T∈ T2,UC), there are no contents in the considered guideline portion which can qualify: the navigational pattern "Myocardial infarction:1" translates into the [3,6] x [8,7] region and the valid elements are therapy(v2), with applicability classes C9 with coordinates (8,5), and therapy(v2)/lifestyle(v1), which inherits applicability to class C9 and is also applicable to class C2 with coordinates (2,1), both laying outside of the region.

Therefore, considering the guideline portion in the right part of Figure 2, a query with navigational pattern "Myocardial infarction:1" returns the first version of the element "therapy" if the temporal selection condition involves a time T∈[T0,T1), retrieves the second version of the element "therapy" (inclusive of the subelement "lifestyle") if the temporal selection condition involves a time T∈[T1,T2) and returns an empty result if the temporal selection involves a time T≥T2.

In order to obtain a fully-fledged efficient and scalable personalization engine, the selection of resource contents based on the semantic indexing described above can be combined with the holistic technology described in (Grandi et al., 2012) and relying on the holistic temporal slicing techniques presented in (Mandreoli et al., 2006). In a few words, the holistic technology is based on a four-level architecture on which stack-based algorithms can be executed for efficient path and twig matching in querying an XML file. Full details on the implemented techniques for efficient personalization query processing can be found in (Grandi et al., 2012).

Finally, we can observe that the query template considered in this section can be easily extended to support other temporal selection operators (e.g., to test overlap or containment of intervals) and to retrieve data valid over temporal intervals (i.e., also belonging to more than one temporal version of the resource). Furthermore, also the applicability constraint can be extended to a more general form, where combinations with "AND" and "OR" logical operators of several navigational patterns in positive or negated form can be specified (in order to qualify for a negated navigational pattern, a resource must have its representative point outside the region defined by the navigational pattern in the plane). Also applicability constraints involving multiple reference ontologies in the same query can be specified and processed as shown in (Grandi et al. 2012).

IMPLEMENTATION NOTES AND PERFORMANCE EVALUATION

The techniques presented in the previous sections have been implemented in a complete prototype of the personalization engine. The engine supports:

- Multi-version ontology management and update, exploiting the insertion/deletion algorithms described in Section "Representation and Management of Multi-version Ontologies" for the modification of the ontology structure;
- Multi-version XML document (i.e. guideline) collection management, exploiting indirect referencing to the ontology as described in Section "Representation and Management of Multi-version Ontologies";
- Query processing capabilities on both ontology (so to retrieve the identifier of the relevant classes) and document collection, in order to fully support the guideline personalization process described in Section "Personalization Query Processing with Multi-version Ontologies".

While the ontology structure evolution is directly managed in relational tables as described in the previous sections, for XML document management we exploit an "XML-native" architecture relying on a Multi-version XML Query Processor we designed on purpose, which is able to manage the XML data repository and to support all the query facilities in a single component. The engine stores and reconstructs on-the-fly the XML guideline versions; personalized access is supported by means of a fast handling of the applicability constraints. Moreover, additional temporal, textual and/or structural constraints are supported. Note that, differently from typical "stratum" approaches (Grandi et al., 2009), our native implementation stores multi-version guidelines as a collection of ad-hoc tuples, each representing one of its multi-version parts. In this way, we do not need to retrieve whole XML documents and build space-consuming structures such as DOM trees to process a query (Mandreoli et al., 2006).

In order to evaluate the performance of our engine in a variety of scenarios, we performed a number of exploratory tests, involving both (a) multi-version ontology and document collection updating (Subsection "Multi-version Ontology and Document Collection Update") and (b) multi-version ontology and document collection querying (Subsection "Multi-version Ontology and Document Collection Querying"). For reference, both kinds of tests will include relevant comparisons with notable baselines.

Experimental Setting

We performed the tests on multi-version ontologies of various sizes: ontologies O1 (approximately containing 130 classes), O2 (600 classes) and O3 (1200 classes). We also performed specific robustness tests on a real-life scale ontology, O4, consisting of 100000 classes.

Our reference guideline collection, D1, contains 10000 XML guidelines; furthermore, we will also test the querying scalability w.r.t. the number of documents with the additional document sets D2 and D3, containing 20000 and 40000 XML guidelines, respectively. The total size of the resulting collections is 250MB (D1), 500MB (D2) and 1GB (D3).

The ontologies and guidelines are synthetically generated. The ontology generator was configured in order to reproduce the characteristics (i.e. tree shape and node distribution) of one of the most established actual medical terminologies, SNOMED-CT, which are also representative of most of the available terminologies. In particular, in a typical SNOMED-CT hierarchy, the tree is very large (i.e. heights of 15-20 with several thousands of classes) and the large majority of the classes are leaf nodes (nearly 73\% in the 2007 version (Bodenreider et al., 2007)). Moreover, the number of children distribution follows an exponential curve (Bodenreider et al., 2007). Our ontologies reproduce, in scale, these characteristics. For instance, Figure 7 shows the exponential curve of the number of children that is found on O3. As to the synthetic guidelines, they have a structure conforming to the GEM guideline schema presented in (Shiffman et al., 2000). As far as the multi-version aspects are concerned, we applied our multi-version encoding scheme to the ontologies and guidelines, using three temporal dimensions, by means of a configurable XML generator (Mandreoli et al., 2006). On average, each document contains 50÷60 nodes, with a depth level of 10, and 15÷20 of these nodes own 2 or 3 time-stamped versions.

All the experiments have been effected on an Intel Core i7 2.3Ghz OS X workstation, equipped with 8 GB RAM and a 256 GB SSD hard drive.

Figure 7. Distribution of the number of children (ontology O3)

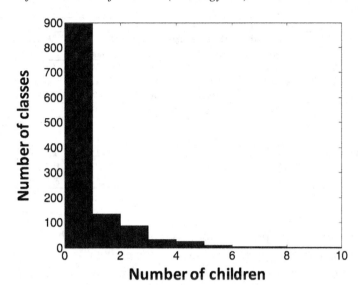

Multi-Version Ontology and Document Collection Update

First of all, we tested the performance of our engine in performing updates (i.e. insertions and deletions of classes) to the available ontology classes and, in case, to propagate such modifications to the document collection. Three ontology update scenarios, U1, U2 and U3, were considered, where several randomly generated updates were successively applied to an initial ontology:

Scenario U1: Starting ontology of 100 classes, modified with 50 update operations (resulting in 5 versions);

Scenario U2: Starting ontology of 500 classes, modified with 250 update operations (resulting in 25 versions);

Scenario U3: Starting ontology of 1000 classes, modified with 500 update operations (resulting in 50 versions).

The scenarios produced the previously introduced ontologies O1, O2 and O3 that have been exploited for the querying tests.

The upper left part of Figure 8 shows the average, total, minimum and maximum update time required to perform the updates. Thanks to our optimized insert/delete algorithms ("Algs" in figure), each modification is performed in a fraction of seconds, also in the larger scenarios. Please also note that the document collection update time is equally low (lower left part of figure). The main reason is that, thanks to the use of indirect referencing ("IndRef" in figure) in the guideline document collection, only a small fraction of collection updates, i.e. only those that refine the annotations referring to newly inserted ontology classes and those due to class deletions, is actually required.

The advantages of our solution is even more evident by comparing update time figures with the following baseline:

Figure 8. Update time for multi-version ontology (top) and guideline document collection (bottom)

	Ontology update (time in secs)					
	With insert/delete algorithms (Algs)				Without (Baseline)	
	avg	tot	min	max	avg	tot
Update Scenario U1	0.026	1.281	0.010	0.046	0.106	5.294
Update Scenario U2	0.135	33.834	0.047	0.322	0.446	111.612
Update Scenario U3	0.266	133.069	0.099	0.571	0.891	445.324
	Document collection update (time in secs)					
	With indirect reference (IndRef)				Without (Baseline)	
	avg	tot	min	max	avg	tot
Update Scenario U1	0.160	7.983	0.103	0.215	17.554	877.693
Update Scenario U2	0.145	36.374	0.095	0.208	109.597	27399.223
Update Scenario U3	0.136	67.754	0.093	0.212	215.980	107990.052

- For updating the ontology, an approach (upper right part of figure) that does not exploit our insert/delete primitives, thus requiring recomputation of the code table from scratch after the creation of each new ontology version. The performance slowdown is very noticeable (nearly 4x slower). Further, Figure 9 illustrates the comparison in terms of number of tuples that need to be modified in the database: note the logarithmic scale and the large gap, especially for larger ontologies, making this an unfeasible solution;
- For updating the document collection, an approach (bottom right in figure) that does not exploit indirect reference, i.e. where preorder codes are directly embedded in the semantic markup of XML documents. In this case, each update to the collection D1 turns out to be a very demanding task, taking more than 3.5 minutes on average in the larger scenario.

Finally, Figure 10 graphically summarizes total (ontology and document collection, when needed) average per-modification update time, showing that exploiting the proposed update primitives together with indirect reference allows us to manage ontology modifications in almost real time (i.e. fraction of

Figure 9. Number of modified ontology tuples in update scenarios U1, U2, U3

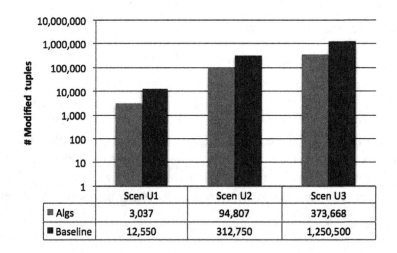

	Scen U1	Scen U2	Scen U3
Algs	3,037	94,807	373,668
Baseline	12,550	312,750	1,250,500

Figure 10. Average per-modification ontology update time in update scenarios U1, U2, U3

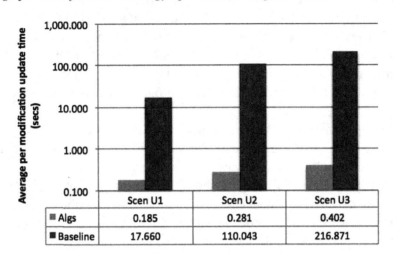

	Scen U1	Scen U2	Scen U3
▦ Algs	0.185	0.281	0.402
■ Baseline	17.660	110.043	216.871

seconds per modification instead of several minutes), an undisputed advantage for practical use of the engine.

Multi-Version Ontology and Document Collection Querying

In order to give a complete picture of the engine performances, we will now investigate its efficiency and scalability in querying the multi-version ontology and guideline collections.

Experiments were conducted by submitting a selection of 100 representative queries and by measuring the engine response time. The queries were designed so to stress the different system capabilities, therefore they contain structural constraints, textual search by keywords, temporal conditions and applicability constraints. Since the system answered all our queries with very uniform performances, we will show summarized processing time for all of them.

Figure 11 shows average, minimum and maximum querying times for both ontology (upper part, ontologies O1, O2 and O3) and document collection (lower part, guidelines sets D1, D2 and D3). As we can see, the time required for querying a multi-version ontology, also in the larger scenarios, is quite negligible (some milliseconds), thanks to the management approach proposed in the chapter.

Figure 11. Ontology and document collection querying time

Ontology querying (time in secs)			
	avg	min	max
Ontology O1	0.001	0.001	0.001
Ontology O2	0.008	0.007	0.011
Ontology O3	0.017	0.001	0.027
Document collection querying (time in secs)			
	avg	min	max
Collection D1	0.529	0.213	1.320
Collection D2	0.989	0.398	2.420
Collection D3	1.583	0.614	3.870

As to guideline querying, our approach shows a good efficiency in every context, providing a short response time (including query analysis, retrieval of the qualifying guideline parts and reconstruction of the result) of less than one or two seconds on average. Therefore, total engine querying time (ontology and guidelines) are confirmed to be in this order of magnitude: Figure 12 makes those times explicit by showing the case of querying the largest ontology (O3) together with the different document sets. The figures of our system are denoted as "Native" in the figure, since they exploit our "XML-native" engine implementation.

Figure 12 is also representative of the good scalability of the system. For instance, the queries executed in 0.53 seconds on the 10,000 documents of collection D1, and took 1.6 seconds on D3, which is four times larger than D1, with a scalability proportion of approximately 0.75:1. This is an important achievement: as also the comparison in figure shows, non-optimized solutions such as a "stratum" implementation on top of a DBMS (Grandi et al., 2009) are not only significantly (more than 10 times) slower, but also do not benefit from larger document sets and scale with a 1:1 proportion. This is due to the post-processing phase necessary to deal with the temporal and applicability aspects, which is forced to work on one document at a time.

Large-Scale Ontology Robustness Tests

We conclude the tests with a specific experiment designed to further stress the system on a large real-life scale ontology. With this setting we reproduce not only the typical characteristics of established medical terminologies (as discussed in Subsection "Experimental Setting"), but also their typical size. For instance, the current version of SNOMED-CT consists of 19 independent hierarchies having different sizes, the largest one reaching nearly 100000 classes; the terminology is updated with a typical number of updates of 1000 modifications per year.

The tests we show in Figure 13 are run on ontology O4, containing exactly 100000 classes, and with a number of 1000 updates. Are the system performances still good enough to guarantee usability? In this case, the total time required to perform a whole annual update cycle is 200 minutes, with an average of 12 seconds per update. This is very acceptable, taking also into account that these updates do not

Figure 12. Average total querying time for guideline collections D1, D2 and D3

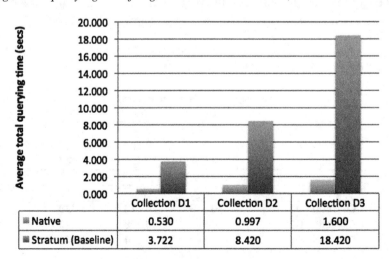

	Collection D1	Collection D2	Collection D3
Native	0.530	0.997	1.600
Stratum (Baseline)	3.722	8.420	18.420

Figure 13. Performance results for large scale ontology O4

	With insert/delete algorithms (Algs)		Without (Baseline)	
	1 upd avg	1000 upd tot	1 upd avg	1000 upd tot
Ontology update	12.0 sec	200.0 min	45.6 sec	760.0 min
	With indirect reference (IndRef)		Without (Baseline)	
	1 upd avg	1000 upd tot	1 upd avg	1000 upd tot
Document collection update	0.1 sec	1.8 min	337.2 min	n/a (~ months)
	avg			
Ontology querying	0.7 sec			

need to be performed in real-time. With an ontology of this size, the use of indirect referencing appears totally crucial: with it, the system is able to update all the documents referenced by the 1000 updates in a very small time (less than 2 minutes total). Without indirect referencing the cost of document updates becomes unbearable, due to the extremely large number of additional modifications to class ids that need to be performed (more than 5 hours for updating the collection for just one of the ontology updates; that would bring to an overall collection update time in the order of months). Finally, the average time for querying the ontology is still kept under a second; document collection querying time is not affected by ontology size and therefore is not shown in figure.

RELATED WORK AND DISCUSSION

Generally speaking, personalization can be defined as the ways in which information and services can be tailored to match the unique and specific needs of an individual or a community. It is based on understanding of the needs of individuals and efficiently and knowledgeably address their needs in a given context (De Bra, 2017). Pretschner (1998) presents a thorough discussion of early ontology-based personalization techniques and systems. More recent proposals of ontology-based personalization solutions, also in various application fields, include (Aroua & Mourad, 2017; Gulzar & Anny Leema, 2017; Lim et al, 2013; Machado et al., 2013; Maleszka, 2017; Nilashi et al., 2018; Sekhar Babu et al., 2018; Sohn et al., 2013; Zhang et al., 2017). When temporal resources are accessed, the necessity of also versioning the ontology used for personalization has been identified (for applications.in the legal domain) in (Grandi & Scalas, 2009).

As far as the medical domain is concerned, several data models and computer tools have been proposed to manage versioning issues and to support adaptable clinical guidelines, including (Boxwala et al., 2002; Fridsma et al., 2006; Gad El-Rab et al., 2017; Groot et al., 2008; Kaiser & Miksch, 2009; Novais et al., 2018; Owens & Nease, 1997; Peleg & Kantor, 2003; Peleg et al., 2017a; Peleg et al., 2017b; Sanders, 1998; Sanders et al., 2001; Scott-Wright et al., 2004; Shahar et al., 1998; Shalom et al., 2016; Terenziani et al., 2004, 2005; Wilk et al., 2017; Zhang & Padman, 2017). In particular, (Riaño et al., 2012; Shahar et al., 2004; Tu et al., 2011; Wang et al., 2013; Zheng et al., 2014) are the proposals more strictly related to our work, which consider the adoption of semantic annotations to support versioning and indexing, and the use of ontologies to support selective querying or adaptation of clinical guidelines (or, more in general, biomedical data). Riaño et al. (2012) propose an approach based on two personalization processes: the former is used to adapt the contents of a medical ontology to a given concrete patient using information available in health-care records; then the latter uses the personalized patient ontology to derive an individual intervention plan in the form of a personalized computer-interpretable guideline. In (Tu et al., 2011), the authors propose a practical method for transforming free-text eligibility criteria specified in clinical trials into computable criteria to support some personalized access (for the "searching for studies enrolling specific patient populations" use case). The DeGeL environment (Shahar et al., 2004) allows assisted conversion of textual guidelines into a computer-interpretable format, semantic annotation (via the Uruz markup tool) and indexing (via the IndexiGuide semantic classifier) of the guidelines to support selective access to the annotated guideline repository (via the Vaidurya context-sensitive search and retrieval tool). The DBOntoLink system (Zheng et al., 2014) allows users to express ontology-based specifications to query semantically annotated biomedical data stored in a traditional database via a Semantic Adapter module. Efficiency is guaranteed by the underlying DBMS capabilities and management of caching for ontology operations. However, all such proposals rely on the query functionalities of a standard relational or XML DBMS for the management of large guideline collections, while adaptation is effected through main-memory processing of the retrieved clinical guidelines. In particular, none of them considered the maintenance of temporal versions of the guidelines, and took into account the proliferation of versions inherent to the management of multiple versioning dimensions. In our previous research (Grandi et al., 2009), we showed how such an approach, in the presence of temporal and semantic versioning, becomes definitely inadequate when the number of resources and versions per resource increases since, in order to select the relevant parts and consistently assemble the personalized versions, one document at a time must be processed and a large amount of main memory is required, which strongly limits scalability and concurrency. In (Grandi et al., 2012), we addressed the efficiency problems in the context of ontology-based access to multi-version clinical guidelines with the introduction of a personalization query engine exploiting technologies developed on purpose. However, by extending (Grandi et al., 2012) with the support of the ontology versioning, the present chapter is, to the best of our knowledge, the first to combine effectiveness and efficiency concerns with the support of a full temporal perspective, in providing personalized access to a large collection of multi-version resources.

Some works deal with computer-aided patient-centered personalization of medical information (Quinn et al. 2014; Weimann et al. 2015) or care plans (González-Ferrer et al., 2013; Quaglini et al. 2009; Sacchi et al. 2013). However, issues concerning temporal versioning and efficient management of large repositories have not been dealt with in such approaches. In our approach, the granted personalization levels rely on the adoption of multiple support ontologies, which can be added in a modular way, for the semantic annotation of guideline contents. Hence, the functionalities of our personalization system can be extended to support patient-centered care plans by adding suitable ontologies modelling non-strictly medical characteristics and preferences of patients as new personalization coordinates. Moreover, the multi-version structure of guidelines enables the authoring and embedding of specific variant parts aimed at delivering recommendations targeted to patients (Enwald, 2013). In particular, (González-Ferrer et al., 2013; Sacchi et al., 2013) present methodologies for automatic extraction of a set of patient-tailored workflow patterns from physician-oriented clinical guidelines. With our approach, such patterns could then be embedded as variant parts when authoring a multi-version guideline to be stored in the repository, such that they can be automatically selected by the personalization engine to match a given patient profile and build a patient-tailored care plan.

The literature presents a large body of works dealing with ontology evolution and management of multiple ontology versions, as witnessed by some recently presented approaches (e.g., Zekri et al., 2016) and by the annotated bibliography published in (Grandi, 2012). Notice that, in this work, we do not deal with ontology evolution in a strict sense but, rather, with evolution of the class IS-A hierarchy extracted from the ontology, which is necessary to support the personalized access to data resources. No other features of the underlying ontologies, including individuals and properties, are of interest for the (XML) data management problem considered here. When the evolution of a fully fledged ontology is required, the proposed approach can be straightforwardly merged with one of the frameworks described in (Zablith et al., 2013). In this case, all modifications involving the class hierarchy can be collected, that is saved as a byproduct of the ontology evolution process or even extracted a posteriori by means of some change detection tool (Grandi, 2012, Sec. 3.4; Zablith et al., 2013, Sec. 7.1.2), to be applied to our accessory data structure, as it has been described in this work.

In order to efficiently manage the evolution of the ontology class hierarchy, as in (Grandi, 2013; Grandi, 2016), we proposed to use a temporal relation. Several papers dealt with efficient storage of ontologies in a relational database (Kwuimi et al., 2017; Zhou & Yongkang, 2013). All these approaches can be adapted to store multi-version ontologies by making temporal the involved relations. Notice that they also provide relations for the storage and management of ontology instances, whereas the ontologies used for personalization as considered in this work (e.g., derived from the SNOMED-CT terminologies) are not equipped with instances. For example, the only table out of the fourteen in the schema of (Zhou & Yongkang, 2013), which is relevant for the personalization method considered in this work, is the one storing the "SubClassOf" information. The TreeRelation considered in this paper substitutes (or complements) the information stored in a "SubClassOf" relation made temporal.

CONCLUSION

In this chapter, we extend the framework for ontology-based personalized access to clinical guidelines introduced in (Grandi et al., 2012) in the direction of multi-version ontologies (Grandi et al., 2017a). The proposal aims at limiting computational and storage costs when the ontologies used for personalized access undergo modifications and there is the need of maintaining all the ontology versions for personalized access. It involves the introduction of a novel numbering scheme and efficient technologies for ontology evolution and query processing. The approach has been evaluated by means of experiments conducted on a prototype of the personalization engine. For the first time, we have shown the good efficiency and scalability of our framework on realistic ontologies sharing both the size and the structural characteristics of widely used medical terminologies.

As a next step, we will remove the limiting hypothesis of dealing with tree-shaped ontologies. In fact, we will consider the managing of graph-like ontologies employing the techniques developed with this aim in (Grandi, 2016). In this way, we will support multiple inheritances among ontology classes, thus including a wide range of healthcare ontologies (Zhang et al., 2004). Extensions in such direction of our personalization query engine are currently under development.

Further work will also include the assessment of our proposal in a concrete working environment, with a repository of real clinical guidelines and real users evaluating the clinical utility of the proposed guideline multidimensional versioning and personalization methods, which is a fundamental step in developing a tool aimed at improving and optimizing healthcare activities.

Research Context, Related Research and Possible Further Developments

Research at the Information Systems Group (ISGroup) at the University of Modena and Reggio Emilia and University of Bologna is focused on the design and development of novel methodologies and tools for efficiently and effectively managing and accessing non-conventional data in a large variety of application contexts. The group expertise covers several research fields, ranging from data sharing and interoperability to approximate search, from real-time querying to semantic knowledge extraction and multi-version information management. Our research has the ultimate ambition of providing answers to the increasingly complex information needs of 21st century applications.

The multi-version ontology-based personalization techniques described in this paper have been developed in the context of several research projects and refined over many years of work in different application scenarios. The original scenario that we considered as inspiration for our research on how to maintain and access multiple versions of data was the legal and e-government one (e.g., Grandi et al., 2009, "Semantic Web techniques for the management of digital identity and the access to norms" and "The dynamics of the norm over time: legal and IT aspects" Italian national projects). In the legal domain laws evolve over time and accessing past versions is necessary for various purposes, while in an e-government scenario citizens would like to retrieve personalized norm versions only containing provisions which are applicable to their personal case. More recently, we tackled the similar problem that rises in the medical context, starting from (Grandi et al., 2012) and going to the present chapter, where the query processor has been refined with several new features and optimizations, including the management of versioned ontologies.

Even if not directly related to the application scenario considered in this chapter, several recent research activities of the group on "hot" research topics will possibly offer in the near future concrete starting points for further expanding the possibilities of the personalization query engine presented in this chapter. In particular, combining streaming data (Carafoli et al., 2017), also in a temporal and versioned context (Grandi et al., 2017b), and IoT (Bujari et al., 2018) technologies will possibly enable the development of a complete health management ecosystem supporting: (a) the acquisition, management and querying of the very large amount of data regarding a patient and coming in real-time from an ever growing number of different sources (e.g., sensors, cameras, etc.); (b) the automatic management and querying of the different versions of the clinical guidelines (and their related ontologies) in order to extract relevant content tailored to the specific use case and actual condition of the patient.

ACKNOWLEDGMENT

This research received no specific grant from any funding agency in the public, commercial or not-for-profit sectors.

REFERENCES

Aroua, E., & Mourad, A. (2017). An ontology-based framework for enhancing personalized content and retrieval information. In *Proceedings of Int. Conf. on Research Challenges in Information Science* (RCIS) (pp. 276–285). Los Alamitos, CA: IEEE Computer Society Press.

Berglund, A., Boag, S., Chamberlin, D., Fernández, M. F., Kay, M., Robie, J. & Jérôme, S. (2016). XML Path Language (XPath) 2.0 (2nd ed.). *W3C Recommendation*. Retrieved April 4, 2018 from http://www. w3.org/TR/xpath20/

Bodenreider, O., Smith, B., Kumar, A., & Burgun, A. (2007). Investigating subsumption in SNOMED CT: An exploration into large description logic-based biomedical terminologies. *Artificial Intelligence in Medicine*, *39*(3), 183–195. doi:10.1016/j.artmed.2006.12.003 PMID:17241777

Boxwala, A. A., Zeng, Q., Tate, D., Greenes, R. A., & Fairchild, D. G. (2002). Applying Axiomatic Design Methodology to Create Guidelines that are Locally Adaptable. In *Proceedings of the AMIA Symposium*. Philadelphia, PA: Hanley & Belfus, Inc.

Bujari, A., Furini, M., Mandreoli, F., Martoglia, R., Montangero, M., & Ronzani, D. (2018). Standards, security and business models: key challenges for the IoT scenario. *Mobile Networks and Applications*, *23*(1), 147–154. doi:10.100711036-017-0835-8

Carafoli, L., Mandreoli, F., Martoglia, R., & Penzo, W. (2017). Streaming tables: native support to streaming data in DBMSs. *IEEE Transactions on Systems, Man, and Cybernetics. Systems*, *47*(10), 2768–2782. doi:10.1109/TSMC.2017.2664585

NEJM Catalyst. (2017). What is Patient-Centred Care? Retrieved April 4, 2018 from https://catalyst. nejm.org/what-is-patient-centered-care/

De Bra, P. (2017). Challenges in User Modeling and Personalization. *IEEE Intelligent Systems*, *32*(5), 76–80. doi:10.1109/MIS.2017.3711638

Enwald, H. (2013). *Tailoring Health Communication* [Doctoral dissertation]. University of Oulu, Finland. Retrieved April 4, 2018 from http://jultika.oulu.fi/files/isbn9789526202792.pdf

Erhardt, L. R., & Gotto, A. Jr. (2006). The evolution of European guidelines: Changing the management of cholesterol levels. *Atherosclerosis*, *185*(1), 12–20. doi:10.1016/j.atherosclerosis.2005.10.001 PMID:16309687

Fridsma, D. B., Gennari, J. H., & Musen, M. A. (1996). Making Generic Guidelines Site-specific. In *Proceedings of the AMIA Symposium*. Philadelphia, PA: Hanley & Belfus, Inc.

Gad El-Rab, W., Zaïane, O. R., & El-Hajj, M. (2017). Formalizing clinical practice guideline for clinical decision support systems. *Health Informatics Journal*, *23*(2), 146–156. doi:10.1177/1460458216632272 PMID:26951569

González-Ferrer, A., ten Teije, A., Fdez-Olivares, J., & Milian, K. (2013). Automated generation of patient-tailored electronic care pathways by translating computer-interpretable guidelines into hierarchical task networks. *Artificial Intelligence in Medicine, 57*(2), 91–109. doi:10.1016/j.artmed.2012.08.008 PMID:23177024

Grandi, F. (2012). Introducing an Annotated Bibliography on Temporal and Evolution Aspects in the Semantic Web. *SIGMOD Record, 41*(4), 18–21. doi:10.1145/2430456.2430460

Grandi, F. (2013). Dynamic Multi-version Ontology-based Personalization. In *Proceedings of the 2nd International Workshop on Querying Graph Structured Data* (GraphQ). New York, NY: ACM Press, pp. 224–232.

Grandi, F. (2016). Dynamic Class Hierarchy Management for Multi-version Ontology-based Personalization. *Journal of Computer and System Sciences, 82*(1), 69–90. doi:10.1016/j.jcss.2015.06.001

Grandi, F., Mandreoli, F., & Martoglia, R. (2009). Issues in Personalized Access to Multi-version XML Documents. In E. Pardede (Ed.), *Open and Novel Issues in XML Database Applications* (pp. 199–230). Hershey, PA: IGI Global. doi:10.4018/978-1-60566-308-1.ch010

Grandi, F., Mandreoli, F., & Martoglia, R. (2012). Efficient management of multi-version clinical guidelines. *Journal of Biomedical Informatics, 45*(6), 1120–1136. doi:10.1016/j.jbi.2012.07.005 PMID:22890019

Grandi, F., Mandreoli, F., & Martoglia, R. (2017a). Multi-version Ontology-based Personalization of Clinical Guidelines for Patient-centric Healthcare. *International Journal on Semantic Web and Information Systems, 13*(1), 104–127. doi:10.4018/IJSWIS.2017010107

Grandi, F., Mandreoli, F., Martoglia, R., & Penzo, W. (2017b). A Relational Algebra for Streaming Tables Living in a Temporal Database World. In *Proceedings of 24th International Symposium on Temporal Representation and Reasoning* (TIME 2017), Dagstuhl, Germany (pp. 15:1–15:17).

Grandi, F., Mandreoli, F., Martoglia, R., Ronchetti, E., Scalas, M. R., & Tiberio, P. (2009). Ontology-Based Personalization of E-Government Services. In P. Germanakos & C. Mourlas (Eds.), *Intelligent User Interfaces: Adaptation and Personalization Systems and Technologies* (pp. 167–187). Hershey, PA: IGI Global. doi:10.4018/978-1-60566-032-5.ch008

Grandi, F., & Scalas, M. R. (2009). The Valid Ontology: a Simple OWL Temporal Versioning Framework. In *Proceedings of the 3rd Int. Conf. on Advances in Semantic Processing (SEMAPRO)*. Los Alamitos, CA: IEEE Computer Society Press, pp. 98–102. 10.1109/SEMAPRO.2009.12

Groot, P., Hommerson, A., & Lucas, P. (2008). Adaptation of Clinical Practice Guidelines. In A. Ten Teije, S. Miksch, & P. Lucas (Eds.), *Computer-based Medical Guidelines and Protocols: A Primer and Current Trends* (pp. 121–139). Amsterdam, The Netherlands: IOS Press.

Gulzar, Z. & Anny Leema, A. (2017). Ontology based classification of computer science domain to support personalization. *Journal of Advanced Research in Dynamical and Control Systems, 9*(6), 493–511.

Jensen, C. S., Dyreson, C. E., Böhlen, M. H., Clifford, J., Elmasri, R., Gadia, S. K., ... Wiederhold, G. (1998). The Consensus Glossary of Temporal Database Concepts - February 1998 Version. In O. Etzion, S. Jajodia, & S. Sripada (Eds.), *Temporal Databases, Research and Practice* (pp. 367–405). Berlin, Germany: Springer Verlag. doi:10.1007/BFb0053710

Kaiser, K., & Miksch, S. (2009). Versioning computer-interpretable guidelines: semi-automatic modeling of 'living guidelines' using an information extraction method. *Artificial Intelligence in Medicine*, *46*(1), 55–66. doi:10.1016/j.artmed.2008.08.009 PMID:18950994

Kwuimi, R., Fonou-Dombeu, J. V., & Tranos, Z. (2017). An empirical analysis of semantic web mechanisms for storage and query of ontologies in relational databases. In *Proceedings of the 3rd International Conference on Advances in Computing, Communication and Engineering (ICACCE)* (pp. 132–136). Dubai, UAE: WASET Open Science.

Lim, G. H., Hong, S.-W., Lee, I., Suh, I. H., & Beetz, M. (2013) Robot recommender system using affection-based episode ontology for personalization. In *Proceedings of the 22nd IEEE International Symposium on Robot and Human Interactive Communication (RO-MAN)*, Gyeongju (pp. 155–160). Los Alamitos, CA: IEEE Computer Society Press.

Machado, J. B., Martins, G. L., Isotani, S., & Barbosa, E. F. (2013) An ontology-based user model for personalization of educational content (S). In *Proceedings of the 25th Int. Conf. on Software Engineering and Knowledge Engineering (SEKE)* (pp. 737–740). Fredericton, NB: KSI Research Inc.

Mackey, T. K., & Liang, B. A. (2011). The Role of Practice Guidelines in Medical Malpractice Litigation. *AMA Journal of Ethics*, *13*(1), 36–41. Retrieved from http://virtualmentor.ama-assn.org/2011/01/hlaw1-1101.html PMID:23121815

Maleszka, B. (2017). A method for ontology-based user profile adaptation in personalized document retrieval systems. In *Proceedings 2016 IEEE International Conference on Systems, Man, and Cybernetics* (SMC) (pp. 3187–3192). Los Alamitos, CA: IEEE Computer Society Press.

Mandreoli, F., Martoglia, R., & Ronchetti, E. (2006). Supporting Temporal Slicing in XML Databases. In *Proceeding of 10th International Conference on Extending Database Technology (EDBT)* (pp. 295–312). Berlin, Germany: Springer Verlag.

Melnick, E. R., Hess, E. P., Guo, G., Breslin, M., Lopez, K., Pavlo, A. J., ... Post, L. A. (2017). Patient-centered decision support: formative usability evaluation of integrated clinical decision support with a patient decision aid for minor head injury in the emergency department. *Journal of Medical Internet Research*, *19*(5), e174. doi:10.2196/jmir.7846 PMID:28526667

Moreno, A., Valls, A., Isern, D., Marina, L., & Borràs, J. (2013). SigTur/E-Destination: Ontology-based personalized recommendation of Tourism and Leisure Activities. *Engineering Applications of Artificial Intelligence*, *26*(1), 633–651. doi:10.1016/j.engappai.2012.02.014

Nilashi, M., Ibrahim, O., & Bagherifard, K. (2018). A recommender system based on collaborative filtering using ontology and dimensionality reduction techniques. *Expert Systems with Applications*, *92*, 507–520. doi:10.1016/j.eswa.2017.09.058

Novais, P., Oliveira, T., Satoh, K., & Neves, J. (2018). The role of ontologies and decision frameworks in computer-interpretable guideline execution. *Advances in Intelligent Systems and Computing, 626*, 197–216. doi:10.1007/978-3-319-64161-4_10

Owens, D. K., & Nease, R. F. Jr. (1997). A normative analytic framework for development of practice guidelines for specific clinical populations. *Medical Decision Making, 17*(4), 409–426. doi:10.1177/0272989X9701700406 PMID:9343799

Peleg, M. (2013). Computer-interpretable clinical guidelines: A methodological review. *Journal of Biomedical Informatics, 46*(4), 744–763. doi:10.1016/j.jbi.2013.06.009 PMID:23806274

Peleg, M., & Kantor, R. (2003). Approaches for Guideline Versioning using GLIF. In *Proceedings of the AMIA Symposium* (pp. 509–513). Philadelphia, PA: Hanley & Belfus, Inc.

Peleg, M., Shahar, Y., Quaglini, S., Shalom, E., & Soffer, P. (2017a). MobiGuide: A personalized and patient-centric decision-support system and its evaluation in the atrial fibrillation and gestational diabetes domains. *User Modeling and User-Adapted Interaction, 27*(2), 159–213. doi:10.100711257-017-9190-5

Peleg, M., Shahar, Y., Quaglini, S., Soffer, P., & van Schooten, B. (2017b). Assessment of a personalized and distributed patient guidance system. *International Journal of Medical Informatics, 101*, 108–130. doi:10.1016/j.ijmedinf.2017.02.010 PMID:28347441

Pretschner, A. (1998). *Ontology based personalized search.* Unpublished Master's thesis, University of Kansas, Lawrence, Kan.

Quaglini, S., Panzarasa, S., Giorgiani, T., Zucchella, C., Bartolo, M., Sinforiani, E., & Sandrini, G. (2009). Ontology-Based Personalization and Modulation of Computerized Cognitive Exercises. In *Proceedings of the 12th Conference on Artificial Intelligence in Medicine* (pp. 240–244). Berlin, Germany: Springer Verlag. 10.1007/978-3-642-02976-9_34

Quinn, S., Bond, R., & Nugent, C. D. (2014). An Ontology Based Approach to the Provision of Personalized Patient Education. In *Proceedings of the 6th Working Conference – IWAAL* (pp. 67–74). Berlin, Germany: Springer Verlag. 10.1007/978-3-319-13105-4_11

Riaño, D., Real, F., López-Vallverdú, J. A. F., Ercolani, S., Mecocci, P., Annicchiarico, R., ... Caltagirone, C. (2012). An ontology-based personalization of health-care knowledge to support clinical decisions for chronically ill patients. *Journal of Biomedical Informatics, 45*(3), 429–446. doi:10.1016/j.jbi.2011.12.008 PMID:22269224

Ruhl, D. S., & Siegal, G. (2017). Medical Malpractice Implications of Clinical Practice Guidelines. *Otolaryngology - Head and Neck Surgery, 157*(2), 175–177. doi:10.1177/0194599817707943 PMID:28585462

Sacchi, L., Fux, A., Napolitano, C., Panzarasa, S., Peleg, M., Quaglini, S., ... Tormene, P. (2013). Patient-tailored workflow patterns from clinical practice guidelines recommendations. In *Proceedings of MedInfo* (pp. 392–396). Amsterdam, The Netherlands: IOS Press.

Sanders, G. D. (1998). *Automated creation of clinical-practice guidelines from decision models.* Unpublished Ph. Doctoral dissertation, Stanford University, Stanford, CA.

Sanders, G. D., Nease, R. F. Jr, & Owens, D. K. (2001). Publishing Web-based Guidelines using Interactive Decision Models. *Journal of Evaluation in Clinical Practice*, 7(2), 175–189. doi:10.1046/j.1365-2753.2001.00271.x PMID:11489042

Scott-Wright, A. O., Fischer, R. P., Denekamp, Y., & Boxwala, A. A. (2004). A Methodology for Modular representation of Guidelines. In *Proceedings of the 11th World Congress on Medical Informatics (MEDINFO)* (pp. 149–153). Amsterdam, The Netherlands: IOS Press.

Sekhar Babu, B., Lakshmi Prasanna, P. & Vidyullatha, P. (2018). Personalized web search on e-commerce using ontology based association mining. *International Journal of Engineering and Technology*, 7(1.1), 286–289.

Shahar, Y., Miksch, S., & Johnson, P. (1998). The Asgaard Project: A Task-specific Framework for the Application and Critiquing of Time-oriented Clinical Guidelines. *Artificial Intelligence in Medicine*, 14(1-2), 29–51. doi:10.1016/S0933-3657(98)00015-3 PMID:9779882

Shahar, Y., Young, O., Shalom, E., Galperin, M., Mayaffit, A., Moskovitch, R., & Hessing, A. (2004). A framework for a distributed, hybrid, multiple-ontology clinical-guideline library, and automated guideline-support tools. *Journal of Biomedical Informatics*, 37(5), 325–344. doi:10.1016/j.jbi.2004.07.001 PMID:15488747

Shalom, E., Shahar, Y., & Lunenfeld, E. (2016). An architecture for a continuous, user-driven, and data-driven application of clinical guidelines and its evaluation. *Journal of Biomedical Informatics*, 59, 130–148. doi:10.1016/j.jbi.2015.11.006 PMID:26616284

Shiffman, R. N., Karras, B. T., Agrawal, A., Chen, R., Marenco, L., & Nath, S. (2000). GEM a Proposal for a More Comprehensive Guideline Document Model using XML. *Journal of the American Medical Informatics Association*, 7(5), 488–497. doi:10.1136/jamia.2000.0070488 PMID:10984468

Sohn, M. M., Jeong, S., & Lee, H. J. (2013). Self-Evolved Ontology-Based Service Personalization Framework for Disabled Users in Smart Home Environment. In *Proceedings of the 7th Int. Confer. on Innovative Mobile and Internet Services in Ubiquitous Computing* (pp. 238–244). Los Alamitos, CA: IEEE Computer Society Press. 10.1109/IMIS.2013.48

Terenziani, P., Montani, S., Bottrighi, A., Molino, G., & Torchio, M. (2005). Clinical Guidelines Adaptation: Managing Authoring and Versioning Issues. In *Proceedings of the 10th Conf. on Artificial Intelligence in medicine (AIME)* (pp. 151–155). Berlin, Germany: Springer Verlag. 10.1007/11527770_22

Terenziani, P., Montani, S., Bottrighi, A., Torchio, M., Molino, G., & Correndo, G. (2004). A Context-adaptable Approach to Clinical Guidelines. In *Proceedings of the 11th World Congress on Medical Informatics (MEDINFO)* (pp. 169–173). Amsterdam, The Netherlands: IOS Press.

Tu, S. W., Peleg, M., Carini, S., Bobak, M., Ross, J., Rubin, D., & Sim, I. (2011). A practical method for transforming free-text eligibility criteria into computable criteria. *Journal of Biomedical Informatics*, 44(2), 239–250. doi:10.1016/j.jbi.2010.09.007 PMID:20851207

Wang, H.-Q., Li, J.-S., Zhang, Y.-F., Suzuki, M., & Araki, K. (2013). Creating personalised clinical pathways by semantic interoperability with electronic health records. *Artificial Intelligence in Medicine*, 58(2), 81–89. doi:10.1016/j.artmed.2013.02.005 PMID:23466439

Weymann, N., Dirmaier, J., von Wolff, A., Kriston, L., & Härter, M. (2015). Effectiveness of a Web-Based Tailored Interactive Health Communication Application for Patients with Type 2 Diabetes or Chronic Low Back Pain: Randomized Controlled Trial. *Journal of Medical Internet Research*, *17*(3), e53. Retrieved from https://www.jmir.org/2015/3/e53/ doi:10.2196/jmir.3904 PMID:25736340

Wilk, S., Fux, A., Michalowski, M., Peleg, M., & Soffer, P. (2017). Using constraint logic programming for the verification of customized decision models for clinical guidelines. In *Proceedings of the 16th Conf. on Artificial Intelligence in Medicine (AIME)* (pp. 37–47). 10.1007/978-3-319-59758-4_4

World Wide Web Consortium. (2018a). Extensible Markup Language (XML) Home Page. Retrieved April 4, 2018 from http://www.w3.org/XML/

World Wide Web Consortium. (2018b). Web Ontology Language (OWL) Home Page. Retrieved April 4, 2018 from http://www.w3.org/2004/OWL/

World Wide Web Consortium. (2018c). XML Query Language (XQuery) Home Page. Retrieved April 4, 2018 from http://www.w3.org/XML/Query/

Zablith, F., Antoniou, G., d'Aquin, M., Flouris, G., Kondylakis, H., Motta, E., ... Sabou, M. (2013). Ontology Evolution: A Process Centric Survey. *The Knowledge Engineering Review*, *30*(1), 45–75. doi:10.1017/S0269888913000349

Zekri, A., Brahmia, Z., Grandi, F., & Bouaziz, R. (2016). τ OWL: A Systematic Approach to Temporal Versioning of Semantic Web Ontologies. *Journal on Data Semantics*, *5*(3), 141–163. doi:10.100713740-016-0066-3

Zhang, L., Perl, Y., Halper, M., Geller, J., & Cimino, J. J. (2004). An enriched unified medical language system semantic network with a multiple subsumption hierarchy. *Journal of the American Medical Informatics Association*, *11*(3), 195–206. doi:10.1197/jamia.M1269 PMID:14764611

Zhang, Y., & Padman, R. (2017). Data-driven Approaches for Developing Clinical Practice Guidelines. In N. Wickramasinghe (Ed.), *Handbook of Research on Healthcare Administration and Management* (pp. 30–46). Hershey, PA: IGI Global. doi:10.4018/978-1-5225-0920-2.ch003

Zhang, Y.-F., Gou, L., Zhou, T.-S., Li, Y., & Li, J.-S. (2017). An ontology-based approach to patient follow-up assessment for continuous and personalized chronic disease management. *Journal of Biomedical Informatics*, *72*, 45–59. doi:10.1016/j.jbi.2017.06.021 PMID:28676255

Zheng, S., Wang, F., & Lu, J. (2014). Enabling Ontology Based Semantic Queries in Biomedical Database Systems. *International Journal of Semantic Computing*, *8*(1), 67–83. doi:10.1142/S1793351X14500032 PMID:25541585

Zhou, Z., & Yongkang, X. (2013). *A study on ontology storage based on relational database. Conference Anthology*. IEEE. doi:10.1109/ANTHOLOGY.2013.6784899

ENDNOTES

[1]   http://www.who.int/classifications/icd/en/

[2]   http://www.ihtsdo.org/snomed-ct/

[3]   Due to this potential adverse side effect, the drug was voluntarily withdrawn from the market by the producer in 2001.

Chapter 12

Learning to Suggest Hashtags:
Leveraging Semantic Features for Time-Sensitive Hashtag Recommendation on the Twitter Network

Fahd Kalloubi
Chouaib Doukkali University, Morocco

El Habib Nfaoui
Sidi Mohamed Ben Abdellah University, Morocco

ABSTRACT

Twitter is one of the primary online social networks where users share messages and contents of interest to those who follow their activities. To effectively categorize and give audience to their tweets, users try to append appropriate hashtags to their short messages. However, the hashtags usage is very small and very heterogeneous and users may spend a lot of time searching the appropriate hashtags. Thus, the need for a system to assist users in this task is very important to increase and homogenize the hashtagging usage. In this chapter, the authors present a hashtag recommendation system on microblogging platforms by leveraging semantic features. Furthermore, they conduct a detailed study on how the semantic-based model influences the final recommended hashtags using different ranking strategies. Moreover, they propose a linear and a machine learning based combination of these ranking strategies. The experiment results show that their approach improves content-based recommendations, achieving a recall of more than 47% on recommending 5 hashtags.

INTRODUCTION

Twitter users broadcast short messages of 140 characters called tweets to users who follow their activities, in this form of communication users often use hashtags (the # symbol concatenated with a short character string) to categorize their posts in order to give meaning or to join communities around particular topics. Thus, users tend to use the appropriate hashtags in their tweets which is crucial for the popularity of their messages, in the measure that hashtags can be seen as a way to give some context to the tweet and

DOI: 10.4018/978-1-5225-7186-5.ch012

Copyright © 2019, IGI Global. Copying or distributing in print or electronic forms without written permission of IGI Global is prohibited.

they make tweets easily exploitable by other users in Twitter sphere. Moreover, they make tweets more accessible by hashtag-based search engines such as hashtags.org[1]. Since hashtags are neither registered nor controlled by any user or group, it will be hard for some users to find appropriate hashtags for their tweets (Kywe Su, Hoang, Lim, & Zhu, 2012). The problem of hashtags suggestions can be defined as follow: given a message entered by a user, retrieve the most reliable hashtags from the top-n similar messages. Indeed, some microbloggers try to create their personalized hashtags in a meaningful way to grant that these hashtags should be widely used for the topic but in many cases the truth may be the contrary, many users add the # symbol prefixed to every word in their tweets; wishing that one of these Hashtags could be widely used by others microbloggers for the topic but that may hinders the quality of the tweet, and the users may be taken as tweet spammers, so it is difficult to users to find the appropriate hashtags for their tweets and they may spend a lot of time to retrieve the appropriate ones, so many efforts have been conducted to assist users in this process, some authors interpreted this problems as a recommender system based on collaborative filtering, other authors have proposed an Information retrieval approaches for hashtags suggestions in Twitter sphere by suggesting hashtags from the most similar tweets using term-based models such as TF-IDF (Zangerle, Gassler, & Specht, 2013) (Zangerle, Gassler, & Specht, 2011) (Mazzia & Juet, 2011). Semantic-based features namely the semantic overlap between the tweet and the query computed using DBpedia are shown to be highly effective for tweet search (Tao, Abel, Hauff, & Houben, 2012).

Previous studies in hashtag suggestions/recommendations use lexical matching between tweets to recommend hashtags to users (Zangerle, Gassler, & Specht, 2013) (Godin, Slavkovikj, De Neve, Schrauwen, & Van de Walle, 2013). Term based models are efficient in term of computation performances and the maturity of term weighting theories make this models very rampant. However, term based approaches often suffer from the problems of polysemy and synonymy and very sensitive to term use variation, especially in the context of micro-posts, due to the limited length of this form of communication, his noisy nature and his highly contextualization. Thus, in their approach the authors leverage semantic features to improve the recommended hashtags by harnessing contextual information which was not studied in previous works.

On the whole, the main contributions of the authors of this chapter are:

- They present an approach for hashtags suggestion based on semantic similarity.
- They use a method for named entity linking for the context of tweets by considering the nature of this form of communication.
- They study the impact of different hashtags ranking strategies on our system.
- They present a linear combination of these ranking strategies.
- They incorporate different hashtag ranking strategies in a learning to rank model, and they study the impact of different combinations on the suggested hashtags, which has not been used in the previous methods.
- They evaluate the effectiveness of our approach with a real data set harvested from twitter.
- Their experiment results show that semantic-based similarity, mainly the overlap score between the semantic meanings of tweets outperforms lexical-based similarity, and using learning to rank model by incorporating different ranking functions with semantic similarity leads to a high performance on the suggested hashtags.

The remainder of this chapter is organized as follows. In section 2, the authors discuss related work pertaining to hashtag recommendations and draw a comparison to their approach; they describe their dataset and the hashtaging behavior within it in section 3. In section 4, they present their approach for hashtags recommendation in microblogging platforms, including their semantic similarity, the ranking functions and their paradigm for learning to recommend hashtags. They give the evaluation results of the proposed approach in section 5. In section 6, they conclude this chapter and give future work.

RELATED WORK

Twitter has not implemented yet any hashtags recommendation system to assist users to choose the appropriate hashtags for their posts which is crucial for the popularity of their micro-posts. Many approaches for tags suggestion in social networking services have been proposed (M. Belém, M. Almeida, & A. Gonçalves, 2016) (Zheng, Yukio Kondo, Zilora, & Yu, 2018) (Yu, Bing, Mingyao, & Feng, 2018). In the context of Twitter hashtag suggestions/recommendations many approaches have been proposed which can be classified into two classes.

One class of these approaches focuses on collaborative filtering (Alvari, 2017). Other approaches use techniques from information retrieval (content-based approaches) to recommend hashtags while there are some problems still existed. (Ben-Lhachemi & Nfaoui, 2018) leveraged the power of word embeddings to address to propose a content-based hashtag recommendation system, they use the DBSCAN (density-based spatial clustering of applications with noise) clustering algorithm to obtain clusters of syntactically and semantically similar tweets. Then, they recommend hahstags of similar centroids. (Jianjun & Tongyu, 2015) proposed a hashtag recommendation system by considering the textual content, user behavior and temporal aspects; they combine long term and short-term user interest in the recommendation process. Also, (Tran, Hwang, & Nguyen, 2018) have addressed the user characteristics and tweet content in the recommendation process by considering the used hahstags and social interactions; they rank the candidate hashtags based on their popularity in short and long period. Furthermore, (Lu & Lee, 2015) proposed a Topic-over-Time Mixed Membership Model (TOT-MMM), which is topic-based hashtag recommendation approach that captures the temporal clustering of latent topics in tweets; also, they state that combining TOT-MMM with a similarity-based approach yield to additional performance improvements. Also, (Kowald, Pujari, & Lex, 2017) have addressed the temporal hashtag usage practices by designing a cognitive-inspired hashtag recommendation algorithm by incorporating the effect of time on individual hashtag reuse and social hashtag reuse. In the same context, (Zhao, Zhu, Jin, & Laurence T., 2016) proposed a personalized hashtag recommendation approach, that represent users by user-topics distribution and finds top-k similar users, then computes all hashtags' frequencies appeared in these users, also, they proposed a *Latent Dirichlet Allocation* (LDA)-based topic model, named *Hashtag-LDA*. (Li, Liu, Jiang, & Zhang, 2016) presented an attention-based LSTM model which incorporates topic modeling into the LSTM architecture through an attention mechanism. (Godin, Slavkovikj, De Neve, Schrauwen, & Van de Walle, 2013) used topic distribution based on Latent Dirichlet Allocation (LDA) to recommend general hashtags based on the underlying topics of the tweets, they try to overcome the problem of tweets based hashtags labeling by applying topic models to recommend general hashtags, they found that TF similarity-based hashtag assignment to hashtag-based pooling outperforms all other pooling strategies.. (She & Lei, 2014) proposed a supervised topic model for hashtags recommendation on Twitter, they treat hashtags as labels and they develop a topic model to discover relationship between words, hashtags and topics, in addition they propose to integrate the user following relationship into the model. Also, (Otsuka, Wallace, & Chiu, 2016) proposed the hashtag Frequency-Inverse hashtag Ubiquity (HF-IHU), which is a variation of TF-IDF ranking scheme, that considers the hashtag relevancy. As reported in (Kalloubi, Nfaoui, & El Beqqali, 2017), using bag-of-words models (e.g. TF-IDF) are no longer effective for recommending Hashtags because contextual information is neglected and hence often leads to synonymy and polysemy problems due to the limited length and the high contextualization of tweets and the chance to select relevant tweets is reduced because their contents have less information. Thus, in this chapter, the authors overcome the problems of semantic gap and high context, in order to improve language understanding in microblogging platforms. In fact, they leverage the semantic feature that has been shown to get best results in microblogging search (Kalloubi, Nfaoui, & El beqqali, 2016). Moreover, they use a system for named entity linking adapted for the context of micro-posts by handling irregular name mentions.

TWITTER DATASET

The authors evaluate the approach presented in this chapter with a real dataset[2] harvested from Twitter (Kalloubi, Nfaoui, & El Beqqali, 2017). The original corpus consists of approximately 284 million following relationships, 3 million user profiles and 50 million tweets. For their needs they use a random sample of 593,582 tweets and they use an existing language detection library[3] to identify English tweets and found 545,515 English tweets in the corpus. Table 1 shows details about the dataset used. As shown in the Table 1, only 16% of the tweets within their dataset contain hashtags.

Table 2 contains information about the hashtagging behavior of users within the dataset. As can be seen in table 1, the majority of hashtags in the dataset occur once, which indicates that the hashtag vocabulary is very heterogeneous and changes consequently, and as such, affects negatively the capabilities of hashtag-based search engine.

Table 1. Data set statistics

Characteristic	Number
Tweets total	545,515
Tweets total without retweets	457,284
Tweets containing hashtags one or more	75,020
Tweets without hashtags	382,264
Retweets	88,231
Retweets containing one or more hashtags	10,901

(Kalloubi, Nfaoui, & El Beqqali, 2017)

Table 2. Hashtags statistics in the data set

Characteristic	Number
Tweets containing hashtags one or more	75,020
Hashtags usage total	173,591
Average number of hashtags per tweet	0.37
Average number of hashtags per tweet (within the set containing at least one hashtags)	2.31
Hashtags occurring < 3 times	20,265
Hashtags occurring < 5 times	22,842
Hashtags occurring >= 5 times	3,110
Hashtags occurring once	15,551
Distinct hashtags	25,952

(Kalloubi, Nfaoui, & El Beqqali, 2017)

PROPOSED SYSTEM FOR HASHTAGS RECOMMENDATION

The recommendations of hashtag assist the user during the creation of new message, for each message top-*k* recommendations are shown to the user, where *k* is the size of the recommended hashtags which is limited to 5-10 recommendations as addressed by (Bollen, Knijnenburg, Willemsen & Graus, 2010) who state that top-5 recommendations are easy to choose by the user. The process of recommending hashtags is described in detail in the following sections.

System Overview

For a given message, the computation of these recommendations based on the underlying data set comprises the following steps which are also illustrated in Figure 1:

1. For a given message posted by a user.
2. Process it using the proposed tweet entity linking approach to obtain a set of DBpedia concepts.
3. Calculate the similarity.
4. Extract the hashtags from similar tweets in order to form a set of candidates hashtags.
5. Ranking the obtained hashtags.
6. Present the top-*k* ranked hashtags to the user.

Tweet Entity Linking Approach

Due to their short, noisy, high contextualization and real-time nature, semantic analysis of micro-posts poses several challenges. Hence, the authors propose a novel method for tweet entity linking in order to tackle polysemy and synonymy problems in lexical methods by leveraging the semantic feature in this form of communications by adding word meaning.

Textual data in social media has the problems of data sparseness and semantic gap. One effective way to solve these problems is to integrate semantic knowledge, which has been found to be useful in dealing

Figure 1. Hashtags recommendations computation
(Kalloubi, Nfaoui, & El Beqqali, 2017)

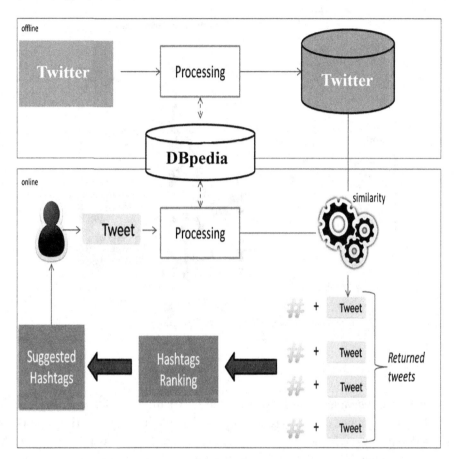

with the semantic gap (Hu, Sun, Zhang, & Chua, 2009) . In this context and given the nature of Twitter posts which are topic specific (Efron, Organisciak, & Fenlon, 2012), enabling the authors to make the assumption that related entities tend to appear together in a tweet. Hence, the authors use DBpedia as knowledge base in order to leverage the linked nature of this knowledge base.

Candidate Generation

The authors filter out determiners, interjections, punctuations, emoticons, discourse markers and URLs in the posts and they select nouns and proper nouns as mentions with a Twitter part-of-speech tagger (Owoputi, et al., 2013) (as depicted in Figure 2). They use many types of sources in DBpedia to generate the candidate sets. These are: rdfs:label, foaf:name, dbpprop:officialName, dbpprop:name, foaf:givenName, dbpprop:birthName, dbpprop:alias, disambiguation that is used to group entities that have various meanings for the same title, and redirect pages that are used to show alternative titles of a given entity (DBpedia ontology properties dbont:wikiPageDisambiguates[4] and dbont:wikiPageRedirects[5]). The candidates that are formed using these resources will be used for the construction of the graph of interlinked entities that depict the context of the document as depicted in the following sections.

Figure 2. An example of candidates' generation for a tweet
(Kalloubi, Nfaoui, & El Beqqali, 2014)

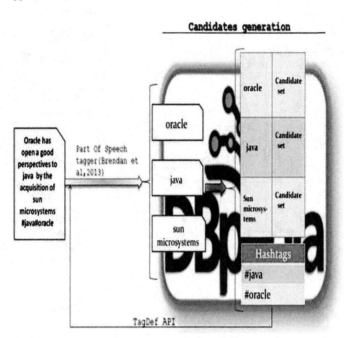

Hashtags

To outside observers, the meaning of hashtags is usually difficult to analyze, as they consist of short, often abbreviated or concatenated concepts (e.g., #Tourdefrance). In this work, the authors consider that hashtags are related to the tweet. In fact, they will be processed separately using the TagDef API[6] to look up the highest-voted hashtag definition and process it (if any), if not the following web service[7] is used to break the hashtags into tokens (e.g., the service will break "#Tourdefrance" into "Tour de france") (Wang, Thrasher, & Paul Hsu, 2011).

Therefore, hashtags are useful to more contextualize the user's posts; the authors process the user's hashtags in order to enrich the user post with more concepts.

Acronym

In order to identify if a mention is an acronym or not the authors use a simple heuristic based method that follow the following conditions as addressed by (Guo, Qin, Li, Liu, & Li, 2013):

- It contains no more than 4 letters.
- It contains no less than 2 upper case letters.
- It contains no more than 2 lower case letters.

They substitute the state abbreviation names[8] in each post into the full forms.
According to their observations, the acronyms and their full names usually satisfy other constraints:

- If it contains more than 3 letters it consists of the initial letters of the full name words (CCP -Chinese Communist Party-).
- If it contains no more than 2 letters then the first letter consists of the initial letter of the full name word and the second letter is contained in the same word (CA (California), fb (facebook)).

These cases can be covered by several regular expressions in order to generate the possible full forms of a given name mention.

Candidate Ranking

Starting from the assumption that related entities tend to appear in the same tweet, which motivate the authors to process the candidates disambiguation task as graph-based problem by leveraging the linked nature of DBpedia as knowledge base.

Graph Construction

After the construction of the candidates entities, the authors search for "dbont:wikiPageWikiLink" links between entities in the constructed candidates set and they use entities and the links found between them to form the graph.

Hence, let's denote $S(T)$ the set of candidate sets for the tweet T that is to be annotated:

$$S(T) = \{s_1, s_2, ..., s_m\}$$

And, $E(s)$ denotes the set of all entities from DBpedia for each mention s in $S(T)$:

$$E(s_i) = \{e_1, e_2, ..., e_k\} \text{ for } s_i \in S(T)$$

The set of all entities for the tweet T is then $E(T)$:

$$E(T) = \cup E(s_i), \ s_i \in S(T)$$

Using the property dbont:wikiPageWikiLink, the authors look if there is a link between any two entities in $E(T)$, then the link is added to the relationships set $R(T)$. Then they build a graph of matched candidate entities and relationship found as a directed edge. The graph is a 3-tuple construct $G = (E(T), R(T), f)$, where f is a centrality factor that the authors use to attribute a weight to the nodes in the next section.

Figure 3 shows a partial graph constructed for the example in figure 2, Java Universal Network Graph (JUNG)[9] is used to construct and visualize the directed graph of entities.

Entities Disambiguation

After the construction of the directed graph of entities, the authors must detect how central a node is in the graph which is a crucial task in their method. They use graph centrality scoring methods that have been shown to be successful because they consider the relationships between nodes.

Figure 3. A partial graph of the example above (see figure 2)

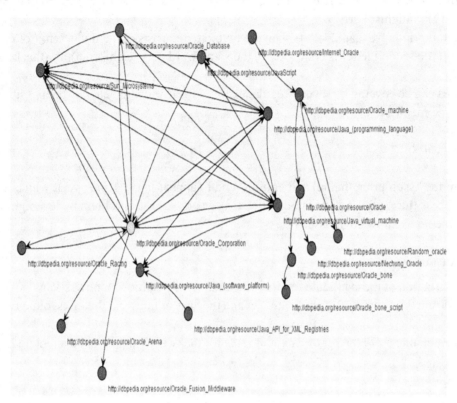

As the constructed graph is directed and disconnected (Figure 3), not all nodes are reachable from other nodes, then for every node, the authors calculate the shortest path using Djikstra's shortest path algorithm from that node to all his successors in the graph. Hence, they use the customized centrality factor used in (Kalloubi, Nfaoui, & El beqqali, 2016) (Kalloubi, Nfaoui, & El Beqqali, 2014). Formally, for node N_a the centrality factor is calculated using the proposed following formula.

$$f\left(N_a\right) = \frac{\Pr\left(N_a\right) + Sc\left(N_a\right)}{\sum_{N_b \in N} sh(N_a, N_b)} \qquad (1)$$

$\sum_{N_b \in N} sh(N_a, N_b)$: Is the sum of the shortest distances between N_a and the reachable nodes from N_a

Pr_{N_a} : Is the number of predecessors' nodes of N_a

Sc_{N_a} : Is the number of successor's nodes of N_a

The centrality factor is used to weight the node as depicted on the following formula (Kalloubi, Nfaoui, & El beqqali, 2016) (Hakimov, Oto, & Dogdu, 2012).

$$W\left(N_a\right) = f\left(N_a\right) * inlinks\left(N_a\right) * outlinks\left(N_a\right) * k \tag{2}$$

$f\left(N_a\right)$ is the customized centrality factor for node N_a, *inlinks* $\left(N_a\right)$ and *outlinks* $\left(N_a\right)$ are respectively the number of incoming and outgoing links for node N_a. k *is* a constant depending on the type of entity N_a. k is set to 1 if the entity is retrieved from disambiguation pages and set to 6 if the entity is from others properties, the attributed values of k is determined by the performance of the tests. Disambiguation pages collect a high number of unrelated entities, which might affect the disambiguation process. Therefore, these entities are given less weight.

The authors extended the named entities extracted by their synonyms using DBpedia redirect pages to form a set of entities that reflect the context of each tweet.

Similarity of Messages

For the lexical feature the authors use cosine similarity (TF-IDF) which is shown to get best results in hashtag recommendations in Twitter network (Zangerle, Gassler, & Specht, 2013).

Cosine Similarity

The cosine similarity function is based on the (weighted) term vectors of both the query and the respective document which is to be compared to the query. The authors choose to evaluate the cosine similarity of weighted term vectors computed by TF-IDF weighting scheme.

Semantic Based Similarity

For the semantic based features the authors use Jaccard similarity coefficient which is a set-based similarity function to compute the overlap score between entities within tweets.

Equation (3) shows the computation of the coefficient, where t_i and t_j are the set of DBpedia entities for the corresponding tweets.

$$Jaccard\left(t_i, t_j\right) = \frac{\left|t_i \cap t_j\right|}{\left|t_i \cup t_j\right|} \tag{3}$$

Ranking

Due to the limited space for displaying the recommended hashtags (in most case a set of 5-10 hashtags) The obtained hashtags set from the most similar tweets have to be ranked to obtain the most suitable top-k hashtags to recommend to the user. Hence, the authors evaluate three ranking strategies as addressed before by (Zangerle, Gassler, & Specht, 2013) and they consider the time feature (Zangerle, Gassler, & Specht, 2011) as a ranking strategy which is important in recommending hashtags in a dynamic social network such as Twitter, where users are interested in fresh and specific hashtags. They observe that specific hashtags tend to appear and disappear according to an event, meaning that his usage frequency is limited to a short period of time.

Let's denote t_c the tweet candidate, t_{input} the user's message, C_T the retrieved tweets and T the dataset.

Score

This ranking method is based on the similarity values of the input tweet and the tweets containing the hashtag recommendation candidates. If the hashtag candidate is present in more than one similar message in the candidate set, the highest similarity score is used for further computations.

$$score(h) = \max(\{sim(t_c, t_{input}) \mid t_c \in C_T \wedge h \in t_c \}) \text{Where } sim \in \{ \text{ tfidf, semantic\_overlap} \} \quad (4)$$

Local

This ranking method is based on the popularity of hashtags within the hashtag recommendation candidate set. This basically means that the more entries in the result set of similar messages contain a certain hashtag, the more suitable the hashtag might be.

$$score(h) = \sum_c contains(t_c, h) \text{ where } t_c \in C_T \quad (5)$$

Global

This ranking method is based on the global popularity of hashtags within the whole underlying data set. As only a few hashtags are used at a high frequency, it is likely that such a popular hashtag matches the message entered by the user.

$$score(h) = \sum_i contains(t_i, h) \text{ where } t_i \in T \quad (6)$$

Time-Sensitive

This ranking method is based on the time popularity of hashtags candidates within the whole underlying data set at the time where the user enters his message, the authors argue this ranking strategy based on the assumption that specific hashtags tend to appear in a short period as a trending topics. Also, this ranking method can be seen as Global method with time sensitive feature. Hence, the authors compute the popularity of a given hashtag in a short period of time

τ rather than computing his popularity in the whole dataset. The authors consider this method as a baseline ranking.

$$score(h) = \sum_i contains(t_i, h) \mid Time_{t_i} \in \left[Time_{t_{input}} - \tau, Time_{t_{input}} \right] \}) \quad (7)$$

where

$t_i \in T$

$Time_{t_i}$ is the time of the candidate tweet.

$Time_{t_{input}}$ is the time of the input tweet.

τ is a period that is set to 10 days.

Combining the Ranking Functions

Linear Based Combination of Ranking Functions

In addition of the aforementioned ranking functions, the authors use a hybrid ranking method based on the presented ranking functions, in order to study the combination between the presented functions. As presented before in (Zangerle, Gassler, & Specht, 2011) (Kalloubi, Nfaoui, & El Beqqali, 2017), the combination between two ranking functions is computed by the following formula:

$$hybrid\left(f_1, f_2\right) = \alpha * f_1 + \left(1 - \alpha\right) * f_2 \tag{8}$$

where $\alpha \in [0, 1]$ is the weight coefficient determining the weight of the respective ranking within the hybrid rank.

Learning to Rank Based Combination for Hashtag Recommendations

Learning to Rank is a data-driven approach which integrates a bag of features in the model effectively. Figure 4 shows the paradigm of learning for hashtag ranking.

Net Based Strategy. ListNet is a multilevel relevance judgment learning to rank model. The goal of the learning in ListNet (Cao, Qin, Liu, Tsai, & Li, 2007) is minimizing ranking errors, rather than minimizing errors in classification of pairs of hashtags or building regression models. ListNet is based on comparing the probability distribution of permutations of lists of candidate hashtags. Specifically, for a set of candidate hashtags to a tweet t, ListNet first defines a permutation probability distribution based on the scores produced by a ranking function for each candidate hashtag.

It then defines another distribution based on the ground truth labels, and measures the inconsistency between these two distributions. The ranking function is defined as a neural network model. Thus, it is possible to iteratively adjust this ranking function according to the measured inconsistency. This adjustment is done at a pre-defined learning rate *lr* during *i* iterations.

As shown in Figure 4, at the first step we use a similarity measure to extract the hashtags candidates C_h. Then, for each couple tweet-hashtag, we construct a set of features using the aforementioned ranking functions.

ListNet (Cao, Qin, Liu, Tsai, & Li, 2007) is used to train a ranking model from the training corpus. Finally, the model is evaluated by the test corpus to obtain the set of ranked hashtags for the user message t_k.

Figure 4. General Paradigm of Learning for hashtag suggestion

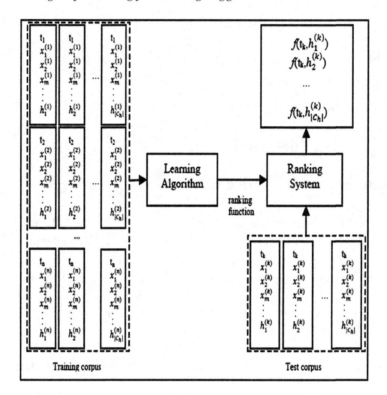

EVALUATION

The evaluation was conducted on the dataset described previously, using an evaluation framework implemented in Java. The evaluation was performed on a 4-core machine with 4 GB of RAM.

The authors performed the leave-one-out test (Cremonesi, Turrin, Lentini, & Matteucci, 2008) in order to evaluate their approach as shown in figure 5. Moreover, they didn't use retweets for the evaluation which can affect negatively the recommendation process, in the measure that they can lead to the recommendation based on the same messages. They also removed tweets that contain more than 6 hashtags which can consist of spam messages. The performed leave-one-out tests are conducted on 1,000 test messages. The authors apply recall value as the most suitable IR-metric to evaluate their system, due to the limited number of the recommended hashtags.

Evaluating the Ranking Methods per Similarity Measures

The authors study the impact of each ranking using semantic similarity and draw a comparison with cosine similarity (TF-IDF) using Lucene[10]. Figures 5, 6, 7 and 8 show the recall@k (k=1, 3, 5, 10, 15, 20) plot of each ranking methods per similarity measures including lexical similarity computed by cosine similarity (*TF-IDF*) and semantic overlapping between entities within messages (*Jaccard similarity*).

As shown in Figures 6, 7, 8, semantic similarity outperforms cosine similarity with TF-IDF using Score, Global and Local Ranking Methods. However, in the case of time-sensitive ranking method as can be seen in figure 9, where semantic similarity perform the cosine similarity in recommending 1,

Figure 5. Basic evaluation algorithm
(Zangerle, Gassler, & Specht, 2013)

```
Data: set T of all tweets within the data set
Result: Evaluation of Recommendation Algorithm
1    begin
2    |   //initialisation
3    |   randomTweet, inputText := null
4    |   hashtagsRecommendation, evaluationResults, hashtags
5    |   numberOfCorrectRecommendations := 0

6    |   // Get random tweets from T
8    |   randomTweet = getRandomTweet(T)
9    |   hashtags = extractHashtags(randomTweet)
10   |   inputText = removeHashtags(randomTweet)
11   |   hashtagsRecommendation=getRecommendedHashtags(inputText)
12   |   // Evaluate Recommended Hahstags
13   |   foreach r within hashtagsRecommendation do
14   |       if r Є hashtags then
15   |       |    numberOfCorrectRecommendations++
16   |       end
17   |   end
18   |   evaluationResult = Metric(
19   |       inputText,
20   |       hashtagsRecommendation,
21   |       numberOfCorrectRecommendations)
22   |   return evaluationResult
23   end
```

Figure 6. Performance of Global ranking method for each similarity measure
(Kalloubi, Nfaoui, & El Beqqali, 2017)

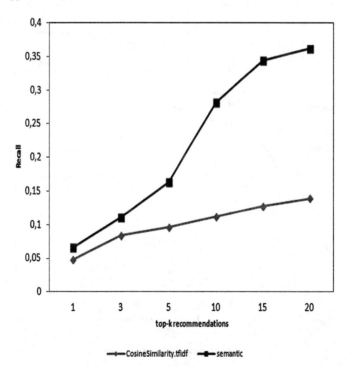

Figure 7. Performance of local ranking method for each similarity measure
(Kalloubi, Nfaoui, & El Beqqali, 2017)

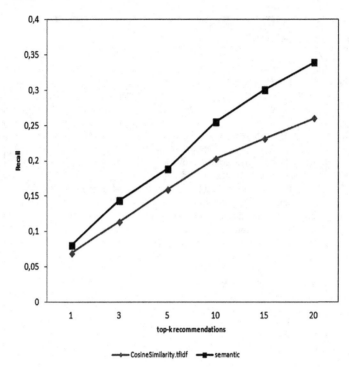

Figure 8. Performance of score ranking method for each similarity measure
(Kalloubi, Nfaoui, & El Beqqali, 2017)

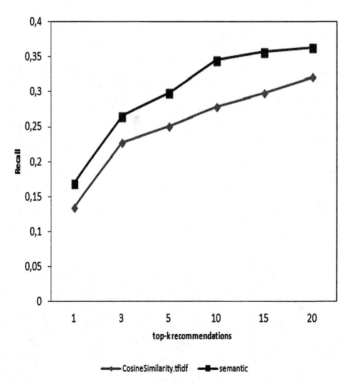

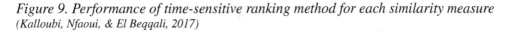

Figure 9. Performance of time-sensitive ranking method for each similarity measure
(Kalloubi, Nfaoui, & El Beqqali, 2017)

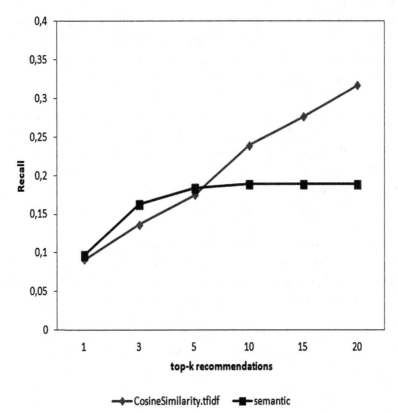

3, 5 hashtags, this performance can be explained by the performance of semantic similarity in which contextual information are not neglected, and often lead to high recall similarity metric, unlike bag-of-words models in which messages are compared based on their lexical content and hence lead to many messages that are not related to the user message. Thus, by using semantic similarity, the number of hashtag candidates is low (i.e. high recall), as the number of relevant hashtags is restricted in a period of times; thus, the recall value doesn't changes when the top-k recommendations are increased. Also, time-sensitive ranking method is more suitable for recommending specific hashtags, and penalizes the suggestion of general hashtags.

The authors explain the good performance of the Score ranking method (as can be seen in Figure 8) by the fact that the relevance of the message is related with the relevance of the hashtags within, meaning that more the message is relevant to the user message more the hashtags embedded in are highly recommended to the user. Moreover, the score ranking method using semantic similarity improves lexical-based score ranking method by more than 4.8% in recall value for recommending 5 hashtags. Figures 6, 7 show the recall@k (k= 1, 3, 5, 10, 15, 20) value of Global and local ranking methods respectively, Score ranking method performs them and proves that the similarity of the messages in which the hashtags are embedded in are more relevant for the quality of the recommendation.

As can be observed from these figures (Figures 6, 7, 8, 9) that semantic similarity, the overlapping named entities within messages, leads to best performance on the suggested hashtags, in the measure that the messages are compared based on their semantics which can explain the good performance of the proposed model compared to TF-IDF.

As can be seen in Figure 10, the time-sensitive ranking method has a reasonable performance in suggesting 5 hashtags compared to Global and Local ranking methods. Furthermore, time-sensitive ranking method is not suitable as a major ranking function, but if no similar tweets are retrieved, the most popular hashtags at the time of user composes his message are proposed as a baseline set of suggested hashtags, this can be seen as not only suggesting global hashtags but in addition hashtags that reflect a trending topics as users are interested by fresh and specific hashtags not only popular ones. Also, like other ranking strategies, time-sensitive ranking method is suitable to build lightweight recommendation interface without overwhelming the user by too many recommendations. Moreover, the performance of time-sensitive ranking strategy can be improved when using a long-term dataset, as the number of hashtags reflecting temporal and local trends can be increased. Furthermore, it is important to note that the recommended hashtags not matching the originals are not necessarily unsuitable as recommended hashtags.

As shown previously, the score ranking strategy using semantic feature have the best performance in recommending hashtags. Moreover, in the hybrid ranking method, the authors chose to study the impact of different combination on their system in order to improve it. The recall@k (k= 1, 3, 5, 10, 15, 20) values for the hybrid ranking methods are displayed in Figure 11.

Figure 10. Performance of all ranking functions on semantic similarity
(Kalloubi, Nfaoui, & El Beqqali, 2017)

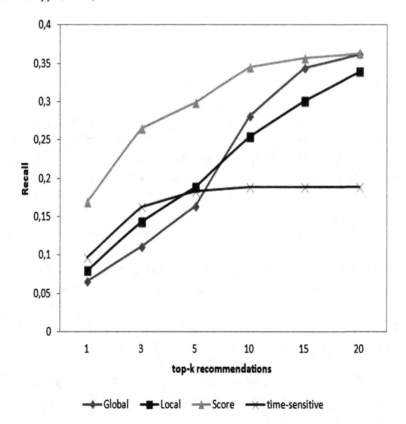

Figure 11. Performance of Hybrid Ranking Methods
(Kalloubi, Nfaoui, & El Beqqali, 2017)

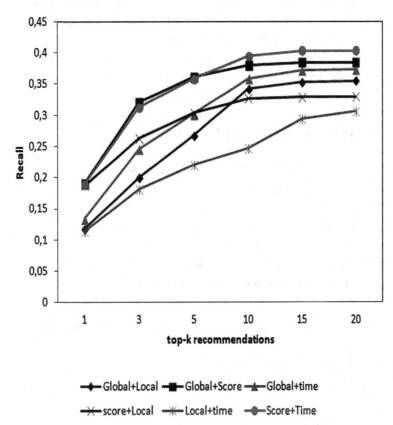

Evaluating the Linear Combination of Ranking Functions

Figure 11, shows that the best hybrid performance is given by combining score ranking method and global ranking method for the recommendation of 5 hashtags, this performance is due to the fact that this combination considers the content of the tweet and the global factor of popularity in the whole dataset. In other words, such combination means that the suggested hashtags are relevant to the tweet entered by a given user and are popular in the Twitter sphere, also, by comparing his performance to the results obtained using lexical and semantic similarity, we can see that such combination improves them by more than 11% and 7% respectively on recommending 5 hashtags . Furthermore, as can be seen, this combination is much correlated with the combination of time-sensitive and score ranking strategies which mean that the suggested hashtags are relevant to the user entered tweet and popular in Twitter sphere at the time which the user compose his tweet. The performance of this combination can be improved when using a long-term dataset. The combination of score ranking method and Local ranking method shows a less performance compared to the aforementioned combinations for recommending 5 hashtags, this less performance is due to the fact that this combination is based on the popularity of hashtags within the set of the relevant hashtags and doesn't involve the context of the hashtags in the dataset (Time-sensitive and Global methods). For the other combinations, the authors argue their less performance by the absence of the relevancy factor which proves that the similarity of the messages in which the hashtags are embedded in are more relevant for the quality of the recommendation process. However, the combination of global popularity ranking and time-sensitive popularity ranking is not suitable as a major combination, but if no similar tweets are retrieved, this combination can be proposed as a baseline. Also, this combination is suitable to build lightweight recommendation interface.

Indeed, Twitter generates a large amount of messages with 9,100 tweets in every second[11], furthermore, due to the fact that the presented system relies only on the content of each tweet, the processing of a user hashtag recommendation can be distributed using MapReduce pattern.

Evaluating the Learning to Rank Based Combination

We use Listnet (Cao, Qin, Liu, Tsai, & Li, 2007) as a multilevel relevance judgment learning to rank model to incorporate different ranking features, we study the impact of different combinations on the recommended hashtags.

We perform leave-one-out cross validation tests as depicted in the algorithm in Figure 12; each of these steps was conducted on 1,000 messages.

Table 3 shows the Pearson correlation between each two ranking strategies using semantic similarity; we found that the less correlation is between Time-sensitive and Global ranking methods. Furthermore,

Figure 12. Basic evaluation algorithm for learning for hashtag recommendation

```
Data: set T of all tweets within the data set
Result: Evaluation of Recommendation Algorithm
1    begin
2        //initialisation
3        randomTweet, inputText := null
4        hashtagsRecommendation, evaluationResults, hashtags, remainingTweets := { }
5        numberOfCorrectRecommendations := 0

6        // Get random tweets from T
8        randomTweet = getRandomTweet(T)
9        hashtags = extractHashtags(randomTweet)
10       inputText = removeHashtags(randomTweet)
11       remainingTweets= T - {randomTweet}
12       model = trainRemainingTweets(remainingTweets)
13       hashtagsRecommendation=testTweet(inputText, model)
14       // Evaluate Recommended Hahstags
15       foreach r within hashtagsRecommendation do
16           if r Є hashtags then
17               numberOfCorrectRecommendations++
18           end
19       end
20       evaluationResult = Metric(
21           inputText,
22           hashtagsRecommendation,
23           numberOfCorrectRecommendation)
24       return evaluationResult
25   end
```

Table 3. Pearson correlation between ranking functions using semantic similarity

	Global	**Local**	**Score**	**Time-Sensitive**
Global	1			
Local	**0,98883567**	1		
Score	0,92246435	0,95014519	1	
Time-sensitive	**0,76590826**	0,82324233	0,95329417	1

Global with Local ranking methods are highly correlated, thus, the combination of these two ranking functions performs the best. Consequently, as shown in figure 11, by incorporating two ranking strategies using semantic similarity in a learning to rank model, we can observe that the best performance is given by incorporating Local and Global methods and the less is given by incorporating Global and Time-sensitive. However, in our approach we study the impact of incorporating more than two ranking functions on the suggested hashtags.

As shown in Figure 13, incorporating the aforementioned ranking functions using semantic similarity in a learning to rank model shows a high improvement on the hashtag recommendations with 18% for semantic similarity and 23% for cosine similarity in recall value for the recommendation of 5 hashtags, this performance is achieved by incorporating Score, Global and Time-sensitive ranking functions and hence proves that the similarity of the messages in which the hashtag recommendation candidates are embedded in are highly relevant for the quality of recommendations. Furthermore, this high performance is due to the fact that this combination involves the context of the hashtags in the dataset (Time-sensitive and Global methods). Moreover, incorporating Global and Time-sensitive ranking functions has the less performance on the recommended hashtags. However, if no similar tweets are retrieved for an input message, the conjunction between popular hashtags (i.e. Global method) and popular hashtags at the time of user composes his message (Time-sensitive method) can be recommended as baseline strategy.

CONCLUSION

In this chapter, the authors presented an approach for hashtag recommendation on microblogging platforms. This recommendation, allow users to use more appropriate hashtags for their message, and therefore to homogenize the hashtagging behavior within microblogging platforms. Furthermore, this recommendation is based on analyzing messages similar to the user's message currently entered and recommending the set of hashtags Candidates from these similar messages. They proposed to leverage the semantic feature of microbblogging posts by taken into account the nature of this form of communication, also they compared their approach with previous approaches using lexical matching between messages. Furthermore, the authors prove that their approach based on semantic similarity between messages outperforms the recommendation based on cosines similarity which has been shown to get best results on recommending hashtags. They also studied the impact of different ranking functions on the recommendation process.

Moreover, the authors proposed a hybrid combination of these ranking strategies and they studied the impact of each combination on the recommended hashtags. The experiment results they conducted showed that their semantic-based similarity, mainly the overlap score between named entities within

Figure 13. The performance of different combinations on the suggested hashtags

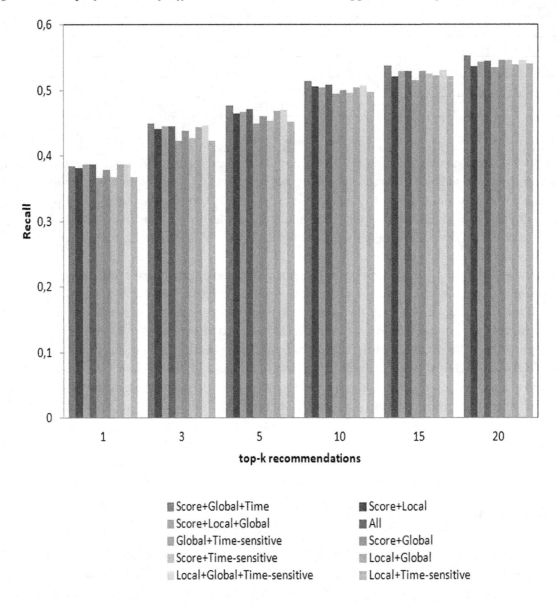

messages, have achieved the best results compared to cosine similarity using TF-IDF, and they found that a combination between the score popularity ranking strategy and the global popularity ranking strategy have the best performance on recommending 5 hashtags. Also, they incorporated different ranking functions using semantic similarity in a learning to rank model, and they showed the impact of different combinations on the recommended hashtags. The evaluation showed that using learning to rank for hashtags recommendation achieve a high performance, improving the cosine similarity using TF-IDF and semantic similarity with respectively 23% and 18% in recall. The approach presented in this chapter was already used to implement a first prototype. Thus, in future work we plan to incorporate user preferences into the recommendation process and the social graph of twitter users. Furthermore, many messages do not contain named entities which are neglected when using only semantic similarity.

Thus, incorporating the lexical feature with semantic feature in the recommendation process is planned, which can solve this issue. Equally important, analyzing the historical hashtagging behavior of users is also planned, as users tend to re-use their hashtags.

REFERENCES

Alvari, H. (2017). Twitter Hashtag Recommendation using Matrix Factorization.

Belém, F. M., Almeida, J. M., & Gonçalves, M. A. (2017). A survey on tag recommendation methods. Journal of the Association for Information Science and Technology, 68(4), 830-844.

Ben-Lhachemi, N., & Nfaoui, E. H. (2018). Using Tweets Embeddings For Hashtag Recommendation in Twitter. *Procedia Computer Science, 127,* 7–15. doi:10.1016/j.procs.2018.01.092

Bollen, D. P., Knijnenburg, B. C., Willemsen, M., & Graus, M. (2010). Understanding choice overload in recommender systems. In *Proceedings of the fourth ACM conference on Recommender systems*, 63-70.

Cao, Z., Qin, T., Liu, T.-Y., Tsai, M.-F., & Li, H. (2007). Learning to Rank: From Pairwise Approach to Listwise Approach. In *Proceedings of the 24th international conference on Machine learning*, Corvallis(pp. 129-136). 10.1145/1273496.1273513

Cremonesi, P., Turrin, R., Lentini, E., & Matteucci, M. (2008, November 17-19). An Evaluation Methodology for Collaborative Recommender Systems. In *International Conference on Automated solutions for Cross Media Content and Multi-channel Distribution, 2008. AXMEDIS '08, Florence*, Italy (pp. 224 – 231). 10.1109/AXMEDIS.2008.13

Efron, M., Organisciak, P., & Fenlon, K. (2012). Improving retrieval of short texts through document expansion. In *SIGIR '12 Proceedings of the 35th international ACM SIGIR conference on Research and development in information retrieval,* Portland, WA.

Godin, F., Slavkovikj, V., De Neve, W., Schrauwen, B., & Van de Walle, R. (2013). Using Topic Models for Twitter Hashtag Recommendation. In *Proceedings of the 22nd International Conference on World Wide Web* (pp. 593-596). 10.1145/2487788.2488002

Guo, Y., Qin, B., Li, Y., Liu, T., & Li, S. (2013). Improving Candidate Generation for Entity Linking. In *18th International Conference on Applications of Natural Language to Information Systems, NLDB 2013*, Salford, UK (pp. 225-236).

Hakimov, S., Oto, S. A., & Dogdu, E. (2012). Named entity recognition and disambiguation using linked data and graph-based centrality scoring. In *Proceedings of the 4th International Workshop on Semantic Web Information Management*. ACM. 10.1145/2237867.2237871

Hu, X., Sun, N., Zhang, C., & Chua, T.-S. (2009). Exploiting Internal and External Semantics for the Clustering of Short Texts Using World Knowledge. In *CIKM '09 Proceedings of the 18th ACM conference on Information and knowledge management* (pp. 919-928).

Jianjun, Y., & Tongyu, Z. (2015). Combining long-term and short-term user interest for personalized hashtag recommendation. *Frontiers of Computer Science, 9*(4), 608–622. doi:10.100711704-015-4284-x

Kalloubi, F., Nfaoui, E. H., & El Beqqali, O. (2014). Graph-based Tweet Entity Linking using DBpedia. In *ACS/IEEE the 11th Conference on computer systems and Applications*, Doha, Qatar (pp. 501-506).

Kalloubi, F., Nfaoui, E. H., & El beqqali, O. (2016). Microblog Semantic context retrieval system based on Linked Open Data and graph-based theory. *Expert Systems with Applications*, *53*, 138–148. doi:10.1016/j.eswa.2016.01.020

Kalloubi, F., Nfaoui, E. H., & El Beqqali, O. (2017). Harnessing semantic features for large-scale content-based hashtag recommendations on microblogging platforms. *International Journal on Semantic Web and Information Systems*, *13*(1), 19. doi:10.4018/IJSWIS.2017010105

Kowald, D., Pujari, S., & Lex, E. (2017). Temporal Effects on Hashtag Reuse in Twitter: A Cognitive-Inspired Hashtag Recommendation Approach. In *26th International Conference on World Wide Web*, Perth, Australia (pp. 1401-1410).

Kywe Su, M., Hoang, T.-A., Lim, E. P., & Zhu, F. (2012). On recommending hashtags in twitter networks. In *SocInfo'12 Proceedings of the 4th international conference on Social Informatics,* Lausanne, Switzerland (pp. 337-350). Springer.

Li, Y., Liu, T., Jiang, J., & Zhang, L. (2016). *Hashtag Recommendation with Topical Attention-Based LSTM. COLING* (pp. 3019–3029). ACL.

Lu, H.-M., & Lee, C.-H. (2015). A Twitter Hashtag Recommendation Model that Accommodates for Temporal Clustering Effects. *IEEE Intelligent Systems*, *30*(3), 18–25. doi:10.1109/MIS.2015.20

Mazzia, A., & Juet, J. (2011). *Suggesting hashtags on Twitter.* Retrieved 01 06, 2016, from http://al-liemazzia.com/pubs/545-final.pdf

Otsuka, E., Wallace, S. A., & Chiu, D. (2016). A hashtag recommendation system for twitter data streams. *Computational Social Networks*, *3*(1), 3. doi:10.118640649-016-0028-9 PMID:29355223

Owoputi, O., O'Connor, B., Dyer, C., Gimpel, K., Schneider, N., & A. Smith, N. (2013). Improved Part-of-Speech Tagging for Online Conversational Text with Word Clusters. In *HLT-NAACL 2013* (pp. 380-390).

She, J., & Lei, C. (2014). TOMOHA: TOpic model-based HAshtag recommendation on twitter. *Proceedings of the companion publication of the 23rd international conference on World wide web companion,* Seoul, Korea (pp. 371-372). 10.1145/2567948.2577292

Tao, K., Abel, F., Hauff, C., & Houben, G.-J. (2012). What makes a tweet relevant for a topic? *In MSM 2012, Proceedings of the workshop on Making Sense of Microposts (MSM2012), workshop at the 21st World Wide Web Conference 2012,* Lyon, France (pp. 49-56).

Tran, v. C., Hwang, D., & Nguyen, N. T. (2018). Hashtag Recommendation Approach Based on Content and User Characteristics. *International Journal of Cybernetics and Systems.*

Wang, K., Thrasher, C., & Paul Hsu, B.-J. (2011). Web scale NLP: a case study on url word breaking. In *WWW '11 Proceedings of the 20th international conference on World wide web* (pp. 357-366).

Yu, H., Bing, Z., Mingyao, D., & Feng, H. (2018). Tag recommendation method in folksonomy based on user tagging status. *Journal of Intelligent Information Systems*, *50*(3), 479–500. doi:10.100710844-017-0468-1

Zangerle, E., Gassler, W., & Specht, G. (2011). Recommending #-tags in Twitter. In *Proceedings of the Workshop on Semantic Adaptive Social Web 2011 in connection with the 19th International Conference on User Modeling, Adaptation and Personalization,* Gerona, Spain.

Zangerle, E., Gassler, W., & Specht, G. (2011). Using Tag Recommendations to Homogenize Folksonomies in Microblogging Environments. In *Proceedings of the Workshop on Semantic Adaptive Social Web 2011 in connection with the 19th International Conference on User Modeling, Adaptation and Personalization,* Singapore. 10.1007/978-3-642-24704-0_16

Zangerle, E., Gassler, W., & Specht, G. (2013). On the impact of text similarity functions on hashtag recommendations in microblogging environments. *Social Network Analysis and Mining*, *3*(4), 889–898.

Zhao, F., Zhu, Y., Jin, H., & Laurence, T. Y. (2016). A personalized hashtag recommendation approach using LDA-based topic model in microblog environment. *Future Generation Computer Systems*, *65*, 196–206. doi:10.1016/j.future.2015.10.012

Zheng, E., Yukio Kondo, G., Zilora, S., & Yu, Q. (2018). Tag-aware dynamic music recommendation. *Expert Systems with Applications*, *106*, 244–251. doi:10.1016/j.eswa.2018.04.014

ENDNOTES

[1] http://www.hashtags.org/

[2] https://wiki.cites.illinois.edu/wiki/display/forward/Dataset-UDI-TwitterCrawl-Aug2012

[3] Language detection, https://github.com/shuyo/language-detection

[4] http://dbpedia.org/ontology/wikiPageDisambiguates

[5] http://dbpedia.org/ontology/wikiPageRedirects

[6] http://tagdef.com/

[7] http://web-ngram.research.microsoft.com/info/break.html

[8] http://en.wikipedia.org/wiki/List_of_U.S._state_abbreviations

[9] http://jung.sourceforge.net/

[10] http://lucene.apache.org/

[11] http://www.statisticbrain.com/twitter-statistics/

Chapter 13
Recent Advances in the Evaluation of Ontology Quality

Niyati Baliyan
Indira Gandhi Delhi Technical University for Women, India

Ankita Verma
Jaypee Institute of Information Technology, India

ABSTRACT

Ontology or domain specific vocabulary is indispensable to a semantic web-based application; therefore, its evaluation assumes critical importance for maintaining the quality. A modular ontology is intuitively preferred to as a monolithic ontology. A good quality modular ontology, in turn, promotes reusability. This chapter is directed at summarizing the efforts towards ontology evaluation, besides defining the process of evaluation, various approaches to evaluation and underlying motivation. In particular, a modular ontology's cohesion and coupling metrics have been discussed in detail as a case study. The authors believe that the body of knowledge in this chapter will serve as a beginning point for ontology quality engineers and at the same time acquaint them with the state-of-art in this field.

INTRODUCTION

Quality is never an accident. It is always the result of intelligent effort. -John Ruskin

Ontology is one of the prominent tools of knowledge representation because of its inherent capability of clear and concise description of the domain knowledge (Gruber, 1995). Ontologies explicitly define domain concepts in a formalized manner in order to facilitate the consensus of understanding among the people and machines. In simpler words, ontologies capture the formal description of a particular domain via relevant concepts (terms) and the relationships between these concepts. Ontologies are the seminal support for the emergence of Semantic Web (Berner-Lee, 2005) as well as other semantically-aware applications (Dou et al., 2005). Ontologies facilitate the interoperability among different web applications of a domain as well as of different domains, hence, establishing the core principle of Semantic Web of breaking the data silos (Maedche & Staab, 2001).Various web languages such Resource Description

DOI: 10.4018/978-1-5225-7186-5.ch013

Copyright © 2019, IGI Global. Copying or distributing in print or electronic forms without written permission of IGI Global is prohibited.

Framework Schema (RDFS) (Brickley, 2000), Web Ontology Language (OWL) (Antoniou & Harmelenn, 2004) and Ontology Inference Layer (OIL) (Fensel et al., 2001), are used to express ontologies. These languages use logic theories to capture the domain knowledge which allows efficient reasoning about the relationships between the objects and concepts.

In Figure 1, a sample ontology for university domain is shown. It comprises of seven classes: Persons, Staff, Students, Faculty, Courses and Subjects, and have five different relations among them. Classes, Staff, and Students are disjoint subclasses of Persons. Similarly, Non-teaching staff and Faculty are the subclasses of Staff class. In Figure 1, only object properties and class hierarchy are shown in an abstract manner.

The OWL code snippet corresponding to Figure 1 is provided below.

```
<?xml version= "1.0"?>
<!DOCTYPE Ontology [
    <!ENTITY owl "http://www.w3.org/2002/07/owl#" >
    <!ENTITY xsd "http://www.w3.org/2001/XMLSchema#" >
    <!ENTITY owl2xml "http://www.w3.org/2006/12/owl2-xml#" >
```

Figure 1. University Ontology Example

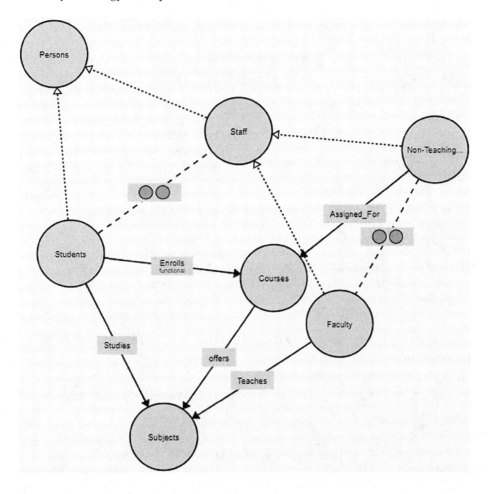

```
    <!ENTITY rdfs "http://www.w3.org/2000/01/rdf-schema#" >
    <!ENTITY rdf "http://www.w3.org/1999/02/22-rdf-syntax-ns#" >
    <!ENTITY Ontology1529057013241 "http://www.semanticweb.org/ontolo-
gies/2018/5/Ontology1529057013241.owl#" >
]>

<Ontology xmlns= "http://www.w3.org/2006/12/owl2-xml#"
    xml:base= "http://www.w3.org/2006/12/owl2-xml#"
    xmlns:owl2xml= "http://www.w3.org/2006/12/owl2-xml#"
    xmlns:xsd= "http://www.w3.org/2001/XMLSchema#"
    xmlns:Ontology1529057013241= "http://www.semanticweb.org/ontolo-
gies/2018/5/Ontology1529057013241.owl#"
    xmlns:rdfs= "http://www.w3.org/2000/01/rdf-schema#"
    xmlns:rdf= "http://www.w3.org/1999/02/22-rdf-syntax-ns#"
    xmlns:owl= "http://www.w3.org/2002/07/owl#"
    URI= "http://www.semanticweb.org/ontologies/2018/5/Ontology1529057013241.
owl">
    <Declaration>
        <Class URI= "&Ontology1529057013241;Courses"/>
    </Declaration>
    <SubClassOf>
        <Class URI= "&Ontology1529057013241;Faculty"/>
        <Class URI= "&Ontology1529057013241;Staff"/>
    </SubClassOf>
    <DisjointClasses>
        <Class URI= "&Ontology1529057013241;Faculty"/>
        <Class URI= "&Ontology1529057013241;Non-Teaching_Staff"/>
    </DisjointClasses>
    <Declaration>
        <Class URI= "&Ontology1529057013241;Faculty"/>
    </Declaration>
    <SubClassOf>
        <Class URI= "&Ontology1529057013241;Non-Teaching_Staff"/>
        <Class URI= "&Ontology1529057013241;Staff"/>
    </SubClassOf>
    <DisjointClasses>
        <Class URI= "&Ontology1529057013241;Non-Teaching_Staff"/>
    </DisjointClasses>
    <Declaration>
        <Class URI= "&Ontology1529057013241;Non-Teaching_Staff"/>
    </Declaration>
    <Declaration>
        <Class URI= "&Ontology1529057013241;Persons"/>
    </Declaration>
```

```
<SubClassOf>
    <Class URI= "&Ontology1529057013241;Staff"/>
    <Class URI= "&Ontology1529057013241;Persons"/>
</SubClassOf>
<DisjointClasses>
    <Class URI= "&Ontology1529057013241;Staff"/>
    <Class URI= "&Ontology1529057013241;Students"/>
</DisjointClasses>
<Declaration>
    <Class URI= "&Ontology1529057013241;Staff"/>
</Declaration>
<SubClassOf>
    <Class URI= "&Ontology1529057013241;Students"/>
    <Class URI= "&Ontology1529057013241;Persons"/>
</SubClassOf>
<Declaration>
    <Class URI= "&Ontology1529057013241;Students"/>
</Declaration>
<Declaration>
    <Class URI= "&Ontology1529057013241;Subjects"/>
</Declaration>
<ObjectPropertyDomain>
    <ObjectProperty URI= "&Ontology1529057013241;Assigned_For"/>
    <Class URI= "&Ontology1529057013241;Non-Teaching_Staff"/>
</ObjectPropertyDomain>
<ObjectPropertyRange>
    <ObjectProperty URI= "&Ontology1529057013241;Assigned_For"/>
    <Class URI= "&Ontology1529057013241;Courses"/>
</ObjectPropertyRange>
<Declaration>
    <ObjectProperty URI= "&Ontology1529057013241;Assigned_For"/>
</Declaration>
<FunctionalObjectProperty>
    <ObjectProperty URI= "&Ontology1529057013241;Enrolls"/>
</FunctionalObjectProperty>
<ObjectPropertyDomain>
    <ObjectProperty URI= "&Ontology1529057013241;Enrolls"/>
    <Class URI= "&Ontology1529057013241;Students"/>
</ObjectPropertyDomain>
<ObjectPropertyRange>
    <ObjectProperty URI= "&Ontology1529057013241;Enrolls"/>
    <Class URI= "&Ontology1529057013241;Courses"/>
</ObjectPropertyRange>
<Declaration>
```

```
        <ObjectProperty URI= "&Ontology1529057013241;Enrolls"/>
    </Declaration>
    <ObjectPropertyDomain>
        <ObjectProperty URI= "&Ontology1529057013241;Studies"/>
        <Class URI= "&Ontology1529057013241;Students"/>
    </ObjectPropertyDomain>
    <ObjectPropertyRange>
        <ObjectProperty URI= "&Ontology1529057013241;Studies"/>
        <Class URI= "&Ontology1529057013241;Subjects"/>
    </ObjectPropertyRange>
    <Declaration>
        <ObjectProperty URI= "&Ontology1529057013241;Studies"/>
    </Declaration>
    <ObjectPropertyDomain>
        <ObjectProperty URI= "&Ontology1529057013241;Teaches"/>
        <Class URI= "&Ontology1529057013241;Faculty"/>
    </ObjectPropertyDomain>
    <ObjectPropertyRange>
        <ObjectProperty URI= "&Ontology1529057013241;Teaches"/>
        <Class URI= "&Ontology1529057013241;Subjects"/>
    </ObjectPropertyRange>
    <Declaration>
        <ObjectProperty URI= "&Ontology1529057013241;Teaches"/>
    </Declaration>
    <ObjectPropertyDomain>
        <ObjectProperty URI= "&Ontology1529057013241;offers"/>
        <Class URI= "&Ontology1529057013241;Courses"/>
    </ObjectPropertyDomain>
    <ObjectPropertyRange>
        <ObjectProperty URI= "&Ontology1529057013241;offers"/>
        <Class URI= "&Ontology1529057013241;Subjects"/>
    </ObjectPropertyRange>
    <Declaration>
        <ObjectProperty URI= "&Ontology1529057013241;offers"/>
    </Declaration>
</Ontology>
```

Ontologies have been categorized as either monolithic or modular. A modular ontology may have numerous partitions or modules identified by high cohesion among a module's concepts (Bateman et al., 2007). If a monolithic ontology is modularized, some links get detached and these inter-modular links contribute to coupling in ontology. The conventional monolithic designs of ontology bear the flaws of poor scalability and difficulty of concept reuse. Further, the reasoning performance in monolithic ontologies is degraded especially when dealing with large and complex ontologies (Ensan & Du, 2013). It has been revealed that collaboratively creating isolated modules that can later be assimilated into one ontology leads to ease of management of the modules as well as better design accuracy (Arpirez et al., 2001; Noy et al., 2006). For the wide adoption of ontologies in the various semantically enabled applications, it becomes crucial to assess the quality of the developed ontology (Brank et al., 2005).

In this chapter, authors comprehensively present the various facets of ontology evaluation. Ontology evaluation is the process of determining the quality of the ontology on the basis of some pre-defined criteria. It is often done to determine which out of all the ontologies developed for the particular domain better conceptualizes the knowledge of the domain. In ontology evaluation, we tend to find the answer of the following question: "How well the developed ontology conceptualizes or models the real world scenario?" The domain specific knowledge of a real-world scenario helps to develop an ontology and in turn the developed ontology is evaluated on the benchmark of how well this knowledge is incorporated, this process of ontology evaluation is shown in Figure 2.

NEED FOR ONTOLOGY EVALUATION

Akin to any scientific or engineering artifact, there must be a systematic and plausible process of quality assessment of ontologies. With the emergence of Semantic Web and other related technologies, more emphasis is laid on better representation of the knowledge for improved reasoning and inference. Under such scenario, efficient knowledge management via ontologies becomes crucial. In a nutshell, evaluation of the ontologies becomes critical due to below mentioned reasons:

- Quality of the ontology has a direct impact on the reusability of the data and effective data exchange among various semantically aware applications.
- Assessing the quality of ontology during its development phase may guide the construction process efficiently resulting in further refinement of the developed ontology.
- By evaluating the quality of the available ontologies, the developer of an application may choose an ontology that best suits some prior-defined criteria. This may promote the reusability of the ontologies and reduce ontology proliferation.
- In semi-automated and automated learning of ontology, effective evaluation metrics can assist in the process of learning at various facets. It may help in parameter tuning of the learning algorithms and also guide the learning process.

Figure 2. Ontology Evaluation

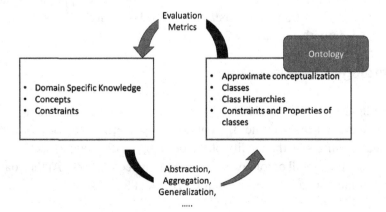

Classification of Ontology Evaluation Approaches

As suggested by G´omez-P´erez (2004), there are two different contexts in which ontology evaluation can be carried out: Ontology Verification and Ontology Validation. Ontology verification refers to development of ontology correctly and checking whether the developed ontology has implemented all the specified requirements. Whereas, ontology validation deals with ensuring how well the developed ontology is modeling the real-world scenario. In this chapter, our focus is on the ontology validation schemes. Ontology validation includes the approaches which fall under the following categories (Raad & Cruz, 2015):

- **Approaches Based on Comparison of an Ontology to Some "Gold Standard":** Under this category, those approaches are included which attempt to align the ontology to be evaluated to some upper ontology (Hovy, 2001; Maedche & Staab, 2002). Ontology engineers while developing ontology often face a scenario in which a core ontology is adapted, modified or enriched with the help of some of the concepts from a larger set of ontologies. Furthermore, it becomes crucial here to measure the similarity between ontologies or ontologies parts. Maedche and Staab (2002) have proposed certain similarity metrics on the basis of which ontology can be evaluated with regards to certain "gold standard".
- **Task Based Evaluation:** These approaches evaluate ontology in the light of an explicit task. Given a suitable task and some algorithms that operate on ontology to solve this task, ontology can be evaluated on the basis of the performance on the given task. Once the performance is evaluated, an ontology can be improved by omitting some of the irrelevant concepts, by including some of the relevant concepts and by substituting the ambiguous concepts with the unambiguous ones. Again, the performance of the improved ontology is computed on the given task (Porzel & Malaka, 2004).
- **Data Driven Evaluation:** Under this approach, ontology is compared with the knowledge about the domain represented in the form of text corpora (Brewster et al., 2004). This approach advocates that the textual documents about the domain of interest is the basic source of information while developing ontology, so the ontology should be evaluated on this as well (Brewster et al., 2001).
- **Approaches Based Human Expertise:** These approaches rely on the judgment of the human experts or the users, about the quality of the ontology. They assess the quality of ontology on the basis of how well it fits certain pre-specified criteria, requirements or standards (Guarino, 1998; Gomez-Perez, 1999; Lozano-Tello & Gómez-Pérez, 2004). The approaches based on this principle are qualitative in nature which depend on the subjectivity of human experts, whereas, the former three are quantitative measures.

Aspects of Ontology Evaluation

Rather than evaluating the ontology as whole, the evaluation can be carried out at various levels separately. This level-wise evaluation facilitates the ontology engineering methods that are based on ontology learning. Evaluator can assess the quality of the ontology at different aspects which can be further integrated or aggregated for overall ontology evaluation (Vrandečić, 2009). At the coarse level, different aspects of ontology evaluation are mentioned below (Brank et al., 2005):

- **Vocabulary or Lexical Level:** Vocabulary is the set of all the terms in the ontology which are used to represent various concepts of the domain of discourse.
- **Hierarchy Level and Other Semantic Relations:** This level is concerned about the evaluation of *is-a* relationship in the ontology. Apart from *is-a* relationship, concepts can be related via other semantic relations which can also be considered.
- **Context Level:** In certain cases, ontology may refer to or be referenced by some concepts defined in another ontologies. Thus, while evaluating such ontologies, the contextual information should also be incorporated.
- **Syntax Level:** As mentioned earlier, various web languages can be used to represent ontology formally and various surface syntaxes can also be adopted. At this level, the concern is to evaluate the whether the different syntaxes can be transformed to one another automatically. Various other concerns such as proper indentation and documentation can also be taken into account.
- **Structural Level:** Semantically similar ontologies can also be represented via different structures of RDF graphs. This aspect is concerned about organization of ontology.

CRITERIA FOR ONTOLOGY EVALUATION

Before embarking on the evaluation process, an important question that needs to be answered is "What is a good ontology?" Thus, first and foremost, the evaluator needs to decide on what criteria ontology will be judged (Vrandečić, 2009). Some of the criteria which are prevalent in the literature are:

- **Accuracy:** It specifies how well ontology is capturing all the aspects of real world scenario as well as the expertise of users (Obrst et al., 2007).
- **Adaptability:** It specifies the capability of ontology to adapt to small changes in the requirements monotonically. Here, it is ensured that the ontology is extendible and flexible enough to incorporate novel information about the domain (G´omez-P´erez, 2004, Gangemi et al., 2005).
- **Clarity:** The terms specified in the ontology should be well defined and effectively communicate the intended meaning of the underlying concept. It should also be specified whether the ontology provides partial description or well-formed definitions of the terms. The dependency of the definitions of the terms on the context should also be considered (Gruber, 1995).
- **Completeness:** This criterion checks if all the relevant concepts of the domain and their representation is included in ontology. This criterion considers the level of granularity and richness of the ontology with respect to the coverage of domain of interest (Vrandečić, 2009).
- **Computational Efficiency:** Under this criterion, an evaluator judges the efficiency and ease of the reasoners while processing the ontology for inference and querying (Obrst et al., 2007).
- **Conciseness:** Ontology should be as precise and concise as possible, including only the relevant axioms with respect to the domain of interest and, discarding irrelevant and redundant axioms (Gómez-P´erez, 2004).
- **Consistency:** It should be ensured that there must not be any logical inconsistency or internal contradictions in the ontology as no meaningful conclusions can be deduced from such ontologies. Usually the ontology becomes inconsistent when new axioms are added afterwards (Horridge et al., 2009). Furthermore, the formal description of the terms must be consistent to the informal description.

- • **Organizational Fitness:** For the better applicability and reuse of the ontologies, it should be ensured that proper process of the ontology development is followed, the ontology is easily deployable in the organization, and it is easily accessible for the potential users for the reuse (Gangemi et al., 2005).

ISSUES WITH EVALUATION OF MODULAR ONTOLOGY

As aforementioned, the modular design of ontology offers several benefits over its monolithic counterparts, such as improved scalability and ease of concepts' reuse. Further, the reasoning performance is upgraded especially while dealing with bulky and complex ontologies (Ensan & Du, 2013). However, the choice among multiple possible modular ontologies is a challenging and critical one task, since it determines the response time of the Semantic Web application backed by ontology. As the Semantic Web movement attains impetus, many large-scale ontologies are being extensively used in real-world applications (Zhang et al., 2010). Nevertheless, only few works are committed to compute the values of modular ontology's cohesion and coupling metrics. In the process of ontology engineering, such metrics assist in the identification of potential issues or incorrect usage of ontology elements, besides providing quality assessment of ontology (Sicilia et al., 2012). Summarizing, the following reasons underpin the requirement of modular ontology evaluation:

- • Increased popularity and utility of Semantic Web applications
- • Increased popularity and utility of Semantic Web applications
- • Ontology forms the basic unit of inference technique on the Semantic Web
- • Many modularizations of a given ontology possible
- • Choice of the best modularization (ontology partition)
- • Users may better understand, maintain, integrate, and reuse ontologies.
- • Better quality of modular ontology leads to better scalability and reusability

The metrics suite proposed for the evaluation of modular ontologies are broadly categorised as the structural and behavioural metrics as shown in Figure 3. Structural metrics are those metrics that are concerned about the structural organization of the ontology at the level of instances as well as concepts. It includes metrics proposed to measure cohesion, coupling and complexity. Conventionally, for software systems, cohesion and coupling are two well-adopted metrics for the evaluating the quality of the software. Chidamber and Kemerer (1994) have defined coupling to exist between two objects if at least

Figure 3. Metrics suite for Modular Ontology Evaluation

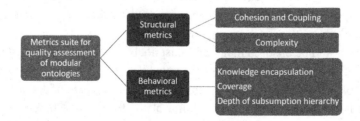

one of them affects the other, while cohesion of any object is calculated by the level of similarity of its methods. Cohesion and coupling are also employed effectively for the assessing the quality of modular ontologies. Metrics that are proposed for the qualifying the complexity of the ontology analyze the concepts and links between them. Usually, various aspects such as distribution of links across concepts, the ratio of actual links to the expected links and cyclomatic complexity are taken into consideration (Baliyan & Kumar, 2016a). Behavioral metrics is concerned about the knowledge embedded in the ontology altogether (Baliyan & Kumar, 2016b). Ontology developer must aim at developing such ontology modules that have higher encapsulation. Higher encapsulation ensures that an ontology can be easily adapted while these changes can remain concealed from foreign ontologies. Coverage specifies the property of ontology to well represent all the relevant concepts and relationships in the domain of discourse. In this chapter, we will focus on the metrics proposed for cohesion and coupling.

Kumar et al. (2017) propose metrics for cohesion and coupling for a modularized ontology, thus facilitating the choice for the most suitable cohesion-coupling trade-off, i.e., high cohesion and low coupling. Subsequently, the most logically consistent modular ontology alternative (among ontologies representing the same domain) is chosen. The proposed metrics for evaluating modular ontologies are based on the semantic definitions of relationships within and across modules, implying cohesion and coupling, respectively. The metrics are based on semantic definitions of ontology links, i.e., they consider all stated and inferred axioms for ontology evaluation. In the subsequent text, we have discussed some of the prior work that have motivated Kumar et al., (2017) to propose this work.

The different kinds of links in the hierarchy are not accounted for in Yao et al. (2005). Similarly, Ouyang et al. (2011); Oh and Ahn (2009) do not consider link types in the ontology hierarchy. In another effort by Orme et al. (2006), coupling of ontology is calculated through the total number of external classes, which are necessary to define concepts and links in the ontology, the total cardinality of the references to external concepts, and the cardinality of the links in the ontology. The work of Orme et al. (2006) merely discusses the coupling measurement, while ignoring cohesion measurement. Moreover, their work has not considered the possible aspects of dependencies based on various types of links. Ma et al. (2009) present a semantic set of metrics for cohesion in ontology, determined by the count of ontology partitions, count of minimal inconsistent subsets, and mean value of axiomatic inconsistencies. However, the work only performs cohesion measurement and ontological semantics, whereas, the coupling and ontological structure has not been accounted for. García et al. (2010a) propose coupling metrics determined by object properties. In García et al. (2010b), the authors' proposal is based on the coupling metric defined in the software engineering field modified to suit ontology needs. In Oh et al. (2011), authors define hierarchical and non-hierarchical relations in a graph and measure the number of relationships among different concepts. Nevertheless, it does not distinguish among different types of relationships and their effect on cohesion and coupling values. The work by Ensan and Du (2013) defines a set of metrics for the measurement of cohesion and coupling, for both monolithic and modular ontologies. They have used semantic definitions to bifurcate relationship types as either strong or not-strong (moderate). However, few relationship types do not lie in either strong or moderate zone, thus, hence their effect remains unmeasured.

To sum up, the existing metrics for analysis of ontology cohesion and coupling and therefore quality are majorly syntax-based, obtained from the graphical representation of the ontology. Even if relationships are considered, they are not categorized on the basis of their relative effect on the ontology; rather, only clearly defined relationships are measured (Vrandecic & Sure, 2007).

Therefore, Kumar et al. (2017) were motivated to facilitate the ontology engineer in choosing the best modularization after performing assessment of ontology modules on the basis of their relationships' type and strength. We will discuss various ontology cohesion and coupling metrics proposed by them in the next section.

COHESION AND COUPLING METRICS FOR MODULAR ONTOLOGY (KUMAR ET AL., 2017)

Kumar et al. (2017) have described the notion of coupling and cohesion using graph theory definitions. Their definitions fit various visualizations of ontologies, i.e., vertices and edges for concepts and relationships, respectively. For coupling and cohesion, authors assign unambiguous, instinctive, and handy formulae.

Figure 4. demonstrates the approach of Kumar et al. (2017) to compute cohesion and coupling values for a particular modular ontology. Firstly, the modular ontology to be evaluated is fed as input, next, the relationships are recognized. Cautious examination of the relationship structure and related dependencies is essential to deduce the type of dependency and strength factor (sf) among every pair of concepts. The sf is calculated through step by step application of rules, such as interpreting the relationship types,

Figure 4. Flowchart for ontology cohesion and coupling computation

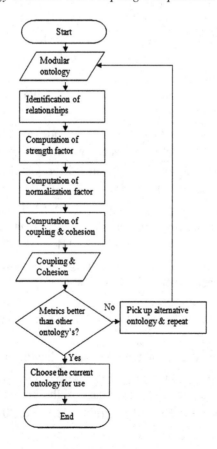

the distance factor, and handling some special cases. After the dependencies between concepts and their respective *sf* have been determined, the normalization factors are computed using the cardinality of module and ontology. Next, the normalized values of cohesion and coupling are determined using the proposed metrics. These values may then be compared for alternative ontologies and the user may choose the best trade-off, i.e., maximum cohesion and minimum coupling.

The rest of this section describes the calculation of cohesion and coupling using the proposed model.

Cohesion Metrics

Let ontology O be divided into n modules $m_1, m_2 \dots m_n$. The cardinality of a module $|m_i|$, is the number of concepts in the module, where $i \in [1, n]$. The cohesion for a module m_i is directly proportional to the combined *sf* of intra-modular dependency (between any two concepts taken at a time). If no dependency exists between two concepts, their *sf* is 0. Hence, the proportionality

$$Cohesion\left(m_i\right) \propto \Sigma C_k \in m_i \Sigma c_j \in m_i \left(sf\left(c_k, c_j\right)\right)$$

holds. This proportionality is also validated by the work in Ensan and Du (2013). In order to find the contribution to cohesion of module per relation, m ($Cohesion\,N\left(m\right)$), a normalization factor needs to be found. Oh et al. (2011) established $|m|\left(|m| - 1\right) / 2$ to be the normalization factor. Therefore,

$$Cohesion\,N\left(m_i\right) = 2 / |m_i|\left(|m_i| - 1\right) \times \Sigma c_k \in m_i \Sigma c_j \in m_i \left(sf\left(c_k, c_j\right)\right)$$

In general, for any module m,

$$Cohesion\left(m\right) = 2 / |m|\left(|m| - 1\right) \times \Sigma c_k \in m \Sigma c_j \in m \left(sf_{\left(c_k, c_j\right)}\right) \tag{1}$$

Coupling Metrics

When a monolithic ontology is modularized, some links are disjointed, these are the inter-modular links that form the coupling of an ontology. Analogous to module cardinality, the cardinality of ontology o is defined as the total number of concepts present in an ontology and is represented by $|o|$. Hence, the coupling for module m_i is directly proportional to the combined *sf* of dependency of any concept in m_i with an outside concept belonging to other modules in o. Few works have also validated this proportionality (Ensan & Du, 2013; Oh et al., 2011).

Let m be a module in an ontology o, then

$$Coupling\left(m\right) \propto \Sigma c_k \in m \Sigma c_j \in \left(o - m_i\right)\left(sf_{\left(c_k, c_j\right)}\right)$$

In order to find the contribution to coupling of module per relation, m (*Coupling* $N(m)$), a normalization factor needs to be found. Ensan and Du (2013) established $|m| \times (|o| - |m|)$ to be the normalization factor. Therefore,

$$Coupling \ N(m) = 1 / |m||o - m| \times \left(\Sigma c_k \in m \Sigma c_j \in (o - m_i) \left(sf_{(c_k, c_j)} \right) \right) \tag{2}$$

Validation

A generic validation framework for software quality metric was given by Kitchenham et al. (1995). A number of criteria were proposed by Briand et al. (1996) for validating specific measurement approaches, for example: size, coupling, and cohesion not specific to any particular software artefact. Thus, we can safely apply it to ontology modules. Moreover, the framework is robust as it is based on well-defined mathematical concepts.

A metric that conforms to the characteristics mentioned in both the frameworks, may be safely inferred to be properly defined, otherwise its validity, consistency and applicability is doubtful (Bieman & Ott, 1994; Dallal, 2010).

Validation by Kitchenham et al.'s Framework

The metric proposed here for cohesion and coupling satisfies Kitchenham et al. (1995) validation framework as in Table 1.

Validation by Briand et al.'s Framework

The metric proposed here for cohesion and coupling satisfies Briand et al. (1996) criteria as in Table 2.

Table 1. Conformance to Kitchenham et al. (1995) framework

Criterion	Conformance of Cohesion	Conformance of Coupling
Unit validity: Is the measurement unit fit to measure the attribute?	Strength factor was assigned to each relationship and such factors were summed to give module cohesion.	Strength factor was assigned to each relationship and such factors were summed to give module coupling.
Attribute validity: Is the attribute of interest reflected in the entity measured, directly or indirectly?	The attribute of interest is relationships among concepts and it is reflected in the intra-modular concepts (entity measured directly).	The attribute of interest is relationships among concepts and it is reflected in the inter-modular concepts (entity measured indirectly).
Instrument validity: Is the model underlying the measuring instrument valid?	The model accurately assigns strength factor to relationships and counts relationship between two concepts, only once.	The model accurately assigns strength factor to relationships and finds the sum of the strength factors between each pair of inter-modular concepts.
Protocol validity: Has an adequate measurement protocol been adopted?	The protocol used is consistent and free from measurement errors.	Totalling the sf of links and then taking its ratio with the total inter-modular links that can possibly exist, ensures dimensional consistency.

Table 2. Conformance to Briand et al. framework

Criterion	Conformance of Cohesion	Conformance of Coupling
Non negativity and Normalization: Is the value of metric non-negative and normalized, to permit comparison among different modules?	Cohesion values are non-negative as they fall in the interval (0,1]. Also, cohesion is normalized for all ontology modules.	Coupling values are non-negative as they fall in the interval (0,1]. Also, cohesion is normalized for all ontology modules.
Null value: In the absence of relationships between modules, is cohesion null?	If a module does not have any intra-modular relations, the value of the cohesion metric is assigned as null.	If a module does not have any inter-modular relations, the value of the coupling metric is assigned as null.
Monotonicity: Does addition of intra-modular relationship increases or maintains cohesion value?	The additive relation among relationships guarantees higher or equal cohesion value, on addition of relationships to the module.	The additive relation among relationships guarantees higher or equal coupling value, on addition of relationships to the module.
Merging of modules: If independent modules are merged, the cohesion of merged module can never be more than the maximum cohesion of merged modules.	The conglomeration of independent modules does not result in increased cohesion, as supported by non-negativity.	The conglomeration of independent modules does not result in increased coupling, as supported by non-negativity.

COMPARATIVE ANALYSIS

Table 3 presents a relative study of the model by Kumar et al. (2017) from the aspect of important features. Many authors such as Ensan and Du (2013), Oh et al. (2011), Abbès et al. (2012) partly cater to the hierarchical ontology's relationships. Furthermore, the intensity and type of the relationship has not been accounted for.

The mathematical formulations of Kumar et al. (2017) for cohesion and coupling add prolifically to a concrete view towards their measurement in partial ontologies whose graph visualizations are visible to the ontology designers. In their work, Kumar et al. (2017) do not assert that their measure is better; rather it is well suited for modular ontologies whose partitions can be handled in size by an average user. Their measures may be applied to cross-domain, domain, application, or task ontology. Their method is applicable to a sufficiently large ontology, as there is no upper limit on the number of concepts, and the number of rows in computation is only limited by the number of relationships.

Table 3. A relative study of the model by Kumar et al. (2017)

Measured Feature	Kumar et al. (2017)	Oh et al. (2011)	Ensan and Du (2013)	Abbes et al. (2012)
Dependence graphs	✓	✓	✓	✓
Type of Relationship	✓	Hierarchical and Non-hierarchical	✓	Hierarchical and Non-hierarchical
Continuous value of strength factor	✓	X	X	X
Indirect Relationships	✓	✓	X	X
Handle concepts in conjunction	✓	X	X	X

LITERATURE ON ONTOLOGY EVALUATION

In the following paragraphs, we discuss some recent works that present ontology evaluation.

The evaluation of biomedical ontologies is a tedious task owing to their complex taxonomy. However, it is crucial to evaluate them for their reuse and interoperability with ontologies and in other applications. Authors propose count of object, annotation and other properties (relations) as a determinant of richness of biomedical domain ontology. For this purpose, SPARQL query is run on Protégé ontology editor. However, the assessment mechanism is limited to biomedical ontologies, additionally it does not embed semantic information or even concepts' assessment while evaluating an ontology on the basis of structural properties alone (Khan et al., 2015).

Verma (2016) presents an abstract framework grounded on a compilation of existing ontology evaluation metrics. It is attempted to point out characteristics of erroneous ontology with intent to rule out poor quality ontologies from being considered for use. This is done prior to ranking similar purpose ontologies, for use. There is, however, no proof of concept to support application of the said framework. Moreover, many recent ontology evaluation metrics are not encompassed (Baliyan & Kumar, 2016a; Baliyan & Kumar, 2016b).

The paper by de Rodrigues et al. (2017) extends and improves OntoClean, a relatively subjective method based on the user's expertise to establish meta properties to the concepts of ontology. Authors' contribution lies in discovering disparities vis-à-vis the real domain. They present an implementation in an all-purpose Constraint Logic-based language, which is applicable even to partially labeled ontologies, and reveals improved scalability and efficiency.

Lantow (2016) has developed a web-based tool, called OntoMetrics to validate and present statistics about ontology in a machine-readable XML format for an input uploaded in RDF/OWL/URL format. OntoMetrics provides free access to metric definition and calculation. The paper provides theoretical background and case studies for OntoMetrics. It has classified and computed ontology metrics as – knowledgebase, class, schema, and graph metrics.

Mohan et al. (2017) propose a light weight approach to evaluate the sufficiency of an ontology by leveraging traditional information retrieval techniques. Currently, the implementation needs to run as a batch process with no interface/tool for end users.

This paper evaluates three popular Cultural Heritage ontologies from the aspect of their potential to represent works of art, using a set of evaluation criteria related to different uses of cultural heritage ontologies. Authors intend to expand this work by taking into account more samples from a wider range of artwork types, as currently their proposition is very small scale and specific (Liu et al., 2017).

The study carried out by Fonou-Dombeu and Kazadi (2017) determined and analyzed both the primitive and advanced complexity features of e-government ontologies in the oeGov repository. The analysis of the primitive complexity metrics of oeGov ontologies showed that only the three top level ontologies in the oeGov have classes, properties and instances; a major portion of the oeGov are instances or datasets of the top-level ontologies. However, classification of e-government ontologies based on their level of complexity has not been carried out.

Tan et al. (2017) consider three quality characteristics as crucial and have evaluated them, namely, usability, correctness, and applicability. The application ontology used by them includes knowledge from software requirements in support of the creation of software test cases. In the future, authors aim to design a generic verbalization process, for rendering their tool fit to evaluate other types of ontologies.

Ontology evaluation has been classified into: self-evaluation, context or domain based, application based, task based by Vrandečić (2009). He discusses the various criteria which a good ontology should meet. These criteria are accuracy, adaptability, clarity, completeness, computational efficiency, conciseness, consistency. Vrandečić (2009) proposed six aspects which should be considered in evaluating ontologies using the above-mentioned criteria as follows: Vocabulary, Syntax, Structure, Semantics, Representation and Context. One of the following four values of metrics is possible: verified, not applicable, deferred, and failed. At the end of the evaluation, the value of each metric is accumulated (from the evaluation of the methods of each aspect) and used to summarize the evaluation of the U Ontology by Ashraf et al. (2018).

Raad and Cruz (2015) present an analysis of advantages and limitations of various ontology evaluation methods in an attempt to find an efficient method. Authors group such methods into four categories: gold standard-based, corpus-based, task-based and criteria based. Additionally, they proposed a hybrid technique out of task-based and the gold-standard approaches, which encompasses the maximum number of ontology evaluation criteria. However, the technique lacks tool support.

Bandeira et al. (2016) employ the Goal Question Metric approach to Vrandečić's (2009) metrics, and call it the FOCA method. However, despite being helpful to guide ontology evaluation, it is cumbersome to implement. The approach's validity rests on the established evaluation metrics that it incorporates.

Hlomani and Stacey (2014) present two perspectives of ontology evaluation – ontology correctness and ontology quality, while mentioning measures for metrics in each perspective. The authors also dissected the existing literature on ontology evaluation measures into these two perspectives. Accuracy (precision and recall), completeness, conciseness, and consistency form a part of ontology correctness, while computational efficiency, adaptability (coupling, cohesion, depth of inheritance tree), and clarity are constituents of ontology quality.

Authors have presented a comparative analysis against approaches for computing similarity in the context of WordNet. The experimental results revealed the highest correlation with the results obtained from human experts, which indicates the ability to capture human notion of similarity. Their novel method is a two-step process; first, to leverage a priori knowledge, a domain ontology expert allocates initial weights to each ontology link. Next, an automatic method for computing the conceptual links revises the weights unless a stable condition is reached. Unlike majority of conventional methods, the proposed algorithm computes similarity between concepts in ontologies that may be hidden in their hierarchical or taxonomic structure (Quintero et al., 2018).

McDaniel et al. (2018) propose quality assessment metrics based on semiotic theory, at four levels, namely, syntactic, semantic, pragmatic, and social. The method is flexible as it permits assignment of weights for each level, as well as individual metrics on each level. This is coupled with an automated support to rank them. The results are compared with those by humans, and Protégé. In the future, ontology reuse may be promoted by applying the approach on ontologies from domains such as, Internet of Things, Big Data, artificial intelligence, and machine learning applications.

Sukalikar et al. (2014) assess quality of modular ontology, particularly from the aspects of cohesion and coupling. They extend their work in Kumar et al. (2017) where an exhaustive framework for coupling and cohesion computation for modular ontology is present, along with case study, and analytical validation against various standards. Most of the previous works do not either handle the structure of the ontological hierarchy or ignore the links' importance in an ontology. Kumar et al. (2017) address the subtle differences among link types. Moreover, the proposed approach is analytically validated, thus rendering it a ready to use comprehensive model. Kumar and Baliyan (2018) is a comprehensive take on modular ontology's quality evaluation.

Baliyan and Kumar (2016a) present a semi-automated framework to measure the structural complexity at various layers of ontology. This is in contrast with existing measures, which either handle complexity at schema and instance levels or define subjective parameters. The framework's metrics have been validated against Briand's and Weyuker's criteria. Additionally, experiments have been carried out to demonstrate relative performance of the framework on public ontologies.

Baliyan and Kumar (2016b) suggested evaluating a modular ontology, not just from the aspect of its structure, rather also on the basis of its inherent characteristics that affect its behavior, considerably. Authors survey existing works on ontology metrics aimed at measuring the knowledge contained in ontology. Knowledge encapsulation, link and concept coverage, and depth of subsumption hierarchy have been identified as such metrics. The IEEE 1061 framework has been used to validate the proposed metrics.

FUTURE RESEARCH DIRECTIONS

Authors aim to use more complex real-world ontologies for experimental validation, and compare the results with those estimated by experts (ontology designers), in the future. Additionally, they intend to fully automate the ontology parsing step of metrics calculation. The domain is likely to see evolutionary growth as modular ontologies offer benefits of reuse and hence reduced efforts. Particularly, an automated framework or comprehensive tool-set for modular ontology's quality assessment could be a plausible area of research.

CONCLUSION

Monolithic ontologies are making way for modular ontologies for use in real-world Semantic Web based applications. This chapter focused on quality aspects of modular ontology and presented state-of-the-art of such evaluation metrics, which may be used by ontology designers as well as end users. The only prerequisite for any novel metrics would be appropriate validation via analytical framework and/or experimental studies through sample ontologies. This work also presents a holistic definition of cohesion and coupling for a modularized ontology. It is an enhancement from earlier works as it uses a continuous scale to highlight the slightest variation in the strength of relationships, a feature missing in earlier models. It interprets indirect links that are not apparent in the ontology structure. The model clearly defines a rule-set to identify the strength of various dependency types, even the ones that were unaccounted for in the previous works. The proposed metrics have been validated through standard validation frameworks and they assist the choice among alternative modular ontologies by favouring decreased coupling between partial ontologies (or modules) and increased cohesion within the partial ontology (or module). Consequentially, decreased coupling and increased cohesion offers benefits such as reduced maintenance time and cost.

Table 4. Summary of recent literature on ontology evaluation

Work	Research Question	Methodology	Tool/Experiment	Contribution	Limitation
Khan et al. (2015)	Evaluation of biomedical ontologies	OBO bioportal for retrieving biomedical ontologies	SPARQL queries on Protégé to extract count of data and object properties	Ontologies with higher component density have high expressivity of domain objects	Only properties are considered for ontology evaluation and not concepts
Verma (2016)	Development of a generic ontology evaluation framework	Comprehensive analysis of existing approaches	None, as the model is abstract	Rank alternatives of ontologies as per suitability	Applicability of framework remains questionable without examples
de Oliveira Rodrigues et al. (2017)	An objective implementation towards ontology evaluation	Subjectivity in ontology evaluation ruled out by logic and extending OntoClean	Constraint Logic-based Language	Improved scalability and efficiency of evaluation method	Familiarity with OntoClean is needed to develop tool for proposed method
Lantow (2016)	Overcome limitations of rule-based ontology evaluation to compute ontology metrics	Code to objectively compute ontology metrics	Developed OnoMetrics – an online tool	Seamless and objective evaluation of ontologies	Tool is not open source and open to code modification for enabling customized choice of metrics
Mohan et al. (2017)	Evaluate ontologies in a light-weight yet effective manner	Concept and relationship coverage extent with respect to domain corpus words	Natural Language Processing, case studies on Education and Security domain	Informal and under evaluated ontologies can be evaluated	Caters to small ontologies only
Liu et al. (2017)	Evaluation of cultural heritage ontologies	Evaluate ontologies based on fulfillment of data modeling requirements	Ten metrics based on six criteria	Small scale evaluation of domain ontologies	Rich metadata is a prerequisite for evaluation using this method
Fonou-Dombeu and Kazadi (2017)	Complexity analysis of e-gGovernment ontologies	Complexity metrics computed at two levels: primitive and advanced	28 ontologies from oeGov repository and Jena API is used	Provides insights for selection, use, and maintenance of e-government ontologies	Other e-government ontologies that are not part of oeGov are excluded
Tan et al. (2017)	Evaluation of application ontology from avionics domain	Validation by domain experts and ontology experts, with requirement specification as reference point	Real world ontology created and analyzed in Protégé.	Gives insights about ontology usability, correctness, applicability	Time overhead for training of domain experts
Ashraf et al. (2018)	Evaluation of U ontology, which conceptualizes the ontology usage analysis domain	Adherence to a set of good practices by Vrandečić (2009) (known as specification of the gold standard)	SPARQL	Checks if the ontology developed for representing ontology usage is of an acceptable quality	Exhaustive list of metrics to be computed, hence complexity of the approach increases
Raad and Cruz (2015)	Survey of ontology evaluation methods	Literature review	None	Defined four categories of ontology evaluation methods	No semi-automatic approach to evaluate an ontology
Bandeira et al. (2016)	Assist subjective assessment through step-by-step procedure to objectively evaluate ontologies	Ontology Type Verification, Questions Verification and Quality Verification	Four ontologies used in evaluation scenario	Guidelines and step by step method to ontology evaluation, supported by statistics	Question answering can be exhaustive and involved prejudice of ontology communities.
Hlomaniand Stacey (2014)	Survey to distinguish ontology correctness and quality in its evaluation	Survey	None	Gap analysis in the area of ontology evaluation	The effect of bias on the measures of ontology correctness may be extended to ontology quality
Quintero et al. (2018)	Evaluate inter-conceptual distance or link-weights in an ontology	Considers ontology topology to compute weight of inter-concept links	GEONTO-MET approach to ontology development	Recognizes a variety of links (meronymy, antonymy, functionality and causality)	Comparative evaluation of complexity with existing approaches is needed
McDaniel et al. (2018)	Layered ontology metrics suite	Semiotic theory	Domain ontology ranking system (DoORs) prototype	Facilitates picking best ontology from candidate domain ontologies	Semi-automated assignment of weights appropriate for a task, remains an open issue
Kumar et al. (2017)	Cohesion and coupling metrics for modular ontology	Mathematical formulae as measures and description logics for metric definition	None. Analytical validation against standard quality criteria	Modular ontology's evaluation easy and objective	Domain knowledge needed for customizing the evaluation framework
Baliyan and Kumar (2016a)	Complexity metrics for ontology	Mathematical formulae	Protégé and Swoogle	Layered complexity metrics to assist evaluation	Semi-automated framework needs working knowledge of ontology editors.
Baliyan and Kumar (2016b)	Quantify the behavior of ontology	Review of existing literature for assimilation of metrics	Java for user interface	Behavioral metrics may be applied on any type of ontology or its partition.	Wide adaptation and use of technique by ontology engineers is missing in nascent stage

REFERENCES

Abbès, S. B., Scheuermann, A., Meilender, T., & d'Aquin, M. (2012).Characterizing modular ontologies. In *Seventh International Conference on Formal Ontologies in Information Systems*, Austria, Vienna (pp. 13-25).

Antoniou, G., & Van Harmelen, F. (2004). Web ontology language: Owl. In *Handbook on ontologies* (pp. 67–92). Berlin, Heidelberg: Springer. doi:10.1007/978-3-540-24750-0_4

Ashraf, J., Hussain, O. K., Hussain, F. K., & Chang, E. J. (2018). Evaluation of U Ontology. In *Measuring and Analysing the Use of Ontologies* (pp. 243–268). Cham: Springer. doi:10.1007/978-3-319-75681-3_9

Baliyan, N., & Kumar, S. (2016a). Towards measurement of structural complexity for ontologies. *International Journal of Web Engineering and Technology, 11*(2), 153–173. doi:10.1504/IJWET.2016.077343

Baliyan, N., & Kumar, S. (2016b). A Behavioral Metrics Suite for Modular Ontologies. In *Proceedings of the Second International Conference on Information and Communication Technology for Competitive Strategies* (p. 133). ACM. 10.1145/2905055.2905193

Bandeira, J., Bittencourt, I. I., Espinheira, P., & Isotani, S. (2016). FOCA: A Methodology for Ontology Evaluation. arXiv:1612.03353

Bieman, J. M., & Ott, L. M. (1994). Measuring functional cohesion. *IEEE Transactions on Software Engineering, 20*(8), 644–657. doi:10.1109/32.310673

Brank, J., Grobelnik, M., & Mladenic, D. (2005). A survey of ontology evaluation techniques. In *Proceedings of the Conference on Data Mining and Data Warehouses*.

Brewster, C., Alani, H., Dasmahapatra, S., & Wilks, Y. (2004). Data Driven Ontology Evaluation. In *Proceedings of the Fourth International Conference on Language Resources and Evaluation (LREC'04)*.

Brewster, C., Ciravegna, F., & Wilks, Y. (2001), Knowledge acquisition for knowledge management: Position paper. In *Proceeding of the IJCAI-2001 Workshop on Ontology Learning*, Seattle, WA.

Briand, L. C., Morasca, S., & Basili, V. R. (1996). Property-based software engineering measurement. *IEEE Transactions on Software Engineering, 22*(1), 68–86. doi:10.1109/32.481535

Brickley, D. (2000). Resource Description Framework (RDF) schema specification 1.0, *W3C candidate recommendation*. Retrieved from http://www.w3.org/TR/2000/CR-rdf-schema-20000327

Chidamber, S. R., & Kemerer, C. F. (1994). A metrics suite for object oriented design. *IEEE Transactions on Software Engineering, 20*(6), 476–493. doi:10.1109/32.295895

de Oliveira Rodrigues, C. M., de Freitas, F. L. G., & de Azevedo, R. R. (2017). An Improved Logic-Based Implementation to Ontology Assessment. In *Brazilian Conference on Intelligent Systems* (pp. 408-413). IEEE.

Dou, D., McDermott, D., & Qi, P. (2005). Ontology translation on the semantic web. *Journal on Data Semantics, II*, 35–57.

Ensan, F., & Du, W. (2013). A semantic metrics suite for evaluating modular ontologies. *Information Systems*, *38*(5), 746–770. doi:10.1016/j.is.2012.11.012

Fensel, D., Van Harmelen, F., Horrocks, I., McGuinness, D. L., & Patel-Schneider, P. F. (2001). OIL: An ontology infrastructure for the semantic web. *IEEE Intelligent Systems*, *16*(2), 38–45. doi:10.1109/5254.920598

Fonou-Dombeu, J. V., & Kazadi, Y. K. (2017). Complexity Based Analysis of eGov Ontologies. In *International Conference on Electronic Government and the Information Systems Perspective* (pp. 115-128). Cham: Springer. 10.1007/978-3-319-64248-2_9

Gangemi, A., Catenacci, C., Ciaramita, M., & Lehmann, J. (2005). Ontology evaluation and validation: an integrated formal model for the quality diagnostic task. Retrieved from http://www.loa-cnr.it/Files/OntoEval4OntoDev_Final.pdf

García, J., García, F., & Therón, R. (2010a). Defining coupling metrics among classes in an OWL ontology. In Trends in Applied Intelligent Systems (pp. 12-17). doi:10.1007/978-3-642-13025-0_2

Garcia, J., Garcia, F., & Theron, R. (2010b). Visualising semantic coupling among entities in an OWL ontology. In Ontology, Conceptualization and Epistemology for Information Systems, Software Engineering and Service Science (pp. 90-106). doi:10.1007/978-3-642-16496-5_7

Gómez-Pérez, A. (2004). Ontology evaluation. In *Handbook on ontologies* (pp. 251–273). Springer. doi:10.1007/978-3-540-24750-0_13

Gomez-Perez, A. (1999). Evaluation of taxonomic knowledge in ontologies and knowledge bases. In *Proceedings of the 12th Bannf Knowledge Acquisition for Knowledge-based Systems Workshop*, Banff, Canada.

Gruber, T. R. (1995). Toward principles for the design of ontologies used for knowledge sharing. *International Journal of Human-Computer Studies*, *43*(5-6), 907–928. doi:10.1006/ijhc.1995.1081

Guarino, N. (1998). Some ontological principles for designing upper level lexical resources. In *First International Conference on language resources & evaluation*: Granada, Spain, May 28-30 (pp. 527-534). European Language Resources Association.

Hlomani, H., & Stacey, D. (2014). Approaches, methods, metrics, measures, and subjectivity in ontology evaluation: A survey. *Semantic Web Journal*, *1*(5), 1–11.

Horridge, M., Parsia, B., & Sattler, U. (2009, September). Explaining inconsistencies in OWL ontologies. In *International Conference on Scalable Uncertainty Management* (pp. 124-137). Springer, Berlin, Heidelberg. 10.1007/978-3-642-04388-8_11

Hovy, E. (2001). *Comparing sets of semantic relations. Semantics of Relations*. Dordrecht, NL: Kluwer Academic Publishers.

Kepler, F. N., Paz-Trillo, C., Riani, J., Ribeiro, M. M., Delgado, K. V., de Barros, L. N., & Wassermann, R. (2006, October). *Classifying Ontologies*. WONTO.

Khan, S., Qamar, U., & Muzaffar, A. W. (2015). A Framework for Evaluation of OWL Biomedical Ontologies Based on Properties Coverage. In *13th International Conference on Frontiers of Information Technology* (pp. 59-64). IEEE. 10.1109/FIT.2015.22

Kitchenham, B., Pfleeger, S. L., & Fenton, N. (1995). Towards a framework for software measurement validation. *IEEE Transactions on Software Engineering*, *21*(12), 930–944. doi:10.1109/32.489070

Kumar, S., & Baliyan, N. (2018). Quality Evaluation of Ontologies. In *Semantic Web-Based Systems* (pp. 19–50). Singapore: Springer.

Kumar, S., Baliyan, N., & Sukalikar, S. (2017). Ontology Cohesion and Coupling Metrics. *International Journal on Semantic Web and Information Systems*, *13*(4), 1–26. doi:10.4018/IJSWIS.2017100101

Lantow, B. (2016). OntoMetrics: Putting Metrics into Use for Ontology Evaluation. In *8th International Joint Conference on Knowledge Discovery, Knowledge Engineering and Knowledge Management* (pp. 186-191). 10.5220/0006084601860191

Liu, D., Bikakis, A., & Vlachidis, A. (2017). Evaluation of Semantic Web Ontologies for Modelling Art Collections. In *Advances in Databases and Information Systems* (pp. 343–352). Cham: Springer. doi:10.1007/978-3-319-67162-8_34

Lozano-Tello, A., & Gómez-Pérez, A. (2004). Ontometric: A method to choose the appropriate ontology. *Journal of Database Management*, *2*(15), 1–18. doi:10.4018/jdm.2004040101

Ma, Y., Jin, B., & Feng, Y. (2009). Semantic oriented ontology cohesion metrics for ontology-based systems. *Journal of Systems and Software*, *83*(1), 143–152. doi:10.1016/j.jss.2009.07.047

Maedche, A., & Staab, S. (2001). Ontology learning for the semantic web. *IEEE Intelligent Systems*, *16*(2), 72–79. doi:10.1109/5254.920602

Maedche, A., & Staab, S. (2002, October). Measuring similarity between ontologies. In *International Conference on Knowledge Engineering and Knowledge Management* (pp. 251-263). Springer, Berlin, Heidelberg.

McDaniel, M., Storey, V. C., & Sugumaran, V. (2018). Assessing the quality of domain ontologies: Metrics and an automated ranking system. *Data & Knowledge Engineering*, *115*, 32–47. doi:10.1016/j.datak.2018.02.001

Mohan, L., Prasad, G. V. S., Chimalakonda, S., Reddy, Y. R., & Choppella, V. (2017). A Lightweight Approach for Evaluating Sufficiency of Ontologies In *29th International Conference on Software Engineering and Knowledge Engineering,* Pittsburgh, PA (pp. 557-561).

Obrst, L., Ceusters, W., Mani, I., Ray, S., & Smith, B. (2007). The evaluation of ontologies. In *Semantic web* (pp. 139–158). Boston, MA: Springer. doi:10.1007/978-0-387-48438-9_8

Oh, S., & Ahn, J. (2009, October). Ontology module metrics. In *IEEE International Conference on e-Business Engineering ICEBE'09* (pp. 11-18).

Oh, S., Yeom, H. Y., & Ahn, J. (2011). Cohesion and coupling metrics for ontology modules. *Information Technology Management*, *12*(2), 81–96. doi:10.100710799-011-0094-5

Orme, A. M., Tao, H., & Etzkorn, L. H. (2006). Coupling metrics for ontology-based system. *IEEE Software, 23*(2), 102–108. doi:10.1109/MS.2006.46

Ouyang, L., Zou, B., Qu, M., & Zhang, C. (2011, July).A method of ontology evaluation based on coverage, cohesion and coupling. In *Eighth International Conference on Fuzzy Systems and Knowledge Discovery* (Vol. 4, pp. 2451-2455). 10.1109/FSKD.2011.6020046

Porzel, R., & Malaka, R. (2004, August). A task-based approach for ontology evaluation. In *ECAI Workshop on Ontology Learning and Population*, Valencia, Spain (pp. 1-6).

Quintero, R., Torres-Ruiz, M., Menchaca-Mendez, R., Moreno-Armendariz, M. A., Guzman, G., & Moreno-Ibarra, M. (2018). DIS-C: Conceptual distance in ontologies, a graph-based approach. *Knowledge and Information Systems*, 1–33.

Raad, J., & Cruz, C. (2015). A Survey on Ontology Evaluation Methods. In *7th International Joint Conference on Knowledge Discovery, Knowledge Engineering and Knowledge Management* (pp. 179-186).

Sicilia, M. A., Rodríguez, D., García-Barriocanal, E., & Sánchez-Alonso, S. (2012). Empirical findings on ontology metrics. *Expert Systems with Applications, 39*(8), 6706–6711. doi:10.1016/j.eswa.2011.11.094

Sukalikar, S., Kumar, S., & Baliyan, N. (2014). Analysing cohesion and coupling for modular ontologies. In *International Conference on Advances in Computing, Communications and Informatics* (pp. 2063-2066). IEEE. 10.1109/ICACCI.2014.6968526

Tan, H., Adlemo, A., Tarasov, V., & Johansson, M. E. (2017). Evaluation of an Application Ontology. In *Proceedings of the Joint Ontology Workshops 2017 Episode 3: The Tyrolean Autumn of Ontology*, Bozen-Bolzano, Italy, September 21–23. Rheinisch-Westfaelische Technische Hochschule Aachen* Lehrstuhl Informatik V.

Verma, A. (2016). An abstract framework for ontology evaluation. In *International Conference on Data Science and Engineering* (pp. 1-6). IEEE.

Vrandečić, D. (2009). Ontology evaluation. In *Handbook on ontologies* (pp. 293–313). Berlin, Heidelberg: Springer. doi:10.1007/978-3-540-92673-3_13

Vrandecic, D., & Sure, Y. (2007). How to design better ontology metrics. *Lecture Notes in Computer Science, 45*(19), 311–325. doi:10.1007/978-3-540-72667-8_23

Yao, H., Orme, A. M., & Etzkorn, L. (2005). Cohesion metrics for ontology design and application. *Journal of Computational Science, 1*(1), 107–113. doi:10.3844/jcssp.2005.107.113

Zhang, H., Li, Y. F., & Tan, H. B. K. (2010). Measuring design complexity of semantic web ontologies. *Journal of Systems and Software, 83*(5), 803–814. doi:10.1016/j.jss.2009.11.735

KEY TERMS AND DEFINITIONS

Cohesion: Defines how close the concepts within a module are, to each other.

Coupling: Defines how dependent the concepts of different modules and hence the modules themselves, are on each other.

Metrics: For which there are mathematical formulae and numeric values, measured directly or indirectly.

Modular Ontology: An ontology, which is disintegrable into components.

Monolithic Ontology: An ontology without any levels or layers, easily disconnected on removal of link(s).

Ontology: A vocabulary particular to a domain, application, or task, visualized as a graph of concepts (nodes) and relationships (edges).

Quality: A non-functional yet desirable requirement of software or application to adhere to a threshold of characteristics, stipulated as well-performing.

Compilation of References

52. North Sensor Web Community. (n.d.). Retrieved from http://52north.org

Abbès, S. B., Scheuermann, A., Meilender, T., & d'Aquin, M. (2012).Characterizing modular ontologies. In *Seventh International Conference on Formal Ontologies in Information Systems*, Austria, Vienna (pp. 13-25).

Abdalla, H. I., Amer, A. A., & Mathkour, H. (2014). A Novel Vertical Fragmentation, Replication and Allocation Model in DDBSs. *Journal of Universal Computer Science*, *20*(10), 1469–1487. Retrieved from http://www.jucs.org/jucs_20_10/a_novel_vertical_fragmentation and https://pdfs.semanticscholar.org/4538/62e6e68f24836fcdfc92f66db14b682adda8.pdf

Abdallaha, H. I., Amer, A. A., & Mathkour, H. (2014). Performance optimality enhancement algorithm in DDBS (POEA). *Computers in Human Behavior*, *30*, 419–426. doi:10.1016/j.chb.2013.04.026

Abdel Raouf, A. E., Badr, N., & Tolba, M. F. (2017). Distributed Database System (DSS) Design Over a Cloud Environment. In Multimedia Forensics and Security (pp. 97-116). Cham: Springer. Retrieved from https://link.springer.com/chapter/10.1007/978-3-319-44270-9_5

Abdel Raouf, A. E., Badr, N. L., & Tolba, M. F. (2018). Dynamic data reallocation and replication over a cloud environment. *Concurrency and Computation*. doi:10.1002/cpe.4416

Abedjan, Z., & Naumann, F. (2013). Improving rdf data through association rule mining. *Datenbank-Spektrum*, *13*(2), 111–120. doi:10.100713222-013-0126-x

Abowd, G. D., Dey, A. K., Brown, P. J., Davies, N., Smith, M., & Steggles, P. (1999). Towards a better understanding of context and context-awareness. In Handheld and ubiquitous computing (pp. 304–307). doi:10.1007/3-540-48157-5_29

Aby, A. T., Guitton, A., Lafourcade, P., & Misson, M. (2015, September). SLACK-MAC: Adaptive MAC protocol for low duty-cycle wireless sensor networks. In *International Conference on Ad Hoc Networks, San Remo, Italy*. Cham: Springer. 10.1007/978-3-319-25067-0_6

Achichi, M., Cheatham, M., Dragisic, Z., Euzenat, J., Faria, D., Ferrara, A., ... & Jiménez-Ruiz, E. (2016). Results of the ontology alignment evaluation initiative 2016. In OM: Ontology Matching (pp. 73–129).

Adomavicius, G., & Tuzhilin, A. (2005). Toward the next generation of recommender systems: A survey of the state-of-the-art and possible extensions. *IEEE Transactions on Knowledge and Data Engineering*, *17*(6), 734–749. doi:10.1109/TKDE.2005.99

Aggarwal, C. C., Ashish, N., & Sheth, A. (2013). The internet of things: A survey from the data-centric perspective. In Managing and mining sensor data (pp. 383-428). Springer US. doi:10.1007/978-1-4614-6309-2_12

Agichtein, E., & Gravano, L. (2009). Snowball: extracting relations from large plain-text collections. In *Proc. of ICDL*, New York, NY (pp. 85-94).

Agoulmine, N., Balasubramaniam, S., Botvich, D., Strassner, J., Lehtihet, E., & Donnelly, W. (2006). Challenges for autonomic network management.

Agrawal, R., Mannila, H., Srikant, R., Toivonen, H., & Verkamo, A. I. (1996). Fast discovery of association rules. *Advances in knowledge discovery and data mining, 12*(1), 307-328.

Ahmadi, H., Viani, F., Polo, A., & Bouallegue, R. (2016). An improved anchor selection strategy for wireless localization of WSN nodes. In *2016 IEEE Symposium on Computers and Communication (ISCC)*, pages 108-113. DOI: 10.1109/ISCC.2016.7543723

Ahmedi, L., Jajaga, E., & Ahmedi, F. (2013, October). An ontology framework for water quality management. In *Proceedings of the 6th International Conference on Semantic Sensor Networks-Volume 1063* (pp. 35-50). CEUR-WS.org.

Ahmedi, L., Sejdiu, B., Bytyçi, E., & Ahmedi, F. (2015). An integrated web portal for water quality monitoring through wireless sensor networks. *International Journal of Web Portals, 7*(1), 28–46. doi:10.4018/IJWP.2015010102

Ahn, J., & Amatriain, X. (2010). Towards Fully Distributed and Privacy-Preserving Recommendations via Expert Collaborative Filtering and RESTful Linked Data. In *2010 IEEE/WIC/ACM International Conference on Web Intelligence and Intelligent Agent Technology* (Vol. 1, pp. 66–73). IEEE. 10.1109/WI-IAT.2010.53

Albowicz, J., Chen, A., & Zhang, L. (2001). Recursive position estimation in sensor networks. In *The 9th International Conference on Network Protocols* (pp. 35–41). doi:10.1109/ICNP.2001.992758

Alec, C., Reynaud-Delaitre, C., & Safar, B. (2016). A model for linked open data acquisition and SPARQL query generation. In O. Haemmerle, G. Stapleton, & C. F. Zucker (Eds.), *Graph-Based Representation And Reasoning* (Vol. 9717, pp. 237–251). Cham: Springer. doi:10.1007/978-3-319-40985-6_18

Alfarhood, S., Labille, K., & Gauch, S. (2017). PLDSD: Propagated linked data semantic distance. In *Proceedings - 2017 IEEE 26th International Conference on Enabling Technologies: Infrastructure for Collaborative Enterprises, WETICE 2017* (pp. 278–283). doi:10.1109/WETICE.2017.16

Alfayez, F., Hammoudeh, M., & Abuarqoub, A. (2015). A Survey on MAC Protocols for Duty-cycled Wireless Sensor Networks. *Procedia Computer Science, 73*, 482–489. doi:10.1016/j.procs.2015.12.034

Al-Ghadhban, D., Alnkhilan, E., Tatwany, L., & Alrazgan, M. (2017). Arabic sarcasm detection in Twitter. In *2017 International Conference on Engineering & MIS (ICEMIS)* (pp. 1-7). IEEE.

Alrababah, S. A. A., Gan, K. H., & Tan, T. P. (2017). Mining opinionated product features using WordNet lexicographer files. *Journal of Information Science, 43*(6), 769–785. doi:10.1177/0165551516667651

Altwaijry, H., Kalashnikov, D. V., & Mehrotra, S. (2017). Qda: A query-driven approach to entity resolution. *IEEE Transactions on Knowledge and Data Engineering, 29*(2), 402–417. doi:10.1109/TKDE.2016.2623607

Alvari, H. (2017). Twitter Hashtag Recommendation using Matrix Factorization.

Amer, A. A., & Sewisy, A. A. (2017). An Extended Approach for Synchronized Data Partitioning and Distribution in Distributed Database Systems (DDBSs). *International Journal of Economics and Management Systems, 2*, 161–170. Retrieved from http://www.iaras.org/iaras/home/caijems/an-extended-approach-for-synchronized-data-partitioning-and-distribution-in-distributed-database-systems-ddbss

Amer, A. A., Sewisy, A. A., & Elgendy, T. M. (2017). An optimized approach for simultaneous horizontal data fragmentation and allocation in distributed database systems (DDBSs). *Heliyon (London), 3*(12). doi:10.1016/j.heliyon.2017.e00487

Angles, R., Boncz, P., Larriba-Pey, J., Fundulaki, I., Neumann, T., Erling, O., ... Toma, I. (2014). The linked data benchmark council: A graph and RDF industry benchmarking effort. *SIGMOD Record, 43*(1), 27–31. doi:10.1145/2627692.2627697

Antonić, A., Marjanović, M., Pripužić, K., & Žarko, I. P. (2016). A mobile crowd sensing ecosystem enabled by CUPUS: Cloud-based publish/subscribe middleware for the Internet of Things. *Future Generation Computer Systems, 56*, 22–607. doi:10.1016/j.future.2015.08.005

Antoniou, G., & Van Harmelen, F. (2004). Web ontology language: Owl. In *Handbook on ontologies* (pp. 67–92). Berlin, Heidelberg: Springer. doi:10.1007/978-3-540-24750-0_4

Aomumpai, S., & Prommak, C. (2011). On the Impact of Reference Node Placement in Wireless Indoor Positioning Systems. *International Journal of Computer, Electrical, Automation. Control and Information Engineering, 5*(12), 1704–1708. doi:10.1109/ECTICon.2014.6839894

Aroua, E., & Mourad, A. (2017). An ontology-based framework for enhancing personalized content and retrieval information. In *Proceedings of Int. Conf. on Research Challenges in Information Science* (RCIS) (pp. 276–285). Los Alamitos, CA: IEEE Computer Society Press.

Arrington, M. (2006). AOL proudly releases massive amounts of private data.

Ashraf, J., Hussain, O. K., Hussain, F. K., & Chang, E. J. (2018). Evaluation of U Ontology. In *Measuring and Analysing the Use of Ontologies* (pp. 243–268). Cham: Springer. doi:10.1007/978-3-319-75681-3_9

Ashton, K. (2009). That 'internet of things' thing. *RFiD Journal, 22*(7), 97–114.

Assaf, A., Senart, A., & Troncy, R. (2016). Towards an objective assessment framework for linked data quality: Enriching dataset profiles with quality indicators. *International Journal on Semantic Web and Information Systems, 12*(3), 111–133. doi:10.4018/IJSWIS.2016070104

Atzori, L., Iera, A., & Morabito, G. (2010). The internet of things: A survey. *Computer Networks, 54*(15), 2787–2805. doi:10.1016/j.comnet.2010.05.010

Auer, S., Bryl, V., & Tramp, S. (2014). *Linked open data-creating knowledge out of interlinked data: Results of the LOD2 Project.* Springer.

Ayala, V. A. A., Przyjaciel-Zablocki, M., Hornung, T., Schätzle, A., & Lausen, G. (2014). Extending SPARQL for Recommendations. In Proceedings of Semantic Web Information Management on Semantic Web Information Management (pp. 1–8). doi:10.1145/2630602.2630604

Baliyan, N., & Kumar, S. (2016a). Towards measurement of structural complexity for ontologies. *International Journal of Web Engineering and Technology, 11*(2), 153–173. doi:10.1504/IJWET.2016.077343

Baliyan, N., & Kumar, S. (2016b). A Behavioral Metrics Suite for Modular Ontologies. In *Proceedings of the Second International Conference on Information and Communication Technology for Competitive Strategies* (p. 133). ACM. 10.1145/2905055.2905193

Bamman, D., & Smith, N. A. (2015). Contextualized sarcasm detection on Twitter. In *International Conference on Web and Social Media 2015* (pp. 574–577). AAAI.

Bandeira, J., Bittencourt, I. I., Espinheira, P., & Isotani, S. (2016). FOCA: A Methodology for Ontology Evaluation. arXiv:1612.03353

Barbieri, F., Saggion, H., & Ronzano, F. (2014). Modelling Sarcasm in Twitter, a Novel Approach. In *Proceedings of the 5th Workshop on Computational Approaches to Subjectivity, Sentiment and Social Media Analysis 2014* (pp. 50–58). ACL.

Barnaghi, P., Wang, W., Henson, C., & Taylor, K. (2012). Semantics for the Internet of Things: Early Progress and Back to the Future. *International Journal on Semantic Web and Information Systems, 8*(1), 1–21. doi:10.4018/jswis.2012010101

Baxter, R., Christen, P., & Churches, T. (2003). A comparison of fast blocking methods for record linkage. In ACM SIGKDD (Vol. 3, pp. 25–27).

Bazoobandi, H. R., Beck, H., & Urbani, J. (2017). Expressive stream reasoning with laser. In *International Semantic Web Conference* (pp. 87-103). Cham: Springer.

Beckett, D. (2002). The design and implementation of the Redland RDF application framework. *Computer Networks, 39*(5), 577–588. doi:10.1016/S1389-1286(02)00221-9

Bedogni, L., Bononi, L., Di Felice, M., D'Elia, A., Mock, R., Morandi, F., ... Vergari, F. (2016). An Integrated Simulation Framework to Model Electric Vehicle Operations and Services. *IEEE Transactions on Vehicular Technology, 65*(8), 5900–5917. doi:10.1109/TVT.2015.2453125

Belém, F. M., Almeida, J. M., & Gonçalves, M. A. (2017). A survey on tag recommendation methods. Journal of the Association for Information Science and Technology, 68(4), 830-844.

Belghith, A., & Abid, M. A. (2009). Autonomic self-tunable proactive routing in mobile ad hoc networks. In *Proceedings of the IEEE International Conference on Wireless and Mobile Computing, Networking and Communications* (pp. 276-281). 10.1109/WiMob.2009.54

Belghith, A., Akkari, W., & Bonnin, J. M. (2008). Traffic Aware Power Saving Protocol in Multi-hop Mobile Ad-Hoc Networks. *Journal of Networks, 2*(4), 1–13. doi:10.4304/jnw.2.4.1-13

Bellavista, P., Corradi, A., Fanelli, M., & Foschini, L. (2012). A survey of context data distribution for mobile ubiquitous systems. *ACM Computing Surveys, 44*(4), 24. doi:10.1145/2333112.2333119

Benatallah, B., Venugopal, S., Ryu, S. H., Motahari-Nezhad, H. R., Wang, W., & ... (2017). A systematic review and comparative analysis of cross-document coreference resolution methods and tools. *Computing, 99*(4), 313–349. doi:10.100700607-016-0490-0

Bendadouche, R., Roussey, C., De Sousa, G., Chanet, J. P., & Hou, K. M. (2012). Extension of the semantic sensor network ontology for wireless sensor networks: The stimulus-WSNnode-communication pattern. In *5th International Workshop on Semantic Sensor Networks in conjunction with the 11th International Semantic Web Conference (ISWC)* (pp. 16-p).

Ben-Lhachemi, N., & Nfaoui, E. H. (2018). Using Tweets Embeddings For Hashtag Recommendation in Twitter. *Procedia Computer Science, 127*, 7–15. doi:10.1016/j.procs.2018.01.092

Berglund, A., Boag, S., Chamberlin, D., Fernández, M. F., Kay, M., Robie, J. & Jérôme, S. (2016). XML Path Language (XPath) 2.0 (2nd ed.). *W3C Recommendation*. Retrieved April 4, 2018 from http://www.w3.org/TR/xpath20/

Berners-Lee, T., Hendler, J., & Lassila, O. (2001). The semantic web. *Scientific American, 284*(5), 28–37. doi:10.1038 cientificamerican0501-34 PMID:11341160

Bharti, S. K., Babu, K. S., & Jena, S. K. (2015). Parsing-based Sarcasm Sentiment Recognition in Twitter Data. In *Proceedings of the 2015 IEEE/ACM International Conference on Advances in Social Networks Analysis and Mining 2015* (pp. 1373-1380). ACM. 10.1145/2808797.2808910

Bharti, S. K., Babu, K. S., & Jena, S. K. (2017c). Harnessing Online News for Sarcasm Detection in Hindi Tweets. In *International Conference on Pattern Recognition and Machine Intelligence* (pp. 679-686). Cham: Springer. 10.1007/978-3-319-69900-4_86

Bharti, S. K., Pradhan, R. K., Babu, K. S., & Jena, S. K. (2017a). Sarcasm Analysis on Twitter Data Using Machine Learning Approaches. *Trends in Social Network Analysis: Information Propagation, User Behavior Modeling, Forecasting, and Vulnerability Assessment*, 51–76. doi:10.1007/978-3-319-53420-6_3

Bharti, S. K., Pradhan, R. K., Babu, K. S., & Jena, S. K. (2017b). Sarcastic Sentiment Detection Based on Types of Sarcasm Occurring in Twitter Data. *International Journal on Semantic Web and Information Systems*, *13*(4), 89–108. doi:10.4018/IJSWIS.2017100105

Bharti, S. K., Vachha, B., Pradhan, R. K., Babu, K. S., & Jena, S. K. (2016). Sarcastic sentiment detection in tweets streamed in real time: A big data approach. *Digital Communications and Networks*, *2*(3), 108–121. doi:10.1016/j.dcan.2016.06.002

Bieman, J. M., & Ott, L. M. (1994). Measuring functional cohesion. *IEEE Transactions on Software Engineering*, *20*(8), 644–657. doi:10.1109/32.310673

Bizer, C., & Seaborne, A. (2004, November). D2RQ-treating non-RDF databases as virtual RDF graphs. In *Proceedings of the 3rd international semantic web conference (ISWC2004)*. Springer.

Bizer, C., Heath, T., & Berners-Lee, T. (2009). Linked data-the story so far. In *Semantic Services, Interoperability and Web Applications: Emerging Concepts* (pp. 205-227).

Bizer, C., Heath, T., & Berners-Lee, T. (2009). Linked Data - The Story So Far. *International Journal on Semantic Web and Information Systems*, *5*, 1–22. doi:10.4018/jswis.2009081901

Bizer, C., & Schultz, A. (2009). The Berlin SPARQL Benchmark. *International Journal on Semantic Web and Information Systems*, *5*(2), 1–24. doi:10.4018/jswis.2009040101

Blanco, R., Cambazoglu, B. B., Mika, P., & Torzec, N. (2013). Entity recommendations in web search. In The Semantic Web–ISWC 2013 (pp. 33–48). doi:10.1007/978-3-642-41338-4_3

Bodenreider, O., Smith, B., Kumar, A., & Burgun, A. (2007). Investigating subsumption in SNOMED CT: An exploration into large description logic-based biomedical terminologies. *Artificial Intelligence in Medicine*, *39*(3), 183–195. doi:10.1016/j.artmed.2006.12.003 PMID:17241777

Bogard, D. (2008). Living a dream. Retrieved from https://www.amazon.com/Living-Dream-D-Bogart/dp/1434380076

Bollacker, K., Cook, R., & Tufts, P. (2007). Freebase: A shared database of structured general human knowledge. In *Proceedings of the 22nd AAAI Conference on Artificial Intelligence*, Vancouver, British Columbia, July 22-26 (pp. 1962-1963). AAAI Press.

Bollegala, D. T., Matsuo, Y., & Ishizuka, M. (2010). Relational duality: unsupervised extraction of semantic relations between entities on the web. In *Proceedings of the International Conference on World Wide Web*, Raleigh, North Carolina, April (pp. 151-160). 10.1145/1772690.1772707

Bollen, D. P., Knijnenburg, B. C., Willemsen, M., & Graus, M. (2010). Understanding choice overload in recommender systems. In *Proceedings of the fourth ACM conference on Recommender systems*, 63-70.

Borges, V., & Jeberson, W. (2013). Survey of context information fusion for sensor networks based ubiquitous systems. arXiv:1309.0598

Botts, M., Percivall, G., Reed, C., & Davidson, J. (2006, October). OGC sensor web enablement: Overview and high level architecture. In *International conference on GeoSensor Networks* (pp. 175-190). Springer Berlin Heidelberg.

Bouhdid, B., Akkari, W., & Belghith, A. (2017). Energy-aware cooperative localization approach for wireless sensor networks. In *Proceedings of the IEEE 13th International Conference on Intelligent Computer Communication and Processing* (pp. 429-435). 10.1109/ICCP.2017.8117043

Bouhdid, B., Akkari, W., & Belghith, A. (2017). Low cost recursive localization scheme for high density wireless sensor networks. *International Journal on Semantic Web and Information Systems*, *13*(3), 68–88. doi:10.4018/IJSWIS.2017070104

Boukerche, A., Oliveira, H. A. B. F., Nakamura, E., & Loureiro, A. A. F. (2007). Localization systems for wireless sensor networks. *IEEE Wireless Communications*, *14*(6), 6–12. doi:10.1109/MWC.2007.4407221

Boxwala, A. A., Zeng, Q., Tate, D., Greenes, R. A., & Fairchild, D. G. (2002). Applying Axiomatic Design Methodology to Create Guidelines that are Locally Adaptable. In *Proceedings of the AMIA Symposium*. Philadelphia, PA: Hanley & Belfus, Inc.

Brank, J., Grobelnik, M., & Mladenic, D. (2005). A survey of ontology evaluation techniques. In *Proceedings of the Conference on Data Mining and Data Warehouses*.

Brewster, C., Alani, H., Dasmahapatra, S., & Wilks, Y. (2004). Data Driven Ontology Evaluation. In *Proceedings of the Fourth International Conference on Language Resources and Evaluation (LREC'04)*.

Brewster, C., Ciravegna, F., & Wilks, Y. (2001), Knowledge acquisition for knowledge management: Position paper. In *Proceeding of the IJCAI-2001 Workshop on Ontology Learning*, Seattle, WA.

Briand, L. C., Morasca, S., & Basili, V. R. (1996). Property-based software engineering measurement. *IEEE Transactions on Software Engineering*, *22*(1), 68–86. doi:10.1109/32.481535

Brickley, D. (2000). Resource Description Framework (RDF) schema specification 1.0, *W3C candidate recommendation*. Retrieved from http://www.w3.org/TR/2000/CR-rdf-schema-20000327

Bröring, A., Stasch, C., & Echterhoff, J. (2012). OGC sensor observation service interface standard. *Open Geospatial Consortium Interface Standard*, 12-006.

Bröring, A., Echterhoff, J., Jirka, S., Simonis, I., Everding, T., Stasch, C., ... Lemmens, R. (2011). New generation sensor web enablement. *Sensors*, *11*(3), 2652–2699. doi:10.3390110302652 PMID:22163760

Bujari, A., Furini, M., Mandreoli, F., Martoglia, R., Montangero, M., & Ronzani, D. (2018). Standards, security and business models: key challenges for the IoT scenario. *Mobile Networks and Applications*, *23*(1), 147–154. doi:10.100711036-017-0835-8

Bytyçi, E., Ahmedi, L., & Kurti, A. (2016). Association Rule Mining with Context Ontologies: An Application to Mobile Sensing of Water Quality. In *Metadata and Semantics Research: 10th International Conference, MTSR 2016 Proceedings*, Göttingen, Germany, November 22-25 (pp. 67-78). Springer International Publishing.

Calbimonte, J. P., Jeung, H., Corcho, O., & Aberer, K. (2011, October). Semantic sensor data search in a large-scale federated sensor network. In *Proceedings of the 4th International Conference on Semantic Sensor Networks* (pp. 23-38). CEUR-WS. org.

Calì, A., Capuzzi, S., Dimartino, M. M., & Frosini, R. (2013). Recommendation of text tags in social applications using linked data. In International Conference on Web Engineering, LNCS (Vol. 8295 LNCS, pp. 187–191). doi:10.1007/978-3-319-04244-2_17

Cantador, I., Castells, P., & Bellogín, A. (2011). An enhanced semantic layer for hybrid recommender systems: application to news recommendation. *International Journal on Semantic Web and Information Systems*, 7(1), 44–78. doi:10.4018/jswis.2011010103

Cantador, I., Konstas, I., & Jose, J. M. (2011). Categorising social tags to improve folksonomy-based recommendations. *Journal of Web Semantics*, 9(1), 1–15. doi:10.1016/j.websem.2010.10.001

Cao, Z., Wang, J., Liu, D., Miao, X., Ma, Q., & Mao, X. (2018). Chase++: Fountain-Enabled Fast Flooding in Asynchronous Duty Cycle Networks. In *IEEE Conference on Computer Communications INFOCOM 2018*, Honolulu, HI. IEEE.

Cao, Z., Liu, D., Wang, J., & Zheng, X. (2017). Chase: Taming concurrent broadcast for flooding in asynchronous duty cycle networks. *IEEE/ACM Transactions on Networking*, 25(5), 2872–2885. doi:10.1109/TNET.2017.2712671

Cao, Z., Qin, T., Liu, T.-Y., Tsai, M.-F., & Li, H. (2007). Learning to Rank: From Pairwise Approach to Listwise Approach. In *Proceedings of the 24th international conference on Machine learning*, Corvallis(pp. 129-136). 10.1145/1273496.1273513

Caraballo, A. A. M., Arruda, N. M., Nunes, B. P., Lopes, G. R., & Casanova, M. A. (2014). TRTML - A Tripleset Recommendation Tool Based on Supervised Learning Algorithms. In V. Presutti, E. Blomqvist, R. Troncy et al. (Eds.), The Semantic Web: ESWC 2014 Satellite Events SE - 58 (pp. 413-417). Springer International Publishing. doi:10.1007/978-3-319-11955-7_58

Carafoli, L., Mandreoli, F., Martoglia, R., & Penzo, W. (2017). Streaming tables: native support to streaming data in DBMSs. *IEEE Transactions on Systems, Man, and Cybernetics. Systems*, 47(10), 2768–2782. doi:10.1109/TSMC.2017.2664585

Carrano, R. C., Passos, D., Magalhaes, L. C., & Albuquerque, C. V. (2014). Survey and taxonomy of duty cycling mechanisms in wireless sensor networks. *IEEE Communications Surveys and Tutorials*, 16(1), 181–194. doi:10.1109/SURV.2013.052213.00116

Carvalho, P., Sarmento, L., Silva, M. J., & De Oliveira, E. (2009). Clues for detecting irony in user-generated contents: oh...!! It's so easy;-). In *Proceedings of the 1st international CIKM workshop on Topic-sentiment analysis for mass opinion* (pp. 53-56). ACM. 10.1145/1651461.1651471

Castano, S., Ferrara, A., & Montanelli, S. (2018). Matching Techniques for Data Integration and Exploration: From Databases to Big Data. In A Comprehensive Guide Through the Italian Database Research Over the Last 25 Years (pp. 61–76). Springer.

Chakravarthy, S., Muthuraj, J., Varadarajan, R., & Navathe, S. B. (1994). An objective function for vertically partitioning relations in distributed databases and its analysis. *Journal Distributed and Parallel Databases*, 2(2), 183-207. Retrieved from http://dl.acm.org/citation.cfm?id=180313

Chan, Y. S., & Roth, D. (2010). Exploiting background knowledge for relation extraction. In *Proceedings of the 23rd International Conference on Computational Linguistics* (pp. 152-160).

Chaudhuri, S., Ganjam, K., Ganti, V., & Motwani, R. (2003). Robust and efficient fuzzy match for online data cleaning. In *Proceedings of the 2003 ACM SIGMOD international conference on Management of data* (pp. 313–324). 10.1145/872757.872796

Chaumartin, F. R. (2007). UPAR7: A knowledge-based system for headline sentiment tagging. In *Proceedings of the 4th International Workshop on Semantic Evaluations* (pp. 422-425). ACL. 10.3115/1621474.1621568

Chawuthai, R., Takeda, H., & Hosoya, T. (2015). Link Prediction in Linked Data of Interspecies Interactions Using Hybrid Recommendation Approach. In T. Supnithi, T. Yamaguchi, J.Z. Pan (Eds.), Semantic Technology SE - 9 (Vol. 8943, pp. 113–128). Springer International Publishing. doi:10.1007/978-3-319-15615-6_9

Cheekula, S. K., Kapanipathi, P., Doran, D., & Jain, P. (2015). Entity Recommendations Using Hierarchical Knowledge Bases. In *Proceedings of the 4th Workshop on Knowledge Discovery and Data Mining Meets Linked Open Data co-located with 12th Extended Semantic Web Conference (ESWC 2015)*. Retrieved from http://ceur-ws.org/Vol-1365/

Chen, H., Finin, T., & Joshi, A. (2005). *Semantic web in the context broker architecture*.

Chen, Y., Zheng, Q., & Chen, P. (2015). Feature assembly method for extracting relations in Chinese. *Artificial Intelligence*, *228*(C), 179-194. Retrieved from http://crfpp.googlecode.com/svn/trunk/doc/index.html

Chen, C., & Lin, T. C. (2013). A Low-Cost Anchor Placement Strategy for Range-Free Localization Problems in Wireless Sensor Networks. *International Journal of Distributed Sensor Networks*, 1–12. doi:10.5121/ijcnc.2011.3607

Cheng, G., & Qu, Y. (2009). Searching linked objects with Falcons: Approach, implementation and evaluation. *Semantic Services Interoperability & Web Applications Emerging Concepts*, *5*(3), 49–70.

Cheng, L., Niu, J., Luo, C., Shu, L., Kong, L., Zhao, Z., & Gu, Y. (2018). Towards minimum-delay and energy-efficient flooding in low-duty-cycle wireless sensor networks. *Computer Networks*, *134*, 66–77. doi:10.1016/j.comnet.2018.01.012

Chen, H., Finin, T., Joshi, A., Kagal, L., Perich, F., & Chakraborty, D. (2004). Intelligent agents meet the semantic web in smart spaces. *IEEE Internet Computing*, *8*(6), 69–79. doi:10.1109/MIC.2004.66

Chicaiza, J., Piedra, N., López-Vargas, J., & Tovar-Edmundo. (2014). Domain Categorization of Open Educational Resources Based on Linked Data. In *Knowledge Engineering and the Semantic Web*, (January).

Chidamber, S. R., & Kemerer, C. F. (1994). A metrics suite for object oriented design. *IEEE Transactions on Software Engineering*, *20*(6), 476–493. doi:10.1109/32.295895

Chirita, P.-A., Idreos, S., Koubarakis, M., & Nejdl, W. (2004). Publish/subscribe for rdf-based p2p networks. In The Semantic Web: Research and Applications (pp. 182–197). Springer.

Chow, J. C. K., Peter, M., Scaioni, M., & Al-Durgham, M. (2018). Indoor tracking, mapping, and navigation: algorithms, technologies, and applications. *Journal of Sensors*, *2018*, 1–89. doi:10.1155/2018/5971752

Christen, P., & Winkler, W. E. (2016). Record Linkage. In Encyclopedia of Machine Learning and Data Mining.

Christen, P. (2008). Febrl-: an open source data cleaning, deduplication and record linkage system with a graphical user interface. In *Proceedings of the 14th ACM SIGKDD international conference on Knowledge discovery and data mining* (pp. 1065–1068). 10.1145/1401890.1402020

Ciobanu, G., Horne, R., & Sassone, V. (2016). A descriptive type foundation for RDF Schema. *Journal of Logical and Algebraic Methods in Programming*, *85*(5), 681–706. doi:10.1016/j.jlamp.2016.02.006

Clark, H. H. (1996). Using language. In *Google books*. Cambridge University Press. doi:10.1017/CBO9780511620539

Codescu, M., Mossakowski, T., & Kutz, O. (2017). A Categorical Approach to Networks of Aligned Ontologies. *Journal on Data Semantics*, *6*(4), 155–197. doi:10.100713740-017-0080-0

Compton, M., Barnaghi, P., Bermudez, L., García-Castro, R., Corcho, O., Cox, S., ... Taylor, K. (2012). The SSN ontology of the W3C semantic sensor network incubator group. *Journal of Web Semantics*, *17*, 25–32. doi:10.1016/j.websem.2012.05.003

Conover, H., Goodman, H. M., Zavodsky, B., Regner, K., Maskey, M., Lu, J., ... Berthiau, G. (2008). Intelligent Assimilation of Satellite Data into a Forecast Model Using Sensor Web Processes and Protocols. In *Earth Science Technology Conference*.

Cox, S. (2011). Observations and measurements-xml implementation (OGC document).

Cremonesi, P., Turrin, R., Lentini, E., & Matteucci, M. (2008, November 17-19). An Evaluation Methodology for Collaborative Recommender Systems. In *International Conference on Automated solutions for Cross Media Content and Multi-channel Distribution, 2008. AXMEDIS '08, Florence*, Italy (pp. 224 – 231). 10.1109/AXMEDIS.2008.13

Cui, L., Xu, C., Li, G., Ming, Z., Feng, Y., & Lu, N. (2018). A high accurate localization algorithm with DV-Hop and differential evolution for wireless sensor network. *Applied Soft Computing, 68*, 39–52. doi:10.1016/j.asoc.2018.03.036

Culotta, A., & Sorensen, J. (2004), Dependency tree kernels for relation extraction. In *Proc. of ACL*, Barcelona, Spain (pp. 423-429).

Cygankiak, R. (2014). *Best practices for publishing linked data*. World Wide Web Consortium.

D'Elia, A., Aguzzi, C., Viola, F., Antoniazzi, F., & Cinotti, T. S. (2017). Implementation and evaluation of the last will primitive in a semantic information broker for IoT applications. In*IEEE 3rd International Forum on Research and Technologies for Society and Industry (RTSI)*, Modena (pp. 1-5) 10.1109/RTSI.2017.8065947

D'Elia, A., Roffia, L., Zamagni, G., Vergari, F., Toninelli, A., & Bellavista, P. (2010). Smart applications for the maintenance of large buildings: How to achieve ontology-based interoperability at the information level. In *Proceedings - IEEE Symposium on Computers and Communications* (pp. 1077–1082).

D'Elia, A., Viola, F., Roffia, L., Azzoni, P., & Cinotti, T. S. (2017). Enabling Interoperability in the Internet of Things: A OSGi Semantic Information Broker Implementation. *Int. J. on Semantic Web and Information Systems, 13*(1), 147–167. doi:10.4018/IJSWIS.2017010109

Damljanovic, D., Stankovic, M., & Laublet, P. (2012). Linked Data-Based Concept Recommendation: Comparison of Different Methods in Open Innovation Scenario. In E. Simperl, P. Cimiano, A. Polleres, O. Corcho, & V. Presutti (Eds.), *The Semantic Web: Research and Applications,* Heraklion, Crete, Greece (pp. 24–38). Springer Berlin Heidelberg. Retrieved from http://link.springer.com/chapter/10.1007/978-3-642-30284-8_9 doi:10.1007/978-3-642-30284-8_9

Dan, B., & Guha, R. V. (2004). RDF vocabulary description language 1.0: RDF schema. *W3C Recommendation 10 February 2004*. Retrieved from http://www.w3.org/TR/2004/REC-rdf- schema-20040210/

Darakeha, F., Khanib, G. R. M., & Azmic, P. (2018). DCRL-WSN: A distributed cooperative and range-free localization algorithm for WSNs. *AEÜ. International Journal of Electronics and Communications*, 1–21. doi:10.1016/j.aeue.2018.05.015

Davidov, D., Tsur, O., & Rappoport, A. (2010). Semi-supervised recognition of sarcastic sentences in twitter and amazon. In *Proceedings of the Fourteenth Conference on Computational Natural Language Learning* (pp. 107-116). ACL.

de Assis Costa, G., & de Oliveira, J. M. P. (2016). A blocking scheme for entity resolution in the semantic web. In *2016 IEEE 30th international conference on Advanced Information networking and applications (AINA)* (pp. 1138–1145).

De Bra, P. (2017). Challenges in User Modeling and Personalization. *IEEE Intelligent Systems, 32*(5), 76–80. doi:10.1109/MIS.2017.3711638

de Oliveira Rodrigues, C. M., de Freitas, F. L. G., & de Azevedo, R. R. (2017). An Improved Logic-Based Implementation to Ontology Assessment. In *Brazilian Conference on Intelligent Systems* (pp. 408-413). IEEE.

De, D., Tang, S., Song, W. Z., Cook, D., & Das, S. K. (2012). ActiSen: Activity-aware sensor network in smart environments. *Pervasive and Mobile Computing, 8*(5), 730–750. doi:10.1016/j.pmcj.2011.12.005

Dell'Aglio, D., Celino, I., & Cerizza, D. (2010). *Anatomy of a Semantic Web-enabled Knowledge-based Recommender System. In 4th international workshop Semantic Matchmaking and Resource Retrieval in the Semantic Web, at ISWC,* Bonn, Germany. (Vol. 667, pp. 115–130). Retrieved from http://citeseerx.ist.psu.edu/viewdoc/download?rep=rep1&type=pdf&doi=10.1.1.204.3679

Devaraju, A., & Kauppinen, T. (2012). Sensors tell more than they sense: Modeling and reasoning about sensor observations for understanding weather events. *International Journal of Sensors Wireless Communications and Control, 2*(1), 14–26. doi:10.2174/2210327911202010014

Di Noia, T., Mirizzi, R., Ostuni, V. C., & Romito, D. (2012). Exploiting the web of data in model-based recommender systems. In *6th ACM conference on Recommender systems - RecSys '12* (p. 253). New York, NY: ACM Press. 10.1145/2365952.2366007

Ding, Y., Tian, H., & Han, G. (2012). A Distributed Node Localization Algorithm for Wireless Sensor Network Based on MDS and SDP. In *Proceedings of the 2012 International Conference on Computer Science and Electronics Engineering* (pp. 624-628). 10.1109/ICCSEE.2012.93

Dinh, T., Kim, Y., Gu, T., & Vasilakos, A. V. (2016). L-MAC: A wake-up time self-learning MAC protocol for wireless sensor networks. *Computer Networks, 105*, 33–46. doi:10.1016/j.comnet.2016.05.015

Dong, C. & Yu, F. (2017). A prediction-based asynchronous MAC protocol for heavy traffic load in wireless sensor networks. *International Journal of Electronics and Communications.*

Dou, D., McDermott, D., & Qi, P. (2005). Ontology translation on the semantic web. *Journal on Data Semantics, II*, 35–57.

Draisbach, U., & Naumann, F. (2010). DuDe: The duplicate detection toolkit. In *Proceedings of the International Workshop on Quality in Databases (QDB).*

Duan, R., Fang, D., & Chen, X. (2015, August). A wakeup adapting traffic and receiver-initiated duty cycle protocol for wsn. In *2015 IEEE Ubiquitous Intelligence and Computing and 2015 IEEE 12th Intl Conf on Autonomic and Trusted Computing and 2015 IEEE 15th Intl Conf on Scalable Computing and Communications and Its Associated Workshops (UIC-ATC-ScalCom),* Beijing, China (pp. 1753-1759). IEEE. 10.1109/UIC-ATC-ScalCom-CBDCom-IoP.2015.318

Duc, T. L., Le, D. T., Zalyubovskiy, V. V., Kim, D. S., & Choo, H. (2017). Towards broadcast redundancy minimization in duty-cycled wireless sensor networks. *International Journal of Communication Systems, 30*(6), e3108. doi:10.1002/dac.3108

Dunning, T. E., Kindig, B. D., Joshlin, S. C., & Archibald, C. P. (2011). *Associating and linking compact disc metadata.* Google Patents.

Echterhoff J. (2011) Open Geospatial Consortium. OpenGIS SWE Service Model Implementation Standard. *Open Geospatial Consoritum*, 155.

Efron, M., Organisciak, P., & Fenlon, K. (2012). Improving retrieval of short texts through document expansion. In *SIGIR '12 Proceedings of the 35th international ACM SIGIR conference on Research and development in information retrieval,* Portland, WA.

Efthymiou, V., Papadakis, G., Papastefanatos, G., Stefanidis, K., & Palpanas, T. (2017). Parallel meta-blocking for scaling entity resolution over big heterogeneous data. *Information Systems, 65*, 137–157. doi:10.1016/j.is.2016.12.001

Elmagarmid, A., Ilyas, I. F., Ouzzani, M., Quiané-Ruiz, J.-A., Tang, N., & Yin, S. (2014). NADEEF/ER: Generic and interactive entity resolution. In *Proceedings of the 2014 ACM SIGMOD international conference on Management of data* (pp. 1071–1074). 10.1145/2588555.2594511

Enríquez, J. G., Domínguez-Mayo, F. J., Escalona, M. J., Ross, M., & Staples, G. (2017). Entity reconciliation in big data sources: A systematic mapping study. *Expert Systems with Applications*, *80*, 14–27. doi:10.1016/j.eswa.2017.03.010

Ensan, F., & Du, W. (2013). A semantic metrics suite for evaluating modular ontologies. *Information Systems*, *38*(5), 746–770. doi:10.1016/j.is.2012.11.012

Enwald, H. (2013). *Tailoring Health Communication* [Doctoral dissertation]. University of Oulu, Finland. Retrieved April 4, 2018 from http://jultika.oulu.fi/files/isbn9789526202792.pdf

Erhardt, L. R., & Gotto, A. Jr. (2006). The evolution of European guidelines: Changing the management of cholesterol levels. *Atherosclerosis*, *185*(1), 12–20. doi:10.1016/j.atherosclerosis.2005.10.001 PMID:16309687

Erling, O., & Mikhailov, I. (2009). RDF Support in the Virtuoso DBMS. In *Networked Knowledge-Networked Media* (pp. 7–24). Springer. doi:10.1007/978-3-642-02184-8_2

Eshghi, K., Rajaram, S. S., Dagli, C., & Cohen, I. (2015). *Identifying related objects in a computer database*. Google Patents.

Esposito, C., Ficco, M., Palmieri, F., & Castiglione, A. (2015). A knowledge-based platform for Big Data analytics based on publish/subscribe services and stream processing. *Knowledge-Based Systems*, *79*, 3–17. doi:10.1016/j.knosys.2014.05.003

Eteläperä, M., Kiljander, J., & Keinänen, K. (2011). Feasibility Evaluation of M3 Smart Space Broker Implementations. In *2011 IEEE/IPSJ 11th International Symposium on Applications and the Internet (SAINT)* (pp. 292–296). 10.1109/SAINT.2011.56

Eugster, P. T., Felber, P. A., Guerraoui, R., & Kermarrec, A.-M. (2003). The many faces of publish/subscribe. *ACM Computing Surveys*, *35*(2), 114–131. doi:10.1145/857076.857078

Felfernig, A., Jeran, M., Ninaus, G., Reinfrank, F., & Reiterer, S. (2013). Toward the Next Generation of Recommender Systems: Applications and Research Challenges. In *Multimedia Services in Intelligent Environments* (pp. 81–98). Springer. Retrieved from http://link.springer.com/chapter/10.1007/978-3-319-00372-6_5#

Fellegi, I. P., & Sunter, A. B. (1969). A Theory for Record Linkage. *Journal of the American Statistical Association*, *64*(328), 1183–1210. doi:10.1080/01621459.1969.10501049

Fensel, D., Van Harmelen, F., Horrocks, I., McGuinness, D. L., & Patel-Schneider, P. F. (2001). OIL: An ontology infrastructure for the semantic web. *IEEE Intelligent Systems*, *16*(2), 38–45. doi:10.1109/5254.920598

Figueroa, C. (2017). *Recommender Systems based on Linked Data*. Politecnico di Torino - Universidad del Cauca; doi:10.6092/polito/porto/2669963

Figueroa, C., Vagliano, I., Rocha, O. R., Torchiano, M., Zucker, C. F., Corrales, J.-C. C., & Morisio, M. (2017). Allied: A framework for executing linked data-based recommendation algorithms. *International Journal on Semantic Web and Information Systems*, *13*(4), 134–154. doi:10.4018/IJSWIS.2017100107

Figueroa, C., Vagliano, I., Rodríguez Rocha, O., & Morisio, M. (2015). A systematic literature review of Linked Data-based recommender systems. *Concurrency and Computation*, *27*(17), 4659–4684. doi:10.1002/cpe.3449

Filatova, E. (2012). Irony and Sarcasm: Corpus Generation and Analysis Using Crowdsourcing. In LREC (pp. 392-398).

Filatova, E. (2017). Sarcasm Detection Using Sentiment Flow Shifts. In *Proceedings of the Thirtieth International Florida Artificial Intelligence Research Society Conference* (pp. 264-269), AAAI.

Fisher, J., Christen, P., Wang, Q., & Rahm, E. (2015). A clustering-based framework to control block sizes for entity resolution. In *Proceedings of the 21th ACM SIGKDD International Conference on Knowledge Discovery and Data Mining* (pp. 279–288). 10.1145/2783258.2783396

Fonou-Dombeu, J. V., & Kazadi, Y. K. (2017). Complexity Based Analysis of eGov Ontologies. In *International Conference on Electronic Government and the Information Systems Perspective* (pp. 115-128). Cham: Springer. 10.1007/978-3-319-64248-2_9

Fridsma, D. B., Gennari, J. H., & Musen, M. A. (1996). Making Generic Guidelines Site-specific. In *Proceedings of the AMIA Symposium*. Philadelphia, PA: Hanley & Belfus, Inc.

Frontini, F., Brando, C., & Ganascia, J.-G. (2015). Domain-adapted named-entity linker using Linked Data. In *Workshop on NLP Applications: Completing the Puzzle co-located with the 20th International Conference on Applications of Natural Language to Information Systems (NLDB 2015)*.

Gad El-Rab, W., Zaïane, O. R., & El-Hajj, M. (2017). Formalizing clinical practice guideline for clinical decision support systems. *Health Informatics Journal*, *23*(2), 146–156. doi:10.1177/1460458216632272 PMID:26951569

Gangemi, A., Catenacci, C., Ciaramita, M., & Lehmann, J. (2005). Ontology evaluation and validation: an integrated formal model for the quality diagnostic task. Retrieved from http://www.loa-cnr.it/Files/OntoEval4OntoDev_Final.pdf

Ganz, F., Barnaghi, P., Carrez, F., & Moessner, K. (2011, July). Context-aware management for sensor networks. In *Proceedings of the 5th International Conference on Communication System software and middleware*, Verona, Italy (p. 6). ACM.

Gao, C., Cheng, Q., Li, X., & Xia, S. (2018). Cloud-assisted privacy-preserving profile-matching scheme under multiple keys in mobile social network. *Cluster Computing*, 1–9.

García, J., García, F., & Therón, R. (2010a). Defining coupling metrics among classes in an OWL ontology. In Trends in Applied Intelligent Systems (pp. 12-17). doi:10.1007/978-3-642-13025-0_2

Garcia, J., Garcia, F., & Theron, R. (2010b). Visualising semantic coupling among entities in an OWL ontology. In Ontology, Conceptualization and Epistemology for Information Systems, Software Engineering and Service Science (pp. 90-106). doi:10.1007/978-3-642-16496-5_7

Garcìa-Castro, R. (2013). *Web Semantics: Science, Services and Agents on the World Wide Web*.

García, M., & Gamallo, P. (2011). Evaluating various linguistic features on semantic relation extraction. *Proc. of RANLP*, Hissar, Bulgaria (pp. 721-726).

Ghrab, D., Jemili, I., Belghith, A., & Mosbah, M. (2016, April). Study of context-awareness efficiency applied to duty-cycled wireless sensor networks. In *2016 IEEE Wireless Communications and Networking Conference (WCNC)*, Doha (pp. 1-6). IEEE. 10.1109/WCNC.2016.7564865

Ghrab, D., Jemili, I., Belghith, A., & Mosbah, M. (2018). Context-aware MAC protocols in Wireless Sensor Networks. *Internet Technologies Letters, e43*.

Ghrab, D., Jemili, I., Belghith, A., & Mosbah, M. (2015, August). ECAB: An Efficient Context-Aware multi-hop Broadcasting protocol for wireless sensor networks. In *2015 International Wireless Communications and Mobile Computing Conference (IWCMC)*, Dubrovnik, Croatia (pp. 1023-1029). IEEE. 10.1109/IWCMC.2015.7289223

Gibbs, R. W., & Colston, H. L. (2007). *Irony in language and thought: A cognitive science reader*. Psychology Press.

Gibbs, R. W. Jr, & O'Brien, J. (1991). Psychological aspects of irony understanding. *Journal of Pragmatics*, *16*(6), 523–530. doi:10.1016/0378-2166(91)90101-3

Giora, R. (1995). On irony and negation. *Discourse Processes*, *19*(2), 239–264. doi:10.1080/01638539509544916

Giusto, D., Iera, A., Morabito, G., & Atzori, L. (Eds.). (2010). *The internet of things: 20th Tyrrhenian workshop on digital communications*. Springer Science & Business Media.

Godin, F., Slavkovikj, V., De Neve, W., Schrauwen, B., & Van de Walle, R. (2013). Using Topic Models for Twitter Hashtag Recommendation. In *Proceedings of the 22nd International Conference on World Wide Web* (pp. 593-596). 10.1145/2487788.2488002

Golbreich, C., Wallace, E. K., Patel-Schneider, P. F., Golbreich, C., Wallace, E. K., & Patel-Schneider, P. F. (2009). OWL 2 Web Ontology Language New Features and Rationale. *W3C Recommendation*. Retrieved from http://www.w3.org/TR/2009/REC-owl2-new-features-20091027/

Gomez-Perez, A. (1999). Evaluation of taxonomic knowledge in ontologies and knowledge bases. In *Proceedings of the 12th Bannf Knowledge Acquisition for Knowledge-based Systems Workshop*, Banff, Canada.

Gómez-Pérez, A. (2004). Ontology evaluation. In *Handbook on ontologies* (pp. 251–273). Springer. doi:10.1007/978-3-540-24750-0_13

Gómez-Pimpollo, J. F., & Otaolea, R. (2010). Smart Objects for Intelligent Applications-ADK. In *2010 IEEE Symposium on Visual Languages and Human-Centric Computing (VL/HCC)* (pp. 267–268). 10.1109/VLHCC.2010.52

González-Ferrer, A., ten Teije, A., Fdez-Olivares, J., & Milian, K. (2013). Automated generation of patient-tailored electronic care pathways by translating computer-interpretable guidelines into hierarchical task networks. *Artificial Intelligence in Medicine*, *57*(2), 91–109. doi:10.1016/j.artmed.2012.08.008 PMID:23177024

González-Ibánez, R., Muresan, S., & Wacholder, N. (2011). Identifying sarcasm in Twitter: a closer look. In *Proceedings of the 49th Annual Meeting of the Association for Computational Linguistics: Human Language Technologies: short papers* (Vol. 2, pp. 581-586). ACL.

Gordea, S., Lindley, A., & Graf, R. (2011). Computing Recommendations for Long Term Data Accessibility basing on Open Knowledge and Linked Data. In *RecSys 2011 Workshop on Human Decision Making in Recommender Systems affiliated with the 5th ACM Conference on Recommender Systems,* Chicago, IL (pp. 1–8). Retrieved from http://ceur-ws.org/Vol-811/paper8.pdf

Grandi, F. (2013). Dynamic Multi-version Ontology-based Personalization. In *Proceedings of the 2nd International Workshop on Querying Graph Structured Data* (GraphQ). New York, NY: ACM Press, pp. 224–232.

Grandi, F., Mandreoli, F., Martoglia, R., & Penzo, W. (2017b). A Relational Algebra for Streaming Tables Living in a Temporal Database World. In *Proceedings of 24th International Symposium on Temporal Representation and Reasoning* (TIME 2017), Dagstuhl, Germany (pp. 15:1–15:17).

Grandi, F. (2012). Introducing an Annotated Bibliography on Temporal and Evolution Aspects in the Semantic Web. *SIGMOD Record*, *41*(4), 18–21. doi:10.1145/2430456.2430460

Grandi, F. (2016). Dynamic Class Hierarchy Management for Multi-version Ontology-based Personalization. *Journal of Computer and System Sciences*, *82*(1), 69–90. doi:10.1016/j.jcss.2015.06.001

Grandi, F., Mandreoli, F., & Martoglia, R. (2009). Issues in Personalized Access to Multi-version XML Documents. In E. Pardede (Ed.), *Open and Novel Issues in XML Database Applications* (pp. 199–230). Hershey, PA: IGI Global. doi:10.4018/978-1-60566-308-1.ch010

Grandi, F., Mandreoli, F., & Martoglia, R. (2012). Efficient management of multi-version clinical guidelines. *Journal of Biomedical Informatics*, *45*(6), 1120–1136. doi:10.1016/j.jbi.2012.07.005 PMID:22890019

Grandi, F., Mandreoli, F., & Martoglia, R. (2017a). Multi-version Ontology-based Personalization of Clinical Guidelines for Patient-centric Healthcare. *International Journal on Semantic Web and Information Systems*, *13*(1), 104–127. doi:10.4018/IJSWIS.2017010107

Grandi, F., Mandreoli, F., Martoglia, R., Ronchetti, E., Scalas, M. R., & Tiberio, P. (2009). Ontology-Based Personalization of E-Government Services. In P. Germanakos & C. Mourlas (Eds.), *Intelligent User Interfaces: Adaptation and Personalization Systems and Technologies* (pp. 167–187). Hershey, PA: IGI Global. doi:10.4018/978-1-60566-032-5.ch008

Grandi, F., & Scalas, M. R. (2009). The Valid Ontology: a Simple OWL Temporal Versioning Framework. In *Proceedings of the 3rd Int. Conf. on Advances in Semantic Processing (SEMAPRO)*. Los Alamitos, CA: IEEE Computer Society Press, pp. 98–102. 10.1109/SEMAPRO.2009.12

Groot, P., Hommerson, A., & Lucas, P. (2008). Adaptation of Clinical Practice Guidelines. In A. Ten Teije, S. Miksch, & P. Lucas (Eds.), *Computer-based Medical Guidelines and Protocols: A Primer and Current Trends* (pp. 121–139). Amsterdam, The Netherlands: IOS Press.

Gruber, T. R. (1995). Toward principles for the design of ontologies used for knowledge sharing. *International Journal of Human-Computer Studies*, *43*(5-6), 907–928. doi:10.1006/ijhc.1995.1081

Guarino, N. (1998). Some ontological principles for designing upper level lexical resources. In *First International Conference on language resources & evaluation*: Granada, Spain, May 28-30 (pp. 527-534). European Language Resources Association.

Gubbi, J., Buyya, R., Marusic, S., & Palaniswami, M. (2013). Internet of Things (IoT): A vision, architectural elements, and future directions. *Future Generation Computer Systems*, *29*(7), 1645–1660. doi:10.1016/j.future.2013.01.010

Gui, L., Val, T., Wei, A., & Dalce, R. (2015). Improvement of range-free localization technology by a novel DV-hop protocol in wireless sensor networks. *Ad Hoc Networks*, *24*, 55–73. doi:10.1016/j.adhoc.2014.07.025

Gulzar, Z. & Anny Leema, A. (2017). Ontology based classification of computer science domain to support personalization. *Journal of Advanced Research in Dynamical and Control Systems, 9*(6), 493–511.

Gündogan, C., Kietzmann, P., Schmidt, T. C. & Wählisch M. (2018). HoPP: Robust and Resilient Publish-Subscribe for an Information-Centric Internet of things.

Guo, S., He, L., Gu, Y., Jiang, B., & He, T. (2014). Opportunistic flooding in low-duty-cycle wireless sensor networks with unreliable links. *IEEE Transactions on Computers*, *63*(11), 2787–2802. doi:10.1109/TC.2013.142

Guo, Y., Pan, Z., & Heflin, J. (2005). LUBM: A Benchmark for OWL Knowledge Base Systems. *Journal of Web Semantics*, *3*(2-3), 158–182. doi:10.1016/j.websem.2005.06.005

Guo, Y., Qasem, A., Pan, Z., & Heflin, J. (2007). A Requirements Driven Framework for Benchmarking Semantic Web Knowledge Base Systems. *Knowledge and Data Engineering. IEEE Transactions on*, *19*(2), 297–309. doi:10.1109/TKDE.2007.19

Guo, Y., Qin, B., Li, Y., Liu, T., & Li, S. (2013). Improving Candidate Generation for Entity Linking. In *18th International Conference on Applications of Natural Language to Information Systems, NLDB 2013*, Salford, UK (pp. 225-236).

Gyrard, A., Patel, P., Datta, S., & Ali, M. (2016, October). Semantic web meets internet of things (iot) and web of things (wot). In *The 15th International Conference on Semantic Web (ISWC)*.

Haag, F., Lohmann, S., Siek, S., & Ertl, T. (2015). QueryVOWL: A visual query notation for linked data. In F. Gandon, C. Gueret, S. Villata et al. (Eds.), Semantic Web: Eswc 2015 Satellite Events (pp. 387-402). Cham: Springer Int. Publishing Ag. doi:10.1007/978-3-319-25639-9_51

Hadj Taieb, M. A., Ben Aouicha, M., Tmar, M., & Hamadou, A. B. (2011). New information content metric and nominalization relation for a new WordNet-based method to measure the semantic relatedness. In *2011 IEEE 10th International Conference on Cybernetic Intelligent Systems (CIS)*. doi:10.1109/CIS.2011.6169134

Hajra, A., Latif, A., & Tochtermann, K. (2014). Retrieving and Ranking Scientific Publications from Linked Open Data Repositories. In *Proceedings of the 14th International Conference on Knowledge Technologies and Data-driven Business* (p. 29:1--29:4). New York, NY: ACM. 10.1145/2637748.2638436

Hakimov, S., Oto, S. A., & Dogdu, E. (2012). Named entity recognition and disambiguation using linked data and graph-based centrality scoring. In *Proceedings of the 4th International Workshop on Semantic Web Information Management*. ACM. 10.1145/2237867.2237871

Halder, S., & Ghosal, A. (2016). A survey on mobility-assisted localization techniques in wireless sensor networks. *Journal of Network and Computer Applications, 60*, 82–94. doi:10.1016/j.jnca.2015.11.019

Hall, P. A. V., & Dowling, G. R. (1980). Approximate string matching. *ACM Computing Surveys, 12*(4), 381–402. doi:10.1145/356827.356830

Hamza, H. S., Enas Ashraf, A. K., Nabih, M. M. A., Ahmed, M., Alaa, S., Hosny, K., … Attallah, A. (2014). SALE--An Innovative Platform for Semantically Enriching Next Generation Advertising Services. *Social Media and Publicity, 53*.

Han, G., Choi, D., & Lim, W. (2009). Reference node placement and selection algorithm based on trilateration for indoor sensor networks. *Wireless Communications and Mobile Computing, 9*(8), 1017–1027. doi:10.1002/wcm.651

Harris, B. S., & Seaborne, A. (2010). SPARQL 1.1 query. *W3C*. Retrieved from http://www.w3.org/TR/2009/WD-sparql11-query-20091022

Harron, K., Goldstein, H., & Dibben, C. (2015). *Methodological developments in data linkage*. John Wiley & Sons. doi:10.1002/9781119072454

Harth, A., Hose, K., & Schenkel, R. (2014). *Linked data management*. CRC Press/Taylor & Francis. doi:10.1201/b16859

Hartig, O. (2013). An overview on execution strategies for linked data queries. *Datenbank-Spektrum, 13*(2), 89–99. doi:10.100713222-013-0122-1

Hartnett, J. (2015). Discogs. com. *The Charleston Advisor, 16*(4), 26–33. doi:10.5260/chara.16.4.26

Hassan, I. Abdalla. (2014). A synchronized design technique for efficient data distribution. *Computers in Human Behavior, 30*, 427–435. Retrieved from http://www.sciencedirect.com/science/article/pii/S0747563213001374

Hayes, P., & McBride, B. (2004). RDF Semantics. *W3C Recommendation*. Retrieved from http://www.w3.org/TR/2004/REC-rdf-mt-20040210/

Hemerly, J. (2011). Making metadata: The case of MusicBrainz.

Henson, C. A., Pschorr, J. K., Sheth, A. P., & Thirunarayan, K. (2009, May). SemSOS: Semantic sensor observation service. In *International Symposium on Collaborative Technologies and Systems CTS'09* (pp. 44-53). IEEE.

Hernández, M. A., & Stolfo, S. J. (1995). The merge/purge problem for large databases. *SIGMOD Record, 24*(2), 127–138. doi:10.1145/568271.223807

He, Y. Q., Xiang, Z. S., Zheng, J., Lin, Y., Overton, J. A., & Ong, E. (2018). The eXtensible ontology development (XOD) principles and tool implementation to support ontology interoperability. *Journal of Biomedical Semantics*, *9*(1), 3. doi:10.118613326-017-0169-2 PMID:29329592

Hlomani, H., & Stacey, D. (2014). Approaches, methods, metrics, measures, and subjectivity in ontology evaluation: A survey. *Semantic Web Journal*, *1*(5), 1–11.

Hoffart, J., Suchanek, F. M., Berberich, K., & Weikum, G. (2013). YAGO2: A spatially and temporally enhanced knowledge base from Wikipedia. *Artificial Intelligence*, *194*, 28–61. doi:10.1016/j.artint.2012.06.001

Honkola, J., Laine, H., Brown, R., & Tyrkko, O. (2010). Smart-M3 information sharing platform. In The IEEE symposium on Computers and Communications (pp. 1041–1046). doi:10.1109/ISCC.2010.5546642

Hopfgartner, F., & Jose, J. M. (2010). Semantic user profiling techniques for personalised multimedia recommendation. *Multimedia Systems*, *16*(4–5), 255–274. doi:10.100700530-010-0189-6

Horridge, M., Parsia, B., & Sattler, U. (2009, September). Explaining inconsistencies in OWL ontologies. In *International Conference on Scalable Uncertainty Management* (pp. 124-137). Springer, Berlin, Heidelberg. 10.1007/978-3-642-04388-8_11

Hovy, E. (2001). *Comparing sets of semantic relations. Semantics of Relations*. Dordrecht, NL: Kluwer Academic Publishers.

Hu, X., Sun, N., Zhang, C., & Chua, T.-S. (2009). Exploiting Internal and External Semantics for the Clustering of Short Texts Using World Knowledge. In *CIKM '09 Proceedings of the 18th ACM conference on Information and knowledge management* (pp. 919-928).

Hyland, B., & Wood, D. (2011). The joy of data-a cookbook for publishing linked government data on the web. In *Linking government data* (pp. 3–26). Springer New York. doi:10.1007/978-1-4614-1767-5_1

IBM. (2015), *Bring big data to the enterprise*. Retrieved from http://www-01.ibm.com/software/data/bigdata/

Ilyas, I. F., Chu, X., & others. (2015). Trends in cleaning relational data: Consistency and deduplication. *Foundations and Trends®in Databases, 5*(4), 281–393.

Ivanko, S. L., & Pexman, P. M. (2003). Context incongruity and irony processing. In *Discourse Processes* (Vol. 35, pp. 241–279). Taylor & Francis.

Jajaga, E., & Ahmedi, L. (2017b). C-SWRL: SWRL for Reasoning over Stream Data information. In *SDI Workshop, IEEE ICSC 2017*.

Jajaga, E., Ahmedi, L., & Ahmedi, F. (2016). StreamJess: Enabling Jess for Stream Data Reasoning and the Water Domain Case (Demo paper). In *20th International Conference on Knowledge Engineering and Knowledge Management (EKAW2016)*, Bologna.

Jajaga, E., Ahmedi, L., & Ahmedi, F. (2017a). (in press). StreamJess: Stream Data Reasoning System for Water Quality Monitoring. *International Journal of Metadata, Semantics and Ontologies*.

Jemili, I., Ghrab, D., Belghith, A., & Mosbah, M. (2017). Context-aware broadcast in duty-cycled wireless sensor networks. *International Journal on Semantic Web and Information Systems*, *13*(3), 48–67. doi:10.4018/IJSWIS.2017070103

Jena, A. (2007). semantic web framework for Java.

Jennings, B., Van Der Meer, S., Balasubramaniam, S., Botvich, D., Foghlú, M. Ó., Donnelly, W., & Strassner, J. (2007). Towards autonomic management of communications networks. *IEEE Communications Magazine*, *45*(10), 112–121. doi:10.1109/MCOM.2007.4342833

Jensen, C. S., Dyreson, C. E., Böhlen, M. H., Clifford, J., Elmasri, R., Gadia, S. K., ... Wiederhold, G. (1998). The Consensus Glossary of Temporal Database Concepts - February 1998 Version. In O. Etzion, S. Jajodia, & S. Sripada (Eds.), *Temporal Databases, Research and Practice* (pp. 367–405). Berlin, Germany: Springer Verlag. doi:10.1007/BFb0053710

Jiang, Y. C., Li, P., & Aftab, A. (2016). A framework for semantic similarity estimation in formal concept analysis. *Journal of South China Normal University*, *48*(3), 44–52.

Jiang, Y. C., Zhang, X. P., Tang, Y., & Nie, R. H. (2015). Feature-based approaches to semantic similarity assessment of concepts using Wikipedia. *Information Processing & Management*, *51*(3), 215–234. doi:10.1016/j.ipm.2015.01.001

Jianjun, Y., & Tongyu, Z. (2015). Combining long-term and short-term user interest for personalized hashtag recommendation. *Frontiers of Computer Science*, *9*(4), 608–622. doi:10.100711704-015-4284-x

Joshi, A., Sharma, V., & Bhattacharyya, P. (2015). Harnessing context incongruity for sarcasm detection. In *Proceedings of the 53rd Annual Meeting of the Association for Computational Linguistics and the 7th International Joint Conference on Natural Language Processing* (Vol. 2, pp. 757–762), ACL.

Juang, Y.-T., Tung, S.-L., & Chiu, H.-C. (2011). Adaptive fuzzy particle swarm optimization for global optimization of multimodal functions. *Information Sciences*, *181*(20), 4539–4549. doi:10.1016/j.ins.2010.11.025

Jurczyk, P., Lu, J. J., Xiong, L., Cragan, J. D., & Correa, A. (2008). FRIL: A tool for comparative record linkage. *AMIA ... Annual Symposium Proceedings - AMIA Symposium. AMIA Symposium*, *2008*, 440. PMID:18998844

Justo, R., Corcoran, T., Lukin, S. M., Walker, M., & Torres, M. I. (2014). Extracting relevant knowledge for the detection of sarcasm and nastiness in the social web. *Knowledge-Based Systems*, *69*, 124–133. doi:10.1016/j.knosys.2014.05.021

Kaiser, K., & Miksch, S. (2009). Versioning computer-interpretable guidelines: semi-automatic modeling of 'living guidelines' using an information extraction method. *Artificial Intelligence in Medicine*, *46*(1), 55–66. doi:10.1016/j.artmed.2008.08.009 PMID:18950994

Kalashnikov, D. V., & Mehrotra, S. (2006). Domain-independent data cleaning via analysis of entity-relationship graph. *ACM Transactions on Database Systems*, *31*(2), 716–767. doi:10.1145/1138394.1138401

Kalloubi, F., Nfaoui, E. H., & El Beqqali, O. (2014). Graph-based Tweet Entity Linking using DBpedia. In *ACS/IEEE the 11th Conference on computer systems and Applications*, Doha, Qatar (pp. 501-506).

Kalloubi, F., Nfaoui, E. H., & El beqqali, O. (2016). Microblog Semantic context retrieval system based on Linked Open Data and graph-based theory. *Expert Systems with Applications*, *53*, 138–148. doi:10.1016/j.eswa.2016.01.020

Kalloubi, F., Nfaoui, E. H., & El Beqqali, O. (2017). Harnessing semantic features for large-scale content-based hashtag recommendations on microblogging platforms. *International Journal on Semantic Web and Information Systems*, *13*(1), 19. doi:10.4018/IJSWIS.2017010105

Kang, H., Getoor, L., Shneiderman, B., Bilgic, M., & Licamele, L. (2008). Interactive entity resolution in relational data: A visual analytic tool and its evaluation. *Visualization and Computer Graphics. IEEE Transactions On*, *14*(5), 999–1014. PMID:18599913

Kaur, H., & Bajaj, B. (2015). Review on localization techniques in wireless sensor. *International Journal of Computers and Applications*, *116*(2), 4–7. doi:10.5120/20306-2348

Kejriwal, M., & Miranker, D. P. (2015). An unsupervised instance matcher for schema-free RDF data. *Journal of Web Semantics*, *35*, 102–123. doi:10.1016/j.websem.2015.07.002

Kepler, F. N., Paz-Trillo, C., Riani, J., Ribeiro, M. M., Delgado, K. V., de Barros, L. N., & Wassermann, R. (2006, October). *Classifying Ontologies*. WONTO.

Keßler, C., & Janowicz, K. (2010, November). Linking sensor data-why, to what, and how? In *Proceedings of the 3rd International Conference on Semantic Sensor Networks* (pp. 48-63). CEUR-WS.org.

Khader, O., Willig, A., & Wolisz, A. (2009, May). Distributed wakeup scheduling scheme for supporting periodic traffic in wsns. In *Wireless Conference, 2009. EW 2009. European*, Leipzig, Germany (pp. 287-292). IEEE. 10.1109/EW.2009.5357978

Khan, S., Qamar, U., & Muzaffar, A. W. (2015). A Framework for Evaluation of OWL Biomedical Ontologies Based on Properties Coverage. In *13th International Conference on Frontiers of Information Technology* (pp. 59-64). IEEE. 10.1109/FIT.2015.22

Khattri, A., Joshi, A., Bhattacharyya, P., & Carman, M. J. (2015). Your sentiment precedes you: Using an author's historical tweets to predict sarcasm. In *6th workshop on computation approaches to subjectivity, sentiment and social media analysis (WASSA, 2015)*,(pp. 25–30), ACL.

Khrouf, H., & Troncy, R. (2013). Hybrid event recommendation using linked data and user diversity. In *Proceedings of the 7th ACM conference on Recommender systems - RecSys '13* (pp. 185–192). New York, NY: ACM Press. 10.1145/2507157.2507171

Kiljander, J., Morandi, F., & Soininen, J.-P. (2012). Knowledge sharing protocol for smart spaces. *International Journal of Advanced Computer Science and Applications*, *3*(9). doi:10.14569/IJACSA.2012.030915

Kirschnick, J., Hemsen, H., & Markl, V. (2016). JEDI: Joint Entity and Relation Detection using Type Inference. In *Proceedings of the Annual Meeting of the Association for Computational Linguistics* (pp. 61-66). 10.18653/v1/P16-4011

Kitaya, K., Huang, H.-H., & Kawagoe, K. (2012). Music Curator Recommendations Using Linked Data. In *Second International Conference on the Innovative Computing Technology (INTECH 2012)*, Casablanca (pp. 337–339). IEEE. 10.1109/INTECH.2012.6457799

Kitchenham, B., Pfleeger, S. L., & Fenton, N. (1995). Towards a framework for software measurement validation. *IEEE Transactions on Software Engineering*, *21*(12), 930–944. doi:10.1109/32.489070

Kjær, K. E., & Hansen, K. M. (2010). Modeling and Implementing Ontology-Based Publish/Subscribe Using Semantic Web Technologies. In *2010 15th IEEE International Conference on Engineering of Complex Computer Systems (ICECCS)* (pp. 63–71).

Klogo, G. S., & Gadze, J. D. (2013). Energy constraints of localization techniques in wireless sensor networks (WSN): A Survey. *International Journal of Computers and Applications*, *75*, 44–52. doi:10.5120/13143-0543

Klyne, G., & Carroll, J. J. (2014). Resource Description Framework (RDF): Concepts and abstract syntax. *W3C Recommendation*. Retrieved from https://www.w3.org/TR/2014/REC-rdf11-concepts-20140225/

Ko, H., Kim, E., Ko, I.-Y., & Chang, D. (2014). Semantically-based recommendation by using semantic clusters of users' viewing history. In *2014 International Conference on Big Data and Smart Computing (BIGCOMP)* (pp. 83–87). IEEE.

Ko, H., & Son, J. (2015). Multi-Aspect Collaborative Filtering based on Linked Data for Personalized Recommendation. In *Proceedings of the 1st Workshop on New Trends in Content-based Recommender Systems co-located with the 8th ACM Conference on Recommender Systems (RecSys 2014)* (pp. 49–50). 10.1145/2740908.2742780

Korzun, D. G., Galov, I. V., Kashevnik, A. M., Shilov, N. G., Krinkin, K., & Korolev, Y. (2011). Integration of Smart-M3 applications: Blogging in smart conference. In Smart Spaces and Next Generation Wired/Wireless Networking (pp. 51–62). Springer.

Kouki, P., Pujara, J., Marcum, C., Koehly, L., & Getoor, L. (2017). Collective entity resolution in familial networks. In *2017 IEEE International Conference on Data Mining (ICDM)* (pp. 227–236). 10.1109/ICDM.2017.32

Kovatsch, M., Hassan, Y. N., & Mayer, S. (2015, October). Practical semantics for the Internet of Things: Physical states, device mashups, and open questions. In *2015 5th International Conference on the Internet of Things (IOT)* (pp. 54-61). IEEE.

Kowald, D., Pujari, S., & Lex, E. (2017). Temporal Effects on Hashtag Reuse in Twitter: A Cognitive-Inspired Hashtag Recommendation Approach. In *26th International Conference on World Wide Web*, Perth, Australia (pp. 1401-1410).

Kreuz, R. J., & Caucci, G. M. (2007). Lexical influences on the perception of sarcasm. In *Proceedings of the Workshop on computational approaches to Figurative Language* (pp. 1-4). ACL. 10.3115/1611528.1611529

Kreuz, R. J., & Glucksberg, S. (1989). How to be sarcastic: The echoic reminder theory of verbal irony. *Journal of Experimental Psychology. General, 118*(4), 374–386. doi:10.1037/0096-3445.118.4.374

Kreuz, R. J., & Link, K. E. (2002). Asymmetries in the use of verbal irony. *Journal of Language and Social Psychology, 21*(2), 127–143. doi:10.1177/02627X02021002002

Kreuz, R. J., & Roberts, R. M. (1995). Two cues for verbal irony: Hyperbole and the ironic tone of voice. *Metaphor and Symbol, 10*(1), 21–31. doi:10.120715327868ms1001_3

Kumar, S., & Baliyan, N. (2018). Quality Evaluation of Ontologies. In *Semantic Web-Based Systems* (pp. 19–50). Singapore: Springer.

Kumar, S., Baliyan, N., & Sukalikar, S. (2017). Ontology Cohesion and Coupling Metrics. *International Journal on Semantic Web and Information Systems, 13*(4), 1–26. doi:10.4018/IJSWIS.2017100101

Kunneman, F., Liebrecht, C., van Mulken, M., & van den Bosch, A. (2014). Signaling sarcasm: From hyperbole to hashtag. *Information Processing & Management, 51*(4), 500–509. doi:10.1016/j.ipm.2014.07.006

Kuo, P. C., Alvarado, F. H. C., & Chen, Y. S. (2018). Facebook Reaction-Based Emotion Classifier as Cue for Sarcasm Detection. arXiv:1805.06510

Kureychik, V., & Semenova, A. (2017). Combined Method for Integration of Heterogeneous Ontology Models for Big Data Processing and Analysis. In *Proceedings of the 15th International Conference on Service Oriented Computing, ICSOC 2017* (pp. 302-311), Springer Publishers. 10.1007/978-3-319-57261-1_30

Kushwaha, N., & Vyas, O. P. (2014). SemMovieRec: Extraction of Semantic Features of DBpedia for Recommender System. In *Proceedings of the 7th ACM India Computing Conference* (p. 13:1--13:9). New York, NY: ACM. 10.1145/2675744.2675759

Kusiak, A. (2017). Smart manufacturing must embrace big data. *Nature, 544*(7648), 23–25. doi:10.1038/544023a PMID:28383012

Kwuimi, R., Fonou-Dombeu, J. V., & Tranos, Z. (2017). An empirical analysis of semantic web mechanisms for storage and query of ontologies in relational databases. In *Proceedings of the 3rd International Conference on Advances in Computing, Communication and Engineering (ICACCE)* (pp. 132–136). Dubai, UAE: WASET Open Science.

Kywe Su, M., Hoang, T.-A., Lim, E. P., & Zhu, F. (2012). On recommending hashtags in twitter networks. In *SocInfo'12 Proceedings of the 4th international conference on Social Informatics,* Lausanne, Switzerland (pp. 337-350). Springer.

Lafferty, J., McCallum, A., & Pereira, F. (2001). Conditional random fields: probabilistic models for segmenting and labeling sequence data. In *Proc. of ICML*, New York, NY (pp. 282-289).

Lamarine, M., Hager, J., Saris, W. H., Astrup, A., & Valsesia, A. (2018). Fuzzy Matching and Machine Learning approaches for large-scale, automated mapping of food diaries on food composition tables. *Frontiers in Nutrition, 5,* 38. doi:10.3389/fnut.2018.00038 PMID:29868600

Lamorte, L., Licciardi, C. A., Marengo, M., Salmeri, A., Mohr, P., & Raffa, G., … Cinotti, T. S. (2007). A platform for enabling context aware telecommunication services. In *Third Workshop on Context Awareness for Proactive Systems,* Guildford, UK.

Lantow, B. (2016). OntoMetrics: Putting Metrics into Use for Ontology Evaluation. In *8th International Joint Conference on Knowledge Discovery, Knowledge Engineering and Knowledge Management* (pp. 186-191). 10.5220/0006084601860191

Le, D. T., Le Duc, T., Zalyubovskiy, V. V., Kim, D. S., & Choo, H. (2017). Collision-tolerant broadcast scheduling in duty-cycled wireless sensor networks. *Journal of Parallel and Distributed Computing, 100,* 42–56. doi:10.1016/j.jpdc.2016.10.006

Lee, T. B. (2006). Linked data. Retrieved from http://www.w3.org/DesignIssues/LinkedData.html

Lee, Y. J., Trevathan, J., Atkinson, I., & Read, W. (2015). The integration, analysis and visualization of sensor data from dispersed wireless sensor network systems using the SWE framework. *Journal of Telecommunications and Information Technology,* (4), 86.

Lefort, L., Henson, C., Taylor, K., Barnaghi, P., Compton, M., Corcho, O., ... & Neuhaus, H. (2011). Semantic sensor network xg final report. *W3C Incubator Group Report, 28.*

Lehmann, J., Isele, R., Jakob, M., Jentzsch, A., Kontokostas, D., Mendes, P. N., ... Bizer, C. (2015). DBpedia-A large-scale, multilingual knowledge base extracted from Wikipedia. *Semantic Web, 6*(2), 167–195.

Le-Phuoc, D., Quoc, H. N. M., Parreira, J. X., & Hauswirth, M. (2011). The linked sensor middleware–connecting the real world and the semantic web. In *Proceedings of the Semantic Web Challenge.*

Liebrecht, C., Kunneman, F., & Bosch, A. (2013). *The perfect solution for detecting sarcasm in tweets\# not. In Proceedings of the Association for Computational Linguistics* (pp. 29–37). ACL.

Liefde, I., Vries, M., & Meijers, B. (2016, June). Exploring the use of the semantic web for discovering, retrieving and processing data from sensor observation services [master thesis]. Delft University of Technology, Netherlands.

Li, J., & Lu, G. (2017). Sparse Anchor Nodes Cooperative Localization Algorithm for WSN. In *Proc. 2017 3rd IEEE International Conference on Computer and Communications (ICCC)* (pp. 368-372). 10.1109/CompComm.2017.8322573

Lim, G. H., Hong, S.-W., Lee, I., Suh, I. H., & Beetz, M. (2013) Robot recommender system using affection-based episode ontology for personalization. In *Proceedings of the 22nd IEEE International Symposium on Robot and Human Interactive Communication (RO-MAN)*, Gyeongju (pp. 155–160). Los Alamitos, CA: IEEE Computer Society Press.

Lin, S., Jin, P., Zhao, X., & Yue, L. (2014). Exploiting temporal information in Web search. *Expert Systems with Applications, 41*(2), 331–341. doi:10.1016/j.eswa.2013.07.048

Li, P., Jiang, Y. C., & Wang, J. (2016). Modular ontology reuse based on conservative extension theory. *Journal of Software, 27*(11), 2777–2795.

Li, P., Jiang, Y. C., Wang, J., & Yin, Z. L. (2017). Semantic Extension of Query for the Linked Data. *International Journal on Semantic Web and Information Systems*, *13*(4), 109–133. doi:10.4018/IJSWIS.2017100106

Li, P., Shi, Y. X., & Jiang, Y. C. (2010). Tourism domain ontology construction based on ε-connections. *Computer Engineering*, *36*(22), 274–276.

Li, P., Xiao, B., Akram, A., Jiang, Y. C., & Zhang, Z. F. (2018). SESLDS: An Extension Scheme for Linked Data Sources Based on Semantically Enhanced Annotation and Reasoning. *International Journal of Intelligent Systems*, *33*(2), 233–258. doi:10.1002/int.21926

Li, P., Xiao, B., Ma, W. J., Jiang, Y. C., & Zhang, Z. F. (2017). A graph-based semantic relatedness assessment method combining wikipedia features. *Engineering Applications of Artificial Intelligence*, *65*, 268–281. doi:10.1016/j.engappai.2017.07.027

Liu, D., Bikakis, A., & Vlachidis, A. (2017). Evaluation of Semantic Web Ontologies for Modelling Art Collections. In *Advances in Databases and Information Systems* (pp. 343–352). Cham: Springer. doi:10.1007/978-3-319-67162-8_34

Liu, P., Chen, W., Ou, G., Wang, T., Yang, D., & Lei, K. (2014). Sarcasm Detection in Social Media Based on Imbalanced Classification. In *Web-Age Information Management* (pp. 459–471). Springer International Publishing. doi:10.1007/978-3-319-08010-9_49

Liu, Y., Jin, P., & Yue, L. (2009). Extracting position relations from the web. In *Proc. of WIDM*, Hong Kong, China (pp. 59-62). 10.1145/1651587.1651601

Li, X., Yan, L., Pan, W., & Luo, B. (2015). Optimization of DV-hop localization algorithm in hybrid optical wireless sensor networks. *Journal of Heuristics*, *21*(2), 177–195. doi:10.100710732-014-9257-y

Li, Y., Liu, T., Jiang, J., & Zhang, L. (2016). *Hashtag Recommendation with Topical Attention-Based LSTM. COLING* (pp. 3019–3029). ACL.

Lo Bue, A., & Machi, A. (2015). Open data integration using SPARQL and SPIN: A case study for the tourism domain. In M. Gavanelli, E. Lamma, & F. Riguzzi (Eds.), *Advances In Artificial Intelligence* (Vol. 9336, pp. 316–326). Berlin: Springer-Verlag Berlin. doi:10.1007/978-3-319-24309-2_24

Lommatzsch, A., Kille, B., Kim, J. W., & Albayrak, S. (2013). An Adaptive Hybrid Movie Recommender Based on Semantic Data. In *Proceedings of the 10th Conference on Open Research Areas in Information Retrieval* (pp. 217–218). Paris, France, Le Centre De Hautes Etudes Internationales D'informatique Documentaire. Retrieved from http://dl.acm.org/citation.cfm?id=2491748.2491795

Lommatzsch, A., Kille, B., & Albayrak, S. (2013). Learning hybrid recommender models for heterogeneous semantic data. In *Proceedings of the 28th Annual ACM Symposium on Applied Computing - SAC '13* (p. 275). New York, NY: ACM Press. 10.1145/2480362.2480420

Lommatzsch, A., Kille, B., Albayrak, S., & Berlin, T. U. (2013). A Framework for Learning and Analyzing Hybrid Recommenders based on Heterogeneous Semantic Data Categories and Subject Descriptors. In *10th Conference on Open Research Areas in Information Retrieval*, Lisbon, Portugal (pp. 137–140). ACM.

Lomov, A. A., Vanag, P. I., & Korzun, D. G. (2011). Multilingual ontology library generator for Smart-M3 application development. In *Proc. 9th Conf. of Open Innovations Framework Program FRUCT and 1st Regional MeeGo Summit Russia--Finland* (pp. 82–91).

Lopes, G. R., André, L., Rabello Lopes, G., Paes Leme, L., Pereira Nunes, B., Casanova, M., & Dietze, S. (2014). Two Approaches to the Dataset Interlinking Recommendation Problem. In Web Information Systems Engineering – WISE 2014 SE (pp. 324–339). doi:10.1007/978-3-319-11749-2_25

Lopes, G. R., Leme, L. A. P. P., Nunes, B. P., & Casanova, M. A. (2014). RecLAK: Analysis and recommendation of interlinking datasets. In CEUR Workshop Proceedings (Vol. 1137).

Lops, P., De Gemmis, M., & Semeraro, G. (2011). Content-based Recommender Systems: State of the Art and Trends. In Recommender Systems Handbook (pp. 73–105). doi:10.1007/978-0-387-85820-3

Lotker, Z., Patt-Shamir, B., & Pettie, S. (2015). Improved distributed approximate matching. *Journal of the Association for Computing Machinery, 62*(5), 38. doi:10.1145/2786753

Lozano-Tello, A., & Gómez-Pérez, A. (2004). Ontometric: A method to choose the appropriate ontology. *Journal of Database Management, 2*(15), 1–18. doi:10.4018/jdm.2004040101

Luan, M., Tsang, I. W., Ming, K., Chai, A., & Hai, L. C. (2014). Robust Domain Adaptation for Relation Extraction via Clustering Consistency. In *Proceedings of the 52nd Annual Meeting of the Association for Computational Linguistics* (pp. 807-817).

Lu, H.-M., & Lee, C.-H. (2015). A Twitter Hashtag Recommendation Model that Accommodates for Temporal Clustering Effects. *IEEE Intelligent Systems, 30*(3), 18–25. doi:10.1109/MIS.2015.20

Lukin, S., & Walker, M. (2013). Really? Well apparently bootstrapping improves the performance of sarcasm and nastiness classifiers for online dialogue. In *Proceedings of the Workshop on Language Analysis in Social Media* (pp. 30-40). ACL

Lunando, E., & Purwarianti, A. (2013). Indonesian social media sentiment analysis with sarcasm detection. In *2013 International Conference on Advanced Computer Science and Information Systems (ICACSIS)* (pp. 195-198). IEEE. 10.1109/ICACSIS.2013.6761575

Luong, V. N., Le, V. S., & Doan, V. B. (2018). Fragmentation in Distributed Database Design Based on KR Rough Clustering Technique. In P. Cong Vinh, N. Ha Huy Cuong, & E. Vassev (Eds.), *Context-Aware Systems and Applications, and Nature of Computation and Communication ICCASA 2017*. Cham: Springer. Retrieved from https://link.springer.com/chapter/10.1007/978-3-319-77818-1_16 doi:10.1007/978-3-319-77818-1_16

Maccatrozzo, V., Ceolin, D., Aroyo, L., & Groth, P. (2014). A Semantic Pattern-Based Recommender. In V. Presutti, M. Stankovic, E. Cambria, I. Cantador, A. Di Iorio, T. Di Noia, … A. Tordai (Eds.), *Semantic Web Evaluation Challenge: SemWebEval 2014 at ESWC 2014, Anissaras, Crete, Greece, May 25-29, 2014, Revised Selected Papers* (pp. 182–187). Cham: Springer International Publishing. 10.1007/978-3-319-12024-9_24

Machado, J. B., Martins, G. L., Isotani, S., & Barbosa, E. F. (2013) An ontology-based user model for personalization of educational content (S). In *Proceedings of the 25th Int. Conf. on Software Engineering and Knowledge Engineering (SEKE)* (pp. 737–740). Fredericton, NB: KSI Research Inc.

Mackey, T. K., & Liang, B. A. (2011). The Role of Practice Guidelines in Medical Malpractice Litigation. *AMA Journal of Ethics, 13*(1), 36–41. Retrieved from http://virtualmentor.ama-assn.org/2011/01/hlaw1-1101.html PMID:23121815

Maedche, A., & Staab, S. (2001). Ontology learning for the semantic web. *IEEE Intelligent Systems, 16*(2), 72–79. doi:10.1109/5254.920602

Maedche, A., & Staab, S. (2002, October). Measuring similarity between ontologies. In *International Conference on Knowledge Engineering and Knowledge Management* (pp. 251-263). Springer, Berlin, Heidelberg.

Mahdisoltani, F., Biega, J., & Suchanek, F. (2014). Yago3: A knowledge base from multilingual Wikipedias. In *Proceedings of the 7th Biennial Conference on Innovative Data Systems Research, CIDR 2015*. Asilomar, CA.

Mahi, M., Baykan, O. K., & Kodaz, H. (2018). A new approach based on particle swarm optimization algorithm for solving data allocation problem. *Applied Soft Computing*, *62*, 571–578. doi:10.1016/j.asoc.2017.11.019

Mahjri, I., Dhraief, A., Belghith, A., Drira, K., & Mathkour, H. (2016). A GPS-less framework for localization and coverage maintenance in wireless sensor networks. *TIIS*, *10*(1), 96–116. doi:10.3837/tiis.2016.01.006

Makris, P., Skoutas, D. N., & Skianis, C. (2013). A survey on context-aware mobile and wireless networking: On networking and computing environments' integration. *IEEE Communications Surveys and Tutorials*, *15*(1), 362–386. doi:10.1109/SURV.2012.040912.00180

Maleszka, B. (2017). A method for ontology-based user profile adaptation in personalized document retrieval systems. In *Proceedings 2016 IEEE International Conference on Systems, Man, and Cybernetics* (SMC) (pp. 3187–3192). Los Alamitos, CA: IEEE Computer Society Press.

Mandreoli, F., Martoglia, R., & Ronchetti, E. (2006). Supporting Temporal Slicing in XML Databases. In *Proceeding of 10th International Conference on Extending Database Technology (EDBT)* (pp. 295–312). Berlin, Germany: Springer Verlag.

Manning, C. D., Raghavan, P. Sch., & Tze, H. (2008). *Introduction to Information Retrieval*. Cambridge University Press. doi:10.1017/CBO9780511809071

Manoj Kumar, S., Anusha, K., & Santhi Sree, K. (2015). Semantic Web-based Recommendation: Experimental Results and Test Cases. *International Journal of Emerging Research in Management & Technology*, *4*(6), 215–222. Retrieved from http://www.ermt.net/docs/papers/Volume_4/6_June2015/V4N6-252.pdf

Manzaroli, D., Roffia, L., Cinotti, T. S., Azzoni, P., Ovaska, E., Nannini, V., & Mattarozzi, S. (2010). Smart-M3 and OSGi: The interoperability platform. In *2010 IEEE Symposium on Computers and Communications (ISCC)* (pp. 1053–1058).

Marcus, M. P., Marcinkiewicz, M. A., & Santorini, B. (1993). Building a large annotated corpus of English: The Penn Treebank. *Computational Linguistics*, *19*(2), 313–330.

Marie, N., Gandon, F., Legrand, D., & Ribière, M. (2013). Discovery Hub: a discovery engine on the top of DBpedia. In *3rd International Conference on Web Intelligence, Mining and Semantics - WIMS '13* (p. 1). New York, NY: ACM Press. 10.1145/2479787.2479820

Masuoka, R., Parsia, B., & Labrou, Y. (2003). Task computing--the semantic web meets pervasive computing. In *The Semantic Web-ISWC 2003* (pp. 866–881). Springer. doi:10.1007/978-3-540-39718-2_55

Matinfar, F., Nematbakhsh, M. A., & Lausen, G. (2014). Discovery of RDFs. *International Journal of Pattern Recognition and Artificial Intelligence*, *28*(2), 17. doi:10.1142/S0218001414500037

Ma, Y., Jin, B., & Feng, Y. (2009). Semantic oriented ontology cohesion metrics for ontology-based systems. *Journal of Systems and Software*, *83*(1), 143–152. doi:10.1016/j.jss.2009.07.047

Maynard, D., & Greenwood, M. A. (2014). Who cares about sarcastic tweets? Investigating the impact of sarcasm on sentiment analysis. *In Proceedings of Language Resources and Evaluation Conference*, (pp. 4238–4243), ACL.

Ma, Z., Sheng, O. R. L., & Pant, G. (2009). Discovering company revenue relations from news: A network approach. *Decision Support Systems*, *4*(47), 408–414. doi:10.1016/j.dss.2009.04.007

Mazzia, A., & Juet, J. (2011). *Suggesting hashtags on Twitter.* Retrieved 01 06, 2016, from http://alliemazzia.com/pubs/545-final.pdf

McCormack, K., & Smyth, M. (2017). A Mathematical Solution to String Matching for Big Data Linking. *Journal of Statistical Science and Application, 5*, 39–55.

McDaniel, M., Storey, V. C., & Sugumaran, V. (2018). Assessing the quality of domain ontologies: Metrics and an automated ranking system. *Data & Knowledge Engineering, 115*, 32–47. doi:10.1016/j.datak.2018.02.001

McGuinness, D. L., & Harmelen, F. (2004). OWL Web ontology language: overview. *W3C Recommendation.* Retrieved from http://www.w3.org/TR/2004/REC-owl- features-20040210/

Medvedev, V., Kurasova, O., Bernatavičienė, J., Treigys, P., Marcinkevičius, V., & Dzemyda, G. (2017). A new web-based solution for modelling data mining processes. *Simulation Modelling Practice and Theory, 76*, 34–46. doi:10.1016/j.simpat.2017.03.001

Melnick, E. R., Hess, E. P., Guo, G., Breslin, M., Lopez, K., Pavlo, A. J., ... Post, L. A. (2017). Patient-centered decision support: formative usability evaluation of integrated clinical decision support with a patient decision aid for minor head injury in the emergency department. *Journal of Medical Internet Research, 19*(5), e174. doi:10.2196/jmir.7846 PMID:28526667

Miranker, D. P., Depena, R. K., Jung, H., Sequeda, J. F., & Reyna, C. (2012). Diamond: A SPARQL query engine, for linked data based on the Rete match. In *Proceedings of the Workshop on Artificial Intelligence meets the Web of Data (AImWD) at ECAI.* IOS Press Amsterdam.

Mohan, L., Prasad, G. V. S., Chimalakonda, S., Reddy, Y. R., & Choppella, V. (2017). A Lightweight Approach for Evaluating Sufficiency of Ontologies In *29th International Conference on Software Engineering and Knowledge Engineering,* Pittsburgh, PA (pp. 557-561).

Morandi, F., Roffia, L., D'Elia, A., Vergari, F., & Cinotti, T. S. (2012). RedSib: a Smart-M3 semantic information broker implementation. In *Proc. 12th Conf. of Open Innovations Association FRUCT and Seminar on e-Tourism* (pp. 86–98). 10.23919/FRUCT.2012.8122091

Moreno, A., Ariza-Porras, C., Lago, P., Jiménez-Guarín, C. L., Castro, H., & Riveill, M. (2014). Hybrid Model Rating Prediction with Linked Open Data for Recommender Systems. In *SemWebEval 2014 at ESWC 2014, Anissaras, Crete, Greece, May 25-29, 2014, Revised Selected Papers* (pp. 193–198). 10.1007/978-3-319-12024-9_26

Moreno, A., Valls, A., Isern, D., Marina, L., & Borràs, J. (2013). SigTur/E-Destination: Ontology-based personalized recommendation of Tourism and Leisure Activities. *Engineering Applications of Artificial Intelligence, 26*(1), 633–651. doi:10.1016/j.engappai.2012.02.014

Morshed, S., Baratchi, M., & Heijenk, G. (2016, March). Traffic-adaptive duty cycle adaptation in TR-MAC protocol for Wireless Sensor Networks. In *Wireless Days (2016 WD)* (pp. 1–6). Toulouse, France: IEEE. doi:10.1109/WD.2016.7461501

Morshed, S., & Heijenk, G. (2014, September). TR-MAC: An energy-efficient MAC protocol exploiting transmitted reference modulation for wireless sensor networks. In *Proceedings of the 17th ACM international conference on Modeling, analysis and simulation of wireless and mobile systems,* Montreal, Canada (pp. 21-29). ACM. 10.1145/2641798.2641804

Moyano, A. N., Sicilia, M. A., & Barriocanal, E. G. (2018). On the graph structure of the web of data. *International Journal on Semantic Web and Information Systems, 14*(2), 70–85. doi:10.4018/IJSWIS.2018040104

Murth, M., & Kühn, E. (2008). A Semantic Event Notification Service for Knowledge-Driven Coordination. In *Proc. of 1st Int'l. workshop on emergent semantics and cooperation in open systems (ESTEEM), cooperation with the 2nd Int'l. Conf. on Distributed Event-Based Systems (DEBS 2008), Rome, Italy.*

Murth, M., & Kühn, E. (2009). A heuristics framework for semantic subscription processing. In The Semantic Web: Research and Applications (pp. 96–110). Springer. doi:10.1007/978-3-642-02121-3_11

Murth, M., & Kuhn, E. (2010). Knowledge-based interaction patterns for semantic spaces. In *2010 International Conference on Complex, Intelligent and Software Intensive Systems (CISIS)* (pp. 1036–1043). 10.1109/CISIS.2010.31

Musto, C., Basile, P., Lops, P., de Gemmis, M., & Semeraro, G. (2017). Introducing linked open data in graph-based recommender systems. *Information Processing & Management, 53*(2), 405–435. doi:10.1016/j.ipm.2016.12.003

Musto, C., Lops, P., de Gemmis, M., & Semeraro, G. (2017). Semantics-aware Recommender Systems exploiting Linked Open Data and graph-based features. *Knowledge-Based Systems, 136,* 1–14. doi:10.1016/j.knosys.2017.08.015

Na, A., & Priest, M. (2007). *Sensor observation service.* Implementation Standard OGC.

Narducci, F., Musto, C., Semeraro, G., Lops, P., & de Gemmis, M. (2013). Exploiting Big Data for Enhanced Representations in Content-Based Recommender Systems. In C. Huemer & P. Lops (Eds.), *14th International Conference, EC-Web 2013, Prague, Czech Republic, August 27-28, 2013. Proceedings* (Vol. 152, pp. 182–193). Springer Berlin Heidelberg. 10.1007/978-3-642-39878-0_17

Nashat, D., & Amer, A. A. (2018). A Comprehensive Taxonomy of Fragmentation and Allocation Techniques in Distributed Database Design. *ACM Computing Surveys, 51*(1), 12.

Nebot, V., & Berlanga, R. (2016). Statistically-driven generation of multidimensional analytical schemas from linked data. *Knowledge-Based Systems, 110,* 15–29. doi:10.1016/j.knosys.2016.07.010

NEJM Catalyst. (2017). What is Patient-Centred Care? Retrieved April 4, 2018 from https://catalyst.nejm.org/what-is-patient-centered-care/

Newcombe, H. B., & Kennedy, J. M. (1962). Record linkage: Making maximum use of the discriminating power of identifying information. *Communications of the ACM, 5*(11), 563–566. doi:10.1145/368996.369026

Nguyen, P. T., Tomeo, P., Di Noia, T., Di Sciascio, E., Di Noia, T., & Di Sciascio, E. (2015). An Evaluation of SimRank and Personalized PageRank to Build a Recommender System for the Web of Data. In *Proceedings of the 24th International Conference on World Wide Web* (pp. 1477–1482). Republic and Canton of Geneva, Switzerland: International World Wide Web Conferences Steering Committee. 10.1145/2740908.2742141

Nguyen, K., & Ichise, R. (2016). Linked data entity resolution system enhanced by configuration learning algorithm. *IEICE Transactions on Information and Systems, 99*(6), 1521–1530. doi:10.1587/transinf.2015EDP7392

Nguyen, K., & Ichise, R. (2017). Automatic schema-independent linked data instance matching system. *International Journal on Semantic Web and Information Systems, 13*(1), 82–103. doi:10.4018/IJSWIS.2017010106

Niculescu, D., & Nath, B., B. (2001). Ad hoc positioning system (APS). In *Proc. of the IEEE GLOBECOM* (pp. 2926-2931). doi:10.1109/GLOCOM.2001.965964

Nilashi, M., Ibrahim, O., & Bagherifard, K. (2018). A recommender system based on collaborative filtering using ontology and dimensionality reduction techniques. *Expert Systems with Applications, 92,* 507–520. doi:10.1016/j.eswa.2017.09.058

Norouzi, M., Fleet, D. J., & Salakhutdinov, R. (2013). Hamming Distance Metric Learning. University of Toronto. Retrieved from https://papers.nips.cc/paper/4808-hamming-distance-metric-learning.pdf

Novais, P., Oliveira, T., Satoh, K., & Neves, J. (2018). The role of ontologies and decision frameworks in computer-interpretable guideline execution. *Advances in Intelligent Systems and Computing, 626*, 197–216. doi:10.1007/978-3-319-64161-4_10

Obrst, L., Ceusters, W., Mani, I., Ray, S., & Smith, B. (2007). The evaluation of ontologies. In *Semantic web* (pp. 139–158). Boston, MA: Springer. doi:10.1007/978-0-387-48438-9_8

Oh, S., & Ahn, J. (2009, October). Ontology module metrics. In *IEEE International Conference on e-Business Engineering ICEBE'09* (pp. 11-18).

Oh, S., Yeom, H. Y., & Ahn, J. (2011). Cohesion and coupling metrics for ontology modules. *Information Technology Management, 12*(2), 81–96. doi:10.100710799-011-0094-5

Oliveira, H. A. B. F., Boukerche, A., Nakamura, E., & Loureiro, A. A. F. (2009). An efficient directed localization recursion protocol for wireless sensor networks. *IEEE Transactions on Computers, 58*(5), 677–691. doi:10.1109/TC.2008.221

Oren, E., Delbru, R., Catasta, M., Cyganiak, R., Stenzhorn, H., & Tummarello, G. (2008). Sindice.com: A document-oriented lookup index for open linked data. *International Journal of Metadata, Semantics and Ontologies, 3*(1), 37–52. doi:10.1504/IJMSO.2008.021204

Orme, A. M., Tao, H., & Etzkorn, L. H. (2006). Coupling metrics for ontology-based system. *IEEE Software, 23*(2), 102–108. doi:10.1109/MS.2006.46

Ostuni, V. C. C., Gentile, G., Di Noia, T., Di Noia, T., Mirizzi, R., Romito, D., & Di Sciascio, E. (2013). Mobile movie recommendations with linked data. In *IFIP WG 8.4, 8.9, TC 5 International Cross-Domain Conference, CD-ARES 2013, Regensburg, Germany, September 2-6, 2013. Proceedings* (Vol. 8127 LNCS, pp. 400–415). 10.1007/978-3-642-40511-2_29

Ostuni, V. C., Di Noia, T., Di Sciascio, E., & Mirizzi, R. (2013). Top-N recommendations from implicit feedback leveraging linked open data. In *Proceedings of the 7th ACM conference on Recommender systems - RecSys '13* (pp. 85–92). New York, NY: ACM Press. 10.1145/2507157.2507172

Ostuni, V. V., Di Noia, T., Mirizzi, R., Di Sciascio, E., & Di Noia, T. (2014). A Linked Data Recommender System Using a Neighborhood-Based Graph Kernel. In M. Hepp & Y. Hoffner (Eds.), *E-Commerce and Web Technologies SE - 10* (pp. 89–100). Springer International Publishing; doi:10.1007/978-3-319-10491-1_10

Otsuka, E., Wallace, S. A., & Chiu, D. (2016). A hashtag recommendation system for twitter data streams. *Computational Social Networks, 3*(1), 3. doi:10.118640649-016-0028-9 PMID:29355223

Ouyang, L., Zou, B., Qu, M., & Zhang, C. (2011, July). A method of ontology evaluation based on coverage, cohesion and coupling. In *Eighth International Conference on Fuzzy Systems and Knowledge Discovery* (Vol. 4, pp. 2451-2455). 10.1109/FSKD.2011.6020046

Ovaska, E., Cinotti, T. S., & Toninelli, A. (2012). The Design Principles and Practices of Interoperable Smart Spaces. In Advanced Design Approaches to Emerging Software Systems: Principles, Methodologies and Tools (pp. 18–47). Hershey, PA: IGI Global. doi:10.4018/978-1-60960-735-7.ch002

Owens, D. K., & Nease, R. F. Jr. (1997). A normative analytic framework for development of practice guidelines for specific clinical populations. *Medical Decision Making, 17*(4), 409–426. doi:10.1177/0272989X9701700406 PMID:9343799

Owoputi, O., O'Connor, B., Dyer, C., Gimpel, K., Schneider, N., & A. Smith, N. (2013). Improved Part-of-Speech Tagging for Online Conversational Text with Word Clusters. In *HLT-NAACL 2013* (pp. 380-390).

Ozdikis, O., Orhan, F., & Danismaz, F. (2011). Ontology-based recommendation for points of interest retrieved from multiple data sources. In *International Workshop on Semantic Web Information Management - SWIM '11* (pp. 1–6). 10.1145/1999299.1999300

Palviainen, M., & Katasonov, A. (2011). Model and ontology-based development of smart space applications. In *Pervasive Computing and Communications Design and Deployment: Technologies, Trends, and Applications* (pp. 126-149).

Pandey, O. M., & Hegde, R. M. (2017). Node localization over small world WSNs using constrained average path length reduction. *Ad Hoc Networks*, *67*, 87–102. doi:10.1016/j.adhoc.2017.10.010

Pang, B., Lee, L., & Vaithyanathan, S. (2002). Thumbs up?: Sentiment classification using machine learning techniques. In *Proceedings of the ACL-02 conference on Empirical methods in natural language processing* (Vol. 10, pp. 79-86). Association for Computational Linguistics. 10.3115/1118693.1118704

Pantsar-Syväniemi, S., Ovaska, E., Ferrari, S., Cinotti, T. S., Zamagni, G., & Roffia, L. … Nannini, V. (2011). Case study: Context-aware supervision of a smart maintenance process. In *Proceedings - 11th IEEE/IPSJ International Symposium on Applications and the Internet, SAINT 2011* (pp. 309-314).

Park, D. H., Kim, H. K., Choi, I. Y., & Kim, J. K. (2012). A literature review and classification of recommender systems research. *Expert Systems with Applications*, *39*(11), 10059–10072. doi:10.1016/j.eswa.2012.02.038

Passant, A. (2010). dbrec - Music recommendations using DBpedia. In International Semantic Web Conference (pp. 209-224). Springer. doi:10.1007/978-3-642-17749-1_14

Paul, A. K., & Sato, T. (2017). Localization in Wireless Sensor Networks: A Survey on Algorithms, Measurement Techniques, Applications and Challenges. *Journal of Sensor and Actuator Networks*, *6*(4), 24. doi:10.3390/jsan6040024

Peleg, M. (2013). Computer-interpretable clinical guidelines: A methodological review. *Journal of Biomedical Informatics*, *46*(4), 744–763. doi:10.1016/j.jbi.2013.06.009 PMID:23806274

Peleg, M., & Kantor, R. (2003). Approaches for Guideline Versioning using GLIF. In *Proceedings of the AMIA Symposium* (pp. 509–513). Philadelphia, PA: Hanley & Belfus, Inc.

Peleg, M., Shahar, Y., Quaglini, S., Shalom, E., & Soffer, P. (2017a). MobiGuide: A personalized and patient-centric decision-support system and its evaluation in the atrial fibrillation and gestational diabetes domains. *User Modeling and User-Adapted Interaction*, *27*(2), 159–213. doi:10.100711257-017-9190-5

Peleg, M., Shahar, Y., Quaglini, S., Soffer, P., & van Schooten, B. (2017b). Assessment of a personalized and distributed patient guidance system. *International Journal of Medical Informatics*, *101*, 108–130. doi:10.1016/j.ijmedinf.2017.02.010 PMID:28347441

Peng, T., Li, L., & Kennedy, J. (2014). A Comparison of Techniques for Name Matching. *Journal of Computers*, *2*(1), 55–61.

Pennebaker, J. W., Francis, M. E., & Booth, R. J. (2001). Linguistic inquiry and word count: LIWC 2001. Lawrence Erlbaum Associates.

Perera, C., Zaslavsky, A., Christen, P., & Georgakopoulos, D. (2014). Context aware computing for the internet of things: A survey. *IEEE Communications Surveys and Tutorials*, *16*(1), 414–454. doi:10.1109/SURV.2013.042313.00197

Ponzetto, S. P., & Strube, M. (2011). Taxonomy induction based on a collaboratively built knowledge repository. *Artificial Intelligence*, *175*(9), 1737–1756. doi:10.1016/j.artint.2011.01.003

Portugal, I., Alencar, P., & Cowan, D. (2018). The use of machine learning algorithms in recommender systems: A systematic review. *Expert Systems with Applications*, *97*, 205–227. doi:10.1016/j.eswa.2017.12.020

Porzel, R., & Malaka, R. (2004, August). A task-based approach for ontology evaluation. In *ECAI Workshop on Ontology Learning and Population*, Valencia, Spain (pp. 1-6).

Pow, C., Iron, K., Boyd, J., Brown, A., Thompson, S., Chong, N., & Ma, C. (2017). Privacy-preserving record linkage: An international collaboration between Canada, Australia and Wales. *International Journal for Population Data Science*, *1*(1). doi:10.23889/ijpds.v1i1.101

Pradilla, J., Palau, C., & Esteve, M. (2016). *SOSLITE: Lightweight Sensor Observation Service (SOS) for the Internet of Things (IOT). ITU Kaleidoscope*. Barcelona: Trust in the Information Society.

Pretschner, A. (1998). *Ontology based personalized search*. Unpublished Master's thesis, University of Kansas, Lawrence, Kan.

Quaglini, S., Panzarasa, S., Giorgiani, T., Zucchella, C., Bartolo, M., Sinforiani, E., & Sandrini, G. (2009). Ontology-Based Personalization and Modulation of Computerized Cognitive Exercises. In *Proceedings of the 12th Conference on Artificial Intelligence in Medicine* (pp. 240–244). Berlin, Germany: Springer Verlag. 10.1007/978-3-642-02976-9_34

Quinn, S., Bond, R., & Nugent, C. D. (2014). An Ontology Based Approach to the Provision of Personalized Patient Education. In *Proceedings of the 6th Working Conference – IWAAL* (pp. 67–74). Berlin, Germany: Springer Verlag. 10.1007/978-3-319-13105-4_11

Quintero, R., Torres-Ruiz, M., Menchaca-Mendez, R., Moreno-Armendariz, M. A., Guzman, G., & Moreno-Ibarra, M. (2018). DIS-C: Conceptual distance in ontologies, a graph-based approach. *Knowledge and Information Systems*, 1–33.

Raad, J., & Cruz, C. (2015). A Survey on Ontology Evaluation Methods. In *7th International Joint Conference on Knowledge Discovery, Knowledge Engineering and Knowledge Management* (pp. 179-186).

Rahmani, H., Ranjbar-Sahraei, B., Weiss, G., & Tuyls, K. (2016). Entity resolution in disjoint graphs: An application on genealogical data. *Intelligent Data Analysis*, *20*(2), 455–475. doi:10.3233/IDA-160814

Rahoman, M. M., & Ichise, R. (2018). A proposal of a temporal semantics aware linked data information retrieval framework. *Journal of Intelligent Information Systems*, *50*(3), 573–595. doi:10.100710844-017-0483-2

Rajadesingan, A., Zafarani, R., & Liu, H. (2015). Sarcasm detection on Twitter: A behavioral modeling approach. In *Proceedings of the Eighth ACM International Conference on Web Search and Data Mining* (pp. 97-106). ACM. 10.1145/2684822.2685316

Rajeswari, K., & ShanthiBala, P. (2018). Recognization of Sarcastic Emotions of Individuals on Social Network. *International Journal of Pure and Applied Mathematics*, *18*(7), 253–259.

Reichartz, F., Korte, H., & Paass, G. (2010). Semantic relation extraction with kernels over typed dependency trees. In *Proceedings of the 16th ACM SIGKDD International Conference on Knowledge Discovery and Data KDD'10* (pp. 773-782). 10.1145/1835804.1835902

Rezvan, M., Barekatain, M., Zaeri, A., & Taghandiki, K. (2015). Applying an innovative semantic sensor network model in internet of things. In *Proceedings of the International Conference on Information and Communication Technology Convergence* (pp. 324–328). 10.1109/ICTC.2015.7354556

Riaño, D., Real, F., López-Vallverdú, J. A. F., Ercolani, S., Mecocci, P., Annicchiarico, R., ... Caltagirone, C. (2012). An ontology-based personalization of health-care knowledge to support clinical decisions for chronically ill patients. *Journal of Biomedical Informatics*, *45*(3), 429–446. doi:10.1016/j.jbi.2011.12.008 PMID:22269224

Ricci, F., Rokach, L., & Shapira, B. (2011). Introduction to Recommender Systems Handbook. In *Recommender Systems Handbook* (pp. 1–35). Springer; doi:10.1007/978-0-387-85820-3_1

Riloff, E., Qadir, A., Surve, P., De Silva, L., Gilbert, N., & Huang, R. (2013). *Sarcasm as Contrast between a Positive Sentiment and Negative Situation* (pp. 704–714). EMNLP.

Risteska, B. S. (2016). A taxonomy of localization techniques based on multidimensional scaling. In *2016 39th International Convention on Information and Communication Technology, Electronics and Microelectronics (MIPRO)*. doi:10.1109/MIPRO.2016.7522221

Ristoski, P., Loza Mencía, E., Paulheim, H., & Menc, E. L. (2014). A Hybrid Multi-strategy Recommender System Using Linked Open Data. In V. Presutti, M. Stankovic, E. Cambria, I. Cantador, A. Di Iorio, T. Di Noia, … A. Tordai (Eds.), Semantic Web Evaluation Challenge SE - 19 (Vol. 475, pp. 150–156). Springer International Publishing. doi:10.1007/978-3-319-12024-9_19

Roffia, L., Azzoni, P., Aguzzi, C., Viola, F., Antoniazzi, F., & Salmon Cinotti, T. (2018). Dynamic Linked Data: A SPARQL Event Processing Architecture. *Future Internet*, *10*(4), 36. doi:10.3390/fi10040036

Rouached, M., Baccar, S., & Abid, M. (2012, June). RESTful sensor web enablement services for wireless sensor networks. In *2012 IEEE Eighth World Congress on Services* (pp. 65-72). IEEE. 10.1109/SERVICES.2012.48

Rowe, M. (2014). Transferring Semantic Categories with Vertex Kernels: Recommendations with SemanticSVD++. In P. Mika, T. Tudorache, A. Bernstein et al. (Eds.), *13th International Semantic Web Conference, Riva del Garda, Italy, October 19-23. Proceedings, Part I* (Vol. 8796, pp. 341–356). Springer International Publishing. doi:10.1007/978-3-319-11964-9_22

Ruhl, D. S., & Siegal, G. (2017). Medical Malpractice Implications of Clinical Practice Guidelines. *Otolaryngology - Head and Neck Surgery*, *157*(2), 175–177. doi:10.1177/0194599817707943 PMID:28585462

Rusu, D., Dali, L., Fortuna, B., Grobelnik, M., & Mladenic, D. (2007). Triplet extraction from sentences. In *Proceedings of the 10th International Multiconference Information Society* (pp. 8-12).

Sacchi, L., Fux, A., Napolitano, C., Panzarasa, S., Peleg, M., Quaglini, S., ... Tormene, P. (2013). Patient-tailored workflow patterns from clinical practice guidelines recommendations. In *Proceedings of MedInfo* (pp. 392–396). Amsterdam, The Netherlands: IOS Press.

Sakuma, J., & Kobayashi, S. (2010). Large-scale k-means clustering with user-centric privacy-preservation. *Knowledge and Information Systems*, *25*(2), 253–279. Retrieved from https://link.springer.com/article/10.1007%2Fs10115-009-0243-x

Salber, D., Dey, A. K., & Abowd, G. D. (1998). *Ubiquitous Computing: Defining an Hci Research Agenda for an Emerging Interaction Paradigm*. Atlanta, GA: Georgia Institute of Technology.

Sande, M. V., Verborgh, R., Dimou, A., Colpaert, P., Mannens, E., & Walle, R. V. D. (2016). Hypermedia-based discovery for source selection using low-cost linked data interfaces. *International Journal on Semantic Web and Information Systems*, *12*(3), 79–110. doi:10.4018/IJSWIS.2016070103

Sanders, G. D. (1998). *Automated creation of clinical-practice guidelines from decision models*. Unpublished Ph. Doctoral dissertation, Stanford University, Stanford, CA.

Sanders, G. D., Nease, R. F. Jr, & Owens, D. K. (2001). Publishing Web-based Guidelines using Interactive Decision Models. *Journal of Evaluation in Clinical Practice*, *7*(2), 175–189. doi:10.1046/j.1365-2753.2001.00271.x PMID:11489042

Santipantakis, G., Kotis, K., & Vouros, G. A. (2017). OBDAIR: Ontology-Based Distributed framework for Accessing, Integrating and Reasoning with data in disparate data sources. *Expert Systems with Applications*, *90*, 464–483. doi:10.1016/j.eswa.2017.08.031

Schifanella, R., de Juan, P., Tetreault, J., & Cao, L. (2016). Detecting sarcasm in multimodal socialplatforms. In *Proceedings of the 2016 ACM on Multimedia Conference* (pp. 1136–1145), ACM. 10.1145/2964284.2964321

Schmachtenberg, M., Bizer, C., & Paulheim, H. (2014). Adoption of the Linked Data Best Practices in Different Topical Domains. In P. Mika, T. Tudorache, A. Bernstein et al. (Eds.), The Semantic Web – ISWC 2014 SE - 16 (Vol. 8796, pp. 245–260). Springer International Publishing. doi:10.1007/978-3-319-11964-9_16

Schmachtenberg, M., Bizer, C., Jentzsch, A. & Cyganiak, R. (2014). Linking open data cloud diagram 2014.

Schmachtenberg, M., Strufe, T., & Paulheim, H. (2014). Enhancing a Location-based Recommendation System by Enrichment with Structured Data from the Web. In *Proceedings of the 4th International Conference on Web Intelligence, Mining and Semantics (WIMS14) - WIMS '14* (pp. 1–12). 10.1145/2611040.2611080

Schmidt, M., Hornung, T., Lausen, G., & Pinkel, C. (2009). SP^ 2Bench: a SPARQL performance benchmark. In *IEEE 25th International Conference on Data Engineering ICDE'09* (pp. 222–233).

Schnell, R., Bachteler, T., & Reiher, J. (2009). Privacy-preserving record linkage using Bloom filters. *BMC Medical Informatics and Decision Making*, *9*(1), 41. doi:10.1186/1472-6947-9-41 PMID:19706187

Scott-Wright, A. O., Fischer, R. P., Denekamp, Y., & Boxwala, A. A. (2004). A Methodology for Modular representation of Guidelines. In *Proceedings of the 11th World Congress on Medical Informatics (MEDINFO)* (pp. 149–153). Amsterdam, The Netherlands: IOS Press.

Seco, N., Veale, T., & Hayes, J. (2004). An Intrinsic Information Content Metric for Semantic Similarity in WordNet. In *European Conference on Artificial Intelligence*.

Sekhar Babu, B., Lakshmi Prasanna, P. & Vidyullatha, P. (2018). Personalized web search on e-commerce using ontology based association mining. *International Journal of Engineering and Technology, 7*(1.1), 286–289.

Sen, S., & Balasubramanian, A. 2018. A highly resilient and scalable broker architecture for IoT applications. In *2018 10th International Conference on Communication Systems & Networks (COMSNETS)* (pp. 336-341).

Sewisy Adel, A., Amer Ali, A., & Abdalla Hassan, I. (2017). A novel query-driven clustering-based technique for vertical fragmentation and allocation in distributed database systems. *International Journal on Semantic Web and Information Systems*, *13*(2). Retrieved from http://www.igi-global.com/article/a-novel-query-driven-clustering-based-technique-for-verti-cal-fragmentation-and-allocation-in-distributed-database-systems/176732

Sha, F., & Pereira, F. (2003). Shallow parsing with conditional random fields. In *Proc. of NAACL*, Edmonton, Canada (pp. 134-141).

Shahar, Y., Miksch, S., & Johnson, P. (1998). The Asgaard Project: A Task-specific Framework for the Application and Critiquing of Time-oriented Clinical Guidelines. *Artificial Intelligence in Medicine*, *14*(1-2), 29–51. doi:10.1016/S0933-3657(98)00015-3 PMID:9779882

Shahar, Y., Young, O., Shalom, E., Galperin, M., Mayaffit, A., Moskovitch, R., & Hessing, A. (2004). A framework for a distributed, hybrid, multiple-ontology clinical-guideline library, and automated guideline-support tools. *Journal of Biomedical Informatics*, *37*(5), 325–344. doi:10.1016/j.jbi.2004.07.001 PMID:15488747

Shalom, E., Shahar, Y., & Lunenfeld, E. (2016). An architecture for a continuous, user-driven, and data-driven application of clinical guidelines and its evaluation. *Journal of Biomedical Informatics*, *59*, 130–148. doi:10.1016/j.jbi.2015.11.006 PMID:26616284

She, J., & Lei, C. (2014). TOMOHA: TOpic model-based HAshtag recommendation on twitter. *Proceedings of the companion publication of the 23rd international conference on World wide web companion,* Seoul, Korea (pp. 371-372). 10.1145/2567948.2577292

Sheth, A., Henson, C., & Sahoo, S. S. (2008). Semantic sensor web. *IEEE Internet Computing*, *12*(4), 78–83. doi:10.1109/MIC.2008.87

Shi, D., Yin, J., Li, Y., Qian, J., & Dong, J. (2007). An RDF-Based Publish/Subscribe System. In *Third International Conference on Semantics, Knowledge and Grid* (pp. 342–345).

Shiffman, R. N., Karras, B. T., Agrawal, A., Chen, R., Marenco, L., & Nath, S. (2000). GEM a Proposal for a More Comprehensive Guideline Document Model using XML. *Journal of the American Medical Informatics Association*, *7*(5), 488–497. doi:10.1136/jamia.2000.0070488 PMID:10984468

Shin, K., Jung, J., Lee, S., & Kang, U. (2015). Bear: Block elimination approach for random walk with restart on large graphs. In *Proceedings of the 2015 ACM SIGMOD International Conference on Management of Data* (pp. 1571–1585). 10.1145/2723372.2723716

Shi, Y. X., Li, P., Xiao, B., Wei, T. T., & Jiang, Y. C. (2010). Semantic query expansion method for tourism domain. *Computer Engineering*, *36*(18), 43–45.

Sicilia, M. A., Rodríguez, D., García-Barriocanal, E., & Sánchez-Alonso, S. (2012). Empirical findings on ontology metrics. *Expert Systems with Applications*, *39*(8), 6706–6711. doi:10.1016/j.eswa.2011.11.094

Singh, R., Rai, B. K., & Bose, S. K. (2017). A joint routing and MAC protocol for transmission delay reduction in many-to-one communication paradigm for wireless sensor networks. *IEEE Internet of Things Journal*, *4*(4), 1031–1045. doi:10.1109/JIOT.2017.2724762

Sivakumara, P., & Radhika, M. (2018). Performance Analysis of LEACH-GA over LEACH and LEACH-C in WSN. *Procedia Computer Science*, *125*, 248–256. doi:10.1016/j.procs.2017.12.034

Skovronski, J. (2007). *An ontology-based publish-subscribe framework*. ProQuest.

Sohn, M. M., Jeong, S., & Lee, H. J. (2013). Self-Evolved Ontology-Based Service Personalization Framework for Disabled Users in Smart Home Environment. In *Proceedings of the 7th Int. Confer. on Innovative Mobile and Internet Services in Ubiquitous Computing* (pp. 238–244). Los Alamitos, CA: IEEE Computer Society Press. 10.1109/IMIS.2013.48

Soldatos, J., Kefalakis, N., Hauswirth, M., Serrano, M., Calbimonte, J. P., Riahi, M., ... Skorin-Kapov, L. (2015). Openiot: Open source internet-of-things in the cloud. In *Interoperability and open-source solutions for the internet of things* (pp. 13–25). Cham: Springer. doi:10.1007/978-3-319-16546-2_3

Song, D., Luo, Y., & Heflin, J. (2017). Linking heterogeneous data in the semantic web using scalable and domain-independent candidate selection. *IEEE Transactions on Knowledge and Data Engineering*, *29*(1), 143–156. doi:10.1109/TKDE.2016.2606399

Song, Z., Cardenas, A., Masuoka, R., & ... (2010). Semantic middleware for the Internet of Things. In *Internet of Things* (pp. 1–8). IOT. doi:10.1109/IOT.2010.5678448

Spahiu, N., Ahmedi, L., & Bouju, A. (2010). Implementation of sensor observation services to monitor moving objects [master thesis]. University of Prishtina, Kosovo, and University of La Rochelle, France.

Stanford NER tool. (2015). Retrieved from http://nlp.stanford.edu/ner/index.shtml

Stanford Postagging Tool. (2015). Retrieved from http://nlp.stanford.edu/software/tagger.shtml

Stankovic, M., Breitfuss, W., & Laublet, P. (2011). Discovering Relevant Topics Using DBPedia: Providing Non-obvious Recommendations. In *2011 IEEE/WIC/ACM International Conferences on Web Intelligence and Intelligent Agent Technology* (pp. 219–222). IEEE. 10.1109/WI-IAT.2011.32

Stanoev, A., Filiposk, S., In, V., & Kocarev, L. (2016). Cooperative method for wireless sensor network localization. *Ad Hoc Networks*, *40*, 61–72. doi:10.1016/j.adhoc.2016.01.003

Strapparava, C., & Valitutti, A. (2004). WordNet Affect: an Affective Extension of WordNet. In LREC (Vol. 4, pp. 1083-1086).

Strobin, L., & Niewiadomski, A. (2014). Recommendations and Object Discovery in Graph Databases Using Path Semantic Analysis. In L. Rutkowski, M. Korytkowski, R. Scherer, R. Tadeusiewicz, L. Zadeh, & J. Zurada (Eds.), *13th International Conference, ICAISC 2014, Zakopane, Poland*, June 1-5, *Proceedings, Part I* (Vol. 8467, pp. 793–804). Springer International Publishing. 10.1007/978-3-319-07173-2_68

Stutzbach, A. R. (2011). MusicBrainz [review]. *Notes*, *68*(1), 147–151. doi:10.1353/not.2011.0134

Suchanek, F. M., Kasneci, G., & Weikum, G. (2008). YAGO: A Large Ontology from Wikipedia and WordNet. *Journal of Web Semantics*, *6*(3), 203–217. doi:10.1016/j.websem.2008.06.001

Sukalikar, S., Kumar, S., & Baliyan, N. (2014). Analysing cohesion and coupling for modular ontologies. In *International Conference on Advances in Computing, Communications and Informatics* (pp. 2063-2066). IEEE. 10.1109/ICACCI.2014.6968526

Sun, Y., Gurewitz, O., Du, S., Tang, L., & Johnson, D. B. (2009, November). ADB: an efficient multihop broadcast protocol based on asynchronous duty-cycling in wireless sensor networks. In *Proceedings of the 7th ACM Conference on Embedded Networked Sensor Systems*, Berkeley, CA (pp. 43-56). ACM. 10.1145/1644038.1644044

Sun, Y., Gurewitz, O., & Johnson, D. B. (2008, November). RI-MAC: a receiver-initiated asynchronous duty-cycle MAC protocol for dynamic traffic loads in wireless sensor networks. In *Proceedings of the 6th ACM conference on Embedded network sensor systems*. Raleigh, NC (pp. 1-14). ACM. 10.1145/1460412.1460414

Suo, H., Wan, J., Zou, C., & Liu, J. (2012). Security in the internet of things: a review. In *2012 International Conference on Computer Science and Electronics Engineering (ICCSEE)* (Vol. 3, pp. 648–651). 10.1109/ICCSEE.2012.373

Sutton, C., & McCallum, A. (2006), An introduction to conditional random fields for relational learning, In L. Getoor & B. Taskar (Eds.), Introduction to Statistical Relational Learning. Cambridge: MIT Press.

Suzuki, S., Orihara, R., Sei, Y., Tahara, Y., & Ohsuga, A. (2017). Sarcasm Detection Method to Improve Review Analysis. In ICAART (Vol. 2, pp. 519-526).

Swami, S., Khandelwal, A., Singh, V., Akhtar, S. S., & Shrivastava, M. (2018). A Corpus of English-Hindi Code-Mixed Tweets for Sarcasm Detection. arXiv:1805.11869

Taelman, R. (2016). Continuously self-updating query results over dynamic heterogeneous linked data. In H. Sack, E. Blomqvist, M. Daquin, C. Ghidini, S. P. Ponzetto, & C. Lange (Eds.), *Semantic Web: Latest Advances And New Domains* (Vol. 9678, pp. 863–872). Cham: Springer Int Publishing Ag. doi:10.1007/978-3-319-34129-3_55

Taherkordi, A., Rouvoy, R., Le-Trung, Q., & Eliassen, F. (2008, December). A self-adaptive context processing framework for wireless sensor networks. In *Proceedings of the 3rd international workshop on Middleware for sensor networks.* Oslo, Norway (pp. 7-12). ACM. 10.1145/1462698.1462700

Talaika, A., Biega, J., Amarilli, A., & Suchanek, F. (2015). IBEX: harvesting entities from the web using unique identifiers. In Proceedings of WebDB (pp. 13-19).

Tan, H., Adlemo, A., Tarasov, V., & Johansson, M. E. (2017). Evaluation of an Application Ontology. In *Proceedings of the Joint Ontology Workshops 2017 Episode 3: The Tyrolean Autumn of Ontology,* Bozen-Bolzano, Italy, September 21–23. Rheinisch-Westfaelische Technische Hochschule Aachen* Lehrstuhl Informatik V.

Tandon, N., Hariman, C., Urbani, J., Rohrbach, A., Rohrbach, M., & Weikum, G. (2016). Commonsense in parts: mining part-whole relations from the web and image tags. In *Proceedings of the Thirtieth AAAI Conference on Artificial Intelligence* (pp. 243-250).

Tao, K., Abel, F., Hauff, C., & Houben, G.-J. (2012). What makes a tweet relevant for a topic? *In MSM 2012, Proceedings of the workshop on Making Sense of Microposts (MSM2012), workshop at the 21st World Wide Web Conference 2012,* Lyon, France (pp. 49-56).

Tayal, D. K., Yadav, S., Gupta, K., Rajput, B., & Kumari, K. (2014, March). Polarity detection of sarcastic political tweets. In *2014 International Conference on Computing for Sustainable Global Development (INDIACom)* (pp. 625-628). IEEE. 10.1109/IndiaCom.2014.6828037

Terenziani, P., Montani, S., Bottrighi, A., Molino, G., & Torchio, M. (2005). Clinical Guidelines Adaptation: Managing Authoring and Versioning Issues. In *Proceedings of the 10th Conf. on Artificial Intelligence in medicine (AIME)* (pp. 151–155). Berlin, Germany: Springer Verlag. 10.1007/11527770_22

Terenziani, P., Montani, S., Bottrighi, A., Torchio, M., Molino, G., & Correndo, G. (2004). A Context-adaptable Approach to Clinical Guidelines. In *Proceedings of the 11th World Congress on Medical Informatics (MEDINFO)* (pp. 169–173). Amsterdam, The Netherlands: IOS Press.

Thomson, G., Bianco, S., Ben Mokhtar, S., Georgantas, N., & Issarny, V. (2008). Amigo aware services. In *Constructing Ambient Intelligence* (pp. 385–390). Springer. doi:10.1007/978-3-540-85379-4_43

Tomeo, P., Fernández-Tobías, I., Cantador, I., & Di Noia, T. (2017). Addressing the Cold Start with Positive-Only Feedback Through Semantic-Based Recommendations. *International Journal of Uncertainty, Fuzziness and Knowledge-based Systems, 25*(Suppl. 2), 57–78. doi:10.1142/S0218488517400116

Tong, F., & Pan, J. (2017). ADC: An adaptive data collection protocol with free addressing and dynamic duty-cycling for sensor networks. *Mobile Networks and Applications, 22*(5), 983–994. doi:10.100711036-017-0850-9

Tran, v. C., Hwang, D., & Nguyen, N. T. (2018). Hashtag Recommendation Approach Based on Content and User Characteristics. *International Journal of Cybernetics and Systems.*

Tran, P. N., & Nguyen, D. T. (2015). Mapping expansion of natural language entities to DBpedia's components for querying linked data. In *Proceedings of the International Conference on Ubiquitous Information Management and Communication* (pp. 1-5). ACM. 10.1145/2701126.2701212

Tran, T., Herzig, D. M., & Ladwig, G. (2011). SemSearchPro-Using semantics throughout the search process. *Journal of Web Semantics, 9*(4), 349–364. doi:10.1016/j.websem.2011.08.004

Tresp, V., Overhage, J., Bundschus, M., Rabizadeh, S., Fasching, P., & Yu, S. (2016). Going digital: A survey on digitalization and large-scale data analytics in healthcare. *Proceedings of the IEEE, 104*(11), 2180–2206. doi:10.1109/JPROC.2016.2615052

Tsur, O., Davidov, D., & Rappoport, A. (2010). ICWSM-A Great Catchy Name: Semi-Supervised Recognition of Sarcastic Sentences in Online Product Reviews. In ICWSM (pp. 162–169). ACL

Tungthamthiti, P., Shirai, K., & Mohd, M. (2014). Recognition of Sarcasm in Tweets Based on Concept Level Sentiment Analysis and Supervised Learning Approaches. In *Proceedings of Pacific Asia Conference on Language, Information and Computing* (pp. 404–413). ACL.

Tu, S. W., Peleg, M., Carini, S., Bobak, M., Ross, J., Rubin, D., & Sim, I. (2011). A practical method for transforming free-text eligibility criteria into computable criteria. *Journal of Biomedical Informatics, 44*(2), 239–250. doi:10.1016/j.jbi.2010.09.007 PMID:20851207

Udayakumar, P., & Indhumathi, M. (2012). Semantic web based Sensor Planning Services (SPS) for Sensor Web Enablement (SWE). arXiv:1207.5310

Umbrich, J., Hose, K., Karnstedt, M., Harth, A., & Polleres, A. (2011). Comparing data summaries for processing live queries over linked data. *World Wide Web, 14*(5-6), 495–544. doi:10.100711280-010-0107-z

Utsumi, A. (2002). Toward a cognitive model of poetic effects in figurative language. In *2002 IEEE International Conference on Systems, Man and Cybernetics* (Vol. 7, pp. 6–11). IEEE.

Utsumi, A. (2000). Verbal irony as implicit display of ironic environment: Distinguishing ironic utterances from nonirony. *Journal of Pragmatics, 32*(12), 1777–1806. doi:10.1016/S0378-2166(99)00116-2

Vagliano, I., Figueroa, C., Rodriguez, O., Torchiano, M., Faron-Zucker, C., & Morisio, M. (2016). *ReDyAl: A Dynamic Recommendation Algorithm based on Linked Data. In 3rd Workshop on New Trends in Content-based Recommender Systems - CBRecSys 2016* (pp. 31–39). Boston, MA, USA: CEUR Workshop Proceedings; Retrieved from http://ceur-ws.org/Vol-1673/paper6.pdf

Valkanas, G., Lappas, T., & Gunopulos, D. (2017). Mining competitors from large unstructured datasets. *IEEE Transactions on Knowledge and Data Engineering, 29*(9), 1971–1984. doi:10.1109/TKDE.2017.2705101

Varga, A. (2010). *OMNeT++ User Manual, Version 4.1*. Retrieved from www.omnetpp.org

Vatsalan, D., Sehili, Z., Christen, P., & Rahm, E. (2017). Privacy-Preserving Record Linkage for Big Data: Current Approaches and Research Challenges. In Handbook of Big Data Technologies (pp. 851–895). Springer.

Vazquez, J. I., de Ipiña, D., & Sedano, I. (2007). Soam: A web-powered architecture for designing and deploying pervasive semantic devices. *International Journal of Web Information Systems, 2*(3/4), 212–224. doi:10.1108/17440080780000301

Vergari, F., Bartolini, S., Spadini, F., D'Elia, A., Zamagni, G., Roffia, L., & Cinotti, T. S. (2010). A smart space application to dynamically relate medical and environmental information. In *Proceedings of the Conference on Design, Automation and Test in Europe* (pp. 1542–1547). 10.1109/DATE.2010.5457056

Vergari, F., Cinotti, T. S., D'Elia, A., Roffia, L., Zamagni, G., & Lamberti, C. (2011). An integrated framework to achieve interoperability in person-centric health management. *International Journal of Telemedicine and Applications, 2011*, 5. doi:10.1155/2011/549282 PMID:21811499

Verma, A. (2016). An abstract framework for ontology evaluation. In *International Conference on Data Science and Engineering* (pp. 1-6). IEEE.

Verma, N., & Bhattacharyya, P. (2004). Automatic lexicon generation through WordNet. *GWC, 2004*, 226–229.

Vidhya, K. A., & Geetha, T. V. (2017). Resolving entity on a large scale: determining linked entities and grouping similar attributes represented in assorted terminologies. *Distributed and Parallel Databases, 35*(3–4), 303–332. doi:10.100710619-017-7205-1

Volz, J., Bizer, C., Gaedke, M., & Kobilarov, G. (2009). *Silk-A Link Discovery Framework for the Web of Data* (Vol. 538). LDOW.

Vrandecic, D., & Sure, Y. (2007). How to design better ontology metrics. *Lecture Notes in Computer Science, 45*(19), 311–325. doi:10.1007/978-3-540-72667-8_23

Wagner, A., Duc, T. T., Ladwig, G., Harth, A., & Studer, R. (2012). Top-k linked data query processing. In *Proceedings of the 9th Extended Semantic Web Conference, ESWC 2012* (pp. 56-712). Springer.

Wang, K., Thrasher, C., & Paul Hsu, B.-J. (2011). Web scale NLP: a case study on url word breaking. In *WWW '11 Proceedings of the 20th international conference on World wide web* (pp. 357-366).

Wang, C., Fan, J., Kalyanpur, A., & Gondek, D. (2011). Relation extraction with relation topics. In *Proceedings of the International Conference on Empirical Methods in Natural Language Processing* (pp. 1426-1436).

Wang, G., Yu, J., Yu, D., Yu, H., Feng, L., & Liu, P. (2015). DS-MAC: An Energy Efficient Demand Sleep MAC Protocol with Low Latency for Wireless Sensor Networks. *Journal of Network and Computer Applications, 58*, 155–164. doi:10.1016/j.jnca.2015.09.007

Wang, H.-Q., Li, J.-S., Zhang, Y.-F., Suzuki, M., & Araki, K. (2013). Creating personalised clinical pathways by semantic interoperability with electronic health records. *Artificial Intelligence in Medicine, 58*(2), 81–89. doi:10.1016/j.artmed.2013.02.005 PMID:23466439

Wang, J., Jin, B., & Li, J. (2004). An ontology-based publish/subscribe system. In *Proceedings of the 5th ACM/IFIP/USENIX international conference on Middleware* (pp. 232–253).

Wang, L., Cao, Z., Melo, G. D., & Liu, Z. (2016). Relation Classification via Multi-Level Attention CNNs. In *Proceedings of the Annual Meeting of the Association for Computational Linguistics* (pp. 1298-1307).

Wang, X., Dong, J. S., Chin, C. Y., Hettiarachchi, S. R., & Zhang, D. (2004). Semantic Space: An infrastructure for smart spaces. *Pervasive Computing, 3*(3), 32–39. doi:10.1109/MPRV.2004.1321026

Wang, Z., Wu, Z., Wang, R., & Ren, Y. (2015). Twitter sarcasm detection exploiting a context-basedmodel. *In International Conference on Web Information Systems Engineering 2015* (pp. 77–91). Springer.

Welling, M. (2011). *A First Encounter with Machine Learning*. Donald Bren School of Information and Computer Science - University of California Irvine. Retrieved from https://www.ics.uci.edu/~welling/teaching/ICS273Afall11/IntroMLBook.pdf

Weymann, N., Dirmaier, J., von Wolff, A., Kriston, L., & Härter, M. (2015). Effectiveness of a Web-Based Tailored Interactive Health Communication Application for Patients with Type 2 Diabetes or Chronic Low Back Pain: Randomized Controlled Trial. *Journal of Medical Internet Research, 17*(3), e53. Retrieved from https://www.jmir.org/2015/3/e53/ doi:10.2196/jmir.3904 PMID:25736340

Wiemann, S., & Bernard, L. (2016). Spatial data fusion in spatial data infrastructures using linked data. *International Journal of Geographical Information Science, 30*(4), 613–636. doi:10.1080/13658816.2015.1084420

Wiese, L., Waage, T., & Bollwein, F. (2017). A Replication Scheme for Multiple Fragmentations with Overlapping Fragments. *The Computer Journal*, *60*(3), 308–328. http://ieeexplore.ieee.org/document/8187838/

Wilk, S., Fux, A., Michalowski, M., Peleg, M., & Soffer, P. (2017). Using constraint logic programming for the verification of customized decision models for clinical guidelines. In *Proceedings of the16th Conf. on Artificial Intelligence in Medicine (AIME)* (pp. 37–47). 10.1007/978-3-319-59758-4_4

World Wide Web Consortium. (2018a). Extensible Markup Language (XML) Home Page. Retrieved April 4, 2018 from http://www.w3.org/XML/

World Wide Web Consortium. (2018b). Web Ontology Language (OWL) Home Page. Retrieved April 4, 2018 from http://www.w3.org/2004/OWL/

World Wide Web Consortium. (2018c). XML Query Language (XQuery) Home Page. Retrieved April 4, 2018 from http://www.w3.org/XML/Query/

Wu, H., Mei, X., Chen, X., Li, J., Wang, J., & Mohapatr, P. (2017). A novel cooperative localization algorithm using enhanced particle filter technique in maritime search and rescue wireless sensor network. *ISA Transactions*, 1–8. doi:10.1016/j.isatra.2017.09.013 PMID:28969856

Xu, L., Yang, G., Xu, J., Wang, L., & Dai, H. (2018). Achieving adaptive broadcasting performance tradeoff for energy-critical sensor networks: A bottom-up approach. *Computer Networks*, *136*, 155–170. doi:10.1016/j.comnet.2018.03.007

Yancey, W. E. (2002). BigMatch: A program for extracting probable matches from a large file for record linkage. *Computing*, *1*, 1–8.

Yang, R., Hu, W., Qu, Y., Li, G., Wang, P., Yu, B., ... Qu, Y. (2013). Using Semantic Technology to Improve Recommender Systems Based on Slope One. *Semantic Web and Web Science*, *2*(1), 11–23. doi:10.1007/978-1-4614-6880-6_2

Yang, F., Wu, D. Z., Lin, L. M., Yang, J., Yang, T. H., & Zhao, J. (2017). The integration of weighted gene association networks based on information entropy. *PLoS One*, *12*(12), 19. doi:10.1371/journal.pone.0190029 PMID:29272314

Yao, H., Orme, A. M., & Etzkorn, L. (2005). Cohesion metrics for ontology design and application. *Journal of Computational Science*, *1*(1), 107–113. doi:10.3844/jcssp.2005.107.113

Yap, W., & Baldwin, T. (2009). Experiments on pattern-based relation learning. In *Proceedings of the 18th ACM Conference on Information and Knowledge Management* (pp. 1657-1660).

Yu, H., Bing, Z., Mingyao, D., & Feng, H. (2018). Tag recommendation method in folksonomy based on user tagging status. *Journal of Intelligent Information Systems*, *50*(3), 479–500. doi:10.100710844-017-0468-1

Yu, M., Li, G., Deng, D., & Feng, J. (2016). String similarity search and join: A survey. *Frontiers of Computer Science*, *10*(3), 399–417. doi:10.100711704-015-5900-5

Zablith, F., Antoniou, G., d'Aquin, M., Flouris, G., Kondylakis, H., Motta, E., ... Sabou, M. (2013). Ontology Evolution: A Process Centric Survey. *The Knowledge Engineering Review*, *30*(1), 45–75. doi:10.1017/S0269888913000349

Zahaf, A., & Malki, M. (2018). Methods for Ontology Alignment Change. In Handbook of Research on Contemporary Perspectives on Web-Based Systems (pp. 214–239). Hershey, PA: IGI Global. doi:10.4018/978-1-5225-5384-7.ch011

Zangerle, E., Gassler, W., & Specht, G. (2011). Recommending #-tags in Twitter. In *Proceedings of the Workshop on Semantic Adaptive Social Web 2011 in connection with the 19th International Conference on User Modeling, Adaptation and Personalization,* Gerona, Spain.

Zangerle, E., Gassler, W., & Specht, G. (2011). Using Tag Recommendations to Homogenize Folksonomies in Microblogging Environments. In *Proceedings of the Workshop on Semantic Adaptive Social Web 2011 in connection with the 19th International Conference on User Modeling, Adaptation and Personalization,* Singapore. 10.1007/978-3-642-24704-0_16

Zangerle, E., Gassler, W., & Specht, G. (2013). On the impact of text similarity functions on hashtag recommendations in microblogging environments. *Social Network Analysis and Mining, 3*(4), 889–898.

Zaveri, A., Maurino, A., & Equille, L.-B. (2014). Web Data Quality: Current State and New Challenges Amrapali. *International Journal on Semantic Web and Information Systems, 10*(2), 1–6. doi:10.4018/ijswis.2014040101

Zekri, A., Brahmia, Z., Grandi, F., & Bouaziz, R. (2016). τ OWL: A Systematic Approach to Temporal Versioning of Semantic Web Ontologies. *Journal on Data Semantics, 5*(3), 141–163. doi:10.100713740-016-0066-3

Zelenko, D., Aone, C., & Richardella, A. (2003). Kernel methods for relation extraction. *Journal of Machine Learning Research, 3*(6), 1083–1166.

Zhang, M., Su, J., & Wang, D., Zhou, g., & Tan. C. (2005). Discovering relations from a large raw corpus using tree similarity based clustering. In *Proc. of IJCNLP,* Jeju Island, Korea (pp. 378-389).

Zhang, Y., Wu, H., Sorathia, V., & Prasanna, V. K. (2014). Event recommendation in social networks with linked data enablement. In *ICEIS 2013 - Proceedings of the 15th International Conference on Enterprise Information Systems* (Vol. 2, pp. 371–379). Retrieved from http://www.scopus.com/inward/record.url?eid=2-s2.0-84887649972&partnerID=tZOtx3y1

Zhang, C., Hoffmann, R., & Weld, D. S. (2012). Ontological smoothing for relation extraction with minimal supervision. In *Proceedings of the Twenty-Sixth AAAI Conference on Artificial Intelligence* (pp. 157-163).

Zhang, H., Li, Y. F., & Tan, H. B. K. (2010). Measuring design complexity of semantic web ontologies. *Journal of Systems and Software, 83*(5), 803–814. doi:10.1016/j.jss.2009.11.735

Zhang, L. Y., Ren, J. D., & Li, X. W. (2017). OIM-SM: A method for ontology integration based on semantic mapping. *Journal of Intelligent & Fuzzy Systems, 32*(3), 1983–1995. doi:10.3233/JIFS-161553

Zhang, L., Perl, Y., Halper, M., Geller, J., & Cimino, J. J. (2004). An enriched unified medical language system semantic network with a multiple subsumption hierarchy. *Journal of the American Medical Informatics Association, 11*(3), 195–206. doi:10.1197/jamia.M1269 PMID:14764611

Zhang, W. E., Sheng, Q. Z., Qin, Y. R., Taylor, K., & Yao, L. N. (2018). Learning-based SPARQL query performance modeling and prediction. *World Wide Web-Internet and Web Information Systems, 21*(4), 1015–1035.

Zhang, Y.-F., Gou, L., Zhou, T.-S., Li, Y., & Li, J.-S. (2017). An ontology-based approach to patient follow-up assessment for continuous and personalized chronic disease management. *Journal of Biomedical Informatics, 72,* 45–59. doi:10.1016/j.jbi.2017.06.021 PMID:28676255

Zhang, Y., & Padman, R. (2017). Data-driven Approaches for Developing Clinical Practice Guidelines. In N. Wickramasinghe (Ed.), *Handbook of Research on Healthcare Administration and Management* (pp. 30–46). Hershey, PA: IGI Global. doi:10.4018/978-1-5225-0920-2.ch003

Zhao, F., Zhu, Y., Jin, H., & Laurence, T. Y. (2016). A personalized hashtag recommendation approach using LDA-based topic model in microblog environment. *Future Generation Computer Systems, 65,* 196–206. doi:10.1016/j.future.2015.10.012

Zhao, J., & Jin, P. (2009). *Towards the extraction of intelligence about competitor from the web.* In *Proc. of The Second World Summit on the Knowledge Society,* Crete, Greece (pp. 118–127). doi:10.1007/978-3-642-04754-1_13

Zhao, J., & Jin, P. (2010a). Conceptual modeling of the competitive intelligence hiding in the internet. *Journal of Software*, *5*(4), 378–386.

Zhao, J., Jin, P., & Liu, Y. (2010b). Business relations in the web: Semantics and a case study. *Journal of Software*, *5*(8), 826–833. doi:10.4304/jsw.5.8.826-833

Zhao, J., Jin, P., Zhang, Q., & Wen, R. (2014). Exploiting location information for web search. *Computers in Human Behavior*, *30*, 378–388. doi:10.1016/j.chb.2013.04.023

Zhao, X., Jin, P., & Yue, L. (2010). Automatic temporal expression normalization with reference time Dynamic-Choosing. In *Proc. of COLING*, Beijing, China (pp. 1498-1506).

Zheng, E., Yukio Kondo, G., Zilora, S., & Yu, Q. (2018). Tag-aware dynamic music recommendation. *Expert Systems with Applications*, *106*, 244–251. doi:10.1016/j.eswa.2018.04.014

Zheng, S., Wang, F., & Lu, J. (2014). Enabling Ontology Based Semantic Queries in Biomedical Database Systems. *International Journal of Semantic Computing*, *8*(1), 67–83. doi:10.1142/S1793351X14500032 PMID:25541585

Zhong, N., Ma, J., Huang, R., Liu, J., Yao, Y., Zhang, Y., & Chen, J. (2016). Research challenges and perspectives on Wisdom Web of Things (W2T). In *Wisdom Web of Things* (pp. 3–26). Cham: Springer. doi:10.1007/978-3-319-44198-6_1

Zhou, G. D., Su, J., Zhang, J., & Zhang, M. (2005). Exploring various knowledge in relation extraction. In *Proc. of ACL* (pp. 427-434).

Zhou, Z., Cui, J. H., & Zhou, S. (2010). Efficient localization for large scale underwater sensor networks. *Ad Hoc Networks*, *8*(3), 267–279. doi:10.1016/j.adhoc.2009.08.005

Zhou, Z., & Yongkang, X. (2013). *A study on ontology storage based on relational database. Conference Anthology.* IEEE. doi:10.1109/ANTHOLOGY.2013.6784899

Zhu, J., Nie, Z., Liu, X., Zhang, B., & Wen, J. R. (2009). StatSnowball: a statistical approach to extracting entity relationships. In *Proceedings of the International Conference on World Wide Web*, Madrid, Spain (pp. 101-110). 10.1145/1526709.1526724

Zhu, L., Ghasemi-Gol, M., Szekely, P., Galstyan, A., & Knoblock, C. A. (2016). Unsupervised Entity Resolution on Multi-type Graphs. In *International Semantic Web Conference* (pp. 649–667).

About the Contributors

Miltiadis D. Lytras, Dr., is an Associate Professor at Deree- ACG with a research focus on semantic web, knowledge management and e-learning, with more than 100 publications. He has co-edited more than 45 special issues in international journals (*IEEE Transaction on Knowledge and Data Engineering*; *IEEE Internet Computing*; *IEEE Transactions on Education*;, *Computers in Human Behaviour*; *Interactive Learning Environments*; *Journal of Knowledge Management*; *Journal of Computer Assisted Learning*) and has authored/edited 42 books (e.g. *Open Source for Knowledge and Learning Management; Ubiquitous and Pervasive Knowledge Management; Intelligent Learning Infrastructures for Knowledge Intensive Organizations; Semantic Web Based Information Systems; China Information Technology Handbook; Real World Applications of Semantic Web and Ontologies; Web 2.0: The Business Model*; etc.). He has served as an Editor in Chief of 8 international journals (e.g. *International Journal on Semantic Web and Information Systems, International Journal of Knowledge Society Research, International Journal of Knowledge and Learning, International Journal of Technology Enhanced Learning*).

***

Naif Radi Aljohani, is an Assistant Professor and Head of Information Systems Department, Faculty of Computing and Information Technology (FCIT), King Abdulaziz University, Jeddah Saudi Arabia. He got his PhD in CS from the University of Southampton. His research interests are human-computer interaction, information science, and computer communications.

Ernesto Damiani joined Khalifa as Director of the Information Security Center. He is on extended leave from the Department of Computer Science, Università degli Studi di Milano, Italy, where he leads the SESAR research lab. Ernesto's research interests include secure service-oriented architectures, privacy-preserving Big Data analytics and Cyber-Physical Systems security. Ernesto has held visiting positions at many international institutions, including George Mason University, US; Tokyo Denki University, Japan; LaTrobe University, Australia; and the Institut National des Sciences Appliquées (INSA) at Lyon, France. He has been Principal Investigator many large-scale research projects funded by the European Commission, the Italian Ministry of Research and by private companies such as British Telecom; Cisco Systems; SAP; Telecom Italia; Siemens Networks (now Nokia Siemens) and others. In 2008, Ernesto was nominated ACM Distinguished Scientist and received the Chester Sall Award from the IEEE Industrial Electronics Society. In 2016 he received the Services Society Stephen Yau Award. Ernesto has co-authored over 400 scientific papers and many books.

Kwok Chui, Dr., received the B.Eng. degree in electronic and communication engineering - Business Intelligence Minor from and Ph.D. degree from City University of Hong Kong in 2013 and 2017, respectively. His research interests include artificial intelligence, data analytics, wireless communication, pattern recognition, healthcare, machine learning algorithms and optimization. He was the recipient of 2nd Prize Award (Postgraduate Category) of 2014 IEEE Region 10 Student Paper Contest. Also, he received Best Paper Award in the IEEE International Conference on Consumer Electronics-China, in both 2014 and 2015. He has around 30 research publications, journal papers, conference papers and book chapters. His research interests include complex network, wireless communication, pattern recognition, healthcare, machine learning algorithms and optimization. He has served as various editorial positions and guest editors in referred international journals and conferences.

Cristiano Aguzzi graduated in Computer Engineering in 2017 at University of Bologna. He is currently a Ph.D. student of Structural and Environmental Health Monitoring and he is working on Linked Data technologies. His research interests are web of things, system software engineering, and software dependability. Other topics are machine learning, AI, computer vision, domain-specific languages and computational models. Technical skills include in Java, C, C++, Go and JavaScript languages.

Lule Ahmedi is a Full Professor at the University of Prishtina, Kosova, Faculty of Electrical and Computer Engineering, where she joined in 2005. She received her PhD in 2004 in Computer Science from University of Freiburg, Germany, where she was also employed as teaching / research staff. She has published papers in renowned international venues in the areas of semantic web, XML and databases, data integration, social network analysis, information retrieval, recommender systems, and is currently also interested in data science, Internet of Things, stream data, and sensor web. She has provided invited lectures in several universities in Europe, as well as implemented some ten projects in ICT, mainly own-authored and as a manager in addition to serving as a lead researcher.

Wafa Akkari, Dr., received her PhD in computer science in 2011 from the National School of Computer Sciences (ENSI), University of Manouba, Tunisia. She is presently a member of HANA Laboratory (Heterogeneous Advanced Networking and Applications) and an Assistant Professor at ENSI since 2012. Her research interests include power saving mechanisms in ad hoc networks, routing, localization and MAC protocols for sensor networks, performance evaluation and simulation.

Ali A. Amer (Ali Abdullah Amer) received his BSc in computer science from Basrah University (IRAQ / 2005) and MSc in computer science from King Saud University (Saudi Arabia / 2013). He had spent four years (2005-2009) as a faculty member (demonstrator) at Taiz University (YEMEN) with an appointments in Computer Science Department, then moved to King Saud University as a Master researcher of computer science in late of 2009. Ali has been currently pursuing his PhD in Assuit University (Egypt / 2015- Present) with an expectation of being graduated at 2019. To present, he has still been serving as doctor assistant in computer science Department at Taiz University since December of 2014. He has been publishing many research papers in highly-ranked and top-tier journals, and refereed International conferences. He has also acted as reviewer for these well-respected Journals. Off these Journals, he has published in, and reviewed for: ACM computing Surveys, Computer in Human behavior, International Journal on Semantic Web and Information Systems, Universal Computer Science and Heliyon, to name a few. His primary interest of research falls into: Database, Distributed and parallel Database Systems, Distributed Systems, Data Integration, Data Mining, Network and Information Retrieval.

Arten Avdiu is currently a PhD Student at South East European University. 15 February 2013–Present, Lecturer at University of Prizren, Prizren (Kosova). 15 February 2012–Present, Lecturer University Institution - VPA, Ferizaj (Kosova). 01 October 2011–Present, Assistant, University of Prishtina, Prishtina (Kosova). 06 October 2007–Present, Solution Architect, Raiffaisen Bank Kosovo, Prishtina (Kosova).

Paolo Azzoni is the Research Program Manager at the Eurotech Group. He is responsible for the international research projects and his main working areas include machine-to-machine (M2M) distributed systems, device to cloud architectures and solutions, semantic M2M and Internet of Things (IoT). He is the chairman of Artemis-IA working group on IoT. Previously, he was involved in academic research and teaching activities in the areas of formal verification, hw/sw co-design and co-simulation for embedded systems and microprocessors. In 2006, he joined ETHLab (Eurotech Research Center) as a Research Project Manager and he has been responsible for international research projects in the area of embedded systems. He holds a master's degree in Computer Science and a second master's degree in Artificial Intelligence both from the University of Verona.

Niyati Baliyan is an Assistant Professor at Indira Gandhi Delhi Technical University for Women, Delhi, India. She received her PhD in the Department of Computer Science and Engineering, Indian Institute of Technology Roorkee, India, in 2016. She has published several research papers in international journals and conferences. During her MTech, she received state funded excellence scholarship to study for one semester in Sheffield (U.K.). She has completed her undergraduate training at Indian Institute of Technology, Kanpur, India. Her areas of interest include semantic web, ontologies, data mining, and software engineering.

Abdelfettah Belghith is currently a full Professor of Computer Science at the College of Computer and Information Sciences, King Saud University, Saudi Arabia. He received his Ph.D. and his Master of Science both in computer science from the University of California at Los Angeles (UCLA) respectively in 1987 and 1982. He is currently the Director of the National School of Conputer Sciences, the Director of the Doctoral School (Gradute School) STICODE of the University of Manouba, the responsible of the Network and Distributed Systems master's degree and the head of the HANA Laboratory at the National School of Computer Sciences. His research and teaching interests focus on advanced Heterogeneous Networking and applications. Particularly, he works on ad hoc networks, sensor networks, mesh networks, WiMax and LTE, inter vehicular communications, management and optimization of hand-off mechanisms, QoS management in wired and wireless networks, performance evaluation and protocol optimization and specification. He is the author of more than 200 journal articles and conference papers. He is currently serving on several reputed international conference Technical Program Committees (IEEE Globecom, IEEE ICC, IEEE LCN, IEEE VTC, IEEE GIIS, IEEE WiMob, IEEE WCNC, etc.). He organized and served as the technical Committee Chair and the organizing committee chair of many international and regional conferences (Africom'98, MCSEI'98, MedHocNet'03, CFIP'06, ICST/CM FTD-DN 2008, CS/IEEE FT-SN 2010, ICWUS 2010, etc.). He has been involved in several national and international collaborative research projects (STIC, CMCU, AUF, PRF, CMPTM, etc.). He has built strong academic and research cooperation with several international institutions (TelecomBretagne, IN-

RIA, IRIS, Labri, LIP6, LAAS, LIA, UCL, LDIOM, SI2M, etc.) with whom several Masters and PhDs have been conducted under joint supervisions. As the head of the HANA Laboratory, he supervised over sixty Master and Ph.D. theses on advanced networking and networking applications.

Abdelfettah Belghith is currently a full Professor at the college of computer and information science, the department of computer science at King Saud University. He is since 1992 a full Professor of Computer Science at the National School of Computer Sciences, University of Manouba, Tunisia. He received his Ph.D. and his Master of Science both in computer science from the University of California at Los Angeles (UCLA) respectively in 1987 and 1982. He was the Director General of the National Agency for Research Promotion (ANPR) (October 2013-June 2014), the Director of the National School of Computer Sciences (August 1st, 2010, November 2013), the Director of the Doctoral School (Graduate School) STICODE of the University of Manouba (October 2009, November 2013), the Chair of the National Doctoral and Habilitation committee in computer science September 2001-September 2008 and August 2010- November 2013). As the Director General of the National Agency for Research Promotion (ANPR) at the Ministry of Higher Education and Scientific Research in Tunisia, he conducted and coordinates several multi-million Euro research and innovation structuring cooperation projects. His research interests focus on Advanced Heterogeneous Networking and Applications. He is the author of more than 300 refereed journal articles and peer reviewed international and regional conference papers. As the head of the HANA Research Laboratory, he has supervised over one hundred Master and Ph.D. theses on advanced networking and networking applications. He is a senior member of IEEE, the past chair of the Tunisian IEEE Section, the current Chair of the IEEE Tunisian ComSoc chapter and the IEEE Tunisian VTS Chapter.

Santosh Kumar Bharti received the BE degree in Computer Science and Engineering from Visveswaraiah Technological University, Karnataka, India in 2007 and M.Tech degree in Computer Science and Engineering from Graphic Era University, Dehradun, India in 2012. He has submitted his PhD thesis in the dept. of Computer Science at National Institute of Technology, Rourkela, India. Currently, he is working as a lecturer at Pandit Deendayal Petroleum University, Gandhinagar. His research interest includes Opinion Mining and Sarcasm Detection.

Badia Bouhdid received the MSc degree in computer science from the National School of Computer Sciences (ENSI), University of Manouba, Tunisia. Currently, she is a PhD student in computer science and member of HANA Research Laboratory, the National School of Computer Sciences (ENSI), University of Manouba. Her main research areas are wireless sensor networks, QoS, localization algorithms, routing approaches and data collection.

Eliot Bytyçi is a teaching assistant in the Department of Mathematics, Faculty of Mathematical and Natural Sciences, University of Prishtina, Kosova. At the same time, he is enrolled in PhD studies at the Faculty of Electrical and Computer Engineering, at the same University.

Juan Carlos Corrales received Dipl-Ing and master's degrees in telematics engineering from the University of Cauca, Colombia, in 1999 and 2004, respectively, and a Ph.D. degree in sciences, specialty computer science, from the University of Versailles Saint-Quentin-en-Yve-lines, France, in 2008. Presently, he is a full professor and leads the Telematics Engineering Group at the University of Cauca. His research interests focus on service composition and data analysis.

Alfredo D'Elia was born in Catanzaro, Italy, in 1981. He received the master's (summa cum laude) degree from the University of Bologna, Bologna, Italy, in 2006, and the Ph.D. degree in information technology from the University of Bologna in 2012, where he was a Research Assistant. He worked in several European projects, such as SOFIA, CHIRON, Internet of Energy, and Arrowhead. He also collaborated with important industries, like Telecom Italia, Rome, Italy, and was an Intern in Nokia, Finland, for six months, where he was a co-inventor of a patent. He also teaches with the University of Bologna and Cesena as an Assistant Professor, where he is responsible for didactic modules. His main topics of interest in research are semantic web, interoperability, information representation techniques, software architecture, and system characterization and optimization.

Lujuan Deng, PhD, is a professor in Software Engineering College, at the Zhengzhou University of Light Industry. Her research interests focus on machine learning, data mining, and knowledge engineering.

Catherine Faron Zucker is an Assistant Professor of Computer Science at University Nice Sophia Antipolis since 2002. She received her PhD in Computer Science from the University Paris 6. She teaches in the Computer Science department of the Engineer School Polytech Nice Sophia where she is responsible of the option of the master's degree IFI entitled "Web Sciences, Technologies, Resources and Applications." She is vice-head of the Wimmics project, a joint research team between Inria, CNRS and University Nice Sophia Antipolis. Her research activity focuses on Knowledge Engineering and Modelling, Graph based Knowledge Representation and Reasoning, Ontologies, Semantic Web and Social Web. Her main application domains are Collective Memories and Intelligent Tutoring Systems.

Daniel Fernández-Álvarez, is a Ph.D. student at the University of Oviedo (Spain), Department of Computer Science. He is a member of WESO (Web Semantics Oviedo) research group since 2014. His thesis aims for an improvement of the available techniques to extract non-ambiguous, structured knowledge from texts written in natural language. He has made research in a variety of topics related to linked data or semantic web technologies, such as benchmarking of Big Open Linked Data, automatic induction of shapes in RDF graphs, record linkage systems using graph-based approaches, or usage of Linked Data in legal environments (Open City).

Cristhian Figueroa is a researcher currently working for the Universidad Antonio Nariño (Colombia). His research interests include the recommender systems, Semantic Web, linked data, mobile information systems, web services retrieval, and business process retrieval. Figueroa has participated in different research projects at Universidad del Cauca, Universidad Antonio Nariño and Politecnico di Torino in collaboration with Telecom Italia and the research group Nexa.

Sofien Gannouni received his master's degree in Computer Science from Paul Sabatier University (Toulouse III - France), and his PhD degree in Computer Science from Pierre & Marie Curie University (Paris VI - France). Currently, he is an Associate Professor at College of Computer and Information Sciences, King Saud University. His main research interests include service-oriented computing, distributed computing, cloud computing and parallel processing.

Daniel Gayo-Avello, in 2000 he started teaching in the University of Oviedo where he got his PhD in 2005. His main area of interest is Web IR but he is now focused on social media research. He has been published in international conferences, journals and magazines, such as Communications of the ACM, IEEE Internet Computing, or IEEE Multimedia. He acted as guest co-editor for a special issue of Internet Research on the predictive power of social media, and he contributed a chapter on Political Opinion to "Twitter: A Digital Socioscope," published by Cambridge University Press.

Dhouha Ghrab, Dr., received an Engineering degree and an PhD degree in computer science both from The National School of Computer Science, University of Manouba, Tunisia, in 2011 and 2017, respectively. Currently, she is an Assistant professor of computer science at the National School of Electronics and Telecommunications (ENET'COM), University of Sfax, Tunisia. Her research focuses on wireless sensor networking. Particularly, she works on exploiting the concept of context-awareness in MAC and routing layers in WSN to optimize resources use and enhance network performance.

Fabio Grandi received from the University of Bologna, Italy, a Laurea degree cum Laude in electronics engineering in 1988 and a Ph.D. in electronics engineering and computer science in 1994. From 1989 to 2002, he worked at the CSITE center of the Italian National Research Council (CNR) in Bologna in the field of neural networks and temporal databases, initially supported by a CNR fellowship. In 1993 and 1994, he was an Adjunct Professor at the Universities of Ferrara, Italy, and Bologna. In the University of Bologna, he was with the Dept. of Electronics, Computers and Systems from 1994 to 1998 as a Research Associate and as an Associate Professor from 1998 to 2012, when he joined the Dept. of Computer Science and Engineering. He is currently an Associate Professor of Information Systems in the School of Engineering and Architecture of the University of Bologna. His scientific interests include temporal, evolution and versioning aspects in data management, WWW and Semantic Web, knowledge representation, storage structures and access cost models.

Peipei Gu, PhD, the lecturer in Software Engineering College, Zhengzhou University of Light Industry. His research mainly focuses on data science.

Imen Jemili is currently an Assistant professor of computer science at the Faculty of sciences of Bizerte, University of Carthage since September 2009. In 2009, she received her PhD degree jointly from the University of Bordeaux 1 (France), where she was also member of the laboratory LaBRI and the University of Mannouba. She received her M.S. degree in Computer Science in 2002 from the National School of Computer Science (ENSI), University of Mannouba, Tunisia. Her research interests include wireless networks, ad hoc and sensor networks, power conservation, synchronization algorithms, routing, QoS management, simulation and performance evaluation. Recent work co supervised with LaBRI concern context awareness in wireless sensor networks and smart cities.

Yuncheng Jiang, PhD, a professor in School of Computer Science, at South China Normal University. His research interests include semantic analysis of Big Data, semantic search, and data sciences. He does very well in the related field such as intelligence science, distributed intelligence, semantic computing, machine learning, and knowledge engineering, and has published several papers in these fields.

Peiquan Jin is an associate professor in the school of computer science and technology at the University of Science and Technology of China.

Fahd Kalloubi is currently an assistant professor in big data and data science at University Chouaib Doukkali. He obtained his PhD in Computer Science from University of Sidi Mohamed Ben Abdellah (GRMS2I Group) in Morocco. He graduated with Msc in computer science in University Sidi Mohamed Ben Abdellah. His research interests are semantic web, social network analysis, social computing, machine learning, social and personalized information retrieval, information extraction and processing.

Korra Sathya Babu is working as an Assistant Professor in the Dept. of CSE, National Institute of Technology Rourkela India. He has obtained his master's and the doctoral degree from the National Institute of Technology Rourkela, India in the year 2008 and 2013, respectively. His research interest includes data engineering, data privacy, opinion mining and sarcasm sentiment detection.

Jose Emilio Labra Gayo obtained his PhD. in Computer Science Engineering in 2001 at the University of Oviedo with distinction. He was the Dean of the School of Computer Science Engineering at the University of Oviedo between 2004 and 2012. He is the founder and main researcher of WESO (Web Semantics Oviedo) research group, which collaborates with different companies around the world applying semantic web technologies to real world problems. Apart of his teaching at the University of Oviedo, His research interests are Semantic Web technologies, Programming Languages and Web Engineering, where he has published a number of papers in selected conferences and journals. He has been part of the W3C Data Shapes working group that developed SHACL and collaborates in the development of the Shape Expressions language.

Pu Li, PhD, the lecturer in Software Engineering College, Zhengzhou University of Light Industry. His researches mainly focus on data intelligence, semantic computing, and semantic search. He does some studies and has published several papers on ontology engineering, semantic similarity computation, and semantic query and search in recent years.

Junxia Ma is a professor in Software Engineering College, Zhengzhou University of Light Industry. His research interests include intelligence science, artificial intelligence, and computer theory.

Federica Mandreoli is an Associate Professor at the FIM Department of the University of Modena and Reggio Emilia. In 2001, she received a Ph.D. in Computer Engineering from the University of Bologna, in 1997, she graduated with honors in Computer Science at the same University. Her current interests are mainly focuses on information sharing in heterogeneous and distributed contexts and graph-oriented data. In the past, she also worked on other non-conventional data, such as text, data streams and XML, on temporal database and schema versioning, and on personalized access. Her research work in these fields has been mainly centered around data and query models for effective access and data structures and algorithmic issues for efficient query processing. On these topics, she participated to various financed projects and published about one hundred papers.

Riccardo Martoglia received his Laurea Degree (cum Laude) and his Ph.D. in Computer Engineering from the University of Modena and Reggio Emilia. He is currently an assistant professor (associate professor habilitated) in the FIM Department of the same university. His research themes are hot topics in the area of databases, information systems, information retrieval and semantic web. In particular, his work concerns the study of new methodologies for managing, storing and querying large amounts of non-conventional information, including textual, XML and graph data. He is author of over 90 publications and has participated to many National and International projects on the above-mentioned topics.

Maurizio Morisio received the PhD degree in software engineering and the MSc degree in electronic engineering from the Politecnico di Torino. He is a full professor at the Politecnico di Torino, Turin, Italy. Previously, he spent two years working as consultant at IGL Technology, Paris. He spent two years as a researcher with the Experimental Software Engineering Group at the University of Maryland, College Park. His interest lies in finding, applying and evaluating the most suitable techniques and processes to produce better software, faster.

Mohamed Mosbah is a Professor in computer science at the Polytechnic Institute of Bordeaux and a holder of a bonus for scientific excellence. He is currently the Director of Industrial Partnerships and Innovation in Computer Science and Engineering. He carries his research in LaBRI, a research Lab. in computer science common with the University of Bordeaux and CNRS, where he is currently the Deputy Director. His research areas include distributed systems and algorithms, simulation tools, security protocols, VANET and wireless networks. In particular, he is leading a project over the last years to develop a new model together with an integrated methodological framework for distributed algorithms. In addition to capturing classical distributed systems concepts, this framework provides methods and software tools to design, prove and implement distributed algorithms and protocols. This platform is used to teach courses in distributed computing for Graduate computer science students, and also to test and prototype algorithms. He wrote more than 60 articles and developed software tools, and he is involved in various technical program committees and organizations of many international conferences. He is also an expert reviewer of national and European projects. He has directed over 52 master's theses and over 17 PhD dissertations. Prof. Mosbah obtained a French-Italian Grant in the PHC Galilee Program (2014) on "Secure Distributed Protocols in Wireless Environments". He also obtained two grants from the French Ministry of Industry for collaborative projects with Aeronautics Companies: RECORDS (2008 – 2010) and SIMID (2010 – 2013) dealing with the safe distributed information processing. He is currently involved in the European-Indian REACH project (2015 – 2018). In 2012, he obtained an academic palm from his institute recognizing his contributions to teaching, research and service.

El Habib Nfaoui is currently an associate Professor of Computer Science at the University of Sidi Mohammed Ben Abdellah. He obtained his PhD in Computer Science from University of Sidi Mohamed Ben Abdellah in Morocco and University of Lyon (LIESP Laboratory) in France under a COTUTELLE (co-advising) agreement. His current research interests are information retrieval, text and web mining, semantic web, web services, social networks, machine learning and multi-agent systems. He is an executive and a co-founder member of the International Neural Network Society Morocco regional chapter. He is a guest editor of the *International Journal of Intelligent Engineering Informatics* (ACM, DBLP, etc.). He co-founded the International Conference on Intelligent Computing in Data Sciences (ICSD2017) and the International Conference on Intelligent Systems and Computer Vision (ISCV2015), and he has served as program committee of various international conferences. He has published several papers in reputed journals and international conferences.

Patricia Ordóñez de Pablos is a professor in the Department of Business Administration and Accountability in the Faculty of Economics at The University of Oviedo (Spain). Her teaching and research interests focus on the areas of strategic management, knowledge management, intellectual capital, and China. She serves as an Associate Editor for the *Behaviour and Information Technology journal*. Additionally, she is Editor-in-Chief of the *International Journal of Learning and Intellectual Capital* (IJLIC) and the *International Journal of Strategic Change Management* (IJSCM). She is also Editor-in-Chief of IGI Global's *International Journal of Asian Business and Information Management* (IJABIM), as well as editor for a number of IGI Global book publications and full book series.

Oscar Rodríguez Rocha is a researcher mainly interested in Artificial Intelligence (AI), Knowledge Representation (KR) in the Semantic Web and Recommender Systems (RS). He started working on linked-data based recommendation systems during his PhD at the SofEng group of the Politecnico di Torino. Currently, he is working for Wimmics, a joint research team between Inria Sophia Antipolis - Méditerranée and I3S (CNRS and Université Nice Sophia Antipolis). Wimmics stands for Web-Instrumented Man-Machine Interactions, Communities, and Semantics, and their challenge is to bridge formal semantics and social semantics on the web.

Luca Roffia received a PhD in Computer Science Engineering in 2005 from the University of Bologna where he is currently a Research Fellow and Adjunct Professor of the Department of Computer Science and Engineering. He has been running bachelor and master courses on computer architecture and information technology and arts organizations. His research interests are mainly focused on investigating interoperable solutions within the linked data and Web of Things domains.

Tullio Salmon Cinotti is an Associate Professor at the "School of Engineering and Architecture" of the University of Bologna, where he is in charge of courses about computer architecture and logic design. His research interest is in the area of semantic interoperability and content-based data-distribution architectures for cyber-physical systems. He is co-author of researchers from Intel Labs, Nokia Research, Siemens Corporate Technology, Centro Ricerche Fiat, Telecom Italia Lab, VTT, Sintef, Politecnico di Milano, University of Kent and other research organizations. Tullio Salmon Cinotti is coordinator of the University of Bologna participation to European research initiatives focused on smart environments and IoT technologies, and on their application to societal challenges like open cultural heritage, electric mobility and water management. He is former director of ARCES, an inter-department research center on electronic systems of the University of Bologna.

Besmir Sejdiu is a teaching assistant at University of Prishtina, Kosova, in the Department of Computer Engineering. He joined the Faculty of Electrical and Computer Engineering in October 2009. He received a Bachelor of Computer Engineering degree from the University of Prishtina in 2008; a Master of Computer Engineering from the same university in 2013, titled *Data stream management system for* *water quality monitoring through wireless sensors* in 2013 under the supervision of Prof. Lule Ahmedi. MSc. Sejdiu has a long experience in a field programming and database design. He is also a teaching assistant at University of Mitrovica, Kosova. Some of courses that he teaches are: databases, programming in internet, algorithms and data structures, Java programming and software engineering. He has published several papers in different International Journal and Conferences.

Marco Torchiano is an associate professor at the Control and Computer Engineering Dept. of Politecnico di Torino, Italy; he has been post-doctoral research fellow at Norwegian University of Science and Technology (NTNU), Norway. He received an MSc and a PhD in Computer Engineering from Politecnico di Torino. He is a Senior Member of the IEEE and a member of the software engineering committee of UNINFO (part of ISO/IEC JTC 1). He is author or co-author of over 140 research papers published in international journals and conferences, of the book 'Software Development—Case studies in Java' from Addison-Wesley, and co-editor of the book 'Developing Services for the Wireless Internet' from Springer. He recently was a visiting professor at Polytechnique Montréal studying software energy consumption. His current research interests are: green software, UI testing methods, open-data quality, and software modeling notations. The methodological approach he adopts is that of empirical software engineering.

Iacopo Vagliano is a postdoctoral researcher in the Knowledge Discovery group at ZBW - Leibniz Information Centre for Economics. His research interests include: recommender systems, semantic web, linked data and deep learning. He obtained his Ph.D. in Computer and Control Engineering from Politecnico di Torino. During his Ph.D. program, he collaborated with the MOBI-Lab group of the Telecom Italia Joint Open Laboratory. Telecom Italia has applied several approaches proposed in his thesis to their use cases. He completed his master's thesis at INRIA, the French national research centre for mathematics and IT, in Sophia Antipolis. He co-authored 4 papers in refereed journals, and 12 papers in international conferences. He also serves regularly as a reviewer for international journals and conferences. He is currently the work package leader of the H2020 EU project MOVING. Previously, he took part in the EU FP7 project CRYSTAL, in the Italian project Decision Theatre, and the French project Datalift.

Ankita Verma is an Assistant Professor at Jaypee Institute of Information Technology, Noida, India. She is currently pursuing Ph.D. (Computer Science and Technology) from the School of Computer and Systems Sciences, Jawaharlal Nehru University (JNU), New Delhi, India. She received her M.Tech degree in Computer Science and Technology from JNU, in 2014. Her current research inclinations include: social network analysis, machine learning, soft computing and semantic web analysis.

Fabio Viola (M'16) was born in Lecce, Italy, in 1986. He received a degree in information engineering from the University of Salento, Lecce, Italy, in 2011, and a master's degree in computer science engineering from the University of Bologna, Bologna, Italy, in 2014, where he is currently pursuing the Ph.D. degree. He was an Assistant Researcher with the Advanced Research Center on Electronic Systems, University of Bologna and is now a 3rd year PhD student.

Jianfei Wang is currently a master student in the school of business at Anhui University.

Fenglong Wu is a professor in Software Engineering College, Zhengzhou University of Light Industry. His research interests include machine learning, artificial intelligence, and computer theory.

Zhifeng Zhang is a professor in Software Engineering College, Zhengzhou University of Light Industry. His research interests include mathematical logic, artificial intelligence, and computer theory.

Jie Zhao is a full professor in the school of business at Anhui University.

Index

Purchase Print, E-Book, or Print + E-Book

IGI Global books are available in three unique pricing formats:
Print Only, E-Book Only, or Print + E-Book. Shipping fees apply.

www.igi-global.com

Recommended Reference Books

ISBN: 978-1-5225-1986-7
© 2017; 309 pp.
List Price: $195

ISBN: 978-1-5225-2209-6
© 2017; 322 pp.
List Price: $195

ISBN: 978-1-5225-0813-7
© 2017; 345 pp.
List Price: $190

ISBN: 978-1-5225-2578-3
© 2018; 296 pp.
List Price: $195

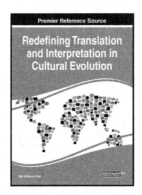

ISBN: 978-1-5225-2832-6
© 2018; 310 pp.
List Price: $195

ISBN: 978-1-5225-3018-3
© 2018; 452 pp.
List Price: $245

Do you want to stay current on the latest research trends, product announcements, news and special offers?
Join IGI Global's mailing list today and start enjoying exclusive perks sent only to IGI Global members.
Add your name to the list at **www.igi-global.com/newsletters.**

Publisher of Peer-Reviewed, Timely, and Innovative Academic Research

www.igi-global.com   Sign up at www.igi-global.com/newsletters   f facebook.com/igiglobal   t twitter.com/igiglobal   t linkedin.com/igiglobal

Ensure Quality Research is Introduced to the Academic Community

Become an IGI Global Reviewer for Authored Book Projects

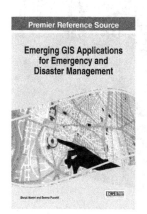
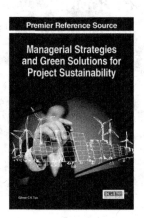

The overall success of an authored book project is dependent on quality and timely reviews.

In this competitive age of scholarly publishing, constructive and timely feedback significantly expedites the turnaround time of manuscripts from submission to acceptance, allowing the publication and discovery of forward-thinking research at a much more expeditious rate. Several IGI Global authored book projects are currently seeking highly qualified experts in the field to fill vacancies on their respective editorial review boards:

Applications may be sent to:
development@igi-global.com

Applicants must have a doctorate (or an equivalent degree) as well as publishing and reviewing experience. Reviewers are asked to write reviews in a timely, collegial, and constructive manner. All reviewers will begin their role on an ad-hoc basis for a period of one year, and upon successful completion of this term can be considered for full editorial review board status, with the potential for a subsequent promotion to Associate Editor.

If you have a colleague that may be interested in this opportunity, we encourage you to share this information with them.

www.igi-global.com

Celebrating 30 Years of Scholarly
Knowledge Creation & Dissemination

InfoSci®-Books

A Collection of 4,000+ Reference Books Containing Over 87,000 Full-Text Chapters Focusing on Emerging Research

This database is a collection of over 4,000+ IGI Global single and multi-volume reference books, handbooks of research, and encyclopedias, encompassing groundbreaking research from prominent experts worldwide. These books are highly cited and currently recognized in prestigious indices such as: Web of Science™ and Scopus®.

Librarian Features:

- No Set-Up or Maintenance Fees
- Guarantee of No More Than A 5% Annual Price Increase
- COUNTER 4 Usage Reports
- Complimentary Archival Access
- Free MARC Records

Researcher Features:

- Unlimited Simultaneous Users
- No Embargo of Content
- Full Book Download
- Full-Text Search Engine
- No DRM

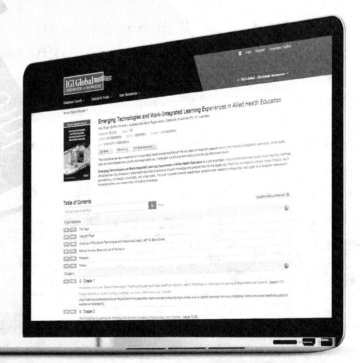

To Find Out More or To Purchase This Database:
www.igi-global.com/infosci-books

eresources@igi-global.com • Toll Free: 1-866-342-6657 ext. 100 • Phone: 717-533-8845 x100

www.igi-global.com

IGI Global Proudly Partners with

Enhance Your Manuscript with
eContent Pro International's Professional
Copy Editing Service

Expert Copy Editing

eContent Pro International copy editors, with over 70 years of combined experience, will provide complete and comprehensive care for your document by resolving all issues with spelling, punctuation, grammar, terminology, jargon, semantics, syntax, consistency, flow, and more. In addition, they will format your document to the style you specify (APA, Chicago, etc.). All edits will be performed using Microsoft Word's Track Changes feature, which allows for fast and simple review and management of edits.

Additional Services

eContent Pro International also offers fast and affordable proofreading to enhance the readability of your document, professional translation in over 100 languages, and market localization services to help businesses and organizations localize their content and grow into new markets around the globe.

IGI Global Authors Save 25% on eContent Pro International's Services!

Scan the QR Code to Receive Your 25% Discount

The 25% discount is applied directly to your eContent Pro International shopping cart when placing an order through IGI Global's referral link. Use the QR code to access this referral link. eContent Pro International has the right to end or modify any promotion at any time.

Email: customerservice@econtentpro.com

econtentpro.com

Printed in the United States
By Bookmasters